THE
NORTH
AFRICAN
COOK
BOOK

THE NORTH AFRICAN COOK BOOK

Jeff Koehler

Introduction

Around the North African Table

Life in North Africa heavily revolves around – and frequently celebrates – that most important of passions, food. Cooking continues to occupy a prominent place in everyday life, and eating with family and friends is both paramount and commonplace. In expressing an unparalleled notion of hospitality, food plays a fundamental role. 'Feed your guests', goes a proverb, 'even if you are starving'.

Such lessons were apparent from the first time I visited the region over two decades ago. I grew up in the American Pacific Northwest, did my postgraduate work in London and then, in 1996, settled in Spain. It wasn't long before I headed to Morocco. Travels around Tunisia and Algeria soon followed. Seduced by North Africa's food culture, deeply fascinated by its traditions and charmed by its people, I have made repeated visits and extended stays continually since then.

Early on, I noticed that the tables are very often round rather than square or rectangular, something both practical and symbolic. The cuisines of North Africa are for sharing and meant to be eaten together – from the same table, even the same dish, with salads, couscous and tagines or long-cooked stews set in the middle of the table. Everyone is equidistant and has a similar reach. With no 'head of the table', there is a natural levelling in hierarchy, at least during mealtimes.

Such tables tend to be chatty, noisy places. But so are the dishes themselves that people have gathered around: the food of North Africa is anything but hushed. It's bold, it's colourful, it's diverse. It's deeply original. And, I quickly learned, it tells both individual and communal stories that are remarkable.

I was just setting out as a writer when I began to travel throughout North Africa. My first published piece – a travel feature for the *Los Angeles Times* – came from a trip there. My career, I like to think, began in Morocco.

Initially, I wrote about travel, architecture and food, and then, before long, almost exclusively about food. I found that through the lens of food I could delve into almost any story. To write about food is to write about culture, place, people, history, politics and geography: food encompasses it all. As well, I loved that everyone was an authority in their own culinary traditions and had much to share.

Arriving somewhere new, the first thing we usually do is eat. (As the American food writer M.F.K. Fisher famously put it, 'First we eat, then we do everything else.') Our initial interactions with a place are frequently through food – the way we begin to experience and understand a culture. I applied that same approach on the page. As a writer, then, I found my way of telling stories, and in North Africa, I found a place to discover them. In the 20-plus years since, I have written about the region for numerous publications.

When I began to write extensively about food back in the early 2000s, I saw that to just write about it was not enough: I needed to cook it as well to fully appreciate it. Over the next few years, I learned to cook through observation, mimicry and countless hours at the stove trying to recreate what I had watched and tasted (learning, simultaneously, just how much the virtue of patience was rewarded in the kitchen). I was soon working on recipes, and in 2006 the first of my cookbooks appeared. While I had been oriented towards food from early on – as a kid I worked on a berry farm in summer, in the kitchen of a hospital during high school and in a supermarket (grocery store) and its butchery in summers during university – I never imagined I would pass so much of my life in kitchens. When I am travelling, I am frequently in someone's kitchen, notebook in hand, trying to stay out of the way, learning what I can. And when I am home, a large part of my day is usually spent at the market, stove or kitchen counter.

I have lived in Barcelona for more than 25 years now, and I am fortunate to have a strong Maghrebi community here to offer advice on North African dishes, as well as a handful of excellent Moroccan butchers, small grocery stores and bakeries in the old city's El Raval neighbourhood to find all the ingredients I need to cook.

While I have friends scattered across North Africa, and plenty of favourite places to eat, shop and visit, I find deep pleasure in the unknown and unexpected, in those tasty surprises that may be just around the next corner. The key for me is to turn off familiar roads and keep pushing ahead to find those less travelled. Satisfaction, of course, goes beyond a delicious meal. It helps you better understand a place. I found that learning about the region's food was to learn about far, far more – and it is this idea that continues to spur me on, corner after corner, meal after meal.

The genesis for this comprehensive, regional cookbook originated two decades ago, not long after my travels widened across North Africa. The culinary similarities that I found from country to country immediately intrigued me. But so did the differences that reside under the unifying bonds of race, religion, history, language and geography.

I finally turned my full-time attention to this long-term project in 2019, when I set out on a few years of dedicated travel, research, eating and cooking to specifically explore those similarities and differences.

One thing is certain: there is no singular way to prepare any one dish, no matter how simple it might be. Watch a half-dozen people make a pot of tea with fresh mint and you will see small but not insignificant differences in each – differences that will often be righteously defended with passion. And that is just tea! In kitchens everywhere as people cook, I continually hear, 'The dish is always done like this!' only to be told across town the next day with equal insistence, 'It is never done like that! It is always done like this!' For *The North African Cookbook*, I was particularly interested in finding more standard versions of both traditional and more contemporary dishes as well as regional variations. That meant tasting something in as many different places as possible, while also consulting various people for every dish. How do you make it? Do you add this or that? How was it cooked at home when you grew up? Have you ever seen it done this way, or with this included? What about in the south of the country? The west? What ingredients are always present? What are some of the options? Is adding this typical – or just the distinctive interpretation of one person?

I was in Oran, Algeria, in 2020 when COVID-19 interrupted my travelling. After returning to Barcelona, my research approach shifted. Instead of sitting in a kitchen in the High Atlas, at a table in Algiers or poking around the weekly market of a southern oasis in Tunisia, I used the full toolbox of modern and digital communication methods to stay connected. There were long hours of video chatting and many photos and videos – of dishes, techniques, ingredients. Insightful information came from a wide net of people in North Africa, plus an extensive diaspora of Maghrebi friends and contacts in New York and Detroit, Marseilles and Paris, Spain, London, even Osaka where an Algerian friend and his Tunisian wife were living. Many times, these dialogues were in real time as I stood at the stove, phone in one hand and wooden spoon in the other. Luckily, the Moroccan stores I frequent in Barcelona's El Raval neighbourhood remained opened, and I could continue to get the ingredients I needed as well as plenty of over-the-counter advice when shopping.

Alongside this web of resources, I frequently returned to my shelf of treasured notebooks. Besides being an obsessive eater and persistent questioner, I am a compulsive notetaker. There is an individual notebook for each journey I have made over the decades along with its companion 'kitchen notebook' filled with what I saw, tasted, observed and learned. From the beginning I kept these, knowing that I could never remember everything when working on a specific article or recipe, but also with an eye on a larger, ongoing and more involved project that I hoped would one day come to fruition.

I also repeatedly consulted my bookshelves. Over the years, I have built up a formidable library of (often locally published) cookbooks and other works about the region's culinary traditions, from encyclopaedic classics like Fatima-Zohra Bouayed's *La Cuisine Algérienne* and Zeinab Kaâk's *La Sofra: Cuisine tunisienne traditionnelle* to smaller ones on more specific themes such as special dishes for Ramadan, Jewish-Moroccan cooking or a regional cuisine. Among my files are also photocopies, photographs and notes from books that I found sitting on the shelves of people's homes, in guest-houses, even restaurants, plus libraries. I went through these over and over, to compare ways I had tasted or seen food prepared, had read about it or had it described to me, or had even glimpsed on social media where the Maghrebi food community is highly active.

As restrictions eased, I returned to travelling, to haunting souqs, or marketplaces, and out-of-the-way kitchen corners, to getting off familiar roads. And to sitting around the North African table.

Another important thing that I learned about tables being round is that others can always squeeze in, no matter how crowded it might be already. There is always room for one more.

---◇---

Drawing a Map

---◇---

Occupying the western half of Africa's crown is the Maghreb: Morocco, Algeria, Tunisia and Libya. Bestowed by seventh-century conquerors from Arabia, the name Maghreb comes from the Arabic word meaning 'the west' or 'the place where the sun sets'. (This is as opposed to Mashriq, the east, where the sun rises.)

It is an area bound together by geography, language, religion and way of life, an original Berber (Amazigh) population and a common history of conquest and colonization. Also, importantly, it shares a signature staple: couscous.

The fourteenth-century Tunisian philosopher, sociologist and historian Ibn Khaldun defined the Maghreb's geographical range as *halq el rouous, lebs el burnous, akl el couscous* – 'where men have shaved skulls, wear burnouses [long, loose hooded cloaks] and consume couscous'. Habib Bourguiba, Tunisia's first president after independence from France in 1956, echoed this by defining the limits of the Maghreb by where people eat couscous.

Couscous refers to both the tiny, hard granules or 'grains' usually rolled from durum wheat semolina or barley and the finished dish. This 'grain' is the region's long-standing staple; as a dish – steamed two or three times in a two-tiered couscoussier over a flavourful stew, which is served on the top – it is the Maghreb's most celebrated and delectable culinary gift. Couscous is so emblematic and important that in parts of Algeria some call it simply *ta'am*, 'food'. It is the most comforting of comfort foods.

Eaten at least weekly, couscous is a meal to share among family and to celebrate life's most important moments, both in joy and sorrow. It is ubiquitous at gatherings and unthinkable for it to be absent from special occasions.

Couscous offers the Maghreb a regional identity – and this book its 'map'. *The North African Cookbook* covers the area where couscous is a staple.

The terms 'Maghreb' and 'North Africa' are generally used interchangeably (as they are in this book), although the former is less common in the United States. The region stretches from the Atlantic coast across the top of Africa to about halfway across the Gulf of Sirte, in the centre of Libya, where an ancient border marks the boundary between Roman Tripolitania and Greek Cyrenaica. This is the boundary between the Maghreb cultural sphere and Egyptian one: the west oriented to the Maghreb, the east to the Mashriq (the eastern part of the Arab world). It is a marker of change. The Maghreb is heavily Berber, while Egypt is not. The spoken Maghrebi dialects are close to each other but quite unintelligible to Egyptians. Libyan Arabic shows this division with two major dialects, a western one and an eastern one. Music in these regions is different, as is food – or more specifically, couscous. Once across that line in Sirte, while couscous is known and prepared, rice becomes the staple.

Some people think that Egypt, Sudan and even the Canary Islands (which lay off the southern Moroccan coast) can also be grouped into this region. I have spent significant time in both Egypt and the Sudan, and I have been several times to the Canary Islands (never Arabicized or Islamicized, and ruled by Spain since the fifteenth century). As I worked on this cookbook, I felt it was not fitting to include them here, even as an extension, for no other reason than them falling so far out of the culinary traditions found in the Maghreb. The definition of the Maghreb was expanded by some from its traditional meaning in the late twentieth century to include Mauritania, the large and largely desert nation to the south of Morocco and Algeria that acts as a cultural bridge between the Maghreb and Mali, Senegal and West Africa. Mauritania has also not been included in this book. Historically, it has largely fallen outside the orbit of the Maghrebi dynasties, rule and groupings. (It was part of French West Africa during the colonial period, for instance.)

Island of the West

At some 5 million km²/2 million square miles and larger than the European Union, the Maghreb is vast but geographically contained. It is surrounded by the Mediterranean on the north, the Atlantic on the west and the great Sahara to the south and east. Some 1,300 years ago, Arab geographers called it *jazirat al-maghrib*, 'island of the west' or 'island of the sunset'.

Within the ample confines of this 'island' exists a wide variety of landscapes and climates. The popular image of North Africa as a parched place with fortified earthen kasbahs (citadels) and oases shrouded in date palms is not necessarily wrong, just woefully incomplete. There are mountain peaks nearly as high as Switzerland's tallest, river gorges and riverine oases, plateaus carpeted in wheat and valleys in barley, cork and holm oak forests with dozens of varieties of wild mushrooms (and even truffles), gnarled olive trees irrigated only by the moisture of the Mediterranean, roses to distil growing in the mountains, hillsides with cumin, wild oregano and vervain, orchards of figs, cherries and plums, citrus groves, fields that turn brilliant red with ripening peppers in summer, meadows with grazing flocks of sheep and dazzling spring flowers, farms producing excellent fresh goat's cheeses, some of the world's finest fishing grounds, islands famed for their octopus or lobster, dates from storied Saharan oases (Biskra! Tozeur! Ghadames!) and a barren mesa where scarlet saffron flowers blossom each morning for a few weeks in autumn. The 'island' offers everything a cook could desire or the larder lacks. For many centuries this fertile land provided not only for its own populations, but also for others elsewhere in a series of ancient empires to which they once belonged.

Mountains are one of North Africa's dominating physical features. Two interlinked ranges cross the Maghreb. The first runs along the coast – it includes the Rif Mountains in Morocco and the Tell Atlas in Algeria and ends with the Kroumirie Mountains in northwestern Tunisia. The second, to its south, includes the Middle Atlas, High Atlas and Anti-Atlas in Morocco, the Saharan Atlas in Algeria and Aurès Mountains in northwestern Tunisia and northeastern Algeria.

To the north (and in Morocco also the west) of these mountain ranges, sandwiched between protective slopes and the coast, runs a fertile, temperate and agricultural-rich strip where most of the Maghreb's population lives. Apart from a handful of notable exceptions – Marrakech, Fès and Meknès in Morocco, Kairouan in Tunisia, Sétif and Constantine in Algeria – the main cities of the Maghreb are on the coast. Many of these have ancient roots that go back thousands of years.

To the east and south of these ranges, the land descends through steppes, into pre-Saharan scrub and then the desert itself, a vast expanse criss-crossed by ancient trade routes. The Sahara is its southern defining characteristic.

A Brief History of North Africa

The Berbers North Africa's storied past opens with its original inhabitants, the Berbers, who have occupied the region since the beginning of recorded history. The term 'Berber' may come from a variation of the Greek word referring to those who did not speak their language that the Romans used for non-Latin speakers. While the name has lost its pejorative connotations (the same root spawned 'barbarian'), some prefer to call themselves Imazighen (singular Amazigh), meaning 'free people' or 'noble people'. In some places, more specific local names such as Kabyle or Chaoui are used.

Berbers are not a homogenous people. There are various Berber (or Amazigh) languages and dialects, with seven major variations used by about 95 per cent of the Berber-speaking population: Shilha (or Tashelhit, in southwestern Morocco), Kabyle (in northern and northeastern Algeria), Central Atlas Tamazight (in the Atlas Mountains of central Morocco), Riffian (in the Rif Mountains of northern Morocco), Shawiya (also spelled Chaoui, in eastern Algeria) and Tuareg (in the southern desert regions). Morocco and Algeria have the largest populations of Berber language speakers. Language is a key touchstone of identity.

To escape successive waves of invasions and occupations, the Berbers retreated to more remote areas, mountainous regions and along the fringes of the desert. (Or, in the case of the Tuaregs, the pastoral Berber ethnic group in the southern regions, the desert itself.) Today they are found predominately in rural parts of the region, where they have retained over the centuries their own language and customs while absorbing influences.

While hard to generalize, Berber cuisine is often rustic, reflecting the austere landscape where they frequently live, as well as once semi-nomadic or even nomadic lifestyles that allowed little time for various courses or culinary flourish. This ancestral cuisine relies heavily on breads and grains, pulses and vegetables, milk and butter, lamb, soups and porridges, honey, fresh herbs and so on.

Yet the Berbers developed some of the region's most prominent dishes, including the most famous of them all, couscous. In an ingenious cooking method, they converted Roman clay pots into perforated baskets to steam the rolled granules from ground barley, wheat and other cereals above the stew simmering below. Berber versions of couscous tend to be hearty with vegetables and often contain less complex spicing than is found in cities. They are also credited with adapting earthenware cooking pots into, for example, tagines in Morocco.

Among numerous other much-loved dishes accredited to the Berbers is the puréed dried broad (fava) bean soup called *bissara* (page 136), various griddle-cooked flatbreads and a trio of breakfast favourites eaten with honey: Layered Msemen Flatbread with Honey (page 65); airy Honeycomb Baghrir Crêpes (page 64); and crumbly *harsha* made with semolina, milk and butter (Crumbly Semolina Flatbread, page 46). In Tunisia, the best-known Berber bread is *tabouna*, baked inside the walls of a traditional clay oven.

The Phoenicians and Carthaginians From a string of trading ports, the Phoenicians and Carthaginians controlled much of North Africa for over 650 years, beginning in about 800 BCE.

The Phoenicians were seafaring merchant-adventurers from Tyre, Sidon and Byblos in modern-day Lebanon who established a chain of safe ports and market towns along the North African coast, for their trade between the Eastern Mediterranean and Spain. As the Phoenicians didn't want more land than they needed for their trade with the Berber tribes of the interior, these settlements often remained relatively small. The major exception was Carthage.

Carthage (from Kart-Hadasht, 'New Town'), founded in 814 BCE in the northeastern corner of modern-day Tunisia by Queen Elissa (aka Dido), grew into an independent empire and power known as Punic. By the fifth century BCE, the Carthaginians ruled across the Mediterranean from the Gulf of Sirte in Libya all the way west to Tangier and over 700 km/435 miles south down Morocco's Atlantic coast to Mogador (modern-day Essaouira). In 300 BCE, Carthage was the largest city in the world and home to as many as 500,000 people.

Sheep, goats and cattle provided milk and, on special occasions, meat, although chickens, rabbits and pigeons were more common in the cooking pot. Red mullet, bream, mackerel and tuna were caught offshore, with salt pans established near fishing centres to preserve them. Cereals were key to the diet and found in soups and porridges. The adjacent Cap Bon peninsula and fertile hinterlands provided garden vegetables and orchards: cabbage, cardoons, artichokes and garlic, apples, pears and grapes, almonds, walnuts and hazelnuts. Figs were famous and exported to Greece and Rome, and pomegranates widespread. In his *Natural History* (77 CE), the Roman naturalist Pliny the Elder called pomegranates 'Punic apples' and wrote that there were nine varieties growing in Carthage.

Trade links with the Berbers increased significantly. By the third century BCE, Berbers of the interior had organized themselves into a handful of large and loosely organized kingdoms. The most powerful was called Numidia, which lay just beyond the coastal area under Carthage's control. Its power peaked under the reign of King Masinissa, who died in 148 BCE.

The Carthaginian Empire began to weaken in the third and second centuries BCE, as it fought a series of wars with the nascent Roman Empire for the control of the Mediterranean. *Carthago delenda est*, went Rome's famous call: 'Carthage must be destroyed'. And it finally was, in 146 BCE during the third and final Punic War.

The Romans When the Romans levelled Carthage, they broke Phoenician supremacy in the region and expanded their dominion of North Africa. They divided the region into four client provinces. The largest was called Africa Proconsularis, roughly modern-day Tunisia, northeastern Algeria and western Libya, with a rebuilt Carthage at its core. Carthage grew back to some 500,000 inhabitants, the largest in the empire after Rome and Alexandria, and by far the largest in Roman North Africa. (Leptis Magna on the Libyan coast was a distant second with 80,000 people. By comparison, Roman London varied between 30,000 and 60,000 people.) From Carthage, the Romans expanded their power to rule from the Nile to the Atlantic.

The six centuries of Roman rule was a time of flourishing urban development in Tunisia, northern Algeria and parts of Morocco, as the Romans managed to control much of the pastoral and nomadic movement. In the vast network linking cities from Alexandria to Tangier, North Africa had about 20,000 km/12,500 miles of roads. During the first two centuries CE, the Maghreb's population was between four and eight million people. (It would fall and not reach that number again until the beginning of the twentieth century.) To keep control of their road network and to extract taxes, Roman officials had to continually negotiate with Berber tribal leaders. Berber traditions were largely left intact as the Roman presence was concentrated in the cities.

Agriculture was the basis of the economy. The area under cultivation increased significantly and strides were made in farming and irrigation techniques. Pliny the Elder wrote of the tradition of multicropping in Tacape (modern-day Gabès) on the southern Tunisian coast: 'Here underneath palms of exceptional size there are olives, under the olives figs, under the figs pomegranates, and under those vines; and underneath the vines is sown legumes, and later leguminous plants, and then garden vegetables, all in the same year, and all nourished in the shade of something else.'

Julius Caesar's policy of rewarding soldiers who fought for the Roman Empire with land in North Africa led many to move to the region and farm. These settlers planted wheat, olives and vines along with fruit orchards, often expanding previous plantings. By the first century CE, Tunisia's wheat fields were satisfying two-thirds of the grain needs of the city of Rome; by the second century CE, olive oil became an important crop in the Sahel along Tunisia's central coast and the northern slopes of the Aurès Mountains in northeastern Algeria and northwestern Tunisia; by the fourth century, the oil was exported throughout the Roman Empire. From North African ports, ships loaded dried fish and clay amphorae (narrow-necked, two-handled clay pots) of garum – a popular fermented fish sauce used as a condiment – and local wine.

Apart from agriculture and fishing, there was little industry except pottery. This, though, keenly influenced the region's cookery. It was likely the Romans that introduced clay cooking vessels, which Berbers adapted into tagines and made into perforated baskets to steam couscous.

The Vandals and Byzantines With the Roman Empire in decline, the Germanic group known as the Vandals crossed into North Africa from Spain in 429 CE and advanced eastward across the region with little opposition, capturing the coastal areas and cutting off Rome's major grain source. Desperate to keep the Vandals from attacking Rome itself, the Romans ceded much of North Africa to them in a 435 treaty. In the agreement, the Vandals were to limit their control to the two westernmost provinces. They reneged, captured Carthage, advanced on Sicily and sacked Rome in 455. They ruled in North Africa for 99 years. This period saw the emergence of independent Berber kingdoms in the mountains and deserts.

In 534, North Africa was conquered again and incorporated in the Byzantine Empire (the Eastern Roman Empire). Incompetence, corruption and Constantinople's general lack of concern for the region marked their time, and, like the Vandals, the Byzantines failed to develop it. They held the coastal cities but remained vulnerable to attacks anytime they ventured outside the fortified city walls. The rural areas were under Berber control. Byzantine rule was short-lived and unable to resist the Arab invasion of the seventh century.

The Arabs After the death of the Prophet Muhammad in 632 CE, Islam swept westward from the Arabian Peninsula, through the Middle East and Egypt and into North Africa. Previous conquerors had come by sea; the Arabs arrived

on horseback. After a series of raids – they took Tripoli in 643 – a renewed push in the 660s saw combatants set out westward to conquer the Maghreb. Under the Arab general Uqba ibn Nafi, they made their first permanent foothold in 670 on the north-central Tunisian plains about 160 km/100 miles south of Carthage, to use as a base for their conquest. They called the town Kairouan, from the Arabic *qayrawan* ('caravan'). Carthage fell to them in 698 and the rest of the Maghreb within a decade, capturing the far-northwestern city of Tangier – the last major holdout – in 710. In less than 65 years they had conquered the entire region. While the Berbers of the hinterlands resisted Arab political domination, they embraced Islam and its doctrines, and some joined Arab armies. In the eleventh century, waves of Arab migration swept across the Maghreb, as around 200,000 nomads from the Banu Hilal and Banu Sulaym tribes of the Arabian Peninsula arrived from Upper Egypt.

The impact of the Arab conquest was profound and lasting. It brought a new language, model of government and politics and social norms. Importantly, it also brought a new religion. With Islam came numerous celebrations with food and dietary restrictions.

The Arab arrivals carried sophisticated new culinary traditions with secrets from the kitchens of Damascus, Baghdad and Cairo. Holding for centuries a monopoly on the spice trade from the east, they brought cinnamon, nutmeg, ginger and turmeric with them to the Maghreb. Cooks drew on spice mixtures and aromatics, and they introduced Persian culinary influences including cooked meats with fresh and dried fruits as well as nuts. *Rfissa* or *trid* – sheets of fine pastry layered with a rich sauce of lentils, onions and fenugreek and topped by stewed chicken – is a Moroccan favourite that derives from a dish of this period (*tharid*, a stew served over pieces of bread that was said to be a favourite of the Prophet Muhammad). Another is *mulukhiya* (page 159), dried and ground mallow simmered for hours that is much loved in Tunisia. They also had an abiding passion for delicate sweetmeats enriched with almonds, sesame seeds and honey, and often aromatized with rose water.

Trans-Sahara Caravans   The Sahara is so vast and rugged that it long formed a seemingly unpassable barrier for trade. From the fifth century BCE, camels finally allowed people to cross it. Perfectly suited for the desert, camels became common by the fourth century CE, when the first caravans reached the Bilad al-Sudan ('Land of Blacks'), a term used by early Arab travellers, historians and geographers to describe the expanse of savannah stretching between the southern edge of the Sahara and the tropical rainforests of Guinea. From the eighth century, annual caravans began crossing the desert to link the Mediterranean with the powerful, medieval Ghana, Mali and the Songhai empires, important sources of gold.

Led by desert Berbers navigating by night stars, the way shadows fell across the dunes, the shape of distant mountains on the horizon and even the smell of the wind, the caravans travelled for 40–60 days. Long columns of laden animals passed through fabled oases such as Timbuktu, Sijilmasa and Ghadames en route to Fès, Tunis or Tripoli. A typical caravan had around 500 animals, although some contained as many as 12,000 loaded camels.

Southbound the caravans carried salt – important as a dietary supplement and for preserving foods – along with glazed pottery cups, lamps and vases, copper wire, ceramics, glassware and olive oil. They returned north with gold, enslaved people, ivory, cloth and spices. In the oases on the way north, the caravans picked up dates.

Among these spices was grains of paradise (also known as melegueta pepper), a peppercorn-like spice from West Africa that offered a piney, pungent and peppery-hot bite alternative to milder black pepper. Overpowered by the arrival of chillies (chiles) from the New World and fallen largely out of favour, today it is most often found in spice blends such as ras el hanout. In Morocco, one spice carries the legacy of this trade to Bilad al-Sudan in its name, *felfla soudania* (cayenne pepper), often just called *soudania*, which came via the West African coast.

The great era of the trans-Saharan trade lasted until the end of the sixteenth century, with the collapse of the Songhai Empire and increased trade by ship as the Portuguese established forts in numerous harbours along Africa's Atlantic coastline. Railways reaching the interior from the coast at the beginning of the twentieth century and then the arrival of rugged, off-road motorized vehicles largely smothered out what remained.

Local Dynasties Following the Arab conquest, North Africa remained under the control of various rulers from the Middle East, but they had difficulty in effectively ruling the region from a distant Damascus or Baghdad, and independent local dynasties eventually gained control. The strongest of these to emerge and rule in the Maghreb were two rival Islamic Berber kingdoms originating in modern-day Morocco.

Initially a religious reform movement from the south, the Almoravids (1060–1147) founded Marrakech in 1062 as their imperial capital. They conquered the Maghreb from the Atlantic coast to Algiers by 1106, and they ruled Spain north to the Ebro River while expanding trans-Saharan trade. At its peak, the Almoravid Empire stretched from Spain to modern-day Mauritania, Mali and northern Senegal.

Next came the Almohad Empire from the Atlas. It conquered Marrakech in 1147, Algiers in 1151 and by 1160 east to Tripoli. Its peak of power came in the last decades of the twelfth century when it controlled a territory that included part of the Iberian Peninsula (moving the Al-Andalus capital from Córdoba to Seville in the process), south into Mauritania and east all the way across modern-day Algeria, Tunisia and Libya. It was the first time the entire Maghreb was ruled by a single local regime. It was also the last time.

After the Almohad Empire's collapse and the fall of Marrakech in 1269, the Maghreb began to take shape closer to today's modern borders.

Al-Andalus In 711 CE, an army of Berber and Arab forces crossed the Strait of Gibraltar in their conquest of Spain and Portugal, and within ten years they controlled almost all the Iberian Peninsula and into Mediterranean France and the Balearic Islands; by the tenth century, a Muslim empire stretched from North Africa across the Mediterranean and included most of the Iberian Peninsula, Sicily, Sardinia and the Balearic Islands. At the core of this European empire was Muslim Spain and Portugal, called Al-Andalus. The region was closely linked with North Africa for about 800 years, until the collapse of the final territory in Spain under Muslim rule at the end of the fifteenth century. The culture of Al-Andalus became known as Moorish. (The term 'Moor' was originally applied to Berbers in the large region of Mauritania in Roman North Africa, and over

time came to signify Muslims in Spain, Portugal and Sicily.) It was a sophisticated, cosmopolitan meeting place of the Orient and Occident where the art of cooking reached lofty heights.

Taking an Arab-Berber fusion of cooking to Spain, these arrivals found familiar, fertile lands that yielded easily to their culinary tastes. What wasn't already growing they introduced with their wide trade network and skilled agriculture techniques. They expanded Roman models of irrigation to new levels of sophistication and increased farming. While the Romans had grown olives, the Moors instigated large-scale planting. Over the centuries, they introduced countless new products, including rice, sugar cane, saffron, artichokes, aubergine (eggplant), hazelnuts, oranges, lemons, pomegranates, watermelons and figs, numerous spices, pasta, couscous and so on. There were new ways to use these ingredients in the kitchen, new combinations, flavours and new cooking techniques, including frying in olive oil, stuffing, marinating in oil and vinegar, thickening with crushed almonds and pounding ingredients. A love of sweet confections – often based on the magical triptych of almonds, sugar and lemon – was heightened. There was even a new art of eating credited to the Baghdad-born musician (and one-time Kairouan resident) named Ziryab, who became an advisor to the emir of Córdoba in 822. Ziryab propagated a concept of eating in an order of courses, starting with lighter ones and ending with something sweet, rather than simply piling everything onto a plate.

Reconquista and Resettling Almost immediately after the eighth-century conquering of Spain began the Reconquista, a long and steady recapturing of the peninsula by Catholic monarchies that was finally completed in 1492 with the fall of Granada. From the mid-thirteenth century (when Catholic forces took Córdoba and Seville) until the early seventeenth century, waves of Muslims living under Christian rule (known as Mudéjars) were driven out. Most went to the Maghreb. So did the Moriscos, former Muslims who had been forcibly converted to Christianity – their choice was either exile or baptism – and still not trusted by the Catholic church, that Spain's King Philip III expelled in 1609. Many Sephardic Jews expelled from the Iberian Peninsula in the fifteenth century also settled and put down roots in North Africa.

Historians estimate up to one million people settled in North Africa from Spain, especially Andalucía, where they added new 'Andalusian' neighbourhoods to Fès, Tunis, Algiers and many other places, and established new cities such as Chefchaouen in Morocco and Sidi Bou Saïd outside Tunis. In Tunisia, many moved to the fertile areas of the Cap Bon peninsula, along the banks of the meandering Medjerda River north of Tunis and to the slopes of Mount Zaghouan to the south of Tunis. One of the most 'Andalusian' cities in North Africa is Tétouan, two hours east of Tangier. Rebuilt from scratch at the end of the fifteenth century under the leadership of the Granada-born military officer Ali al-Mandri, it was significantly enlarged in the sixteenth century with the arrival of Moriscos from Spain. Nicknamed the 'White Dove' and 'Daughter of Granada', dense, tiered layers of whitewashed buildings spread from just inland up through a valley known for its orange, pomegranate and almond orchards.

These arrivals brought to their adopted homes in North Africa a new level of sophistication with cooking that had been refined in Al-Andalus, sparking something of a culinary renaissance. A fresh nobility in the cuisine could be tasted in dishes like chicken topped with *tfaya* (caramelized onions and raisins, page 208), *pastilla* (a savoury 'pie' filled with pigeon, eggs, almonds and cinnamon, page 62) and Almond Ghriba Cookies (page 369) with their chewy, cracked surfaces. Techniques for preserving fruits and vegetables were improved and the use of distilled orange blossom water was popularized. They also carried with them products that recently arrived in Spain from the New World: tomatoes, peppers, potatoes, corn, pumpkins, squash and courgettes (zucchini). These became so deeply absorbed into the local cuisines that it is unthinkable to imagine them without these ingredients.

Jewish Communities North Africa's Jewish population was once formidable. Each North African nation had flourishing communities until the mid-twentieth century. Jews lived in the region since antiquity, although waves of expulsions from Spain, beginning in the twelfth century, and then fleeing the Spanish Inquisition with Muslims in the fifteenth and sixteenth centuries increased their numbers significantly.

In 1948, the first exodus of Jews left North Africa for Israel. That year there were around 265,000 Jews living in Morocco (about 3 per cent of the population). There were large communities in Fès and Marrakech and along the coast in Casablanca, Rabat and, most famously, Essaouira. Developed in the mid-eighteenth century at the behest of the Alaouite ruler Sultan Sidi Mohammed Ben Abdellah (also known as Mohammed III) on the site of a sixteenth-century Portuguese fortress, Essaouira was established as a royal port and major trading post to link Morocco and its hinterland with Africa and Europe. The thriving Jewish community accounted for about 40 per cent of the cosmopolitan city's population, with over three dozen synagogues in Essaouira's Jewish Quarter. In 1948, the Jewish population in Tunisia and Libya was equal to Morocco's at 3 to 4 per cent, while Algeria's was half. In Algeria in the mid-twentieth century, Algiers, Oran and Constantine had the largest Jewish communities, with notable others found in Sétif, Tlemcen in the far northwest and Ghardaïa in the M'zab Valley in the Sahara. By 1962, when Algeria became the last country in the Maghreb to gain independence, nearly the entire remaining Jewish community had departed, largely for Israel, France and the Americas. The flavours of North Africa travelled with them and can still be tasted in many diaspora homes today.

In North Africa, Jewish influences are seen in certain stews and pastries and methods of preserving foods. Jewish communities were particularly associated with saffron, preserved lemons, garlic and spices – cinnamon, nutmeg and ginger – and mixing the savoury and sweet. Kosher dietary restrictions stipulating that dairy and meat could not be mixed meant a wide use of olive oil. Of their culinary legacies found today, one of the most important is a range of dishes with vegetables, pulses, grains and meats that were slow-cooked overnight on Friday to eat on Saturday, the Jewish Sabbath. These were known as *dafina* (or *tfina* or *skina*), meaning 'covered'. Among the popular classics today and not considered strictly Jewish is *hargma*, with calves' feet. In Tunisia, *mekbouba* (a confit of tomatoes and peppers eaten as a salad, page 74) is another dish generally considered Jewish though still commonly prepared today.

The Ottomans   The Ottoman Empire spanned from 1299 to 1922 and at its peak in 1683 covered 5.2 million km²/2 million square miles across Turkey, the Balkans, the Middle East, Arabia, Egypt and the coastal strip of Africa's northern crown excluding Morocco. Founded in western Anatolia, Turkey, it gradually expanded its territory in Anatolia and the Balkans and in 1453, conquered the Byzantine Empire's capital of Constantinople (modern-day Istanbul). From there it pushed onward, capturing Algiers in 1516, Tripoli in 1551 and Tunis in 1574. Ottoman North Africa was formally divided into three 'regencies' – Tripoli, Tunis and Algiers. Ottoman rule in the Maghreb lasted for over three centuries – until 1830 in Algeria, 1881 in Tunisia and 1912 in Libya.

The sprawl of that vast empire can be traced today in food. *Boureks* (flaky, stuffed pastries, pages 56–57), *kefta* (spiced minced/ground meat, page 272), stuffed vegetables (collectively known as *dolma*, pages 166–167) and most notably thick Turkish-style coffee (page 425) are all Ottoman hallmarks.

European Colonialism   While Spanish and Portuguese presence in North Africa dates back to the fifteenth century, with the occupation of the coastal enclaves of Ceuta and Melilla, European colonization began in 1830 when France invaded Algiers, and soon after made Algeria officially part of France and converted it into a settler colony. Tunisia became a French Protectorate (without being a direct possession) in 1881 and Morocco in 1912. Morocco and Tunisia gained independence in 1956. Algeria remained under French rule until 1962.

The marks of French colonialism are evident in the layout of many cities, urban architecture style and rows of pavement (sidewalk) café tables, and the wide use of the French language. Most noticeable are morning *café au lait* and croissants, long baguettes baked alongside traditional round loaves in bakeries and desserts such as flan. French-style pastry-making techniques joined elaborate traditional ones. *Confiture* (jam) is another French influence, suited to the plentiful fruits growing in the region (fig and apricot are two favourites).

France was not the only colonial power in the region. Spain governed Morocco's Mediterranean north during the Protectorate, with Tétouan as its capital. It also controlled the deep south for much

of the twentieth century, including the Western Sahara (1884–1976) and, for periods, the Tarfaya Strip on Cape Juby to its north and the seaside town of Sidi Ifni. In these northern and southern areas, small fish are floured and deep-fried without the *chermoula*, and there are local versions of paella and the frequent inclusion of a classic Spanish sofrito base of onions and tomatoes in many dishes – usually with the very Moroccan addition of cumin.

In the colonial period, there were also about 100,000 Italian residents in Tunisia, outnumbering French nearly three to one, and three-quarters were Sicilian. Not until 1930 would the French population overtake the Italian one. Italian settlers made a significant impact with pasta, which began to replace couscous as a daily meal in Tunisia. In Algeria, Italians opened the first commercial couscous factories.

Italy's presence was strongest in Libya. In 1911, Italy declared war on the Ottoman Empire and seized ports in Libya, including Tripoli. At the end of the Italo-Turkish War in 1912, the Ottomans pulled out. Italy annexed the territory, then gained full control in 1931 (lasting until 1943), with a quarter of Libya's population killed.

Algerian-born French Citizens   In the mid-twentieth century, Algeria had a population of around nine million. About one million were Algerian-born French with French citizenship, known as *pieds-noirs* (literally 'black feet'). Some had families who had settled in Algeria generations ago. (The term came to include other Europeans as well.) One heard various languages on the street from communities of Muslim Algerians of Arab and Berber descent, Jews, French, Spanish and Italians who often lived side-by-side. One significant *pied-noir* culinary tradition was *la kémia*, a series of hors d'oeuvres – pickled vegetables, hunks of preserved tuna fish, almonds, chickpeas (garbanzo beans) with cumin and paprika, olives – often served with anisette liqueur.

Independence and Today   Independence came to North Africa in the mid-twentieth century. Algeria fought the War of Independence from 1954 to 1962 and at independence over 10 per cent of the population were Algerian-born Europeans, nearly all departed, settling mostly in southern France and Corsica. They took with them a hybrid cuisine

that reflected the multicultural roots that blended North African flavours with French, Spanish and Sephardic Jewish traditions.

Relations among Maghrebi neighbours since independence have not always been smooth, especially between Morocco and Algeria. They fought a brief war in 1963 and have had their land border closed since 1994. Much of their disagreement is over the status of the Western Sahara, the disputed coastal desert region largely under Moroccan control. In 1989, the Arab Maghreb Union was formed by Morocco, Algeria, Tunisia, Libya and Mauritania as a geographic and regional block of over 100 million people in order to promote economic integration and security, and bolster trading power.

Historically ostracized, the Berber people began a cultural revival in the mid-1970s, marked in part by the Algerian singer Idir (Hamid Cheriet) releasing an album in the Berber language. Calls for a greater celebration of Berber traditions and language followed, as well as a unified written script called Tifinagh, which happened in the 1980s. Eventually, both Morocco and Algeria officially recognized Berber languages, which are now taught in some schools.

Cuisines are alive, always changing, always adapting. They begin with landscape and gain layers through its people and history, with each seam in the every-growing strata adding its culinary imprint. From *tacos français* – 'French tacos', a wrap stuffed with meat or chicken, a cheesy sauce and fried potatoes – on the streets of urban Algeria and aluminium foil-wrapped triangles of cheese in the kitchen to restaurants like chef Najat Kaanache's celebrated Nur in Fès, where she draws on her training around the world to offer a highly creative approach to Morocco's seasonal bounty, the region continues to incorporate new influences, tastes and foods. Just as it has done for the past 3,000 years.

———————◇———————

Country Snapshots

———————◇———————

Morocco   Morocco has one of the world's most refined cuisines. Marked by sweet-and-savoury

combinations and spicing, it is colourful, sensual and sophisticated. Its distinction stems from a varied and fertile landscape, rich history and the long presence of a royal court. From a series of Moroccan dynasties that have ruled for more than a thousand years – including, for some centuries, also north across Spain, east to Libya and south into West Africa – the country has had four imperial cities (Marrakech, Fès, Meknès and Rabat) with vital royal kitchens. This has ensured that the finest ingredients have always been available to palace chefs, traditions upheld but innovation expected and nothing short of perfection required. In homes, artful presentation on the table is fundamental.

If cuisine is a marriage of land and history, then this one begins on the most varied ground in North Africa. Occupying the northwest corner of the continent, al-Maghrib al-Aqsa – 'the farthest Maghreb' – includes diverse landscapes that can grow the ingredients that make the cuisine of this country of 37 million stand out. Citruses, quince and melons, plums for prunes, grapes for raisins, almonds, dates. Vegetable gardens. Wheat and olives. Seafood from the Atlantic as well as the Mediterranean. Gentle pastures for livestock. But it is also home to other ingredients that elsewhere in the Maghreb are less common, such as saffron, which grows in the Anti-Atlas Mountains and makes Morocco one of the world's largest producers. Trout are farmed in Middle Atlas streams outside Azrou. Gnarled argan trees in the Anti-Atlas produce a rich oil. The pink petals of the Damask rose are used to make *ma ward*, distilled rose water, used in countless confections and desserts and even savoury dishes. The roses grow in the rugged Dadès Gorge, on the eastern slopes of the High Atlas, where they climb along stone walls, among fig and pomegranate trees and in hedges between fields of barley. Collected in the morning while their fragrance is strongest, between 3,000 and 4,000 tons of petals are gathered during April and May in the Valley of the Roses. How they first arrived in this remote valley is not known. One legend credits a merchant coming from Damascus in the twelfth century, another of local pilgrims bringing them back on the return journey from Mecca.

Morocco began to take shape a thousand years ago. After being part of a larger Islamic empire ruled from the Middle East, the far western region of the Maghreb fragmented into a patchwork of independent states that were unified with the rise of Berber dynasties from the south. From their capital Marrakech, the Almoravid (1060–1147) and Almohad (1147–1248) empires showed Morocco at its most potent, with control reaching north, south and east. (The names of the country in many languages – Morocco, Maroc, Marruecos and so on – derive from the name of the city of Marrakech.) The succeeding Berber Marinid dynasty (mid-thirteenth-century to 1465) lacked the sprawling geographic range of its predecessors but managed from its capital Fès to hold Morocco together for two centuries and also rule at times parts of Algeria and Tunisia. In the mid-sixteenth century, a local dynasty of Arab origin took control for the first time when the Saadians captured Fès in 1554. They traced their lineage back to the Prophet Muhammad, as did their successors, the Alaouites (1665–), who united a fracturing country, established a unified Moroccan state and remain in power today.

When the Marinids made Fès their capital in the mid-thirteenth century, they initiated the city's Golden Age. Fès was a crossroads and meeting place, a city where people from elsewhere settled. Over the next five or so centuries, until the French shifted the capital to Rabat in 1912, Fès exerted a dominant role in Morocco's religious, cultural and educational life. With its 9,400 streets, alleys and lanes and 40,000 dead ends, it is the greatest medieval city in the world. It is home to the oldest existing and continually operating educational institution in the world, Al-Qarawiyyin University (or Al-Karaouine), founded by 859 CE by the Tunisian-born Fatima al-Fihri. Fès also retains the reputation among Moroccans for having the highest standards of culinary arts in the country.

While the Ottoman Empire conquered the rest of North Africa, Morocco managed to keep it from expanding into its territory. The French controlled Algeria from 1830, but only gained power in Morocco much later, occupying Casablanca in 1907, then making most of the country a Protectorate in 1912.

The north and far south of Morocco were governed by Spain, while Tangier was designated an international zone. Tangier was an important commercial city, the country's diplomatic gateway and a key port on one of the world's busiest maritime routes. It was cosmopolitan and had been for centuries. Tangier, at the very northwestern edge of Africa, is a meeting point of two seas, two continents and various cultures.

France moved the country's capital to Rabat, developed ports in Casablanca and Kénitra and built a *ville nouvelle* (new town) in the major cities, often abutting the ancient walled city (the medina). The French period saw the popularity of baked morning pastries and baguettes and a new style of café culture with terraces set out on the wide boulevards of the *ville nouvelle*. Green salads common today are a French influence, as are the jams on breakfast breads.

Since independence in 1956, the country has been led by a series of monarchs – Mohammed V, Hassan II and Mohammed VI (since 1999). In 1979, Hassan II set up a cooking school on the royal palace grounds in Rabat that was run by women for palace employee daughters. It then opened to women under 25, and the Centre de Qualification Professionnelle Hôtelière et Touristique de Touarga selects a few dozen women for the two-year degree to receive rigorous training in classical Moroccan cooking: no writing or books, just preparing the dishes over and over again until perfected.

Traditional Moroccan cuisine is frequently meat-rich. While Seven Vegetable Couscous (page 194) is considered a national dish and includes seven vegetables, it is usually flavoured with bone-in meat. *Harira* (page 118), the famous silky tomato-based soup with pulses and fresh herbs eaten nightly during the holy month of Ramadan, usually has small pieces of meat in it. This can be said for numerous dishes dominated by vegetables though not vegetarian.

This isn't usually the case, though, with the assortment of fresh and cooked 'salads' that can open meals. Depending on the season, these might include jammy, caramelized tomatoes with orange blossom water, prunes and fried almonds; chilled cubes of caramelized butternut squash dusted with cinnamon; oranges segments with black olives; mashed aubergine (eggplant) *zaâlouk* (pages 87–88) with plenty of garlic, cumin and paprika; and cucumbers in a sweetened marinade and scattered with local wild oregano called *zaâtar* (see page 61). Such a variety of salads – of different colours, different flavours, different textures – is one of the country's greatest culinary traditions, offering not just a showcase for a cook's creativity but also the cuisine's originality and penchant for blending disparate ingredients.

From palaces to humble homes, though, the tagine – the name of both the succulent, slow-cooked stew braised with very little liquid and the low, terracotta pot with a conical lid where it cooks – holds pride of place at the table, and its importance to the Moroccan kitchen can hardly be overstated. Whether for a festive occasion or a midweek meal, whether a goat tagine with dried figs in the damp Rif Mountains, a chicken one with slices of preserved lemon peel cut into the shape of leaves in Marrakech or one of monkfish topped by a caramelized onion and raisin compote called *tfaya* in coastal Essaouira, the tagine lies quite literally at the heart of the family meal. When ready, the tagine is set in the centre of the table and everyone eats directly from it.

The flavours in a tagine are layered and complex and produce an aromatic stew that never fails to nourish or satisfy. It often feels that what is most important is not the pieces of lamb or chicken or fish, but the saucy goodness at the bottom of the tagine.

In the winter in the High Atlas, one delicious vegetable tagine, with wedges of quince added for its aroma and hints of sweetness, is called *tatajine douze* in Berber. *Douze* means that it is something to be eaten with bread, a fitting name for this tagine – or really any tagine. Wiping the last of those concentrated flavours from the tagine with a piece of bread is the ultimate reward.

Algeria   Blending Berber, Arabic and Ottoman influences with French, Spanish and Mediterranean ones, Algerian cuisine is an eclectic mélange of flavours and aromas, deeply original and highly satisfying. It lacks the consistent heat of Tunisia and the frequent sweet-and-savoury combinations of Morocco, yet Algerian food is certainly not bland. And while it can be robust, subtle and even frugal, it is a lively cuisine that pleases all of the senses.

Algeria is Africa's largest country. At nearly 2.4 million km²/926,000 square miles, it is four times the size of France. Algeria became a political entity in the sixteenth century under Ottoman occupation, although they only controlled the north. In the twentieth century, under French colonial rule, Algeria's borders extended south into the desert. While 80 per cent of the country is covered by the Sahara, most of the population (45 million) lives along the Mediterranean coast and in the mountainous Kabylia region to the east of Algiers.

Algeria is a land of cereal and the heartland of *kuskus* (couscous). From fish couscous in coastal Jijel, chicken couscous in Algiers with *marka baida* ('white sauce', perfumed with cinnamon) and the sauceless couscous with peas and broad (fava) beans of Kabylia, the variations of couscous on offer here are unmatched. What goes into the stew changes from season to season and house to house.

Except for when couscous is served, Algeria's other key staple is always on the table – bread. Loaves are both leaven and unleavened, with round loaves and baguettes from bakeries alongside traditional flat loaves such as pan-cooked *kesra* (semolina flatbreads, page 45), which are often prepared at home. A symbol of generosity, bread retains the highest level of respect, and is considered sacred; it is also used to pick up morsels and mop up sauces.

Algerian cuisine offers plenty of vegetables, dozens of traditional dishes with chicken and countless ones with lamb. The Mediterranean Sea plays an important role, and markets burst with seafood: tuna, rays, red mullet, mackerel, bonito in spring, sardines and anchovies with warmer weather, cuttlefish and prawns (shrimp). Snails are popular in the north, especially Oran. Eggs are devoured frequently, often in a range of straightforward omelettes with seasonal produce. Fried potatoes (Frites, page 164) top stews, stuff sandwiches and are made into an omelette that is a comforting classic eaten in a baguette. While Tunisian harissa has become a favourite condiment across Algeria, the country has its own distinctive chilli (chile) paste, *dersa* (page 441), made by pounding fresh or dried chillies (or even a spoonful of cayenne pepper), a number of cloves of garlic, cumin or caraway and salt in a mortar, and used as a base for sauces and marinades.

Chorba (soup) could be considered a national dish. From *chorba hamra* ('red', with tomatoes, page 123) to *chorba baida* ('white', without tomatoes, often with turnips and courgettes/zucchini and a generous pinch of cinnamon, page 124) and about everything in between, there are enough soups to have a different one each night for weeks.

Usually served alongside *chorba* is another emblem of the Algerian kitchen, savoury stuffed *bourek* pastries (pages 56–57). The most popular filling is meat and onion, seasoned with cinnamon and blended with some egg. While a legacy of the Ottoman period, *bourek* are made with *diouls*, paper-thin cooked sheets of pastry that give *boureks* their lovely flakiness when fried.

The Ottoman era in Algeria lasted over three centuries. There were, though, some pockets of exception to their rule. Oran was founded in the tenth century by Moorish Andalusian traders on a wide crescent of the Mediterranean at the closest point between Spain and Algeria. It was ruled by Berber and Muslim dynasties until 1509, when the Spanish gained control for the next nearly three hundred years. Even after Algeria was a French colony, Spanish outnumbered French in this sun-lit port city of long boulevards and whitewashed buildings, nicknamed 'The Radiant'. The Spanish left a distinct imprint on the city's food, as is clear in the names of numerous dishes, including rabbit *frita* (ragoût with peppers, page 308, from the Spanish for 'fried') and cut-out cookies known in much of Algeria as *halwat tabaa* ('cookie cutter sweet', page 373) but in Oran called *tornos* from the Spanish 'to turn' (as in a lathe).

Oran is also the home to *calentica* (or *karantika*, Chickpea Flour Tart, page 66), a simple, soft tart made with chickpea (garbanzo bean) flour that is the country's iconic street food. The story of its origin dates to the 1500s, when Spanish soldiers besieged the Santa Cruz Fort that overlooks Oran. Told by the governor to make something for the starving group, the cook pounded chickpeas to powder, mixed it with water and baked it in the oven. He then warned the famished soldiers to wait a moment, supposedly saying *Está caliente* ('It's hot.') A variant stuck as a name, and a barely modified version of the dish – usually chickpea flour, olive oil, salt and water – eventually became the country's most beloved snack. Generations of school kids have eaten this snack during the mid-morning break or later in the day. Thicker than the *socca* of Nice, *calentica* has two distinct layers of texture – a firmer bottom one with a creamy, flan-like one at the top – and a blackened, gratinated surface. Baked in large sheet pans, *calentica* is sold in slices, either alone on a sheet of paper or filling a foot-long portion of baguette. These get a generous sprinkling of cumin and salt and often a drizzle of diluted harissa.

Around the country, creamy delicacies like *mhalbi* (Rice Flour Pudding with Pistachios, page 380), *palouza* (Milk Pudding, page 382) and flan with orange blossom water are popular, and home kitchens usually have cookies and sweetmeats on trays for visitors. Algerians retain a devotion to traditional confectionery. Among the most adored sticky treats are *makrout* (semolina cookies filled with date paste, cut into diamond-shaped lozenges, fried and dipped into warm honey, page 362), gazelle horns filled with orange blossom water-scented almond paste (page 366) and triangular *samsa* pastries stuffed with almonds (page 352). These are often served between meals with tea or coffee, or for guests.

Meals end with fresh fruit. The country's orchards are bountiful with apricots and peaches, apples and pears, melons and watermelons, figs, cherries, strawberries, pomegranates, quince and plenty of oranges. The citrus industry is substantial – Algeria produces over 1.5 million tons of citrus a year. The oranges of Boufarik, southwest of Algiers, are particularly famous, while Algeria's clementines – first bred in the early twentieth century in Oran – are duly celebrated. And, of course, there are Algeria's legendary dates that are grown in the south. The main date-producing regions are the province of Biskra, on the northern cusp of the Sahara, and El Oued, near the Tunisian border, where date palms grow (as the popular saying goes) with their feet in water and heads in the sun.

Algeria is typically the fourth or fifth largest producer of dates in the world, harvesting over 1 million tons of soft, translucent deglet nour, *ghars* and hundreds of other varieties of dates a year, but only a small percentage is exported because local demand is so high. They are a staple as well as a symbol, offered to guests and eaten first when breaking the fast during Ramadan. Dates also get stuffed with almond paste and are served as a rich delicacy; halved and used to decorate mounds of sweet couscous; or mashed to a paste, seasoned and used to fill various types of semolina cookies.

French rule in Algeria began in 1830, and in 1962, after eight years of fighting, Algeria gained independence. There was an exodus of Algerian-born Europeans and Sephardic Jews, who settled largely along the French Mediterranean, carrying with them the unique blend of flavours from Algeria.

Ultimately, the culinary influences from the French in Algeria are relatively limited. Potatoes were grown on a large scale during the French period, and Algeria has a love of frites today. Also, neighbourhood patisseries place incredible attention on the design and display of both traditional Algerian pastries and those introduced under the French like croissants, éclairs and *pain au chocolat*. Both styles are prepared with equal patience and attention to detail.

Tunisia In between Algeria and Libya, halfway across Africa's Mediterranean crown, nearly equidistant from the Atlantic and the Nile, Tunisia is the smallest country in the Maghreb. It has long functioned as a crossroads for disparate worlds, with influences and ingredients arriving by sea, overland and on caravans across the Sahara. What is found in the kitchens and on the plates of this country of 12 million is an eloquent (and often spicy) recounting of that cosmopolitan past and bountiful land.

Over the centuries, the country's 1,150-km-/ 715-mile-long coastline and fertile land have attracted waves of conquerors; each left a fresh layer on Tunisia's original Berber culinary foundation. For centuries, it was the centre of a string of ancient empires that ruled the western Mediterranean.

The Phoenicians founded nearly every significant port in southern Europe and North Africa, and Tunisia was home to Carthage, the greatest port of them all, and which became an empire. The Romans sacked and then rebuilt Carthage, making it the capital of the largest of the Roman provinces in North Africa, Africa Proconsularis.

During the Roman era, farmers cultivated wheat, olives and grape vines, and workers built countless roads with posts marking every thousand paces, bridges and aqueducts, and numerous cities. The most impressive of these was the Zaghouan Aqueduct that carried some 30 million litres/66 million gallons of water a day to Carthage from the springs of Zaghouan 132 km/82 miles away. During the first century of the modern era, these plains supplied 60 per cent of Rome's grain requirement. They produced more olive oil than Italy and nearly as much wine. Prosperous and peaceful, the region drew settlers and retired soldiers from across the vast Roman Empire,

many of whom turned to farming. The province eventually gifted its name to the entire continent.

When Arab troops swept across the Maghreb in the seventh century, they made their first permanent settlement at Kairouan, 160 km/100 miles south of Carthage, then under control of the Byzantine Empire. Kairouan became an important centre of Islamic learning and is widely considered the fourth holiest city in the Muslim world. (Seven pilgrimages to Kairouan's Great Mosque – founded in 670, it's the oldest mosque in the Maghreb – is considered to be the equivalent of one pilgrimage to Mecca.) After conquering Carthage in 698, Arabs established themselves in the small nearby settlement of Tunis, developing it into the country's most important city. They called the province Ifrīkiya.

At the core of Tunis's ancient medina is the Al-Zaytuna Mosque ('Olive Tree Mosque'), with its vast courtyard and stone-pillared hall. The souqs (markets), radiate outwards by guild: the trades such as perfumers, booksellers and spicemongers are housed under vaulted roofs near the mosque; others are on the edges of the medieval city and along the outside of ancient walls. In the peripheries, open doors reveal craftsmen tapping brass plates with pin-headed hammers or soldering ornate serving trays or teapots; the smell of scorched metals, sweet sawdust and freshly cured leather lingers in the air.

Found in the medina's quiet lanes are the building blocks of the cuisine. Tubs of olives and preserved lemons bump against cans of *double concentré* tomato purée (paste), bonito tuna and pickled vegetables, bottles of olive oil that glow lemony-yellow and emerald green and orange blossom water. Mounds of caraway, cumin and coriander seeds. Wreaths of garlic and dried red chillies (chiles) dangle over baskets of lentils, couscous in various sizes and numerous shapes of pasta, dried fruits and dark roasted Arabica coffee beans.

Located in the heart of the Mediterranean, Tunisia is the most Mediterranean country in Africa. With the exception of Kairouan, its main cities are on the sea. From the northeast, the Cap Bon peninsula juts towards Sicily, 140 km/87 miles away. Between Tunisia and Sicily runs the Strait of Sicily. Dividing the western Mediterranean Sea from the eastern Mediterranean, it is one of the richest and most important fishing grounds in the region. Fleets of Tunisian trawlers go after anchovies, sardines, hake, bream and tuna, octopus, cuttlefish and squid, and prawns (shrimp). From seafood salads and fried red mullet to cracked barley soup with octopus and couscous with grouper, the sea's bounty is more dominant on Tunisian tables than elsewhere in the Maghreb.

There are many shared hallmarks between the cuisine on the Italian side of the Strait and the Tunisian one, including an abundance of olive oil, tomatoes, garlic, capers, lemons and pasta. Tunisians eat the second most amount of pasta in the world behind Italians, although its pasta dishes are far from Italian copies. Other dishes on the Tunisian table always have their own unique accents: whole roasted fish with tomatoes, but also black olives, wild capers from hills in the north and pungent preserved lemons in a stunning dish called *kabkabou*; or even freshly squeezed lemonade which gets puréed with fresh mint leaves before being strained into glasses (page 430).

The most distinct accent in Tunisian cuisine comes from the omnipresent chilli paste called harissa. Robust and spicy, there is a nutty, pungent earthiness behind the heat from garlic, caraway, coriander and often cumin. Few savoury dishes in Tunisia seem complete without a spoonful or two (or more) of harissa. Home cooks stir it into couscous broth, fish soups and tomato sauce for pasta, add it to cooked 'salads' made from roasted peppers or boiled carrots, and slather it on sardines and red mullet. Tuna-stuffed *fricassé* sandwiches (page 51) sold on the street get a generous dollop, as do bowls of *lablabi* (page 147), the widely popular dish of chickpeas (garbanzo beans) served over pieces of day-old bread and topped with an egg and flakes of canned tuna. Harissa is often added as a condiment: there is usually a dish of it on the table.

From Cap Bon – home to the country's harissa and tomato production – Tunisia's coast makes an abrupt turn south, giving it a second face to the Mediterranean. Here are the famous olive groves along the Tunisian Sahel ('seashore'). Despite the low rainfall, the heavy dew from the Mediterranean is enough to cultivate olives without irrigation.

Along the Sahel on the Gulf of Gabès is Sfax, the country's second city, with its fleet of fishing boats that head out at dusk, bringing in a quarter of Tunisia's catch. (The area also produces about 40 per cent of its olive oil and 30 per cent of its almonds.) Ferries from Sfax frequently cross to the Kerkennah Islands, a string of seven low-lying islands well known for octopus (both fresh and dried) and fish stews. Drawing on their knowledge of local sea currents and the topography of offshore shallows, Kerkennah fisherman still practise a traditional method of fishing called *charfia*. Using an intricate system of palm fronds embedded in the seabed, they create a series of traps that block fish – sea bream are the main catch – from exiting once they are brought in by the tide. Each June, the traps are raised and rebuilt in autumn.

Further down the gulf, past ancient Gabès and close to the Libyan border, is Djerba. At roughly 500 km²/200 square miles, it is the largest island in North Africa. The squarish-shaped island is tethered to the mainland by a 6-km-/4-mile-long causeway that dates back to the Roman era. Moist sea breezes and a network of underground wells make the fields bountiful, and farmers cultivate pomegranates, sweet grapes, figs, grenadines, apricots, date palms and hundreds of thousands of olive trees. Farmhouses and whitewashed mosques with square-topped minarets are scattered sparsely among the fields and orchards. The dry, dusty sirocco winds that blow from the Sahara can appear at a moment's notice, filling the horizon with a golden glow and covering every surface with fine grit.

Inland from the fertile southern coast, the land becomes arid and gives way to *chotts* (salt flats) and then the desert, with oases and extensive *palmeraies* (palm groves) fed by artesian springs producing dates along the northern fringes of the Sahara. This part of the country is the Djerid (fully Bled el Djerid, 'Land of Palms'). 'Date palms form a large and dark massif around the city', wrote the eleventh-century Arab-Andalusian historian and geographer al-Bakri of Tozeur, one of the region's important oases. 'There is no other place in Ifrīkiya that produces so many dates; almost every day a thousand camels, or even more, are loaded with this fruit.' Today the sprawling palmeraie of Tozeur contains 400,000 date palms and is famous for its deglet nour dates. The name means 'finger of light' because of their appearance when held up to the sun. The amber-coloured, nearly translucent variety that may have originated in Algeria has a soft texture and honey-like taste. Deglet nour account for three-quarters of Tunisia's production.

Unlike Algeria, Tunisia exports most of its dates. While the country harvests only around 3 per cent of the global production, Tunisia is the world's leading date exporter in value. A thousand years ago, according to al-Bakri, Tozeur's dates reached Al-Andalus and Egypt. Today they reach much further.

Libya The name 'Libya' comes from the Egyptian (and Berber) term 'Libu', indicating the region west of the Nile. The ancient Greeks referred to Berbers as Libyans and the Romans used the word to describe Africans living in Carthage's territories. The name then fell out of favour until the Italians resurrected it in the 1920s, when they formally linked the provinces they ruled into one colony named Libya. The shape of the modern nation took form, and the name stuck.

Libya has a 1,770-km-/1,100-mile-long Mediterranean coastline between Tunisia and Egypt, with borders that run far south into the Sahara. At 1.7 million km²/655,000 square miles, or three times the size of France, the country is large. But 93 per cent is desert or semi-desert. It is largely a flat, undulating plain. The small percentage of arable land is on the Jifara Plain, a semi-circular area equally split between northwestern Libya and eastern Tunisia, and in the Jebel Akhdar region near Benghazi in the east. The low Jebel Nafusa range southwest of Tripoli is known for its apricots, figs, almonds and olives, and goats.

Tripoli is home to nearly half of the country's 7 million people. Founded by Phoenicians on a rocky point of land in the seventh century BCE, it has been an important city under a succession of rulers. During the sixteenth century, Tripoli was controlled by the Spanish and then the Knights of St John from Malta, who were ousted by the Ottomans in 1551. Ottoman rule lasted until 1911, followed by Italian control until 1943. Independence, with King Idris on the throne, came in 1951.

The first oil wells pumped in 1960, transforming Libya into a wealthy monarchy with a fast-growing economy. At the end of the 1960s, the king was overthrown by a small, shadowy group of military officers led by the young Muammar Gaddafi, who converted it to an Islamic socialist state and ruled for over four decades, until his 2011 ousting and death during the Arab Spring uprising.

Tripoli sat at the end of three major trans-Saharan routes, linking Timbuktu, Lake Chad and the south with the Mediterranean. One key stop on the route was Ghadames, the great oasis and caravan town 550 km/340 miles southwest of Tripoli, near Libya's border with Algeria. Known as the Pearl of the Desert, Ghadames was a centre of the medieval trans-Saharan trade that peaked between the thirteenth and sixteenth centuries.

Along with the traditional staples of grains, olive oil, dates and milk, Libya's cuisine draws on the sea as well as the land. It is generally spicy, with fresh green chillies (chiles) often adding extra heat. Two spice blends dominate. One is called *bzaar* (page 446), with significant amounts of turmeric combined with cinnamon, black pepper, ginger, coriander, caraway, clove, ginger-like galangal and occasionally nutmeg. *Hararat* is similar, though less dominated by turmeric. While there is overlap, home cooks sometimes add both blends to the same dish.

Favourite ways to begin a meal include stuffed vegetables, filled potato wedges called *m'battan* and, in summer, a chunky, juicy tomato and onion salad eaten with plenty of bread. In autumn, pomegranate seeds moistened with orange blossom water often come at the beginning or end of a meal. Flaky filled *bourek* pastries are popular and spicy, lamb-based *shorbas* (soups) with onions, tomatoes and small pasta are beloved. Cooks usually stir in parsley and dried mint at the end and serve the *shorba* with lemon wedges. The typical version is so popular that it is considered a national dish and called *shorba libiya*, 'Libyan soup' (page 127).

Couscous remains a Friday staple and stands out for the quantity of onions used. *Busla* (page 203) is the name of the onion and chickpea (garbanzo bean) topping frequently spooned on before serving. Pasta dishes tend to be one-pot and usually spicy. The pasta is boiled in the sauce rather than in water and then tossed with the sauce.

The abundance of pasta is the most obvious legacy of four decades as an Italian colony. In 1911, Italy, desiring more power in the Mediterranean, declared war on the Ottoman Empire and invaded Tripoli. After a year of fighting, the Ottomans surrendered control to the Italians. After two decades, the Italians gained control of the country. Benito Mussolini called Libya Italy's Quarta Sponda ('Fourth Shore').

In October 1938, a group of 20,000 Italian settlers (known as *ventimilli*) were brought to Libya in a single convoy. By 1940, over 100,000 Italians had settled in Libya, about 12 per cent of the population. While olives had been growing since antiquity, most of the groves today date from the large agricultural settlements created by Italians in the 1930s. Gaddafi protected the olive trees and forbid cutting them down.

As elsewhere in the Maghreb, lamb is the meat of choice, while fish and seafood are also popular. Fish is often grilled or marinated and cooked in a sauce of garlic, parsley, onion and tomatoes. Cumin is the spice most associated with fish – dusted on before grilling or stirred into the stew or sauce during cooking.

Since ancient times, the Gulf of Sirte has been an important tuna fishing ground. Libyan fishermen also catch red mullet, breams and groupers in their nets. While most of the fishing boats are gillnetters, there is a fleet of lampara fishing boats in the western gulf towards the Tunisian border. In a method of fishing that dates back 2,000 years, *dhgaissa* (lamp boats) with bright lights mounted on them illuminate the sea's surface to attract shoals of sardines, anchovies, mackerel and a large-eyed variety of bream known as boops boops or (in Libyan Arabic) *bougah*.

Meals often end with fruit. Watermelons and melons, grapes, apricots, peaches, strawberries, nectarines and citrus fruits became more plentiful in the markets in the early 1990s with the ambitious Great Man-Made River project that taps underground reservoirs of water in the desert and pipes it north for drinking water and irrigation. Dates from the oases are deeply important.

Confections and sticky, honey-rich pastries are as popular as elsewhere in the region. One local treat is *abambar*, a macaroon cookie with bitter almonds (page 370). And coffee is deeply entrenched in the culture. Especially in the south, *shay* – strong, sweet tea – is also commonplace. Ceremonial Libyan tea (page 424) is known for the foamy head made from pouring the tea back and forth between a couple of mugs dozens of times. There are traditionally three rounds served in small glasses. For that third round, whole almonds or peanuts are often added to the glass.

Couscous

If a single item on the table can bind the region it is couscous, an emblem of shared heritage. Couscous is more than a meal. It is an ancient and important tradition, a symbol of culture and a deep point of pride that shows no sign of losing popularity.

Couscous is both the name for the small dried 'grains' or granules, as well as the name of the dish. The name borrows from the Maghrebi Arabic *kuskus*, derived from the Berber (or Amazigh) word *seksu* (or *keskesu*). Some historians say the original Berber meaning was 'well rolled', while others believe *seksu* comes from the sound steam makes coming through the cooking grains, or that of the fingers winnowing and raking in a circular motion when rolling dry ones.

Associated with the area's original inhabitants, couscous predates the nation states that form the Maghreb. Utensils similar to those used in preparing couscous have been found in tombs from the reign of Masinissa, a powerful Berber king and ally of Rome in the Second Punic War (218–201 BCE) against the Phoenicians. Berbers likely began making couscous using barley, millet and sorghum flour before hard durum wheat became the predominant cereal to grind and roll into dry granules. It was an ingenious method that utilized the steam of the stew, also imparting flavour to the couscous grains.

Neither constrained by class nor geography, couscous is found from urban centres to rural hamlets, from the mountains to the desert, and from high-rise apartments and humble homes to palatial kitchens. In Morocco and Libya, eating couscous after midday Friday prayers is an important tradition. In Algeria, Friday or Saturday couscous is typical, while for many in Tunisia Sunday is the most common day to prepare the family couscous.

Couscous is also a celebratory dish, served at weddings and holidays, though it is also prepared in times of mourning. At Algiers weddings, for instance, guests traditionally get couscous with a sauce that includes lamb and plenty of turnips. In Berber weddings in northern Morocco's Rif

Mountains, sweet couscous usually follows meat tagines. In Tunisia, it is customary to offer newly-weds couscous (in Nabeul, at the edge of Cap Bon, the couscous is adorned with sweets/candies, candied almonds and hard-boiled eggs), while three days after a death, couscous is prepared with freshly butchered lamb and chickpeas (garbanzo beans).

Shop- or market-bought couscous now dominates pantries, and fewer people hand roll the grains themselves any longer. Hand rolling is done using two sizes of (usually) semolina (milled durum wheat) sprinkled with water and salt, then rolled to form tiny granules. These are separated and sieved to uniform size and then spread out to dry in the sun.

While the couscous might now be shop-bought, the manner of cooking it remains little changed. The grains are moistened with water and oil, then steamed two or three times in the perforated basket of a couscoussier above a pot of simmering sauce. Between steamings, the couscous is dumped into a wide dish, any lumps broken up and the grains moistened with cool water. The final results are light, fluffy grains that are tender though not mushy, and they remain individual and separate from each other. Mounded on a platter, steamed couscous is drizzled with broth and topped with vegetables and meat or fish.

There are as many couscous recipes as there are households, reflecting the landscape, the season and a family's economic resources. While nearly all include seasonal vegetables and often a handful of chickpeas, the meat varies. Lamb is the most popular, but goat, beef and even, in the south of the Maghreb, camel can be found. Chicken is also common and, along the coast, fish and octopus, while some communities top couscous with stewed snails. There are complex versions with dozens of ingredients, but also sauceless ones. The most famous of these is *mesfouf* from Algeria's Kabylia region with fresh peas and broad (fava) beans and sometimes raisins, drizzled with deep-green olive oil from the area's groves and served with *lben* (buttermilk).

There are also popular sweetened versions of couscous, too, with honey or icing (confectioners') sugar and topped with dried fruits, dates and nuts. Sweet couscous can be a snack, dessert or even in Morocco follow a tagine. A mound of sweet couscous can also be part of the *suhur* breakfast before beginning a day's fast during Ramadan. Some like to moisten it with milk. One rustic favourite is *seikouk*, barley couscous with chilled *lben* poured over the top.

Regional differences with couscous reside less in the steamed grains or methods of preparing than in the flavourings of the stew.

To generalize, Algerian couscous is robust, replete with vegetables – turnips, carrots, courgettes (zucchini), pumpkin, potatoes – and seasoned with a relatively limited array of spices. Lamb might be considered king of meats here, but chicken couscous is common and fish couscous widely popular along the coast. The sauce is often red from tomatoes (and sometimes tomato purée/paste) but there are popular 'white' versions with onions, turnips and courgettes and seasoned with cinnamon and occasionally a touch of freshly grated nutmeg. Algerian cooks often use a more generous hand when adding butter or olive oil to the steamed grains before topping with sauce.

Moroccan couscous often includes complex spice flavourings, blending saffron or turmeric, ginger, cinnamon, sweet paprika and cumin, and sometimes sweetness from dried fruits. The sweetest of toppings is *tfaya* (page 208), a lush, caramelized onion and raison compote spooned over the top when serving.

Couscous in Tunisia always has a red broth from the double concentrated tomato purée liberally stirred into the sauce, and a bite of heat from added fiery harissa chilli (chile) paste. A dish of harissa always comes alongside to add more as desired. One difference to their neighbours is how Tunisians liberally soak the steamed grains with sauce before mounding it on the platter and arranging the other elements from the stew on top. Especially inland, lamb couscous is typical, but couscous with fish or octopus is common. In fact, many would call couscous with grouper a national dish in Tunisia.

In western Libya, couscous has chunks of lamb, beef or, in the south, camel to help flavour the sauce. Fish couscous is also very popular along the coast. Libyan versions tend to be spicy, often use a lot of onions and frequently include some potatoes. One distinctive and favourite addition before serving is *busla* (page 203), a topping of onions and chickpeas with cinnamon and cloves.

Beginning with the first wave of immigration after World War I, the Maghrebi diaspora carried their beloved staple with them to Europe and beyond. With Algeria's independence in 1962, around one million Algerian-born Europeans and Sephardic Jews settled largely in southern France, bringing a keen taste for the dish. By the end of the twentieth century, couscous had become a favourite food in France.

But couscous had previously travelled north. The first mention of couscous comes in *The Anonymous Andalusian Cookbook* from the thirteenth century. So common was the dish at the time that the author did not even give a recipe for the standard version, and simply wrote: 'The usual moistened couscous is known by the whole world.'

In December 2020, UNESCO inscribed the 'knowledge, know-how and practices related to the production and consumption of couscous' to its list of Intangible Cultural Heritage. Traditionally, the know-how for preparing couscous was passed down orally by women, a transmission considered 'intangible'.

Couscous is a sign of hospitality and generosity, meeting and sharing. It brings families and friends, neighbours and even communities together.

Arabesque

North Africa has a highly developed sense of visual artistic expression, with a long tradition of arabesque – geometrically repeating and interlacing patterns with elaborate detail and bold colours used for decoration – and in the flowing forms in Arabic calligraphy. These emerged in part from Islam's prohibition of figurative depictions. Such design is integrated into architecture and community life, and found in mosques and palaces, on glazed tiles, pottery and jewellery, in carpets and so on.

From constantly being surrounded by such patterns, home cooks have effectively internalized and often subconsciously extended such ornamentation to the kitchen and presentation of the food. The pattern is used to align stuffed dates on the plate, place a fried almond at the precise centre of each piece of square-cut

basbousa semolina cake (page 375) or decorate a mound of sweet couscous with perfect lines of cinnamon. 'First we eat with our eyes,' goes the fitting expression.

Islam and Food

Islam plays a fundamental role in the culinary traditions and dietary habits of North Africa. And food plays an essential part in the celebrations of Muslim holidays. The Islamic (or Hijri) calendar is lunar, alternating months of 29 and 30 days that begin with each new moon. On the (solar) Gregorian calendar (the most widely used one in the world today), the year is about 11 days longer than on the Islamic one, which means that most Islamic holidays shift ahead that amount each year on the Gregorian calendar.

According to Islamic dietary guidelines, Muslims can only eat permitted food, called halal. Most meat is halal if the animal is slaughtered in the manner as prescribed in the Qur'an. Pork is forbidden, or haram. Alcohol – including cooking food with wine – is also forbidden.

Ramadan   The holy month of Ramadan marks the time when the Qur'an was revealed to the Prophet Muhammad. Muslims refrain from eating, drinking and smoking between sunrise and sunset during this period. As one of the five pillars of the Islamic faith, fasting (*sawn*) during Ramadan is an obligatory act for all of those who are able. (The elderly, children, pregnant women, people who are ill and those travelling are not required to fast.) Fasting teaches self-discipline, shows obedience to God and atoning for one's sins and errors, while the feeling of hunger helps to develop compassion for the less fortunate. During this period, communities feel closer as they celebrate the collective experience.

While Ramadan is a time of spiritual renewal and reflection, contemplation and celebration, it is also a month-long culinary extravaganza. Kitchens are busy. Culinary skills are exhibited and traditional dishes reign supreme. The pantry is stocked with dates, dried fruit and nuts, semolina, sugar and other staples in advance. Special tableware is used for Ramadan, while the house is thoroughly cleaned in preparation. Markets are crowded all month, as people place an emphasis on what they put into their shopping baskets and on their tables. It is a time when the main ingredients for popular dishes such as soups are piled in larger stacks, and a wider selection of breads can be found.

Walking around in the late afternoon, the smell of cooking emanates from homes as people need to have the meals on the table before it is time to break the fast. As in much of the Muslim world, North Africans follow the example of Muhammad and break the fast with dates and a glass of milk or *lben* (buttermilk), or water or juice. Soothing on the empty stomach, dates are easy to digest, quickly restore blood sugar and quell the initial pangs of hunger. Dates are generally eaten in odd numbers (one, three or five).

The *iftar* (or *ftour*) meal follows. It is a festive moment and moods are high. As the popular local expression goes, 'When the stomach is full it commands the head to sing.' While dishes vary from home to home, there are some regional favourites.

In Algeria, the *iftar* meal usually starts with a bowl of *chorba*, a thick soup with herbs and tomatoes plus *frik* (freekeh, roasted and coarsely ground green wheat), small pieces of pasta or barley. The soup is easy on the stomach and helps prepare the body for the large meal that follows. Alongside the *chorba* are stuffed and fried *bourek* pastries, salads, and then the main course, which can be just about anything, although couscous is rare. On the first day of Ramadan, many Algerian families prepare a sweet, aromatic lamb dish with prunes and dried apricots. Plenty of sweet desserts follow. Date-filled Semolina Cookies (*makrout*, page 362) and fried, floral-shaped cookies soaked in honey (*griwach*, page 374) are two Ramadan classics. While Algerians drink coffee, mint tea (pages 417–421) frequently accompanies these sweetmeats.

Soup also kicks off the *iftar* in Tunisia, followed by *brick*, a filled triangular pastry – classically with tuna, potato, parsley and a fresh egg – quickly fried until golden. (It is tricky to fry so that the pastry is crispy and the egg perfectly runny, and even trickier at first to eat without getting egg yolk all over.) These are the two givens of the Tunisian *iftar*, although sometimes a baked frittata-like *tajine* (page 177) replaces the *brick*. The main course has more variety. Dishes range from pasta in tomato sauce to sautéed cuttlefish with peas (but rarely couscous). For desserts, one beloved creamy pudding is *assida zgougou* made from Aleppo pine nuts (page 387). With trays of different sweetmeats comes mint tea with a few pine nuts dropped into it (page 418) or cups of strong coffee.

In Libya, following the dates and milk, families eat a selection of starters – *boureks*, *dolma*, *m'battan* (stuffed and fried potato wedges, page 164), small pizzas, stuffed buns, and so on – with soup followed by a main dish that, on the first day of Ramadan, is often fresh *rechta* pasta (page 231) topped with lamb and plenty of steamed onions.

In Morocco, by far the most famous Ramadan dish is *harira* (page 118), a nourishing tomato- and vegetable-based soup loaded with pulses, fresh herbs and spices and thickened with flour to give it a characteristic silky texture. Many home cooks prepare it most evenings during the month of Ramadan. This is served with honey-dipped *chebakia* pastries. Joining *harira* are plenty of replenishing liquids – tea and coffee, milk, juices and fruit purées thickened with avocado. There are hard-boiled eggs to be dipped into ground cumin, fresh cheeses, and marmalades and honey to eat with various breads. Typical breads include puffed, pitta bread-like rounds (*batbout*, page 40), layered *msemen* (page 65) flatbread cooked in a frying pan and crumbly, unleavened *harsha* (page 46) made with fine semolina, butter and milk. Among the favourite sweets are hard, biscotti-like *fekkas* (page 370), *briouat bel louz* (Honeyed Triangles Stuffed with Almonds, page 352) and *sellou* (or *sfouf*) (page 357) made with roasted flour and ground nuts and eaten with a spoon.

Moroccans often break the meal there, head to the mosque, go for a stroll, sit in cafés, browse the shops that have reopened and so on, returning to the table for a late dinner. Depending on the time of year that Ramadan falls, this is between 10 p.m. and 1 a.m., and it might include salads and starters, a hearty tagine of fish, chicken or lamb, and plenty of fruit.

Then, after a few hours of sleep, it's time to eat again. People across North Africa rise in the predawn darkness for a light meal. According to the Qur'an, eating is permitted 'until the white thread of dawn becomes distinct to you from the black thread of night'. The meal before the day's fast commences is called *suhur*, literally 'of the dawn'. When Ramadan falls in summer, the days are long and often hot, and the fast can lasts for up to 16 hours in North Africa. The *suhur* usually includes various types of breads, pastries, sometimes thick *assida* porridge and always plenty of juices to hydrate the body for the fast ahead. While couscous might be absent from the evening meal, sweet couscous is a popular *suhur* dish across the region. The steamed couscous grains get tossed with melted butter and sugar, topped with nuts, raisins and often dates and served with glasses of *lben* (buttermilk) or milk. When pomegranates are in season, these are also sometimes added.

The last meal before fasting is considered a blessed one, as the Qu'ran says: 'Eat *suhur*, for in *suhur* there is blessing.'

The last week of Ramadan is a busy time for shopping for gifts and new clothes (which kids must save until Eid to wear), for performing acts of charity (called *zakat*; one of the five pillars of Islam) and for baking for the impending guests during the Eid al-Fitr holiday that follows.

Eid al-Fitr   Following the end of Ramadan is the multi-day Eid al-Fitr celebration. People travel home to be with family, they dress up, give gifts and visit friends and relatives.

Eid al-Fitr is the time to pay social calls. The abundance of these visits means plenty of cookies and pastries, whether bought from the bakery or made at home in the days leading up to Eid. Visits tend to be short, as it is important to wish *all* your family, friends and relatives a happy Eid in person. Every visit means offering – or being offered – a glass of mint tea, coffee or juice along with an array of sweet indulgences. From the crescent-shaped, almond paste-filled *kaab el ghazal* (Gazelle Horns, page 366) to the date-stuffed *makrout* semolina cookies (page 362), the list of options is long and the trays always piled high. Visitors are often sent on their way with a box of these treats to enjoy later. In Tunisia, the first big meal of Eid is frequently *mulukhiya* (page 159), made from dried and ground mallow, and a vegetable-laden soup with small, wiry twists of *hlalem* pasta (page 231).

Eid al-Adha   About two months after Ramadan, the region celebrates Eid al-Adha, which means 'feast of the sacrifice', one of the most important holidays on the Muslim calendar. (It is sometimes called Eid al-Kabir, or 'the great feast'.) It commemorates God testing the faith of Ibrahim by commanding him to sacrifice his son, Ismail. As Ibrahim was about to kill his son, God stopped him and gave him a lamb to sacrifice instead.

Today, many families butcher a sheep – or goat, cow or, in the deep south, camel – for Eid. (One-third of the meat should be donated to the poor.) Cooks first prepare the offal (variety or organ meats): the heart, liver, tripe and more, including brain (generally cooked in tomato sauce). Over the next few days, various lamb dishes grace festive tables, from grilled cuts to slow-cooked stews. In many Moroccan families, *boulfaf* (seasoned cubes of lamb liver individually wrapped in caul fat before being threaded onto a skewer, page 281) is prepared on the first day of Eid, followed on the next days by *mrouzia* (Spicy Honeyed Lamb with Raisins and Almonds, page 256), grilled lamb chops or skewers of marinated leg of lamb. Tunisians traditionally prepare part of the lamb to use during the year. The ribs are the most common to season with spices and salt and hang out to dry in the sun.

Islamic New Year   The Islamic (or Hijri) New Year is celebrated on the first day of the month of Muharram. In Tunisia, where it is called the Ras el-Am holiday, many eat the viscous, deep-green *mulukhiya* (Simmered Mallow, page 159), as green is the colour associated with Islam. Another dish associated with the day is couscous with *kaddid* (seasoned, salted and air-dried meat, see page 206) and dried broad (fava) beans garnished with hard-boiled eggs.

Yennayer, the Berber (Amazigh) New Year
Yennayer celebrations take place on 12–13 January to mark the beginning of the Berber (Amazigh) calendar. (Yennayer lends its name to the year's first month.) The ancient holiday celebrates abundance and nature's generosity. Among the dishes typically prepared are couscous with plenty of vegetables, thick soups with dried broad (fava) beans and wheat, and stewed chicken. Baskets of nuts and sweets are plentiful. These foods embody hope for a fruitful and prosperous year ahead.

Mawlid al-Nabi: Birthday of the Prophet Muhammad The twelfth day of the third month on the Islamic calendar is the birthday of the Prophet Muhammad. For breakfast, people across North Africa eat *assida* (see page 242), a thick, pasty dish prepared with cooked semolina. Served mounded in a communal bowl, a piece is pinched off with the fingers and dipped in butter or olive oil and sweetened with honey, sugar or *ruub* (date syrup). In Tunisia, cooks often prepare *assida zgougou*, a creamy, dark pudding made from Aleppo pine nuts (page 387). Especially in eastern Algeria, fried fritters called *sfenj* (page 361) are typical, while many Algerian families prepare chicken with turnips and chickpeas (garbanzo beans). A sweet dish of toasted semolina, honey and butter called *tamina* (or *taknetta*) (page 356) is also common. In Morocco, a beef or chicken tagine with prunes and almonds is a popular choice to prepare for the family.

Languages

Arabic is the official language of North Africa. Modern Standard Arabic is used for writing, in the media and government. The spoken vernacular is significantly different. Maghrebi (or Western) Arabic – called Darija or Derja – borrows from the various cultural layers that have influenced the region over the years, including Berber, Latin, Turkish and French. Each country has its own dialect – Moroccan Arabic, Algerian Arabic, Tunisian Arabic and Libyan Arabic. (Tunisians also call theirs Tounsi.) These are largely understood among Maghrebis, but not necessarily to those in Egypt or the Middle East who speak Mashriqi (or Eastern) Arabic.

Transliterating Arabic into the written Latin alphabet generates numerous difficulties. Variances in spelling occur because words can be transliterated in different ways. Transliteration in North Africa generally follows a French phonetic system. For this book, the spelling of Maghrebi words tries to best reflect not just pronunciation but also what one commonly finds in books, online, and on menus, signs and packaging.

There are also many who speak one of the Berber (Amazigh) languages or their dialects. Morocco and Algeria have the largest number of speakers, with some pockets in Tunisia (in Djerba and Matmata in the south) and in Libya (Jebel Nefoussa, a mountain range in the northwest). The region's main European language is French, while some Spanish and Italian are used. English has become increasingly important for a new generation of North Africans.

Icon Legend

Vegetarian

Vegan

Dairy-free

Gluten-free

30 minutes
or less

One pot

5 ingredients
or fewer

BREADS
AND
SAVOURY
PASTRIES

Pan-cooked Bread Pockets

MOROCCO
PREPARATION TIME: 30 minutes,
plus rising and resting time
COOKING TIME: 20 minutes
MAKES: 20 small (10-cm/4-inch) breads

These small pockets of bread known as *batbout* are cooked on the stove rather than in the oven like many similar pitta-like breads in the Middle East. Commonly eaten at breakfast with honey and butter (or jam or fresh cheese, or olives and olive oil), *batbout* are also prepared for other meals, too, and they go particularly well with grilled meats.

250 g/9 oz (1⅔ cups) plain (all-purpose) flour, plus extra for dusting
250 g/9 oz (1½ cups) fine semolina, plus extra for dusting
7 g/¼ oz (2¼ teaspoons) instant yeast or fast-action active dry yeast granules
1½ teaspoons salt
olive oil, to serve, optional
olives, to serve, optional

◇ Sift the flour and semolina into a large, wide bowl and add the yeast and salt. Using your fingers, gradually work in about 250 ml (8 fl oz/1 cup) warm water or enough to form a moist but not overly sticky dough. Transfer to a lightly floured work counter and patiently knead for 10 minutes, or until supple and elastic. Or use a dough hook in a stand mixer. Cover with cling film (plastic wrap) and leave to rise in a warm place for 1 hour, or until doubled in size.

Roll out the dough on a lightly floured work counter to 5 mm/¼ inch thick. Using a round 10-cm/4-inch cookie cutter or inverted glass, cut into 20 circles and dust with semolina. Cover with a clean dish towel and leave to rest in a warm place for 30 minutes.

Heat a large frying pan or griddle over a high heat until very hot. Reduce the heat to medium. Working in batches, carefully lay the breads in the pan and cook for 4 minutes, turning occasionally, until puffy and browned on each side. Transfer the breads to a clean dish towel-lined plate to cool. The breads are best eaten when warm. Serve with olive oil for dipping and the olives on the side (if using).

SEMOLINA

Most of the world's wheat is common wheat or bread wheat (*Triticum aestivum*), which yields fine, velvety-soft flour. Common wheat accounts for about 95 per cent of the total global production.

In North Africa, the classic variety of wheat is durum (*Triticum durum*), with smaller, harder kernels. Milling the endosperm of durum wheat, also known as hard wheat, yields a more granular and yellower product called semolina (*smida* in Maghrebi Arabic and *semoule*

in French). It is higher in gluten and protein than soft wheat flour and has less starches. That means semolina dough is less stretchy, stiffer and harder to work. But it is able to absorb more moisture and holds its shape better when cooked, making it perfect for couscous and dried pasta. Semolina is also used to make various types of leaven and unleavened breads, biscuits (cookies) and cakes, added to soups to thicken and used as a coating for frying fish. In certain breads, some cooks blend softer

wheat flour with semolina for a more elastic texture.

There are three calibres of semolina: fine, medium and coarse. Fine semolina is sometimes called semolina flour. Even when finely ground, milled durum wheat always retains 'semolina' in its name. Note that the word 'semolina' is sometimes attached to other grains, such as corn semolina or rice semolina. In these cases, it simply refers to size.

Olive Bread

MOROCCO, TUNISIA
PREPARATION TIME: 30 minutes,
plus rising and resting time
COOKING TIME: 10 minutes
MAKES: 4 medium round loaves

This *khobz zeytoun* is made from a blend of fine
semolina and plain (all-purpose) flour and some
olives in the dough. It is excellent eaten with
cheese and strong olive oil.

300 g/11 oz (2 cups) fine semolina
300 g/11 oz (2 cups) plain (all-purpose) flour, plus
    extra for dusting
1 tablespoon instant yeast or fast-action active dry yeast
    granules
1½ teaspoons salt
1 tablespoon olive oil, plus extra for oiling
1 egg yolk
1 teaspoon milk
150 g/5 oz sliced black olives (about 1 heaped cup)

Put the semolina, flour, yeast and salt into a wide
bowl and mix together. Using your fingers, gradually
work in the oil and about 300 ml (10 fl oz/1¼ cups)
warm water or enough to form a slightly sticky dough.
Transfer to a lightly floured work counter and
patiently knead for 10 minutes, or until supple
and elastic. Or use a dough hook in a stand mixer.
Place in a lightly oiled bowl, cover with cling film
(plastic wrap) and leave to rise in a warm place for
1–2 hours until doubled in size.

Line 2 baking sheets with baking (parchment)
paper. Make an egg wash by putting the egg
yolk and milk into a small dish and, using a fork,
beating together.

Divide the dough into 4 pieces (about 250 g/9 oz
each). Using either your fingers or a rolling pin,
spread each out to a disc about 20 cm/8 inches in
diameter. Place on the prepared baking sheets, brush
with the egg wash and decorate with olives. (There
might be some remaining.) Cover with cling film
and leave to rest in a warm place for 30 minutes.

Meanwhile, preheat the oven to 200°C/400°F/
Gas Mark 6.

Prick the bread in a few places with the tines of a
fork or a cocktail stick (toothpick). Transfer to the
hot oven and bake for 10 minutes, or until golden,
rotating the baking sheets about halfway through
baking. Remove from the oven and leave to cool
on wire racks. The breads are best eaten when warm.

Classic Round Loaf

MOROCCO
PREPARATION TIME: 30 minutes,
plus resting and rising time
COOKING TIME: 20 minutes
MAKES: 2 loaves

Khobz (bread) is served with virtually every meal.
This is the classic Moroccan round, slightly domed
loaf, prepared with plain (all-purpose) flour. (Some
cooks like to mix in some fine semolina.) The
outside should be firm enough to hold together
when using a piece to scoop up some chicken
tagine, say, while the inside of the loaf is fluffy
enough to soak up all of the sauce.

500 g/1 lb 2 oz (3⅓ cups) plain (all-purpose) flour,
    plus extra for dusting
7 g/¼ oz (2¼ teaspoons) instant yeast or fast-action
    active dry yeast granules
1 tablespoon sugar
2 teaspoons salt
2 tablespoons mild olive oil
cornmeal or coarse semolina for sprinkling, optional

Sift the flour into a large, wide bowl and make
a mound. Add the yeast, sugar, salt and oil, and,
using your fingers, gradually work in about 250 ml
(8 fl oz/1 cup) warm water or enough to form a
compact ball.

Transfer the dough to a lightly floured work
counter and patiently knead for 10 minutes until
supple, elastic and slightly tacky to touch. Or use a
dough hook in a stand mixer. Divide the dough into
2 even pieces and press into slightly flattened balls.
Put into 2 large bowls, lightly dust the tops with
flour, then cover with a clean dish towel and leave
to rest for 1 hour.

Line a baking sheet with baking (parchment) paper
or dust lightly with flour. Transfer the loaves to the
sheet, spacing them at least 5 cm/2 inches apart. With
the palm of your hand, flatten to about 1 cm/½ inch
thick. Lightly dust the tops with flour if needed.
Cover the loaves with a clean dish towel, then cover
with cling film (plastic wrap) and leave in a warm
place to rise for 1–2 hours until it has doubled in size.

Meanwhile, preheat the oven to 220°C/425°F/
Gas Mark 7.

Prick the loaves with the tines of a fork or a cocktail
stick (toothpick). Sprinkle with cornmeal (if using),
then transfer to the hot oven and bake for 20 minutes,
or until golden and hollow sounding when tapped on
the bottom. Rotate the baking sheet halfway through
baking. Remove from the oven and leave to cool on
wire racks. The breads are best eaten when warm.

Round Loaves with Nigella Seeds

ALGERIA
PREPARATION TIME: 20 minutes,
plus rising time
COOKING TIME: 15 minutes
MAKES: 2 × 20-cm/8-inch round loaves

This oven-baked bread mixes plain (all-purpose) flour with semolina. The semolina should be medium calibre, which adds texture to the loaves. The small, black nigella seeds (called *sanoudj* in Maghrebi Arabic) give the bread a lovely earthy and nutty aroma.

- 250 g/9 oz (1⅔ cups) plain (all-purpose) flour, plus extra for dusting
- 250 g/9 oz (1½ cups) medium semolina
- 7 g/¼ oz (2¼ teaspoons) instant yeast or fast-action active dry yeast granules
- 2 teaspoons nigella seeds, plus extra to decorate
- 1 teaspoon salt
- 2 tablespoons olive oil
- 1 egg yolk, beaten

Line a baking sheet with baking (parchment) paper and set aside. Sift the flour and semolina into a wide bowl, then add the yeast, nigella seeds and salt. Using your fingers, gradually work in the olive oil and about 250 ml (8 fl oz/1 cup) warm water or enough to form a moist but not overly sticky dough. Transfer to a lightly floured work counter and knead for 10 minutes, or until supple and elastic. Or use a dough hook in a stand mixer. Divide the dough into 2 pieces.

Press out each piece of dough on a lightly floured work counter to a disc, about 20 cm/8 inches in diameter and 1 cm/½ inch thick. Transfer to the prepared baking sheet, then brush with egg yolk and sprinkle with nigella seeds. Loosely cover with a clean dish towel and leave to rise in a warm place for 2 hours.

Preheat the oven to 180 °C/350 °F/Gas Mark 4.

Transfer to the hot oven and bake for 15 minutes, or until golden. Remove from the oven and leave to cool on a wire rack. The breads are best eaten when warm.

Round Semolina Loaves with Aniseed and Fennel Seeds

ALGERIA
PREPARATION TIME: 20 minutes,
plus rising time
COOKING TIME: 15 minutes
MAKES: 2 medium loaves

These soft loaves have a blend of semolina and plain (all-purpose) flour, as well as some butter, which imparts a richness to the dough. The aniseed and fennel seeds give these loaves their striking flavour.

- 375 g/13 oz (2¼ cups) fine semolina
- 125 g/4¼ oz (generous ¾ cup) plain (all-purpose) flour, plus extra for dusting
- 7 g/¼ oz (2¼ teaspoons) instant yeast or fast-action active dry yeast granules
- 1 tablespoon sugar
- 1 teaspoon salt
- 1 teaspoon aniseed, plus extra for sprinkling
- 1 teaspoon fennel seeds, plus extra for sprinkling
- 25 g/1 oz (2 tablespoons) butter, melted
- 1 egg yolk, beaten

Line a baking sheet with baking (parchment) paper and set aside. Sift the semolina and flour into a large, wide bowl, then stir in the yeast, sugar, salt, aniseed and fennel seeds. Using your fingers, gradually work in the melted butter and about 250 ml (8 fl oz/1 cup) warm water or enough to form a moist but not overly sticky dough. Transfer to a lightly floured work counter and patiently knead for 10 minutes, or until supple and elastic. Or use a dough hook in a stand mixer. Divide the dough into 2 pieces.

Shape the dough on a lightly floured work counter to 2 round loaves, about 1 cm/½ inch thick and 18 cm/ 7 inches in diameter. Transfer to the prepared baking sheet, then cover with a clean dish towel and leave to rise in a warm place for 2 hours.

Preheat the oven to 180 °C/350 °F/Gas Mark 4.

Brush the breads with egg yolk and sprinkle with some aniseed and fennel seeds. Transfer to the hot oven and bake for 15 minutes, or until golden. Remove from the oven and leave to cool on wire racks. The breads are best eaten when warm.

Semolina Kesra Galette

ALGERIA
PREPARATION TIME: 20 minutes,
plus resting time
COOKING TIME: 8 minutes per batch
MAKES: 3–4 medium breads

Kesra are Algerian flatbreads cooked on a *tajine*, a round griddle pan with raised, circular ridges that leave distinctive marks. Traditionally unleavened, they have just a quartet of ingredients: fine semolina, plenty of olive oil, salt and water. They are eaten with saucy stews, soups and salads – especially *hmiss* salad made with roasted peppers and tomatoes (page 72). *Kesra* are also delicious slathered with butter, honey or jam.

500 g/1 lb 2 oz (3 cups) fine semolina
2 teaspoons salt
6 tablespoons olive oil, plus extra for coating

Put the semolina and salt into a large bowl and mix together, then add the oil and work with your fingers until coated. Still using your fingers, gradually work in about 200 ml (7 fl oz/generous ¾ cup) warm water or enough to form a soft, compact dough, allowing the semolina to absorb the water as you work. There might be some water remaining, or it might require a touch more. Patiently knead for 10 minutes until supple. Spread some oil over the top and leave to rest for 5–10 minutes.

Divide the dough into 3 or 4 pieces, then roll out each piece on a clean work counter to a thickness of about 7.5 mm/⅓ inch and 20 cm/8 inches in diameter. Prick the surface with a fork in numerous places.

Heat a large or medium *tajine*, griddle pan or frying pan over a high heat. Lay a dough in the pan, pricked-side down. Prick the top with a cocktail stick (toothpick) in a number of places and cook until browned on both sides, spinning or rotating and using a folded clean dish towel to put slight pressure as needed to cook evenly, turning a few times, 5–8 minutes per batch. Remove and repeat with the remaining dough. The breads are best eaten when warm.

Kabyle Kesra Galette with Fresh Herbs

ALGERIA
PREPARATION TIME: 20 minutes,
plus resting time
COOKING TIME: 20 minutes
MAKES: 2 large breads

This version of *kesra* – the popular unleavened semolina flatbreads cooked on a *tajine* (round ridged griddle pan) – comes from the Kabylia region, a mountainous Berber area in north-central Algeria. The texture of this *kesra* is a touch crumblier than others because of the amount of oil used. This recipe also adds fresh *naânaâ* (mint) and *hbek* (basil) into the dough. For added flavour, melt some lamb suet (the fat around the kidneys) and add to the dough. Serve with good extra-virgin olive oil to dip the bread into.

500 g/1 lb 2 oz (3 cups) medium semolina
4 tablespoons olive oil, plus extra for oiling
1 teaspoon salt
2 heaped tablespoons finely chopped mint
1 heaped tablespoon finely chopped basil
extra-virgin olive oil, to serve

Put the semolina, olive oil and salt into a wide dish or bowl. Using your fingers, gradually work in about 200 ml (7 fl oz/generous ¾ cup) warm water, allowing the semolina to gradually absorb the water. (There might be water left over.) Once it begins to form a dough, add the mint and basil. Patiently knead for 10 minutes until smooth. Spread some oil over the top and leave to rest for 5–10 minutes.

Divide the dough in half, then roll out each piece on a clean work counter until it is 1 cm/½ inch or less thick. Prick both sides of the dough with the tines of a fork or a cocktail stick (toothpick) in several places.

Heat a medium *tajine*, griddle pan or frying pan over a high heat. Lay a dough in the pan and cook until browned on both sides, turning from time to time, about 10 minutes. Hold with a clean dish towel and brown the edges as needed and use the towel to press down on the bread to cook evenly. Remove and repeat with the remaining dough. Serve warm with extra-virgin olive oil for dipping.

Crumbly Semolina Flatbread

ALGERIA, MOROCCO
PREPARATION TIME: 15 minutes,
plus resting time
COOKING TIME: 10 minutes per batch
MAKES: 4–6 small round breads

Crumbly *harsha* is deeply popular in Morocco, especially the north. Markets sell wide, flat sheets of the coarsely grained *harsha*, although at home it is more common to make individual-size patties cooked in a frying pan. They are easy to make and kids are often allowed to prepare them in the family kitchen. The only tricky part comes in turning them in the pan as *harsha* can crumble easily. Use a wide spatula and turn just once if possible. Generally served with honey, they are also excellent with local fresh cheese such as *jben*, jam or butter.

250 g/9 oz (1½ cups) fine semolina
2 tablespoons sugar
2 teaspoons baking powder
1 teaspoon salt
100 g/3½ oz (7 tablespoons) butter, softened
90 ml/3 fl oz (6 tablespoons) milk, or extra as needed
coarse semolina, for dusting and sprinkling on top
oil, for oiling
honey, to serve

Mix the fine semolina, sugar, baking powder and salt together in a large bowl, then work in the butter with your fingers. Still using your fingers, gradually add the milk to form a sticky dough without working too much. Add a touch more milk if needed. Loosely cover the bowl with a clean dish towel and leave to rest for 15 minutes for the semolina to fully absorb the milk.

Press the dough out with your fingers on a clean work counter that has been lightly dusted with coarse semolina until it is about 1 cm/½ inch thick. Use a bowl or cookie cutter to form patties, about 10 cm/4 inches in diameter. (They can be smaller or larger – between 7.5 and 13 cm/3 and 5 inches across.) Sprinkle coarse semolina across the top.

Heat a frying pan or griddle pan over a medium-low heat. Lightly oil, then carefully set 1 or 2 patties in the pan, depending on size, and cook for 10 minutes, or until golden and cooked through. They are delicate and can crumble, so flip just once by placing a hand on top and a wide spatula underneath. Serve warm with honey.

Crumbly Semolina Flatbread with Olives, Cheese and Dried Herbs

MOROCCO
PREPARATION TIME: 20 minutes,
plus resting time
COOKING TIME: 15 minutes per batch
MAKES: 6 small stuffed breads

While *harsha* (see left) can be split open and filled with a range of ingredients, sometimes the fillings get added directly to the dough itself. This is often the case with olives and cheese. In Fès, *harsha* with some pieces of *khlii* (a seasoned confit of dried meat, see page 206) is another local favourite.

250 g/9 oz (1½ cups) fine semolina
1 tablespoon sugar
2 teaspoons baking powder
1 teaspoon salt
60 g/2¼ oz (4 tablespoons) butter, softened
90 ml/3 fl oz (6 tablespoons) milk, or extra as needed
5 creamy cheese wedges or 100 g/3½ oz another
    soft cheese
50 g/2 oz pitted and chopped black olives (about
    ½ cup)
1 tablespoon dried thyme, oregano or *zaâtar* (see
    page 61)
coarse semolina, for dusting
oil, for oiling

Put the fine semolina, sugar, baking powder and salt into a large bowl and mix together, then work in the butter with your fingers. Still using your fingers, gradually add the milk to form a sticky dough without working too much. Add a touch more milk if needed. Loosely cover the bowl with a clean dish towel and leave to rest for 15 minutes for the semolina to fully absorb the milk.

Mix the cheese, olives and thyme together in a small bowl.

Divide the dough into 6 equal portions, then roll each piece into a ball on a clean work counter, about the size of a tangerine. Flatten the balls with your fingers to about 13 cm/5 inches across and 5 mm/¼ inch thick. Put about 1 tablespoon of the filling into the centre and pull the sides up and around to close. Gently press out to about 1-cm-/½-inch-thick patties. Dust both sides with coarse semolina.

Heat a frying pan or griddle pan over a medium-low heat. Lightly oil, then carefully set 1 or 2 patties in the pan, depending on size, and cook for 10–15 minutes until golden and cooked through. They are delicate and can crumble, so flip just once by placing a hand on top and a wide spatula underneath. Serve warm.

Flatbread Stuffed with Shallots and Suet

MOROCCO
PREPARATION TIME: 30 minutes,
plus resting time
COOKING TIME: 8 minutes per batch
MAKES: 8 stuffed breads

Simple, frugal, filling and flavourful, this *khobz bi chehma* ('fat bread') comes from the Berber-dominated High Atlas Mountains. If possible, use the suet of lamb rather than of beef, as it becomes more tender. This version calls for shallots, but home cooks along Morocco's coast might add prawns (shrimp), while those inland may add some minced (ground) meat instead. Serve with sweet, piping hot Mint Tea (pages 417–421).

    100 g/3½ oz (1 cup) chopped lamb or beef suet,
        finely chopped
    3 shallots, finely chopped
    2 packed tablespoons finely chopped coriander
        (cilantro)
    1 teaspoon sweet paprika
    ½ teaspoon ground cumin
    generous pinch of cayenne pepper
    400 g/14 oz (2⅔ cups) plain (all-purpose) flour,
        plus extra for dusting
    2 teaspoons instant yeast or fast-action active dry yeast
        granules
    neutral oil, for oiling
    salt
    Mint Tea (pages 417–421), to serve

Put the suet, shallots, coriander (cilantro), paprika, cumin and cayenne pepper into a large bowl and mix together, then season with salt.

Sift the flour into a wide, large bowl, add the yeast and season with salt. Using your fingers, gradually work in about 250 ml (8 fl oz/1 cup) warm water or enough to form a compact ball. (There might be some water remaining.) Transfer to a lightly floured work counter and patiently knead for 10 minutes until supple and elastic. Moisten your hands with oil. Take a piece of dough and squeeze it in the palm of your hand, forcing out a piece the size of a large plum, about 80 g/3 oz (¼ cup), through your thumb and forefinger. Twist to pinch off. There should be 8. Alternatively, cut the dough into 8 equal pieces and roll into balls.

Working with one piece of dough at a time on a lightly oiled work counter, flatten out the dough to about 18 cm/7 inches in diameter and place 3 tablespoons of the stuffing mix on top. Pull the sides around the top like a money bag to enclose the filling and pinch closed, pressing as much air out as possible. Gently flatten out by smoothing the sides and working outwards with your fingers until it is about 15 cm/6 inches in diameter with the filling evenly spread around inside the dough. If the dough tears, simply stretch over to repair. Cover with a clean dish towel and leave to rest for 30 minutes.

Line a platter with paper towels. Heat a medium heavy frying pan or griddle pan over a medium heat. Lightly oil, then lay a stuffed bread on the pan and cook over a medium-low heat, turning from time to time, until patchy golden, about 8 minutes. Transfer to the paper towels to absorb any excess oil. Cook the remaining breads. Serve with very hot mint tea.

Saharan Folded Flatbread

ALGERIA, TUNISIA
PREPARATION TIME: 30 minutes,
plus resting time
COOKING TIME: 50 minutes
SERVES: 6

The name of this filled bread is *mtabga*, which frequently gets translated for visitors as 'Berber pizza'. It is a favourite across the northern Sahara in Tunisia and Algeria. The filling often consists of ingredients at hand, from carrots, tomatoes and long sweet peppers to the fat of lamb or camel.

- 200 g/7 oz (1¼ cups) fine semolina, plus extra for sprinkling
- 200 g/7 oz (1⅓ cups) plain (all-purpose) flour, plus extra for dusting
- 5 tablespoons olive oil, plus extra for oiling
- 2 red or yellow onions, finely chopped
- 2 cloves of garlic, minced
- 2 long sweet green peppers, cored, seeded and finely chopped
- 3 tomatoes, halved crosswise and grated, peel discarded (see page 445)
- 1 heaped tablespoon double concentrated tomato purée (paste)
- harissa (page 409), to taste, optional
- 2 tablespoons finely chopped flat-leaf parsley
- ½ teaspoon ground caraway
- salt and pepper

Sift the semolina and flour into a wide bowl, then add ½ teaspoon salt and 2 tablespoons of the oil. Using your fingers, gradually work in about 200 ml (7 fl oz/generous ¾ cup) warm water to form a moist but not overly sticky dough. Transfer to a lightly floured work counter and patiently knead for 10 minutes, or until supple and elastic. Or use a dough hook in a stand mixer. Put the dough into a lightly oiled bowl, cover with cling film (plastic wrap) and leave to rest for 30 minutes.

Heat the remaining 3 tablespoons of oil in a sauté pan over a medium heat, add the onions and cook for 10 minutes, or until soft and pale. Add the garlic and peppers and cook for 5 minutes. Stir in the tomatoes, tomato purée (paste) and 4 tablespoons warm water, the harissa (if using), parsley and caraway, and season with salt and pepper. Cook for 10 minutes, or until the tomato is darker and reduced. Remove from the heat.

Divide the dough into 6 pieces, about 100 g/ 3½ oz each. Spread each piece of dough out on a lightly floured work counter using either your hands or a rolling pin to discs, about 20 cm/8 inches in diameter. For each disc, place about 70 g/2¾ oz (¼ cup) of the filling on one side, then spread around one half of the disc, leaving a space along the round edges. Fold the empty half over to cover and seal by pressing the tines of a fork around the edges.

Heat a medium frying pan over a medium heat. Lightly brush the pan with oil, lay a stuffed bread in the pan and cook for about 2 minutes. Brush the top with oil and turn. Cook for another 2 minutes, or until golden. Transfer to a plate and cook the remaining stuffed breads. Serve hot.

Sandwich Merguez-frites

ALGERIA, MOROCCO, TUNISIA
PREPARATION TIME: 15 minutes
COOKING TIME: 30 minutes
SERVES: 4

This iconic Parisian street sandwich has its roots in North Africa, where it is quintessential fast food. A baguette filled with spicy grilled merguez sausages gets slathered in harissa and topped with Frites (fries, page 164). Usually made of lamb (beef ones are less common), merguez have a signature reddish colour from the spices in the sausage stuffing. Some Tunisians garnish the baguettes with slices of Hard-boiled Egg (page 443), cheese, olives, lettuce and tomatoes. Add a touch of olive oil or water to the harissa if needed to make it more spreadable.

- neutral oil, for deep-frying and oiling
- 400 g/14 oz white potatoes, peeled and cut lengthwise into 1-cm-/⅓-inch-thick fries
- 500 g/1 lb 2 oz merguez sausages
- 2 baguettes
- mayonnaise
- harissa (page 409)

Heat an abundant amount of oil in a deep frying pan over a medium heat until the surface shimmers. Line a baking sheet with paper towels. Working in batches that don't crowd the pan or bring down the temperature of the oil, add the potatoes and fry for 10 minutes, or until golden. Transfer with a slotted spoon to the paper towels to briefly drain.

Meanwhile, lightly oil a medium frying pan, add the merguez and cook over a medium heat for 10 minutes, or until blistered and cooked through.

Cut the baguettes into 2 lengths and slice open along one side. Remove some of the soft inside part if desired to make more room for the filling. Slather with mayonnaise and harissa, then fill with the merguez and top with the frites. Serve immediately.

Fricassé Stuffed Sandwich Rolls

TUNISIA
PREPARATION TIME: 20 minutes,
plus rising and resting time
COOKING TIME: 35 minutes
MAKES: about 12 rolls

Tunisia's iconic snack, *fricassé* fried buns get stuffed
(or rather, overstuffed) with everything from potatoes
to tuna to olives and capers – and always a dollop
of harissa. While popular to buy from small shops,
they are also frequently made at home when there
is a big gathering.

For the dough:
500 g/1 lb 2 oz (3⅓ cups) plain (all-purpose) flour,
  plus extra for dusting
1 tablespoon sugar
2 teaspoons instant yeast or fast-action active dry yeast
  granules
1 teaspoon salt
1 large egg
2 tablespoons olive oil
neutral oil, for oiling and frying

For the fillings:
2 white potatoes, peeled and cut into 1.5-cm/⅔-inch
  pieces
harissa (page 409), to taste
1 (150-g/5-oz) can of tuna in olive oil, drained
2 Hard-boiled Eggs (page 443), peeled and cut into
  wedges
pitted black or green olives
capers, rinsed, optional
salt

TO MAKE THE DOUGH: Put the flour, sugar,
yeast and salt into a large bowl and mix together
with your fingers. Work in the egg and olive oil,
then begin adding about 200 ml (7 fl oz/generous
¾ cup) warm water, working the dough into a ball.
Transfer to a lightly floured work counter and
patiently knead for 10 minutes, or until supple and
elastic. Or use a dough hook in a stand mixer. Put
the dough into a lightly oiled bowl, cover with cling
film (plastic wrap) and leave to rise in a warm place
for 2 hours, or until doubled in size.

MEANWHILE, PREPARE THE FILLINGS: Put the
potatoes into a large pot or saucepan of lightly salted
water, bring to the boil and boil for 12–15 minutes
until tender. Drain. If needed, loosen the harissa
with a touch of water to make it more spreadable.

Press down to deflate the dough, then roll it into a
log on a clean work counter and cut it into 12 pieces.
Roll each piece into a ball and then slightly oval in
shape, about 4 × 6 cm/1½ × 2½ inches. Lightly dust
with flour, cover with cling film (plastic wrap) and
leave to rest for 20 minutes.

Heat at least 2 cm/¾ inch of oil in a large frying
pan over a medium heat until the surface shimmers.
Line a plate with paper towels. Working in batches,
gently place the dough in the pan and fry for
5 minutes, or until golden brown on both sides,
using a spoon to keep oil on the top and turning
from time to time. Transfer with a slotted spoon
to the paper towels to drain and repeat with the
remaining dough.

Once cooled, cut open in half. Dab with harissa,
then generously fill with potato, tuna, egg, olives and
capers (if using).

Sweet Constantine Brioche

ALGERIA
PREPARATION TIME: 20 minutes,
plus rising time
COOKING TIME: 15 minutes
MAKES: about 12 buns

Known as *chrik* or *brioche constantinoise* after the Algerian coastal city of Constantine where they are popular, these breads, with less butter, are not quite as rich as classic French brioche.

    2 large eggs
    80 g/3 oz (6 tablespoons) sugar
    100 g/3½ oz (7 tablespoons) butter, melted,
        or olive oil
    200 ml/7 fl oz (generous ¾ cup) warm milk
    1 teaspoon salt
    1 tablespoon orange blossom water
    500 g/1 lb 2 oz (3⅓ cups) plain (all-purpose) flour,
        plus extra for dusting
    1 tablespoon instant yeast or fast-action active dry
        yeast granules
    1 egg yolk
    sesame seeds, to decorate

Put the eggs and sugar into a large bowl and beat together, then add the butter and beat until combined. Stir in the milk, salt and orange blossom water. Sift in the flour, add the yeast and patiently knead for 10 minutes to a smooth, supple dough that does not stick to the fingers and peels away from the sides of the bowl. Cover with a clean dish towel and leave to rise in a warm place for 1 hour, or until it has doubled in size.

Line 2 baking sheets with baking (parchment) paper. Put the egg yolk and a couple of drops of water into a bowl and beat together.

Gently deflate the dough by pressing it down, then put it onto a lightly floured work counter. Cut the dough into pieces about the size of an egg, then gently roll into round balls and place on the prepared baking sheets. Gently press down on the top of each to slightly flatten. Brush with the egg yolk and sprinkle with sesame seeds. Leave to rise in a warm place for 30 minutes.

Meanwhile, preheat the oven to 180 °C/350 °F/ Gas Mark 4.

Put the buns into the hot oven and bake for 15 minutes, or until golden brown. Remove from the oven and leave to cool on wire racks. The buns are best eaten when warm.

Sweet Buns with Aniseed and Sesame Seeds

MOROCCO
PREPARATION TIME: 20 minutes,
plus rising time
COOKING TIME: 15–20 minutes
MAKES: about 10 generous buns

This Moroccan *krachel* is similar to Algerian *chrik* (see left). They are delicious with butter and jam.

    500 g/1 lb 2 oz (3⅓ cups) plain (all-purpose) flour,
        plus extra for dusting
    100 g/3½ oz (½ cup) sugar
    1 tablespoon instant yeast or fast-action active dry yeast
        granules
    ½ teaspoon salt
    2 tablespoons toasted sesame seeds, plus extra
        to decorate
    1 tablespoon aniseed
    100 ml/3½ fl oz (generous ⅓ cup) milk, warmed
    100 ml/3½ fl oz (generous ⅓ cup) vegetable oil
    1 tablespoon orange blossom water
    2 large eggs
    1 egg yolk

Sift the flour into a large bowl, add the sugar, yeast, salt, sesame seeds and aniseed and mix together with your fingers. Add the milk, oil, orange blossom water and the 2 eggs and work to a slightly sticky dough. Add a touch of water or more flour as needed. Transfer to a lightly floured work counter and patiently knead for 10 minutes to a smooth, supple dough that does not stick to the fingers and peels away from the sides of the bowl. Cover with a clean dish towel and leave to rise in a warm place for 1–2 hours until it has doubled in size. Line 2 baking sheets with baking (parchment) paper.

Punch down to deflate the dough, then roll into a log on a lightly floured work counter and cut into 10 or so pieces, about 100 g/3½ oz each. Gently roll under the palm of your hand into round balls. Gently flatten and arrange on the prepared baking sheets. Cover with a dish towel and leave to rise in a warm place for 30–90 minutes, until almost doubled in size.

Meanwhile, preheat the oven to 180 °C/350 °F/ Gas Mark 4. Put the egg yolk and a couple of drops of water into a bowl and beat together.

Gently brush the buns with the egg yolk and sprinkle the tops with sesame seeds. Put the buns into the hot oven and bake for 15–20 minutes until golden brown and the bases sound hollow when tapped. Remove from the oven and leave to cool on wire racks. The buns are best eaten warm.

French Toast with Almonds and Honey

ALGERIA, MOROCCO
PREPARATION TIME: 10 minutes
COOKING TIME: 15 minutes
SERVES: 4–6

In North Africa, this regional favourite goes by the French name *pain perdu*, which means 'lost bread'. It is also called *syour bel beid*, literally 'laces with eggs'. It's a popular way to use bread that is too dry to eat.

    3 large eggs
    250 ml/8 fl oz (1 cup) milk
    icing (confectioners') sugar, for dusting
    ground cinnamon, for dusting
    3 tablespoons neutral oil for frying
    1 stale baguette, cut into 1.5-cm-/⅔-inch-thick slices
    chopped or sliced almonds, to decorate
    honey, to serve

Put the eggs into a wide bowl and beat together, then mix in the milk. Put some sugar and cinnamon into a small bowl and mix together, then set aside.

Heat the oil in a medium frying pan over a medium heat. Working in batches, dip the bread into the egg-and-milk mixture, turning over and allowing to absorb. Lift above the bowl and leave to drain for a moment before setting in the pan. Cook until golden brown on both sides, turning as needed, 2–3 minutes in total. Transfer to paper towels. Prepare the remaining slices of bread.

Arrange on a platter, and lightly dust with the sugar-cinnamon mixture. Scatter over the almonds and serve immediately with honey to drizzle over as desired.

French Toast with Orange Blossom Syrup

ALGERIA
PREPARATION TIME: 10 minutes
COOKING TIME: 25 minutes
SERVES: 4

This version of *pain perdu* turns out more like small, fried cakes. Soaked in orange blossom water syrup, they make a delicious treat.

    200 g/7 oz (1 cup) sugar
    2 teaspoons orange blossom water
    3 large eggs
    250 ml/8 fl oz (1 cup) milk
    2 large pinches of ground cinnamon
    3 tablespoons neutral oil, for frying
    1 stale baguette, cut into 1.5-cm-/⅔-inch-thick slices

Put the sugar and 250 ml (8 fl oz/1 cup) water into a large saucepan and bring to the boil over a high heat, stirring to dissolve the sugar. Reduce the heat to low and simmer for 5 minutes, or until it has reduced to a light, clear syrup. Stir in the orange blossom water, remove from the heat and cover to keep warm.

Put the eggs into a wide bowl and beat together, then mix in the milk and cinnamon.

Heat the oil in a medium frying pan over a medium heat. Working in batches, dip the bread into the egg-and-milk mixture, turning over and allowing to absorb. Lift above the bowl and leave to drain for a moment before setting in the pan. Cook until golden brown on both sides, turning as needed, 2–3 minutes in total. Transfer to paper towels. Prepare the remaining slices of bread.

Arrange on a platter and generously drizzle with the syrup. Serve.

Brioche French Toast

ALGERIA
PREPARATION TIME: 10 minutes
COOKING TIME: 10 minutes
SERVES: 4

This is the richest version of *pain perdu* as it is made with slices of *pain brioche* (made with eggs, milk and plenty of butter) or its slightly less buttery cousin *pain viennois*.

    2 large eggs
    250 ml/8 fl oz (1 cup) milk
    sugar, for dusting
    ground cinnamon, for dusting
    butter, for greasing
    8 thick slices of stale brioche or Vienna loaf

Put the eggs into a wide bowl and beat together, then mix in the milk. Put some sugar and cinnamon into a small bowl and mix together, then set aside.

Heat a large frying pan over a medium heat and grease with butter. Working with a few slices at a time, dip the brioche into the egg-and-milk mixture, turning over and allowing to absorb. Lift above the bowl and leave to drain for a moment before setting in the pan. Cook for 3–4 minutes until a rich golden brown, turning as needed. Transfer to paper towels. Prepare the remaining slices of brioche.

Arrange on a platter, dust with the sugar-cinnamon mixture and serve immediately.

Minced Meat Boureks

ALGERIA
PREPARATION TIME: 20 minutes,
plus cooling time
COOKING TIME: 30 minutes
MAKES: 8–10 pastries

There are many versions of stuffed *bourek* pastries in Algeria, but the favourite might be with seasoned minced (ground) meat, plenty of onions, some cooked egg and a bit of ground cinnamon for a touch of aroma. These *boureks* are sometimes called *bourek dioul*, referring to the thin pastry sheets (known as *dioul*) used to roll them. They are a staple of the Ramadan table alongside a bowl of *chorba* (soup) (pages 122–129 and 132). Any other time of year, they make a perfect hot starter on their own.

3 tablespoons olive oil
2 red or yellow onions, finely chopped
2 cloves of garlic, minced
250 g/9 oz minced (ground) lamb or beef
1 tablespoon finely chopped flat-leaf parsley
¼ teaspoon ground cinnamon
3 large eggs
dioul, warka or *brick* pastry leaves (see below), spring
   roll wrappers or filo (phyllo) sheets
neutral oil, for frying
salt and pepper
lemon wedges, to serve

Heat 2 tablespoons of the olive oil in a sauté pan or frying pan over a medium heat, add the onions and garlic and cook for 10 minutes, or until the onions are pale and soft. Stir in the meat, parsley and cinnamon, season with salt and pepper and moisten with 2 tablespoons water. Cook for 10 minutes, or until the meat is browned and the moisture has evaporated. Transfer to a bowl and leave to cool completely.

Heat the remaining 1 tablespoon of olive oil in a small frying pan over a medium heat. Beat 2 of the eggs, pour into the pan and make a simple omelette. Transfer to a plate and coarsely chop.

Separate the yolk from the remaining 1 egg, put the yolk into a small bowl and beat.

Unroll the pastry sheets on a clean, flat work counter. If round, cut the sheets in half into semi-circles. If rectangular, cut into pieces about 20 cm/8 inches wide and at least 25 cm/10 inches in length. Place 2 heaped tablespoons of the filling at the bottom and set a piece of omelette on top of it. Fold the sides overlapping in the centre, then roll like a cigar almost to the end. Brush some egg yolk on the end and finish rolling. Repeat with the remaining pastry pieces, filling and omelette. Place the rolls on a plate without letting them touch.

Heat at least 1 cm/½ inch of oil for frying in a large frying pan over a medium heat until the surface shimmers. Line a plate with paper towels. Working in batches, gently place the rolls in the oil and fry, turning as needed, until golden brown and crispy, 1½–2 minutes. Transfer to the paper towels to briefly drain. Serve immediately with lemon wedges.

WARKA, BRICK, MALSOUKA AND DIOUL PASTRY SHEETS

Paper-thin pastry sheets are used across North Africa for savoury and sweet stuffed and fried pastries and some desserts.

These pastry sheets go by various names across the region, including *warka, brick, malsouka* and *dioul*. They are generally made by tapping or smearing a fine coating of damp, sticky dough across a wide, hot griddle pan, before being peeled off after about 15 seconds in a single, fluid motion. These sheets are difficult to prepare, and most people now buy them either in commercial packages or freshly made in the market.

They are usually made from a blend of fine semolina and flour, giving them a higher gluten content than filo (phyllo). They are also quite resistant to cracking and breaking when filled, folded and fried, and they acquire a lovely, crispy texture.

For commercial leaves, look for packages labelled (in French) 'Feuilles de Brick' or sometimes 'Feuilles de Pastilla'. They can be found in refrigerated or frozen sections.

While they are often compared to filo pastry, there are some significant differences. Filo is stretched, uncooked dough rather than cooked like *warka* or *brick*. Filo is also slightly thicker and made of plain (all-purpose) flour, rather than a semolina blend.

To substitute: Filo pastry is a good alternative. Thin and delicate Filipino lumpia wrappers make an excellent substitution, as do Chinese spring roll wrappers.

Spinach and Cheese Boureks

ALGERIA
PREPARATION TIME: 20 minutes,
plus cooling
COOKING TIME: 45 minutes
MAKES: about 20 pastries

Another popular *bourek* (stuffed pastry), this is a vegetarian version filled with spinach, cheese and egg. As other types of *boureks*, these are commonly served with bowls of *chorba* (soup) (pages 122–129 and 132).

2 tablespoons olive oil
450 g/1 lb spinach leaves
1 clove of garlic, minced
1 red or yellow onion, finely sliced
4 large eggs
5 creamy cheese wedges or 100 g/3½ oz cream cheese
dioul, warka or *brick* pastry leaves (see page 56), spring roll wrappers or filo (phyllo) sheets
neutral oil, for frying
salt and pepper
lemon wedges, to serve

Heat the olive oil in a deep saucepan over a medium heat, add the spinach and cook for 2–4 minutes until it begins to wilt. Add the garlic and onion, season with salt and pepper and cook for 30 minutes, or until the onion is soft and all of the water has evaporated from the pan. Add 3 of the eggs, and cook for 1–2 minutes, stirring to scramble. Transfer the mixture to a bowl and leave to cool completely. Add the cheese and mix with a fork.

Separate the yolk from the remaining 1 egg, put the yolk into a small bowl and beat.

Unroll a few pastry sheets on a clean, flat work counter. If round, cut the sheets in half into semi-circles. If rectangular, cut into pieces about 18 cm/7 inches wide and at least 25 cm/10 inches in length. Place the straight edge of one piece facing you (or short edge if rectangular). Place 2 tablespoons of the filling along the bottom. Fold the sides overlapping in the centre, then roll like a cigar almost to the end. Brush some egg yolk on the end and finish rolling. Repeat with the remaining pastry pieces and filling. Place the rolls on a plate without letting them touch.

Heat at least 1 cm/½ inch of oil for frying in a large frying pan over a medium heat until the surface shimmers. Line a plate with paper towels. Working in batches, gently place the rolls in the oil and fry, turning as needed, until golden brown and crispy, 2–3 minutes. Transfer with a slotted spoon to the paper towels to briefly drain. Serve immediately with lemon wedges.

Cheese Boureks

ALGERIA, MOROCCO
PREPARATION TIME: 20 minutes
COOKING TIME: 5 minutes
MAKES: about 10 pastries

These fried cheese-filled *boureks* (stuffed pastries) are a favourite of many families, especially during Ramadan when they are served with soup. They can also be rolled into cigars (see page 58 for directions). There is a similar version in Morocco made with fresh cheese that is called *briouat bel jben* (Triangular Stuffed Briouats with Fresh Cheese and Herbs, page 61).

5 creamy cheese wedges or 100 g/3½ oz cream cheese
1 large egg
25 g/1 oz (packed ¼ cup) shredded white cheese, such as Emmental or Gruyère
1 heaped tablespoon finely chopped flat-leaf parsley
dioul, warka or *brick* pastry leaves (see page 56), spring roll wrappers or filo (phyllo) sheets
1 egg yolk, beaten
neutral oil, for frying
salt and pepper
lemon wedges, to serve

Put the creamy cheese and egg into a large bowl and mash together, then stir in the shredded cheese and parsley. Season with salt and pepper. Set aside.

Unroll a few pastry sheets on a clean, flat work counter, then cut into strips, about 7.5 cm/3 inches wide and at least 23 cm/9 inches in length. Arrange a couple of the strips facing away from you; cover the remaining strips with cling film (plastic wrap) to keep from drying out.

Place scant 1 tablespoon of the cheese filling on the end of each strip closest to you. Fold over to form a triangle, then turn again to form another triangle, and so on to the end. Brush with beaten egg yolk and tuck over the loose end. Repeat with the remaining pastry and cheese filling. Place the triangles on a plate without letting them touch.

Heat at least 1 cm/½ inch of oil for frying in a large frying pan over a medium heat until the surface shimmers. Line a plate with paper towels. Working in batches, gently place the triangles in the oil and fry, turning once, until golden brown, 1–2 minutes per batch. Transfer with a slotted spoon to the paper towels to briefly drain. Serve hot with lemon wedges.

Stuffed Brick Pastries with Tuna and Runny Egg

TUNISIA
PREPARATION TIME: 15 minutes
COOKING TIME: 40 minutes
MAKES: 6 pastries

Tunisia's best-known starter, *brick* is a crispy fried pastry filled with tuna, potato, herbs and a runny egg. The name comes from the thin, round sheets of pastry that are used (see page 56). The trick with this dish is to get the pastry crispy and keep the egg runny, then serve immediately (the pastry will get soggy if it stands). If preparing a number of *bricks* that you want to serve together, you could always place them in a warm oven after they have been fried. Cheese has become a popular, modern addition to the mixture, while a few capers will add a pleasing tang.

  1 white potato
  1 (150–175-g/5–6-oz) can of tuna in olive oil, drained
  ½ red or yellow onion, grated
  3 tablespoons finely chopped flat-leaf parsley
  neutral oil, for frying
  6 *brick*, *warka* or *dioul* pastry leaves (see page 56), spring roll wrappers or filo (phyllo) sheets
  6 eggs
  salt and pepper
  lemon wedges, to serve

Put the potato into a large pot or saucepan of lightly salted water, bring to the boil and boil for 20–30 minutes until just tender. Drain in a colander. When cool enough to handle, peel and put into a large bowl. Add the tuna, onion and parsley, season with salt and pepper and mash together with a fork.

Heat at least 2 cm/¾ inch of oil for frying in a medium frying pan over a medium heat until the surface shimmers. Line a plate with paper towels.

Place a pastry sheet on a clean work counter. Working quickly so that the sheet doesn't get soggy, place 2 tablespoons of the filling in a row along the edges of 2 sides to form a border that will keep the egg in place in the centre. Crack an egg inside the barrier of filling. Gently fold in half to form a triangle or semi-circle depending on the shape of the pastry sheet. With the help of a plate, gently slide the *brick* into the oil. Tap down the edges to seal with a slotted spoon and fry until golden, turning with the help of 2 slotted spoons or spatulas, 30 seconds–1 minute on each side. Transfer with a slotted spoon to the paper towels to briefly drain. Repeat to make 6 pastries. Serve immediately with lemon wedges.

Cigar-shaped Stuffed Briouats with Spiced Minced Meat and Onion

MOROCCO
PREPARATION TIME: 30 minutes, plus cooling time
COOKING TIME: 30 minutes
MAKES: 15–18 pastries

This recipe is for cigar-shaped *briouats*, though they can be rolled into triangles following the folding directions for Triangular Stuffed Briouats with Fresh Cheese and Herbs (page 61).

  2 tablespoons olive oil
  1 red or yellow onion, finely chopped
  2 cloves of garlic, minced
  450 g/1 lb minced (ground) beef or lamb
  1 heaped tablespoon finely chopped flat-leaf parsley
  1 heaped tablespoon finely chopped coriander (cilantro)
  1 teaspoon sweet paprika
  ½ teaspoon ground cumin
  ¼ teaspoon ground cinnamon
  warka, *brick* or *dioul* pastry leaves (see page 56), spring roll wrappers or filo (phyllo) sheets
  1 egg yolk, beaten
  neutral oil, for frying
  salt and pepper

Heat the olive oil in a sauté pan or frying pan over a medium heat, add the onion and cook for 10 minutes, or until pale and soft. Stir in the garlic, meat, parsley, coriander (cilantro), paprika, cumin and cinnamon, season with salt and pepper and cook for 5 minutes, or until the meat is browned. Transfer to a bowl and leave to cool.

Unroll a few pastry sheets on a clean, flat work counter and cut into strips, about 15 cm/6 inches wide and at least 23 cm/9 inches in length. Arrange a couple of the strips facing away from you; cover the remaining strips with cling film (plastic wrap) to keep from drying out.

Place 1 heaped tablespoon of the filling at the bottom of one of the pastry strips closest to you and fold over. Fold the sides overlapping in the centre, then roll like a cigar almost to the end. Brush some egg yolk on the end and finish rolling. Repeat with the remaining pastry strips and filling. Place the rolls on a plate without letting them touch.

Heat at least 1 cm/½ inch of oil for frying in a large frying pan over a medium heat until the surface shimmers. Line a plate with paper towels. Working in batches, gently place the rolls in the oil and fry, turning once, until golden brown and crispy, 30–45 seconds. Transfer with a slotted spoon to the paper towels to briefly drain. Serve immediately.

Cigar-shaped Stuffed Briouats with Spiced Minced Meat and Onion ➤➤

Triangular Stuffed Briouats with Fresh Cheese and Herbs

MOROCCO
PREPARATION TIME: 20 minutes
COOKING TIME: 5 minutes
MAKES: about 15 pastries

Filled with fresh cheese (*jben*) and some fresh herbs, these triangular *briouat* pastries are a perfect combination of flavours, especially when lightly brushed with honey. For an earthier version, use some dried *zaâtar* (wild oregano, see below), thyme or oregano instead of coriander (cilantro).

225 g/8 oz Moroccan *jben*, ricotta or another fresh semi-soft farmer's cheese (about 1 cup)
1 large egg
1 heaped tablespoon finely chopped coriander (cilantro)
warka, *brick* or *dioul* pastry leaves (see page 56), spring roll wrappers or filo (phyllo) sheets
1 egg yolk, beaten
neutral oil, for frying
honey, for brushing
toasted sesame seeds, to garnish

Put the cheese, egg and coriander (cilantro) into a large bowl and mix together with a fork. Set aside.

Unroll a few pastry sheets on a clean, flat work counter, then cut into strips, about 7.5 cm/3 inches wide and at least 23 cm/9 inches in length. Arrange a couple of the strips facing away from you; cover the remaining strips with cling film (plastic wrap) to keep from drying out.

Place 1 tablespoon of the cheese filling on the end of each strip closest to you. Fold over to form a triangle, then turn again to form another triangle, and so on to the end. Brush with beaten egg yolk and tuck over the loose end. Repeat with the remaining pastry and cheese filling. Place the triangles on a plate without letting them touch.

Heat at least 1 cm/½ inch of oil for frying in a large frying pan over a medium heat until the surface shimmers. Line a plate with paper towels. Working in batches, gently place the triangles in the oil and fry, turning once, until golden brown, about 1 minute per batch. Transfer with a slotted spoon to the paper towels to briefly drain.

Divide the rolls among plates, brush with honey and sprinkle with sesame seeds. Serve hot.

ZAÂTAR

In the Middle East, *zaâtar* is an aromatic and somewhat tart spice blend of thyme, sesame seeds, sumac and salt that is particularly popular in the cuisines of Syria, Jordan, Lebanon, Palestine and Israel. In North Africa it is something altogether different.

In Moroccan Arabic, *zaâtar* is the common name for oregano, but there are nearly 70 species. When home cooks in Morocco buy it in the market, they are usually referring to the stronger local variety with a hint more bitterness and notes of thyme.

Often collected from wild populations, this shrubby herb has slender leaves and tight clusters of deep-pink flowers. Used in dried form, the tiny, flaky green leaves can flavour soups, occasionally salads and other dishes such as fresh cheese in stuffed *briouat* pastries (see above). Some in southern Morocco use *zaâtar* when preparing preserved butter (*smen*, see pages 120 and 412) for the herb's natural preservation properties and flavour. The finest, most aromatic *zaâtar* in Morocco grows in the High Atlas Mountains.

The name is not without regional confusion, though. In Algeria *zaâtar* usually refers to thyme. (In Morocco *zaitra* is more commonly used for thyme.)

To substitute: Use a blend of oregano and thyme.

Pastilla with Chicken and Almonds

MOROCCO
PREPARATION TIME: 45 minutes,
plus cooling time
COOKING TIME: 1 hour 45 minutes
SERVES: 6

Pastilla (or *bastella/b'stilla*) is a sophisticated celebration of the sweet and savoury with three distinct layers wrapped inside a layered pastry case (shell): braised pigeon or chicken; eggs and some of the onion sauce from the meat; and ground, sweetened almonds. Some divide the layers with pastry sheets, though the final crispy pastry is better if omitted. If using filo (phyllo) pastry, be sure to brush each of the sheets with oil or melted butter to ensure that they don't crack or break.

For the chicken filling:
2 tablespoons olive oil
1 red or yellow onion, finely chopped
1 clove of garlic, minced
4 bone-in chicken thighs and/or drumsticks
    (about 700 g/1 lb 8½ oz total), skin removed
2 tablespoons finely chopped flat-leaf parsley
2 tablespoons finely chopped coriander (cilantro)
1 teaspoon sugar
1 teaspoon ground ginger
1 teaspoon ground cinnamon
pinch of saffron threads, crumbled
salt and pepper

For the egg filling:
4 large eggs, beaten

For the almond filling:
150 g/5 oz (1 cup) whole almonds
neutral oil, for frying
2 tablespoons sugar
15 g/½ oz (1 tablespoon) butter
1 teaspoon orange blossom water
¼ teaspoon ground cinnamon

For assembling:
neutral oil or melted butter, for brushing
9 round *warka*, *brick* or *dioul* pastry leaves
    (see page 56) or filo (phyllo) sheets
1 egg yolk, beaten
icing (confectioners') sugar, to decorate
ground cinnamon, to decorate

PREPARE THE CHICKEN FILLING: Heat the olive oil in a large pot or saucepan over a medium heat, add the onion and cook for 5 minutes, or until the onion begins to soften. Add the garlic and chicken and cook for another 5 minutes, or

until it changes colour. Add the parsley, coriander (cilantro), sugar, ginger, cinnamon and saffron, then season with salt and pepper. Stir in 200 ml (7 fl oz/generous ¾ cup) water, cover and cook for 45 minutes, or until the chicken is tender and comes away from the bone. It should be a thick sauce; remove the lid at the end to reduce if needed. Remove the chicken from the sauce and leave to cool. Transfer half of the sauce to a large bowl. Shred the meat and put into the bowl. Set aside.

PREPARE THE EGG FILLING: Add the eggs to the pot with the remaining sauce and cook, uncovered, over a low heat for 5–10 minutes until set and the mixture is 'dry', stirring frequently. Spoon into a clean bowl and leave to cool.

PREPARE THE ALMOND FILLING: Blanch, peel and fry the almonds in oil until golden following the directions on page 445. Transfer with a slotted spoon to paper towels to drain and cool. Put the cooled almonds, sugar, butter, orange blossom water and cinnamon into a blender and pulse to a grainy (not smooth) consistency. Set aside.

Preheat the oven to 180°C/350°F/Gas Mark 4. Put oil for brushing into a small bowl.

TO ASSEMBLE: Brush a round 23-cm/9-inch pie dish or cake pan with oil. Lay 1 pastry sheet over the top, leaving about a third of the sheet hanging over the edge of the dish. Lightly brush with oil and lay another pastry sheet on top of the first, somewhat overlapping and with about a third overhanging the edge. Lightly brush with oil and repeat with 2 more sheets, with each one somewhat overlapping the other. Lay 1 sheet in the very centre as the base. Spread the chicken filling evenly over the centre. On top, spread the egg filling and finally cover with the almond filling. Place a round pastry sheet over the top, then fold the corners of the overhanging pastry over the top, keeping its circular shape. Smooth out the folded edges so that the *pastilla* is even and flat. Brush with oil. Top with 1 pastry sheet and tuck around the sides and under the edges. Brush the top with oil. Lay another sheet on top and tuck around the sides and under the edges. Brush the top with oil. Lay a final sheet on top and tuck around the sides and under the edges. Brush with oil and then the beaten egg yolk.

Transfer to the hot oven and bake for 30 minutes, or until the *pastilla* is golden and the edges are slightly crispy. Remove from the oven and leave to cool. Before serving, generously dust the top with icing (confectioners') sugar and decorate with some lines of cinnamon.

Seafood Pastilla

MOROCCO
PREPARATION TIME: 45 minutes,
plus cooling time
COOKING TIME: 55 minutes
SERVES: 4–6

While the classic *pastilla* (or *bastella*) has chicken or pigeon in the filling (page 62), this modern version with seafood has become extremely popular. Chinese vermicelli rice noodles are used as a filler along with the seafood. The pastry leaves are brushed with oil, but they can also be brushed with butter or a blend of oil and butter.

3 tablespoons olive oil, plus extra for brushing
200 g/7 oz cleaned squid (calamari), cut into
   small pieces
2 cloves of garlic, minced
1 heaped tablespoon finely chopped flat-leaf parsley
1 heaped tablespoon finely chopped coriander
   (cilantro)
½ teaspoon sweet paprika
½ teaspoon ground cumin
pinch of saffron threads, crumbled
200 g/7 oz peeled and deveined raw prawns (shrimp)
200 g/7 oz firm white-fleshed fish fillets such as cod,
   bream or monkfish, skinned
80 g/3 oz thin Asian rice stick (vermicelli) noodles
2 tablespoons fresh lemon juice
1 teaspoon grated lemon zest, or ½ preserved lemon,
   flesh scraped out and discarded, peel finely
   chopped (see page 292)
9–10 round *warka*, *brick* or *dioul* pastry leaves
   (see page 56) or filo (phyllo) sheets
1 egg yolk, beaten
salt and pepper
1 lemon, cut into wedges, to serve

Heat the oil in a large frying pan or sauté pan over a high heat. Add the squid (calamari) and cook for 5–10 minutes until it has released its moisture and is golden and tender. Stir in the garlic, parsley, coriander (cilantro), paprika, cumin and saffron, and season with salt and pepper. Add the prawns (shrimp) and cook for 2 minutes, or until they have released their moisture. Add the fish and cook for 5–8 minutes, depending on the thickness of the fillets, breaking the fish into flakes as it turns opaque. Transfer to a large bowl.

Bring a large saucepan of lightly salted water to the boil, add the vermicelli noodles and boil for 5 minutes, or until tender but not mushy. Drain in a colander and rinse with cool water. Cut with kitchen scissors into shorter lengths, then transfer to the

bowl with the fish. Add the lemon juice and zest and toss the mixture to blend well. Leave to cool.

Preheat the oven to 180 °C/350 °F/Gas Mark 4. Put oil for brushing into a small bowl.

Brush a round 20-cm/8-inch pie dish or cake pan with oil. Lay 1 pastry sheet over the top, leaving about a third of the sheet hanging over the edge of the dish. Lightly brush with oil and lay another pastry sheet on top of the first, somewhat overlapping and with about a third overhanging the edge. Lightly brush with oil and repeat with 2 or 3 more sheets, with each one somewhat overlapping the other. Lay 1 sheet in the very centre as the base. Spoon the seafood mixture evenly over the centre. Place a round pastry sheet over the top, then fold the corners of the overhanging pastry over the top, keeping its circular shape. Smooth out the folded edges so that the *pastilla* is even and flat. Brush with oil. Top with 1 pastry sheet and tuck around the sides and under the edges. Brush the top with oil. Lay another sheet on top and tuck around the sides and under the edges. Brush the top with oil. Lay a final sheet on top and tuck around the sides and under the edges. Brush with oil and then the beaten egg yolk.

Transfer the *pastilla* to the hot oven and bake for 30 minutes, or until golden and the edges are slightly crispy. Transfer to a serving plate and serve hot in wedges with lemon wedges on the side.

Honeycomb Baghrir Crêpes

ALGERIA, MOROCCO
PREPARATION TIME: 10 minutes,
plus resting time
COOKING TIME: 30 minutes
MAKES: 12 × 13-cm/5-inch *baghrir*

Spongy *baghrir* are akin to a large crêpe or pancake cooked only on one side. On the surface is a honeycombed web made from bubbles forming, merging then popping, giving them their distinctive sponginess. Sometimes in French they are called *crêpe mille trous*, 'thousand-holes crêpe'. While the batter was once left overnight to ferment and form bubbles, most cooks now blend for 1–2 minutes to thoroughly aerate and then leave it to stand for a shorter time. A couple of warm *baghrir* with melted butter and honey drizzled over the top is a wonderful way to start the day. Snugly wrapped in cling film (plastic wrap) and stored in the refrigerator, cooked *baghrir* keep well for a few days. Reheat in a frying pan for a few minutes.

325 g/11½ oz (2 cups) fine semolina
1 heaped tablespoon plain (all-purpose) flour
2 teaspoons baking powder
1½ teaspoons instant yeast or fast-action active dry
    yeast granules
1 teaspoon sugar
1 teaspoon salt
butter, to serve
honey, to serve

Put the semolina, flour, baking powder, yeast, sugar and salt into a blender. Add 500 ml (18 fl oz/2 cups) lukewarm water and blend at high speed for at least 1 minute to get a smooth, bubbly and well-aerated batter. Pour into a bowl, cover tightly with cling film (plastic wrap) and leave in a warm place for 30 minutes to rest. There should be a foamy layer on top.

Heat a non-stick crêpe pan over a medium heat, ladle 60 ml (2 fl oz/¼ cup) of the batter into the centre of the pan and allow it to spread. Do not tilt or swirl the pan. Cook for 1½ minutes, or until set, the top isn't wet and feels spongy, and the bottom is golden. Do not flip. Transfer with a wide spatula to a clean dish towel to cool.

Make the remaining baghrir. Do not stack the cooked *baghrir* on top of one another until completely cool.

Melt some butter and honey in a small saucepan over a low heat. Serve the *baghrir* with the butter and honey to drizzle over the top.

Layered Msemen Flatbread with Honey

ALGERIA, MOROCCO, TUNISIA
PREPARATION TIME: 30 minutes,
plus resting time
COOKING TIME: 1 hour
MAKES: about 12 breads

Msemen is an enormously popular layered flatbread cooked in a frying pan or on a griddle pan. With honey it is a breakfast favourite. While generally unleavened, some cooks add a bit of yeast to the dough as it will keep better, ideal for a larger batch to be eaten over a few days. In Tunisia they are called *mlaoui*.

250 g/9 oz (1½ cups) fine semolina
250 g/9 oz (1¾ cups) plain (all-purpose) flour,
    plus extra for dusting
1 teaspoon salt
pinch of sugar
neutral oil, for oiling and brushing

75 g/2¾ oz (½ cup) coarse or medium semolina,
    for sprinkling
60 g/2¼ oz (¼ cup) butter
honey, to serve

Sift the fine semolina and flour into a large, wide bowl, add the salt and sugar and, using your fingers, work in about 280 ml (9 fl oz/1 cup plus 2 tablespoons) warm water to form a moist but not overly sticky dough. Transfer to a lightly floured work counter and patiently knead for 10 minutes, or until supple and elastic. Or use a dough hook in a stand mixer. Put the dough into a lightly oiled bowl, cover with cling film (plastic wrap) and leave to rest at room temperature for 10 minutes.

Put the coarse semolina into a small bowl. Put about 60 ml (2 fl oz/¼ cup) of oil and the butter into a small saucepan and heat over a medium-low heat until the butter melts. Stir and remove from the heat.

Moisten your hands with the oil-butter mixture and divide the dough into 12 balls, about 5 cm/2 inches in diameter. Cover with cling film and leave to rest for 10 minutes.

Using oiled hands, press each ball flat on a flat, lightly oiled work counter and begin working the dough outwards with your fingers to form an even, thin sheet, about 23 cm/9 inches in diameter, without tearing. It should be thin enough to be almost transparent. Brush with the oil-butter mixture and sprinkle with some coarse semolina. Fold into thirds like a sheet for a letter by doubling the 2 sides so that they overlap in the centre. Fold in the other 2 sides in the same manner of thirds to form a 6-cm/2½-inch square. Place on a lightly oiled platter. Once all the balls have been rolled, cover with cling film and leave to rest for 5 minutes.

Line a platter with paper towels. Heat a griddle pan or large, heavy frying pan over a medium heat and brush with the oil-butter mixture.

Working with one at a time, place a piece of folded dough on the oiled work counter and press out to 13–15 cm/5–6 inches square. Lightly sprinkle with semolina and lay, semolina-side down, in the pan. Brush with the oil-butter mixture and lightly sprinkle the top with semolina. Cook for 3–5 minutes, turning from time to time, until golden. Transfer to the paper towels to absorb any excess oil and repeat with the remaining dough.

Serve warm with honey.

Spiral Meloui Flatbread

MOROCCO
PREPARATION TIME: 45 minutes–1 hour,
plus resting time
COOKING TIME: 20 minutes
MAKES: about 12 small breads

These flaky, spiral Moroccan breads called
meloui (or *mlaoui*) are rolled like a snail and then
flattened, giving a spiral grain to the finished bread.
The dough is the leavened version of *msemen*
(flatbread, page 65).

- 250 g/9 oz (1½ cups) fine semolina
- 250 g/9 oz (1⅔ cups) plain (all-purpose) flour,
  plus extra for dusting
- 1 teaspoon instant yeast or fast-action active dry yeast
  granules
- 1 teaspoon salt
- neutral oil, for oiling and brushing
- 75 g/2¾ oz (½ cup) medium or fine semolina,
  for sprinkling
- 2 teaspoons baking powder
- 2 tablespoons olive oil
- 25 g/1 oz (2 tablespoons) butter

Sift the fine semolina and flour into a wide bowl, add
the yeast and salt and, using your fingers, gradually work
in about 280 ml (9 fl oz/1 cup plus 2 tablespoons)
warm water to form a moist but not overly sticky
dough. Transfer to a lightly floured work counter
and patiently knead for 10 minutes, or until supple
and elastic. Or use a dough hook in a stand mixer.
Put the dough into a lightly oiled bowl, cover with
cling film (plastic wrap) and leave to rest at room
temperature for 10 minutes.

Put the medium semolina and baking powder into
a small bowl and mix together. Put the olive oil and
butter into a small saucepan and heat over a medium-
low heat until the butter melts. Stir and remove from
the heat.

Moisten your hands with the oil-butter mixture and
divide the dough into 12 balls, about 5 cm/2 inches
in diameter. Cover with cling film and leave to
rest for 10 minutes. Re-moisten your hands with
the oil-butter mixture and press each ball flat on a
flat, lightly oiled work counter and begin working
the dough outwards with your hands to about
25 cm/10 inches in diameter and thin enough to be
almost transparent. Brush with the oil-butter mixture
and sprinkle with some semolina mixture.

Fold in half, sprinkle with semolina mixture, then
fold the bottom up to form a long, 6-cm/2½-inch-
wide strip. Rub with the oil-butter mixture and
sprinkle with semolina mix. Roll into a fat cylinder

and push the centres in with your thumbs. Place
on a lightly oiled platter and prepare the remaining
dough and filling.

Heat a griddle pan or large, heavy frying pan
over a high-medium heat. Lightly oil.

Working with 1 or 2 at a time, on the lightly
oiled work counter, flatten the dough, pushing out
from the centre, to about 12–13 cm/4½–5 inches in
diameter. Lay on the pan and cook for 3 minutes,
turning from time to time, until golden. Transfer to
a platter lined with paper towels to absorb any excess
oil, then wrap in a clean dish towel to keep warm.
Repeat with the remaining dough. The breads are
best eaten when warm.

Chickpea Flour Tart

ALGERIA, MOROCCO
PREPARATION TIME: 5 minutes,
plus resting time
COOKING TIME: 30–40 minutes
SERVES: 8–12

The local name for Algeria's iconic snack, which is
especially popular in the city of Oran, is *calentica*,
kalinti or *karantika*. In northern Morocco it is called
caliente, the Spanish word for 'hot'. It has distinctive
layers: the firmer bottom, a soft, flan-like top and
a gratinated surface. Slices or squares cut from the
pan can be dusted with salt and cumin, but it is also
common to put pieces inside a baguette, sprinkled
with salt and cumin and with a dollop of harissa.

- 250 g/9 oz (2 cups) chickpea (garbanzo bean) flour
- 1 teaspoon salt, plus extra to serve
- 2 tablespoons olive oil, plus extra for oiling
- 2 baguettes, optional
- ground cumin, for dusting
- harissa (page 409), optional

Put the chickpea (garbanzo bean) flour, salt and
1 litre (34 fl oz/4¼ cups) warm water into a blender
or electric mixer and blend well. Leave to rest for
1 hour. Add the oil and blend well again.

Preheat the oven to 245°C/475°F/Gas Mark 9
with both the top and bottom elements.

Oil a 20-cm/8-inch round deep baking dish or
20 × 20-cm/8 × 8-inch square one and add the batter.
It should be about 2 cm/¾ inch deep. Transfer to
the hot oven and bake for 30–40 minutes until the
bottom half is set, the top half is flan-like and the
surface has some dark spots. Remove from the oven,
loosen the edges with a spatula and cut into wedges.
Serve hot either by itself or inside a baguette (if
using). Season with cumin and a dollop of harissa
(if using).

FRESH
AND COOKED
SALADS

Grilled Salad

TUNISIA
PREPARATION TIME: 20 minutes,
plus cooling time
COOKING TIME: 40 minutes
SERVES: 4–6

Slata mishwiya – 'grilled salad' – is one of Tunisia's best-known dishes, and a much beloved opener to many meals. While cooks traditionally pounded the peppers and tomatoes in a large mortar, most now finely chop with a knife. The peppers can be grilled on embers, over a gas flame or, as in this recipe, under a grill (broiler). This version comes from Nabeul, on the Cap Bon peninsula, home to the country's important pepper industry. Caraway gives this classic salad a pleasing nutty and slightly pungent flavour, while garnishing it with a spoonful of capers can make a zesty addition. Serve with a small dish of harissa – and plenty of bread.

2 red bell peppers
2 long sweet green peppers or 1 green bell pepper
3 ripe tomatoes
neutral oil, for brushing
2 cloves of garlic, unpeeled
½ teaspoon ground caraway
extra-virgin olive oil, for drizzling
½ lemon
1 (150-g/5-oz) can of tuna in olive oil, drained, optional
salt
12 black olives, to garnish
2 Hard-boiled Eggs (page 443), peeled and cut into wedges, to garnish
harissa (page 409), to serve

Preheat the oven grill (broiler). Brush the peppers and tomatoes with neutral oil and arrange on a large baking sheet. Scatter the garlic around the sheet. Grill (broil) for 30–40 minutes, turning from time to time, until the vegetables are charred in places and tender and the garlic is soft. Remove from the oven, cover the tray with aluminium foil and leave to cool in the steam to make peeling easier.

Once cool enough to handle, peel, core and seed the peppers and tomatoes, reserving the juices. Pinch the garlic from its skin. Finely chop the peppers, tomatoes and garlic, put into a large bowl, add the caraway and a tablespoonful of the reserved juices, and season with salt. Mix well.

Spoon into a salad bowl, generously drizzle with olive oil and squeeze over the lemon. Arrange the tuna (if using) on top and the olives and hard-boiled eggs around the edges. Serve with harissa to add as desired.

'SALADS'

The concept of 'salad' in North Africa is quite loose and has few rules. While some salads are prepared with fresh produce and served raw, many first require cooking the vegetables – grilling, frying, steaming or boiling – before using in a salad that can be served at the beginning of a meal either warm or chilled. Algerian *hmiss* with roasted peppers and tomatoes (page 72), Tunisian *omek houria* of boiled and mashed carrots (page 81) and smooth Moroccan aubergine (eggplant) *zaâlouk* salad (page 87–88) are iconic. In Morocco, salads frequently showcase the penchant for combining disparate flavours.

The ideal opening to lunch or dinner is a handful of diverse salads. Rather than serving just one, prepare a couple and eat them over the course of a few days, adding a fresh one or two prepared at the moment.

When choosing which to prepare, the key is to contrast flavours, colours and textures. One way to highlight this is using a selection with the same principal ingredient. A dish of tangy beetroot (beets) with plenty of fresh herbs (page 97) might appear beside a sweet one of beetroot tossed with orange segments and a hint of orange blossom water (page 94). Or a salad with chilled circles of boiled carrots tossed with olive oil, sweet paprika and plenty of cumin (page 78) is an ideal companion to a bowl of grated raw carrots steeped in fresh orange juice, scattered with raisins and scented with orange blossom water and ground cinnamon (page 81). This playful linking chain of ingredients can continue with a bowl of orange segments tossed in olive oil and garnished with black olives (page 105) and then maybe a salad of beetroot and oranges.

While salads with fresh produce are generally served cool, ones that used cooked vegetables can be served either chilled (typical in summer) or warm. Serve them as a first course or starter, but keep them on the table when the main course arrives, and they convert into side dishes.

Grilled Salad ➤

Grilled Pepper and Tomato Salad

ALGERIA
PREPARATION TIME: 15 minutes,
plus cooling time
COOKING TIME: 40 minutes
SERVES: 4

Hmiss is Algeria's best-known – and best-loved – salad. This version from Constantine and the northeast includes peppers, tomatoes and garlic. Elsewhere around the country it might have coriander (cilantro) or caraway or come garnished with Hard-boiled Eggs (page 443). Served warm or chilled, it is frequently eaten with *kesra* flatbread (page 45). Depending on the peppers used, *hmiss* can be very spicy. Such popularity means that there are many ways to prepare it. This version roasts and peels the peppers. (Some purists don't rinse while removing the blackened skin, arguing that the water washes away some of that lovely smoky flavour.) While peeling, it helps to frequently rinse your hands to remove the clingy bits.

  4 long sweet green peppers or 2 green bell peppers
  3 tablespoons extra-virgin olive oil, plus extra for
    drizzling
  2 cloves of garlic, minced
  3 ripe tomatoes, halved crosswise and grated,
    peel discarded (see page 445)
  salt and pepper
  1 green chilli (chile), cored, seeded and sliced,
    to garnish, optional

Roast the peppers over a gas flame on the stove, under an oven grill (broiler) or on a barbecue for 5–15 minutes, turning as the skin blackens and blisters. Put into a paper sack or put into a bowl, cover with aluminium foil and leave to cool in the steam to soften and make peeling easier. Once cool enough to handle, remove the stems and seeds, reserving the juices. Rub off the blackened skin and finely chop the flesh. Set aside.

Heat the oil in a medium sauté pan or frying pan over a medium heat, add the garlic and cook for 30 seconds, or until aromatic. Add the tomatoes and 60 ml (2 fl oz/¼ cup) of the reserved juices from the peppers or water. Season with salt and pepper and cook for 12 minutes, or until darker and reduced. Add the peppers, reduce the heat to low and cook for about 15 minutes, or until very soft. Add a few spoonfuls more of the reserved pepper juice or water if needed. Spoon into a salad bowl. Before serving, generously drizzle with oil and garnish with the chilli (chile), if desired.

Grilled Green Pepper and Tomato Salad

MOROCCO
PREPARATION TIME: 15 minutes,
plus cooling time
COOKING TIME: 15 minutes
SERVES: 4

This classic Moroccan salad combines the smokiness of grilled peppers with the summery freshness of raw tomatoes. It is called *taktouka* for the sizzling sound it makes while cooking. Roast the peppers over a gas flame, on a charcoal barbecue or under an indoor grill (broiler). Serve the salad warm, at room temperature or chilled. Stir in a tablespoon of finely chopped preserved lemon (page 410) for a zesty touch.

  2 green bell peppers
  2 ripe tomatoes, peeled (see page 445) and diced
  1 small clove of garlic, minced
  1 tablespoon finely chopped flat-leaf parsley
  1 tablespoon finely chopped coriander (cilantro)
  ¼ teaspoon sweet paprika
  pinch of ground cumin
  2 tablespoons extra-virgin olive oil
  1 tablespoon fresh lemon juice
  salt and pepper

Roast the peppers over a gas flame on the stove, under an oven grill (broiler) or on a barbecue for 5–15 minutes, turning as the skin blackens and blisters. Place in a paper sack or put into a bowl, cover with aluminium foil and leave to cool in the steam to soften and make peeling easier. Once cool enough to handle, rub off the blackened skin. Remove the stems and seeds, reserving the juices, then cut the peppers into 1-cm/½-inch square pieces.

Put the peppers, tomatoes, garlic, parsley, coriander (cilantro), paprika and cumin into a salad bowl, season with salt and pepper and drizzle over the oil. Toss. Before serving, add the lemon juice and toss again. Serve warm, at room temperature or even chilled.

Caramelized Tomatoes with Prunes and Almonds

MOROCCO
PREPARATION TIME: 15 minutes
COOKING TIME: 1 hour
SERVES: 4–6

Serve this sweet, caramelized tomato salad warm, at room temperature or slightly chilled – but always with plenty of bread. Prunes with stones (pits) tend to hold together better when cooking and are preferable to use here.

3 tablespoons olive oil
1.5 kg/3¼ lb ripe tomatoes, peeled (see page 445) and cut into small pieces, reserving all juices
3 tablespoons sugar
1¼ teaspoons ground cinnamon
2 tablespoons honey
100 g/3½ oz (⅔ cup) prunes, preferably with stones (pits)
salt and pepper
30 g/1 oz (scant ¼ cup) roasted almonds (see page 445), chopped, to garnish
toasted sesame seeds, to garnish

Heat the oil in a frying pan or sauté pan over a medium heat, add the tomatoes and their juices, 1 tablespoon of the sugar and 1 teaspoon of the cinnamon, and season with salt and pepper. Bring to a simmer, cover and cook over a medium-low heat, stirring from time to time, about 30 minutes. Add the honey and cook, uncovered, for 15–20 minutes, stirring frequently, until jammy.

Meanwhile, bring 250 ml (8 fl oz/1 cup) water to a simmer in a small saucepan. Add the prunes, the remaining 2 tablespoons sugar and ¼ teaspoon of cinnamon. Simmer, uncovered, over a low heat until tender but not mushy and the liquid is syrupy, carefully stirring from time to time, about 30 minutes. Remove from the heat.

Spoon the tomatoes into a wide dish. Remove the prunes with a spoon and arrange on top. Drizzle some syrup from the saucepan over the top, sprinkle with the chopped almonds and sesame seeds and serve.

Fresh Summer Salad with Tomatoes, Cucumber and Chilli

LIBYA
PREPARATION TIME: 10 minutes
SERVES: 4

Slatha is a popular Libyan summer salad. It can be quite herby – add some coriander (cilantro) or mint leaves if desired – and can be eaten as a light, summertime meal with plenty of bread rather than as a side dish. Serve with crusty bread and perhaps some high-quality tuna preserved in olive oil.

6 tomatoes, coarsely chopped, all juices reserved
1 red onion, cut into thin slices
1 cucumber, peeled and diced
1 green chilli (chile), seeded and cut into small pieces
12 green olives
4 tablespoons extra-virgin olive oil
2 tablespoons fresh lemon juice
salt
crusty bread, to serve

Put the tomatoes and all their juices, the onion, cucumber, chilli (chile) and olives into a large salad bowl and season with salt. Add the oil and lemon juice and loosen with a few tablespoons of cold water if desired to make it juicier. Toss to blend. Serve with crusty bread.

Tomato and Pepper Confit Salad

TUNISIA
PREPARATION TIME: 15 minutes,
plus cooling time
COOKING TIME: 2 hours
SERVES: 4–6

Considered a dish that originated in the country's Jewish community, *mekbouba* remains popular to prepare at home in Tunisia. There are different ways that cooks cut the tomatoes and peppers, but leaving the tomatoes in quarters and the peppers in long strips gives a pleasing final texture to the salad. Add a small, whole fresh chilli (chile), if desired. There are two key points when cooking *mekbouba*. The first is to make sure the heat is very low. The second is to not stir the tomatoes and peppers for the first 1½ hours or so, and then stir only very little.

4 tablespoons olive oil
4 cloves of garlic, peeled
5 ripe tomatoes, cored and quartered
1 red bell pepper, cored, seeded and cut into 2-cm-/
  ¾-inch-thick strips
1 chilli (chile), optional
salt

Add the oil and garlic to a large frying pan or sauté pan and cook over a low heat for 1 minute, or until aromatic. Add the tomatoes, peppers and chilli (chile) (if using), season with salt and cook, uncovered, over a low heat for 2 hours, or until the moisture has evaporated and the tomatoes and peppers are very sweet. Stir only after about 1½ hours, then only a few times to turn the pieces. Spoon into a wide dish and leave to cool. Serve at room temperature or chilled.

Tomato Salad with Anchovies and Capers

TUNISIA
PREPARATION TIME: 10 minutes
SERVES: 4

The bold flavours of anchovies and capers make a perfect duo. Here they combine delightfully with tomatoes in a simple and vibrant Tunisian salad. This is perfect to serve in the summer.

8 anchovy fillets
4 ripe tomatoes, cored and diced
3 tablespoons extra-virgin olive oil, for drizzling
1 tablespoon fresh lemon juice
1 heaped tablespoon finely chopped flat-leaf parsley
2 tablespoons capers, rinsed
salt and pepper

Rinse the anchovies under cold running water, pat dry with paper towels and set aside.

Put the tomatoes into a salad bowl. Put the oil and lemon juice into a small bowl and whisk together, then stir in the parsley and season with salt and pepper. Pour over the tomatoes and turn with a spoon until coated. Scatter over the capers and arrange the anchovies across the top. Serve.

Tozeur Mashed Summer Salad

TUNISIA
PREPARATION TIME: 10 minutes
SERVES: 3–4

Known as *radhkha de Tozeur*, this summer salad refers to Tozeur, an oasis along the northern edge of the Sahara in southern Tunisia. Once a major trans-Saharan trading post and important waystation, Tozeur is today best known for the deglet nour dates grown in its sprawling palmeraie. While the tomatoes in this dish were once pounded in a mortar, most home cooks now grate them on a box grater. Some add a dash of vinegar or fresh lemon juice to the salad.

6 ripe plum tomatoes
2 small green chillies (chiles), seeded and deribbed
2 cloves of garlic, minced
4 tablespoons extra-virgin olive oil
white vinegar or fresh lemon juice, for dashing,
  optional
salt

Trim the end of the tomatoes, then seed and grate on a box grater (see page 445). Put into a bowl. Grate the chillies (chiles) and the garlic (or mince with a knife) and add to the bowl. Season with salt, add the oil and stir to blend. Add a dash of vinegar (if using), stir again and divide among bowls. Serve with spoons.

Tomato and Pepper Confit Salad ➤

Tomato, Cucumber and Onion Salad

TUNISIA
PREPARATION TIME: 15 minutes
SERVES: 4

This salad of tomatoes, cucumber and onion tossed in a vinaigrette with dried mint is so identified with the country that people call it *slata tounsia*, 'Tunisian salad'. This version includes some pieces of tart green apple for a delightful acidic tang.

    4 ripe tomatoes, peeled (see page 445) and diced
    1 cucumber, peeled and diced
    1 small red onion, finely chopped
    ½ tart green apple, cored and diced, optional
    1½ teaspoons dried mint
    3 tablespoons extra-virgin olive oil
    1 tablespoon fresh lemon juice
    salt
    black olives, to garnish
    2 Hard-boiled Eggs (page 443), peeled and cut into
        wedges, to garnish

Put the tomatoes, cucumber, onion and apple (if using) into a large bowl and sprinkle over the mint. Whisk the oil and lemon juice together in a small bowl with a generous pinch of salt, pour over the salad and toss to blend. Spoon onto a serving plate. Garnish with olives and the hard-boiled eggs and serve.

Spiced Carrot Salad

ALGERIA
PREPARATION TIME: 10 minutes,
plus cooling and chilling time
COOKING TIME: 35 minutes
SERVES: 4

This popular cooked carrot salad is a year-round favourite in Algeria. During Ramadan, it is a typical one to prepare among the salads for the fast-breaking *iftar* meal in the evening. While they can be boiled, the carrots are steamed here so that none of their natural sweetness leaches out into the boiling water. The salad can be served lukewarm, although the flavours are denser and sweeter when chilled.

    6 carrots, cut into 5-mm-/¼-inch-thick circles
    2 cloves of garlic, minced
    1 teaspoon sweet paprika
    ½ teaspoon ground caraway or cumin
    2 tablespoons olive oil
    white vinegar, for dashing
    salt and pepper
    finely chopped coriander (cilantro) or flat-leaf parsley,
        to garnish

Bring a large steamer pot or couscoussier to the boil with about 5 cm/2 inches water. Put the carrots into the steamer basket, snugly cover with a lid and steam for about 30 minutes, or until tender. Alternatively, boil in a large saucepan of lightly salted water for 10–15 minutes, then drain. Put the carrots into a salad bowl.

Meanwhile, put the garlic, paprika and caraway into a mortar and pound with a pestle. Season with salt and pepper, then stir in a small amount of water to form a loose paste. Heat the oil in a small frying pan over a low heat, add the paste and cook for 2–3 minutes, stirring constantly, until aromatic and the garlic has lost its raw bite. Do not let it burn. Spoon over the carrots, dash with vinegar and turn to coat while still warm. Leave to cool, then cover with cling film (plastic wrap) and refrigerate until chilled. Before serving, add the coriander (cilantro) and toss to mix.

Caramelized Carrot Salad with Golden Sultanas and Fried Almonds

MOROCCO
PREPARATION TIME: 10 minutes,
plus cooling and chilling time
COOKING TIME: 30 minutes
SERVES: 4

In this sweet cooked carrot salad, cinnamon and ginger add lovely aromatic notes, the sultanas (golden raisins) a boost of sweetness and the fried almonds a contrast in flavour as well as texture in their pleasing crunch.

500 g/1 lb 2 oz carrots
50 g/2 oz (⅓ cup) golden sultanas (golden raisins) or seedless raisins
3 tablespoons sugar
¼ teaspoon ground cinnamon, plus extra to garnish
¼ teaspoon ground ginger
1 tablespoon olive oil
½ small lemon
75 g/2¾ oz (½ cup) whole almonds
neutral oil, for frying
salt

Halve the carrots lengthwise. Remove the cores if thick, then cut crosswise into 5-mm-/¼-inch-thick pieces.

Put the carrots, a pinch of salt and 250 ml (8 fl oz/ 1 cup) water into a large saucepan and bring to the boil. Cover with a lid, reduce the heat and gently boil for about 10 minutes, or until starting to become tender. Add the sultanas (golden raisins), sugar, cinnamon, ginger and olive oil and cook, uncovered, for 15 minutes, or until the carrots are tender, the sultanas plump and the sauce has reduced to a glaze. Squeeze the lemon over the top and stir. Transfer to a salad bowl and leave to cool. Cover with cling film (plastic wrap) and refrigerate until chilled.

Put the almonds into a small saucepan of water, bring to the boil and boil for 3–5 minutes, then drain and leave to cool. Once cool enough to handle, slip off the skins by rubbing them with your fingers. Spread the almonds out on paper towels to dry. Heat about 7 mm/⅓ inch of neutral oil in a small frying pan over a medium heat until the surface shimmers. Line a plate with paper towels. Add the almonds and fry for 1–2 minutes until just golden. Transfer with a slotted spoon to the paper towels to drain.

Before serving, toss the carrots, add a pinch of cinnamon and top with the fried almonds.

Carrot and Cumin Salad

ALGERIA, MOROCCO
PREPARATION TIME: 10 minutes,
plus cooling and chilling time
COOKING TIME: 12 minutes
SERVES: 4

One of Morocco's most popular cooked salads, this dish offers an ideal combination of the chilled sweetness of carrots and earthiness of cumin and paprika. Prepare in advance to allow them time to fully chill and the flavours to blend. It is also commonly found in Algeria.

450 g/1 lb carrots, cut into 5-mm-/¼-inch-thick circles
4 tablespoons olive oil
1 teaspoon ground cumin
½ teaspoon sweet paprika
½ teaspoon sugar
1 small lemon, halved
2 heaped tablespoons finely chopped flat-leaf parsley
salt and pepper

Put the carrots into a large saucepan of lightly salted water, bring to the boil and boil for 8–10 minutes until just tender. Transfer with a slotted spoon to a bowl of cold water to stop further cooking. Once the carrots have cooled, drain and spread out on paper towels to dry.

Heat the oil in a large frying pan or sauté pan over a medium heat, add the carrots, cumin, paprika and sugar and season with salt and pepper. Cook, turning the carrots over, for 1 minute. Remove from the heat. Squeeze ½ of the lemon over the carrots and turn to coat evenly. Transfer to a bowl and leave to cool. Cover with cling film (plastic wrap) and refrigerate until chilled. Before serving, squeeze the remaining lemon half over the carrots, scatter over the parsley and turn to mix.

Grated Carrot Salad with Orange Juice, Raisins and Cinnamon

MOROCCO
PREPARATION TIME: 10 minutes,
plus soaking and chilling time
SERVES: 4–6

This delicious, popular salad can do double duty and be served as a dessert. It is fresh, with a delightful texture and juiciness. While the raisins can be omitted, they add a lovely sweet chewiness to the salad. If the carrots have large, bitter cores, remove them before grating.

2 oranges
35 g/1¼ oz (¼ cup) seedless raisins
2 carrots (225 g/8 oz), grated
1 tablespoon sugar
dash of orange blossom water
ground cinnamon, for dusting

Juice the oranges into a large bowl. There should be about 250 ml (8 fl oz/1 cup) of juice. Add the raisins and leave to soak for 15 minutes to soften.

Put the carrots into a serving bowl, add the orange juice, raisins, sugar and orange blossom water and turn to mix. Cover with cling film (plastic wrap) and refrigerate until well chilled. Divide among small bowls, generously dust with cinnamon and serve.

Mashed Carrot Salad

TUNISIA
PREPARATION TIME: 10 minutes,
plus cooling and chilling time
COOKING TIME: 20 minutes
SERVES: 4

The name of this famous Tunisian mashed carrot salad is *omek houria*, which roughly translates to 'the carrot's mother'. Home cooks prepare it in various degrees of consistency – some very soft, even mushy, while others give it more of a minced texture. It can be garnished with a broad variety of items including Hard-boiled Eggs (page 443), shredded white cheese, anchovy fillets, tuna, olives and capers. It is best served chilled, although it doesn't need to be.

5–6 carrots (about 600 g/1 lb 5 oz), cut into
    2-cm/¾-inch circles
harissa (page 409), to taste
1 clove of garlic, minced
¼ teaspoon ground caraway
3 tablespoons olive oil
juice of ½ lemon
salt
black olives, to garnish
2 Hard-boiled Eggs (page 443), peeled and cut
    into wedges, to garnish
capers, to garnish, optional
canned tuna, drained, to garnish, optional

Put the carrots into a large saucepan of lightly salted water, bring to the boil and boil for 15–20 minutes until tender. Drain, reserving about 60 ml (2 fl oz/¼ cup) of the liquid.

Put the still warm carrots into a large bowl and mash with a fork. Put harissa, to taste, into a small bowl and stir in 2 tablespoons of the reserved carrot liquid. Add to the carrots together with the garlic and caraway. Drizzle with the olive oil and lemon juice, season with salt and stir to blend well. Add a touch more of the reserved liquid if needed to loosen. Leave to cool. Cover with cling film (plastic wrap) and refrigerate until chilled.

Garnish with the olives and hard-boiled eggs, and capers and tuna (if using). Serve chilled.

Chilled Sweet Butternut Squash Salad with Cinnamon

MOROCCO
PREPARATION TIME: 10 minutes,
plus cooling and chilling time
COOKING TIME: 20 minutes
SERVES: 4

A dash of aromatic distillation gives a pleasant floral touch to this salad. The recipe calls for rose water, but the salad is also lovely with orange blossom water, especially when garnished with orange slices.

    1 kg/2¼ lb butternut, acorn or pumpkin squash, or
        another firm-fleshed, hard-skinned squash
    3 tablespoons olive oil
    50 g/2 oz (¼ cup) sugar
    2 pinches of salt
    ½ teaspoon rose water or orange blossom water,
        or extra as desired
    ground cinnamon, for dusting
    ½ orange, cut into thin slices, optional

Remove the skin from the squash, scoop out the seeds and cut the flesh into 1–1.5-cm/½–⅔-inch cubes. There should be about 675 g (1½ lb/4 cups) of cubes.

Heat the oil in a large frying pan or sauté pan over a medium-high heat, add the squash, sugar and salt, and cook, stirring from time to time, for 10 minutes. Sprinkle in the rose water, reduce the heat to medium and cook for about 10 minutes, or until the squash is tender but not mushy.

Transfer the squash to a serving bowl and leave to cool. Cover with cling film (plastic wrap) and refrigerate until chilled. Before serving, lightly dust with cinnamon and arrange the orange slices (if using) around the bowl.

Mashed Pumpkin Squash with Dates

MOROCCO
PREPARATION TIME: 20 minutes,
plus cooling and chilling time
COOKING TIME: 20 minutes
SERVES: 4

This delicious salad can be scented with a dash of orange blossom water. For a lovely contrast to the dish's smooth texture, garnish with chopped almonds.

    1 kg/2¼ lb pumpkin, butternut or acorn squash,
        or another firm-fleshed, hard-skinned squash
    2 tablespoons olive oil
    50 g/2 oz (¼ cup) sugar
    ½ teaspoon ground cinnamon, plus extra for dusting
    2 pinches of salt
    sesame seeds, to garnish
    12–16 soft, sweet dates, such as deglet nour or medjool

Remove the skin from the squash, scoop out the seeds and cut the flesh into about 2-cm/¾-inch cubes. There should be about 675 g (1½ lb/4 cups) of cubes.

Bring a large steamer pot or couscoussier to the boil with about 5 cm/2 inches water. Put the pumpkin into the steamer basket, snugly cover with a lid and steam for about 12 minutes, or until tender.

Heat the oil in a large frying pan or sauté pan over a medium-high heat, add the pumpkin, sugar, cinnamon and salt, and cook for about 5 minutes, while stirring and mashing down the pumpkin with a wooden spoon or potato masher, until it is a paste-like consistency.

Transfer to a serving bowl and leave to cool. Cover with cling film (plastic wrap) and refrigerate until chilled. Just before serving, lightly dust with cinnamon, sprinkle with sesame seeds and arrange the dates along the edges of the bowl.

Caramelized Pumpkin Salad

MOROCCO
PREPARATION TIME: 10 minutes,
plus cooling time
COOKING TIME: 50 minutes
SERVES: 2–3

This is a dense, sweet pumpkin salad, cooked until the moisture has largely evaporated. It's quite thick and pasty. The concentrated flavours go especially well with grilled meat dishes or strongly seasoned stews. It is called *garaa mderbla* or *m'aassla*, literally 'sweetened (or caramelized) pumpkin'. (*Garaa* can mean both pumpkin and courgette/zucchini.)

- 1 kg/2¼ lb pumpkin, butternut or acorn squash, or another firm-fleshed, hard-skinned squash
- 2 tablespoons olive or vegetable oil
- 1 tablespoon honey
- 1 tablespoon sugar
- 1 teaspoon orange blossom water, or to taste
- 2 pinches of ground cinnamon, plus extra for dusting
- salt
- fried almonds (page 445), to garnish

Remove the skin from the pumpkin, scoop out the seeds and cut the flesh into 2.5-cm/1-inch pieces. There should be about 675 g (1½ lb/4 cups) of cubes.

Put the pumpkin into a large saucepan of lightly salted water, bring to the boil and gently boil for about 20 minutes, or until tender. Drain in a colander for 15 minutes, jiggling the colander from time to time to drain as much moisture as possible.

Heat the oil in a medium frying pan or sauté pan over a medium-high heat, add the pumpkin and 1 teaspoon salt and cook for about 15 minutes, while stirring and mashing down the ingredients with the back of a fork or potato masher, to a paste-like consistency and the moisture has evaporated. Add the honey and sugar and cook for another 15 minutes, while stirring and mashing, until denser and darker. Stir in the orange blossom water and cinnamon and cook for a final 1 minute. Transfer to a serving bowl and leave to cool to room temperature. Garnish with fried almonds before serving.

Savoury Pumpkin Salad

MOROCCO
PREPARATION TIME: 10 minutes
COOKING TIME: 50 minutes
SERVES: 4

While there are plenty of delicious, cooked pumpkin salads in Morocco, not all of them are sweet. This savoury version has a bite of spice – yet it still carries some sweet, aromatic notes of cinnamon.

- 1 kg/2¼ lb pumpkin, butternut or acorn squash, or another firm-fleshed, hard-skinned squash
- 3 tablespoons olive oil
- 3 cloves of garlic, grated
- 2 heaped tablespoons finely chopped flat-leaf parsley
- 2 heaped tablespoons finely chopped coriander (cilantro)
- 1 small cinnamon stick or piece of cinnamon bark
- cayenne pepper, to taste
- salt

Remove the skin from the pumpkin, scoop out the seeds and cut the flesh into 1.5-cm/⅔-inch cubes. There should be about 675 g (1½ lb/4 cups) of cubes.

Add the pumpkin, oil and garlic to a large frying pan or sauté pan and cook over a medium heat for 2–3 minutes, stirring frequently, until the garlic is aromatic. Add the parsley, coriander (cilantro), cinnamon and cayenne pepper, season with salt and cover with 150 ml (5 fl oz/⅔ cup) water. Bring to the boil, reduce the heat and gently cook, uncovered, stirring from time to time until tender but not mushy and the sauce reduced, about 45 minutes. Spoon into a serving dish and serve warm or at room temperature.

Spicy Artichoke Salad with Capers, Olives and Hard-boiled Eggs

TUNISIA
PREPARATION TIME: 15 minutes,
plus cooling and chilling time
COOKING TIME: 10 minutes
SERVES: 4

Tunisia is one of the world's largest producers of artichokes. Artichoke season runs from early October until the end of May there, and during this period the long-stemmed, violet-tinged variety and the more familiar green ones are found abundantly in markets – and often on tables.

½ lemon
4 artichokes
2 tablespoons extra-virgin olive oil, plus extra if needed
2 cloves of garlic, minced
harissa (page 409), to taste
1 tablespoon capers, rinsed
salt and pepper
black olives, to garnish
2 Hard-boiled Eggs (page 443), peeled and cut into wedges, to garnish

Fill a large bowl with cool water. Squeeze in the lemon, then drop into the water. Working with one artichoke at a time, cut or pull away the toughest outer petals, then cut off the stem and trim away the top section. Cut into quarters, then remove the choke and drop into the lemon water to keep from discolouring. Repeat with the remaining artichokes. Drain only when ready to cook.

Heat the oil in a large frying pan or sauté pan over a medium heat, add the garlic and cook for about 30 seconds, or until aromatic, without browning. Add the artichokes and harissa, season with salt and pepper and cover with 120 ml (4 fl oz/½ cup) water. Partly cover the pan with a lid and simmer over a medium heat until tender and the liquid has evaporated, about 10 minutes. Add a touch more water if needed, or remove the lid towards the end to evaporate. Transfer to a salad bowl, leave to cool, then cover with cling film (plastic wrap) and refrigerate until chilled.

Before serving, toss the artichokes, adding more olive oil if needed. Scatter the capers over the top, then garnish with olives and the hard-boiled eggs and serve chilled.

Spinach and Preserved Lemon Salad

MOROCCO
PREPARATION TIME: 20 minutes
COOKING TIME: 5 minutes
SERVES: 4–6

This classic salad is prepared with spinach or with fresh mallow (*bakoula*; *mauve* in French), a spinach-like plant found in springtime in Morocco. (It is virtually impossible to find fresh outside of the country.) If using mallow, steam it first for 15–30 minutes before adding to the pot as it is tougher than spinach. You can also prepare this dish using fresh chard. Serve anywhere from hot to cooled.

½ preserved lemon (page 410)
3 tablespoons olive oil
4 cloves of garlic, finely chopped
2 heaped tablespoons finely chopped flat-leaf parsley
2 heaped tablespoons finely chopped coriander (cilantro)
2 heaped tablespoons finely chopped celery leaves
500 g/1 lb 2 oz spinach leaves, coarsely chopped
1 teaspoon ground cumin
1 teaspoon sweet paprika
pinch of cayenne pepper
½ lemon
salt
olives, to garnish

Cut the preserved lemon into 2 pieces and remove any seeds. Scrape out the pulp, chop and put into a small bowl. Chop the peel, put half into the bowl and set the remaining half aside to garnish.

Heat the oil in a large pot or saucepan over a medium heat, add the garlic and cook for about 1 minute, or until aromatic. Immediately stir in the parsley, coriander (cilantro), celery and reserved preserved lemon pulp and peel. Cook, stirring constantly, for 1 minute. Add the spinach, cumin, paprika and cayenne pepper, season with salt, then increase the heat to high and cook for about 3 minutes, or until the spinach is wilted, the flavours combined and the liquid has evaporated. Squeeze the lemon over the top and stir.

Transfer to a serving dish and garnish with the olives and the remaining reserved preserved lemon peel. Serve hot, warm or even cool.

Spicy Mashed Aubergine, Tomato and Garlic Zaâlouk Salad

MOROCCO
PREPARATION TIME: 10 minutes
COOKING TIME: 30 minutes
SERVES: 4

This cooked aubergine (eggplant) salad known as *zaâlouk* is a Moroccan classic. Served warm, cold or at room temperature, it is ideal as part of a spread of salads and pairs nicely with grilled meats or fish. This recipe has a slightly less spicy bite than many versions, especially those from the south of the country. A potato masher is the easiest method to mash the aubergine. There are various ways to prepare this classic; a few of them follow.

2 aubergines (eggplant) (about 800 g/1¾ lb total)
5 tablespoons olive oil
2 cloves of garlic, finely chopped
2 tomatoes, halved crosswise and grated, peel discarded (see page 445)
1 heaped tablespoon finely chopped flat-leaf parsley
1 heaped tablespoon finely chopped coriander (cilantro)
1 teaspoon sweet paprika
1 teaspoon ground cumin
cayenne pepper, to taste
salt and pepper
bread, to serve

Using a vegetable peeler or knife, peel the aubergine (eggplant) skin lengthwise in strips, leaving about a third of the skin on the flesh. Cut the aubergines into 1.5–2-cm/ ⅔–¾-inch cubes.

Heat the oil in a large frying pan or sauté pan over a medium heat, add the aubergines, cover and cook, stirring frequently, for about 10 minutes, or until soft. Stir in the garlic, then add the tomatoes, parsley, coriander (cilantro), paprika, cumin and cayenne pepper and season with salt and pepper. Cover with a lid, reduce the heat to medium-low and cook, stirring and mashing down the ingredients with a wooden spoon or potato masher until it has a paste-like consistency, the tomatoes have reduced and the flavours combined, about 20 minutes. Add a couple of tablespoons of water if needed. Transfer to a serving bowl and serve warm or at room temperature with bread.

Mashed Aubergine, Tomato and Garlic Zaâlouk Salad (Steamed Version)

MOROCCO
PREPARATION TIME: 15 minutes
COOKING TIME: 40 minutes
SERVES: 4

This steamed version of *zaâlouk* (see left) is a bit smoother and mellower in both texture and taste. Because there is less oil, it is also slightly lighter, though equally tasty.

2 aubergines (eggplant) (about 800 g/1¾ lb total)
4 cloves of garlic, unpeeled
3 tablespoons olive oil
3 ripe tomatoes, halved crosswise and grated, peel discarded (see page 445)
½ teaspoon sweet paprika
1 heaped tablespoon finely chopped flat-leaf parsley
1 heaped tablespoon finely chopped coriander (cilantro)
½ teaspoon ground cumin
cayenne pepper, to taste
salt and pepper

Using a vegetable peeler or knife, peel the aubergine (eggplant) skin lengthwise in strips, leaving about a third of the skin on the flesh. Cut the aubergines into about 3-cm/1¼-inch pieces.

Bring a large steamer pot or couscoussier to the boil with at least 5 cm/2 inches water. Put the aubergine and garlic into the steamer basket, snugly cover with a lid and steam for about 25 minutes, or until tender. Remove from the heat. Leave the garlic to cool, then squeeze from the skins, discarding the skins.

Heat the oil in a large frying pan or sauté pan over a medium heat, add the tomatoes, paprika, parsley, coriander (cilantro), cumin and cayenne pepper, then season with salt and pepper. Cook, stirring frequently, for about 8 minutes, or until the tomatoes are a deeper red and pulpy. Stir in the aubergines and garlic and cook for another 5 minutes, stirring and mashing down the ingredients frequently with a wooden spoon or potato masher until it has a paste-like consistency and the flavours are mixed together. Transfer to a serving bowl and serve warm or at room temperature.

Smoky Mashed Aubergine Zaâlouk Salad

MOROCCO
PREPARATION TIME: 15 minutes,
plus cooling time
COOKING TIME: 15 minutes
SERVES: 4

Many cooks prefer to grill aubergines (eggplant) over a flame so their *zaâlouk* salad has hints of smoke. This version omits tomato to allow the lovely smokiness of the aubergine to dominate.

  2 aubergines (eggplant) (about 800 g/1¾ lb total)
  2 tablespoons extra-virgin olive oil, plus extra
    for drizzling
  2 cloves of garlic, grated
  dash of white vinegar
  ¼ teaspoon ground cumin
  salt and pepper
  finely chopped flat-leaf parsley, to garnish
  finely chopped coriander (cilantro), to garnish

Grill the aubergines (eggplant) over a flame on the stove or on embers on a barbecue for 10–15 minutes, turning as needed, being careful not to break the skin, until blackened. Leave to cool, then peel, removing all of the blackened skin. Chop the aubergines and put into a large bowl.

Add the oil and garlic to a small frying pan over a low heat and cook for 1–2 minutes until aromatic. Transfer to the bowl. Add the vinegar and cumin to the bowl, drizzle with oil and season with salt and pepper. Mix well. Spoon into a serving bowl, garnish with parsley and coriander (cilantro) and serve.

Cucumbers with Fresh Mint

MOROCCO
PREPARATION TIME: 5 minutes,
plus chilling time
SERVES: 4

This tasty salad is easy to put together and especially delicious during summer when the cucumber season is at its peak. For a delicious, earthier version, substitute the mint with dried wild Moroccan oregano (*zaâtar*, see page 61).

  2 cucumbers, peeled and cut into thin rounds
  4 tablespoons extra-virgin olive oil
  1 tablespoon fresh lemon juice
  2 heaped tablespoons finely chopped mint
  salt and pepper

Put the cucumbers into a salad bowl. Put the oil and lemon juice into a small bowl and whisk together, then season with salt and pepper. Pour over the cucumbers and turn until the slices are well coated. Cover and refrigerate for at least 30 minutes to chill. Just before serving, sprinkle over the mint and turn the slices to coat.

Cucumber and Onion Salad with Capers

TUNISIA
PREPARATION TIME: 5 minutes,
plus salting time
SERVES: 4–6

This simple salad also makes a lovely starter or side dish. Use the sweetest onion possible. Soaking the onion in a medium bowl of ice-cold water for 15 minutes will remove some of its raw bite.

  2 cucumbers
  ½ sweet onion, very thinly sliced
  1 tablespoon fresh lemon juice or white vinegar
  2 heaped tablespoons capers, rinsed
  salt and pepper

Peel the cucumbers and cut into thin circles or batons. Put into a salad bowl and lightly season with salt and pepper. Leave the cucumbers to sweat some of their moisture for 15 minutes. Do not drain. Add the onion and lemon juice and toss. Scatter the capers over the top and serve.

Cucumbers with Dried Mint, Lemon and Capers

TUNISIA
PREPARATION TIME: 10 minutes
SERVES: 4–6

This is another simple Tunisian salad that is very popular when cucumbers are in season. Capers and some minced preserved lemons (page 410) are a frequent pairing. If you don't have preserved lemons, use fresh lemon juice instead.

    2 cucumbers
    ¼ small preserved lemon (page 410)
    2 teaspoons dried mint
    2 heaped tablespoons capers, rinsed
    white vinegar, for dashing
    extra-virgin olive oil, for drizzling
    salt and pepper

Peel the cucumbers and cut into thin circles. Put into a salad bowl. Rinse the preserved lemon in water, scrape out the pulp and discard. Mince the peel and add to the bowl along with the mint. Season with salt and pepper and toss. Add the capers, generously dash with vinegar and toss again. Spoon onto a salad plate, drizzle with oil and serve.

Fennel Salad with Olives

TUNISIA
PREPARATION TIME: 10 minutes
SERVES: 4

In winter, when cucumbers are hard to find in Tunisian markets, fennel can stand in as a substitute. While other ingredients often join the fennel (see Winter Fennel Salad, right, for a fuller version), a delightful, easy-to-make salad can be prepared with just the addition of a simple vinaigrette to fully appreciate the fennel's crunch and anise flavours.

    2 small fennel bulbs (about 700 g/1 lb 8½ oz total)
    3 tablespoons extra-virgin olive oil
    1½ tablespoons fresh lemon juice
    salt and pepper
    black olives, to garnish

Trim off the stalks of the fennel. (Discard or use for another dish.) Quarter the bulbs and clean any grit. Slice crosswise as thinly as possible and put into a salad bowl. Put the oil and lemon juice into a small bowl and whisk together, then pour over the top of the fennel. Season with salt and pepper and toss well. Garnish with olives and serve.

Winter Fennel Salad

TUNISIA
PREPARATION TIME: 15 minutes
SERVES: 4

This is a more elaborate version of Fennel Salad with Olives (see left). In Tunisia, apples sometimes replace fennel or cucumbers in salads, and here they make a lovely cold-season variation on the classic 'Tunisian salad' (page 77) of tomatoes, cucumbers and onions.

    2 small fennel bulbs (about 700 g/1 lb 8½ oz total),
        or 2 crisp apples, cored
    1 small red onion, thinly sliced
    1 ripe tomato, finely chopped
    3 tablespoons extra-virgin olive oil
    1 tablespoon fresh lemon juice
    salt and pepper

Trim off the stalks of the fennel. (Discard or use for another dish.) Quarter the bulbs and clean any grit. Slice crosswise as thinly as possible and put into a salad bowl. Add the onion and tomato and toss. Put the oil and lemon juice into a small bowl and whisk together, then pour over the top of the fennel. Season with salt and pepper and toss well. Serve.

Courgette and Tomato Salad with Black Olives

MOROCCO
PREPARATION TIME: 10 minutes
COOKING TIME: 20 minutes
SERVES: 4

To keep the contrasts in this salad distinct, cook the tomatoes until pulpy and rich, adding the courgettes (zucchini) at the end, so they retain a nice bite. The coriander (cilantro) and cumin contribute an earthiness, while the black olives offer a vibrancy. For an added punch of flavour, add 1 tablespoon of double concentrated tomato purée (paste) with the fresh tomatoes.

    2 courgettes (zucchini) (about 700 g/1 lb 8½ oz total)
    4 tablespoons olive oil
    4 ripe plum tomatoes, peeled (see page 445) and
        chopped
    2 cloves of garlic, minced
    1 tablespoon finely chopped flat-leaf parsley
    1 tablespoon finely chopped coriander (cilantro)
    ¼ teaspoon ground cumin
    ¼ teaspoon sweet paprika
    pinch of cayenne pepper
    16 black olives
    salt and pepper
    1 lemon wedge, to serve

Peel the courgettes (zucchini), then quarter lengthwise and cut into 1-cm/½-inch cubes.

Heat the oil in a large frying pan or sauté pan over a medium heat, add the tomatoes and garlic, season with salt and pepper and cook, stirring frequently, for about 10 minutes, or until the tomatoes are pulpy and deeper red. Stir in the parsley, coriander (cilantro), cumin, paprika and cayenne pepper. Add the courgettes (zucchini) and olives. Cook for 5–8 minutes, stirring from time to time, until the courgettes are just done and still have a bite. Transfer to a serving bowl and serve warm or at room temperature. Before serving, squeeze over the lemon.

Courgette Saffron Salad

MOROCCO
PREPARATION TIME: 10 minutes
COOKING TIME: 30 minutes
SERVES: 4

This simple, stunning salad (or side dish) of cooked courgettes (zucchini) bursts with flavour and has a dazzling golden colour from saffron. If in season, use the small, pale-green variety of courgettes.

    2 courgettes (zucchini) (about 700 g/1 lb 8½ oz total)
    4 tablespoons mild olive oil
    1 red onion, grated
    ½ teaspoon ground ginger
    pinch of saffron threads, crumbled
    salt

Quarter the courgettes (zucchini) lengthwise, then cut each crosswise into 3 or 4 pieces. Cut away some of the core. Set aside.

Add the oil, onion, ginger and saffron to a medium saucepan and season with salt. Cook over a medium heat for about 5 minutes, or until the onion is golden brown. Add the courgettes, cover with 250 ml (8 fl oz/1 cup) water and cook, uncovered, until tender but not limp and the sauce reduced, about 25 minutes. Transfer to a serving bowl and serve warm or at room temperature.

Courgette Zaâlouk

MOROCCO
PREPARATION TIME: 10 minutes
COOKING TIME: 40 minutes
SERVES: 4

This version of the mashed aubergine (eggplant) salad known as *zaâlouk* (pages 87–88) is made with courgettes (zucchini). Leave some skin to add an appealing green colour to the dish.

> 2 courgettes (zucchini) (about 700 g/1 lb 8½ oz total)
> 2 tablespoons extra-virgin olive oil
> 2 cloves of garlic, grated
> 2 tomatoes, halved crosswise and grated, peel discarded (see page 445)
> 2 tablespoons finely chopped flat-leaf parsley
> 3 generous pinches of ground cumin
> ½ teaspoon sweet paprika
> cayenne pepper or harissa (page 409), to taste
> juice of ¼ lemon
> salt

Peel most of the skin off the courgettes (zucchini), leaving a small amount, then thinly slice crosswise. Bring a steamer pot or couscoussier to the boil with at least 5 cm/2 inches water, put the courgettes into the steamer basket, snugly cover with a lid and steam for 15–20 minutes until tender. Alternatively, put the courgettes into a large saucepan of lightly salted water, bring to the boil and boil for about 15 minutes, or until soft, then drain well.

Heat the oil in a large frying pan or sauté pan over a medium heat, add the garlic, tomatoes, parsley, cumin, paprika and cayenne pepper and season with salt. Cook, stirring frequently, for about 10 minutes, or until the tomatoes are pulpy and a deeper red. Add the courgettes. Cook, stirring and mashing down, until a paste-like consistency, the flavours are mixed and the moisture evaporated, about 10 minutes. Stir in the lemon juice and cook for another 1–2 minutes. Spoon into a serving bowl and serve warm or at room temperature.

Courgette Ajlouk

TUNISIA
PREPARATION TIME: 10 minutes
COOKING TIME: 20 minutes
SERVES: 4

The Tunisian version of the Moroccan courgette (zucchini) *zaâlouk* (see left) is called *ajlouk*. For this salad, courgettes are best steamed rather than boiled, as they get less soggy and retain more flavour. If boiling, drain them well. Directions for both methods are included.

> 2 courgettes (zucchini) (about 700 g/1 lb 8½ oz total)
> juice of ¼ lemon
> 1 clove of garlic, minced
> harissa (page 409), to taste
> ½ teaspoon ground caraway, optional
> 2 tablespoons extra-virgin olive oil
> salt and pepper
> 12 black olives, to garnish

Peel most of the skin off the courgettes (zucchini), leaving a small amount, then thinly slice crosswise. Bring a steamer pot or couscoussier to the boil with at least 5 cm/2 inches water, put the courgettes into the steamer basket, snugly cover with a lid and steam for 15–20 minutes until tender. Gently press out the excess moisture with the back of a spoon. Alternatively, put the courgettes into a large pot or saucepan of lightly salted water, bring to the boil and boil for about 15 minutes, or until tender. Transfer to a colander to drain, then gently press out the excess moisture with the back of a spoon.

Transfer the courgettes to a salad bowl and mash with the back of a fork. Stir in the lemon juice, garlic, harissa and caraway (if using), and season with salt and pepper. Mix well, then drizzle with the oil, garnish with the olives and serve.

Cauliflower Zaâlouk

MOROCCO
PREPARATION TIME: 5 minutes
COOKING TIME: 35 minutes
SERVES: 4

This dish is another popular mashed cooked *zaâlouk* salad, made with cauliflower. It is an excellent way to utilize a vegetable that is available throughout much of the year. Serve it as a salad or a side dish.

½ cauliflower (about 800 g/1¾ lb), cut into florets
2 tablespoons extra-virgin olive oil
2 cloves of garlic, grated
½ teaspoon ground cumin
½ teaspoon sweet paprika
cayenne pepper, to taste
1 heaped tablespoon finely chopped flat-leaf parsley
1 heaped tablespoon finely chopped coriander (cilantro)
juice of ½ lemon
salt and pepper

Put the cauliflower into a large pot or saucepan of lightly salted water, bring to the boil and boil for about 20 minutes, or until tender. Drain in a colander.

Heat the oil in a medium frying pan over a medium-low heat, add the garlic and cook for about 1 minute, or until aromatic. Add the cauliflower, cumin, paprika, cayenne pepper, parsley, coriander (cilantro) and lemon juice and season with salt and pepper. Cook, stirring and mashing with the back of a fork, 10–15 minutes. Spoon into a serving bowl and serve warm or at room temperature.

Radish Salad

TUNISIA
PREPARATION TIME: 10 minutes, plus chilling time
SERVES: 4

Forming the heart of a range of raw salads, radishes combine well with everything from celery and olives to oranges. This salad is so simple and keeps the focus on the radishes. It's quick to prepare and can be served as a starter.

12 round red radishes
1 heaped tablespoon finely chopped flat-leaf parsley
1 heaped tablespoon finely chopped celery leaves
2 tablespoons extra-virgin olive oil
2 tablespoons fresh lemon juice
salt and pepper

Cut the radishes in half, then slice each half into a couple of pieces. Put into a salad bowl, add the parsley and celery leaves, drizzle with the oil and lemon juice and season with salt and pepper. Toss well. Cover with cling film (plastic wrap) and refrigerate for at least 30 minutes to chill. Toss before serving.

Radish and Celery Salad with Olives

TUNISIA
PREPARATION TIME: 10 minutes
SERVES: 4

Popular in Tunisia, this herby, vibrant and colourful version of Radish Salad (see above) is delightfully crunchy. Serve fresh or chilled.

15 round red radishes (about 225 g/8 oz total)
1 celery stalk, finely chopped
2 heaped tablespoons finely chopped flat-leaf parsley
2 tablespoons extra-virgin olive oil
1 tablespoon fresh lemon juice
salt and pepper
black olives, to garnish

Cut the radishes in half, then slice each half into a couple of pieces. Put into a salad bowl with the celery and parsley. Put the oil and lemon juice into a small bowl and whisk together, then pour over the vegetables, season with salt and pepper and toss well. Garnish with olives. Refrigerate until serving, if desired.

Radish and Orange Salad

MOROCCO
PREPARATION TIME: 10 minutes,
plus chilling time
SERVES: 4

This is a delicious and original salad that's quick to prepare. Add a pinch of sugar to the oranges if needed to sweeten them. A bit of shaved fresh fennel bulb will add a pleasing hint of aniseed.

1 plump navel or Valencia orange
6 round red radishes (about 120 g/4 oz total)
pinch of salt
pinch of white pepper
extra-virgin olive oil, for drizzling
1 tablespoon finely chopped mint, to garnish

Peel the orange and separate into segments. Cut the segments crosswise into 1-cm-/½-inch-thick pieces and put into a salad bowl. Remove any pips. Thinly slice the radishes, put into the bowl, add the salt and white pepper and turn to coat. Cover with cling film (plastic wrap) and refrigerate for at least 30 minutes to chill. Transfer to a serving bowl, drizzle with oil and toss. Scatter the mint over the top and serve.

Roasted Beetroot Salad with Oranges and Orange Blossom Water

MOROCCO
PREPARATION TIME: 15 minutes,
plus cooling and chilling time
COOKING TIME: 45 minutes
SERVES: 4

Roasting draws out a deeper and earthier sweetness from the beetroot (beets), a flavour that pairs nicely with the oranges in this colourful salad. Depending on the beetroot, roasting time can vary from 30 minutes to 1 hour. The beetroot can be boiled instead. See Beetroot Salad with Herb Vinaigrette (page 97) for directions on boiling them.

3 beetroot (beets) (about 600 g/1 lb 5 oz total), unpeeled
neutral oil, for rubbing
2 plump oranges
3 tablespoons extra-virgin olive oil
dash of orange blossom water
1 teaspoon sugar
salt
finely chopped flat-leaf parsley, to garnish

Preheat the oven to 190°C/375°F/Gas Mark 5.
 To prevent the beetroot (beets) from 'bleeding' while cooking, leave the root end and at least 2.5 cm/1 inch of stem. Rub with neutral oil, season with salt and snugly wrap in aluminium foil. Roast in the hot oven for about 45 minutes, or until tender and a knife tip poked into the centre enters with little resistance. Remove from the oven and leave to cool for a few moments before carefully unwrapping. Leave to cool completely, about 15–20 minutes, then trim the ends and peel off the skin. Cut the beetroot lengthwise in half, then cut crosswise into thin slices or small cubes. Put into a large bowl.
 Trim the top and bottom ends of the oranges and set aside. Peel the oranges, remove any white pith with a sharp knife and cut crosswise into 1-cm-/½-inch-thick slices, catching any juice. Pull the segments into triangular pieces.
 Arrange a layer of beetroot in a shallow serving dish, then top with pieces of orange and then another layer of beetroot and oranges.
 Squeeze the juice from the reserved orange ends into a small bowl, then add the olive oil, orange blossom water, sugar and a pinch of salt and whisk to combine. Pour over the salad, then cover with cling film (plastic wrap) and refrigerate for 1 hour to chill. Garnish with parsley before serving.

Beetroot Salad with Herb Vinaigrette

ALGERIA, MOROCCO
PREPARATION TIME: 15 minutes,
plus cooling and chilling time
COOKING TIME: 55 minutes
SERVES: 4

Another simple, lovely salad with beetroot (beets), this version is earthy and herby. For denser flavours, the beetroot can be roasted (see Roasted Beetroot Salad with Oranges and Orange Blossom Water on page 94 for directions on doing this). When in season, garnish the salad with some thinly sliced spring onions (scallions).

3 beetroot (beets) (about 600 g/1 lb 5 oz total)
3 tablespoons extra-virgin olive oil
1 tablespoon fresh lemon juice or white vinegar
1 heaped tablespoon finely chopped flat-leaf parsley
1 heaped tablespoon finely chopped coriander
   (cilantro)
salt and pepper

Wash the beetroot (beets) but do not peel. To prevent them from 'bleeding' while cooking, leave the root end and at least 2.5 cm/1 inch of stem. Put the beetroot into a large saucepan of abundant water, bring to the boil and gently boil for about 45 minutes, or until tender and a knife tip poked into the centre enters with little resistance. Drain in a colander and leave to cool, about 15–20 minutes, then trim the ends and peel off the skin. Cut the beetroot in half lengthwise, then cut crosswise into slices no thicker than 5 mm/¼ inch. Put into a large bowl.

Put the oil and lemon juice into a small bowl and whisk together, then stir in the parsley and coriander (cilantro) and season with salt and pepper. Pour over the beetroot and turn with a spoon until coated. Cover with cling film (plastic wrap) and refrigerate for 1 hour before serving.

Beetroot Salad with Onions

ALGERIA
PREPARATION TIME: 15 minutes,
plus cooling and chilling time
COOKING TIME: 55 minutes
SERVES: 4

The natural sweetness of cooked beetroot (beets) allows for them to be tossed in a vinaigrette with bold flavours, as in this lovely Algerian salad. It's a colourful and tasty addition to any table.

3 beetroot (beets) (about 600 g/1 lb 5 oz total)
3 tablespoons extra-virgin olive oil
1 tablespoon fresh lemon juice or white vinegar
1 clove of garlic, minced
1 heaped tablespoon finely chopped flat-leaf parsley
½ teaspoon sweet paprika
1 small red or yellow onion, thinly sliced
salt and pepper

Wash the beetroot (beets) but do not peel. To prevent them from 'bleeding' while cooking, leave the root end and at least 2.5 cm/1 inch of stem. Put the beetroot into a large saucepan of abundant water, bring to the boil and boil for about 45 minutes, or until tender and a knife tip poked into the centre enters with little resistance. Drain in a colander and leave to cool, about 15–20 minutes, then trim the ends and peel off the skin. Cut the beetroot into cubes and put into a large bowl.

Put the oil and lemon juice into a small bowl and whisk together, then stir in the garlic, parsley and paprika and season with salt and pepper. Pour over the beetroot and turn with a spoon until coated. Scatter over the onion and toss again. Cover with cling film (plastic wrap) and refrigerate for 1 hour before serving. Serve chilled.

Swede Salad with Bitter Oranges and Harissa

TUNISIA
PREPARATION TIME: 15 minutes,
plus salting and marinating time
SERVES: 4–6

Swedes (rutabaga) are a roundish, purple-topped cousin of the turnip, with a denser texture, sharper flavour and more yellowish colour than their white-fleshed counterparts. The name of the dish is *torchi larange*, referring to the bitter or Seville orange (*larange*; in French *bigarade*) used for its marinating juice. When they can't find bitter oranges in the market, some home cooks substitute a regular orange, while others use half a grapefruit and a touch of lemon juice. Serve with other salads or as a starter.

500 g/1 lb 2 oz swedes (rutabaga) or purple turnips, trimmed
1 bitter (Seville) orange or standard orange
2 tablespoons extra-virgin olive oil
harissa (page 409), to taste, optional
salt
2 heaped tablespoons finely chopped celery leaves, to garnish

Peel the swedes (rutabaga), halve lengthwise and cut into thin slices. (If using turnips, do not peel.) Put into a colander, toss with salt and leave to drain for 20–30 minutes. Thoroughly rinse in water, rubbing away all of the salt, then put into a salad bowl.

Squeeze the orange and pour into a small bowl. Add the oil and a dollop of harissa (if using) and whisk together. Pour over the swede and toss. Leave to marinate for 30 minutes. Transfer to a serving bowl, garnish with the celery leaves and serve.

HARISSA

Tunisia's famed harissa chilli (chile) paste is robust, with a nutty, pungent earthiness behind its heat. Garlic and ground caraway and coriander seeds that go into harissa give it more complexity than most other hot sauces. While Tunisia is the largest producer and consumer of harissa in North Africa, it is widely popular in Algeria, Libya and Morocco.

In Tunisia, harissa is omnipresent. It is both a condiment and an ingredient. It flavours eggs, seafood, pasta, soup, meat dishes, couscous, vegetables, salads and stuffed sandwiches. Seemingly every savoury item prepared in the Tunisian kitchen gets a dollop of the deep-red paste. As well, a generous spoonful of harissa on a dish drizzled with local olive oil is set on the table. Dipping a piece of bread into harissa is the best way to fully appreciate its expressive flavours.

Cap Bon is the heartland of harissa. Locals call the fertile peninsula 'red land' not only for the rich soil that deepens in colour in the softening late-afternoon light, but also for the peppers that ripen and turn bright red across its fields in autumn. Capsicum peppers brought from the Americas likely reached Tunisia in the sixteenth century from Spain, perhaps during the Spanish occupation of Tunis (1535–1574) or by Spanish Muslims who fled Spain and settled in Cap Bon. The plant adapted particularly well to the peninsula's climate and soil, and Cap Bon remains the main area of pepper production. At its tip, outside the quiet, isolated town of Al Haouaria and reached only on foot, is Le Phare du Cap Bon, the lighthouse that lends the world's most famous harissa its name and its likeness on the logo.

Farmers in Cap Bon grow a couple of different varieties

of peppers today, including *baklouti*, a waxy-skinned, conical and slightly curving pepper 15–20 cm/6–8 inches in length. After being harvested, the peppers are sun-dried, turning from bright red to ruddy-crimson and taking on a smooth, leathery sheen. Garlands of dried peppers are a common sight across the country.

When using commercial paste: For the smooth and sometimes dense store-bought harissa, whisk a touch of water or olive oil to loosen slightly if desired before serving as a condiment.

To substitute: Cayenne pepper can replace the heat of harissa but not the other nuances. Add some ground cumin, a pinch of ground caraway and coriander if possible and perhaps some dried garlic. You can moisten with a touch of water or olive oil to form a simple paste.

Warm Turnip Salad

MOROCCO
PREPARATION TIME: 10 minutes
COOKING TIME: 50 minutes
SERVES: 4

Turnips help flavour many soups, stews and slow-cooked meat dishes. But they also star in some salads. This lovely 'cooked' salad is easy to prepare and teeming with flavours.

- 3 tablespoons olive oil
- 1 small red onion, grated
- ½ teaspoon ground ginger
- ¼ teaspoon ground turmeric
- 2 cloves of garlic, grated
- 500 g/1 lb 2 oz small turnips, peeled and cut into long, 1-cm-/½-inch-thick pieces
- salt
- black olives, to garnish

Add the oil, onion, ginger and turmeric to a large saucepan and season with salt. Cook over a medium heat for about 5 minutes, or until the onion is golden brown. Add the garlic and cook for about 1 minute, or until aromatic. Add the turnips, cover with 300 ml (10 fl oz/1¼ cups) water and cook, uncovered, until tender and the sauce reduced, about 40 minutes. Transfer to a serving bowl, garnish with olives and serve warm or at room temperature.

Winter Salad with Cabbage, Carrot and Radishes

TUNISIA
PREPARATION TIME: 15 minutes, plus standing time
SERVES: 6

If the iconic 'Tunisian salad' (page 77) is a summer dish, then this is a winter version from coastal Sfax. It is prepared in late winter when the cabbages are still in season and the radishes are arriving in the market. The cabbage should have a nice crunch to it. If preparing in advance of serving, salt the cabbage first to draw out some of the moisture to help keep it crunchy. Put the shredded cabbage into a colander, sprinkle with 1–2 teaspoons of salt and leave to drain in the sink for 1 hour to remove excess moisture. Rinse thoroughly, drain and continue making the recipe.

- ½ head white cabbage (about 500 g/1 lb 2 oz)
- 1 carrot
- 6 red radishes (about 120 g/4 oz total)
- 3 tablespoons extra-virgin olive oil
- 1 tablespoon white vinegar
- 1 tablespoon fresh lemon juice
- 2 teaspoons dried mint
- 1 heaped tablespoon finely chopped coriander (cilantro)
- salt

Remove the woody core from the cabbage and discard the tough outer leaves. Shred as finely as possible. Grate the carrots on a box grater or use a peeler to cut into long, thin strips. Thinly slice the radishes. Put the vegetables into a salad bowl and toss. Put the oil, vinegar, lemon juice, mint and coriander (cilantro) into a small bowl and whisk together, then season with salt. Pour over the vegetables and toss to mix. Leave to stand for 15 minutes to allow the flavours to meld before serving.

Potato Salad with Cumin Vinaigrette

ALGERIA, MOROCCO, TUNISIA
PREPARATION TIME: 15 minutes,
plus cooling time
COOKING TIME: 15 minutes
SERVES: 3–4

Boiled potatoes tossed in vinaigrette are popular across North Africa. Be sure to toss while the potatoes are still warm in order to fully absorb the flavours. In Tunisia, for the vinaigrette, many add spicy harissa (page 409) instead of sweet paprika. Serve warm in the winter.

- 4 white potatoes (about 900 g/2 lb), peeled and cut into 1.5-cm/⅔-inch cubes
- 1 small clove of garlic, peeled
- 4 tablespoons extra-virgin olive oil
- 1 tablespoon fresh lemon juice
- 1 tablespoon minced flat-leaf parsley
- 1 teaspoon ground cumin
- ½ teaspoon sweet paprika or dollop of harissa (page 409)
- salt and pepper

Put the potatoes into a large pot or saucepan of lightly salted water, bring to the boil and boil for 12–15 minutes until just tender. Drain in a colander and leave to cool for about 10 minutes until still warm.

Put the garlic and a generous pinch of salt into a mortar and pound to a paste with a pestle. Transfer to a small bowl, add the olive oil, lemon juice, parsley, cumin and paprika and whisk together, then season with salt and pepper. Pour over the potatoes and very gently turn without breaking. Serve at room temperature or, once completely cool, cover and refrigerate until chilled. Before serving, gently toss.

Potato Salad with Tomatoes and Tuna

ALGERIA
PREPARATION TIME: 15 minutes,
plus cooling and chilling time
COOKING TIME: 15 minutes
SERVES: 4

There are lots of variations of this potato, tomato and tuna salad today. Some like to add capers, which grow around the region, to give it a zesty punch. Substitute the tuna for eight or so anchovy fillets, cut into pieces, if desired.

- 3 white potatoes (about 500 g/1 lb 2 oz), peeled and cut into 1-cm/½-inch cubes
- 150 g/5 oz (1 cup) cherry tomatoes, halved, or 3 tomatoes, chopped
- 24 pitted black olives, halved
- 2 tablespoons capers, rinsed, optional
- 4 tablespoons extra-virgin olive oil
- 1 tablespoon white vinegar
- 1 tablespoon minced flat-leaf parsley
- 1 (150–175-g/5–6-oz) can of tuna in olive oil, drained
- salt and pepper
- 2 Hard-boiled Eggs (page 443), peeled and cut into wedges, to garnish, optional

Put the potatoes into a large pot or saucepan of lightly salted water, bring to the boil and gently boil for 12–15 minutes until just tender. Drain, gently rinse under cold running water to cool and thoroughly drain in a colander.

Put the potatoes into a salad bowl with the tomatoes, olives and capers (if using).

Prepare a vinaigrette by putting the oil and vinegar into a small bowl and whisking together until cloudy and blended. Stir in the parsley, season with salt and pepper and whisk again. Pour over the salad and gently toss. Cover with cling film (plastic wrap) and refrigerate for 30 minutes–1 hour until chilled. Before serving, toss again and top with the tuna, then arrange the hard-boiled eggs (if using) along the sides.

Golden Potato Salad with Tuna and Capers

TUNISIA
PREPARATION TIME: 10 minutes,
plus cooling and chilling time
COOKING TIME: 15 minutes
SERVES: 2–3

The potatoes in this Tunisian salad are yellow from boiling them with ground turmeric. Add some grated or very finely chopped onion, if desired. A delightful, colourful salad.

- 3 white potatoes (about 500 g/1 lb 2 oz), peeled and cut into 1-cm/½-inch cubes
- ½ teaspoon ground turmeric
- 80 g/3 oz (½ cup) drained canned tuna
- 3 tablespoons capers, rinsed
- 1 tablespoon minced flat-leaf parsley
- 2 tablespoons extra-virgin olive oil
- salt and pepper

Put the potatoes into a large pot or saucepan of lightly salted water, bring to the boil and boil for 12–15 minutes until just tender. Drain in a colander.

Put the potatoes into a salad bowl with the tuna, capers and parsley, season with salt and pepper and add the oil. Gently turn to mix.

Cover with cling film (plastic wrap) and refrigerate for 30 minutes–1 hour until chilled. Before serving, gently mix.

Sweet Potato Salad

MOROCCO
PREPARATION TIME: 15 minutes
COOKING TIME: 30 minutes
SERVES: 4–6

At its simplest, this sweet-and-savoury salad can be prepared with little more than sweet potatoes, sugar, saffron, salt and pepper. But the savoury side of the dish can be nicely drawn out with some cumin, garlic, onions or even preserved lemon peel (page 410). To make the sweetness jump, some Moroccan cooks include a handful of raisins when adding the sweet potato.

- 3 tablespoons olive oil
- 1 red or yellow onion, finely chopped
- 2 cloves of garlic, minced
- 1 kg/2¼ lb orange-fleshed sweet potatoes, peeled and cut into 1.5-cm/⅔-inch cubes
- ½ teaspoon sweet paprika
- ½ teaspoon ground ginger
- pinch of saffron threads, crumbled
- ½ cinnamon stick or piece of cinnamon bark
- 2 tablespoons sugar
- 12 sprigs flat-leaf parsley
- 12 sprigs coriander (cilantro)
- salt and pepper
- black olives, to garnish

Heat the oil in a large, deep frying pan or sauté pan over a medium heat, add the onion and cook for about 5 minutes, or until pale. Stir in the garlic, then add the sweet potatoes, paprika, ginger, saffron, cinnamon stick and sugar and season with salt and pepper. Tie the parsley and coriander (cilantro) into a bundle and add to the pan, then pour in 500 ml (18 fl oz/2 cups) water and bring to a low boil. Cook, uncovered, until the sweet potatoes are tender and the sauce reduced, about 20 minutes. Be very careful when turning to keep the pieces from crumbling. Remove and discard the coriander and parsley bundle and the cinnamon stick. Carefully transfer the sweet potatoes to a serving dish. If the sauce is too watery, reduce the sauce over a high heat for a couple of minutes until glazy. Spoon the glazy sauce over the potatoes, garnish with olives and serve warm or at room temperature.

Orange Salad with Black Olives

MOROCCO
PREPARATION TIME: 10 minutes,
plus chilling time
SERVES: 4

Dazzling in its colours, bold in its flavours and simple to prepare, this salad makes a perfect winter salad. It is delightful when tossed in a nutty oil such as walnut or hazelnut or even argan oil. Pressed from the seeds of a spiny tree native to south-western Morocco, argan oil is commonly found in health and beauty products. Be sure to use culinary (rather than cosmetic) argan oil. See page 358 for more about this oil.

- 2 ripe oranges
- 1½ tablespoons extra-virgin olive, walnut, hazelnut or culinary-grade argan oil
- 2 teaspoons minced flat-leaf parsley
- salt and pepper, optional
- 16 pitted black olives, halved, to garnish

Trim off the top and bottom ends of the oranges and set aside. Peel the oranges with a knife, remove any of the white pith and cut crosswise into 1-cm-/½-inch-thick slices, catching any juice in a bowl. Pull the segments into triangular pieces over a medium bowl, then drop into the bowl. Squeeze the reserved ends into the bowl. Add the oil and parsley, season with salt and pepper (if using) and toss to blend well. Cover with cling film (plastic wrap) and refrigerate for 30 minutes, or until chilled. To serve, toss again, put into a salad bowl and garnish with the olives.

Clementine and Red Onion Salad

ALGERIA
PREPARATION TIME: 10 minutes,
plus soaking and chilling time
SERVES: 4

Clementines are a reddish-orange hybrid of mandarin with a bright, glossy peel that was developed outside Oran in the late nineteenth century and named in 1902 after a French missionary, Brother Clément Rodier. Soaking the onion in a bowl of cold water will lessen some of its snap and allow more natural sweetness to shine. The salad can be garnished with dates, nuts and/or olives.

- 1 small red onion
- 6 clementines, tangerines or mandarin oranges
- juice of ½ lemon
- 3 tablespoons extra-virgin olive oil, for drizzling
- pinch of salt
- fresh dates, to garnish, optional
- walnuts, almonds or pine nuts, to garnish, optional
- black olives, to garnish, optional

Halve the onion crosswise and cut into very thin slices. Separate the layers, put into a small bowl and cover with cold or iced water. Leave to soak for 20 minutes, then drain and arrange in the bottom of a serving plate or salad bowl. Peel the clementines, separate the segments and cut in half. Add to the plate.

Put the lemon juice, olive oil and salt into a small bowl and whisk together, then pour over the top of the clementines and onion. Toss. Cover with cling film (plastic wrap) and refrigerate for 30 minutes, or until chilled. Serve chilled, and garnished with dates, nuts and olives (if using).

Chickpea Salad with Cumin and Paprika

ALGERIA, MOROCCO
PREPARATION TIME: 10 minutes,
plus cooling time
COOKING TIME: 5 minutes
SERVES: 4

This easy and earthy salad of chickpeas (garbanzo beans) was especially popular Algerian-born French or other Europeans, see page 19 in Algeria. It can be made by soaking dried chickpeas overnight and boiling (see page 443), although using canned ones makes it quite quick to prepare. In this recipe, the canned chickpeas are steamed to soften in order to keep as much flavour as possible, but they can also be boiled for a couple of minutes (see right).

500 g/1 lb 2 oz (3 cups) canned chickpeas
  (garbanzo beans), rinsed
3 tablespoons extra-virgin olive oil
1 tablespoon white vinegar or lemon juice
1 teaspoon ground cumin
1 teaspoon sweet paprika
salt and pepper

Bring a large steamer pot or couscoussier to the boil with about 5 cm/2 inches water. Put the chickpeas into the steamer basket, snugly cover with a lid and steam for about 5 minutes, or until tender. Transfer the chickpeas to a salad bowl. Put the oil, vinegar, cumin and paprika into a small bowl and whisk together until cloudy. Season with salt and pepper and pour over the chickpeas while still they are still warm. Toss and leave to cool to room temperature. Toss again before serving.

Chickpea Salad with Red Pepper, Cucumber and Fresh Mint

MOROCCO
PREPARATION TIME: 10 minutes,
plus cooling time
COOKING TIME: 5 minutes
SERVES: 4

A vibrant, easy salad full of body, texture and colours. The tang and minty herbal aromas with the earthiness of the chickpeas (garbanzo beans) and crunch of fresh peppers is a delightful combination. This recipe uses canned chickpeas. Bringing them to a quick boil will remove their canned flavours and allow them to soften. To use dried chickpeas, see page 443 for how to cook them.

500 g/1 lb 2 oz (3 cups) canned chickpeas
  (garbanzo beans), rinsed
¼ red bell pepper, seeded and diced
1 cucumber, peeled and finely diced
5 tablespoons extra-virgin olive oil
1 tablespoon fresh lemon juice
4 packed tablespoons finely chopped mint
salt and pepper

Put the chickpeas (garbanzo beans) into a large saucepan with about 500 ml (18 fl oz/2 cups) water and bring to the boil. Drain in a colander and leave to cool to room temperature. Put the cooled chickpeas into a salad bowl with the diced pepper and cucumber. Put the oil and lemon juice into a small bowl and whisk together until cloudy. Season with salt and pepper and pour over the chickpeas. Scatter over the mint and toss well. Serve.

Sweet Onion and Caper Salad

TUNISIA
PREPARATION TIME: 10 minutes,
plus standing time
COOKING TIME: 40 minutes
SERVES: 4

The sweetness of the onions gets a delightful contrasting tang from the vinaigrette and capers. Serve warm, at room temperature or even chilled. For deeper flavours, the onions can be roasted whole in the oven or cooked in embers, as they were in the past.

- 2 red or sweet white onions, unpeeled
- 2 tablespoons extra-virgin olive oil
- 2 teaspoons white vinegar
- 1 heaped tablespoon capers, rinsed
- salt

Have a large bowl of cold water ready nearby. Put the onions into a large pot or saucepan of water, bring to the boil and boil for 30–40 minutes until tender. Transfer with a slotted spoon to the bowl of cold water and leave until cool enough to handle. Drain, trim the ends and gently squeeze the onions to extract as much water as possible. Peel and cut lengthwise into eighths and put into a large bowl.

Put the oil, vinegar and salt to taste into a small bowl and whisk together, then pour over the onions and toss to mix well. Leave to stand for 15 minutes to allow the flavours to meld. Arrange the onions on a platter or salad plate, scatter the capers across the top and serve.

Fresh Broad Bean Salad with Preserved Lemon

MOROCCO
PREPARATION TIME: 10 minutes
COOKING TIME: 15 minutes
SERVES: 4

The tasty, slightly bitter flavours of steamed fresh broad (fava) beans get a bold counterpunch from the preserved lemon (page 410). Directions for both fresh beans in the pod and shelled ones are included.

- 1 kg/2¼ lb fresh broad (fava) beans in their pods or 300 g/11 oz (2 generous cups) shelled fresh or frozen beans
- 4 tablespoons olive oil
- 1 tablespoon fresh lemon juice, plus extra if needed
- 1 clove of garlic, minced, optional
- ½ teaspoon sweet paprika
- ¼ teaspoon ground cumin
- 1 tablespoon minced flat-leaf parsley
- 1 tablespoon minced coriander (cilantro)
- peel of ¼ preserved lemon (page 410), finely chopped
- salt and pepper
- 12 red olives, to garnish

If using whole broad (fava) beans in their pods, bring a large steamer pot or couscoussier to the boil with about 5 cm/2 inches water. Put the beans into the steamer basket, snugly cover with a lid and steam for 10–15 minutes until tender. Remove from the heat and leave until cool enough to handle, then shell, discarding the pods.

If using shelled broad beans, put the beans into a large saucepan, cover with water and some lemon juice, bring to the boil and boil for about 5 minutes, or until tender. Drain.

Put the oil, lemon juice, garlic (if using), paprika, and cumin into a small bowl and whisk together, then season with salt and pepper. Put the broad beans into a salad bowl, pour over the mixture, add the parsley, coriander (cilantro) and preserved lemon and toss. Garnish with the olives and serve warm.

Fresh Broad Bean Salad with Tomatoes

MOROCCO
PREPARATION TIME: 15 minutes,
plus cooling time
COOKING TIME: 20 minutes
SERVES: 4

In this simple and delightful salad, the spiced, cooked tomatoes balance the slightly bitter flavour of the broad (fava) beans.

- 1 kg/2¼ lb fresh broad (fava) beans in their pods, shelled, or 300 g/11 oz (2 generous cups) shelled fresh or frozen beans
- 3 ripe tomatoes, halved crosswise and grated, peel discarded (see page 445)
- 3 tablespoons olive oil
- 1 tablespoon minced flat-leaf parsley
- 1 tablespoon minced coriander (cilantro)
- ½ teaspoon sweet paprika
- ½ teaspoon ground cumin
- ¼ lemon
- extra-virgin olive oil, for drizzling
- salt and pepper

Put the shelled broad (fava) beans, tomatoes, olive oil, parsley, coriander (cilantro), paprika and cumin into a large pot or saucepan and season with salt and pepper. Add 120 ml (4 fl oz/½ cup) water, cover with a lid and cook over a medium heat until the beans are tender and sauce darker and reduced, 15–20 minutes. Spoon into a salad bowl and leave to cool. Serve at room temperature. Before serving, squeeze over the lemon and drizzle with extra-virgin olive oil.

Spiced Lentil Salad with Carrots

MOROCCO
PREPARATION TIME: 10 minutes
COOKING TIME: 30 minutes
SERVES: 4

In restaurants, this widely popular dish is served as a salad, often at room temperature. For many families, it is served warm as a main dish at home. The carrots in this recipe are boiled apart, drained and rinsed to keep their texture tender but not mushy.

- 200 g/7 oz (1 cup) dried green or pale brown lentils, picked over for any stones or debris and rinsed
- 2 cloves of garlic, crushed in their skin
- 1 small onion, peeled
- 2 carrots, cut into 5-mm-/¼-inch-thick circles
- 3 tablespoons extra-virgin olive oil, plus extra, optional
- 1 tablespoon fresh lemon juice
- 1 tablespoon minced flat-leaf parsley
- ¼ teaspoon ground cumin
- ¼ teaspoon sweet paprika
- salt and pepper

Put the lentils into a large saucepan, add the garlic and onion, then pour in 1.5 litres (50 fl oz/generous 6 cups) water and bring to the boil. Season with salt, cover with a lid, reduce the heat and gently boil for about 30 minutes, or until the lentils are just tender. Drain in a colander and leave to cool for few minutes. Transfer the lentils to a large bowl.

Meanwhile, put the carrots into a medium saucepan of lightly salted water, bring to the boil and boil for about 15 minutes, or until tender but not mushy. Transfer with a slotted spoon to a bowl of cold water to stop further cooking. Drain.

Put the oil, lemon juice, parsley, cumin and paprika into a small bowl and whisk together, then season with salt and pepper. Pour over the lentils and stir well to combine. Fold in the carrots.

Spoon into a salad bowl and serve warm or leave to cool and serve at room temperature. Toss before serving, adding a touch more oil if needed.

Seafood Salad

TUNISIA
PREPARATION TIME: 20 minutes,
plus chilling time
COOKING TIME: 15 minutes
SERVES: 2–4

This is a delightful salad of *fruits de mer* from Tunisia's lengthy coastline. Add some pieces of cooked and chilled octopus, if desired (see page 444 for boiling octopus) or small steamed clams. (Steam the clams in a large covered saucepan over a medium-high heat until all the clams have opened, about 5 minutes, shaking the pan from time to time. Discard any that do not open.)

    350 g/12 oz cleaned squid (calamari) or cuttlefish,
        cut into bite-size pieces
    350 g/12 oz raw prawns (shrimp) with heads and shells
    1 spring onion (scallion), chopped
    3 tablespoons extra-virgin olive oil
    1 tablespoon fresh lemon juice
    1 clove of garlic, minced
    1 teaspoon ground cumin
    1 tablespoon finely chopped flat-leaf parsley
    1 tablespoon finely chopped coriander (cilantro)
    salt and pepper
    black olives, to garnish
    1 or 2 Hard-boiled Eggs (page 443), peeled and cut
        into wedges, to garnish, optional

Have a large bowl of cold water ready nearby. Bring a saucepan of lightly salted water to the boil, add the squid (calamari) and boil for 5–10 minutes until tender, depending on their size. Transfer with a slotted spoon to a plate to cool. Add the prawns (shrimp) to the pan and boil for 1–2 minutes until just opaque throughout. Transfer with a slotted spoon to the bowl of cold water to stop any further cooking and leave to cool, then drain. Peel and, if desired, devein. Cut the prawns in half, if desired. Put the squid and prawns into a large bowl and add the onion.

Put the oil, lemon juice, garlic, cumin, parsley and coriander (cilantro) into a small bowl and whisk together, then season with salt and pepper. Pour over the seafood and toss. Cover with cling film (plastic wrap) and refrigerate for 30 minutes, or until chilled. Before serving toss again, then garnish with olives and hard-boiled eggs (if using). Serve.

Octopus Salad

TUNISIA
PREPARATION TIME: 10 minutes
SERVES: 4

Among the many ways you find octopus on Tunisian tables is as a salad. It's quite simple and allows the flavours of octopus to dominate. Add some capers for a pungent hint, minced garlic and olives, or, in winter, some dill. To fill out the salad, add some boiled and cubed potatoes. Look in advance at the directions for preparing octopus on page 444.

    450 g/1 lb cooked octopus (page 444)
    1 small red onion, thinly sliced
    2 ripe tomatoes, diced
    3 heaped tablespoons finely chopped flat-leaf parsley
    1 tablespoon fresh lemon juice
    4 tablespoons olive oil
    salt and pepper

Leave the octopus to cool if needed. Using kitchen scissors, cut the octopus into bite-size pieces and put into a salad bowl. Scatter over the onion and tomatoes. Put the parsley, lemon juice and oil into a small bowl and whisk together, then season with salt and pepper and mix well. Pour over the salad and toss. Arrange on a serving platter and serve. Or put into the refrigerator to chill before serving.

Algerian Anchovy, Onion and Tomato Salad

ALGERIA
PREPARATION TIME: 10 minutes
SERVES: 2–3

This simple salad of anchovies, onions and tomatoes called *n'tchouba* is ubiquitous on Ramadan tables in Algiers alongside various hot and cold starters. Mop up the flavours that remain on the serving dish with bread.

12 anchovy fillets
2 tomatoes, halved, cored and sliced crosswise
1 red onion, sliced crosswise
14 olives
extra-virgin olive oil, for drizzling
white vinegar, for dashing
finely chopped flat-leaf parsley, to garnish

Rinse the anchovies under cold running water, pat dry with paper towels and arrange on a plate without overlapping. Lay slices of tomatoes and onion on top of the anchovies and the olives around them. Generously drizzle with oil and add a dash of vinegar. Scatter over some parsley and serve.

Anchovies with Capers

ALGERIA
PREPARATION TIME: 5 minutes
SERVES: 4

Preserved anchovies are deeply popular in Algeria. When they are good, there is little reason to do much to them. But adding some garlic, parsley and capers to the fillets makes for a perfect starter. Anchovies now usually come packed in oil, although they can still be found packed in salt. For those in salt, rinse thoroughly, soak in a bowl of cold water for 2 hours, rinse again and pat dry with paper towels.

16 anchovy fillets packed in oil
2 teaspoons capers, rinsed
2 cloves of garlic, coarsely chopped
1 tablespoon chopped flat-leaf parsley
¼ lemon
extra-virgin olive oil, for drizzling
pepper

Rinse the anchovies under cold running water and pat dry with paper towels. If needed, separate into individual fillets and trim.

Neatly arrange the anchovies on a small plate. Sprinkle over the capers, garlic and parsley. Grind some black pepper over the top and squeeze over the lemon. Generously drizzle with oil and serve.

Summer Rice Salad with Tuna and Fresh Peas

ALGERIA, MOROCCO
PREPARATION TIME: 20 minutes,
plus chilling time
COOKING TIME: 15 minutes
SERVES: 6

In recent years, rice salads have become popular across North Africa. In summertime they often have a lighter vinaigrette (like this version), although in winter many prefer mayonnaise. Season providing, just about anything can be added to the salad, from grated carrots to cooked beetroot (beets) to some steamed green beans. From the can, sweetcorn and tuna are popular additions. Short- or medium-grain white rice is fine, although long-grain is the most common. In Algeria, some like to add mustard to the vinaigrette.

    400 g/14 oz (2 cups) long-grain white rice
    120 g/4 oz shelled fresh peas (about 1 cup)
    2 ripe plum tomatoes, cored and chopped
    1 cucumber, peeled and cubed
    160 g/5¾ oz (⅔ cup) canned sweetcorn, drained
        and rinsed
    1 (150-g/5-oz) can of tuna in olive oil, drained
    24 pitted black or green olives, sliced
    6 tablespoons extra-virgin olive oil
    2 tablespoons white vinegar
    1 shallot, minced
    1 teaspoon wholegrain or Dijon mustard
    salt and pepper
    2 Hard-boiled Eggs (page 443), peeled and cut into
        wedges, to garnish

Put the rice into a large pot or saucepan of lightly salted water, bring to the boil and boil for about 15 minutes, or until tender. Drain the rice, rinse under cold running water to stop any further cooking and drain well.

Meanwhile, put the peas into a small saucepan of lightly salted water, bring to the boil and boil for 5 minutes, or until just tender. Drain and rinse under cold running water to stop any further cooking.

Put the rice, peas, tomatoes, cucumber, sweetcorn, tuna and olives into a large salad bowl and toss to blend well. Cover with cling film (plastic wrap) and refrigerate for 30 minutes–1 hour until chilled.

When ready to serve, prepare the vinaigrette. Put the oil, vinegar, shallot and mustard into a small bowl and whisk together until cloudy. Season with salt and pepper and pour over the rice. Toss well. Divide among plates, garnish with hard-boiled eggs and serve.

Rice Salad with Pickled Vegetables, Tuna and Olives

TUNISIA
PREPARATION TIME: 15 minutes,
plus chilling time
COOKING TIME: 15 minutes
SERVES: 6

Especially during Ramadan, rice salads have become commonplace in Tunisia. They generally include some pickled vegetables called *merrket mellah* or *variantes* (page 171). Along with the crunchy pickled carrots, cauliflower, turnips and so on, many cooks add tuna and olives plus, depending on the season, some diced fresh tomatoes, cucumbers and perhaps some red pepper.

    400 g/14 oz (2 cups) long-grain white rice
    120 g/4 oz mixed pickled vegetables (*variantes*,
        page 171) (about 1 cup)
    2 ripe plum tomatoes, cored and chopped
    1 cucumber, peeled and cubed
    24 black or green pitted olives, sliced
    6 tablespoons extra-virgin olive oil
    2 tablespoons fresh lemon juice
    salt and pepper
    1 (150-g/5-oz) can of tuna in olive oil, drained,
        to garnish

Put the rice into a large pot or saucepan of lightly salted water, bring to the boil and boil for about 15 minutes, or until tender. Drain the rice, rinse under cold running water to stop any further cooking and drain well. Rinse the pickled vegetables well with hot water.

Put the rice, pickled vegetables, tomatoes, cucumber and olives into a large salad bowl and toss to mix well. Cover with cling film (plastic wrap) and refrigerate for 30 minutes–1 hour until chilled.

When ready to serve, prepare the vinaigrette. Put the oil, lemon juice with salt and pepper to taste into a small bowl and whisk until cloudy. Pour over the rice and toss well. Divide among plates, garnish with tuna and serve.

SOUPS

Harira Soup

MOROCCO
PREPARATION TIME: 15 minutes
COOKING TIME: 1 hour 20 minutes
SERVES: 6

Morocco's iconic *harira* is prepared across the country during Ramadan, when it is a key part of the fast-breaking meal (see page 32). There are endless variations on this soup, but all are soothing and nourishing. Whisking flour into the soup towards the end gives the dish its quintessential velvety texture. The traditional spoon to eat *harira* with is carved from lemon or orange wood into a deep, ladle-like shape. Outside of Ramadan *harira* remains a favourite for dinner but also breakfast, and it is typically the last thing served at the end of Moroccan weddings that last until dawn.

3 tablespoons olive oil
250 g/9 oz boneless lamb or stewing beef, cut into small cubes
2 red or yellow onions, finely chopped
1 celery stalk with leaves, finely chopped
3 heaped tablespoons finely chopped flat-leaf parsley, plus extra leaves to garnish
3 heaped tablespoons finely chopped coriander (cilantro), plus extra to garnish
15 g/½ oz (1 tablespoon) butter or 1 teaspoon *smen* (page 412)
4 ripe tomatoes, halved crosswise and grated, peel discarded (see page 445)
2 tablespoons double concentrated tomato purée (paste)
¼ teaspoon ground turmeric
¼ teaspoon ground ginger
¼ teaspoon ground cinnamon
100 g/3½ oz (½ cup) dried brown lentils, picked over for any stones or debris and rinsed
100 g/3½ oz (½ cup) canned chickpeas (garbanzo beans), rinsed, or cooked dried chickpeas (page 443)
2 tablespoons uncooked rice
70 g/2¾ oz (½ cup) plain (all-purpose) flour
salt and pepper
lemon wedges, to serve
dates, to serve

Add the oil, lamb, onions, celery, parsley, coriander (cilantro) and butter to a soup pot, cover with a lid and cook over a medium heat for 10 minutes. Add the tomatoes, tomato purée (paste) and 3 tablespoons water and cook, stirring frequently, for 5 minutes. Stir in the turmeric, ginger and cinnamon, season with salt and pepper and add 1.5 litres (50 fl oz/ generous 6 cups) water. Bring to a simmer, cover with a lid and cook over a medium-low heat for 20 minutes. Add the lentils and chickpeas (garbanzo beans) and cook for 15 minutes. Add the rice and cook for another 15 minutes.

Pour 250 ml (8 fl oz/1 cup) cold water into a large bowl, add the flour and whisk until smooth. Leave to stand for 5 minutes, then whisk again. While steadily stirring, slowly add to the soup. Reduce the heat to low and cook, uncovered, stirring frequently, for about 10 minutes, allowing the soup to thicken. Thin with some water if it becomes too thick.

Ladle into soup bowls and garnish with parsley, coriander and pepper. Serve with lemon wedges to squeeze over and the dates on the side.

A RAMADAN SYMBOL

Soup plays an important role during the month of Ramadan, when it is consumed every night after breaking the fast. It's rich, filling and soothing on the empty stomach, preparing it for the meal ahead. It is also quenching. The word *chorba* comes from the verb meaning 'to drink'.

In Morocco, by far the most famous soup is *harira*, a symbol of the Ramadan table and eaten by many households nightly for the entire month of sunrise-to-sunset fasting. Cooks begin preparing it in the afternoon and the simmering aromas of *harira* emanate from homes across the country. Onions, tomatoes, pulses and usually some small pieces of lamb or beef for flavour, plus plenty of chopped fresh herbs – parsley, coriander (cilantro), often celery leaves – are found in most versions. But beyond these, there is little agreement, and certainly no unified version of the dish. There are those with nuances of cinnamon, ginger or caraway, ground cumin or the potent cubeb (tailed) pepper (see opposite). Some versions are more yellow from turmeric or saffron, others a deep red from abundant tomatoes (and tomato purée/paste). Some cooks add both lentils and chickpeas (garbanzo beans), others just one or the other. Skinny pieces of vermicelli pasta, or rice, get added towards the end. Usually, a spoonful of flour gets stirred in at the end to give *harira* its characteristic silkiness. Some stir in beaten egg at the very end.

Moroccan *harira* (page 118) is traditionally served with *chebakia*, a flower-shaped, fried and honey-dipped cookie. Its sweet notes perfectly complement the soup, while the honey offers some restorative energy. Dates and, when in season, fresh figs are also common companions. In Oran, there is a popular version called *harira oranaise* (see opposite). As in the rest of Algeria with *chorba*, it gets a savoury pairing – stuffed and fried *boureks* (stuffed pastries, pages 56–57). Yet despite differences found in *harira*, the result is the same: a soup rich, substantial and comforting. Prepared in generous-size batches, it's also festive.

SMEN

Preserved salted butter known as *smen* (page 412) adds a depth of savoury earthiness to many dishes in Morocco and Algeria. Its aroma, usually described as somewhat cheesy, gives dishes a distinctive flavour. But it also lends them a richer, lusher texture. *Smen* is never used as a spread for bread, for instance, as is butter sometimes: it is always an ingredient. Cooks rub it into steamed couscous and on roasting lamb, add it to stewed white beans with tomato sauce (page 140) and soups such as *harira* (page 118). It is called for in various chicken tagines, including a Fès speciality with copious onions and almonds called *djaj khadra* (Fès-style Chicken in Buttery Onion Sauce with Almonds, page 302). In Algeria, it is found in numerous dishes from *chorba* (soup) to garlicky meatballs (*mtewem*) and couscous.

There are two main methods for making *smen*. One clarifies the butter. Removing the milk solids and moisture from the butter allows for significantly longer storage, a key preserving point, especially in pre-refrigeration days. Salt is mixed into the golden liquid, poured into (traditionally ceramic) jars and left to take on *smen*'s characteristic aromas. A second method kneads salt and a blend of dried herbs – in southern Morocco, one with wild oregano known as *zaâtar* (see page 61) is classic – into the butter. Packed into containers, the liquid gets drained off the butter repeatedly over the next few months until it is ready.

Usually made from the milk of cows, *smen* remains common to use. Supermarkets sell commercial brands while merchants in the markets sell freshly made versions. Especially in cities, it is becoming uncommon to prepare at home.

To substitute: Use salted butter. For a hint of the cheesiness, add a small crumbled piece of blue cheese with the butter.

Oran Harira

ALGERIA
PREPARATION TIME: 20 minutes
COOKING TIME: 1 hour 30 minutes
SERVES: 6–8

Harira (page 118) is also popular in Algeria, especially in Oran, where it is known as *harira oranaise*. Flour is stirred in to thicken and for a silky texture. It is also soothing on the stomach, important when the soup opens the fast-breaking *iftar* meal (see page 33). If preparing the soup in advance, do not stir in the flour until just before serving. A key to that silkiness is to continue stirring once the mixture is added. Use a piece of meat with a generous bone. The goal is flavour rather than the meat itself. Some canned or precooked chickpeas (garbanzo beans) can be added after the flour has been stirred into the soup. This puréed version from Oran has the aromas of caraway, coriander (cilantro) and cubeb pepper. Also known as tailed pepper or Java pepper (*kababa*), cubeb resembles a black peppercorn with a little stalk or tail protruding from one end, and it carries hints of fresh pepper and pine. During Ramadan, when *harira* is prepared frequently, *boureks* (stuffed pastries, pages 56–57) are often served alongside.

3 tablespoons olive oil
15 g/½ oz (1 tablespoon) butter or *smen* (page 412)
1 × 225-g/8-oz piece bone-in lamb or beef
2 red or yellow onions, finely chopped
2 cloves of garlic, minced
3 ripe tomatoes, peeled (see page 445) and coarsely chopped
2 tablespoons double concentrated tomato purée (paste)
3 celery stalks with leaves, coarsely chopped
1 carrot, coarsely chopped
1 courgette (zucchini), coarsely chopped
1 turnip, peeled and coarsely chopped
3 heaped tablespoons finely chopped coriander (cilantro) or flat-leaf parsley, plus extra to garnish
½ teaspoon ground ginger
¼ teaspoon ground turmeric
3 tablespoons plain (all-purpose) flour
¼ teaspoon ground cinnamon
¼ teaspoon ground caraway, plus extra to garnish
generous pinch of ground cubeb (tailed pepper or Java pepper) or ras al hanout (page 446)
1 lemon, cut into wedges
salt and pepper

Add the oil, butter and lamb to a soup pot, then season with salt and pepper and brown the lamb on each side over a medium heat for about 5 minutes. Add the onions and cook for another 5 minutes, or until they begin to soften. Stir in the garlic, then add the tomatoes, tomato purée (paste) and 4 tablespoons water, the celery, carrot, courgette (zucchini), turnip, coriander (cilantro), ginger and turmeric, and cook for 10 minutes, stirring from time to time. Pour in 1.2 litres (40 fl oz/5 cups) water, cover with a lid and bring to the boil. Reduce the heat and simmer for 45 minutes, or until the lamb is cooked. Remove the lamb and set aside.

In a mixing bowl, whisk the flour into 250 ml (8 fl oz/1 cup) water until smooth. Set aside.

Purée the soup in the pot using a hand blender, or carefully in a food processor, in batches, returning to the pot. Stir in a touch of water to loosen, if desired. Remove any meat from the lamb, shred by hand and set aside.

Add a ladle of soup to the flour mixture and stir. With the soup pot over a medium heat, add the flour mixture to the soup while stirring constantly. Reduce the heat to low and cook, uncovered, stirring frequently, until it returns to the boil and thickens, about 15 minutes. Stir in the cinnamon, caraway, cubeb and reserved lamb meat and cook for another 1–2 minutes. Remove from the heat, cover with a lid and leave to stand for 5 minutes. Ladle into bowls. Give each bowl a small squeeze of lemon juice and garnish with a pinch of caraway and some coriander (cilantro). Serve with the remaining lemon wedges.

Harira with Lentils and Short Vermicelli Pasta

MOROCCO
PREPARATION TIME: 15 minutes
COOKING TIME: 1 hour 20 minutes
SERVES: 8

This is one of countless versions of Morocco's iconic *harira* (page 118). For extra richness, stir in some butter or *smen* before serving.

3 tablespoons olive oil
2 red or yellow onions, finely chopped
2 ripe tomatoes, halved crosswise and grated, peel discarded (see page 445)
2 tablespoons double concentrated tomato purée (paste)
1 celery stalk with leaves, finely chopped
3 heaped tablespoons finely chopped flat-leaf parsley, plus extra to garnish
3 heaped tablespoons finely chopped coriander (cilantro), plus extra to garnish
½ teaspoon ground cinnamon
¼ teaspoon ground ginger
pinch of saffron threads, crumbled
150 g/5 oz (¾ cup) dried brown lentils, picked over for any stones or debris and rinsed
70 g/2¾ oz (½ cup) plain (all-purpose) flour
50 g/2 oz (½ cup) short vermicelli pasta, crushed angel hair pasta, *tlitli* (birds' tongues, see page 227) or another small soup pasta
salt and pepper
lemon wedges, to serve

Add the oil and onions to a soup pot and cook for about 5 minutes, or until they begin to soften. Add the tomatoes, tomato purée (paste) and 3 tablespoons water and cook, stirring frequently, for 5 minutes. Stir in the celery, parsley, coriander (cilantro), cinnamon, ginger and saffron. Season with salt and pepper and pour in 1.75 litres (60 fl oz/ generous 7 cups) water. Bring to the boil. Add the lentils, then cover with a lid and cook over a medium-low heat for 40 minutes.

In a large bowl, whisk the flour into 250 ml (8 fl oz/1 cup) cold water until smooth. Leave to stand for 5 minutes and whisk again. While steadily stirring, slowly add to the soup. Reduce the heat to low and cook, uncovered, stirring frequently, for 10 minutes, allowing the soup to thicken. Add the vermicelli and cook until the pasta is tender, about 10 minutes. Thin with some hot water if the soup becomes too thick.

Ladle into soup bowls and garnish with some parsley and coriander. Serve with lemon wedges to squeeze over.

Chorba with Cracked Freekeh

ALGERIA, TUNISIA
PREPARATION TIME: 10 minutes
COOKING TIME: 1 hour 30 minutes
SERVES: 4

An ancient Mediterranean grain, *frik* – freekeh in English – is green durum wheat that has been roasted and then rubbed, giving it a smoky, nutty flavour. (The name *frik* comes from the Arabic word meaning 'rubbed'.) It is sold either whole grain or cracked; the latter, which cooks faster, is preferable here in this soup. While this version has lamb, some cooks use beef or chicken, and often add a handful of chickpeas (garbanzo beans). In Algeria, cooks sometimes add small meatballs seasoned with dried mint, or stir in some *smen* (page 412) at the end, while Tunisians usually give it a dollop of harissa. The pinch of dried mint or ground cinnamon at the end offers a lovely aromatic final touch. Some add a few drops of lemon juice before serving.

3 tablespoons olive oil
250 g/9 oz boneless lamb, trimmed and cut into small cubes
2 cloves of garlic, minced
2 tablespoons finely chopped flat-leaf parsley
1 celery stalk, finely chopped
cayenne pepper or harissa (page 409), to taste
1 teaspoon tabil spice blend (page 446) or a mix of ground coriander and caraway seeds
2 heaped tablespoons double concentrated tomato purée (paste)
120 g/4 oz (⅔ cup) cracked freekeh
salt and pepper
dried mint, to garnish, optional
ground cinnamon, to garnish, optional
lemon wedges, to serve, optional

Add the oil and lamb to a soup pot or casserole dish (Dutch oven), season with salt and pepper and brown over a medium heat for about 5 minutes. Add the garlic, parsley, celery, cayenne pepper and tabil spice blend and cook for about 2 minutes until aromatic. Add the tomato purée (paste) and 6 tablespoons water and cook for 5 minutes, stirring frequently. Pour in 1 litre (34 fl oz/4¼ cups) water, bring to the boil and stir in the freekeh. Reduce the heat to low, partly cover the pot with a lid and cook until the freekeh is tender and the soup has thickened, 1 hour–1 hour 15 minutes. Add a touch more water if needed. Sprinkle with pinches of dried mint and cinnamon (if using), then ladle into bowls and serve with lemon wedges (if using).

Red Chorba Vegetable Soup with Vermicelli

ALGERIA
PREPARATION TIME: 15 minutes
COOKING TIME: 50 minutes
SERVES: 6–8

The name of this deeply popular Algerian dish is *chorba hamra*, literally 'red soup', a colour it takes from the tomatoes, double concentrated tomato purée (paste), paprika and cayenne pepper. Vermicelli or crumbled angel hair pasta are common options to add to it, as is *tlitli* (shaped like orzo or 'birds' tongues', see page 227). Some add rice or bulgur wheat, while cooks in the mountainous Kabylia region may add *frik* (freekeh). If in season, add shelled fresh peas or broad (fava) beans. Serve with *boureks* (stuffed pastries, pages 56–57) and, whenever possible, fresh figs.

2 tablespoons olive oil
250 g/9 oz boneless lamb, cut into small pieces
1 red or yellow onion, finely chopped
4 ripe tomatoes, halved crosswise and grated,
    peel discarded (see page 445)
2 tablespoons double concentrated tomato purée
    (paste)
4 tablespoons finely chopped coriander (cilantro)
1 teaspoon sweet paprika
2 pinches of cayenne pepper
150 g/5 oz (¾ cup) canned chickpeas
    (garbanzo beans), rinsed, or cooked dried
    chickpeas (page 443)
1 white potato, peeled and diced
1 courgette (zucchini), diced
1 carrot, diced
1 celery stalk, finely chopped
1 stalk or fronds fennel, finely chopped, optional
25 g/1 oz (¼ cup) short vermicelli pasta, crushed angel
    hair pasta, *tlitli* (birds' tongues) or another small
    soup pasta
pinch of ground cinnamon
salt and pepper
lemon wedges, to serve

Heat the oil in a soup pot over a medium heat, add the lamb and onion, then season with salt and pepper and cook, stirring frequently, until the meat is browned and the onion begins to soften, about 5 minutes. Add the tomatoes, tomato purée (paste) and 4 tablespoons water, the coriander (cilantro), paprika and cayenne pepper and cook for 5 minutes. Pour in 1.5 litres (50 fl oz/generous 6 cups) water and bring to the boil. Add the chickpeas (garbanzo beans), potato, courgette (zucchini), carrot, celery and fennel (if using). Reduce the heat to low, cover with a lid and simmer for about 30 minutes, or until the meat and vegetables are tender. Add the pasta and cinnamon and cook for about 5 minutes, or until tender. Ladle into bowls, give each a generous grinding of pepper and serve with lemon wedges to squeeze over the top.

White Chorba Chicken Soup with Egg and Lemon

ALGERIA
PREPARATION TIME: 10 minutes
COOKING TIME: 1 hour
SERVES: 4

The classic version of Algeria's famous *chorba baida* ('white soup') is prepared with chicken, small vermicelli pasta and cinnamon. Some versions have meatballs (see right). This recipe is bound at the end with some beaten egg and lemon juice.

2 bone-in chicken thighs, skin removed
1 onion, grated
2 tablespoons olive oil
15 g/½ oz (1 tablespoon) butter or *smen* (page 412)
150 g/5 oz (¾ cup) canned chickpeas (garbanzo beans), rinsed, or cooked dried chickpeas (page 443)
50 g/2 oz (½ cup) short vermicelli pasta or crushed angel hair pasta
pinch of cinnamon
1 egg yolk
1 tablespoon fresh lemon juice
1 tablespoon minced flat-leaf parsley, plus extra to garnish
salt and pepper

Put the chicken, onion, oil and butter into a soup pot and season with salt and pepper. Cook over a medium heat until the chicken changes colour and the onion begins to soften, about 5 minutes. Do not let it brown. Pour in 1 litre (34 fl oz/4¼ cups) of hot water and bring to the boil. Cover the pot with a lid, reduce the heat slightly and gently boil for 45 minutes.

Remove the chicken from the pot and leave until cool enough to handle, then debone, discarding the bones. Shred the pieces of meat and return to the pot. Add the chickpeas (garbanzo beans). Return the soup to the boil, add the pasta and cinnamon and cook for about 5 minutes, or until tender. Remove the pot from the heat and leave to cool for a moment.

Put the egg, lemon juice and parsley into a small bowl and, using a fork, beat together. Slowly add a ladleful of soup to the mix, stirring constantly, then slowly add the mixture to the soup, stirring constantly. Ladle into bowls, scatter over some parsley to garnish and serve.

Algiers White Chorba with Meatballs

ALGERIA
PREPARATION TIME: 20 minutes
COOKING TIME: 1 hour
SERVES: 4

This version of Algeria's *chorba baida* ('white soup') with meatballs and rice is especially popular in Algiers and Constantine. These days, some cooks add a chicken, lamb or vegetable stock (bouillon) cube to boost the flavour.

3 tablespoons olive oil
2 red or yellow onions, finely chopped
1 celery stalk, finely chopped
100 g/3½ oz (½ cup) canned chickpeas (garbanzo beans), rinsed, or cooked dried chickpeas (page 443)
1 chicken, lamb or vegetable stock (bouillon) cube, crumbled, optional
250 g/9 oz minced (ground) beef or lamb
2 tablespoons finely chopped flat-leaf parsley
50 g/2 oz (¾ cup) dry breadcrumbs
1 egg
pinch of ground cinnamon
3 tablespoons uncooked white rice
1 egg yolk
1 lemon, cut into wedges
salt and pepper
2 tablespoons finely chopped coriander (cilantro), to garnish

Heat the oil in a large casserole dish (Dutch oven) or wide soup pot over a medium heat, add the onions, season with salt and pepper and cook, stirring frequently, until softened but not browned, about 5 minutes. Add the celery, chickpeas (garbanzo beans) and stock (bouillon) cube (if using). Pour in 1.2 litres (40 fl oz/5 cups) water, bring to a simmer, cover with a lid and simmer for 15 minutes.

Meanwhile, prepare the meatballs. Put the meat, parsley, breadcrumbs, egg and cinnamon into a large bowl and season with salt and pepper. Mix well with your hands. With moistened hands, roll into 2.5-cm-/1-inch-diameter balls from 1 tablespoon of the mixture for each one.

Set the meatballs in the pan, cover with a lid and simmer for 15 minutes. Add the rice and cook for 15–20 minutes until tender. Put the egg yolk, 1 tablespoon of fresh lemon juice from 1 of the wedges and a ladleful of broth from the pan into a medium heatproof bowl and beat until combined. While stirring, slowly add it to the soup. Ladle into bowls, garnish with coriander (cilantro) and serve with the remaining lemon wedges.

White Chorba Chicken Soup with Egg and Lemon ➤➤

Winter Chorba with Lentils

ALGERIA
PREPARATION TIME: 15 minutes
COOKING TIME: 1 hour
SERVES: 4–6

Another popular Algerian *chorba* (soup), this warm, homey version with lentils is perfect for a cold winter's night.

2 tablespoons olive oil
1 red or yellow onion, finely chopped
225 g/8 oz boneless lamb or stewing beef, cut into 1-cm/½-inch pieces
2 tomatoes, halved crosswise and grated, peel discarded (see page 445)
2 tablespoons double concentrated tomato purée (paste)
1 teaspoon sweet paprika
2 pinches of cayenne pepper
100 g/3½ oz (½ cup) dried brown lentils, picked over for any stones or debris and rinsed
1 carrot, diced
50 g/2 oz (½ cup) short vermicelli pasta, angel hair pasta or another small soup pasta
3 heaped tablespoons finely chopped flat-leaf parsley
salt and pepper
lemon wedges, to serve

Heat the oil in a soup pot over a medium heat, add the onion and meat, season with salt and pepper and cook, stirring frequently, until the meat is browned and the onion begins to soften, about 5 minutes. Add the tomatoes, tomato purée (paste), 4 tablespoons water, the paprika and cayenne pepper and cook for 5 minutes. Stir in the lentils, add the carrot and pour in 1.2 litres (40 fl oz/5 cups) of hot water. Bring to the boil, cover with a lid, reduce the heat to low and simmer for about 45 minutes, or until the lentils and meat are tender.

Avoiding any pieces of meat, scoop out about 250 ml (8 fl oz/1 cup) of the lentils and purée in a blender or food processor, then return to the soup. Add the pasta and cook for about 5 minutes, or until tender, then stir in the parsley. Ladle into bowls, give each a generous grinding of pepper and serve with lemon wedges to squeeze over the top.

Chorba with Lamb and Dried Mint

LIBYA
PREPARATION TIME: 15 minutes
COOKING TIME: 1 hour 20 minutes
SERVES: 4

This soup with lamb, dried mint and plenty of spices is considered something of a national dish and often referred to as *shorba libiya*, 'Libyan soup'. Versions vary from kitchen to kitchen, but one of the key constants is adding a generous amount of dried mint at the very end, and it is usually spicy. During Ramadan, it can be found almost nightly on tables.

3 tablespoons olive oil
175 g/6 oz trimmed stewing lamb or beef, cut into about 1-cm/½-inch pieces
1 red or yellow onion, finely chopped
2 cloves of garlic, minced
3 ripe tomatoes, halved crosswise and grated, peel discarded (see page 445)
2 heaped tablespoons double concentrated tomato purée (paste)
½ teaspoon ground cinnamon
½ teaspoon ground ginger
½ teaspoon ground turmeric
cayenne pepper, to taste
100 g/3½ oz (½ cup) canned chickpeas (garbanzo beans), rinsed, or cooked dried chickpeas (page 443)
2 heaped tablespoons finely chopped flat-leaf parsley
2 tablespoons finely chopped coriander (cilantro)
100 g/3½ oz orzo or another small soup pasta (about ½ cup)
1 heaped tablespoon dried mint
salt and pepper
lemon wedges, to serve

Add the oil, lamb and onion to a soup pot, season with salt and pepper and cook over a high heat for 8–10 minutes until the meat is browned and the onion begins to soften. Stir in the garlic, then add the tomatoes, tomato purée (paste) and 4 tablespoons water. Add the cinnamon, ginger, turmeric and cayenne pepper and cook for 2–3 minutes. Pour in 750 ml (25 fl oz/3 cups) of hot water, cover with a lid and simmer for 30 minutes. Add the chickpeas (garbanzo beans), parsley and coriander (cilantro). Pour in 500 ml (18 fl oz/2 cups) of hot water, cover again and simmer for 15–30 minutes until the meat is tender. Add the pasta, increase the heat slightly and boil for 8–10 minutes until tender. Stir in the mint. Ladle the soup into bowls and serve with lemon wedges to squeeze over the top.

Vegetable Chorba with Hlalem Pasta

TUNISIA
PREPARATION TIME: 15 minutes,
plus soaking time
COOKING TIME: 1 hour
SERVES: 6

This hearty Tunisian soup calls for *hlalem*, a type of popular, fresh and often homemade pasta. The pieces of pasta are small, wiry twists about 1 cm/½ inch long, similar to Italian *trofie*. The recipe for fresh *hlalem* can be found on page 231.

50 g/2 oz (¼ cup) dried brown lentils, picked over for any stones or debris and rinsed
3 tablespoons olive oil
1 red or yellow onion, finely chopped
175 g/6 oz trimmed stewing beef, cut into 1-cm/½-inch pieces
2 cloves of garlic, minced
1 ripe tomato, halved crosswise and grated, peel discarded (see page 445)
2 heaped tablespoons double concentrated tomato purée (paste)
cayenne pepper or harissa (page 409), to taste
100 g/3½ oz (½ cup) canned chickpeas (garbanzo beans), rinsed, or cooked dried chickpeas (page 443)
1 carrot, finely chopped
1 celery stalk, finely chopped
4 tablespoons finely chopped flat-leaf parsley
225 g/8 oz Hlalem Pasta (page 231) or *trofie* pasta
salt and pepper
lemon wedges, to serve

Put the lentils into a large bowl, cover with abundant water and leave to soak for 1 hour. Drain and set aside.

Add the oil, onion and meat to a medium soup pot, season with salt and pepper and cook for 8–10 minutes until the meat is browned and the onion has softened. Stir in the garlic, tomato, tomato purée (paste) and 6 tablespoons water, then season with cayenne pepper and cook for 5 minutes. Stir in the lentils, chickpeas (garbanzo beans), carrot, celery and parsley, then pour in 2 litres (68 fl oz/ generous 2 quarts/8½ cups) of hot water and bring to the boil. Partly cover with a lid and gently boil for 30 minutes.

Add the pasta, reduce the heat to low and cook for about 15 minutes, or until the pasta is tender. The soup should be loose but not watery. Ladle into bowls and serve with lemon wedges to squeeze over the top.

Spicy Soup with Small Meatballs

TUNISIA
PREPARATION TIME: 20 minutes
COOKING TIME: 35 minutes
SERVES: 4

A popular winter soup, *hsou* is also a Ramadan favourite. While adding small meatballs is most common, there are also popular versions with *kaddid* (seasoned, salted and air-dried meat, see page 206) and cuttlefish. It has plenty of black pepper and some capers that add a tangy note.

250 g/9 oz minced (ground) beef
3 teaspoons dried mint
4 tablespoons olive oil
1 yellow onion, finely chopped
2 cloves of garlic, minced
4 tomatoes halved crosswise and grated, peel discarded (see page 445)
1 heaped tablespoon double concentrated tomato purée (paste)
cayenne pepper, to taste
2 tablespoons capers, rinsed
3 tablespoons plain (all-purpose) flour
salt and pepper

Put the minced (ground) meat and 1½ teaspoons of the mint into a large bowl, season with salt and pepper and mix well. Roll the mixture into small meatballs, about 2.5 cm/1 inch in diameter. There should be about 32 of them.

Heat the oil in a soup pot over a medium heat, add the meatballs and cook for about 4 minutes, or until browned. Transfer with a slotted spoon to a plate. Add the onion to the pot and cook for about 8 minutes, or until pale and soft. Add the garlic and cook for about 1 minute, or until aromatic. Add the tomatoes, tomato purée (paste) and 4 tablespoons water, then season with cayenne pepper and salt. Reduce the heat to low and cook until thickened and the oil rises to the surface, about 10 minutes. Stir in 1 litre (34 fl oz/4¼ cups) of hot water and bring to the boil. Add the meatballs with the remaining 1½ teaspoons of mint, the capers and a generous grinding of pepper. Reduce the heat to low and simmer for about 5 minutes, or until the meatballs are cooked through.

Whisk the flour into 3 tablespoons water in a small bowl. While stirring, very slowly add to the soup, then cook for a few minutes over a low heat, stirring constantly, until the soup has a silky consistency. Ladle into bowls and serve hot.

Chorba Fish Soup

ALGERIA
PREPARATION TIME: 15 minutes
COOKING TIME: 1 hour
SERVES: 4

Use whatever fish looks good in the market for this *chorba* (soup), although white-fleshed fish are preferable to darker, oily ones like sardines, mackerel or tuna. Generous pieces of grouper or sea bream, for instance, are ideal. There are many options for additional flavourings to this rather straightforward recipe. Add some fennel, carrots, sweet green peppers, saffron or, for a piney, pepperiness, a pinch of ground cubeb pepper (see page 121). For a creamier soup, purée before adding the pasta and returning the pieces of deboned fish to the pot.

- 2 tablespoons olive oil
- 2 cloves of garlic, finely chopped
- 1 onion, finely chopped
- 3 tomatoes, peeled (see page 445) and finely chopped
- 1 tablespoon double concentrated tomato purée (paste)
- 1 small celery stalk, coarsely chopped
- 3 tablespoons coarsely chopped flat-leaf parsley
- 3 tablespoons coarsely chopped coriander (cilantro)
- 1 kg/2¼ lb mixed white-fleshed fish, cleaned, scaled and cut into large pieces as needed
- 75 g/2¾ oz (¾ cup) short vermicelli pasta, crushed angel hair pasta or another small soup pasta
- salt and pepper

Heat the oil in a soup pot over a medium heat, add the garlic, onion, tomatoes, tomato purée (paste) and 3 tablespoons water, the celery, parsley and coriander (cilantro), then season with salt and pepper. Cook, stirring frequently, until darker and reduced, about 10 minutes. Pour in 1.5 litres (50 fl oz/generous 6 cups) water and add the fish. Bring to a gentle boil, reduce the heat, mostly cover the pot with a lid and simmer for 20 minutes. Remove from the heat and, using a slotted spoon, remove the fish. Once cool enough to handle, flake the fish into pieces, discarding the skin and bones. Set aside.

Return the soup to a simmer. Add the pasta and the reserved fish meat and cook for about 5 minutes, or until the pasta is tender. Ladle into bowls and serve.

Silky Fish Soup

ALGERIA
PREPARATION TIME: 20 minutes
COOKING TIME: 1 hour 30 minutes
SERVES: 4

Among the influences from 130 years of French rule in Algeria is this style of *soupe de poisson* with croutons, a staple of fish restaurants.

- 750 g/1⅔ lb mixed white-fleshed fish, cleaned and scaled as needed
- 3 tablespoons olive oil, plus extra for rubbing
- 3 cloves of garlic, peeled
- 1 onion, coarsely chopped
- 1 leek, white part only, coarsely chopped
- 2 ripe tomatoes, peeled (see page 445) and coarsely quartered
- 1 tablespoon double concentrated tomato purée (paste)
- 1 white potato, peeled and coarsely chopped
- 1 carrot, coarsely chopped
- 1 courgette (zucchini), peeled and coarsely chopped
- 1 celery stalk, coarsely chopped
- ½ teaspoon sweet paprika
- pinch of saffron threads, crumbled
- pinch of cayenne pepper, optional
- 8–12 slices of baguette
- salt and pepper

Add the fish to a soup pot, season with salt and pepper and pour in 1.5 litres (50 fl oz/generous 6 cups) water. Bring to a simmer and simmer for 30 minutes. Strain the fish stock (broth) through a sieve into a large jug (pitcher) or bowl, gently pressing out the liquid from the fish. Set aside. Once cool enough to handle, remove some pieces of fish if desired, being careful to avoid any bones.

Put the oil, garlic, onion and leek into a clean soup pot and cook over a medium heat for 10 minutes. Add the tomatoes, tomato purée (paste) and 3 tablespoons water, then season with salt and pepper and cook for 5 minutes. Add the potato, carrot, courgette (zucchini), celery, paprika, saffron and cayenne pepper (if using) and pour in the reserved fish stock. Bring to the boil, cover with a lid and gently boil for 30 minutes, or until the vegetables are tender. Purée in the pot using an immersion hand blender, or transfer to a blender or food processor and purée in batches until smooth. Stir in the reserved fish meat and bring to a simmer.

Meanwhile, preheat the oven grill (broiler), then rub the bread with oil, add a pinch of salt and toast under the grill, turning as needed.

Serve the soup with the croutons on the side.

Spicy Fish Soup with Red Mullet

TUNISIA
PREPARATION TIME: 20 minutes
COOKING TIME: 1 hour
SERVES: 4

This popular Tunisian soup can also be prepared with *frik* (freekeh, roasted and cracked or coarsely ground green wheat), which requires about 30 minutes to cook. Add a touch more water if needed and stir in some ground cumin or coriander, if desired. This recipe calls for red mullet, though any firm, white-fleshed fish will work.

   750 g/1⅔ lb small red mullet or a white-fleshed
      soup fish, cleaned and scaled
   3 tablespoons olive oil
   1 onion, finely chopped
   3 cloves of garlic, minced
   harissa (page 409), to taste
   3 ripe tomatoes, halved crosswise and grated,
      peel discarded (see page 445)
   2 tablespoons double concentrated tomato purée
      (paste)
   1 celery stalk, finely chopped
   1 heaped tablespoon finely chopped flat-leaf parsley
   ½ teaspoon sweet paprika
   150 g/5 oz (¾ cup) *langues d'oiseaux* (birds' tongues)
      or orzo pasta, short vermicelli pasta or another
      soup pasta
   salt and pepper
   lemon wedges, to serve

Add the fish to a soup pot, season with salt and pepper and pour in 1.5 litres (50 fl oz/generous 6 cups) water. Bring to a simmer and simmer for 20 minutes. Strain the fish through a sieve into a large jug (pitcher) or bowl, reserving the liquid. Once cool enough to handle, flake the fish into pieces, discarding the skin and bones. Set aside.

Put the oil and onion into a soup pot and cook over a medium heat for about 10 minutes, or until golden and tender. Stir in the garlic, then add the harissa, tomatoes, tomato purée (paste) and 4 tablespoons water, the celery, parsley and paprika and cook for 10 minutes, stirring frequently. Add the reserved fish broth and bring to the boil. Add the pasta and cook for 15–20 minutes until tender. Stir the reserved fish meat into the soup, then ladle into bowls and serve with lemon wedges.

Cracked Barley and Octopus Soup

TUNISIA
PREPARATION TIME: 10 minutes
COOKING TIME: 1 hour 10 minutes
SERVES: 6

Tchich bel karnit – cracked barley (or barley grits) with octopus – is a classic of the Tunisian coastal kitchen. The dried mint at the end is a lovely touch. The tradition of salting and air-drying octopus is popular in the Kerkennah Islands off Sfax and on Djerba, and when fresh octopus isn't readily available cooks there use the dried version in this dish. If using dried octopus, soak overnight in a large bowl of cold water. The next day, drain and rinse, then cut into bite-size pieces with kitchen scissors. In some homes, cooks add pickled capers and some cayenne pepper at the end of cooking.

   250 g/9 oz cleaned octopus, thawed if frozen
   2 tablespoons olive oil
   1 red or yellow onion, finely chopped
   3 tablespoons double concentrated tomato purée
      (paste)
   harissa (page 409), to taste
   2 cloves of garlic, minced
   ½ teaspoon ground coriander
   ½ teaspoon ground cumin
   ½ teaspoon sweet paprika
   90 g/3¼ oz (½ cup) *tchich* or cracked barley
   salt and pepper
   ½ teaspoon dried mint, to garnish

Rinse the octopus, removing any grit in the tentacles. Cut into generous bite-size pieces.

Heat the oil in a soup pot over a medium heat, add the onion and cook for 5 minutes. Add the octopus and cook for another 5 minutes. Add the tomato purée (paste) and 4 tablespoons water, the harissa, garlic, coriander, cumin and paprika, then season with salt and pepper and cook for 5 minutes. Pour in 1.2 litres (40 fl oz/5 cups) of hot water. Reduce the heat to low, bring to a gentle boil, cover with a lid and gently boil for 30 minutes. Stir in the barley, cover with a lid and cook until both the octopus and barley are tender, about 20 minutes. Ladle into bowls, sprinkle with some dried mint and serve.

Chorba with Prawns and Rice

ALGERIA
PREPARATION TIME: 5 minutes
COOKING TIME: 35 minutes
SERVES: 4

While adding cumin to this prawn (shrimp) soup lends some earthiness, substituting it with a generous pinch or two of ground cinnamon will turn the dish into something more sweetly aromatic.

 2 tablespoons olive oil
 1 red or yellow onion, finely chopped
 3 cloves of garlic, minced
 3 tablespoons double concentrated tomato purée (paste)
 1 teaspoon paprika
 ½ teaspoon ground cumin, optional
 1 sprig thyme
 1 bay leaf
 3 tablespoons uncooked white rice
 400 g/14 oz peeled raw prawns (shrimp)
 2 heaped tablespoons finely chopped coriander (cilantro)
 salt and pepper
 lemon wedges, to serve

Heat the oil in a soup pot over a medium heat, add the onion and cook for about 8 minutes, or until pale and soft. Stir in the garlic, then add the tomato purée (paste) and 4 tablespoons water, the paprika, cumin (if using), thyme and bay leaf, then season with salt and pepper. Cover with a lid and cook for 2–3 minutes, stirring frequently. Add 1 litre (34 fl oz/ 4¼ cups) of hot water and bring to the boil. When the soup returns to the boil, sprinkle in the rice. Cover, reduce the heat to low and cook until the rice is tender, about 15 minutes, adding the prawns (shrimp) partway through cooking. Stir in the coriander (cilantro). Ladle into soup bowls and serve with lemon wedges.

Velvety Semolina Soup

TUNISIA
PREPARATION TIME: 5 minutes
COOKING TIME: 40 minutes
SERVES: 4–5

Sder is a smooth semolina soup that is enormously popular in many Tunisian households during Ramadan (see page 32). The semolina gives a soothing, nourishing quality that is easy on the stomach. As with any popular soup – especially one made with such frequency – there are many variations of it. This is a simple vegetarian one, but you can add some small meatballs with dried mint (see the recipe for a similar Tunisian soup, *hsou*, page 128). Outside of Ramadan, when salty food is usually avoided, you can add some pieces of *kaddid* (seasoned, salted and air-dried meat, see page 206). Garnish the soup with chopped celery, capers and, if desired, lemon wedges. In Tozeur, an oasis known for its dates, cooks often add an herb called *el figel* (*rue*, also known as herb-of-grace).

 3 tablespoons olive oil
 1 red or yellow onion, finely chopped
 2 cloves of garlic, minced
 1 celery stalk, finely chopped
 1 tablespoon finely chopped flat-leaf parsley
 2 tablespoons double concentrated tomato purée (paste)
 harissa (page 409) or cayenne pepper, to taste
 1 teaspoon ground caraway
 70 g/2¾ oz (6 tablespoons) medium semolina
 2 tablespoons capers, rinsed
 salt and pepper
 dried mint, to garnish

Heat the oil in a soup pot over a medium heat, add the onion and cook for about 8 minutes, or until pale and soft. Add the garlic, celery and parsley and cook for 5 minutes. Add the tomato purée (paste) and 4 tablespoons water, the harissa and caraway, then season with salt and pepper. Reduce the heat to low and cook for 5 minutes, stirring frequently. Pour in 1.5 litres (50 fl oz/generous 6 cups) of hot water and bring to the boil. Stir in the semolina and cook for 10 minutes, stirring frequently. Add the capers and cook for a final 10 minutes until silky. Ladle into bowls, add a pinch of dried mint to each and serve hot.

Puréed Mushroom Soup

MOROCCO
PREPARATION TIME: 20 minutes
COOKING TIME: 35 minutes
SERVES: 4–6

Puréed mushroom soup makes a change from traditional *harira* (page 118) during Ramadan. This recipe uses button mushrooms, though can also be prepared with wild mushrooms. If using foraged wild mushrooms, brush and wipe clean. If using cultivated mushrooms, quickly dunk them in cold water, drain and pat dry with paper towels. See below for more on Morocco's wild mushrooms.

2 tablespoons olive oil
2 red or yellow onions, thinly sliced
2 cloves of garlic, minced
500 g/1 lb 2 oz button mushrooms, coarsely chopped
2 medium–small white potatoes (about 350 g/12 oz total), peeled and coarsely chopped
15 g/½ oz (1 tablespoon) butter
small bunch flat-leaf parsley, tied together
salt and pepper

Heat the oil in a soup pot over a medium heat, add the onions and cook for about 5 minutes, or until they become tender. Stir in the garlic, then the mushrooms. Add the potatoes and butter and season with salt and pepper. Cover with a lid and cook over a medium heat, stirring from time to time, for 10 minutes. Pour in 500 ml (18 fl oz/2 cups) of hot water, add the parsley, cover and bring to the boil. Reduce the heat to low and cook until the mushrooms and potatoes are tender, about 15 minutes.

Remove the pot from the heat, uncover and leave to cool for a few minutes. Discard the parsley. Purée the soup in the pot using an immersion hand blender, or transfer to a blender or food processor and purée in batches until smooth. Thin with 250 ml (8 fl oz/1 cup) water or as desired and return to a simmer. Ladle into bowls and serve with a grinding of pepper.

WILD MUSHROOMS

The Rif Mountains stretch from Morocco's northwestern tip 300 km/186 miles east towards the Algerian border. In the centre of the range near Ketama, they reach about 2,500 m/8,000 feet in elevation. In Arabic, Rif means 'edge' or 'border'. With a backbone of limestone, Africa's northernmost range forms a protective, almost impenetrable arc at the country's Mediterranean coast.

With few towns and relatively few roads, the Rif feels isolated, and even in large parts inaccessible. Hamlets, grassy grazing hills and intense cultivation form mosaics around patches of dense forest whose trees change with the elevation. Scrub, oaks, Mediterranean pine trees, wild olives and orchards of figs, plums and almonds give way to Aleppo pine, tall maritime pine, thuya (an indigenous cypress beloved by woodworkers for its grain) and fir as the hills ascend, with magnificent stands of cedars.

In the rich loam under these trees grow 35 varieties of edible wild mushrooms and truffles. The western Rif, with wet winters and more rainy days than anywhere along Africa's Mediterranean coast, is particularly rich in fungi. Sought-after varieties found here include fluted, golden chanterelles (*Cantharellus cibarius*), porcini (*Boletus edulis*), funnel-shaped black trumpets (*Craterellus cornucopioides*, also called horn of plenty), a large variety of coral fungi the size of cauliflower, valuable matsutake (*Tricholoma magnivelare*) and Caesar's mushroom (*Amanita caesarea*, one of the few edible *Amanita* mushrooms).

There is traditionally not much of a culinary culture for wild mushrooms in Morocco – most in the market are button mushrooms – and many of these varieties are sold to brokers and exported. Local Berbers pick them up when grazing livestock or gathering firewood or fodder for animals. While most go to brokers, they do eat some of what they collect, usually boiled or fried, or preserved in olive oil to eat later in the year.

Wild mushrooms are one of the many things gathered in nature's pantry. Well before innovative restaurant chefs began plundering nature's wild largesse, people in places like the Jbala in the western part of the Rif Mountains have been utilizing what grows in the hills around them for nourishment and medicinal purposes – and the pleasures of flavour and variety.

Aromatic Carrot and Leek Soup

MOROCCO
PREPARATION TIME: 10 minutes
COOKING TIME: 35 minutes
SERVES: 4–6

Puréed vegetable soups have become very popular in Morocco. Drawing on the classic combination of carrots and oranges in salads (page 81), this soup adds some orange zest for a tasty, sophisticated touch to a nourishing soup. Add a dash of orange blossom water for an even greater punch.

60 g/2¼ oz (4 tablespoons) butter
3 leeks, finely chopped, or 2 red or yellow onions, finely chopped
450 g/1 lb carrots, cut into 8 or so pieces
1 white potato, peeled and cut into 8 or so pieces
finely grated zest of ½ orange, plus extra to garnish
pinch of white pepper
salt
freshly ground nutmeg, to garnish, optional

Melt the butter in a soup pot over a medium-low heat, add the leeks, cover with a lid and cook for about 8 minutes, or until soft, stirring from time to time. Add the carrots, potato and orange zest, then pour in 1 litre (34 fl oz/4¼ cups) of hot water. Bring to the boil, reduce the heat, cover with a lid and boil until the carrots and potatoes are tender, about 20 minutes.

Remove the pot from the heat, uncover and leave to cool for a few minutes. Purée the soup in the pot using an immersion hand blender or transfer to a blender or food processor and purée in batches until smooth. Add a touch of water if desired to loosen the consistency. Stir in the white pepper, season with salt and return to a simmer. Ladle into bowls, garnish with a pinch of orange zest and some nutmeg (if using) and serve.

Velvety Butternut Squash Soup

ALGERIA, MOROCCO, TUNISIA
PREPARATION TIME: 15 minutes
COOKING TIME: 35 minutes
SERVES: 4

Another smooth, puréed soup that has become popular recently, this makes an autumn treat. Some cooks like to add a pinch of ground nutmeg at the end rather than – or even alongside – the cumin. Stir in a touch of crème fraîche, if desired.

1 tablespoon olive oil
1 red or yellow onion, thinly sliced
750 g/1⅔ lb peeled and seeded butternut squash, cut into about 3.5-cm/1⅓-inch cubes
1 white potato, peeled and quartered
generous pinch of ground cumin
salt and pepper
crème fraîche, to garnish, optional

Heat the oil in a soup pot over a medium heat, add the onion and cook for about 5 minutes, or until softened. Add the squash and potato and season with salt and pepper. Stir well. Pour in 600 ml (20 fl oz/2½ cups) water and bring to the boil. Reduce the heat, cover with a lid and gently boil until the squash and potatoes are tender, about 20 minutes.

Remove the pot from the heat, uncover and leave to cool for a few minutes. Purée the soup in the pot using an immersion hand blender, or transfer to a blender or food processor and purée in batches until smooth. Add the cumin and return the soup to a simmer. Thin with water if desired or simmer uncovered to thicken. Ladle into bowls, garnish with crème fraîche (if using) and serve.

Puréed Vegetable Chorba

ALGERIA
PREPARATION TIME: 15 minutes
COOKING TIME: 1 hour
SERVES: 8

This is a hearty soup made with a range of vegetables in the pantry. Some home cooks add a stock (bouillon) cube to boost flavour, though it is not necessary with a wide selection of good vegetables added to the pot.

 1 tablespoon olive oil
 1 red or yellow onion, coarsely chopped
 2 leeks, coarsely chopped
 2 celery stalks, coarsely chopped
 3 carrots, coarsely chopped
 2 courgettes (zucchini), peeled and coarsely chopped
 2 white potatoes, peeled and coarsely chopped
 2 tomatoes, cored and coarsely chopped
 2 turnips, peeled and coarsely chopped
 2 fennel bulbs, coarsely chopped
 1 long sweet green pepper, cored, seeded and coarsely chopped
 salt and pepper
 finely chopped flat-leaf parsley, to garnish
 finely chopped coriander (cilantro), to garnish

Heat the oil in a soup pot over a medium heat, add all the vegetables, season with salt and pepper and cook, stirring frequently, for 5 minutes. Pour in 1.5 litres (50 fl oz/generous 6 cups) of hot water and bring to the boil. Reduce the heat, cover with a lid and gently boil until all the vegetables are tender, about 45 minutes.

Remove the pot from the heat, uncover and leave to cool for a few minutes. Purée the soup in the pot using an immersion hand blender or transfer to a blender or food processor and purée in batches until smooth. Return the soup to a simmer. Thin with water if desired or simmer uncovered to thicken. Ladle into bowls and garnish with parsley and coriander (cilantro). Serve.

Puréed Broad Bean Soup with Garlic, Cumin and Olive Oil

MOROCCO
PREPARATION TIME: 10 minutes, plus soaking time
COOKING TIME: 40 minutes
SERVES: 4–5

Bissara is one of Morocco's most iconic, rustic dishes. While this hearty purée of dried broad (fava) beans is eaten across the country, in the Rif Mountains it is a much-beloved staple. Use the small, split and peeled broad beans, not the large ones often called *ful*. Some Moroccans use a blend of broad beans and dried green peas. And in Fès and elsewhere, *bissara* made with dried and split green peas (page 137) is popular.

 400 g/14 oz (2 cups) small peeled and split dried broad (fava) beans
 3 cloves of garlic, peeled
 1 teaspoon ground cumin, plus extra to garnish
 1 teaspoon sweet paprika, plus extra to garnish
 generous pinch of cayenne pepper
 extra-virgin olive oil, for drizzling
 ½ lemon
 salt

Put the broad (fava) beans into a large colander and pick over to remove any stones or debris. Rinse under cold running water, then put into a large bowl. Cover with cold water and leave to soak for at least 8 hours. Drain.

Put the beans and garlic into a large soup pot or pot, pour in 1 litre (34 fl oz/4¼ cups) water and bring to the boil, skimming off any foam that rises to the surface with a slotted spoon. Reduce the heat to low, cover with a lid and gently boil until the beans are very tender, about 30 minutes.

Remove the pot from the heat, uncover and leave to cool for a few minutes. Add the cumin, paprika and cayenne pepper. Purée in the pot using an immersion hand blender until creamy, or transfer to a blender or food processor in batches to purée. Bring back to a simmer. If the soup is too thin, reduce over a medium heat for a few minutes to the desired consistency, or, for looser *bissara*, stir in a touch of hot water. The soup should be silky and creamy.

Ladle into bowls, drizzle with oil, squeeze some lemon juice over the top and generously garnish with cumin and paprika. Serve hot.

Puréed Split Pea Soup with Cumin and Paprika

MOROCCO
PREPARATION TIME: 10 minutes
COOKING TIME: 1 hour 10 minutes
SERVES: 6

This is another popular version of *bissara* prepared with split peas rather than broad (fava) beans (page 136). To shorten cooking time, soak the split peas for an hour or two, or even overnight in a bowl of cold water. To give it more texture, mash rather than purée. This *bissara* goes particularly nicely with grilled sardines (page 331).

500 g/1 lb 2 oz (2¼ cups) dried split green peas
4 cloves of garlic, peeled
1 teaspoon ground cumin, plus extra to garnish
½ teaspoon sweet paprika, plus extra to garnish
pinch of cayenne pepper
extra-virgin olive oil, for drizzling
salt

Put the split peas into a large colander and pick over to remove any stones or debris. Rinse under cold running water.

Put the peas and garlic into a large soup pot or pot, pour in 1.75 litres (60 fl oz/generous 7 cups) water and bring to the boil, skimming off any foam that rises to the surface with a slotted spoon. Reduce the heat to low, cover with a lid and gently boil until the split peas are very tender, 50 minutes–1 hour.

Remove the pot from the heat, uncover and leave to cool for a few minutes. Purée in the pot using an immersion hand blender until creamy, or transfer to a blender or food processor in batches to purée. For a more textured soup, mash by hand. Stir in the cumin, paprika and cayenne pepper, season with salt and bring back to a simmer. If the soup is too thin, reduce over a medium heat for a few minutes to the desired consistency, or, for a looser *bissara*, stir in a touch of hot water. The soup should be silky and creamy.

Ladle into bowls, add a drizzled circle of oil and a generous pinch of cumin and paprika to each. Serve hot.

Puréed Lentil Soup with Toasted Garlic Bread

TUNISIA
PREPARATION TIME: 10 minutes
COOKING TIME: 35 minutes
SERVES: 4

This winter favourite called *tbikha* from southeastern Tunisia is usually prepared with reddish-orange lentils, which gives it a delightful creaminess. You can serve it with some slices of toasted bread with harissa or olive spread on them, or even rubbed with garlic and drizzled with olive oil. Note that in Algeria *tbikha* refers to a vegetable potage.

3 tablespoons olive oil
1 red or yellow onion, thinly sliced
3 cloves of garlic, minced
250 g/9 oz (1¼ cups) split red lentils, picked over
    for any stones or debris and rinsed
1 teaspoon ground cumin
1 white potato, peeled and cut into pieces
1 carrot, cut into small pieces, optional
salt and pepper
thin slices of bread, to serve
harissa (page 409), to serve, optional
1 tablespoon extra-virgin olive oil, or extra as desired,
    to serve
1 clove of garlic, peeled, for rubbing bread, optional

Heat the oil in a large soup pot or pot over a medium heat, add the onion and cook for about 5 minutes, or until soft. Stir in the garlic and cook for about 30 seconds, or until aromatic. Stir in the lentils and cumin, season with salt and pepper and pour in 750 ml (25 fl oz/3 cups) water. Bring to the boil, add the potato, cover with a lid, reduce the heat to low and gently boil until the lentils have largely disintegrated and the potato is tender, about 25 minutes. Add a touch more water if needed.

Remove the pot from the heat, uncover and leave to cool slightly. Purée in the pot with an immersion hand blender or transfer to a blender or food processor and purée in batches until smooth. Bring back to a simmer. Thin with a touch of water or leave to simmer for a few minutes to get the desired consistency. Divide among soup bowls.

Before serving, toast the bread. Loosen the harissa with some oil and spread on the toast, or rub the bread with garlic and drizzle with oil. Serve alongside the lentils.

PULSES
AND
VEGETABLES

Stewed White Beans in Tomato Sauce (Quick Version)

MOROCCO
PREPARATION TIME: 10 minutes
COOKING TIME: 35 minutes
SERVES: 2–4

White beans stewed in tomato sauce is the epitome of popular comfort food in Morocco. This is a relatively quick version using canned white beans. You can also prepare it using about 150 g/5 oz (¾ cup) dried beans soaked overnight and cooked following the directions on page 443.

- 25 g/1 oz (2 tablespoons) butter, *smen* (page 412) or olive oil
- 2 cloves of garlic, grated
- 1 onion, grated
- 2 ripe tomatoes, halved crosswise and grated, peel discarded (see page 445)
- 1 (425-g/15-oz) can of white beans, such as cannellini or white haricot (navy) (about generous 2 cups), rinsed
- 1 heaped tablespoon finely chopped coriander (cilantro)
- 1 heaped tablespoon finely chopped flat-leaf parsley
- 1 teaspoon sweet paprika
- ½ teaspoon ground cumin
- ¼ teaspoon ground turmeric
- salt and pepper

Melt the butter in a pot over a medium-low heat, add the garlic and onion and cook for about 10 minutes, or until the onion is pale and soft. Add the tomatoes and cook, stirring from time to time, until they are deeper red and pulpy, about 10 minutes. Add a spoonful or two of water if needed to keep it from scorching.

Meanwhile, put the beans into a large saucepan. Pour in 500 ml (18 fl oz/2 cups) cool water and bring to the boil. Remove from the heat and do not drain.

Add the coriander (cilantro), parsley, paprika, cumin and turmeric to the pot of onion and tomato sauce. Drain the beans, reserving the liquid, then add the beans to the pot with about 350 ml (12 fl oz/1½ cups) of the reserved liquid. Season with salt and pepper. Bring to the boil, reduce the heat to low and simmer, uncovered, for 10–15 minutes to thicken the sauce. Ladle into bowls and serve.

Stewed White Beans in Tomato Sauce

MOROCCO
PREPARATION TIME: 10 minutes,
plus overnight soaking time
COOKING TIME: 1 hour 45 minutes–
2 hours 15 minutes
SERVES: 6–8

This is a popular version of *loubia* using dried white beans and common for any time of day, even breakfast. In simple eateries and snack bars, it is served alongside dishes like rotisserie chicken.

- 500 g/1 lb 2 oz dried white beans, such as cannellini or white haricot (navy) (about 2½ cups)
- 3 tablespoons olive oil
- 2 onions, grated
- 2 cloves of garlic, grated
- 3 ripe tomatoes, halved crosswise and grated, peel discarded (see page 445)
- 1 teaspoon sweet paprika
- 1 teaspoon ground ginger
- 1 teaspoon ground turmeric
- ½ teaspoon ground cumin
- 2 heaped tablespoons double concentrated tomato purée (paste)
- 1 heaped tablespoon finely chopped flat-leaf parsley
- 1 heaped tablespoon finely chopped coriander (cilantro)
- salt and pepper
- bread, to serve

Put the beans into a large bowl, cover with abundant water and leave to soak for 12 hours. The next day, drain and rinse.

Heat the oil in a large heavy pot or casserole dish (Dutch oven) over a medium heat, add the onions and cook for about 5 minutes, or until they begin to soften. Stir in the garlic, then the tomatoes. Add the beans, paprika, ginger, turmeric and cumin, then turn to coat the beans well and cook for 10 minutes, stirring from time to time. Pour in 1.5 litres (50 fl oz/ generous 6 cups) of hot water. Bring to the boil, then cover with a lid, reduce the heat to low and gently boil for 1 hour. Stir in the tomato purée (paste), parsley and coriander (cilantro), then cover again and cook until the beans are tender, 30 minutes– 1 hour, depending on the beans. It should be loose and saucy but not watery. Add more hot water if necessary, or uncover completely and cook until it is reduced to your desired consistency. Season with salt and pepper and serve in wide bowls with bread.

Stewed White Beans with Lamb

ALGERIA, LIBYA, MOROCCO, TUNISIA
PREPARATION TIME: 10 minutes,
plus overnight soaking time
COOKING TIME: 1 hour 45 minutes–
2 hours 15 minutes
SERVES: 4–5

Among the many versions of *loubia* across
North Africa, more complete ones with lamb
are commonplace. This one calls for dried beans
that have been soaked overnight. For canned
beans, use 500 g/1 lb 2 oz (generous 2½ cups).
Rinse thoroughly, put into a large saucepan with
cool water and bring to the boil, then remove from
the heat and leave in the water until ready to add.
Add to the stew and cook for 10 minutes. In Libya,
the dish is called *fasolia bel lham*.

  250 g/9 oz dried white beans, such as cannellini
    or white haricot (navy) (about 1¼ cups)
  3 tablespoons olive oil
  3 cloves of garlic, minced
  1 red or yellow onion, finely chopped
  500 g/1 lb 2 oz bone-in lamb or beef, cut into
    4–8 pieces
  1 tomato, halved crosswise and grated, peel discarded
    (see page 445)
  2 tablespoons double concentrated tomato purée
    (paste)
  cayenne pepper or harissa (page 409), to taste
  ½ teaspoon sweet paprika
  ½ teaspoon ground turmeric
  ½ teaspoon ground ginger, optional
  ½ teaspoon ground cumin or coriander seeds,
    optional
  2 green chillies (chiles), sliced crosswise
  salt and pepper
  finely chopped flat-leaf parsley, to garnish

Put the beans into a large bowl, cover with abundant
water and leave to soak overnight or for 12 hours.
The next day, drain and rinse.
  Heat the oil in a large pot or casserole dish (Dutch
oven) over a medium heat, add the garlic, onion
and meat and cook for 6–8 minutes until the meat
is browned and the onion is soft. Stir in the tomato,
tomato purée (paste) and 4 tablespoons water, then
cook for 5 minutes to reduce the sauce. Stir in
the cayenne pepper, paprika, turmeric and ginger
(if using). Add the beans and pour in 1.2 litres
(40 fl oz/5 cups) of hot water. Bring to the boil,
reduce the heat to low, mostly cover the pan with
a lid and cook until the meat and beans are tender,
1½–2 hours. It should be loose but not watery. Add

some hot water if necessary, or uncover completely and
cook until it is reduced to your desired consistency.
Stir in the cumin (if using), add the chillies (chiles)
and season with salt and pepper. Cook for a final
few minutes. Sprinkle with parsley, ladle into bowls
and serve.

Stewed Lentils with Lamb

ALGERIA
PREPARATION TIME: 10 minutes
COOKING TIME: 55 minutes
SERVES: 4–5

This stewed lentil potage is perfect for winter. It
should be soupy but not watery. Some cooks like
to stir in a generous pinch of ground cinnamon at
the end for aroma.

  3 tablespoons olive oil
  225 g/8 oz boneless lamb or beef, trimmed and cut
    into small pieces
  3 cloves of garlic, finely chopped
  1 onion, finely chopped
  1 celery stalk, finely chopped
  2 bay leaves
  300 g/11 oz (1½ cups) dried brown or green lentils,
    picked over for any stones or debris and rinsed
  2 tablespoons double concentrated tomato purée
    (paste)
  1 teaspoon sweet paprika
  1 teaspoon ground cumin
  2 carrots, cut into 1.25-cm/½-inch circles
  2 white potatoes, peeled and cut into bite-size pieces
  1 long sweet green pepper or ½ green bell pepper,
    cored, seeded and cut into 1.5-cm/⅔-inch pieces
  salt and pepper
  finely chopped flat-leaf parsley, to garnish

Heat the oil in a large, heavy pot or casserole dish
(Dutch oven) over a medium heat, add the lamb,
garlic, onion and celery, season with salt and pepper
and cook, stirring frequently, until the meat has
browned, about 5 minutes. Add the bay leaves,
then pour in 1.2 litres (40 fl oz/5 cups) of hot water
and bring to the boil. Add the lentils, cover with
a lid, reduce the heat to low and gently boil for
15 minutes. Stir in the tomato purée (paste) and
4 tablespoons water, the paprika, cumin, carrots,
potatoes and green pepper. Cover again and gently
boil until the lentils are tender but not mushy and
the carrots and potatoes done, about 25 minutes.
Add more water if necessary to keep the lentils
soupy, or uncover to reduce if too watery. Ladle
into bowls, sprinkle with the parsley and serve.

Stewed Lentils with Pumpkin

MOROCCO
PREPARATION TIME: 10 minutes,
plus soaking time
COOKING TIME: 1 hour
SERVES: 6

To this popular warm lentil dish cooks sometimes add *khlii* (a seasoned confit of dried meat, see page 206) and, rather than olive oil, some of its fat to punch up the flavours. It can also be served as a salad.

    400 g/14 oz (2 cups) dried brown or green lentils,
        picked over for any stones or debris and rinsed
    700 g/1 lb 8½ oz pumpkin, butternut or acorn squash,
        or another firm-fleshed, hard-skinned squash
    2 tablespoons olive oil
    1 red or yellow onion, finely chopped
    2 teaspoons sweet paprika
    ½ teaspoon cayenne pepper
    12 sprigs coriander (cilantro) and parsley tied together
    2 tomatoes, peeled (see page 445) and chopped
    1 small sweet or hot green pepper, cored, seeded
        and cut into bite-size pieces
    salt

Put the lentils into a large bowl, cover with abundant water and leave to soak for 1 hour. Drain and set aside. Remove the skin from the pumpkin, scoop out the seeds and cut the flesh into 1–2-cm/½–¾-inch cubes; set aside.

Add the oil and onion to a medium soup pot and cook over a medium heat for about 8 minutes, or until pale and soft. Stir in the paprika and cayenne pepper, then pour in 1.2 litres (40 fl oz/5 cups) of hot water and bring to the boil. Add the lentils and coriander (cilantro) and parsley bundle, cover with a lid, reduce the heat to medium-low and gently boil for 15 minutes. Add the pumpkin, tomatoes and green pepper, then season with salt. Cover again and cook until the lentils are tender but not mushy and the pumpkin done, 25–30 minutes. Add more water if necessary to keep the lentils soupy, or uncover to reduce if too watery. Remove and discard the bundle of coriander and parsley. Ladle into bowls and serve.

Creamy Red Lentils with Chewy Fried Onions

LIBYA
PREPARATION TIME: 15 minutes
COOKING TIME: 1 hour
SERVES: 6

The combination of creamy red lentils with the chewy, sweet fried onions makes this a perfect comfort food. When frying the onions, be sure to watch carefully towards the end so that they do not burn.

    3 red or yellow onions
    2 tablespoons olive oil
    2 cloves of garlic, minced
    1½ teaspoons ground cumin, plus extra to serve
    400 g/14 oz (2 cups) split red lentils, picked over
        for any stones or debris and rinsed
    1 tomato, peeled (see page 445) and chopped
    1 carrot, coarsely chopped
    180 ml/6 fl oz (¾ cup) neutral oil, for frying
    salt

Finely chop 1 of the onions. Heat the olive oil in a soup pot over a medium heat, add the finely chopped onion and cook for about 5 minutes, or until soft. Stir in the garlic and cumin, then add the lentils, tomato and carrot. Pour in 1.2 litres (40 fl oz/5 cups) of hot water and bring to the boil. Cover with a lid, reduce the heat to low and gently boil until the lentils have largely disintegrated and the carrots are soft, about 40 minutes. Add a touch more water if needed. Season with salt, then remove from the heat and leave to cool slightly. Purée in the pot with an immersion hand blender, or in batches in a food processor. Reduce the purée over a low heat to thicken, if desired.

Meanwhile, thinly slice the remaining 2 onions and separate the segments. Line a plate with paper towels. Heat the neutral oil in a small frying pan over a medium heat, add the onions, cover with a lid, reduce the heat to low and cook until they become soft and translucent, about 20 minutes. Increase the heat to high and cook, uncovered, for 8–10 minutes until the onions are caramel brown. Watch carefully at the end that the onions do not burn. Transfer with a slotted spoon to the paper towels to drain.

Ladle the lentils into bowls, top with some fried onions and serve with a dish of cumin to add as desired.

Stewed Lentils with Tomato

MOROCCO
PREPARATION TIME: 10 minutes
COOKING TIME: 1 hour
SERVES: 5–6

This lentil dish is rich and deeply satisfying. Serve it as a soup course or a main dish. You can use either dried brown lentils or the greenish variety.

2 tablespoons olive oil
2 cloves of garlic, minced
1 red or yellow onion, grated
2 tomatoes, halved crosswise and grated, peel discarded (see page 445)
1 teaspoon sweet paprika
½ teaspoon ground turmeric
½ teaspoon ground ginger
400 g/14 oz (2 cups) dried brown or green lentils, picked over for any stones or debris and rinsed
1 tablespoon double concentrated tomato purée (paste)
1 heaped tablespoon finely chopped flat-leaf parsley
1 heaped tablespoon finely chopped coriander (cilantro)
salt and pepper

Add the oil, garlic, onion and tomatoes to a medium soup pot and cook over a medium heat for 5–10 minutes until the onion begins to soften and the tomatoes darken. Stir in the paprika, turmeric and ginger, pour in 1.2 litres (40 fl oz/5 cups) of hot water and bring to the boil. Cover with a lid, reduce the heat to low and gently boil for 20 minutes. Stir in the lentils, tomato purée (paste) and 4 tablespoons water, then cover again and cook until the lentils are tender but not mushy, 20–25 minutes. It should be loose and saucy but not watery. Add some water if necessary, or uncover completely and cook until it is reduced to your desired consistency. Stir in the parsley and coriander (cilantro) and season with salt and pepper. Ladle into bowls and serve.

Market Stall Chickpeas

TUNISIA
PREPARATION TIME: 10 minutes, plus overnight soaking time
COOKING TIME: 1 hour 35 minutes
SERVES: 4–6

Lablabi is Tunisia's quintessential comfort food: stewed chickpeas (garbanzo beans) ladled over torn pieces of day-old bread, generously seasoned with cumin and harissa, topped with an egg (or two), some capers, olives and tuna and finally given a good lug of heady extra-virgin olive oil. It is found in simple eateries, on street corners or along busy lanes in the medina, where it is a breakfast favourite during winter. (A stack of upturned ceramic bowls indicates that it is available.) It is also prepared at home.

500 g/1 lb 2 oz (3 cups) dried chickpeas (garbanzo beans)
2 cloves of garlic, crushed in the peel
1 day-old (or lightly toasted) baguette, torn into pieces
harissa (page 409), to taste
ground cumin, to taste
extra-virgin olive oil, for drizzling
100–150 g/3½–5 oz drained high-quality canned tuna in olive oil
4–6 large eggs
salt and pepper
lemon wedges, to serve

Put the dried chickpeas (garbanzo beans) into a large bowl, cover with abundant cold water and leave to soak overnight or for about 12 hours. The next day, drain and rinse.

Put the chickpeas and garlic into a large pot or casserole dish (Dutch oven), pour in about 3 litres (101 fl oz/generous 3 quarts/12½ cups) water and bring to the boil. Cover with a lid, reduce the heat slightly and gently boil until tender, about 1½ hours. Add a generous pinch of salt once the chickpeas begin to soften. If the pot needs more water during cooking, add boiling water. There should be about 1 kg (2¼ lb/6 cups) cooked chickpeas. Do not drain. Keep hot.

Prepare large soup bowls. Fill each about half with bread. (There might be some bread leftover.) Ladle in about 250 g (9 oz/1 cup) chickpeas with a small amount of hot broth. Season with harissa, cumin and salt and pepper, then drizzle with oil and add some tuna. Crack 1 egg into each bowl, then ladle in some more hot broth. Serve each bowl with a pair of spoons to mix up and combine, and with harissa and lemon wedges on the side.

Spicy Biskra Chickpeas

ALGERIA
PREPARATION TIME: 10 minutes, plus
overnight soaking time if using dried beans
COOKING TIME: 1 hour 45 minutes,
less if using canned beans
SERVES: 4

The name of this spicy chickpea (garbanzo bean)
dish is *doubara de Biskra*. *Doubara* means to fend for
yourself. Lore has it that a woman in Biskra (an oasis
south of Algiers) needed to feed an unexpected
visitor and could not find any meat to offer, so she
cooked this chickpea dish. The simple, inexpensive
creation is now Biskra's iconic dish. In the spirit
of the story, this version uses canned chickpeas
for a particularly quick preparation. That said, it
also gives directions for using dried chickpeas,
recommended if there is time – and no unexpected
visitor is anxiously awaiting a meal.

    200 g/7 oz (1 cup) dried chickpeas (garbanzo
        beans) or 400 g/14 oz (2 cups) cooked or canned
        chickpeas
    2 teaspoons ground cumin
    1 bay leaf
    2 tablespoons olive oil, plus extra for drizzling
    2 cloves of garlic, minced
    1 tablespoon double concentrated tomato purée
        (paste)
    1 teaspoon sweet paprika
    cayenne pepper or harissa (page 409), to taste
    3 ripe tomatoes, peeled (see page 445) and coarsely
        chopped
    2 tablespoons finely chopped flat-leaf parsley
    2 tablespoons finely chopped coriander (cilantro)
    salt and pepper
    lemon wedges, for squeezing and to serve

If using dried chickpeas (garbanzo beans), put them
into a large bowl, cover with abundant cold water
and leave to soak overnight or for about 12 hours.
The next day, drain and rinse. Put the chickpeas
into a large pot or saucepan, pour in about 3 litres
(101 fl oz/generous 3 quarts/12½ cups) water, add
1 teaspoon of the cumin and the bay leaf and bring
to the boil. Cover with a lid, reduce the heat slightly
and gently boil until tender, about 1½ hours. Add a
generous pinch of salt once the chickpeas begin to
soften. If the pot needs more water during cooking,
add boiling water. Remove from the heat and leave
the chickpeas in the water until ready to use.
    If using canned chickpeas, rinse, then put them
into a large saucepan, add 1 teaspoon of the cumin,
the bay leaf and a pinch of salt. Pour in 1 litre

(34 fl oz/4¼ cups) water and bring to the boil.
Gently boil for 10 minutes. Remove from the heat
and leave the chickpeas in the water until ready
to use.
    Add the oil, the garlic, tomato purée (paste)
and 4 tablespoons of liquid from the chickpeas,
the paprika, cayenne pepper and the remaining
1 teaspoon of cumin to a medium pot. Season with
salt and pepper and cook over a medium heat for
3–5 minutes until aromatic and a touch thicker.
Transfer the chickpeas with a slotted spoon to the
pot with about 250 ml (8 fl oz/1 cup) of their liquid
and bring to the boil. Stir in the tomatoes, parsley
and coriander (cilantro) and cook for 10 minutes.
It should be quite loose and soupy but not watery.
Add a touch more of the reserved liquid from the
chickpeas, if desired. Ladle into bowls, give each a
drizzle of olive oil and a squeeze of lemon juice and
serve with lemon wedges.

Chickpea and Onion Stew

TUNISIA
PREPARATION TIME: 15 minutes,
plus overnight soaking time
COOKING TIME: 2 hours 5 minutes–
2 hours 35 minutes
SERVES: 4–5

Tunisia's popular chickpea (garbanzo bean) stew
called *mermez* calls for plenty of onions and some
meat as well. Substitute the ground coriander and
caraway seeds in this recipe for ground cumin,
if desired.

    200 g/7 oz (1 cup) dried chickpeas (garbanzo beans)
    3 tablespoons olive oil
    500 g/1 lb 2 oz boneless beef or lamb, cut into
        generous cubes
    4 red or yellow onions, sliced
    3 cloves of garlic, minced
    3 tomatoes, halved crosswise and grated,
        peel discarded (see page 445)
    1 heaped tablespoon double concentrated tomato
        purée (paste)
    harissa (page 409) or cayenne pepper, to taste
    1 teaspoon sweet paprika
    ½ teaspoon ground turmeric
    ¼ teaspoon ground coriander
    ¼ teaspoon ground caraway
    1 long sweet green pepper
    salt

Put the dried chickpeas (garbanzo beans) into a
large bowl, cover with abundant cold water and

leave to soak overnight or for about 12 hours. The next day, drain and rinse.

Add the oil and meat to a heavy, wide pot and brown over a high heat for about 5 minutes. Add the onions and cook for another 5 minutes until they begin to soften. Stir in the garlic, then add the tomatoes, tomato purée (paste) and 4 tablespoons water, the harissa, paprika, turmeric, coriander and caraway and cook for 5 minutes, stirring from time to time. Add the chickpeas, pour in 600 ml (20 fl oz/2½ cups) water and bring to the boil. Cover with a lid, reduce the heat to low and simmer until the chickpeas are tender, 1½–2 hours. Add more water if needed, or remove the lid towards the end. It should be quite loose and soupy but not watery. Add the green pepper, season with salt and cook for about 15 minutes, or until tender. Ladle into bowls and serve.

Winter Chickpea Stew

ALGERIA
PREPARATION TIME: 10 minutes,
plus overnight soaking time
COOKING TIME: 1 hour 35 minutes–
2 hours 5 minutes
SERVES: 4

Comforting, filling and economical, this simple, satisfying Algerian chickpea (garbanzo bean) dish is a winter morning favourite. Some like to stir in 1 or 2 generous tablespoons of double concentrated tomato purée (paste) into the pan for the final 10 minutes of cooking.

    250 g/9 oz (1½ cups) dried chickpeas
        (garbanzo beans)
    1 bay leaf
    2 cloves of garlic, unpeeled
    ½ teaspoon ground cumin, plus extra to garnish
    salt and pepper
    2 ripe tomatoes, halved crosswise and grated,
        peel discarded (see page 445), to garnish
    1 red or yellow onion, grated, to garnish
    finely chopped flat-leaf parsley or coriander (cilantro),
        to garnish
    extra-virgin olive oil, for drizzling
    harissa (page 409), to garnish, optional
    4 Hard-boiled Eggs (page 443), peeled and cut in half,
        to garnish
    4 lemon wedges, to serve

Put the chickpeas (garbanzo beans) into a large bowl, cover with abundant cold water and leave to soak overnight or for about 12 hours. The next day, drain and rinse.

Put the chickpeas into a large pot or casserole dish (Dutch oven), pour in 750 ml (25 fl oz/3 cups) water, add the bay leaf, garlic and cumin and bring to the boil. Cover with a lid, reduce the heat slightly and gently boil until the chickpeas are tender, 1½–2 hours. Add a generous pinch of salt once the chickpeas begin to soften. If the pot needs more water during cooking, add boiling water. There should be about 360 ml (12 fl oz/1½ cups) of liquid at the end.

Ladle the chickpeas into bowls with some of the liquid. Garnish with grated tomatoes, onion and some parsley, then season with cumin, salt and pepper. Add a drizzle of oil and a dollop of harissa (if using), then add a boiled egg and a lemon wedge to each bowl and serve immediately.

'Cooked and Soft' Chickpeas

MOROCCO
PREPARATION TIME: 5 minutes
COOKING TIME: 5 minutes
SERVES: 4

Street vendors selling hot chickpeas (garbanzo beans) sprinkled with cumin and paprika in paper cones call them *tayb wa hari*, which means 'cooked and soft'. These make a perfect snack or starter. This is the quick version prepared by boiling canned chickpeas (garbanzo beans). Steam them if desired. To prepare using dried beans, follow the directions on page 443 for soaking and boiling chickpeas.

    400 g/14 oz (2 cups) canned chickpeas
        (garbanzo beans), drained and rinsed
    ½ teaspoon ground cumin
    ½ teaspoon sweet paprika
    ¼ teaspoon cayenne pepper
    salt and pepper

Put the chickpeas (garbanzo beans) into a large saucepan, cover with cold water and bring to a rolling boil. The chickpeas should be tender and easily pinched between your thumb and forefinger; if not, leave to boil for a few minutes. Drain and put into a large bowl. Sprinkle with the cumin, paprika and cayenne pepper, season with salt and pepper and toss well to blend. Spoon into individual bowls and serve hot.

Berber Winter Vegetable Tagine

MOROCCO
PREPARATION TIME: 15 minutes
COOKING TIME: 1 hour 10 minutes
SERVES: 2

In Morocco's High Atlas Mountains, this vegetable tagine is called *tatajine douze* in the Berber language. *Douze* means that it is something to be eaten with bread, a fitting name for this dish. The quince here is treated as a vegetable rather than a fruit, and it brings a sweet, aromatic note to the tagine. Most families use whatever is in season or in the vegetable larder, with the longer-cooking ones on the bottom layer.

- 3 tablespoons olive oil
- 2 small red onions, cut crosswise into slices
- 2 cloves of garlic, finely chopped
- ¼ teaspoon ground turmeric
- ¼ teaspoon ground ginger
- ¼ teaspoon sweet paprika
- 4 carrots, halved crosswise, then halved lengthwise
- 2 turnips, peeled and quartered lengthwise
- 1 small quince, peeled, cored and cut lengthwise into 8 wedges
- 1 fennel bulb, quartered lengthwise
- 1 small aubergine (eggplant), cut crosswise into 1-cm/½-inch circles
- 225 g/8 oz cauliflower, cut into small florets
- 1 tomato, peeled (see page 445) and quartered
- 2 tablespoons finely chopped flat-leaf parsley
- 2 tablespoons finely chopped coriander (cilantro)
- ¼ teaspoon ground cumin
- salt and pepper
- bread, to serve

Add the oil, onions, garlic, turmeric, ginger and paprika to a medium tagine (see page 250) and moisten with 4 tablespoons water. Cover the tagine with the lid and cook over a medium-low heat for 5 minutes, stirring from time to time. Remove from the heat. Spread the onions evenly across the bottom of the tagine. Arrange the carrots and turnips like spokes on top of the onions, then build a pyramid with the vegetables by stacking the quince, fennel, aubergine (eggplant), cauliflower and finally the tomato. Sprinkle over the parsley, coriander (cilantro) and cumin, then season with salt and pepper. Pour 120 ml (4 fl oz/½ cup) water around the edge, cover the tagine and cook over a low heat until all of the vegetables are tender, about 1 hour. Add a touch of water if needed, or remove the lid to reduce the sauce if watery. Serve from the tagine with bread.

Shakshuka

LIBYA
PREPARATION TIME: 10 minutes
COOKING TIME: 50 minutes
SERVES: 4

The roots of the widely popular shakshuka are hotly contested. Possibly originating in Tripoli, it was brought by Libyan (and Tunisian) Jews in the mid-twentieth century to Israel, where it has become widespread, even iconic. Shakshuka is one-pot comfort food and a classic breakfast dish in Libya and beyond. Some versions include *gueddid* (seasoned, salted and air-dried lamb, see page 206). If adding to this recipe, be frugal with the salt and soak the *gueddid* beforehand and add at the first step. In Tunisia, it is popular to prepare with merguez sausages (page 152). Serve with plenty of bread.

- 2 tablespoons olive oil
- 1 red or yellow onion, chopped
- 2 chillies (chiles), seeded and diced
- 3 cloves of garlic, minced
- 4 ripe tomatoes, diced
- 2 tablespoon double concentrated tomato purée (paste)
- ½ teaspoon ground turmeric
- ½ teaspoon ground cumin
- cayenne pepper, to taste
- 4 large eggs
- salt and pepper
- bread, to serve

Heat the oil in a large frying pan or sauté pan over a medium-high heat, add the onion and chillies (chiles), and cook for 5 minutes, stirring frequently. Stir in the garlic and cook for about 1 minute, or until aromatic. Add the tomatoes, tomato purée (paste) and 4 tablespoons water, then season with salt and pepper and cook for 2–3 minutes. Stir in the turmeric, cumin and cayenne pepper and add 250 ml (8 fl oz/1 cup) water. Bring to a simmer, reduce the heat to low and simmer until saucy, 20–30 minutes. Stir in a touch more water if needed.

Make 4 spaces in the sauce. Without breaking the yolks, crack the eggs directly into the pan. Cover with a lid and cook the eggs to the desired level of yolk runniness, 5–10 minutes. Serve hot directly from the pan with bread.

Shakshuka with Peppers and Merguez Sausages

ALGERIA, TUNISIA
PREPARATION TIME: 10 minutes
COOKING TIME: 40 minutes
SERVES: 4

Adding merguez makes a fuller version of this one-pot tomato and pepper dish. It's lovely for breakfast. Many Tunisians like to season their shakshuka with *tabil* (page 446), a spice blend based on ground coriander and caraway seeds with dried garlic, chilli (red pepper) flakes and salt.

4 tablespoons olive oil
2 red or yellow onions, chopped
1 clove of garlic, minced
4 merguez sausages (about 200 g/7 oz), cut into
    5-cm/2-inch pieces
4 ripe tomatoes, peeled (see page 445) and diced
2 tablespoons double concentrated tomato purée
    (paste)
1 red bell pepper, cored, seeded and cut into strips
1 green bell pepper, cored, seeded and cut into strips
1 green chilli (chile), seeded and finely chopped
¼ teaspoon ground cumin
harissa (page 409), to taste
4 large eggs
salt and pepper
bread, to serve

Heat the oil in a large frying pan or sauté pan over a medium-high heat, add the onions and cook for 5 minutes, stirring frequently. Stir in the garlic and cook for about 30 seconds, or until aromatic. Add the merguez sausages, tomatoes, tomato purée (paste) and 4 tablespoons water, the peppers, chilli (chile), cumin and harissa, then season with salt and pepper and pour in 120 ml (4 fl oz/½ cup) water. Reduce the heat to low, cover with a lid and cook until the vegetables are tender and the sauce thickened, about 25 minutes.

    Make 4 spaces in the sauce. Without breaking the yolks, crack the eggs directly into the pan. Cover and cook until the eggs are just set, 8–10 minutes. Serve hot directly from the pan with bread.

Shakshuka with Fresh Broad Beans and Chard

TUNISIA
PREPARATION TIME: 10 minutes
COOKING TIME: 50 minutes
SERVES: 4

This version of shakshuka includes both broad (fava) beans and chard. To prepare with only broad beans, simply double the amount. When young and tender, you can leave the broad beans in the pod without shelling them. If using frozen and thawed broad beans, reduce the amount of water added. Some Tunisians like to add some *kaddid* (seasoned, salted and air-dried meat, see page 206). This is the vegan version, but you can crack a few eggs directly into the pan, if desired.

3 tablespoons olive oil
1 large onion, finely chopped
2 cloves of garlic, minced
1 tomato, halved crosswise and grated, peel discarded
    (see page 445)
1 heaped tablespoon double concentrated tomato
    purée (paste)
cayenne pepper or harissa (page 409), to taste
400 g/14 oz shelled fresh or thawed frozen broad
    (fava) beans (about 2¾ cups)
450 g/1 lb Swiss chard, coarsely chopped
½ teaspoon ground caraway
1 tablespoon finely chopped flat-leaf parsley
salt and pepper
bread, to serve

Heat the oil in a large frying pan or sauté pan over a medium heat, add the onion and cook for 5–10 minutes until pale and soft. Stir in the garlic, then add the tomato, tomato purée (paste) and 3 tablespoons water. Season with cayenne pepper, salt and pepper and cook for about 5 minutes to thicken. Add the broad (fava) beans and chard, pour in 175 ml (6 fl oz/ ¾ cup) water, cover with a lid and cook until the beans are tender, 20–30 minutes. Stir in a touch more water if needed or remove the lid to reduce. It should be moist but not overly runny. Stir in the caraway and parsley and cook for 5 minutes. Serve warm with bread.

Aubergine Shakshuka with Eggs

ALGERIA
PREPARATION TIME: 10 minutes
COOKING TIME: 30 minutes
SERVES: 2–3

This Algerian shakshuka with aubergine (eggplant) and fresh peppers makes an easy meal. This version adds the eggs, lightly beaten, to the pan, though you can crack them whole directly into the pan, if desired.

    5 tablespoons olive oil
    1 aubergine (eggplant), cut into 1.5-cm/⅔-inch cubes
    1 green or red bell pepper, cored, seeded and cut into
        1.5-cm/⅔-inch pieces
    1 red chilli (chile), seeded and finely chopped,
        optional
    3 cloves of garlic, minced
    3 tomatoes, halved crosswise and grated,
        peel discarded (see page 445)
    1 tablespoon double concentrated tomato purée
        (paste)
    3 large eggs
    salt and pepper

Heat the oil in a large frying pan or sauté pan over a medium-high heat, add the aubergine (eggplant), pepper and chili (chile), stir well, cover with a lid and cook until they are becoming tender, about 10 minutes. Stir in the garlic and cook for about 1 minute, or until aromatic. Add the tomatoes, tomato purée (paste) and 120 ml (4 fl oz/½ cup) water, then season with salt and cook, uncovered, until the aubergine and peppers are tender and the tomato sauce reduced, about 15 minutes. Add a touch of water to keep it from scorching if needed. Spread the mixture evenly across the pan.

Crack the eggs into a bowl and season with salt and pepper. Break the yolks with a fork, stir a few times (do not beat) and pour evenly over the top of the mixture. Don't stir. Cover the pan with a lid or aluminium foil and cook until the eggs have set but are still a touch runny, about 3 minutes. Serve immediately.

Aubergine in Escabeche

ALGERIA
PREPARATION TIME: 10 minutes,
plus cooling and marinating time
COOKING TIME: 30 minutes
SERVES: 6

Preparing aubergine (eggplant) in *skabitch* (escabeche) makes an excellent alternative to the better-known version with sardines (page 335). The aubergine is boiled and then the moisture gently pressed out, before being covered with the oil-and-vinegar marinade.

    2 aubergines (eggplant) (about 800 g/1¾ lb total)
    120 ml/4 fl oz (½ cup) olive oil, plus extra as needed
        for covering
    1 red onion, thinly sliced
    6 cloves of garlic, gently crushed in the skin
    pinch of cayenne pepper
    60 ml/2 fl oz (¼ cup) white vinegar
    salt

Peel the aubergines (eggplant), then cut crosswise into 1-cm-/½-inch-thick circles. Bring a large pot or saucepan of salted water to the boil, then add the aubergines and boil for about 20 minutes, or until they take on a translucent shine. Transfer with a slotted spoon to a colander to drain. Very gently, without breaking, press with the bottom of the slotted spoon to extract more moisture.

Meanwhile, add the oil, onion, garlic, cayenne pepper and a pinch of salt to a small saucepan and cook for 3–4 minutes until the onions begin to soften. Remove from the heat, leave to cool for a few minutes, then carefully pour in the vinegar and 120 ml (4 fl oz/½ cup) of hot water. Bring to the boil and boil for 5 minutes. Remove from the heat.

Arrange half of the aubergines in a wide bowl, spoon over some of the marinade, then add the remaining aubergines. Cover with the remaining marinade. Add more oil if needed to cover and leave to cool to room temperature. Cover with cling film (plastic wrap) and refrigerate for at least 24 hours to fully absorb the flavours. Remove about 30 minutes before serving and serve slightly chilled (but not cold) with some of the marinade spooned over the top. Store in the refrigerator and use within 4 days.

Saucy Fresh Broad Beans

ALGERIA
PREPARATION TIME: 20 minutes
COOKING TIME: 40 minutes
SERVES: 4

Ros bratel – saucy broad (fava) beans with plenty of coriander (cilantro) – is popular across Algeria, although it is largely considered a dish from the east of the country. Home cooks like to prepare this dish at the beginning of the season when broad beans are tender. Some add tomatoes and a little diluted double concentrated tomato purée (paste) to thicken the sauce or chopped onions for flavour. This is the straightforward version that keeps the focus on the fresh broad beans. It is also excellent if using mint instead of coriander (cilantro).

500 g/1 lb 2 oz tender fresh broad (fava) beans
   in their pods
3 cloves of garlic, peeled
1 teaspoon sweet paprika
dried chilli (chile) or cayenne pepper, to taste
3 tablespoons olive oil
15 g/½ oz (loosely packed ½ cup) finely chopped
   coriander (cilantro)
1 teaspoon fresh lemon juice or white vinegar
salt and pepper

Trim the ends of the broad (fava) bean pods and the strand that runs along the base. Cut into pieces about 2.5 cm/1 inch long. Rinse and set aside. Put the garlic, paprika and chilli (chile) into a mortar and pound with a pestle, then season with salt and pepper. Loosen with a few tablespoons of water to make it paste-like.

Add the oil and garlic paste to a large wide frying pan or sauté pan and cook over a medium heat for about 1 minute, or until aromatic. Add the broad beans, stir to coat in the paste and cook for 2 minutes. Pour in 180 ml (6 fl oz/¾ cup) water, cover with a lid, reduce the heat to low and cook until the beans are tender, about 30 minutes. Stir in the coriander (cilantro) and lemon juice, add some water if needed to keep it loose and cook, uncovered, for 5 minutes. It should be saucy. Serve.

Steamed Broad Beans with Cumin

ALGERIA, MOROCCO
PREPARATION TIME: 10 minutes
COOKING TIME: 15 minutes
SERVES: 4

A dish of steamed broad (fava) beans with salt and cumin makes a perfect starter alongside a bowl of olives in early spring, when pods of the vegetable arrive in the market. Some homes like them even simpler when the beans are so tender, and they are served with just a drizzle of good, extra-virgin olive oil or a squeeze of lemon juice.

500 g/1 lb 2 oz (4 cups) shelled fresh broad (fava)
   beans
ground cumin, for seasoning
extra-virgin olive oil, for drizzling, optional
salt
lemon wedges, to serve, optional

Season the broad (fava) beans with salt. Fill the bottom of a couscoussier or a large pot fitted with a steamer basket with about 5 cm/2 inches water and bring to the boil. Put the beans into the steamer basket, snugly cover with a lid and steam for about 10–15 minutes, or until just tender.

Transfer the beans to a serving bowl, season with cumin and salt and toss. Drizzle over some olive oil (if using) and serve with lemon wedges (if using).

Fried Peppers and Tomatoes with Eggs

TUNISIA
PREPARATION TIME: 15 minutes
COOKING TIME: 30 minutes
SERVES: 2–3

Across Tunisia, *gargottes* (small eateries) serve popular favourites like this *tastira*, a mix of peppers and tomatoes with egg. The vegetables are fried separately and then chopped in this dish. While it's preferable to remove the skin of the fried peppers and tomatoes before chopping, some *gargottes* skip this step. *Tastira* traditionally has *tabil*, a spice blend that includes ground coriander and caraway seeds (page 446). Serve hot or at room temperature.

2 tablespoons olive oil
500 g/1 lb 2 oz long sweet red and green peppers or red and green bell peppers, cored
500 g/1 lb 2 oz ripe plum tomatoes, halved lengthwise
2 cloves of garlic, grated
½ teaspoon tabil spice blend (page 446) or a mix of ground coriander and caraway seeds
2–3 large eggs
salt and pepper

Heat the oil in a large frying pan or sauté pan over a high heat. Line a plate with paper towels. Add the peppers to the pan, cover the pan with a lid and fry, turning as needed, until the skin blisters and softens, 10–15 minutes. Transfer to the paper towels to absorb some of the oil and leave to cool. Add the tomatoes to the pan and fry, turning as needed, until tender and the skin comes away, about 10 minutes. Transfer to the plate to cool.

Remove the skin and seeds from the peppers and tomatoes. Put into a large bowl, add the garlic and tabil spice blend and season with salt and pepper.

In the same pan over a medium heat, adding more oil if necessary, fry the eggs for 3–4 minutes until the yolk sets. Transfer to the bowl with the vegetables. Chop into small pieces using 2 knives in swift, criss-crossing motions. Divide among plates and serve.

Smoky Grilled Peppers in Olive Oil

MOROCCO
PREPARATION TIME: 15 minutes, plus cooling and standing time
COOKING TIME: 40 minutes
SERVES: 4–6

This is a quicker version than Preserved Grilled Red Peppers (page 412). Delicious in salads or on breads, they are also a perfect accompaniment to grilled lamb, chicken or fish.

500 g/1 lb 2 oz long sweet red peppers or red bell peppers
500 g/1 lb 2 oz long sweet green peppers or green bell peppers
2 cloves of garlic, halved lengthwise
1 tablespoon fresh lemon juice or white vinegar
4 tablespoons extra-virgin olive oil
salt

Prepare the charcoal on a barbecue or preheat an indoor oven grill (broiler). Set the peppers on the grill above the charcoal or arrange the peppers on a baking sheet if using an oven grill. Cook, turning as needed, until charred in places and tender, about 20–40 minutes. (They will take less time on the barbecue.) Put into a bowl, cover with aluminium foil and leave to cool in the steam to make peeling easier.

Peel, core and seed the peppers, then tear into long strips. Lay in a large shallow serving dish, tuck the garlic among the strips and season with salt. Drizzle over the lemon juice and cover with the oil. Jiggle to settle. Leave to stand for at least 1 hour for the flavours to penetrate before serving.

Kerkennah Islands Tomato 'Sauce'

TUNISIA
PREPARATION TIME: 10 minutes
COOKING TIME: 2 minutes
SERVES: 2–4

The Kerkennah Islands are a 30-minute ferry ride from Sfax off Tunisia's central coast. Called *sauce kerkénaise*, this gazpacho-like sauce can be served with a range of items, from the Kerkennah flatbread *galette*, which is more akin to a cracker than bread, to couscous. Some versions include very thinly sliced or finely chopped onion.

    4 ripe tomatoes
    1 small red onion, finely chopped
    1 small sweet long green pepper, cored, seeded and
        finely chopped
    1 clove of garlic, minced
    2 tablespoons extra-virgin olive oil
    1½ tablespoons fresh lemon juice
    1 tablespoon finely chopped flat-leaf parsley
    1 teaspoon dried mint
    harissa (page 409), to taste, optional
    salt and pepper

Core the tomatoes, then score an X in the bottom with the tip of a knife. Fill a large bowl with cold water. In a saucepan, bring enough water to cover the tomatoes to a rolling boil, add the tomatoes and blanch until the skins begin to split, 20–60 seconds, depending on the ripeness of the tomatoes. Transfer with a slotted spoon and plunge into the cold water. Drain. Working over a bowl to catch all of the juice, peel and seed the tomatoes. Chop, then mash them with a fork and put into a salad bowl with the juice.

Add the onion, green pepper, garlic, olive oil, lemon juice, parsley and mint, then season with salt and pepper and harissa (if using). Stir to mix. Serve at room temperature or cover with cling film (plastic wrap) and refrigerate for 30 minutes–1 hour until chilled. Serve chilled.

Cauliflower Beignets

TUNISIA
PREPARATION TIME: 10 minutes,
plus cooling time
COOKING TIME: 20 minutes
SERVES: 4

These batter-dipped and fried cauliflower florets make a perfect starter or side dish. Turmeric in the batter gives them a lovely golden colour – and a touch more flavour.

    1 cauliflower (about 1 kg/2¼ lb), cut into
        medium florets
    3 eggs
    75 g/2¾ oz (½ cup) plain (all-purpose) flour
    ½ teaspoon ground turmeric
    2 tablespoons finely chopped flat-leaf parsley
    neutral oil, for frying
    salt
    lemon wedges, to serve

Put the cauliflower into a large pot or saucepan of lightly salted water, bring to the boil and boil until just tender, about 10 minutes. Transfer to a colander to drain and cool.

Put the eggs into a wide bowl and, using a fork, beat together, then work in the flour, turmeric, parsley and salt to taste until it is a smooth, thick batter. Add 1 tablespoon of water to loosen if necessary.

Heat at least 2.5 cm/1 inch of oil in a medium, deep frying pan over a medium heat until the surface shimmers. Line a plate with paper towels. Working in batches, dip the cauliflower florets into the batter, then carefully add to the hot oil and fry until golden, about 45 seconds, turning to ensure even cooking. Remove with a slotted spoon or tongs and place on the paper towels to briefly drain. Serve immediately with lemon wedges to squeeze over the top.

Simmered Mallow

TUNISIA
PREPARATION TIME: 5 minutes
COOKING TIME: 5 hours 15 minutes
SERVES: 6

Mulukhiya is one of the country's ancient and iconic dishes. It is prepared with *Corchorus olitorius*, commonly known as Jew's mallow or, in Tunisia, *mulukhiya* (*corète potagère* in French). The leaves are dried and ground into a green powder. As it cooks, it becomes a deep, very dark green; when it is done, oil forms a sheet on the surface. It is thick and silky and should just dribble off the spoon. Despite its natural bitterness, and the five or so hours it takes to prepare, it remains deeply beloved. It usually has some pieces of bone-in beef, which are added about halfway through cooking, and is served with plenty of bread. During Muslim New Year, many houses prepare the dish, since green is the colour of Islam. You can smell it cooking as you stroll through neighbourhoods across the country.

120 ml/4 fl oz (½ cup) olive oil
100 g/3½ oz (1 cup) *mulukhiya* (mallow) powder
6 pieces boneless stewing or braising beef (about 350 g/12 oz total)
4 cloves of garlic, finely chopped
½ teaspoon ground coriander seeds
½ teaspoon ground caraway
1 tablespoon double concentrated tomato purée (paste)
harissa (page 409), to taste
1 red onion, peeled, optional
salt and pepper
lemon wedges, to serve

Bring 2 litres (68 fl oz/generous 2 quarts/8½ cups) water to the boil in a large saucepan. Heat the oil in a large, heavy pot or casserole dish (Dutch oven) over a medium heat and stir in the *mulukhiya* (mallow) powder. Cook for about 1 minute until bubbly, then work in the hot water, a ladle at a time, adding more only when it has been incorporated. Reduce the heat to low and cook, stirring from time to time, for 2½ hours.

Meanwhile, put the meat into a large bowl with the garlic, coriander and caraway, season with salt and pepper and toss. Cover with cling film (plastic wrap) and refrigerate until ready to add.

Stir the tomato purée (paste) and harissa into the casserole dish, then add the onion (if using) and the meat with all of the spices in the bowl. Cover with a lid and gently simmer, stirring from time to time, until it thickens, turns a deep, dark green and the oil separates and forms a sheet on the surface, about 2½ hours. The final consistency should be silky and just dribble off the spoon. If it gets too thick, stir in 250 ml (8 fl oz/1 cup) water and cook for another 15 minutes. Remove and discard the onion. Ladle into wide bowls with a piece of meat in each and serve with lemon wedges on the side.

Spicy Mashed Carrots

TUNISIA
PREPARATION TIME: 10 minutes
COOKING TIME: 30 minutes
SERVES: 4

This version of the popular Mashed Carrot Salad (*omek houria*, page 81) comes from Sfax, along the central Tunisian coast, where it is often served alongside fried fish.

6 carrots (about 600 g/1 lb 5 oz), cut into 2-cm/¾-inch circles
3 tablespoons olive oil
3 cloves of garlic, minced
1 ripe tomato, halved crosswise and grated, peel discarded (see page 445)
1 heaped tablespoon double concentrated tomato purée (paste)
¼ teaspoon ground caraway
½ teaspoon sweet paprika
harissa (page 409), to taste
salt and pepper
finely chopped flat-leaf parsley, to garnish

Put the carrots into a large pot or saucepan of lightly salted water, bring to the boil and boil until tender, about 20 minutes. Drain, reserving about 120 ml (4 fl oz/½ cup) of the liquid. Put the carrots into a large bowl and mash with the back of a fork or potato masher. Tip in some of the reserved liquid if needed.

Heat the oil in a large frying pan or sauté pan over a medium heat, add the garlic, tomato, tomato purée (paste) and 4 tablespoons of the reserved liquid, the caraway, paprika and harissa, then season with salt and pepper. Cook for 5 minutes to reduce. Add the mashed carrots and cook for 5 minutes, stirring frequently to fully blend. Add a touch more of the reserved liquid if needed while cooking. Transfer to a serving dish, garnish with parsley and serve.

Braised Fennel
in Tangy Tomato Sauce

TUNISIA
PREPARATION TIME: 15 minutes,
plus cooling time
COOKING TIME: 40 minutes
SERVES: 4–6

The anise-flavour of fennel combines well with this tangy tomato sauce. Adding a spoonful of double concentrated tomato purée (paste) gives the sauce a denser, richer quality. It is lovely chilled. This dish can be easily served as a 'cooked' salad.

4 fennel bulbs (about 1 kg/2¼ lb total)
3 tablespoons olive oil
2 red or yellow onions, finely chopped
4 tomatoes, halved crosswise and grated,
    peel discarded (see page 445)
1 tablespoon double concentrated tomato purée
    (paste), optional
2 tablespoons sugar
juice of 1 lemon
salt and pepper

Trim the fennel bulbs at the base, cut away any hard stems and remove the outer layer if hard and stringy. Quarter lengthwise. Put the fennel into a large pot or saucepan of lightly salted water, bring to the boil and boil for 5 minutes. Drain.

Heat the oil in a large frying pan or sauté pan over a high heat, add the onions, tomatoes, tomato purée (paste) and 4 tablespoons water (if using) and cook for 5 minutes to thicken the sauce. Add the reserved fennel, sugar and lemon juice, then season with salt and pepper. Reduce the heat to low, cover and simmer until tender, about 30 minutes. Add a touch of water if needed to keep the sauce moist. Transfer to a serving bowl and leave to cool. Serve at room temperature or cover with cling film (plastic wrap) and refrigerate. Serve chilled.

Spinach in Tomato Sauce

ALGERIA
PREPARATION TIME: 15 minutes
COOKING TIME: 40 minutes
SERVES: 4

One way to give this lovely spinach dish more kick is to stir some *dersa* (garlic-chilli paste, page 441) into the tomato sauce. Cooks often add a spoonful of double concentrated tomato purée (paste) to intensify the tomato flavour. To make into a fuller dish, crack a couple eggs into the pan at the end, then cook until the egg whites are set but the yolks still runny, about 5 minutes.

3 tablespoons olive oil
1 red or yellow onion, grated
3 cloves of garlic, minced
3 tomatoes, halved crosswise and grated,
    peel discarded (see page 445)
1 teaspoon sweet paprika
½ teaspoon ground cumin
750 g/1⅔ lb fresh spinach
salt and pepper

Heat the oil in a large, wide pot or saucepan over a medium heat, add the onion and cook for about 10 minutes, or until translucent. Add the garlic, tomatoes, paprika and cumin, season with salt and pepper and cook for 10 minutes, adding a few spoonfuls of water if needed to keep it from drying out. Add the spinach, cover with a lid, reduce the heat to low and cook until the spinach is wilted, 10–15 minutes. Uncover and cook, stirring frequently, for 5 minutes to reduce the liquid. Spoon into a serving dish and serve warm.

Saharan Potato and Chicken Fritters

TUNISIA
PREPARATION TIME: 20 minutes
COOKING TIME: 35 minutes
SERVES: 2–4; MAKES: 10 fritters

These fritters are very popular in the south of Tunisia, where it is often called *kefta du Sahara* ('Saharan kefta'). They are similar to *maakouda* (Potato Fritters, see right) but the addition of chicken and cheese makes them richer.

  2 white potatoes, peeled and quartered
  2 tablespoons olive oil
  1 smallish skinless, boneless chicken breast
     (about 250 g/9 oz), cut into generous cubes
  1 red or yellow onion, finely chopped
  2 cloves of garlic, minced
  ½ teaspoon ground turmeric
  ½ teaspoon ground ginger
  2 tablespoons finely chopped flat-leaf parsley
  50 g/2 oz (packed ½ cup) shredded white cheese,
     such as Emmental or Gruyère
  1 large egg, separated
  dry breadcrumbs, for coating
  neutral oil, for frying
  salt and pepper

Put the potatoes into a large saucepan of lightly salted water, bring to the boil and boil until tender, about 15 minutes. Drain, then return to the pan and mash with the back of a fork or a potato masher.

Meanwhile, heat the oil in a frying pan or sauté pan over a medium-high heat, add the chicken, onion, garlic, turmeric and ginger and cook until the chicken is cooked through and the onion has softened, about 10 minutes. Transfer to a food processor and grind using pulses until it is a notch coarser than smooth.

Add the potatoes, ground chicken mixture, the parsley, cheese and egg yolk to a large bowl, season with salt and pepper and mix well with a fork.

Using moistened hands, take about 50 g (2 oz/ scant ¼ cup) of the mixture, form into a ball, then gently flatten into a thick patty, about 2 cm/¾ inch thick and 6 cm/2½ inches in diameter. Repeat with the remaining mixture.

Put enough breadcrumbs for coating into a shallow bowl. In another bowl, whisk the egg white with 1 tablespoon water. Line a plate with paper towels.

Heat at least 1 cm/½ inch of oil in a large, deep frying pan over a medium heat until the surface shimmers. Working in batches, dip the patties into the breadcrumbs until coated all over, then into the egg white, then gently place in the pan and fry until golden brown on both sides, 2–3 minutes. Transfer to the paper towels to briefly drain. Serve hot.

Potato Fritters

ALGERIA, MOROCCO
PREPARATION TIME: 20 minutes
COOKING TIME: 45 minutes
SERVES: 4; MAKES: 16 fritters

Maakouda (potato fritters) are one of Morocco and Algeria's great savoury treats. They are popular street food but also commonly made at home and served alongside soup.

  5 white potatoes (about 1 kg/2¼ lb total), unpeeled
  1 small onion, grated
  2 cloves of garlic, minced
  1 large egg
  4 heaped tablespoons finely chopped flat-leaf parsley
     or coriander (cilantro)
  ½ teaspoon ground turmeric
  plain (all-purpose) flour, for coating
  neutral oil, for frying
  salt and pepper

Put the potatoes into a large pot or saucepan of lightly salted water, bring to the boil and gently boil for 20–30 minutes until a knife tip penetrates the potatoes with little resistance. Transfer to a colander to drain and cool. Peel.

Put the potatoes into a large bowl and mash with the back of a fork or a potato masher. Add the onion, garlic, egg, parsley and turmeric. Season with salt and pepper and, using a wooden spoon, mix to a smooth consistency. Take about 50 g (2 oz/¼ cup) of the mixture and carefully flatten into a thick patty, about 2.5 cm/1 inch thick. Repeat with the remaining mixture. There should be about 16 fritters.

Put enough flour for coating into a shallow bowl. Line a plate with paper towels. Heat at least 1 cm/ ½ inch of oil in a large, deep frying pan over a medium heat until the surface shimmers. Working in batches, dip the patties into the flour until coated, then gently set in the pan and fry until golden brown on both sides, about 3 minutes. Transfer with a slotted spoon to the paper towels to briefly drain. Serve hot.

Frites

ALGERIA, LIBYA, MOROCCO, TUNISIA
PREPARATION TIME: 10 minutes
COOKING TIME: 30 minutes
SERVES: 4

Frites – *pommes frites*, although usually just called frites – are not just eaten on the side but often form an intrinsic part of a dish: covered with tomato sauce (page 442), topping merguez sandwiches (page 50) or used for the popular *frites-omelette* in Algeria (page 184), alongside grilled fish in Tunisia and rotisserie chicken in Morocco, or even scattered across a chicken tagine before serving. Ideally, use at least 1.5 litres (50 fl oz/ generous 6 cups) neutral oil for a batch of 450 g/1 lb potatoes. In Morocco, it remains popular to dip frites into strong, nose-tickling mustard.

1 kg/2¼ lb white potatoes
neutral oil, for frying
salt

Scrub the potatoes or peel and cut lengthwise into 1-cm-/½-inch-thick fries.

Heat an abundant amount of oil in a deep frying pan over a medium heat until the surface shimmers. Line a baking sheet with paper towels. Working in batches that don't crowd the pan or bring down the temperature of the oil, add the potatoes and fry until golden, about 10 minutes. Transfer with a slotted spoon to the paper towels to briefly drain. Season with salt and serve hot.

Stuffed Potato Wedges

LIBYA
PREPARATION TIME: 30 minutes
COOKING TIME: 1 hour
SERVES: 4

M'battan is a beloved Libyan speciality of potato slices stuffed with seasoned minced (ground) meat and then fried. The trick is in cutting the slices in half while leaving them connected at the bottom. Cooks generally fill the pan with stuffed potatoes and reduce the oil temperature, giving them time to cook through without the outside burning.

2 tablespoons olive oil
1 red or yellow onion, finely chopped
2 cloves of garlic, minced
500 g/1 lb 2 oz minced (ground) beef or lamb
1 tablespoon double concentrated tomato purée (paste)
½ teaspoon ground cinnamon
½ teaspoon ground ginger
¼ teaspoon ground turmeric
2 heaped tablespoons finely chopped flat-leaf parsley
3 large eggs
3 tablespoons dry breadcrumbs, plus extra for coating
3 large white potatoes
neutral oil, for frying
salt and pepper

Heat the olive oil in a wide saucepan over a medium heat, add the onion and cook for about 5 minutes, or until soft and pale. Stir in the garlic and meat and brown for about 5 minutes. Add the tomato purée (paste) and 4 tablespoons water and cook for 2–3 minutes. Add the cinnamon, ginger and turmeric, season with salt and pepper and pour in 120 ml (4 fl oz/½ cup) water. Cook for 5–10 minutes until the moisture has evaporated. Transfer to a bowl and leave to cool for a few minutes. Add the parsley, 1 of the eggs and the 3 tablespoons of breadcrumbs and, using your hands, mix well.

Meanwhile, fill a large bowl with water. Peel the potatoes and cut crosswise into 1-cm-/½-inch-thick slices. Cut each of these in half down the middle, but leaving the base intact so that they remain attached at the bottom. Place in the water until ready to use.

Put enough breadcrumbs for coating into a medium bowl. Put the remaining 2 eggs into another bowl and, using a fork, beat together.

Drain the potatoes. Open a wedge and holding by the joined end, fill it with 1 heaped tablespoon of filling (about 25 g/1 oz) using a small teaspoon and your fingers. Press the filling down firmly so that there are no gaps. Running a finger around the edges, remove any filling that hangs out. Dip the end (not the whole potato) into the breadcrumbs and set on a plate. Repeat with the remaining potatoes.

Heat at least 2 cm/¾ inch of neutral oil in a medium, deep frying pan over a medium heat until the surface shimmers. Line a plate with paper towels. Working in batches, coat the filled potatoes in egg and carefully set in the oil. Fill the pan and cook until the filled potatoes are golden brown and the tip of a knife easily slides into the potatoes, about 20 minutes per batch. Transfer to the paper towels to drain and cool. Serve.

Fried Potatoes with Tomato Sauce

ALGERIA
PREPARATION TIME: 15 minutes
COOKING TIME: 40 minutes
SERVES: 4

A kids' favourite, *frites en sauce tomate* tops homemade fries with tomato sauce. For some savoury earthiness in the tomato sauce, add a pinch of thyme or oregano.

  2 tablespoons olive oil
  5 cloves of garlic, minced
  4 tomatoes, halved crosswise and grated,
    peel discarded (see page 445)
  2 tablespoons finely chopped flat-leaf parsley,
    plus extra to garnish
  1 tablespoon sweet paprika
  pinch of dried thyme or oregano
  1 kg/2¼ lb white potatoes
  neutral oil, for frying
  salt and pepper

Heat the olive oil and garlic in a medium saucepan over a medium heat for about 1 minute, or until aromatic. Add the tomatoes, parsley, paprika and thyme and season with salt. Cook, stirring frequently, until darker and reduced, about 15 minutes. Add a touch of water to loosen the sauce at the end. Remove from the heat.

Meanwhile, scrub the potatoes but do not peel. Cut them lengthwise into 1-cm-/½-inch-thick fries.

Heat about 5 cm/2 inches of neutral oil in a large, deep frying pan or saucepan over a medium heat until the surface shimmers. Line a baking sheet with paper towels. Working in batches that don't crowd the pan or bring down the temperature of the oil, add the potatoes and fry until golden, about 10 minutes. Transfer with a slotted spoon to the paper towels to briefly drain.

Put the fries into a large sauté pan, spoon over the tomato sauce and cook for 1–2 minutes to combine the flavours. Grind some pepper over the top and garnish with parsley. Serve.

Courgettes Stuffed with Meat

ALGERIA
PREPARATION TIME: 30 minutes
COOKING TIME: 2 hours
SERVES: 4

One culinary imprint of the Ottoman rule of Algeria, Tunisia and Libya is *dolma* – stuffed vegetables. Some cooks add grated onion to the filling mixture.

  3 tablespoons olive oil
  250 g/9 oz boneless lamb, cut into pieces
  3 red or yellow onions, finely chopped
  3 tomatoes, peeled (see page 445) and finely chopped
  ½ teaspoon sweet paprika
  2 generous pinches of ground cinnamon
  175 g/6 oz (1 cup) canned chickpeas (garbanzo beans),
    rinsed, or 100 g/3½ oz (½ cup) cooked dried
    chickpeas (page 443)
  2 tablespoons long-grain white rice
  350 g/12 oz minced (ground) beef
  1 large egg
  2 tablespoons finely chopped flat-leaf parsley
  4 courgettes (zucchini) (about 1.2 kg/2½ lb total)
  salt and pepper

Heat the oil in a large frying pan or sauté pan over a medium heat, add the lamb and cook for about 5 minutes, or until browned on each side. Add the onions, tomatoes, paprika and cinnamon, then season with salt and pepper and cook until the sauce has reduced, about 20 minutes. Add the chickpeas and 250 ml (8 fl oz/1 cup) water, then cover with a lid and simmer for 45 minutes.

Meanwhile, parboil the rice by putting it into a small saucepan of lightly salted water, bringing to the boil and boiling for 5 minutes. Drain and set aside.

Put the minced (ground) beef, egg, parsley and rice into a large bowl, season with salt and pepper and, using your hands, mix to a paste.

Trim off the ends of the courgettes (zucchini) and cut crosswise into 3 lengths of about 6 cm/2½ inches. Hollow each segment from one end, leaving a cup-like bottom. Season the inside with salt and fill with the meat mixture. If there is any mixture remaining, roll into small meatballs.

Lay the stuffed courgettes in the pan of sauce on their sides, tucking under the sauce as much as possible, as well as any meatballs. Cover the pan with a lid and cook over a low heat until the courgettes are tender and the filling is cooked through, about 40 minutes. Uncover and cook for 5 minutes to reduce the sauce at the end if necessary. Serve on a large tray surrounded by the meat and sauce.

Stuffed Cabbage Rolls

ALGERIA, LIBYA
PREPARATION TIME: 30 minutes,
plus standing time
COOKING TIME: 1 hour 40 minutes
SERVES: 6–8; MAKES: about 30 rolls

This recipe for *dolma krombit* (stuffed cabbage rolls) has a Libyan tang with the dried mint. In Algeria, many cooks add caraway instead of mint, and even prepare a much fuller sauce with meat and chickpeas (garbanzo beans) to stew the cabbage rolls. Place the cabbage rolls snugly in the pan and cover with a plate to keep them from unravelling while cooking.

  1 head green cabbage
  350 g/12 oz minced (ground) or finely chopped beef or lamb
  1 onion, finely chopped
  200 g/7 oz (1 cup) uncooked short- or medium-grain white rice
  1 small long sweet green pepper, cored, seeded and finely chopped
  4 heaped tablespoons finely chopped flat-leaf parsley
  4 heaped tablespoons finely chopped coriander (cilantro)
  1 tablespoon dried mint
  ½ teaspoon ground turmeric
  ¼ teaspoon ground cinnamon
  ¼ teaspoon ground paprika
  4 tablespoons olive oil
  2 tablespoons double concentrated tomato purée (paste)
  salt and pepper

Bring a large, wide pot or casserole dish (Dutch oven) of water to a rolling boil. Set the cabbage into the water, letting it boil in the water, gradually removing the leaves layer by layer with tongs as they can be peeled away, about 10 minutes total.

Set the tough outer leaves aside. From the other leaves, trim away the hard core – a triangular piece of fibrous raised centre vein – and cut the leaves in half.

Put the meat, onion, rice, green pepper, parsley, coriander (cilantro), mint, turmeric, cinnamon and paprika into a large bowl. Season with salt, moisten with the oil and, using your hands, mix well.

Put 1 cabbage leaf on a flat work counter so that the edges naturally curl upwards. Place about 1 heaped tablespoon (25 g/1 oz) of filling along the widest part of the leaf, fold the sides over and roll down to the end. Set on a plate with the fold facing downwards to keep from unravelling and repeat with the remaining leaves and filling.

Line the bottom of a large pot with some of the reserved outer leaves to form a bed. Put the rolls into the pot, pressed snugly against one another. Stir the tomato purée (paste) into 500 ml (18 fl oz/2 cups) water and pour over the rolls. Layer the remaining cabbage leaves snugly over the top. Cover the pot with a lid and cook over a low heat until the rolls and their filling are tender, about 1½ hours. Check from time to time that there is some water in the pot. Remove from the heat and leave to stand for at least 15 minutes before serving.

To serve, gently remove the rolls and arrange on a serving platter. Spoon some juice over the top and serve.

Stuffed Vine Leaves

ALGERIA, LIBYA
PREPARATION TIME: 30 minutes
COOKING TIME: 1 hour 30 minutes
MAKES: about 28 rolls

Lebrak (stuffed vine leaves) are a favourite in Libya and Algeria. This is a delightful vegetarian version.

225 g/8 oz vine (grape) leaves in brine, rinsed
75 g/2¾ oz (½ cup) seedless raisins
4 tablespoons olive oil
2 red or yellow onions, finely chopped
2 cloves of garlic, minced
100 g/3½ oz (½ cup) uncooked short- or medium-
   grain white rice
2 heaped tablespoons finely chopped mint
salt
lemon wedges, to serve

Bring a large, wide pot or casserole dish (Dutch oven) of water to the boil, add the leaves and boil for 5–10 minutes until the leaves are tender and limp. Drain and rinse under cold running water. Put the raisins into a small heatproof bowl, cover with lukewarm water and leave to soak for 10 minutes to soften, then drain.

Add 2 tablespoons of the oil and the onions to a large saucepan and cook over a medium heat for 10 minutes, or until pale and soft. Stir in the garlic, then the rice, season with salt and cook until translucent, about 3 minutes. Add 250 ml (8 fl oz/ 1 cup) water and bring to the boil. Cover with a lid, reduce the heat to low and cook until the liquid is absorbed, about 5 minutes. Stir in the mint and raisins, then spoon into a bowl and leave to cool.

Trim off the stem of the vine leaves. Lay one out with the shiny side down. Depending on the size of the leaf, place 1–2 heaped tablespoons (15–25 g/ ½–1 oz) of the stuffing near the end of the stem. Fold the sides over the stuffing and roll tightly up into a compact packet. Roll the remaining vine leaves.

In a wide pot, spread 1 tablespoon of the oil across the bottom and arrange the rolls end-to-end in a circular form starting at the outside of the pot and working towards the centre. Add 250 ml (8 fl oz/ 1 cup) water, then place an inverted dinner plate on top of the rolls to keep them from unravelling. Cover with a lid and cook over a low heat until the moisture has been largely absorbed and the leaves and rice are tender, 45 minutes– 1 hour. Add a touch more water if needed.

Arrange the vine leaves on a serving plate and drizzle over the remaining 1 tablespoon of oil. Serve warm or cooled with lemon wedges.

Green Peppers Stuffed with Fish

TUNISIA
PREPARATION TIME: 30 minutes
COOKING TIME: 1 hour 15 minutes
SERVES: 4

Stuffing vegetables with fish might be less common than with meat, but it is a modern and lovely alternative.

200 g/7 oz white-fleshed fish fillets such as whiting,
   bream or hake
8 tablespoons olive oil
1 red or yellow onion, finely chopped
3 cloves of garlic, minced
½ teaspoon sweet paprika
½ teaspoon ground coriander seeds
½ teaspoon ground turmeric
harissa (page 409) or cayenne pepper, to taste
50 g/2 oz (¾ cup) dry breadcrumbs
4 tablespoons finely chopped flat-leaf parsley
2 eggs
4 long sweet green peppers
plain (all-purpose) flour, for coating
salt and pepper

Poach the fish by putting it into a large saucepan of lightly salted water and cooking over a low heat until opaque throughout, 3–5 minutes, depending on the thickness of the fillets. Using a slotted spoon, transfer to a plate to drain and cool. Remove any skin or bones and break into small flakes.

Heat 2 tablespoons of the oil in a frying pan or sauté pan over a medium heat, add the onion and cook for about 8 minutes, or until pale and soft. Stir in the garlic and cook for about 1 minute, or until aromatic. Transfer to a large bowl, add the paprika, coriander, turmeric and harissa, then season with salt and pepper. Stir and leave to cool. Add the breadcrumbs, parsley and eggs, and, using your hands, mix to a paste. Fold in the flaked fish.

Remove the caps of the peppers. Without tearing the peppers, remove and discard the seeds. Using a narrow spoon, fill the peppers with about 100 g (3½ oz/½ cup) of the filling.

Heat the remaining 6 tablespoons of oil over a medium heat. Put enough flour for coating into a shallow bowl.

Dip the stuffed end of the peppers into the flour. Using tongs to hold upright, fry the floured end for about 30 seconds, then lay the pepper flat in the pan and cook, turning as needed, over a medium-low heat until tender and the stuffing is cooked through, 10–15 minutes. Transfer to paper towels to drain and repeat with the remaining peppers. Serve warm.

Spiced Olives

MOROCCO
PREPARATION TIME: 10 minutes,
plus soaking and chilling time
MAKES: 500 g/1 lb 2 oz (about 4 cups)

Souq (market) stalls sell a wide variety of spiced olives, but many make home versions to their own taste. You can prepare this Moroccan version with any type of olive, but pitted green ones are nice as they allow the flavours to penetrate. Soaking the olives first in hot water will remove some of the briny tang and showcase the marinade's herb and spice flavours.

  500 g/1 lb 2 oz green olives (about 4 cups),
    preferably pitted
  ¼ preserved lemon (page 410)
  1 clove of garlic, grated
  2 teaspoons minced flat-leaf parsley
  2 teaspoons minced coriander (cilantro)
  ¼ teaspoon ground cumin
  cayenne pepper, to taste
  3 tablespoons extra-virgin olive oil
  2 tablespoons fresh lemon juice
  salt and pepper

Rinse the olives, put into a large bowl and cover with hot water. Leave to soak for 10 minutes, then drain and spread out on paper towels to dry. Transfer to another large bowl.

Scrape out the pulp of the preserved lemon and discard. Mince the peel. Put the preserved lemon peel, garlic, parsley, coriander (cilantro), cumin and cayenne pepper into a small bowl and mix together, then season with salt and pepper and loosen with the oil. Pour over the olives and toss to evenly coat. Cover with cling film (plastic wrap) and refrigerate for 30 minutes–1 hour until chilled. Before serving, add the lemon juice and toss. Store in a sterilized 1-litre (34-fl oz) glass jar (see page 462) in the refrigerator for up to 3 weeks.

Pickled Turnips with Harissa

TUNISIA
PREPARATION TIME: 10 minutes,
plus pickling time
SERVES: 4

Torchi are a favourite starter, and they go perfectly with anything from grilled meats, *lablabi* (page 147) to *fricassé* sandwiches (page 51) or as a side to couscous or pasta. While best to macerate for 3–4 hours before serving, they can be eaten after a handful of minutes if needed. Leftover ones are best eaten within 1 week.

  2 turnips, preferably white ones
  2 teaspoons harissa (page 409), or to taste
  1 tablespoon white vinegar
  1 tablespoon fresh lemon juice
  ½ teaspoon salt
  extra-virgin olive oil, for drizzling

Cut the turnips crosswise into thin, almost translucent slices and put into a salad bowl. Put the harissa, vinegar, lemon juice and salt into a small bowl and whisk together, then pour over the turnips and toss to mix. It can be served immediately, but it is preferable to cover with clingfilm (plastic wrap) and refrigerate for 3–4 hours before doing so. Drizzle with oil before serving. These are best eaten within 1 week.

Pickled Vegetables

TUNISIA
PREPARATION TIME: 15 minutes,
plus cooling and pickling time
MAKES: 1-litre/34-fl oz jar

Known as *merrket mellah* or *variantes*, these pickled vegetables are eaten nearly daily in Tunisia. While carrots, cauliflower florets and turnips are classic, add peppers or fennel if in season. A 1-litre/34-fl oz jar will hold about 500 g/1 lb 2 oz chopped vegetables. They are best left a few days before using.

  3 tablespoons fine or pickling salt
  200 g/7 oz carrots
  150 g/5 oz small turnips
  150 g/5 oz cauliflower
  ½ lemon, scrubbed and cut into wedges

Put the salt and 500 ml (18 fl oz/2 cups) of hot water into a large heatproof container and stir to dissolve, then leave to cool to room temperature.

Cut the carrots and turnips preferably with a waffle-shaped cutter, into bite-size pieces. Cut the cauliflower into bite-size florets. Pack snugly into a sterilized 1-litre (34-fl oz) glass jar (see page 462). Squeeze the lemon juice over the top and put the wedges into the jar. Pour in the salt water. Loosely cover or set the lid on the jar, then put into a cool spot or the refrigerator to macerate for 2–3 days before using. Tighten the lid. Rinse thoroughly with warm water before serving. Store in the refrigerator and eat within a few months.

EGGS

Berber Egg Tagine

MOROCCO
PREPARATION TIME: 10 minutes
COOKING TIME: 20 minutes
SERVES: 2

This easy-to-make egg tagine is an ideal option when you don't have time to prepare something more complex. This version comes from the Berber area on the eastern slopes of Morocco's High Atlas Mountains. It is common to blend cooking oils in a single dish, including at least a spoonful of high-quality extra-virgin olive oil for its flavour.

1 red or yellow onion, finely chopped
1 clove of garlic, minced
2 plum tomatoes, ends trimmed and grated, peel discarded (see page 445)
1 tablespoon finely chopped flat-leaf parsley
½ teaspoon ground cumin, plus extra for sprinkling
¼ teaspoon sweet paprika
¼ teaspoon ground turmeric
2 tablespoons vegetable oil
1 tablespoon extra-virgin olive oil
4 large eggs, lightly beaten
salt and pepper

Put the onion, garlic, tomatoes, parsley, cumin, paprika and turmeric into a small tagine (see page 250), season with salt and pepper and drizzle over both the oils. Stir, cover with the lid and cook over a medium heat until the onions are tender, about 15 minutes. Spread the vegetables evenly across the bottom of the tagine, then pour the eggs evenly over the top. Cover and cook over a low heat until the eggs are just set, about 5 minutes. Generously sprinkle with cumin and serve in the tagine.

Fried Eggs with Khlii

MOROCCO
PREPARATION TIME: 2 minutes
COOKING TIME: 10 minutes
SERVES: 1

A classic winter breakfast in Morocco, especially around Fès, fried eggs with *khlii* (a spiced confit of dried meat, see page 206) is rich, filling and bursting with savoury flavours. Traditionally, this dish is cooked and served in a small terracotta tagine, which will hold its heat after being removed from the stove. If using a small frying pan, cook for

another 30 seconds or so after breaking the yolks. It is always served with hot Mint Tea (pages 417–421).

4–5 tablespoons *khlii* (spiced confit of dried meat, see page 206), some fat removed and meat trimmed
2 large eggs
salt
Mint Tea (pages 417–421), to serve

Add the *khlii* to a small tagine (see page 250) or frying pan over a medium heat and cook over a low heat until the meat has softened and the oil is bubbling, about 5 minutes. Crack the eggs into the tagine and add a pinch of salt. Reduce the heat to low, cover with a lid and cook until the egg whites are set but the yolks still runny, about 5 minutes. Break the yolks and remove from the heat. Serve from the tagine with Mint Tea.

Eggs in Harissa-laced Tomato Sauce

TUNISIA
PREPARATION TIME: 5 MINUTES
COOKING TIME: 15 minutes
SERVES: 1–2

The most basic version of Tunisia's famous *ojja* (egg dishes) has little more than double concentrated tomato purée (paste), harissa and olive oil – even if some purists claim it needs pieces of tomatoes and peppers to qualify as an *ojja*. This quick dish of eggs in a spicy, harissa-laced tomato sauce is served with plenty of bread. If substituting the harissa with cayenne pepper, add in a bit of minced garlic and a few generous pinches of ground coriander, caraway or cumin if possible.

1 tablespoon olive oil
2 tablespoons double concentrated tomato purée (paste)
harissa (page 409), to taste
pinch of salt
2 large eggs
crusty bread, to serve

Mix the oil, tomato purée (paste) and 4 tablespoons water, the harissa and salt in a small stovetop low, flat casserole dish or sauté pan. Cover with a lid and cook over a low heat for 10 minutes. Crack the eggs into the sauce, break the yolks by making a criss-cross motion with two knives, cover and cook until the egg whites are set and the yolks still runny, 4–5 minutes. Serve immediately in the dish with plenty of bread.

Eggs with Tomatoes and Peppers

TUNISIA
PREPARATION TIME: 10 minutes
COOKING TIME: 25 minutes
SERVES: 2

This is a classic version of Tunisia's iconic *ojja* (egg dishes). Prepared with tomatoes and peppers, it's simple, vegetarian and always spicy. Restaurants often add merguez sausage or even peeled prawns (shrimp) (page 177) for a more complete dish. Typically, the yolks are broken in the pan before cooking, though some prefer their eggs intact on the plate.

3 cloves of garlic, peeled
½ teaspoon ground caraway
3 tablespoons olive oil
½ red bell pepper, seeded and cut into generous
  bite-size pieces
½ green bell pepper, seeded and cut into generous
  bite-size pieces
1 green chilli (chile), seeded and finely chopped
4 ripe tomatoes, peeled (see page 445) and diced
1 tablespoon double concentrated tomato purée
  (paste)
harissa (page 409), to taste
2 large eggs
salt

In a mortar, pound the garlic with the caraway and a pinch of salt with a pestle.

Heat the oil in a large frying pan or sauté pan over a high heat, add the garlic paste, peppers, chilli (chile), tomatoes, tomato purée (paste) and 3 tablespoons water and cook for 2–3 minutes, stirring frequently. Generously season with harissa and add 120 ml (4 fl oz/½ cup) water. Reduce the heat to low, cover with a lid and cook until the peppers are tender, about 15 minutes. Crack the eggs directly into the pan. If desired, break the yolks by making a criss-cross motion with two knives. Cover with a lid and cook until the egg whites are set but the yolks still runny, about 5 minutes. Serve from the pan.

DOUBLE CONCENTRATED TOMATO PURÉE (PASTE)

Along with harissa (page 409), tomatoes are one of the defining characteristics of Tunisian cuisine – more specifically the abundant use of tomato purée (paste). Cans and jars of double concentrated tomato purée (*double concentré de tomates*) are among the most essential items in the Tunisian pantry and used in cooking all manner of sauces and stews. Industry statistics put local consumption at 10 kg/22 lb per person per year – that's 30 g/1 oz (2 tablespoons) of tomato purée (paste) a day for every person in the country. The rest of the Maghreb frequently adds tomato purée to the cooking pot, too, but not with the same frequency as Tunisia. Algeria was once a large producer of tomato purée, although today it imports most of its supply.

Tomatoes likely came to Tunisia with the Andalusians who settled on the Cap Bon peninsula and just north of Tunis in the sixteenth century. The first commercial processing plant for tomato purée was set up on Cap Bon in 1903, and production of *concentré de tomates* remains centred on the fertile peninsula.

Tomato purée is generally diluted with a touch of water and cooked for at least a couple of minutes to cut its acidity. Cooks often use it in tandem with fresh tomatoes. The purée gives bolder, denser tomato flavours to sauces, and enriches them with a silkier texture. It also turns the dish a deep reddish colour, an important aesthetic consideration, as many Tunisians freely admit that they prefer colourful food. Even the country's beloved staple couscous gets soaked with red broth before serving, to give it a lovely tone.

Eggs in Tomato Sauce with Prawns

TUNISIA
PREPARATION TIME: 10 minutes
COOKING TIME: 30 minutes
SERVES: 2–3

In Tunisia, there are a handful of popular ways to eat prawns (shrimp), including in seafood pasta (page 234) and in Seafood Salad (page 110). Cooked in an *ojja* (egg dish) with tomato sauce is another.

3 tablespoons olive oil
½ red bell pepper, seeded and finely chopped
1 long sweet green pepper, cored, seeded and finely chopped
2 cloves of garlic, grated
4 ripe tomatoes, halved crosswise and grated, peel discarded (see page 445)
1 heaped tablespoon double concentrated tomato purée (paste)
harissa (page 409), to taste
½ teaspoon ground caraway
200 g/7 oz peeled raw large prawns (shrimp)
4 large eggs
salt and pepper

Heat the oil in a large frying pan or sauté pan over a high heat, add the peppers and cook for about 5 minutes, or until aromatic and softening. Stir in the garlic, then add the tomatoes, tomato purée (paste) and 6 tablespoons water, the harissa and caraway, and season with salt and pepper. Reduce the heat to low, cover with a lid and cook until the sauce has thickened, about 15 minutes. Add the prawns (shrimp) and cook for 3–4 minutes until they turn translucent. Crack the eggs directly into the pan. Break the yolks and loosely scramble. Cover with a lid and cook until the eggs are set, about 5 minutes. Divide among plates and serve.

Parsley Frittata

TUNISIA
PREPARATION TIME: 20 minutes, plus cooling time
COOKING TIME: 1 hour 10 minutes
SERVES: 4–6

Tajine in Tunisia refers not to the conical earthenware cookware as in Morocco, or a round ridged griddle pan for cooking flatbreads in Algeria, but frittata-like baked egg dishes. One of the most famous is *tajine madnous* ('parsley tajine'). Its name is a bit misleading as it has chicken and cheese as well as plenty of parsley. Substitute the hard-boiled eggs with some boiled or fried cubes of potatoes, if desired.

1 tablespoon olive oil, plus extra for oiling
400 g/14 oz skinless, boneless chicken breasts
8 large eggs
½ teaspoon ground turmeric
15 g/½ oz flat-leaf parsley leaves (about 2 unpacked cups)
2 Hard-boiled Eggs (page 443), peeled and coarsely chopped
150 g/5 oz (1½ cups) shredded white cheese, such as Emmental or Gruyère
salt and pepper
lemon wedges, to serve

Preheat the oven to 180 °C/350 °F/Gas Mark 4.
Heat the oil in a small frying pan over a medium heat, add the chicken and cook until cooked through, 7–12 minutes depending on the thickness. Remove from the heat and leave to cool, then coarsely chop into pieces no larger than 1 cm/½ inch.

Put the eggs and turmeric into a large bowl and, using a fork, beat together. Season with salt and pepper and fold in the chicken, parsley, hard-boiled eggs and cheese.

Oil a 15-cm-/6-inch-round cake pan, silicone mould or deep baking dish and spoon in the mixture. Jiggle to evenly settle, then bake in the oven until cooked through and a knife poked into the centre comes out dry, 45–55 minutes. Remove from the oven and leave to cool for a few minutes, then unmould with a spatula or knife. Transfer to a large serving plate and cut into wedges. Serve with lemon wedges.

Potato and Chicken Frittata

LIBYA
PREPARATION TIME: 20 minutes
COOKING TIME: 1 hour
SERVES: 6–8

In Libya, frittata-like baked egg dishes tend to be similar to their Tunisian counterparts (*tajine*, see page 177), though usually they are thinner, and while they also include turmeric, they often have different spicing. In this recipe, the chicken is cooked with rosemary and thyme.

> 3 white potatoes (about 500 g/1 lb 2 oz), peeled and cut into 1-cm/½-inch cubes
> 350 g/12 oz skinless, boneless chicken breasts
> ½ teaspoon dried thyme
> ½ teaspoon dried rosemary
> 2 tablespoons olive oil, plus extra for oiling
> 1 red or yellow onion, finely chopped
> 8 large eggs
> ½ teaspoon ground turmeric
> 100 g/3½ oz (1 cup) shredded white cheese, such as Emmental or Gruyère
> 2 heaped tablespoons flat-leaf parsley leaves
> salt and pepper
> lemon wedges, to serve

Put the potatoes into a large pot or saucepan of lightly salted water and boil until just tender, about 10 minutes. Drain in a colander.

Meanwhile, season the chicken with the thyme, rosemary and salt and set aside.

Heat 1 tablespoon of the oil in a small–medium frying pan over a medium heat, add the onion and cook for about 8 minutes until pale and soft. Spoon into a bowl and leave to cool. Add the remaining 1 tablespoon of oil to the pan, add the chicken and cook until cooked through, 7–12 minutes depending on the thickness. Remove from the heat and leave to cool.

Meanwhile, preheat the oven to 180 °C/350 °F/Gas Mark 4.

Once the chicken is cool enough to handle, coarsely chop into pieces no larger than 1 cm/½ inch. Put the eggs and turmeric into a large bowl and, using a fork, beat together. Season with salt and pepper, then fold the chicken, onion, potatoes, cheese and parsley into the eggs.

Oil a 23 × 23-cm-/9 × 9-inch-square baking pan, silicone mould or baking dish and spoon in the mixture. Jiggle to evenly settle. It should not be more than 2 cm/¾ inch deep. Bake in the oven until cooked through and a knife poked into the centre comes out dry, about 30 minutes. Remove

from the oven and leave to cool for a few minutes, then unmould with a spatula or knife. Transfer to a large serving plate and cut into pieces. Serve with lemon wedges.

Aubergine and Potato Frittata

TUNISIA
PREPARATION TIME: 20 minutes
COOKING TIME: 1 hour 15 minutes
SERVES: 6–8

Another one of Tunisia's popular frittata-like egg *tajine* (see page 177), this includes aubergines (eggplant) and potatoes. After frying the aubergines, be sure to drain well on paper towels to keep the dish less oily. Serve with a variety of salads.

> 2 white potatoes (about 700 g/1 lb 8½ oz), peeled and cut into 1.5-cm/⅔-inch cubes
> 6 tablespoons olive oil, plus extra for oiling
> 2 aubergines (eggplant), cut into 1.5-cm/⅔-inch cubes
> 1 large red or yellow onion, finely chopped
> 10 large eggs
> ½ teaspoon ground turmeric
> 200 g/7 oz (2 cups) shredded white cheese, such as Emmental or Gruyère
> 3 tablespoons finely chopped flat-leaf parsley
> salt and pepper
> lemon wedges, to serve

Preheat the oven to 180 °C/350 °F/Gas Mark 4.

Put the potatoes into a large pot or saucepan of lightly salted water and boil until just tender, about 12 minutes. Drain in a colander.

Heat the oil in a large frying pan or sauté pan over a high heat, add the aubergines (eggplant) and fry until tender, about 15 minutes. Using a slotted spoon, transfer to paper towels. Add the onion to the pan, reduce the heat to medium and cook until tender and pale, about 10 minutes. Remove from the heat.

Put the eggs and turmeric into a large bowl and, using a fork, beat together. Season with salt and pepper and stir in the cheese and parsley. Fold the aubergine, potatoes and onion into the mixture.

Oil a 20-cm-/8-inch-round cake pan, silicone mould or deep baking dish and spoon in the mixture. Bake in the oven until cooked through and a knife poked into the centre comes out dry, about 35 minutes. Remove from the oven and leave to cool for a few minutes before unmoulding with a spatula or knife. Transfer to a large serving plate and cut into wedges. Serve with lemon wedges.

Frittata Wrapped in Pastry Leaves

TUNISIA
PREPARATION TIME: 20 minutes
COOKING TIME: 1 hour
SERVES: 4–5

Perhaps the most famous *tajine* (see page 177) in Tunisia, *tajine malsouka* comes wrapped in fine pastry leaves known as *brick* or *malsouka* (see page 56). While this recipe calls for minced (ground) meat, there are versions with chicken and with hunks of preserved tuna. This makes a deep (4–5-cm/1½–2-inch) round *tajine* about 20 cm/8 inches in diameter. Use a wider baking dish if desired, reducing the baking time slightly.

    3 tablespoons olive oil, plus extra for oiling
        and brushing
    2 red or yellow onions, finely chopped
    400 g/14 oz minced (ground) beef or lamb
    4 large eggs
    small pinch of saffron threads, crumbled
    2 tablespoons finely chopped flat-leaf parsley
    100 g/3½ oz (1 cup) shredded white cheese, such as
        Emmental or Gruyère
    5 Hard-boiled Eggs (page 443), peeled and diced
    4–5 round *brick*, *warka* or *dioul* leaves (see page 56),
        spring roll wrappers or filo (phyllo) sheets
    salt and pepper
    lemon wedges, to serve

Preheat the oven to 180 °C/350 °F/Gas Mark 4.

Heat the oil in a large frying pan or sauté pan over a medium-high heat, add the onions and cook for about 10 minutes, or until pale and soft. Stir in the meat and cook for about 10 minutes, or until browned all over. Remove from the heat, drain off any liquid from the meat and set aside.

Put the eggs and saffron into a large bowl and, using a large fork, beat together. Season with salt and pepper and fold in the meat, parsley, cheese and hard-boiled eggs.

Oil a 20-cm-/8-inch-round cake pan or baking dish. Brush the pastry sheets with oil, then lay 3 sheets in the pan so that they overlap each other and hang over the edges of the pan. Spoon in the mixture, drizzle with some of the reserved liquid from browning the meat, then fold the overhanging leaves across the top. Top with 1 or 2 more leaves, trimming a touch if needed, and tuck the edges into the side.

Bake in the oven until cooked through, 35–40 minutes. Unmould onto a serving dish, cut into wedges and serve with lemon wedges.

Spinach Omelette

ALGERIA
PREPARATION TIME: 10 minutes
COOKING TIME: 15 minutes
SERVES: 2

In Algeria, omelettes are a quick and popular lunch or dinner. One of the most common is this simple omelette with spinach. This version isn't flipped, although some prefer to do so.

    2 tablespoons olive oil
    250 g/9 oz baby spinach leaves
    3 large eggs
    2 cloves of garlic, minced
    salt and pepper

Heat 1 tablespoon of the oil in a large, deep sauté pan over a medium heat, add the spinach and cook, stirring frequently, until wilted, about 5 minutes. Transfer to a colander to drain, gently pressing out any excess liquid.

Put the eggs into a large bowl and, using a fork, beat together, then season with salt and pepper.

Heat the remaining 1 tablespoon of oil in a 20-cm/8-inch non-stick frying pan over a medium heat, add the garlic and cook for about 30 seconds, or until aromatic. Add the spinach and stir to blend with the garlic, then spread it evenly across the bottom of the pan. Pour in the egg mixture. Using a wooden spoon, distribute the egg among the spinach so that it isn't simply pooled on top. Cover the pan with a lid and cook over a low heat for 8–10 minutes until the eggs are set. Loosen the omelette with a thin spatula and slide onto a plate. Serve immediately.

Classic Tuna and Cheese Omelette

TUNISIA
PREPARATION TIME: 5 minutes
COOKING TIME: 5 minutes
SERVES: 1

This omelette with tuna and cheese is so popular in Tunis that people there refer to it as an *omelette classique*. With some Frites (fries, page 164) and a small salad, it makes a full meal.

  2 large eggs
  25 g/1 oz (packed ¼ cup) shredded white cheese, such as Emmental or Gruyère
  40 g/1½ oz (¼ cup) drained canned tuna
  1 tablespoon olive oil
  salt and pepper

Put the eggs into a large bowl and, using a fork, beat together. Season with salt and pepper and beat again. Add the cheese, then break the tuna into flakes and fold into the eggs.

 Heat the oil in a 25-cm/10-inch non-stick frying pan over a medium heat. Pour the egg mixture into the pan and cook until it begins to set, about 1 minute. Using a thin spatula, fold over one-third towards the centre and then the opposite third and cook until the centre is set enough to turn, about 1 minute. Turn the omelette using a plate for help if needed, and cook for a final 1 minute, or until the egg in the centre is set. Slide onto a plate and serve.

Saffron Omelette

MOROCCO
PREPARATION TIME: 2 minutes,
plus steeping time
COOKING TIME: 4 minutes
SERVES: 1

Moroccan saffron has long grown on the Taliouine plain (see page 183). Locals there use it in soups and stews, plus to prepare Saffron Tea (page 422) and even steep a few threads in hot milk added to an omelette. This recipe is for an individual omelette. Double the recipe and use a 25-cm/10-inch frying pan to serve two people.

  2 tablespoons milk
  2–3 saffron threads
  2 large eggs
  1 tablespoon olive oil
  salt

Heat the milk in a small saucepan over a low heat, add the saffron, remove from the heat and leave to steep for 10–15 minutes. Put the eggs, milk and saffron into a large bowl and, using a large fork, beat together, then season with salt.

 Heat the oil in a small non-stick frying pan over a medium heat, pour in the eggs and cook until set, about 2 minutes. Loosen the edge with a thin spatula and fold in half. Cook, turning once or twice, until cooked through, 1–2 minutes. Slide onto a plate and serve.

MOROCCAN SAFFRON

The village of Taliouine sits along a rock-strewn *wadi* (seasonal riverbed) on the Souktana plateau of Morocco's southern Anti-Atlas Mountains. It's an arid, undulating landscape jagged with eroded, mineral-rich hills etched in geological whorls like fingerprints. During the night for a few weeks each autumn, delicate purple saffron blossoms push up through the soil in the patchwork of fields around town. Tucked within the petals of these solitary purple flowers are three precious bright-orange to reddish-purple stigma.

Just after dawn, women – mostly but not exclusively – carrying a wicker basket hooked over an arm begin moving across the fields, before the petals open and the sun can wilt and diminish the colour and aroma of the saffron threads within. They pinch off new blooms at the base and place in their baskets. Once the field has been picked, the women take the blooms back to the family home and dump them out onto a large table.

Nimbly extracting the trio of stigma is tedious and repetitive work. It requires 150,000 or so individually plucked flowers – around 300 kg/660 lb – to get 5 kg/11 lb of stigmas (or threads) that will yield 1 kg/2¼ lb of dried saffron.

Brought from Asia Minor where it originated, saffron arrived in Morocco as far back as the ninth century. Grown almost exclusively by smallholder farmers in Taliouine, entire families pitch in during the intense harvesting time to cultivate, pick and process saffron. It has recently been planted elsewhere in Morocco, but Taliouine remains Morocco's undisputed saffron capital. The brutally hot summers and bitter cold winters give strength to the colour and pungency to the aroma, and the centuries of tradition assure that the highest-quality finished saffron gets to the market.

It's no surprise that saffron makes more frequent appearances in the kitchens of Taliouine. Along with going into tagines, couscous and soups, it is used for a fragrant Saffron Tea (page 422) and a Saffron Omelette (page 182). In both cases, a couple of saffron threads transform the simple into something more refined – and far more delicious.

'There is nothing so much adulterated as saffron,' Pliny the Elder wrote 2,000 years ago in *Natural History*. Little has changed. The world's most expensive spice is also its most falsified, with safflower petals and dyed coconut fibres substituted for *Crocus sativus* stigmas and turmeric sold as ground saffron.

For centuries, Spain was the world's largest producer of saffron. Today at least 90 per cent of the world's saffron is grown by Iran. Spain is the top buyer and it imports, repackages and sells the Iranian-grown spice. Morocco now produces more saffron than Spain.

BUYING AND USING SAFFRON

When buying saffron, purchase from a trusted source. Threads are more difficult to adulterate than ground saffron, making them the preferable option. Look for long, unbroken threads that are bright red to reddish-purple in colour.

Store saffron in a dark, cool place. Light will damage its potency.

When using high-quality saffron, just a small pinch of threads is required for most dishes. Using too much will give an unpleasant medicinal flavour to the food.

Saffron threads can be lightly dry-toasted in a small, ungreased frying pan over a medium-low heat for 1–3 minutes until aromatic and a darker shade of red. Leave to cool. Crumble with dry fingers or crush in a mortar with a pestle or the back of a spoon in a bowl to release their full potency. Be sure to rinse out the mortar and pestle or bowl with water to get every speck.

Especially when using in pastries and breads, some cooks prefer to steep the threads in warm water, milk or even oil and then incorporate the golden, aromatic liquid into the dough or dish. You can either discard the threads or use them in the recipe.

Rustic Omelette

MOROCCO
PREPARATION TIME: 5 minutes
COOKING TIME: 10 minutes
SERVES: 1

This simple omelette draws on the flavours of the Moroccan countryside – farm-fresh eggs, garlic, bay leaf and a generous pinch of cumin. With bread, some chewy black olives and a pot of Mint Tea (pages 417–421), it makes a hearty meal at any time of the day.

3 large eggs
ground cumin, for seasoning
2 tablespoons extra-virgin olive oil, plus extra
    for drizzling
3 cloves of garlic, crushed in the skin
1 bay leaf
salt and pepper

Put the eggs into a large bowl and, using a fork, beat together. Season with cumin, salt and pepper and beat again.

Heat the oil in a 25-cm/10-inch non-stick frying pan over a medium heat, add the garlic and cook, stirring frequently, for about 1 minute, or until aromatic and beginning to soften.

Pour the eggs into the pan, swirling the pan to keep the eggs from sticking. Lay the bay leaf in the centre. Cover the pan with a lid and cook over a low heat until the eggs are set, 3–5 minutes. Loosen the omelette with a thin spatula and slide onto a plate. Sprinkle with a pinch of cumin, drizzle with oil and serve immediately.

Frites-omelette

ALGERIA
PREPARATION TIME: 15 minutes
COOKING TIME: 25 minutes
SERVES: 2

Frites-omelette is one of Algeria's legendary and affordable fast foods. It's simple to make at home, especially if there are leftover Frites (fries, page 164). If using leftover Frites, cook long enough in the butter to warm them throughout. Stuffed into a baguette, this omelette makes a popular and inexpensive sandwich.

neutral oil, for frying
4 white potatoes (about 700 g/1 lb 8½ oz total),
    peeled and cut lengthwise into 1-cm-/½-inch-thick
    fries
4 large eggs
10 g/¼ oz (2 teaspoons) butter
salt and pepper

Heat an abundant amount of oil in a large, deep frying pan over a medium heat until the surface shimmers. Line a baking sheet with paper towels. Working in batches that don't crowd the pan or bring down the temperature of the oil, add the potatoes and fry until golden, about 10 minutes. Using a slotted spoon, transfer the potatoes to the paper towels to briefly drain.

Put the eggs into a large bowl and, using a fork, beat thoroughly until frothy, then season with salt and pepper.

Melt the butter in a 25-cm/10-inch non-stick frying pan over a medium heat, add the frites in an even layer in the pan, then pour in the egg mixture. Using a wooden spoon, distribute the egg evenly among the pan by lifting the frites and allowing the egg to flow under them. Cook until the eggs are set, about 3 minutes. Cover with a plate or lid and carefully flip, sliding the omelette gently back into the pan. Cook until the eggs are cooked through, about 2 minutes. Slide onto a plate and serve.

COUSCOUS,
PASTA,
RICE
AND GRAINS

COUSCOUS

Couscous is the Maghreb's iconic culinary staple. It is the name for both the 'grains' or granules of rolled and dried semolina and the dish itself.

From the Mediterranean shoreline to Saharan oases, mounds of steamed couscous moistened with a flavourful (and sometimes spicy) broth, topped with vegetables and pieces of meat or fish are devoured with gusto. Couscous is the biggest symbol of the North African kitchen.

VARIETIES OF COUSCOUS

There are different types and sizes of couscous. There are numerous popular commercial brands of couscous throughout the region that produce durum wheat couscous and sometimes barley couscous.

Durum wheat: Most couscous today is prepared from milled durum wheat called semolina (*smida* in Maghrebi Arabic). Durum wheat has a high gluten content, which helps couscous keep its shape while cooking. (See page 40 for more on semolina.)

Barley couscous (*belboula*): One of the original cereals used by Berbers to make couscous, barley continues to be popular, especially in Berber regions of Morocco and Algeria, where it is known in some Berber languages as *sksou n'timzin* or *sksou n'ibrine*. In Maghrebi Arabic it is called *belboula*, although in Tunisia and Libya it is generally called *malthouth*. Rather than being rolled from ground barley, it is made from pounded or crushed barley sieved for consistent size. It is darker and earthier than couscous made from semolina and takes slightly longer to steam. Look for packages that read *couscous al belboula, sakssou al belboula* or (in French) *couscous d'orge*. See page 192 for preparing barley couscous.

Other varieties: Couscous made from corn (called *baddaz* in Maghrebi Arabic) and millet tend to be hand-rolled and found mostly in rural Berber areas. They are very difficult to find commercially.

Sizes: The most common size is medium (look for the French *moyen* on packaging), followed by fine (*fin*), although some dishes might typically use a particular size, such as fine for sweet couscous (pages 218–221) or with the Moroccan caramelized onion and raisin topping called *tfaya* (page 208). The choice usually comes down to personal preference.

Quick cooking: Outside North Africa, much of the couscous sold in supermarkets (grocery stores) is touted as 'quick-cooking', 'instant' or 'precooked' (in French, *précuit*). Directions usually call for adding boiling water. This, though, can result in mushy, clumpy couscous. Follow the directions on page 191 for lighter, fluffier results.

COUSCOUSSIER

Couscous is steamed in a two-level pot called a couscoussier. The stew or water goes in the pot-bellied bottom, known as either *gedra* or *makfoul*. The grains are steamed in the perforated top section – the *keskas* or *kiskes* – that fits tightly over the top. The steam from the stew cooks the couscous grains above while bestowing them with flavour. Originally made of terracotta, today couscoussiers are usually of a light, inexpensive metal.

Filling the basket: It is key that the steaming basket is not overloaded. The goal is to have light, fluffy grains, so too much will compact down the bottom layer. The steaming basket should be no more than three-quarters full when adding the uncooked couscous, as it will expand. Steam in batches if needed.

Multiple steamings: The grains are steamed multiple times to ensure that all the grains cook evenly. Three steamings is typical. (Fine-size couscous often just needs two.) Between steamings, the couscous is sprinkled with water and any clumps are broken up.

Sealing the joint between the pot and steamer basket: All the steam needs to be forced up through the couscous grains in the perforated basket, so it is important that the two parts of the couscoussier have a good seal between them. To keep any steam from escaping, the traditional method painted a band of flour and water paste around the joint. Today it is more common to use a strip of aluminium foil or cling film (plastic wrap), set atop the rim of the bottom pot with the basket pressed snugly down over it.

Covering: In Morocco, couscous is nearly always steamed uncovered. Elsewhere in the region, some cooks cover the steaming basket – which means reducing the amount of time of each steaming and watching the final steaming to ensure the grains do not get gummy.

To substitute: A large saucepan with a colander or steamer basket fitted over the top will work. If the holes in the colander are too large and the couscous falls through, line it with a piece of muslin (cheesecloth) or a loosely woven muslin cloth. Be sure that there is a good seal between the bottom pot and basket and that steam does not escape around the edges.

COOKING WITH COUSCOUS

Cooking: The goal is light, fluffy and individual grains. Dry couscous needs to be moistened with cool water and left to stand and swell before being steamed two or three times in a two-tiered steamer pot called a couscoussier (see page 188). Between steamings, the grains are moistened with cool water and any clumps broken up. See pages 190–191 for steaming couscous in the traditional manner.

Quantities: As a general rule, calculate 80–115 g (3–4 oz/scant ½–½ cup) dry couscous per person. These recipes call for 500 g (1 lb 2 oz, about 3 cups) for 4–6 people, 600 g (1 lb 5 oz, about 3½ cups) for 6 people and 750 g (1⅔ lb, about 4½ cups) for 6–8 people. That said, there are many in the region who prepare a 1 kg (2¼ lb) bag for a family of 6. A generous mound is always impressive, and couscous is excellent leftover. So, without overloading the steamer basket (see page 188), make plenty.

Adding sauce to the steamed grains: After being steamed, couscous grains generally get just a ladle or two of brothy sauce before being topped with the vegetables, pulses and meat or fish, with bowls of remaining sauce served on the side to add as desired. Within families, though, there is often little agreement on just how much sauce to add. Some prefer the couscous drier with little sauce, others like it moistened well. As a result, it is common to find couscous spooned directly in individual bowls, with the sauce served on the side to add as desired.

Tunisian style: Tunisia has a different couscous treatment. The steamed grains are well soaked with sauce and absorb the liquid before being put on the serving platter and topped with vegetables and meat. There should be enough liquid to fully moisten and colour the couscous, but not leave it drenched. Dragging a spoon across the bottom of the bowl should show that the grains have a reddish colour but that there is not a layer of liquid underneath. Some Tunisians even use all the brothy sauce for the couscous and do not serve more on the side.

Serving: The traditional method of serving couscous is to form a generous single mound, make a well in the top for the meat or fish and arrange the vegetables along the sides in a decorative manner. Some houses, though, serve it in deep, individual bowls.

Steamed Medium Semolina Couscous

ALGERIA, LIBYA, MOROCCO, TUNISIA
PREPARATION TIME: 20 minutes,
plus resting time
COOKING TIME: 45 minutes
MAKES: 1.5 kg/3 lb (10 cups)
SERVES: 4–6

The three steamings required for medium couscous are generally for 15 minutes, 15 minutes and then 5–15 minutes or until done (the count begins when the steam comes up through the couscous). This method soaks with grains initially with plenty of liquid and then quickly drains it off. In another method for 500 g (1 lb 2 oz/3 cups) dry couscous, some cooks use 500 ml (18 fl oz/2 cups) salted water that they sprinkle on the grains in three parts, one-third before steaming, one-third after the first steaming and one-third after the second steaming. For 600 g (1 lb 5 oz/generous 3½ cups) of couscous, increase the water to 600 ml (20 fl oz/2½ cups). (See the directions for steaming barley couscous on page 192 for this method.) The final results of the two methods are similar. This recipe steams the grains over water, but the timing and process is the same if done over a simmering stew.

- 500 g/1 lb 2 oz (3 cups) medium semolina couscous
- 2 tablespoons olive oil
- 2 teaspoons salt
- 25 g/1 oz (2 tablespoons) butter, *smen* (page 412) or olive oil

Put the couscous into a large, wide bowl and cover with about 500 ml (18 fl oz/2 cups) cool water. Swirl and sift with your fingers in a circular motion for a few moments, then drain the water off completely by cupping a hand against the side of the bowl. Add 1 tablespoon of the oil and the salt, and work in using your fingers. Let the grains absorb the moisture for 10 minutes. Toss the grains with both hands, lifting the grains and letting them fall through your fingers. Work out any clumps by rubbing the palms of your hands together, letting the grains drop back into the bowl.

Meanwhile, fill the bottom part of a couscoussier with at least 7.5 cm/3 inches of lightly salted water, place a strip of aluminium foil or cling film (plastic wrap) around the rim to ensure a good seal between the sections and bring the water to a rolling boil.

Transfer the couscous to the steaming basket, handful by handful, rubbing out any clumps. Don't pack down. Place the basket snugly on top of the bottom section of the couscoussier so that no steam escapes from the seal in the joint from the first steaming. Steam, uncovered, for 15 minutes, starting the counting once the steam rises up through the couscous.

Turn the couscous out into the bowl. Break up any larger clumps with a wooden spoon. Leave to cool for a few minutes. Add the remaining 1 tablespoon of oil and sprinkle over 120 ml (4 fl oz/½ cup) cool water. Once the grains are cool enough to handle, rub them between the palms of your hands and lift and let them fall through your fingers. Once they have cooled completely, transfer the grains a handful at a time back to the steaming basket, rubbing them between the palms of your hands to work out any clumps.

Place the basket snugly on top of the bottom section of the couscoussier. Steam the couscous, uncovered, for 15 minutes, starting the counting once the steam rises up through the grains.

Turn the couscous out into the bowl. Break up any larger clumps with a wooden spoon and leave to cool for 5 minutes. Slowly sprinkle with 120 ml (4 fl oz/½ cup) cool water. Mix well with your hands, rubbing the grains gently between the palms of your hands and lifting and letting them fall through your fingers. Leave to stand for 5 minutes, or until cool. Check the water level in the couscoussier and add more if needed.

Transfer the grains a handful at a time back to the steaming basket, rubbing them between the palms of your hands to work out any clumps. Place the basket snugly on top of the bottom section of the couscoussier. Steam the couscous, uncovered, for 5–15 minutes, starting the counting once the steam rises up through the grains. Check the couscous for doneness. The grains should be tender not mushy.

Turn the couscous back out into the bowl and break up any larger clumps with a wooden spoon. Once the couscous is cool enough to handle, rake through the grains a final time with your fingers, making sure there are no clumps. Work in the butter with your fingers. Serve immediately or cover with a clean dish towel until serving.

Steamed Fine Semolina Couscous

ALGERIA, LIBYA, MOROCCO, TUNISIA
PREPARATION TIME: 20 minutes,
plus resting time
COOKING TIME: 30 minutes
MAKES: about 1 kg/2¼ lb (7 cups)
SERVES: 4–6

For the traditional steaming method, fine-size (calibre) couscous needs to be worked with more oil than medium size to ensure that it does not clump together. Two steamings is usually sufficient. This recipe steams the grains uncovered over water, but the timing is the same if done over a simmering stew. For 600 g (1 lb 5 oz/generous 3½ cups) of couscous, increase the water to 600 ml (20 fl oz/2½ cups).

2 teaspoons salt
500 g/1 lb 2 oz (3 cups) fine semolina couscous
3 tablespoons olive oil
25 g/1 oz (2 tablespoons) butter, *smen* (page 412)
    or olive oil

Pour 500 ml (18 fl oz/2 cups) water into a large jug (pitcher) and stir in the salt.

Put the couscous into a large, wide bowl, add 2 tablespoons of the oil and work with your fingers to coat all the grains. Pour in 250 ml (8 fl oz/1 cup) of the salty water and sift with your fingers in a circular motion for a few moments. Let the grains absorb the water for 5 minutes. Work out any clumps with your fingers and by rubbing the palms of your hands together.

Meanwhile, fill the bottom part of a couscoussier with at least 5 cm/2 inches of lightly salted water, place a strip of aluminium foil or cling film (plastic wrap) around the rim to ensure a good seal between the sections and bring the water to a rolling boil.

Transfer the couscous to the steaming basket, handful by handful, making sure that there are no clumps. Do not pack down. Place the basket snugly on top of the bottom section of the couscoussier so that no steam escapes from the seal in the joint for the first steaming. Steam, uncovered, for 15 minutes, starting the counting once the steam rises up through the couscous.

Turn the couscous out into the bowl. Break up any larger clumps with a wooden spoon. Add the remaining 1 tablespoon of oil and sprinkle over the remaining 250 ml (8 fl oz/1 cup) of salty water. Once the grains are cool enough to handle, rub them between the palms of your hands and lift and let them fall through your fingers. Once they have cooled completely, transfer the grains a handful at a time back to the steaming basket, rubbing them

between the palms of your hands to work out any clumps.

Place the basket snugly on top of the bottom section of the couscoussier. Steam the couscous, uncovered, for 15 minutes, starting the counting once the steam rises up through the grains. Check the couscous for doneness. The grains should be tender not mushy. Steam longer if needed.

Turn the couscous back out into the bowl and break up any larger clumps with a wooden spoon. Once the couscous is cool enough to handle, rake through the grains a final time with your fingers, making sure there are no clumps. Work in the butter. Serve immediately or cover with a clean dish towel until serving.

Quick Couscous

ALGERIA, LIBYA, MOROCCO, TUNISIA
PREPARATION TIME: 10 minutes,
plus resting time
COOKING TIME: 10 minutes
SERVES: 4–6

While most directions on packages of quick-cooking or 'instant' couscous call for covering the dry grains in boiling water, that generally leads to mushy couscous. Rather, use an equal volume of salted tepid water and allow the couscous to stand and absorb it for 15–20 minutes.

500 g/1 lb 2 oz (3 cups) medium or fine couscous
1 teaspoon fine salt
1 tablespoon olive oil
15 g/½ oz (1 tablespoon) butter or *smen* (page 412),
    optional

Pour the couscous into a very wide, shallow dish. Pour 750 ml (25 fl oz/3 cups) tepid water into a large jug (pitcher), add the salt and stir to dissolve, then pour over the couscous. Jiggle the dish to settle and leave to stand undisturbed for 15–20 minutes until tender.

Meanwhile, preheat the oven to 180°C/350°F/ Gas Mark 4.

Rake the couscous with a fork and fluff, then drizzle with the oil. Using both hands, lift the grains and let them fall through your fingers. Work out any clumps by rubbing the grains gently between the palms of your hands. Transfer to a large baking dish and place in the oven until it begins to steam, about 10 minutes. Toss with the butter (if using).

Pile the grains onto a serving platter and fluff with a fork.

Barley Couscous

ALGERIA, LIBYA, MOROCCO, TUNISIA
PREPARATION TIME: 20 minutes,
plus resting time
COOKING TIME: 1 hour
MAKES: 1.2 kg/2½ lb (8 cups);
SERVES: 4–6

While the method for steaming barley couscous (*belboula*) is the same as with semolina couscous, it takes an additional 5 minutes or so for each steaming. This recipe steams the grains uncovered over water, but the timing is the same if done over a simmering stew. For 600 g (1 lb 5 oz/generous 3½ cups) of couscous, increase the water to 650 ml (22 fl oz/2¾ cups).

2 teaspoons salt
500 g/1 lb 2 oz (scant 3 cups) barley couscous
2 tablespoons olive oil
25 g/1 oz (2 tablespoons) butter, *smen* (page 412) or olive oil

Pour 525 ml (18 fl oz/2¼ cups) water into a large jug (pitcher), add the salt and stir to dissolve.

Put the couscous into a large, wide bowl, add 1 tablespoon of the oil and work into the grains with your fingers. Add 175 ml (6 fl oz/¾ cup) of the salted water and sift with your fingers in a circular motion for a few moments. Let the grains absorb the water for 5 minutes, then work out any clumps with your fingers and by rubbing the palms of your hands together.

Meanwhile, fill the bottom part of a couscoussier with at least 7.5 cm/3 inches of lightly salted water, place a strip of aluminium foil or cling film (plastic wrap) around the rim to ensure a good seal between the sections and bring the water to a rolling boil.

Transfer the couscous to the steaming basket, handful by handful, rubbing out any clumps. Don't pack down. Place the basket snugly on top of the bottom section of the couscoussier so that no steam escapes from the seal in the joint for the first steaming. Steam, uncovered, for 20 minutes, starting the counting once the steam rises up through the couscous.

Turn the couscous out into the bowl. Break up any larger clumps with a wooden spoon. Add the remaining 1 tablespoon of oil and sprinkle over 175 ml (6 fl oz/¾ cup) of the salted water. Once the grains are cool enough to handle, rub them between the palms of your hands and lift and let them fall through your fingers. Once they have cooled completely, transfer the grains a handful at a time back to the steaming basket, rubbing them between the palms of your hands to work out any clumps.

Place the basket snugly on top of the bottom section of the couscoussier. Steam the couscous, uncovered, for 20 minutes, starting the counting once the steam rises up through the grains.

Turn the couscous out into the bowl and break up any larger clumps with a wooden spoon. Leave to cool for 5 minutes. Slowly sprinkle over the remaining 175 ml (6 fl oz/¾ cup) of the salted water. Once cool enough to handle, mix well with your hands, rubbing the grains gently between the palms of your hands and lifting and letting them fall through your fingers. Leave to cool for about 5 minutes. Check the water level in the couscoussier and add more if needed.

Transfer the grains a handful at a time back to the steaming basket, rubbing them between the palms of your hands to work out any clumps. Place the basket snugly on top of the bottom section of the couscoussier. Steam the couscous, uncovered, for 10–20 minutes, starting the counting once the steam rises up through the grains. Check the couscous for doneness. The grains should be tender not mushy.

Turn the couscous back out into the bowl. Break up any larger clumps with a wooden spoon. Once the couscous is cool enough to handle, rake through the grains a final time with your fingers, making sure there are no clumps. Work in the butter. Serve immediately or cover with a clean dish towel until serving.

Winter Vegetarian Couscous

TUNISIA
PREPARATION TIME: 30 minutes,
plus overnight soaking and resting time
COOKING TIME: 1 hour 30 minutes
SERVES: 4

This vegetarian Tunisian couscous is especially popular in winter when lots of good root vegetables fill market stalls. It's hearty, healthy and flavourful. Use the vegetables that the season offers.

100 g/3½ oz (½ cup) dried chickpeas (garbanzo beans)
500 g/1 lb 2 oz (3 cups) medium couscous
3 tablespoons olive oil, plus extra for preparing the couscous
1 red or yellow onion, finely chopped
4 cloves of garlic, minced
2 tomatoes, halved crosswise and grated (see page 445), peel discarded
1 heaped tablespoon double concentrated tomato purée (paste)
harissa (page 409), to taste, plus extra to serve
1 fennel bulb, quartered
3 carrots, halved crosswise and then lengthwise
3 turnips, peeled and halved lengthwise
6 sprigs flat-leaf parsley, tied together
2 generous pieces of seeded pumpkin or butternut squash, with the peel (about 500 g/1 lb 2 oz)
1 wedge green cabbage (about 175 g/6 oz)
2 long sweet green peppers, halved lengthwise, cored and seeded
1 teaspoon sweet paprika
2 pinches of ground caraway
2 pinches of ground coriander seeds
salt and pepper

Put the chickpeas into a large bowl, cover with abundant water and leave to soak overnight. The next day, drain and rinse and set aside.

If steaming the couscous in a couscoussier over the stew, see the directions on page 190, adding ingredients to the stew before and between steamings as needed and omitting the butter. For other methods of preparing couscous, see page 189. For details on cooking with a couscoussier, including alternatives, see page 188. For quick-cooking couscous, prepare it following the directions on page 191.

Heat the oil in the bottom of a couscoussier over a high heat, add the onion and cook for 5 minutes, stirring frequently. Stir in the garlic, then add the tomatoes, tomato purée (paste), 4 tablespoons water and harissa and cook for 5 minutes. Add the chickpeas (garbanzo beans), fennel, carrots, turnips

and parsley. Pour in 1 litre (34 fl oz/4¼ cups) of hot water, bring to the boil and gently boil for 45 minutes. (If there is no steaming basket on top, loosely cover the pot.) Add the pumpkin, cabbage, peppers, paprika, caraway and coriander, season with salt and pepper and cook until all of the vegetables are tender, about 30 minutes.

To serve, put the couscous into a large bowl. Gradually moisten with about 500 ml (18 fl oz/ 2 cups) of the broth, turning the couscous to mix well. Cover and leave to stand for 5–10 minutes. Add a touch more broth if the couscous can absorb it without becoming too soggy. Mound the couscous and arrange some of the vegetables attractively around it. Serve with the remaining vegetables on a platter, the broth in a bowl on the side and some harissa in a dish to add as desired.

Seven Vegetable Couscous

MOROCCO
PREPARATION TIME: 30 minutes,
plus soaking and resting time
COOKING TIME: 1 hour 30 minutes
SERVES: 6–8

Many in Morocco would call this couscous with
seven vegetables the country's national dish. This
is especially true in urban areas, where a wide
choice of vegetables is always available, or on
the fertile plains in the west that are well known
for their agriculture. The choice of vegetables
varies throughout the season, from fresh broad
(fava) beans and artichokes in spring to fennel in
winter and pumpkin or squash in autumn. While
the number seven is auspicious throughout Islam,
couscous aux sept légumes often has – season allowing
– more than seven different types of vegetables (as
in this recipe). If using canned chickpeas (garbanzo
beans) rather than dried ones, rinse and add with
the pumpkin and courgettes (zucchini).

100 g/3½ oz (½ cup) dried chickpeas
   (garbanzo beans)
750 g/1⅔ lb (4½ cups) medium couscous
500 g/1 lb 2 oz bone-in lamb leg, shoulder or neck,
   or beef shanks, cut into 6–8 pieces
2 red or yellow onions, quartered
1 tablespoon sweet paprika
pinch of saffron threads, crumbled
2 tablespoons olive oil, plus extra for preparing the
   couscous
4 carrots, halved crosswise and lengthwise
2 turnips, peeled and halved lengthwise
4 ripe tomatoes, quartered
12 sprigs flat-leaf parsley
12 sprigs coriander (cilantro)
2 wedges green cabbage (about 250 g/9 oz total)
2 white potatoes, peeled and quartered lengthwise
400 g/14 oz pumpkin or butternut squash, peeled,
   seeded and cut into 7.5 × 5-cm/3 × 2-inch pieces
2 courgettes (zucchini), scrubbed but not peeled,
   halved lengthwise and then crosswise
2 long sweet green peppers, halved lengthwise and
   seeded
25 g/1 oz (2 tablespoons) butter, cut into small pieces
salt and pepper

Put the dried chickpeas (garbanzo beans) into
a large bowl, pour in abundant water to cover
and leave to soak overnight. The next day, drain
and rinse.

If steaming the couscous in a couscoussier
over the stew, see the directions on page 190,
adding ingredients to the stew before and between
steamings as needed. For other methods of preparing
couscous, see page 189. For details on cooking with
a couscoussier, including alternatives, see page 188.
For quick-cooking couscous, prepare it following
the directions on page 191, warming it until steaming
in the oven before serving.

Put the lamb, onions, paprika and saffron into the
bottom of a large couscoussier. Season with salt and
pepper and add the oil. Swirl to coat, then cook over
a medium heat for 5 minutes. Add 1.5 litres (50 fl oz/
generous 6 cups) of hot water and bring to the boil.
Add the chickpeas, carrots, turnips and tomatoes.
Fold the parsley and coriander (cilantro) sprigs,
tie into a tight bundle with kitchen string and add.
Cook for 30 minutes. (If there is no steaming basket
on top, loosely cover the pot.) Add the cabbage
and cook for 20 minutes. Add the potatoes, squash,
courgettes (zucchini) and peppers and cook for a
final 30 minutes. Remove and discard the parsley
and coriander, then carefully transfer the vegetables
and meat to a large platter with a slotted spoon.

To serve, fluff the warm couscous, add the butter
and toss the couscous until coated. Either on a large
round serving platter or in individual bowls, gently
mound the couscous and make a well in the centre.
Place the meat in the well surrounded by vegetables.
Scatter chickpeas around the edges and ladle over
some broth. Serve with the remaining broth in a bowl
to add as desired and, if needed, the remaining
vegetables on the side.

Kabyle Couscous with Steamed Vegetables

ALGERIA
PREPARATION TIME: 30 minutes,
plus resting time
COOKING TIME: 1 hour 20 minutes
SERVES: 4

Known as a*makfoul* (or sometimes *mesfouf*), this rustic Berber couscous from Algeria's mountainous Kabylia region is a famous sauceless one: the vegetables are steamed under a layer of couscous in the steamer basket and then tossed with olive oil.

500 g/1 lb 2 oz (3 cups) medium couscous
1 red onion, finely sliced
1 white potato, peeled and diced
1 turnip, peeled and diced
1 courgette (zucchini), diced
1 carrot, diced
250 g/9 oz green beans, cut into bite-size pieces
1 teaspoon sweet paprika
extra-virgin olive oil, for drizzling
salt and pepper
2 Hard-Boiled Eggs (page 443), peeled and cut into wedges, to garnish
lben (buttermilk) or milk, to serve

Put the couscous into a large, shallow bowl, sprinkle with 120 ml (4 fl oz/½ cup) water, toss and leave to swell for 10 minutes. Rake with your fingers through the grains and break up any clumps. Transfer to the steaming basket.

Meanwhile, in the bottom of a couscoussier, bring about 2 litres (68 fl oz/generous 2 quarts/8½ cups) lightly salted water to the boil.

Place the basket firmly over the couscoussier and steam, uncovered, for 15 minutes, beginning the timing when the steam rises up through the surface of the couscous. Dump the couscous into the bowl and sprinkle with about 120 ml (4 fl oz/½ cup) water. Once cool enough, rake the grains with your fingers to break up any clumps.

Put the onion, potato, turnip, courgette (zucchini), carrot and green beans into the bottom of the empty steamer basket. Sprinkle with the paprika and season with salt and pepper. Cover the vegetables with the couscous. Place the basket snugly back on top of the couscoussier and steam, uncovered, until the vegetables and couscous are both done, 30–40 minutes.

Tip the couscous and vegetables into a wide serving bowl, drizzle with olive oil and toss. Divide among bowls and garnish with hard-boiled eggs. Serve with glasses of *lben*.

Couscous with Fresh Peas and Broad Beans

ALGERIA
PREPARATION TIME: 30 minutes,
plus resting time
COOKING TIME: 45 minutes
SERVES: 4

Mesfouf is another beloved sauceless couscous, especially around Algiers. This version has both peas and fresh broad (fava) beans but is often made with only peas. For that, simply double the amount of peas in the recipe below. For a hint of sweetness, add a small handful of raisins. Soften the raisins in a small heatproof bowl of warm water for about 10 minutes before adding with the couscous for the final steaming. This dish is usually served with a glass of *lben* (buttermilk).

350 g/12 oz (2 cups) medium couscous
150 g/5 oz shelled fresh peas (about 1¼ cups)
150 g/5 oz shelled fresh broad (fava) beans (about 1¼ cups)
40 g/1½ oz (3 tablespoons) butter, cut into small pieces
extra-virgin olive oil, for drizzling
salt
lben (buttermilk) or milk, to serve

Fill a couscoussier or a large pot fitted with a steamer basket with at least 5 cm/2 inches of lightly salted water. Steam the couscous until tender following the directions on page 190.

Meanwhile, in another steamer basket over a large pot or saucepan with at least 5 cm/2 inches of boiling water, steam the peas and broad (fava) beans until tender, about 15 minutes.

Turn the couscous out into a large serving dish. Season with salt, add the butter and turn to coat. Add the peas and broad beans to the couscous and toss to blend. Transfer to a serving platter and drizzle with olive oil. Serve with glasses of *lben*.

Spring Couscous with Lamb

TUNISIA
PREPARATION TIME: 30 minutes,
plus resting and soaking time
COOKING TIME: 2 hours
SERVES: 6

Full of spring's bounty, this seasonal couscous
with broad (fava) beans, artichokes and courgettes
(zucchini) has lamb to give it flavour. If catching the
fennel season in Tunisia – December to April – add
a quartered fennel bulb with the artichokes.

600 g/1 lb 5 oz (generous 3½ cups) medium couscous
3 tablespoons olive oil, plus extra for preparing the
    couscous
1 red or yellow onion, finely chopped
6 generous pieces of bone-in lamb
4 cloves of garlic, minced
2 tomatoes, halved crosswise and grated,
    peel discarded (see page 445)
1 heaped tablespoon double concentrated tomato
    purée (paste)
harissa (page 409), optional
500 g/1 lb 2 oz fresh broad (fava) beans in their pods,
    shelled, or 125 g/4¼ oz (1 cup) shelled beans
2 celery stalks, cut into 5-cm/2-inch pieces
6 sprigs flat-leaf parsley, tied together
1 lemon wedge
2 artichokes
2 white potatoes, peeled and quartered
2 long sweet green peppers, halved lengthwise, cored
    and seeded
1 courgette (zucchini), cut into 4-cm-/1½-inch-long
    pieces
1 teaspoon sweet paprika
2 pinches of ground caraway
2 pinches of ground coriander seeds
pinch of grated nutmeg
salt and pepper

If steaming the couscous in a couscoussier over
the stew, see the directions on page 190, adding
ingredients to the stew before and between
steamings as needed and omitting the butter. For
other methods of preparing couscous, see page 189.
For details on cooking with a couscoussier, including
alternatives, see page 188. For quick-cooking
couscous, prepare it following the directions on
page 191.

Heat the oil in the bottom of a couscoussier over
a high heat, add the onion and lamb and cook,
uncovered, for 5 minutes, stirring frequently. Stir in
the garlic, then the tomatoes, tomato purée (paste),
4 tablespoons water and harissa (if using) and cook

for 2–3 minutes. Add 1 litre (34 fl oz/4¼ cups)
of hot water, bring to the boil and gently boil for
45 minutes. (If there is no steaming basket on top,
loosely cover the pot.) Add the broad (fava) beans,
celery and parsley and cook for 30 minutes.

Meanwhile, fill a large bowl with cool water.
Squeeze in the lemon wedge, then drop into the
water. Working with one artichoke at a time, cut
or pull away the toughest outer petals, then cut off
the stem and trim away the top section. Quarter
lengthwise, then remove the choke and drop into
the lemon water to keep from discolouring. Repeat
with the remaining artichokes. Leave in the water
until ready to use.

Drain the artichokes and add to the pot together
with the potatoes, peppers, courgette (zucchini),
paprika, caraway, coriander and nutmeg. Season with
salt and pepper and cook until the vegetables are
tender, about 30 minutes.

To serve, put the couscous into a large bowl.
Gradually moisten with about 600 ml (20 fl oz/
2½ cups) of the broth, turning the couscous to mix
well. Cover and leave to stand for 5–10 minutes.
Add a touch more broth if the couscous can absorb
it without becoming too soggy. Mound the couscous
and make a well in the centre. Place some of the
meat in the well and arrange some of the vegetables
attractively around it. Serve with the remaining
vegetables and meat on a platter, with the broth
in a bowl on the side to add as desired.

Couscous with Lamb and Meatballs

ALGERIA
PREPARATION TIME: 30 minutes,
plus overnight soaking if using dried
beans and resting time
COOKING TIME: 2 hours
SERVES: 4–6

A favourite in Constantine and Annaba, *keskkou mhawer* is made from fine (rather than medium) couscous, presented with cinnamon-scented 'white sauce' – no paprika, tomatoes or tomato purée (paste) – and topped with meatballs and hard-boiled eggs. Directions for using both dried chickpeas (garbanzo beans) and canned ones are included.

100 g/3½ oz (½ cup) dried chickpeas (garbanzo beans) or 175 g/6 oz (1 cup) canned, rinsed
500 g/1 lb 2 oz (3 cups) fine couscous
3 tablespoons olive oil, for preparing the couscous
40 g/1½ oz (3 tablespoons) butter
1 tablespoon *smen* (page 412), optional
700 g/1 lb 8½ oz bone-in lamb leg or shoulder, cut into generous pieces
3 red or yellow onions, grated
2 cloves of garlic, minced
250 g/9 oz minced (ground) beef
½ teaspoon ground cinnamon
25 g/1 oz (2 tablespoons) butter, *smen* (page 412) or olive oil, for finishing the couscous
salt and pepper
4 Hard-boiled Eggs (page 443), peeled and cut into wedges, to garnish

If using dried chickpeas (garbanzo beans), put them into a large bowl, pour in abundant water to cover and leave to soak overnight. The next day, drain and rinse. Set aside.

If steaming the couscous in a couscoussier over the stew, see the directions on page 191, adding ingredients to the stew before and between steamings as needed. For other methods of preparing couscous, see page 189. For details on cooking with a couscoussier, including alternatives, see page 188. For quick-cooking couscous, prepare it following the directions on page 191, warming it until steaming in the oven before serving.

Put 25 g (1 oz/2 tablespoons) of the butter, the *smen* (if using), the lamb and two-thirds of the onions into the bottom of a couscoussier. Season with salt and pepper and brown over a medium heat for about 10 minutes. Stir in half of the garlic, add the soaked chickpeas (if using dried) and pour in 1 litre (34 fl oz/4¼ cups) of hot water. Bring to a low

boil and gently boil for 1 hour 15 minutes. (If there is no steaming basket on top, loosely cover the pot.)

Meanwhile, prepare the meatballs. Put the minced (ground) beef, remaining onion, remaining garlic and ¼ teaspoon of the cinnamon into a large bowl and season with salt and pepper. Using moistened hands, roll the mixture into meatballs about 3 cm/1¼ inches in diameter. There should be about 16 meatballs. Melt the remaining 15 g (½ oz/1 tablespoon) of the butter in a large frying pan over a medium-high heat, add the meatballs and cook for about 5 minutes until browned. Remove from the heat and set aside until ready to add.

Add the meatballs, chickpeas (if using canned) and remaining ¼ teaspoon of cinnamon to the pot and gently boil for 30 minutes.

To serve, fluff the warm the couscous, add the butter and toss until coated. Either on a large round serving platter or in individual bowls, gently mound the couscous and make a well in the centre. Place the meat in the well, surround with meatballs and chickpeas and ladle over some broth. Garnish with hard-boiled eggs and serve with the remaining broth in a bowl on the side to add as desired.

Festive Lamb Couscous with Nuts and Raisins

TUNISIA
PREPARATION TIME: 30 minutes,
plus resting and soaking time
COOKING TIME: 2 hours 20 minutes
SERVES: 6

This is an elegant lamb couscous with plenty of nuts. The combination of textures and flavours is exquisite. If desired, at the beginning of cooking, add a handful of dried chickpeas (garbanzo beans) that have been soaked overnight. If it is for a special occasion, garnish with peeled but still whole Hard-boiled Eggs (page 443).

600 g/1 lb 5 oz (generous 3½ cups) medium couscous
1.5 kg/3¼ lb bone-in lamb leg or shoulder, cut into 8–12 pieces
2 tablespoons olive oil, plus extra for preparing the couscous
2 red or yellow onions, quartered
pinch of saffron threads, crumbled
½ teaspoon ground ginger
½ teaspoon ground turmeric
1 heaped tablespoon double concentrated tomato purée (paste)
1 carrot, halved lengthwise
1 turnip, peeled and halved lengthwise
1 cinnamon stick or piece of cinnamon bark
35 g/1¼ oz (¼ cup) seedless raisins, preferably golden sultanas (golden raisins)
25 g/1 oz (2 tablespoons) butter
35 g/1¼ oz (¼ cup) roasted almonds (see page 445)
30 g/1 oz (¼ cup) pine nuts
25 g/1 oz (¼ cup) shelled pistachios
salt and pepper
harissa (page 409), to serve, optional

If steaming the couscous in a couscoussier over the stew, see the directions on page 190, adding ingredients to the stew before and between steamings as needed and omitting the butter. For other methods of preparing couscous, see page 189. For details on cooking with a couscoussier, including alternatives, see page 188. For quick-cooking couscous, prepare it following the directions on page 191.

Generously season the lamb with salt and pepper. Add the oil, onions and lamb to the bottom of a large couscoussier and cook over a medium-high heat, stirring frequently, until the onions have softened and the lamb browned, about 15 minutes. Stir in the saffron, ginger, turmeric, tomato purée (paste) and 4 tablespoons water and cook for 5 minutes. Add the carrot, turnip and cinnamon, pour in 1 litre (34 fl oz/4¼ cups) of hot water and bring to the boil. Reduce the heat to medium-low and gently boil until the lamb is very tender, about 2 hours. (If there is no steaming basket on top, loosely cover the pot.) Add more water if needed.

Meanwhile, put the raisins into a small heatproof bowl, cover with lukewarm water and leave to soak for 10 minutes to soften. Drain. Melt the butter in a small saucepan over a low heat, add the almonds, pine nuts, pistachios and soaked raisins and cook until the nuts are browned and the raisins plump, 3–5 minutes. Transfer to a bowl.

To serve, put the couscous into a large bowl. Gradually moisten with about 500 ml (18 fl oz/2 cups) of the broth, turning the couscous to mix well. Cover and leave to stand for 5–10 minutes. Add a touch more broth if the couscous can absorb it without becoming too soggy. Mound the couscous and make a well in the centre. Place the lamb in the well and top with the raisins and nuts. Serve with the remaining broth in a bowl on the side to add as desired along with a dish of harissa (if using).

Spicy Lamb Couscous with Onion and Chickpea Topping

LIBYA
PREPARATION TIME: 30 minutes,
plus resting time
COOKING TIME: 1 hour 45 minutes
SERVES: 6

Libyan couscous often has a kick of cayenne pepper in it and a lot of onions. The most famous version is topped with a savoury onion and chickpea (garbanzo bean) sauce called *busla* (Libyan Arabic for onion). While some cooks steam the onion slices before finishing in the pan with a bit of sauce, this recipe cooks them in a large frying pan. The dish calls for *bzaar* (page 446), a spice blend centred on turmeric, ginger, cinnamon and black pepper.

600 g/1 lb 5 oz (generous 3½ cups) medium couscous
3 tablespoons olive oil, plus extra for preparing the couscous
3 red or yellow onions, sliced
1 kg/2¼ lb bone-in lamb, cut into 6 or so generous pieces
2 tablespoons double concentrated tomato purée (paste)
1 tablespoon bzaar spice blend (page 446)
1 teaspoon cayenne pepper or to taste
2 carrots, halved lengthwise and then crosswise
2 white potatoes, peeled and quartered
2 courgettes (zucchini), halved lengthwise and then crosswise
salt and pepper
2 Hard-boiled Eggs (page 443), to garnish

For the busla topping:
2 tablespoons olive oil
8 red or yellow onions, sliced
175 g/6 oz (1 cup) canned chickpeas (garbanzo beans), rinsed, or cooked dried chickpeas (page 443)
½ teaspoon ground cinnamon
5 cloves

If steaming the couscous in a couscoussier over the stew, see the directions on page 190, adding ingredients to the stew before and between steamings as needed and omitting the butter. For other methods of preparing couscous, see page 189. For details on cooking with a couscoussier, including alternatives, see page 188. For quick-cooking couscous, prepare it following the directions on page 191.

Heat the oil in the bottom of a couscoussier over a medium-high heat, add the onions and cook until they begin to soften, about 5 minutes. Add the meat and cook for 5 minutes, or until browned on each side. Stir in the tomato purée (paste) and 4 tablespoons water and cook for 2–3 minutes stirring frequently. Add the bzaar spice blend, cayenne pepper and carrots. Pour in 1.2 litres (40 fl oz/5 cups) of hot water and bring to the boil. Reduce the heat to medium-low and gently boil for 1 hour. (If there is no steaming basket on top, loosely cover the pot.) Add the potatoes and cook for 15 minutes. Add the courgettes (zucchini) and cook for a final 15 minutes.

MEANWHILE, PREPARE THE BUSLA TOPPING: Add the oil and onions to a large frying pan, cover with a lid and cook first over a medium heat, then over a low heat until translucent, about 30 minutes. Make sure the onions don't burn. Add the chickpeas (garbanzo beans), cinnamon, cloves and 2 ladles of the sauce from the couscoussier. Season with salt and pepper and cook, uncovered, until very tender and saucy, about 10 minutes. Remove from the heat and keep covered until ready to serve.

To serve, put the couscous into a large, shallow serving bowl and moisten with about 250 ml (8 fl oz/1 cup) of the broth, turning the couscous to mix well. Mound the couscous and make a well in the centre. Place the meat in the well and some sauce and arrange the vegetables around the sauce. Drizzle over a ladle of broth. Cover with the busla topping and arrange the hard-boiled eggs around the edges. Serve with the remaining broth in a bowl on the side to add as desired.

Barley Couscous
with Vegetables and Lamb

ALGERIA, MOROCCO
PREPARATION TIME: 30 minutes,
plus resting time
COOKING TIME: 1 hour 45 minutes
SERVES: 6

This ancestral dish with one of the original cereals that Berbers used for rolling couscous is hearty and satisfying. *Berboula* is darker, has denser and nuttier flavours and takes slightly longer to steam than its durum wheat sibling. If in season, add some fresh broad (fava) beans.

600 g/1 lb 5 oz (3½ cups) barley couscous
750 g/1⅔ lb bone-in lamb neck, ribs, leg and/or
   shoulder, cut into generous pieces
2 red or yellow onions, quartered
4 ripe tomatoes, quartered
1 tablespoon sweet paprika
1 teaspoon ground ginger
1 teaspoon ground cumin
pinch of saffron threads, crumbled
3 tablespoons olive oil, plus extra for preparing the
   couscous
2 carrots, halved lengthwise and then crosswise
2 turnips, peeled and quartered lengthwise
2 white potatoes, peeled and quartered
500 g/1 lb 2 oz pumpkin or butternut squash, peeled,
   seeded and cut into generous pieces
1 small aubergine (eggplant), halved lengthwise
2 courgettes (zucchini), halved lengthwise and then
   crosswise
12 sprigs coriander (cilantro), tied together
25 g/1 oz (2 tablespoons) butter or *smen* (page 412), cut
   into small pieces
salt and pepper

If steaming the couscous in a couscoussier over the stew, see the directions on page 192, adding ingredients to the stew before and between steamings as needed. For other methods of preparing couscous, see page 189. For details on cooking with a couscoussier, including alternatives, see page 188.

Add the lamb, onions, tomatoes, paprika, ginger, cumin and saffron to the bottom of a couscoussier. Season with salt and pepper and moisten with the oil. Swirl to coat, then cook over a medium heat for 10 minutes, stirring from time to time. Add 1 litre (34 fl oz/4¼ cups) of hot water, bring to the boil and cook for 30 minutes. (If there is no steaming basket on top, loosely cover the pot.) Add the carrots, turnips and potatoes and cook for 30 minutes. Add the pumpkin, aubergine (eggplant), courgettes (zucchini), coriander (cilantro) and 250 ml (8 fl oz/1 cup) water and cook for a final 30 minutes.

To serve, fluff the warm couscous, add the butter and toss until coated. Either on a large round serving platter or in individual bowls, gently mound the couscous and make a well in the centre. Place the meat in the well surrounded by vegetables and ladle over some broth. Serve with the remaining broth in a bowl on the side to add as desired.

Lamb Couscous with 'Red Sauce'

ALGERIA
PREPARATION TIME: 30 minutes, plus overnight
soaking if using dried chickpeas and resting time
COOKING TIME: 2 hours
SERVES: 6

This classic Algerian recipe is particularly popular
in the east of the country. Depending on the season,
home cooks might add fresh broad (fava) beans
or squash. If fresh ripe tomatoes aren't available,
use whole canned ones. Add a generous pinch of
cinnamon at the end, if desired.

100 g/3½ oz (½ cup) dried chickpeas (garbanzo
beans) or 175 g/6 oz (1 cup) canned, rinsed
600 g/1 lb 5 oz (generous 3½ cups) medium couscous
3 tablespoons olive oil, plus extra for preparing the
couscous

◇

1 kg/2¼ lb bone-in lamb leg or shoulder, cut into
generous pieces
1 onion, grated
3 ripe tomatoes, halved crosswise and grated, peel
discarded (see page 445)
1 heaped tablespoon double concentrated tomato
purée (paste)
½ teaspoon sweet paprika
2 carrots, halved lengthwise
2 turnips, peeled and quartered lengthwise
2 courgettes (zucchini), cut into 2.5-cm/1-inch pieces
25 g/1 oz (2 tablespoons) butter, cut into small pieces
salt and pepper

If using dried chickpeas (garbanzo beans), put them
into a large bowl, pour in abundant water to cover
and leave to soak overnight. The next day, drain and
rinse. Set aside.

If steaming the couscous in a couscoussier over
the stew, see the directions on page 190, adding
ingredients to the stew before and between

PRESERVED MEAT

Salted, seasoned and sun-dried strips of lamb or beef
are an ancient way of keeping butchered meat longer. Once
prepared for practical reasons, preserving meat now is largely
done for the unique flavour that it adds to a dish. In Morocco,
khlii (or *khlea*) – a confit of seasoned, salted and air-dried
meat – is a quintessential and still popular preserve.

To make *khlii*, the meat has to first be dried. Strips of beef (also
camel in the south) are rubbed in salt and spices – garlic, sweet
paprika, ground cumin and ground coriander – and left to
season overnight. Hung out in the sun for a couple of days, they
get brought inside in the evening to avoid night-time moisture.
Once fully dried, the preserved meat is called *gueddid* or *kaddid*,
depending on the area. The strips, with their long fibres, are
cut with kitchen scissors into pieces. These can be rehydrated
and used to season soups and so on.

Often *gueddid* is used to make *khlii*. The dried pieces are
cooked in olive oil, some fat (usually suet, the hard fat from
around the kidneys) and water until the moisture has completely
evaporated and the meat tender. It is then submerged in rendered
fat and olive oil in a sealed jar, and *khlii* can be kept like this
for a long time. The region of Fès generally gets credit for
perfecting the art of making *khlii*, and it remains deeply
popular in the city, where it is widely available in the markets.
Agriss is a less expensive version with small shreds of meat. *Khlii*
imparts its unique flavour most commonly in lentils (page 144),
certain tagines, couscous and, in Fès, most famously with fried
eggs (page 174) for breakfast or a quick meal. In stews, it is treated
just like meat, although less salt is needed in the dish. Some cooks
add a bit of the conserving fat in the jar to the pan with *khlii*.

In Tunisia and Algeria, preserved meat is called *kaddid*,
while in Libya it is usually spelled *gueddid*. In Tunisia it is common
to prepare using part of the lamb butchered for the Eid al-Adha
celebration (see page 34). The meat typically gets seasoned with
a blend of salt, garlic, ground coriander, dried mint, harissa
and olive oil in Tunisia, while many Algerians favour a blend of
salt, garlic, caraway, coriander, cumin and paprika. The strips of
meat are hung on clotheslines in the sun to dry and then stored in
sealed jars with olive oil or, these days, in the freezer. Especially
in winter, it is typical to find it in soups, potages with small,
pellet-shaped pasta called *mhamsa* or *berkoukès* (page 228) and in
couscous. For the Islamic New Year, many Tunisians prepare a
couscous with *kaddid* and dried broad (fava) beans (page 207).

steamings as needed. For other methods of preparing couscous, see page 189. For details on cooking with a couscoussier, including alternatives, see page 188. For quick-cooking couscous, prepare it following the directions on page 191, warming it until steaming in the oven before serving.

Put the oil and meat into the bottom of a large couscoussier, season with salt and pepper and swirl the pot. Cook the meat over a high heat for about 5 minutes until brown. Add the onion, tomatoes, tomato purée (paste) and 4 tablespoons water and cook for 5 minutes. Add the paprika, soaked chickpeas (if using dried), carrots and turnips. Pour in 1 litre (34 fl oz/4¼ cups) of hot water and bring to the boil. Reduce the heat to medium-low and gently boil for 1 hour. (If there is no steaming basket on top, loosely cover the pot.) Add the courgettes (zucchini) and chickpeas (if using canned) and gently boil until tender, about 40 minutes.

To serve, fluff the warm couscous, add the butter and toss until coated. Either on a large round serving platter or in individual bowls, gently mound the couscous and make a well in the centre. Place the meat in the well, surround with the vegetables and chickpeas and ladle over some broth. Serve with the remaining broth in a bowl on the side to add as desired.

New Year Couscous with Preserved Meat and Dried Broad Beans

TUNISIA
PREPARATION TIME: 45 minutes,
plus overnight soaking and resting time
COOKING TIME: 1 hour 20 minutes
SERVES: 4–6

For the Ras el-Am el-Hijri holiday – the Islamic New Year also known as Muharram – many Tunisians prepare a couscous with seasoned, salted and air-dried meat (*kaddid*, see page 206) and often either dried broad (fava) beans or chickpeas (garbanzo beans). Some add raisins as well. Versions in Nabeul put bean-size sweets (candies) in different colours on top as well. Peeling the broad beans is time consuming but necessary, as the outer skins of large beans remain tough, even with long cooking. The peeled beans are easily split in half, which helps reduce their cooking time to about 1 hour. Some people omit the tomato purée (paste) and present a rather white-coloured couscous, a symbol of the new.

250 g/9 oz (1½ cups) dried large broad (fava) beans
    or chickpeas (garbanzo beans)
500 g/1 lb 2 oz seasoned, salted, air-dried meat
    (*kaddid*, see page 206), cut into generous pieces
500 g/1 lb 2 oz (3 cups) medium couscous
2 tablespoons olive oil , plus extra for preparing the
    couscous
2 long sweet green peppers
1 red or yellow onion, quartered
4 heaped tablespoons double concentrated tomato
    purée (paste)
harissa (page 409), to taste
1 teaspoon ground turmeric
1 teaspoon sweet paprika
salt and pepper
4 Hard-boiled Eggs (page 443), peeled and left whole

Put the dried broad (fava) beans into a large bowl, cover with abundant water and leave to soak overnight. The next day, drain, then peel the beans and discard the skins. Split the peeled beans in half. Put the preserved meat into a large bowl, cover with hot water and leave to soak for 10 minutes. Drain.

If steaming the couscous in a couscoussier over the stew, see the directions on page 190, adding ingredients to the stew before and between steamings as needed and omitting the butter. For other methods of preparing couscous, see page 189. For details on cooking with a couscoussier, including alternatives, see page 188. For quick-cooking couscous, prepare it following the directions on page 191.

Heat the oil in the bottom of a couscoussier over a medium-high heat, add the green peppers and fry for about 3 minutes, or until tender, turning as needed. Transfer to a plate. Add the preserved meat and onion and cook, stirring frequently, until the onion has begun to soften, about 5 minutes. Stir in the tomato purée (paste) and 120 ml (4 fl oz/½ cup) water and cook for 2–3 minutes. Add the broad beans, harissa, turmeric and paprika, then season with salt and pepper. Pour in 1.2 litres (40 fl oz/5 cups) of hot water and bring to the boil. Reduce the heat to medium-low and gently boil until the meat and broad beans are tender, about 1 hour. (If there is no steaming basket on top, loosely cover the pot.)

To serve, put the couscous into a large bowl. Gradually moisten with about 500 ml (18 fl oz/ 2 cups) of the broth, turning the couscous to mix well. Cover and leave to stand for 5–10 minutes. Add a touch more broth if the couscous can absorb it without becoming too soggy. Mound the couscous and make a well in the centre. Place the meat in the well and top with the broad beans. Lay the peppers across the top and arrange the hard-boiled eggs along the edges. Serve with the remaining broth in a bowl on the side to add as desired.

Chicken Couscous with Caramelized Onion and Raisin Tfaya

MOROCCO
PREPARATION TIME: 30 minutes,
plus soaking and resting time
COOKING TIME: 1 hour 30 minutes
SERVES: 6

One of the classics of the Moroccan kitchen, *kuskus tfaya* exemplifies both sophistication and a harmonious blending of the sweet with the savoury. The spice-laden sauce and chicken that top the couscous are given a crowning garland of caramelized onion and raisin *tfaya*. Add a handful of chickpeas (garbanzo beans) if desired. It is perfect served with cold glasses of *lben* (buttermilk). Fine-size (calibre) couscous is generally used for this dish. It can be done with bone-in lamb as well – increase the cooking time by about 1 hour and add a touch more water if needed.

600 g/1 lb 5 oz (generous 3½ cups) fine couscous
1.2 kg/2½ lb bone-in chicken thighs or legs,
    skin removed and fat trimmed
½ teaspoon ground ginger
pinch of saffron threads, crumbled
6 cloves
1 small cinnamon stick or piece of cinnamon bark
1 tablespoon olive oil, plus extra for preparing the
    couscous
10 sprigs coriander (cilantro), tied together
10 sprigs flat-leaf parsley, tied together
40 g/1½ oz (3 tablespoons) butter
150 g/5 oz (¾ cup) canned chickpeas
    (garbanzo beans), rinsed, or cooked dried
    chickpeas (page 443)
75 g/2¾ oz (½ cup) whole almonds
neutral oil, for frying
salt and white pepper
3 Hard-boiled Eggs (page 443), peeled and cut into
    wedges, to garnish

For the tfaya:

75 g/2¾ oz (½ cup) seedless raisins
40 g/1½ oz (3 tablespoons) butter or olive oil
1 kg/2¼ lb red onions, sliced lengthwise
1 teaspoon ground ginger
½ teaspoon ground cinnamon
4 tablespoons honey

PREPARE THE TFAYA: Put the raisins into a small heatproof bowl, cover with lukewarm water and leave to soak for 10 minutes to soften. Drain. Add the butter, onions, soaked raisins, ginger, cinnamon and 120 ml (4 fl oz/½ cup) water to a large heavy frying pan or sauté pan, cover with a lid and cook over a medium heat, stirring frequently, until the onions soften, 30–45 minutes. Stir in the honey and cook, uncovered, over a low heat, letting the onions gently bubble while stirring frequently until caramelized, about 10 minutes. Remove from the heat and set aside.

If steaming the couscous in a couscoussier over the stew, see the directions on page 191, adding ingredients to the stew before and between steamings as needed. For other methods of preparing couscous, see page 189. For details on cooking with a couscoussier, including alternatives, see page 188. For quick-cooking couscous, prepare it following the directions on page 191, warming it until steaming in the oven before serving.

Put the chicken, ginger, saffron, cloves and cinnamon stick into the bottom of a couscoussier. Season with salt and white pepper, add the olive oil and swirl to coat. Fold the coriander (cilantro) and parsley in half, tie into a tight bundle with kitchen string and add 15 g (½ oz/1 tablespoon) butter and the chickpeas (garbanzo beans). Pour in 1 litre (34 fl oz/4¼ cups) of hot water and bring to the boil. Reduce the heat to medium-low and gently boil until the chicken is very tender, about 45 minutes. (If there is no steaming basket on top, loosely cover the pot.)

Meanwhile, boil the almonds in a small saucepan of water for 3–5 minutes, then drain. Once cool enough to handle, slip off the skins. Spread the almonds out on paper towels to dry. Heat at least 1 cm/½ inch of neutral oil in a small frying pan over a medium heat until the surface shimmers. Line a plate with paper towels. Fry the almonds until just golden, 1–2 minutes. Transfer with a slotted spoon to the paper towels to drain.

To serve, fluff the warm couscous, add the remaining 25g (1 oz/2 tablespoons) butter and toss until coated. Either on a large round serving platter or in individual bowls, gently mound the couscous and make a well in the centre. Place the meat in the well and ladle over some broth. Cover with the *tfaya* and top with the almonds. Garnish the edges with hard-boiled eggs. Serve with the remaining broth in a bowl on the side to add as desired.

Chicken Couscous with Vegetables

MOROCCO
PREPARATION TIME: 30 minutes,
plus resting time
COOKING TIME: 1 hour
SERVES: 4–6

This is a delicious, homey and vegetable-filled chicken couscous flavoured by saffron, ginger and pepper. If there is time, marinate the chicken in advance with this trio. The saffron gives the broth a lovely golden colour.

500 g/1 lb 2 oz (3 cups) medium couscous
6 bone-in chicken thighs and/or drumsticks,
    skin removed
6 tablespoons olive oil, plus extra for preparing the
    couscous
1 teaspoon ground ginger
pinch of saffron threads, crumbled
2 red or yellow onions, sliced
2 tomatoes, quartered
100 g/3½ oz (½ cup) canned chickpeas
    (garbanzo beans), rinsed, or cooked dried
    chickpeas (page 443)
2 wedges green cabbage (about 250 g/9 oz total)
3 carrots, halved lengthwise and then crosswise
2 turnips, peeled and quartered lengthwise
2 white potatoes, peeled and quartered lengthwise
400 g/14 oz seeded pumpkin or butternut squash,
    with the skin, cut into large wedges
10 sprigs coriander (cilantro), tied together
1 small aubergine (eggplant), halved lengthwise
1 small green chilli (chile), optional
1 courgette (zucchini), halved lengthwise and then
    crosswise
15 g/½ oz (1 tablespoon) butter, cut into pieces
salt and pepper

If steaming the couscous in a couscoussier over the stew, see the directions on page 190, adding ingredients to the stew before and between steamings as needed. For other methods of preparing couscous, see page 189. For details on cooking with a couscoussier, including alternatives, see page 188. For quick-cooking couscous, prepare it following the directions on page 191, warming it until steaming in the oven before serving.

Put the chicken, oil, ginger and saffron into the bottom of a large couscoussier. Season with salt and a generous amount of pepper. Prick the chicken with the tip of a knife to better absorb the spices. Turn to coat. Add the onions and tomatoes and cook over a high heat until the chicken turns pale, 5–10 minutes. Pour in 500 ml (18 fl oz/2 cups) water

and bring to the boil. As it comes to the boil, add the chickpeas (garbanzo beans), cabbage, carrots, turnips, potatoes, pumpkin, coriander (cilantro), aubergine (eggplant) and chilli (chile) (if using). Pour in 750 ml (25 fl oz/3 cups) of hot water and return to the boil. (If there is no steaming basket on top, loosely cover the pot.) Gently boil, swirling the pot from time to time, until the chicken is done and the vegetables tender, about 45 minutes. Add the courgette (zucchini) for the last 10 minutes or so.

To serve, fluff the warm couscous, add the butter and toss until coated. Either on a large round serving platter or in individual bowls, gently mound the couscous and make a well in the centre. Place the chicken surrounded by some of the vegetables and chickpeas into the well and ladle over some broth. Serve with the remaining vegetables on a plate and the broth in a bowl on the side to add as desired.

Chicken Couscous with Fresh Broad Beans

ALGERIA
PREPARATION TIME: 30 minutes,
plus marinating and resting time
COOKING TIME: 1 hour
SERVES: 4–6

If the broad (fava) beans are young and tender, you do not need to shuck them. Simply trim the pods into 2.5-cm/1-inch segments and add directly to the stew for the final 20–30 minutes.

6 bone-in chicken pieces, skin removed
3 cloves of garlic, minced
1 teaspoon sweet paprika
½ teaspoon cayenne pepper
½ teaspoon ground coriander seeds
3 tablespoons olive oil, plus extra for preparing the
    couscous
500 g/1 lb 2 oz (3 cups) medium couscous
1 onion, finely chopped
2 tomatoes, halved crosswise and grated, peel
    discarded (see page 445)
1 tablespoon double concentrated tomato purée
    (paste)
1 kg/2¼ lb fresh broad (fava) beans in their pods,
    shelled (generous 2 cups shelled beans)
25 g/1 oz (2 tablespoons) butter, smen (see page 412)
    or extra-virgin olive oil
salt and pepper

Put the chicken into a large bowl with the garlic, paprika, cayenne pepper and coriander and season with salt and pepper. Add the oil and turn the chicken until coated. Cover with cling film (plastic wrap), refrigerate and leave to marinate for at least 1 hour.

If steaming the couscous in a couscoussier over the stew, see the directions on page 190, adding ingredients to the stew before and between steamings as needed. For other methods of preparing couscous, see page 189. For details on cooking with a couscoussier, including alternatives, see page 188. For quick-cooking couscous, prepare it following the directions on page 191, warming it until steaming in the oven before serving.

Put the chicken with its marinade, the onion, tomatoes, tomato purée (paste) and 4 tablespoons water into the bottom of a couscoussier. Swirl to coat and cook over a medium-high heat for 5 minutes. Pour in 1 litre (34 fl/4¼ cups) of hot water and bring to the boil. Reduce the heat to medium-low and gently boil for 30 minutes. (If there is no steaming basket on top, loosely cover the pot.) Add the broad (fava) beans and cook until the beans and chicken are tender, 10–15 minutes.

To serve, fluff the warm couscous, add the butter and toss until coated. Either on a large round serving platter or in individual bowls, gently mound the couscous and make a well in the centre. Place the chicken in the well surrounded by broad beans and ladle over some of the broth. Serve with the remaining broth in a bowl on the side to add as desired.

Chicken Couscous with Aromatic 'White Sauce'

ALGERIA
PREPARATION TIME: 30 minutes, plus resting time
COOKING TIME: 1 hour 15 minutes
SERVES: 4–6

Widespread across much of northern Algeria, chicken couscous with 'white sauce' is particularly popular in Constantine. The tomato-less sauce, with turnips, carrots and courgettes (zucchini) along with chicken is cooked with a cinnamon stick. It is straightforward but tasty. Replace some of the butter for *smen* (page 412) for bolder flavours.

500 g/1 lb 2 oz (3 cups) medium couscous
3 tablespoons olive oil, for preparing the couscous
4 bone-in chicken thighs or legs, skin removed
70 g/2½ oz (5 tablespoons) butter
2 red or yellow onions, grated
pinch of saffron threads, crumbled
2 carrots, halved crosswise and then lengthwise
2 turnips, peeled and halved lengthwise
1 cinnamon stick or piece of cinnamon bark
2 small courgettes (zucchini), halved crosswise and then lengthwise
175 g/6 oz (1 cup) canned chickpeas (garbanzo beans), rinsed, or cooked dried chickpeas (page 443)
salt and pepper

If steaming the couscous in a couscoussier over the stew, see the directions on page 190, adding ingredients to the stew before and between steamings as needed. For other methods of preparing couscous, see page 189. For details on cooking with a couscoussier, including alternatives, see page 188. For quick-cooking couscous, prepare it following the directions on page 191, warming it until steaming in the oven before serving.

Put the chicken, 40 g (1½ oz/3 tablespoons) of the butter, the onions and saffron into the bottom of a couscoussier. Season with salt and pepper and cook over a medium heat until the chicken turns pale, about 10 minutes. Add 1 litre (34 fl oz/4¼ cups) of hot water and bring to the boil. Add the carrots, turnips and cinnamon stick and gently boil for 30 minutes. (If there is no steaming basket on top, loosely cover the pot.) Add the courgettes (zucchini) and chickpeas (garbanzo beans) and cook until the chicken and vegetables are done, 20–30 minutes. Carefully transfer the vegetables and chicken to a platter. Remove and discard the cinnamon stick.

To serve, fluff the warm couscous, add the remaining 25 g (1 oz/2 tablespoons) of the butter and toss until coated. Either on a large round serving platter or in individual bowls, gently mound the couscous and make a well in the centre. Place the chicken in the well surrounded by vegetables and chickpeas and ladle over some of the broth. Serve with the remaining broth in a bowl on the side to add as desired.

Couscous with Grouper

TUNISIA
PREPARATION TIME: 30 minutes,
plus resting time
COOKING TIME: 1 hour 10 minutes
SERVES: 4–5

Fish couscous is one of the defining dishes of coastal Tunisia. Grouper (locally called *manani*) is the fish of choice, both for its flavour as well as that it can be cooked a little longer than many other species. Substitute three medium sea bream cut into thirds (the head and then the body into two halves), adding the head in the beginning. If pomegranates are in season, serve a bowl of pomegranate seeds alongside to spoon over the top of the couscous. The contrast in flavours and textures is perfect.

500 g/1 lb 2 oz (3 cups) medium couscous
4 tablespoons olive oil, plus extra for preparing the couscous
2 green chillies (chiles)
1 large red or yellow onion, thinly sliced
6 cloves of garlic, minced
4 ripe tomatoes, halved crosswise and grated, peel discarded (see page 445)
3 tablespoons double concentrated tomato purée (paste)
1 tablespoon sweet paprika
½ teaspoon ground cumin
1 generous piece grouper head
3 carrots, halved crosswise and then lengthwise
2 white potatoes, peeled and halved
2 generous pieces of seeded pumpkin or butternut squash, with the skin (about 500 g/1 lb 2 oz)
1 × 1 kg/2¼ lb grouper, cleaned, scaled and cut into 4 or so large pieces
100 g/3½ oz (½ cup) canned chickpeas (garbanzo beans), rinsed, or cooked dried chickpeas (page 443)
salt and pepper
harissa (page 409), to serve, optional

If steaming the couscous in a couscoussier over the stew, see the directions on page 190, adding ingredients to the stew before and between steamings as needed and omitting the butter. For other methods of preparing couscous, see page 189. For details on cooking with a couscoussier, including alternatives, see page 188. For quick-cooking couscous, prepare it following the directions on page 191.

Add the oil and chillies (chiles) to the bottom of a couscoussier and cook over a medium heat until tender, about 3 minutes. Remove the chillies and set aside. Add the onion and cook until it begins to soften, about 5 minutes. Stir in the garlic. Add the tomatoes, tomato purée (paste) and 4 tablespoons water. Season with salt and pepper and cook for 5 minutes. Stir in the paprika and cumin, add the grouper head, carrots, potatoes and pumpkin. Pour in 1 litre (34 fl oz/4¼ cups) of hot water, bring to the boil and gently boil for 30 minutes. (If there is no steaming basket on top, loosely cover the pot.) Remove the head and pumpkin if needed for space. Add the grouper pieces and chickpeas (garbanzo beans) and cook until the fish is done and vegetables are tender, about 15 minutes. Remove the pot from the heat and leave to stand for a few minutes. Carefully transfer the fish to a platter with a slotted spoon and then the vegetables.

To serve, put the couscous into a large bowl. Gradually moisten with about 500 ml (18 fl oz/ 2 cups) of the broth, turning the couscous to mix well. Cover and leave to stand for 5–10 minutes. Add a touch more broth if the couscous can absorb it without becoming too soggy. Mound the couscous in a serving dish and make a well in the centre. Place the fish in the well surrounded by some of the vegetables. Serve with the remaining broth in a bowl on the side as well as harissa to add if desired.

Couscous
with Chermoula-marinated Fish

MOROCCO
PREPARATION TIME: 30 minutes,
plus marinating and resting time
COOKING TIME: 1 hour 15 minutes
SERVES: 4–6

This recipe calls for either fish steaks or skin-on fillets, but you can also use 1.5 kg/3¼ lb cleaned whole fish – such as a sea bream. If using whole fish, trim the head and tail and add to the pot to help flavour the sauce.

3 tablespoons olive oil, plus extra for preparing the couscous
1 tablespoon fresh lemon juice
2 small cloves of garlic, minced
2 tablespoons finely chopped flat-leaf parsley
2 tablespoons finely chopped coriander (cilantro)
1 teaspoon ground cumin
2 teaspoons sweet paprika
1.5 kg/3¼ lb bone-in bream, hake or grouper steaks, or 1 kg/2¼ lb large skin-on bream, sea bass, cod or grouper fillets, cut into 4 portions
500 g/1 lb 2 oz (3 cups) medium couscous
1 onion, finely chopped
3 ripe tomatoes, halved crosswise and grated, peel discarded (see page 445)
pinch of saffron threads, crumbled
2 carrots, halved lengthwise and then crosswise
2 small turnips, peeled and halved lengthwise
2 courgettes (zucchini), halved lengthwise and then crosswise
25 g/1 oz (2 tablespoons) butter, cut into small pieces
salt and pepper

Put 1 tablespoon of the oil and the lemon juice with the garlic, parsley, coriander (cilantro), cumin and 1 teaspoon of the paprika into a large bowl and mix together. Season with salt and pepper. Trim the head and tail is using a whole fish and set aside. Add the fish to the marinade and turn to coat. Cover with cling film (plastic wrap) and leave to marinate in the refrigerator until ready to add.

If steaming the couscous in a couscoussier over the stew, see the directions on page 190, adding ingredients to the stew before and between steamings as needed. If the fish is done before the couscous, remove the fish from the pot, add a touch of water if needed and continue to steam until ready. For other methods of preparing couscous, see page 189. For details on cooking with a couscoussier, including alternatives, see page 188. For quick-cooking couscous, prepare it following the directions on page 191, warming it until steaming in the oven before serving.

Put the remaining 2 tablespoons of the oil in the bottom of a couscoussier, add the onion and tomatoes and cook over a medium heat until the tomatoes are a deeper red and pulpy, about 10 minutes. Stir in the remaining 1 teaspoon paprika and the saffron, then season with salt and add the carrots, turnips and reserved head and tail of the fish. Pour in 1.2 litres (40 fl oz/5 cups) of hot water and bring to the boil. Reduce the heat to medium-low and gently boil for 30 minutes. (If there is no steaming basket on top, loosely cover the pot.) Add the courgettes (zucchini) and cook for 20 minutes.

Remove the fish from the marinade and discard the marinade. Gently lay the fish in the broth, pushing down to cover with liquid. (Remove the head and tail and some of the vegetables if needed to have room.) Cook until opaque throughout, 5–15 minutes depending on the thickness and cut of the fish, basting from time to time with the broth. Carefully transfer the fish to a platter with a slotted spoon and then the vegetables. If needed, strain the broth through a colander to remove any bones.

To serve, fluff the warm couscous, add the butter and toss until coated. Either on a large round serving platter or in individual bowls, gently mound the couscous and make a well in the centre. Place the fish in the well surrounded by vegetables and ladle over some broth. Serve with the remaining broth in a bowl on the side to add as desired.

Fish Couscous with Quince

TUNISIA
PREPARATION TIME: 30 minutes,
plus resting time
COOKING TIME: 1 hour 35 minutes
SERVES: 4–5

When quince – called *sfarjel* in Tunisia – are in
season during late autumn and winter, home cooks
like to add them to couscous. This sweet-and-
savoury fish version is an elegant and delicious treat.

4 thick bream, sea bass or grouper fillets or generous
    steaks
1 teaspoon ground cumin
3 cloves of garlic, minced
500 g/1 lb 2 oz (3 cups) medium couscous
4 tablespoons olive oil, plus extra for preparing the
    couscous
1 red or yellow onion, finely chopped
4 tomatoes, halved crosswise and grated, peel
    discarded (see page 445)
1 heaped tablespoon double concentrated tomato
    purée (paste)
harissa (page 409), to taste, plus extra to serve
1–2 quince, peeled, seeded and quartered
4 long sweet green peppers, side slit and seeded,
    or 2 green bell peppers, cored, seeded and halved
    lengthwise
generous pinch of saffron threads, dry-roasted
    and ground
175 g/6 oz (1 cup) canned chickpeas (garbanzo beans),
    rinsed, or cooked dried chickpeas (page 443)
75 g/2¾ oz (½ cup) seedless raisins
salt and pepper

Liberally season the fish with salt and pepper and
rub ½ teaspoon of the cumin and half the garlic
into the steaks. Cover with cling film (plastic wrap)
and leave to marinate in the refrigerator until ready
to add.

If steaming the couscous in a couscoussier over
the stew, see the directions on page 190, adding
ingredients to the stew before and between steamings
as needed and omitting the butter. If the fish is done
before the couscous, remove the fish from the pot,
add a touch of water if needed and continue to
steam until ready. For other methods of preparing
couscous, see page 189. For details on cooking with
a couscoussier, including alternatives, see page 188.
For quick-cooking couscous, prepare it following
the directions on page 191.

Add the oil and onion to the bottom of a
couscoussier and cook over a medium heat until
the onion begins to soften, about 5 minutes. Add the
tomatoes, tomato purée (paste) and 4 tablespoons
water, and harissa, the remaining ½ teaspoon cumin
and garlic, then season with salt. Stir and cook for
10 minutes until the mixture reduces and darkens.
Add the quince, peppers and saffron, then pour in
1 litre (34 fl oz/4¼ cups) of hot water and bring to
the boil. Reduce the heat to medium-low and gently
boil for 30 minutes. (If there is no steaming basket
on top, loosely cover the pot.) Add the chickpeas
(garbanzo beans) and raisins and gently simmer
for 30 minutes. Carefully remove the peppers and
set aside. Lay the fish in the broth and cook until
opaque throughout, 5–15 minutes depending on the
thickness and cut of the fish, basting from time to
time. Carefully transfer the fish and quince with a
slotted spoon to a plate without breaking. Strain the
broth through a colander to remove any bones.

To serve, put the couscous into a large bowl
and gradually moisten with about 500 ml (18 fl oz/
2 cups) of the broth, turning the couscous to mix
well. Cover and leave to stand for 5–10 minutes.
Add a touch more broth if the couscous can absorb
it without becoming too soggy. On a large serving
platter, or in individual bowls, mound the couscous
and make a well in the centre. Place the fish in the
well surrounded by the quince, green peppers,
chickpeas and raisins. Serve the remaining broth
on the side with harissa to add as desired.

Fish Couscous with 'Red Sauce'

ALGERIA
PREPARATION TIME: 30 minutes,
plus marinating and resting time
COOKING TIME: 45 minutes
SERVES: 4

This couscous with *sauce rouge* ('red sauce') is highly popular among the coastal communities of Algeria. It highlights the flavours of fresh fish found in area markets.

1 kg/2¼ lb grouper, scorpion fish, swordfish, bonito or another fish
2 cloves of garlic, minced
¾ teaspoon ground cumin
¾ teaspoon sweet paprika
500 g/1 lb 2 oz (3 cups) medium couscous
2 tablespoons olive oil, plus extra for preparing the couscous
2 red or yellow onions, finely chopped
3 ripe tomatoes, peeled (see page 445) and chopped
1 heaped tablespoon double concentrated tomato purée (paste)
15 g/½ oz (1 tablespoon) butter, cut into pieces
salt and pepper

If using whole fish, scale by holding by the tail and scraping at the scales with the back edge of a knife. Remove and discard the entrails. Remove and set the heads and tails aside. If using a large fish, cut into generous steaks. Leave smaller fish whole. Rinse thoroughly under cold running water.

Put half of the garlic, ½ teaspoon of the cumin and ½ teaspoon of paprika into a large bowl and mix together, then season with salt and pepper. Stir in a touch of water to loosen. Add the fish and turn to coat. Cover with cling film (plastic wrap) and leave to marinate in the refrigerator for 1 hour, or until ready to add.

If steaming the couscous in a couscoussier over the stew, see the directions on page 190, adding ingredients to the stew before and between steamings as needed. If the fish is done before the couscous, remove the fish from the pot, add a touch of water if needed and continue to steam until ready. For other methods of preparing couscous, see page 189. For details on cooking with a couscoussier, including alternatives, see page 188. For quick-cooking couscous, prepare it following the directions on page 191, warming it until steaming in the oven before serving.

Add the oil and onions to the bottom of a couscoussier and cook over a medium heat until the onions begin to soften, about 5 minutes. Add the

remaining garlic, ¼ teaspoon cumin and ¼ teaspoon paprika, the tomatoes, tomato purée (paste) and 4 tablespoons water. Season with salt and pepper and cook for 10 minutes to reduce. Add the fish and any spices in the bowl, then pour in 750 ml (25 fl oz/3 cups) water. Bring to a slow boil and gently boil for 20–30 minutes. Strain the broth through a colander. Remove the pieces of fish and discard the rest.

To serve, fluff the warm couscous, add the butter and toss until coated. Either on a large round serving platter or in individual bowls, gently mound the couscous and make a well in the centre. Place the fish in the well and ladle broth over the couscous. Serve with the remaining broth in a bowl on the side to add as desired.

Couscous with Octopus

TUNISIA
PREPARATION TIME: 30 minutes,
plus resting time
COOKING TIME: 1 hour
SERVES: 4–5

Couscous with *karnit* (octopus) is a speciality of coastal Tunisia, especially around Sfax and the Kerkennah Islands. The easiest way to tenderize octopus before cooking is to freeze it for a day or two and then thaw it. If using small octopus, add it about halfway through cooking the sauce. Some cooks in Djerba and the Kerkennah Islands use dried octopus, which they boil in water to remove the salt and to soften before adding. You can add a small handful of dried chickpeas (garbanzo beans) that have been soaked overnight in the beginning of cooking, or canned ones towards the end. If desired, add other vegetables than those included here, such as a piece of pumpkin or a courgette (zucchini).

500 g/1 lb 2 oz (3 cups) medium couscous
3 tablespoons olive oil, plus extra for preparing the
    couscous
2 green chillies (chiles)
1 red or yellow onion, thinly sliced
500 g/1 lb 2 oz cleaned octopus
3 cloves of garlic, finely chopped
2 ripe tomatoes, halved crosswise and grated,
    peel discarded (see page 445)
3 tablespoons double concentrated tomato purée
    (paste)
1 teaspoon sweet paprika
½ teaspoon ground turmeric
harissa (page 409) or cayenne pepper, to taste
2 white potatoes, peeled and quartered
2 carrots, halved crosswise and then lengthwise
1 turnip, peeled and quartered
salt and pepper

If steaming the couscous in a couscoussier over the stew, see the directions on page 190, adding ingredients to the stew before and between steamings as needed and omitting the butter. For other methods of preparing couscous, see page 189. For details on cooking with a couscoussier, including alternatives, see page 188. For quick-cooking couscous, prepare it following the directions on page 191.

Add the oil and chillies (chiles) to the bottom of a couscoussier and cook over a medium heat until tender, about 3 minutes. Remove the chillies and set aside. Add the onion and cook until pale and soft, about 5 minutes. Add the octopus. Stir in the garlic, add the tomatoes, tomato purée (paste), 4 tablespoons water, the paprika and turmeric and season with harissa, salt and pepper. Cook for 5 minutes. Pour in 1.2 litres (40 fl oz/5 cups) water and bring to the boil. Add the potatoes, carrots and turnip and gently boil until the octopus and vegetables are tender, about 45 minutes. (If there is no steaming basket on top, loosely cover the pot.)

To serve, put the couscous into a large bowl and gradually moisten with about 500 ml (18 fl oz/2 cups) of the broth, turning the couscous to mix well. Cover and leave to stand for 5–10 minutes. Add a touch more broth if the couscous can absorb it without becoming too soggy. On a large serving platter, or in individual bowls, mound the couscous and make a well in the centre. Place the octopus in the well surrounded by the vegetables and fried chillies. Serve with the remaining brothy sauce in a bowl on the side to add as desired.

Sweet Couscous
with Dates, Nuts and Raisins

ALGERIA, MOROCCO, TUNISIA
PREPARATION TIME: 10 minutes,
plus soaking time
COOKING TIME: 10 minutes
SERVES: 4

Across the Maghreb, people prepare sweet versions of couscous, usually with raisins, dates and nuts, and dusted with sugar and cinnamon. It makes a filling dessert or snack. The names of such couscous change from place to place – from *mesfouf* in Tunisia to *seffa* in Morocco – and versions from kitchen to kitchen. Add walnuts if desired. Pound a handful in a mortar and toss with the couscous. If the couscous is freshly steamed and still hot, skip the oven step.

75 g/2¾ oz (½ cup) seedless raisins
500 g/1 lb 2 oz (4¼ cups) prepared fine couscous
    (see page 191)
25 g/1 oz (2 tablespoons) butter, cut into small pieces,
    or olive oil
icing (confectioners') sugar, for sweetening and
    dusting
12 large dates, pitted and halved lengthwise,
    to decorate
roasted almonds (see page 445), to decorate
ground cinnamon, for dusting
cold milk or *lben* (buttermilk), to serve

Preheat the oven to 180°C/350°F/Gas Mark 4.
 Put the raisins into a small heatproof bowl, cover with warm water and leave to soak for 10 minutes. Drain.
 Put the couscous into a large baking dish with the raisins, toss to blend and heat in the oven until warm, about 10 minutes. Add the butter to the couscous and work it in with your hands, then sweeten with icing (confectioners') sugar, to taste and fluff with a fork.
 On a large serving platter, mound the couscous into a dome, decorate with the date halves and almonds and dust with cinnamon and icing sugar. Serve with glasses of milk.

Sweet Couscous
with Cinnamon-scented Milk

MOROCCO
PREPARATION TIME: 10 minutes,
plus soaking time
COOKING TIME: 10 minutes
SERVES: 4

This recipe soaks the warm, steamed couscous with cinnamon-infused milk. In addition to this, some cooks like to moisten the grains with milk (rather than water) between – and even before – the two steamings. Add a dash of orange blossom water to the milk, if desired. The recipe calls for fine-size (calibre) couscous. Follow the directions on page 191 for steaming these small grains.

500 g/1 lb 2 oz (4¼ cups) prepared fine couscous
    (see page 191)
250 ml/8 fl oz (1 cup) milk
1 cinnamon stick or piece of cinnamon bark
dash of orange blossom water, optional
25 g/1 oz (2 tablespoons) butter, cut into small pieces,
    or olive oil
75 g/2¾ oz (½ cup) seedless raisins, optional
50 g/2 oz (scant ½ cup) icing (confectioners') sugar,
    plus extra for dusting
ground cinnamon, for dusting
toasted almonds, to decorate
2 Hard-boiled Eggs (page 443), peeled and cut into
    wedges, to decorate

If the couscous is not already warm, preheat the oven to 180°C/350°F/Gas Mark 4. Put the couscous into a large baking dish and heat in the oven until warm, about 10 minutes.
 Meanwhile, put the milk, cinnamon stick and orange blossom water (if using) in a large saucepan and bring to a simmer over a medium-low heat. Remove from the heat.
 Turn the warm couscous out into a large dish. Gradually mix in the milk with your fingers or a wooden spoon, then add the raisins (if using) and icing (confectioners') sugar and work with your hands to mix. Leave the couscous to stand for a few minutes to absorb the milk.
 On a large serving platter, mound the couscous into a dome, dust with cinnamon and icing sugar and decorate with almonds. Decorate with hard-boiled eggs and serve.

Sweet Couscous with Pomegranate Seeds

ALGERIA, TUNISIA
PREPARATION TIME: 10 minutes,
plus cooling time
COOKING TIME: 10 minutes
SERVES: 4

This simple, sweet couscous studded with ruby-like pomegranate seeds and perfumed with orange blossom or rose water is popular when the fruit fills the markets in October. If the couscous is freshly steamed and still warm, skip the oven step. It is important that it is allowed to cool before adding the pomegranate seeds, as they will lose their vibrant colour and turn brownish if mixed with warm couscous. Add a pinch of cinnamon, if desired. It goes well with *lben* (buttermilk) or milk.

500 g/1 lb 2 oz (4¼ cups) prepared fine couscous (see page 191)
15 g/½ oz (1 tablespoon) butter, cut into small pieces
150 g/5 oz (generous 1 cup) pomegranate seeds
1 teaspoon icing (confectioners') sugar, plus extra for dusting
4–6 drops of orange blossom water or rose water
ground cinnamon, for dusting

Preheat the oven to 180°C/350°F/Gas Mark 4.
Put the couscous into a large baking dish and heat in the oven until warm, about 10 minutes. Work in the butter, then leave the couscous to cool completely.
Put the pomegranate seeds, sugar and orange blossom water into a small bowl and toss. Add to the couscous and mix well.
On a serving platter, mound the pomegranate-studded couscous into a dome, dust with icing (confectioners') sugar and a few pinches of cinnamon. Serve.

Couscous with Honey

ALGERIA
PREPARATION TIME: 10 minutes,
plus soaking time
COOKING TIME: 10 minutes
SERVES: 4

Still sometimes served on special occasions in Algeria's interior, this dish received a fitting description in an 1896 colonial French travelogue *En Algérie: La Kabylie et les oasis du Sud* ('In Algeria: Kabylia and the southern oases'): 'After the lamb, the *caïd* [the village leader] serves us another no less sought-after dish, couscous with honey. The couscous is inside a large earthen bowl and the honey is in a saucer. We take a little honey with a wooden spoon and mix it with pearled grains, and it makes an exquisite dish.' This recipe assumes the couscous is leftover and chilled, or at least room temperature. If it is hot and freshly steamed, skip the oven step included below. Be sure to use high-quality honey.

75 g/2¾ oz (½ cup) seedless golden sultanas (golden raisins), optional
500 g/1 lb 2 oz (4¼ cups) prepared fine couscous (see page 191)
15 g/½ oz (1 tablespoon) butter, softened
honey, to serve

Preheat the oven to 180°C/350°F/Gas Mark 4.
Put the sultanas (golden raisins) (if using) into a small bowl, cover with lukewarm water and leave to soak for 15 minutes. Drain.
Put the couscous into a large baking dish and heat in the oven until warm, about 10 minutes. Add the butter and work it in with your fingers or a wooden spoon, then add the sultanas (if using) and toss until combined. Divide the couscous among bowls. Put honey into individual saucers. To eat, dip a spoon into the honey and take a spoonful of couscous.

Sweet Couscous with Milk, Dates and Raisins

TUNISIA
PREPARATION TIME: 10 minutes
COOKING TIME: 10 minutes
SERVES: 4

The Tunisian version of *koskosi halib* (couscous with milk) usually includes pieces of pitted dates as well as raisins. It should be milky enough to need a spoon to eat. Add some almonds, hazelnuts or walnuts if desired, and maybe a pinch of cinnamon to each bowl.

500 g/1 lb 2 oz (4¼ cups) prepared fine couscous
  (see page 191)
granulated or icing (confectioners') sugar,
  for sweetening
8 dates, pitted and cut into pieces
35 g/1¼ oz (¼ cup) seedless raisins
500 ml/18 fl oz (2 cups) lukewarm milk, or as desired

If the couscous is not already warm, preheat the oven to 180°C/350°F/Gas Mark 4. Put the couscous into a large baking dish and heat in the oven until warm, about 10 minutes.

Divide the couscous among bowls. Sprinkle over sugar to sweeten, add the dates and raisins, then pour in the milk. Serve.

Sweet Couscous with Milk

ALGERIA, MOROCCO, TUNISIA
PREPARATION TIME: 5 minutes
COOKING TIME: 5 minutes
SERVES: 4

Couscous leftover from the midday meal with *lben*, a thick, lightly fermented buttermilk, makes a simple snack or even light dinner. This is a hot, slightly more elaborate (and sweeter) version. Some people serve the milk on the side, rather than poured over the top. If you don't have leftover couscous, prepare it following the directions on page 190.

350 g/12 oz (3 cups) prepared medium couscous
  (see page 190)
icing (confectioners') sugar, for dusting
ground cinnamon, for dusting
500 ml/18 fl oz (2 cups) full-fat (whole) milk
pinch of salt
orange blossom water, for dashing

Divide the couscous among 4 soup or *café au lait* bowls and generously dust with icing (confectioners') sugar and cinnamon.

Add the milk, salt and a couples of dashes of orange blossom water to a large saucepan and bring to a simmer over a medium-low heat, stirring so that it does not scorch. Pour into the bowls over the couscous. There should be enough milk to require a spoon to eat. Serve.

Italy is only a short distance across the Mediterranean, but pasta dishes in North Africa are far from copies of Italian ones. That is clear from the spicy heat of harissa in Tunisian and Libyan recipes, the sweet and savoury notes in Morocco ones and the cinnamon in certain Algerian ones. It is also clear in the ingredients, with chicken, potatoes and chickpeas (garbanzo beans) used in various beloved pasta sauces.

Sometimes the uniqueness of the region's traditions resides in the pastas themselves. In Tunisia, *nwasser* are square thumbnails of flat pasta about the size of a postage stamp. Rather than being boiled, *nwasser* get steamed in a two-tiered couscoussier – the top level holds the pasta, the bottom a brothy stew of chicken, chickpeas and vegetables (page 226). Fresh Algerian skinny *rechta* (page 231) is also steamed and served with a sauce of chicken and turnips. In Libya, *rechta* often gets topped with a stew of onions and chickpeas. In Morocco, short, skinny pasta called *shariya* are steamed, tossed with cinnamon and sugar and either eaten alone (page 238) or used to bury a succulent braised chicken (page 224). One of the region's unique pastas is peppercorn-shaped bullets variously called *mhamas, mhamsa* or *berkoukès*, found in soups or potages. There is even a popular dish in Morocco of pasta cooked in sweetened milk and scented with cinnamon (page 238).

Classical shapes like spaghetti also receive their own touches. While much of the Mediterranean considers the ideal texture of cooked pasta to be al dente – firm but not brittle – many in North Africa prefer their pasta softer. After boiling and draining spaghetti, cooks often finish cooking it in the sauce itself. The pasta is more tender but also more flavourful from absorbing the sauce. In Libya – with the strongest Italian influence in the region – pasta is usually boiled directly in the sauce. If it is spaghetti, cooks usually break it up first before adding to the sauce.

Pasta with Chicken in Tomato Sauce

LIBYA
PREPARATION TIME: 10 minutes
COOKING TIME: 1 hour
SERVES: 4

The Italian influence in Libya is featured in the popularity of pasta dishes, especially around Tripoli. The most famous of these is called *mbakbaka*. It often has pieces of lamb or beef, although chicken, as in this version, is also common. Some home cooks like to add chickpeas (garbanzo beans) and diced seasonal vegetables. The spaghetti in this recipe is broken into a few sections and boiled directly in the sauce, but use pasta elbows or short tubes, if desired. Some even use small pasta, turning the dish into an almost minestrone-like stew.

3 tablespoons olive oil
2 small green chillies (chiles), seeded and chopped
4 bone-in chicken thighs or legs, skin removed
1 red or yellow onion, finely chopped
2 cloves of garlic, minced
4 tablespoons double concentrated tomato purée (paste)
1 teaspoon sweet paprika
½ teaspoon ground turmeric
cayenne pepper, to taste
400 g/14 oz spaghetti
salt and pepper
finely chopped flat-leaf parsley, to garnish

Heat the oil in a large pot or casserole dish (Dutch oven) over a medium-high heat, add half the chillies (chiles) and cook for about 1 minute, or until aromatic. Add the chicken, onion and garlic and cook until the onion has softened and the chicken browned on each side, about 5–10 minutes. Stir in the tomato purée (paste), paprika, turmeric and cayenne pepper. Season with salt and pepper, cover with a lid and cook for 2–3 minutes. Pour in 1.5 litres (50 fl oz/generous 6 cups) of hot water, bring to the boil, mostly cover the pan with a lid and gently boil until the chicken is cooked through, 30–40 minutes. Break the spaghetti into 3 or 4 pieces and add to the sauce. Cover again and boil, stirring frequently to keep it from sticking, until the pasta is tender. Add more boiling water if necessary. The sauce should be moist at the end, not overly watery. Remove the pot from the heat and leave to stand for a few minutes. Divide among bowls, sprinkle parsley over the top and serve.

Pasta with Chicken, Potato and Chickpeas

TUNISIA
PREPARATION TIME: 10 minutes
COOKING TIME: 1 hour 5 minutes
SERVES: 4

Known as *makrouna arbi*, it is pure Tunisian comfort food. The classic pasta shape for this dish is one locally called *fell*, which are short, smooth tubes.

2 tablespoons olive oil
4 bone-in chicken drumsticks and/or thighs, skin removed
2 cloves of garlic, minced
3 heaped tablespoons double concentrated tomato purée (paste)
1 teaspoon tabil spice blend (page 446) or a blend of ground coriander and caraway seeds
1 bay leaf
harissa (page 409), to taste
1 white potato, peeled and quartered lengthwise
125 g/4¼ oz (¾ cup) canned chickpeas (garbanzo beans), rinsed, or cooked dried chickpeas (page 443)
1 long sweet green pepper, quartered and seeded
400 g/14 oz *fell*, *mezzi tubetti lisci*, macaroni or penne pasta
salt and pepper

Heat the oil in a large pot, saucepan or casserole dish (Dutch oven) over a medium-high heat, add the chicken and lightly brown for about 5 minutes on each side. Stir in the garlic and cook for about 30 seconds, or until aromatic. Add the tomato purée (paste) and 4 tablespoons water, the tabil, bay leaf and harissa. Season with salt and pepper and cook for 2–3 minutes. Pour in 175 ml (6 fl oz/¾ cup) water, add the potato, cover with a lid and simmer until the potato has softened and the chicken is nearly done, about 45 minutes. Add the chickpeas (garbanzo beans), arrange the green pepper on the top, cover again and cook for a final 10 minutes. It should be loose and saucy but not watery. Add a touch more water if needed or remove the lid to evaporate.

Meanwhile, bring a large pot or saucepan of salted water to a rolling boil, add the pasta and boil until al dente, or firm but not brittle.

Gently remove the chicken, potato and green pepper from the sauce and set aside.

Drain the pasta and transfer to the pan. Cook for a final few minutes until the pasta is tender. Transfer to a serving bowl, arrange the chicken, potato and green pepper on the top and serve.

Pasta with Chicken in Spicy Tomato Sauce

TUNISIA
PREPARATION TIME: 10 minutes
COOKING TIME: 1 hour
SERVES: 4

This is a slightly simpler but spicier version of Tunisian pasta with chicken. Be generous in adding the harissa or cayenne pepper. The pasta finishes cooking in the sauce, absorbing some of the liquid.

6 cloves of garlic, peeled
4 tablespoons olive oil
2 long sweet green peppers
4 heaped tablespoons double concentrated tomato purée (paste)
harissa (page 409) or cayenne pepper, to taste
1 teaspoon tabil spice blend (page 446) or a blend of ground coriander and caraway seeds
4 bone-in chicken drumsticks and/or thighs, skin removed
3 small bay leaves
400 g/14 oz macaroni or elbow pasta
salt and pepper
grated hard white cheese, to serve

Put the garlic with a generous pinch of salt into a mortar and pound with a pestle.

Heat the oil in a large wide pot or casserole dish (Dutch oven) over a medium-high heat, add the peppers and cook until blistered, turning as needed, about 5 minutes. Transfer to a plate. Spoon the garlic into the pan, add the tomato purée (paste), 120 ml (4 fl oz/½ cup) water, the harissa, tabil and chicken. Season with salt and pepper and cook until the chicken changes colour, about 5 minutes. Pour in 250 ml (8 fl oz/1 cup) water, add the bay leaves, cover with a lid and simmer until the chicken is done, 30–40 minutes. It should be quite loose and saucy but not watery. Add a touch more water if needed or remove the lid to evaporate.

Meanwhile, bring a large pot or saucepan of salted water to a rolling boil, add the macaroni and boil for 8–12 minutes until al dente, or firm but not brittle, but follow the timings on the package.

Gently remove the chicken from the sauce, cover with aluminium foil and keep warm.

Drain the pasta and transfer to the pan. Cook for a final few minutes until the pasta is tender. Transfer to a serving dish, arrange pieces of the reserved chicken and fried peppers on top and serve with the cheese to generously sprinkle over the top.

Braised Chicken Buried Under Sweetened Vermicelli Pasta

MOROCCO
PREPARATION TIME: 30 minutes,
plus marinating time
COOKING TIME: 1 hour 30 minutes
SERVES: 6

Hidden under a mound of sweetened, short vermicelli dusted with cinnamon is a braised chicken bursting with savoury flavours. The dish is called *shariya medfouna* – *shariya* is the name of the pasta, and *medfouna* means 'buried'. It is a spectacular mix of flavours but also originality. This dish can also be made with steamed couscous instead of pasta. Many homes like to serve it with glasses of cold milk that has been scented with orange blossom water (page 428).

2 large red onions, 1 grated and 1 chopped
2 heaped tablespoons finely chopped flat-leaf parsley
2 heaped tablespoons finely chopped coriander
   (cilantro)
1 teaspoon ground cinnamon, plus extra for dusting
1 teaspoon ground ginger
2 pinches of saffron threads, crumbled
6 tablespoons olive oil
1 whole chicken (about 1.8 kg/4 lb), trimmed of excess
   fat
40 g/1½ oz (3 tablespoons) butter
500 g/1 lb 2 oz short vermicelli or crushed angel hair
   pasta
6 tablespoons icing (confectioners') sugar, plus extra
   for sprinkling
100 g/3½ oz (⅔ cup) roasted almonds (page 445)
salt and pepper

Put the grated onion, parsley, coriander (cilantro), cinnamon, ginger and saffron into a large bowl and mix together. Season with salt and pepper and moisten with 2 tablespoons of the oil. Mix and rub over the chicken. Cover with cling film (plastic wrap), refrigerate and leave to marinate for 30 minutes.

Put the chicken, breast-side down, into a large casserole dish (Dutch oven) or pot and spoon over the remaining marinade from the bowl. Add the chopped onion and 25 g (1 oz/2 tablespoons) of the butter, cover with a lid and cook over a medium heat for 15 minutes. Turn the chicken breast-side up, add 120 ml (4 fl oz/½ cup) water, reduce the heat to low, cover with a lid and cook until the chicken is done, about 1 hour.

Meanwhile, steam the pasta. Fill the bottom of a couscoussier or a large pot fitted with a steamer basket with about 7.5 cm/3 inches lightly salted water and bring to the boil. Toss the vermicelli with 2 tablespoons of the oil in a large, wide heatproof bowl until well coated. Transfer to the steaming basket and place the basket firmly over the couscoussier. Steam, uncovered, for 15 minutes, beginning the timing when the steam rises up through the surface of the pasta.

Bring about 2 litres (68 fl oz/generous 2 quarts/8½ cups) water to a rolling boil in a large saucepan. Preheat the oven to 180 °C/350 °F/Gas Mark 4.

Put the pasta into the bowl and cover with the boiling water. Leave to stand and swell for 1 minute, then drain. Drizzle the remaining 2 tablespoons of oil over the vermicelli, mixing until coated. Return to the steamer basket and put the basket back on top of the couscoussier. Steam the pasta, uncovered, for a second time until pleasantly al dente or firm but not brittle, about 10 minutes, beginning to count once the steam rises through the surface. Tip the pasta into the bowl, add the icing (confectioners') sugar and remaining 15 g (½ oz/1 tablespoon) of butter and gently break up any clumps of pasta with a fork.

Meanwhile, gently lift the chicken out of the casserole and set on a baking sheet. Set the sauce in the pot aside and then reheat just before serving. Roast the chicken in the hot oven until the skin is golden brown, about 15 minutes.

To serve, put the chicken into the centre of a large serving platter, spoon over some of the sauce and completely bury under a mound of vermicelli. Sprinkle with icing sugar and draw a pattern of lines with cinnamon over the pasta. Arrange the almonds around the mound in a decorative fashion and serve with the remaining sauce in a bowl.

Small Nwasser Pasta Squares with Chicken

TUNISIA
PREPARATION TIME: 20 minutes
COOKING TIME: 1 hour
SERVES: 6

One of the unique pastas in Tunisia is *nwasser* (also spelled *nouasser*), which are tiny, thin pasta squares similar in shape to Italian *quadrettini* and Greek *hilopites*. They are not boiled but steamed in a couscoussier, tossed in the sauce and then finished in the oven, where they soak up and absorb all the flavours. This dish is always served with *lben* (buttermilk). *Nwasser* are hard to find outside Tunisia, so you can use *quadrettini* or *hilopites* instead.

  5 tablespoons olive oil
  1 onion, finely chopped
  6 bone-in chicken thighs or drumsticks, skin removed
  2 heaped tablespoons double concentrated tomato
      purée (paste)
  harissa (page 409), to taste
  175 g/6 oz (1 cup) canned chickpeas (garbanzo beans),
      rinsed, or cooked dried chickpeas (page 443)
  3 white potatoes, peeled and halved lengthwise
  2 carrots, halved crosswise and then lengthwise
  1 courgette (zucchini), halved crosswise
      and then lengthwise
  500 g/1 lb 2 oz *nwasser*, *quadrettini* or *hilopites*
  15 g/½ oz (1 tablespoon) butter
  ¼ teaspoon ground cinnamon
  salt and pepper

In the bottom of a couscoussier, add 3 tablespoons of the oil, the onion and chicken and cook over a medium heat until the chicken is browned on each side, about 5 minutes. Stir in the tomato purée (paste) and 6 tablespoons warm water, and the harissa. Add the chickpeas (garbanzo beans), season with salt and pepper and cook for 2–3 minutes. Pour in 1.5 litres (50 fl oz/generous 6 cups) of hot water and bring to the boil. Add the potatoes, carrots and courgette (zucchini) and cook until just tender and the chicken is cooked through, about 30 minutes.

Meanwhile, put the *nwasser* into a large bowl, drizzle over the remaining 2 tablespoons of the oil, season with salt and toss with your hands to coat. Transfer to the steamer basket and place on top of the couscoussier. Cover the basket with a lid and steam, fluffing the pasta from time to time, for 20 minutes. Ladle over 250 ml (8 fl oz/1 cup) of the broth from below and gradually drizzle over the top while tossing. Cover the basket and continue steaming the *nwasser* until tender, about 5 minutes.

Meanwhile, preheat the oven to 180 °C/350 °F/Gas Mark 4.

Transfer the *nwasser* to a large ovenproof baking dish, add the butter and cinnamon and toss. Ladle over about 600 ml (20 fl oz/2½ cups) of the sauce with chickpeas and turn the pasta to coat. Place in the oven and let the *nwasser* absorb the sauce for about 10 minutes.

Arrange the chicken and vegetables on top and serve.

Constantine-style Tlitli Pasta with Chicken and Meatballs

ALGERIA
PREPARATION TIME: 30 minutes
COOKING TIME: 1 hour 15 minutes
SERVES: 6

Algerian *tlitli* pasta are a short, slender ovoid pasta similar to *langues d'oiseaux* ('birds' tongues') or orzo. Some home cooks first steam the pasta in a couscoussier. Others brown it in butter, bring to the boil, then absorb it into the sauce, finishing with a velvety texture and aromas of cinnamon and black pepper. This *tlitli* recipe is a speciality of Constantine and includes chicken and often, as here, also meatballs.

3 tablespoons olive oil
2 red or yellow onions, finely chopped
6 chicken bone-in thighs or drumsticks, skin removed
2 cloves of garlic, minced
1 large egg
pinch of ground cinnamon
350 g/12 oz minced (ground) beef or lamb
50 g/2 oz (¾ cup) dry breadcrumbs
2 tablespoons finely chopped flat-leaf parsley
175 g/6 oz (1 cup) canned chickpeas (garbanzo beans), rinsed, or cooked dried chickpeas (page 443)
15 g/½ oz (1 tablespoon) or *smen* (page 412)
salt and pepper
500 g/1 lb 2 oz *tlitli*, *langues d'oiseaux* (birds' tongues) or orzo pasta
2 Hard-boiled Eggs (page 443), peeled and cut into wedges, to garnish

Add the oil, onions and chicken to a large casserole dish (Dutch oven) or large, heavy pot and cook over a medium heat until the onions are softening and the chicken has browned on each side, about 10 minutes. Stir in the garlic, then pour in 750 ml (25 fl oz/3 cups) water and bring to the boil. Cover with a lid, reduce the heat to low and gently boil for 30 minutes.

Meanwhile, prepare the meatballs. Put the egg and cinnamon into a large bowl and beat together. Season with salt and pepper and work in the meat, breadcrumbs and parsley to form a smooth paste. Using moistened hands, roll the mixture into meatballs that are about 3 cm/1¼ inches in diameter. There should be about 20.

Set the meatballs in the pot, add the chickpeas (garbanzo beans) and cook, uncovered, until the chicken and the meatballs are cooked through, about 20 minutes.

Meanwhile, bring a large saucepan of lightly salted water to the boil. Melt the butter in a large frying pan, add the pasta and brown over a medium heat, stirring frequently for about 5 minutes. Transfer to the boiling water and boil for 10–15 minutes until just tender. Drain and return to the saucepan. Scoop out about 500 ml (18 fl oz/2 cups) of the broth and pour over the pasta. Cook over a low heat until the pasta is very tender and the sauce absorbed, 5–10 minutes.

Spoon the pasta into a shallow serving dish, top with the chicken, meatballs and chickpeas and garnish with hard-boiled eggs. Serve hot with the remaining broth in a bowl on the side to moisten as desired.

Stewed Pasta Pellets with Vegetables and Chicken

ALGERIA
PREPARATION TIME: 20 minutes,
plus resting time
COOKING TIME: 1 hour 30 minutes
SERVES: 5–6

There are plenty of different recipes with *berkoukès*, large-size couscous or pasta pellets called *mhamas* or *mhamsa* elsewhere in the region and *petits plombs* in French. This is a hearty dish, popular in winter and eaten very hot. It is also traditional in northern Algeria to serve it for lunch after a baby is born. Before being added to the stew, the *berkoukès* are steamed in a couscoussier – two steamings of 15 minutes – so they do not absorb all the broth. (It also speeds up cooking time and gives them a perfect final texture.) If you skip the steaming step and add them directly to the stew, increase the cooking time by 5–10 minutes and add a touch more liquid. You can add a courgette (zucchini), some freshly shelled broad (fava) beans, green beans, green peas or another seasonal vegetable. Serve with harissa to stir into the bowls as desired.

3 tablespoons olive oil
4 bone-in chicken thighs, skin removed
1 onion, grated
2 cloves of garlic, minced
2 tomatoes, halved crosswise and grated,
    peel discarded (see page 445)
1 tablespoon double concentrated tomato purée
    (paste)
¼ teaspoon sweet paprika
¼ teaspoon cayenne pepper, optional
¼ teaspoon ground cumin
¼ teaspoon ground ginger
¼ teaspoon ground turmeric
1 white potato, peeled and diced
2 carrots, diced
1 celery stalk, diced
175 g/6 oz (1 cup) canned chickpeas (garbanzo beans),
    rinsed, or cooked dried chickpeas (page 443)
200 g/7 oz (1 cup) *berkoukès*, *mhammas*, *petits plombs* or
    peppercorn-size pasta bullets
2 tablespoons finely chopped flat-leaf parsley
salt and pepper
1 lemon, cut into wedges, to serve
harissa (page 409), to serve, optional

Heat 2 tablespoons of the oil in a large pot or casserole dish (Dutch oven) over a medium heat, add the chicken and brown on each side for about 5 minutes. Transfer to a plate. Add the onion to the pot and cook for 5 minutes. Stir in the garlic, then add the tomatoes, tomato purée (paste) and 3 tablespoons water. Cook for 5 minutes. Stir in the paprika, cayenne pepper (if using), cumin, ginger and turmeric and season with salt and pepper. Return the chicken to the pot, add the potato, carrots, celery and chickpeas (garbanzo beans) and pour in 1.5 litres (50 fl oz/generous 6 cups) of hot water. Bring to the boil, cover with a lid and cook until the chicken is very tender and beginning to come away from the bone, about 50 minutes. Remove the chicken and leave to cool, then remove the meat, shred using your fingers and set aside.

Meanwhile, bring an abundant amount of water to the boil in the bottom of a couscoussier or in a large pot with a steaming basket. Rinse the *berkoukès* in hot water. Put into the steaming basket, add the remaining 1 tablespoon of the oil and toss to coat the pasta. Once the water is boiling, place the basket firmly over the couscoussier. Cover the basket with a lid and steam for 15 minutes, starting the timing when the steam rises up through the *berkoukès*. Dump into a large bowl, sprinkle over some tablespoons of water and leave to absorb for 5 minutes. Return to the steamer basket, cover and steam for a second time for 15 minutes.

Transfer the *berkoukès* to the stew and cook, uncovered, until the *berkoukès* are tender, 10–20 minutes. Add more liquid if needed to keep it loose and soupy. Stir in the parsley and reserved shredded chicken, remove from the heat and leave to rest for 5 minutes. Ladle into wide bowls and serve hot with lemon wedges to squeeze over the top and harissa (if using).

Potage with Small Mhamas Pasta Pellets, Vegetables and Pulses

TUNISIA
PREPARATION TIME: 15 minutes,
plus overnight soaking time
COOKING TIME: 2 hours
SERVES: 8

The hearty, pulse- and vegetable-laden potage has *mhamas*, small pasta pellets akin to large couscous. They are also called *berkoukès* or (in French) *petits plombs*. Squeeze lemon over the top and then stir in some harissa chilli paste. To use canned chickpeas (garbanzo beans) instead of dried ones that have been soaked overnight, rinse and add to the pot about 15 minutes before the end of cooking.

100 g/3½ oz (½ cup) dried chickpeas
   (garbanzo beans)
3 tablespoons olive oil
1 red or yellow onion, finely chopped
4 cloves of garlic, minced
2 ripe tomatoes, halved crosswise and grated,
   peel discarded (see page 445)
2 tablespoons double concentrated tomato purée
   (paste)
1 celery stalk, diced
1 heaped tablespoon finely chopped flat-leaf parsley
1 teaspoon caraway seeds, ground
100 g/3½ oz (½ cup) dried lentils or small peeled
   and split dried broad (fava) beans
2 carrots, diced
1 white potato, peeled and diced
1 turnip, peeled and diced
150 g/5 oz (¾ cup) *mhammas*, *berkoukès*, *petits plombs*
   or peppercorn-size pasta bullets
250 g/9 oz spinach leaves, shredded
harissa (page 409), to taste, plus extra to serve
salt and pepper
1 lemon, cut into wedges, to serve

Put the dried chickpeas (garbanzo beans) into a large bowl, cover with abundant water and leave to soak overnight. The next day, drain and rinse.
   Add the oil and onion to a soup pot and cook over a medium heat until it begins to soften, about 5 minutes. Stir in the garlic, tomatoes, tomato purée (paste), celery, parsley and caraway. Season with salt and pepper and cook for 5 minutes. Add the chickpeas (garbanzo beans) and 1.5 litres (50 fl oz/generous 6 cups) of hot water. Bring to the boil, cover with a lid and gently boil for 45 minutes. Add the lentils, carrots, potato and turnip, stir in the *mhamsa* and add the spinach. Cover and cook until the chickpeas and *mhamsa* are tender, about 1 hour.

The consistency should be loose, so add more water if necessary. Stir in some harissa. Serve hot in wide bowls with lemon wedges to squeeze over the top and a bowl of harissa to spoon in as desired.

Steamed Fresh Rechta Pasta with Chicken and Turnips

ALGERIA
PREPARATION TIME: 15 minutes,
plus overnight soaking time
COOKING TIME: 1 hour 20 minutes
SERVES: 6–8

Rechta (or *rishda*) is a type of fresh pasta made from hard durum semolina and cut into skinny ribbons (see the recipe opposite). They give this famous dish its name. The pasta gets steamed atop a couscoussier and then topped with a 'white sauce' laden with chicken (or sometimes lamb), turnips, chickpeas (garbanzo beans) and when in season courgettes (zucchini). It's hearty, tasty and a keen favourite. It is also considered a special dish and frequently prepared for the birth of a child and religious holidays, such as the Mawlid al-Nabi, the birthday of the Prophet Muhammad.

200 g/7 oz (1 cup) dried chickpeas (garbanzo beans)
2 tablespoons olive oil, plus extra for oiling
25 g/1 oz (2 tablespoons) butter
2 red or yellow onions, finely chopped
6–8 bone-in chicken drumsticks and/or thighs
6 turnips, peeled and quartered lengthwise
½ teaspoon ground cinnamon, plus extra for dusting
750 g/1⅔ lb fresh *rechta* pasta (page 231) or another
   type of thin, fresh pasta
salt and pepper

Put the dried chickpeas (garbanzo beans) into a large bowl, cover with abundant water and leave to soak overnight. The next day, drain and rinse.
   In the bottom of a couscoussier or a large casserole dish (Dutch oven), add the oil, 15 g (½ oz/1 tablespoon) of the butter and the onions and cook over a medium heat until the onions have begun to soften, about 5 minutes. Add the chicken, season with salt and pepper and cook until the chicken has browned on each side, about 10 minutes. Add the chickpeas and turnips and pour in 750 ml (25 fl oz/3 cups) water. Bring to a simmer and simmer until the chicken is done and the chickpeas and turnips tender, about 1 hour. Add the cinnamon towards the end of cooking. If the chickpeas are not yet tender, remove the chicken and turnips and simmer until ready, adding a touch of water

if needed. Return the chicken and turnips to the sauce for a moment to warm. Season with salt and pepper.

Meanwhile, steam the *rechta*. Put the pasta onto a wide platter and rub with oil. Put into the top basket of the couscoussier, cover the basket with a lid and steam for 15 minutes. Transfer to the platter, rub with oil and separate. If the pasta is not done, return to the steamer basket, cover and steam for 5–10 minutes until tender.

Put the pasta into a wide serving bowl and toss with the remaining 15 g (½ oz/1 tablespoon) of butter. Moisten with some broth, lightly dust with cinnamon and arrange the pieces of chicken and the turnips on top. Serve with the remaining broth on the side.

Fresh Rechta Pasta

ALGERIA, LIBYA
PREPARATION TIME: 30 minutes,
plus resting and drying time
MAKES: 860 g/1 lb 14 oz pasta

This version of the thin strands of *rechta* pasta uses a standard three-to-one ratio of fine semolina to plain (all-purpose) flour and calls for a pasta machine. *Rechta* is also prepared in Libya, where it is called *rishda*, and sometimes gets served with an onion and chickpea (garbanzo bean) topping called *busla* (see page 203).

    450 g/1 lb (2¾ cups) fine semolina
    150 g/5 oz (1 cup) plain (all-purpose) flour
    1 teaspoon salt
    cornflour (cornstarch), for dusting

Put the semolina, flour and salt into a large bowl and mix together with your fingers. Work in about 300 ml (10 fl oz/1¼ cups) tepid water, little by little, to form a consistent ball. (There might be some water leftover, or it might take a touch more.) Transfer the dough to a clean work counter and patiently knead for about 10 minutes, or until smooth and elastic. Cover with cling film (plastic wrap) and leave to rest for 30 minutes.

Cut the dough into 4–6 pieces. Working with one piece at a time, flatten the dough and run through a pasta machine, gradually stepping down notches, to one of the thin settings. Cut the pasta in half if it becomes unwieldy and long. Spread out the thin sheets to dry for 15 minutes, then cut the sheets into ribbons using the fine setting on the pasta machine. Lightly dust with cornflour (cornstarch) to keep from sticking. Leave to dry on a cornflour-dusted clean dish towel for 15 minutes. Cover with a clean dish towel until ready to steam.

Fresh Hlalem Pasta

TUNISIA
PREPARATION TIME: 30 minutes,
plus resting and drying time
MAKES: 225 g/8 oz pasta

Hlalem is a type of fresh and often homemade pasta that Tunisians like to add to soup (page 128). The wiry, tapering twists are similar in shape to Italian *trofie*. Often made in a big batch by a couple of people in the kitchen (it is laborious), the pasta is air-dried and kept in jars to use during the winter. This version uses pasta that is left to dry for only a short period before using in the soup. If time allows, leave it to dry for at least a few hours.

    115 g/4 oz (⅔ cup) fine durum wheat semolina
    30 g/1 oz (¼ cup) plain (all-purpose) flour
    1 tablespoon olive oil
    pinch of salt
    cornflour (cornstarch), for dusting

Put the semolina and flour into a large bowl, add the oil and salt and gradually work in about 75 ml (2½ fl oz/⅓ cup) water with your fingers to form a single ball of dough. (There might be some water leftover.) Transfer the dough to a clean work counter and patiently knead for about 10 minutes, or until supple and elastic. Cover with cling film (plastic wrap) and leave to rest for 30 minutes.

Pinch off a piece about the size of a golf ball and roll out with your hands to a thin, long rope. Twist off pieces about 1 cm/½ inch in length into skinny twists or roll under the palms of your hands to thin shapes with tapered ends. Place on a clean dish towel dusted with cornflour (cornstarch) to keep them from sticking and repeat with the remaining dough, tossing from time to time with cornflour. Leave to dry on the towel for at least 1 hour before using.

Spaghetti with Octopus

TUNISIA
PREPARATION TIME: 20 minutes
COOKING TIME: 1 hour
SERVES: 4

Karnit (octopus) is deeply popular in Tunisia, especially in the Kerkennah Islands, a tight group of small, very flat islands in the Gulf of Gabès, a one-hour ferry ride from Sfax. One way to prepare it is *makrouna bel karnit*, with pasta. As with other Tunisian pasta sauces, it should be loose, since the pasta finishes cooking in it. While the recipe that follows (Pasta with Small Octopus, see right) cooks the raw octopus directly in the sauce, this version starts with boiling it apart and cutting it into pieces before adding it to the sauce. See the directions for cooking octopus on page 444 beforehand.

- 250 g/9 oz cleaned medium octopus tentacle(s), thawed if frozen
- 5 tablespoons olive oil
- 2 long sweet green peppers
- 3 cloves of garlic, finely chopped
- 2 tomatoes, halved crosswise and grated, peel discarded (see page 445)
- 2 heaped tablespoons double concentrated tomato purée (paste)
- 1 teaspoon ground coriander
- harissa (page 409) or cayenne pepper, to taste
- 400 g/14 oz spaghetti
- salt and pepper

Cook the octopus following the directions on page 444. Do not drain. Remove the pan from the heat and leave the octopus in the water until ready to add to the sauce.

Line a plate with paper towels. Heat 2 tablespoons of the oil in a large pot or saucepan over a medium heat, add the peppers and fry until tender, turning as needed, about 3 minutes. Transfer to the lined plate. Add the remaining 3 tablespoons of oil, the garlic, tomatoes, tomato purée (paste), 6 tablespoons of liquid from cooking the octopus, the coriander and harissa, then season with salt and pepper. Cook over a medium heat to thicken the sauce, about 10 minutes. Stir in 120 ml (4 fl oz/½ cup) of liquid from cooking the octopus. Cut the octopus with kitchen scissors into bite-size pieces and add to the sauce.

Meanwhile, bring a large pot or saucepan of salted water to a rolling boil, add the spaghetti and boil for 8–12 minutes until al dente, or firm but not brittle, but follow the timings on the package. Drain and immediately add the pasta to the sauce, stirring to

blend. Cover the pan with a lid and finish cooking the pasta over a medium heat for about 2 minutes. Add a touch more of the octopus liquid if needed. Transfer to a serving platter, arrange the octopus on top and serve with the fried peppers.

Pasta with Small Octopus

TUNISIA
PREPARATION TIME: 20 MINUTES
COOKING TIME: 1 hour
SERVES: 4

In this version of pasta with octopus, the fresh *karnit* gets cooked directly in the sauce. It is typically prepared with spaghetti, but some home cooks also make it with penne pasta.

- 350 g/12 oz small octopus
- 3 tablespoons olive oil
- 1 onion, finely chopped
- 2 cloves of garlic, finely chopped
- 3 ripe tomatoes, halved crosswise and grated, peel discarded (see page 445)
- 2 heaped tablespoons double concentrated tomato purée (paste)
- harissa (page 409) or cayenne pepper, to taste
- 400 g/14 oz penne pasta or spaghetti
- salt and pepper

Clean the octopus. If needed, remove and discard the mouth, eyes and ink sack and rinse well under cold running water, checking the suction cups for any sand or grit. Cut the octopus into generous pieces and set aside.

Heat the oil in a large pot or saucepan over a medium heat, add the onion and cook for 5 minutes. Add the octopus and cook for another 5 minutes. Stir in the garlic, then add the tomatoes, tomato purée (paste) and 6 tablespoons water, and harissa. Season with salt and pepper and cook for 10 minutes to reduce the sauce. Stir in 250 ml (8 fl oz/1 cup) water, cover with a lid, reduce the heat to low and cook until the octopus is tender, about 40 minutes. It should be loose and saucy but not watery. Add a touch more water if needed or remove the lid to evaporate.

Meanwhile, bring a large pot or saucepan of salted water to a rolling boil, add the pasta and boil for 10–12 minutes until al dente, or firm but not brittle, but follow the timings on the package. Drain and immediately add the pasta to the sauce, stirring to blend. Cover the pot and cook the pasta over a medium heat until tender, about 2 minutes. Add a touch of water if needed. Divide among bowls, arrange the octopus on top and serve.

Spaghetti with Octopus ➤➤

Spicy Seafood Spaghetti

TUNISIA
PREPARATION TIME: 20 minutes
COOKING TIME: 35 minutes
SERVES: 4–5

Four of Tunisia's most beloved ingredients come together in this local favourite: harissa, tomato purée (paste), seafood and pasta. Start with a teaspoon of harissa, and towards the end of cooking, taste the sauce and stir in more until just the right level of heat is reached.

- 16–20 live mussels
- 2 tablespoons olive oil
- 12 large raw prawns (shrimp), peeled with tails left on
- 350 g/12 oz cleaned squid (calamari) or cuttlefish with tentacles, cut into bite-size pieces
- 1 small long sweet green pepper or ½ green bell pepper, cored, seeded and cut into 1-cm/½-inch pieces
- 225 g/8 oz small peeled raw prawns (shrimp), thawed if frozen
- 1 plum tomato, cored and cut into 1-cm/½-inch pieces
- 3 tablespoons double concentrated tomato purée (paste)
- harissa (page 409), to taste
- 500 g/1 lb 2 oz spaghetti
- salt and pepper

Trim and debeard the mussels, then scrape the outside of the shells with a paring knife if needed. Rinse under cold running water.

Put the mussels and 120 ml (4 fl oz/½ cup) water into a small saucepan, cover the pan with a lid and steam over a medium-high heat, shaking the pan from time to time, until the mussels have opened, about 2 minutes. Discard any that do not open. Set aside.

Heat the oil in a large sauté pan over a medium-high heat, add the large prawns (shrimp) and cook until pink, 3–4 minutes, turning as needed. Transfer to a platter. Add the squid (calamari) to the pan and cook for 5–8 minutes until becoming tender. Add the green pepper and cook until it begins to soften, about 5 minutes. Add the small prawns (shrimp) and cook, stirring, for 1 minute. Stir in the tomato, tomato purée (paste) and 3 tablespoons water, then the harissa and cook for 2–3 minutes. Add 250 ml (8 fl oz/1 cup) water, bring to a simmer and simmer for 5 minutes.

Meanwhile, drain the liquid from the mussels, then strain it through a muslin- (cheesecloth-) lined sieve into a large bowl or jug and set aside. Twist off the empty half of each shell and discard.

Taste the sauce for spiciness and add more harissa as desired. If the squid is not completely tender, tip in a touch of the reserved mussel liquid and simmer for a little longer. Add the reserved prawns and mussels to the sauce and turn to coat. Season with salt and pepper.

Meanwhile, bring a large pot or saucepan of salted water to a rolling boil, add the spaghetti and boil for 8–12 minutes until al dente or firm but not brittle, but follow the timings on the package. Drain and transfer to the sauce. Cook for a final few minutes until the pasta is tender. Divide among warmed bowls, arrange the seafood on top and serve.

Pasta with Lobster

TUNISIA
PREPARATION TIME: 20 minutes
COOKING TIME: 35 minutes
SERVES: 4

From 1540 to 1742, Tabarka, on Tunisia's far northwestern coast near the Algerian border, was controlled by the maritime Republic of Genoa, which built a still-standing fort on an island outcrop. Today the town is most famous for its diving, red coral and seafood – namely lobsters. One favourite way to enjoy its fine lobsters is with spaghetti. A dollop of harissa perfectly balances the sweetness of the lobster. This version cuts the lobster tail into pieces for easy access to the meat when eating, although some like to serve the tails simply halved for a more striking presentation.

- 1 fresh lobster (about 600 g/1 lb 5 oz)
- 3 tablespoons olive oil
- 3 cloves of garlic, finely chopped
- 1 red or yellow onion, finely chopped
- 3 ripe tomatoes, halved crosswise and grated, peel discarded (see page 445)
- 2 tablespoons double concentrated tomato purée (paste)
- harissa (page 409) or cayenne pepper, to taste
- 1 teaspoon sweet paprika
- 400 g/14 oz spaghetti or another pasta
- 1 tablespoon minced flat-leaf parsley
- salt and pepper

If required, place the lobster in the freezer for 15 minutes (this numbs the lobster), then kill the lobster quickly and humanely by placing the tip of a large, heavy knife on the line just behind the lobster's head and firmly plunge it through the shell. Turn the lobster over on its back and split in half lengthwise, cutting along the belly. Generously season with salt and pepper. Gently crack the large claws so that they remain intact but the meat will be easily accessible when eating.

Heat the oil in a large casserole dish (Dutch oven) or large frying pan over a medium heat, add the lobster and cook until it changes its colour from pearly to white, about 5 minutes. Transfer to a platter and remove and discard the stomach, sac, intestinal tract and head.

Add the garlic and onion to the pan and cook for about 5 minutes, or until the onion begins to soften. Add the tomatoes, tomato purée (paste) and 120 ml (4 fl oz/½ cup) water, the harissa and paprika and cook until darker and reduced, about 15 minutes. Cut the lobster tail crosswise into pieces with a heavy knife or kitchen scissors leaving the meat

attached to the shell, then return to the pan. Stir in 120 ml (4 fl oz/½ cup) water, cover with a lid and cook for 5 minutes.

Meanwhile, bring a large pot or saucepan of salted water to a rolling boil, add the spaghetti and boil for 10–12 minutes until al dente, or until firm but not brittle, but follow the timings on the package. Drain, reserving some of the water, and immediately add the pasta to the sauce. Cook over a medium heat until the pasta is tender and has absorbed some flavours of the sauce, about 2 minutes. Loosen with a touch of reserved water from the pasta if necessary. Divide among bowls, arrange the lobster pieces on top, sprinkle over the parsley and serve.

TUNISIA'S PASTA OBSESSION

While couscous is Tunisia's national dish and eaten weekly, pasta has become its daily meal. According to the International Pasta Organization, Tunisians devour 17 kg/37½ lb per person a year, an amount only surpassed by its pasta-obsessed neighbours in Italy (23 kg/51 lb). That is about twice as much as the US (8.8 kg/19½ lb), France (8.3 kg/18¼ lb) and Germany (7.9 kg/17½ lb) and five times the UK (3.5 kg/7¾ lb).

Even though Tunisia was under French control from 1881 to 1956, at the beginning of the twentieth century there were three times more Italian residents than French ones. Most were Sicilians. With them came spaghetti and different types of makrouna, the generic local name for all shapes of pasta. While couscous remains the beloved cultural touchstone that is prepared for the week's

most important meal with family, pasta is easier and quicker to make than couscous and is more frequently found on the table.

Tunisian pasta dishes do not mimic those in Sicily. The difference is first tasted in the notable tenderness of the pasta, which is often boiled and then finished by cooking in the sauce beyond al dente – firm though not brittle. Next, are the flavours, as the earthy spiciness of harissa floods the palate. Some of the pasta shapes are unique, and rather than being boiled they get steamed in the basket of a couscoussier. A tiny, square type called nwasser is such a pasta (page 226): after being steamed it is covered in sauce, which it absorbs. Yet even pasta dishes that appear more similar to those in Sicily have their own unique Tunisian stamp. The sauce usually has tomato purée (paste) and harissa but also tabil

(page 446) – a spice blend of ground coriander and caraway seeds, chilli (red pepper) flakes and dried garlic.

With Tunisia's long coastline, there are plenty of pasta dishes that draw on the sea's generous bounty. Spaghetti with a piquant tomato sauce of seafood (page 234) or octopus (page 232) is popular, a pasta dish from the northwest with lobster (page 234) is a sublime treat and another with clams in a spicy red sauce (page 236) is both simple and lovely. For ease, there is the quick, everyday favourite of pasta with tuna and black olives (page 236).

The most famous local pasta is makrouna arbi with chicken, potatoes and chickpeas in a spicy tomato sauce (page 223). The name literally means 'Arabic pasta' and is a way of saying it is Tunisia's own and not an Italian import.

Spaghetti with Tuna, Black Olives and Cayenne Pepper

TUNISIA
PREPARATION TIME: 5 minutes
COOKING TIME: 15 minutes
SERVES: 2

This very popular dish tops pasta with tuna, tomatoes and black olives. It is quick, easy and extremely flavourful. To make the tomato sauce a bit denser, add 1–2 tablespoons double concentrated tomato purée (paste) with 4–6 tablespoons water with the tomatoes.

  2 tablespoons olive oil
  1 onion, finely chopped
  1 clove of garlic, minced
  2 plum tomatoes, cored and finely chopped
  50 g/2 oz (½ cup) pitted black olives, sliced
  1 tablespoon finely chopped flat-leaf parsley
  pinch of cayenne pepper or hot chilli (chile) flakes
  225 g/8 oz spaghetti
  1 (150–175-g/5–6-oz) can of tuna in olive oil, drained
  salt

Heat the oil in a medium frying pan over a medium-high heat, add the onion and cook for about 3 minutes, or until blondish. Stir in the garlic and immediately add the tomatoes. Season with salt and cook until the tomatoes begin to soften and lose their rawness, about 2 minutes. Stir in the olives, parsley and cayenne pepper and remove from the heat.

Meanwhile, bring a large pot or saucepan of salted water to a rolling boil, add the spaghetti and boil for 10–12 minutes until al dente, or firm but not brittle, but follow the timings on the package. Drain, but do not rinse, then put into a large bowl. Add the sauce and toss to coat. Divide the pasta among 2 warmed pasta bowls, then top with the tuna and serve immediately.

Pasta with Clams in Spicy Red Sauce

TUNISIA
PREPARATION TIME: 10 minutes,
plus soaking time
COOKING TIME: 20 minutes
SERVES: 4

This pasta, with its signature harissa-laced tomato sauce, is simple, lovely and quick to make. Before adding to the pan, be sure to soak the clams in advance to expel all sand.

  500 g/1 lb 2 oz live clams in the shell, preferably a small-shelled variety
  6 tablespoons olive oil
  3 cloves of garlic, finely chopped
  2 heaped tablespoons double concentrated tomato purée (paste)
  4 ripe tomatoes, halved crosswise and grated, peel discarded (see page 445)
  harissa (page 409), to taste
  1 teaspoon sweet paprika
  ½ teaspoon ground caraway
  400 g/14 oz spaghetti, linguine or another long pasta
  salt and pepper
  finely chopped flat-leaf parsley, to garnish

Scrubs the clams, then put into a large bowl and cover with cold, salted water. Leave to soak for at least 2 hours to release any sand. Drain and rinse under cold running water.

Heat the oil in a large casserole dish (Dutch oven) or another heavy pot or saucepan over a medium heat, add the garlic and cook for about 30 seconds, or until aromatic. Add the tomato purée (paste) and 120 ml (4 fl oz/½ cup) water and cook for 2 minutes, stirring constantly. Add the tomatoes and cook until reduced and the oil rises to the surface, about 10 minutes. Stir in the harissa, paprika and caraway, then season with salt and pepper. Add the clams, cover with a lid and cook, stirring frequently, until the clams open, about 5 minutes. Discard any that do not open.

Meanwhile, bring a large pot or saucepan of salted water to a rolling boil, add the spaghetti and boil for 10–12 minutes until al dente, or firm but not brittle, but follow the timings on the package. Scoop out about 120 ml (4 fl oz/½ cup) of the pasta water and set aside.

Drain the pasta and add to the sauce. Cover with a lid and cook until the pasta is tender and has absorbed the flavours of the sauce, 1–2 minutes. Loosen with some reserved pasta water if needed. Divide among bowls, top with the clams, sprinkle over some parsley and serve.

Sweet Vermicelli Pasta

MOROCCO
PREPARATION TIME: 5 minutes
COOKING TIME: 25 minutes
SERVES: 4

Sweet dishes with rice or couscous are common across North Africa. Sweet ones with pasta are less so. In northern Morocco, there are a couple made with *shariya* – short, thin vermicelli noodles. For this one, called *shariya seffa*, pasta is steamed in a couscoussier, then tossed in cinnamon and sugar. The pasta can be boiled in water until al dente instead, but the steaming gives it a more pleasing texture. Some home cooks sprinkle it with water between steamings and let the water be absorbed, in the same manner as couscous, though others cover with hot water for 1 minute, then drain, speeding up the cooking and removing some sticky starches, making it easier to toss. You can add a handful of soaked seedless raisins to the last steaming and some butter at the end to make it richer, if desired. In a stunning and original sweet-and-savoury dish called *shariya medfouna* (Braised Chicken Buried Under Sweetened Vermicelli Pasta, page 224), a whole braised chicken gets covered in sweet vermicelli.

250 g/9 oz short vermicelli pasta or crushed angel hair pasta
3 tablespoons extra-virgin olive oil
15 g/½ oz (1 tablespoon) butter, cut into pieces
icing (confectioners') sugar, for sweetening
ground cinnamon, for dusting
salt

Fill the bottom of a couscoussier or a large pot fitted with a steamer basket with 1.5 litres (50 fl oz/generous 6 cups) lightly salted water and bring to the boil.

Put the vermicelli and 1 tablespoon of the oil into a large heatproof bowl and toss until well coated. Transfer to the steaming basket. Place the basket firmly over the couscoussier and steam, uncovered, for 15 minutes, beginning the timing when the steam rises up through the surface of the pasta.

Meanwhile, bring about 1.5 litres (50 fl oz/generous 6 cups) of water to a rolling boil in a large saucepan.

Put the pasta into the bowl and cover with the boiling water. Leave to stand and swell for 1 minute, then drain. Drizzle the remaining 2 tablespoons of oil over the vermicelli, mixing until coated. Return to the steamer basket and place the basket back on top of the couscoussier. Steam the pasta, uncovered, for a second time until pleasantly al dente,

5–10 minutes, beginning the timing once the steam rises through the surface of the pasta.

Transfer the vermicelli to a wide serving bowl, add the butter and break up any clumps of pasta with a fork. Divide among bowls, generously sweeten with the sugar, dust with cinnamon and serve warm.

Vermicelli Pasta with Milk and Cinnamon

MOROCCO
PREPARATION TIME: 2 minutes
COOKING TIME: 10 minutes
SERVES: 4

A speciality of northern Morocco, this simple pasta dish gets served for a snack, as a dessert or even soup-like for a light dinner. The amount of milk and sugar used are personal preferences – some people add plenty of milk, others less so; some add lots of sugar, others omit the cinnamon. Serve warm in bowls with a spoon.

1 litre/34 fl oz (4¼ cups) full-fat (whole) milk
3 tablespoons sugar, optional
pinch of salt
100 g/3½ oz short vermicelli pasta or crushed angel hair pasta
orange blossom water, for dashing
ground cinnamon, for dusting, optional

Bring the milk to a simmer in a large saucepan over a medium heat, stirring so that it does not scorch. Stir in the sugar (if using) and salt, then add the vermicelli. Reduce the heat to low and cook, stirring frequently, until the vermicelli is tender, about 5 minutes. Stir in a dash of orange blossom water and remove from the heat. Divide evenly among bowls, generously dust with cinnamon (if using) and serve warm with spoons.

Aromatic Rice
with Liver, Raisins and Almonds

LIBYA
PREPARATION TIME: 20 minutes,
plus soaking time
COOKING TIME: 45 minutes
SERVES: 5–6

This Libyan favourite with steamed rice known
as *roz khalta* – *roz* means rice, *khalta* refers to the
raisins and almonds that top it – is prepared with
liver. Add some toasted pine nuts to the *khalta* mix,
if desired.

400 g/14 oz (2 cups) long-grain white rice
10 cardamom pods
5 whole cloves
4 tablespoons olive oil
35 g/1¼ oz (¼ cup) seedless raisins
75 g/2¾ oz (½ cup) whole almonds
1 lamb liver (about 450 g/1 lb), trimmed and cut into
    1.5-cm/⅔-inch cubes
generous pinch of ground cinnamon
generous pinch of ground ginger
generous pinch of ground cardamom seeds
generous pinch of ground cloves
1 yellow or red onion, finely chopped
salt and pepper

Rinse the rice in a few changes of water until the
water runs clearish. Put into a large bowl, cover with
water and leave to soak for 15 minutes.

Fill the bottom of a couscoussier or a large pot fitted
with a steamer basket with at least 10 cm/4 inches
water and bring to the boil.

Drain the rice and return to the bowl. Add the
cardamom pods and whole cloves, then season with salt
and pepper and drizzle over 1 tablespoon of the oil.
Mix well. Transfer the mixture to the steamer basket.
Place the basket snugly on top of the couscoussier.
Cover tightly with a lid and steam for about 45 minutes,
or until done. During steaming, sprinkle the rice
with about 120 ml (4 fl oz/½ cup) warm water every
10 minutes or so, then turn the rice over with a large
spoon. Check to make sure that the pot has enough
water and doesn't go dry.

Meanwhile, put the raisins into a small heatproof
bowl, cover with lukewarm water and leave to soak
for 10 minutes to soften; drain and spread out to
dry on a clean dish towel or paper towels. Put the
almonds into another heatproof bowl, cover with
boiling water and leave to soak for 5 minutes, or
until the skins slip off easily. Remove the skins with
your fingers and spread the almonds out to dry on
paper towels. Heat 1 tablespoon of the oil in a small
saucepan over a low heat, add the almonds and cook
for 2–3 minutes until they are just turning brown.
Add the raisins and cook until the raisins are plump,
about 1 minute. Transfer to a bowl and set aside.

Put the liver into a large bowl, season with the
ground cinnamon, ginger, cardamom and cloves
and turn to coat. Set aside.

Heat the remaining 2 tablespoons of oil in a sauté
pan or frying pan over a medium-high heat, add the
onion and cook for about 8 minutes, or until soft.
Add the liver and cook, stirring frequently, until
cooked through, about 5 minutes.

Transfer the rice to a large bowl, add the liver,
almonds and raisins and toss. Serve.

Steamed Djerbian Rice with Chard and Chicken

TUNISIA
PREPARATION TIME: 15 minutes,
plus soaking time
COOKING TIME: 1 hour 15 minutes
SERVES: 6

Rouz jerbi (Djerbian rice) is one of the few traditional rice dishes from Tunisia. A speciality of the southern island of Djerba but now found along the southern coast, the rice is steamed atop a couscoussier with chicken or minced (ground) lamb, vegetables (often including chard) and spices. There is a similar version from the nearby Kerkennah Islands that calls for cuttlefish with *besbes* (wild fennel) and chard.

  400 g/14 oz (2 cups) long-grain white rice
  1 heaped tablespoon double concentrated tomato
    purée (paste)
  harissa (page 409), to taste
  1 heaped teaspoon dried mint
  ½ teaspoon sweet paprika
  ¼ teaspoon ground turmeric
  2 tablespoons olive oil
  1 skinless, boneless chicken breast, cut into bite-size
    pieces
  1 red or yellow onion, finely chopped
  1 carrot, chopped
  1 white potato, peeled and cut into bite-size pieces
  450 g/1 lb Swiss chard or spinach, finely chopped
  2 tablespoons finely chopped flat-leaf parsley
  2 tablespoons finely chopped coriander (cilantro)
  100 g/3½ oz (½ cup) canned chickpeas
    (garbanzo beans), rinsed, or cooked dried
    chickpeas (page 443)
  salt and pepper

Rinse the rice in a few changes of water until the water runs clearish. Put into a large bowl, cover with water and leave to soak for 15 minutes. Drain.

Fill the bottom of a couscoussier or a large pot fitted with a steamer basket with about 15 cm/ 6 inches water and bring to the boil.

Put the drained rice, tomato purée (paste) and 3 tablespoons water, the harissa, mint, paprika and turmeric into a large bowl. Season with salt and pepper, drizzle over the oil and mix well. Add the chicken, onion, carrot, potato, chard, parsley and coriander (cilantro) and turn to mix.

Transfer the mixture to the steamer basket. Place the basket snugly on top of the couscoussier, cover tightly with a lid and steam for 45 minutes. Turn the rice once or twice with a large spoon. Fold in the chickpeas (garbanzo beans), cover and steam until the rice is tender, 20–30 minutes, turning the rice from time to time with a large spoon. Check to make sure that the pot has enough water and doesn't go dry. Divide among plates and serve.

Sweet Rice with Raisins

MOROCCO
PREPARATION TIME: 5 minutes,
plus standing and soaking time
COOKING TIME: 20 minutes
SERVES: 6–8

While using short vermicelli, crushed angel hair pasta or couscous is more popular in this sweet dish studded with raisins and perfumed with cinnamon and orange blossom water, some Moroccans now prepare it with rice. It is lovely following a tagine of lamb or chicken. The rice is rich and should be followed by a bowl of fresh fruit.

  400 g/14 oz (2 cups) long-grain white rice
  100 g/3½ oz (¾ cup) seedless raisins
  1 tablespoon orange blossom water
  25 g/1 oz (2 tablespoons) butter, cut into small pieces
  2 heaped tablespoons icing (confectioners') sugar,
    plus extra for dusting
  ground cinnamon, for dusting

Put the rice into a large pot or saucepan and rinse with various changes of water, swishing around, until the water runs clear. Drain well and return to the pot. Pour in 600 ml (20 fl oz/2½ cups) water and bring to the boil. Cover the pot snugly with a lid, reduce the heat to low and simmer without lifting the lid until the rice is tender and water evaporated, about 15 minutes. Remove from the heat and leave to stand for 5 minutes without lifting the lid.

Meanwhile, put the raisins into a medium heatproof bowl, cover with 250 ml (8 fl oz/1 cup) lukewarm water, add the orange blossom water and leave to soak for 10 minutes. Drain.

Add the butter and sugar to the rice, fluff with a fork and fold in the raisins. Transfer to a large platter and leave to cool for a few minutes. Mound into a dome, then decorate with cinnamon and sugar and serve.

Bulgur with Lamb

TUNISIA
PREPARATION TIME: 5 minutes
COOKING TIME: 1 hour 15 minutes
SERVES: 5–6

This popular Tunisian *borghol* (bulgur) dish calls for coarse-size bulgur that are nearly whole grains. It is cooked on the stove and then finished in the oven. You can fry whole long sweet green peppers at the beginning and add them at the end as a tasty garnish.

3 tablespoons olive oil
6 pieces bone-in lamb shoulder or leg
    (about 750 g/1⅔ lb total)
1 red or yellow onion, grated
3 tablespoons concentrated tomato purée (paste)
harissa (page 409) or cayenne pepper, to taste,
    optional
1 teaspoon sweet paprika
½ teaspoon ground turmeric
400 g/14 oz (2 cups) coarse-size bulgur wheat
100 g/3½ oz (½ cup) canned chickpeas
    (garbanzo beans), rinsed, or cooked dried
    chickpeas (page 443)
salt and pepper

Heat the oil in a heavy, wide pot, saucepan or casserole dish (Dutch oven) over a medium heat, add the lamb and brown on each side for about 5 minutes. Add the onion and cook until pale and soft, about 5 minutes. Add the tomato purée (paste) and 4 tablespoons water, the harissa (if using), paprika and turmeric. Season with salt and pepper. Stir in the bulgur wheat and chickpeas (garbanzo beans), pour in 1.2 litres (40 fl oz/5 cups) of hot water and bring to the boil. Cover with a lid, reduce the heat to low and simmer until the bulgur is tender, about 45 minutes. Add a touch more water if it threatens to dry out.

Meanwhile, preheat the oven to 180 °C/350 °F/ Gas Mark 4.

Transfer everything in the pot to a large baking dish and cook, uncovered, in the hot oven for 10 minutes until bubbly. Serve.

Doughy Semolina Assida with Butter and Honey

ALGERIA, LIBYA, MOROCCO, TUNISIA
PREPARATION TIME: 5 minutes
COOKING TIME: 25 minutes
SERVES: 3–4

For breakfast across the region on Mawlid al-Nabi, the celebration of the birth of the Prophet Muhammad, people eat a Berber dish called *assida* (*tarwait* in the Berber language), a thick, pasty dish made from semolina or another flour. This is the classic stiffer version of *assida*, topped with butter and honey and traditionally eaten with the fingers from a shared bowl. Pinch off a piece, dip it into the melted butter and honey and enjoy.

15 g/½ oz (1 tablespoon) butter
175 g/6 oz (1 cup) fine or medium semolina
salt
melted butter, to serve
honey, to serve

Bring 1 litre (34 fl oz/4¼ cups) water to the boil in a large, heavy pot or saucepan. Season with salt, add the butter, then pour in the semolina in a slow, steady stream. Cook, stirring constantly with a wooden spoon, until thick, creamy and elastic, 15–20 minutes.

Drizzle a small amount of the melted butter into a large serving bowl. Transfer the *assida* to the bowl. Dip a spoon into the melted butter, then smooth out the *assida* using the back of the spoon. Form a well in the centre and pour melted butter into it. Serve with honey on the side. Eat directly from the bowl with your fingers or use a spoon.

Semolina Porridge Assida with Butter and Honey

ALGERIA, LIBYA, MOROCCO, TUNISIA
PREPARATION TIME: 3 minutes
COOKING TIME: 25 minutes
SERVES: 6

Among the different versions of *assida* is this porridge-like version eaten with a spoon, particularly popular in the rural countryside for breakfast. (A thicker-style that can be pinched off and eaten with the fingers is on page 242.) Add some ground aniseed or saffron, or savoury herbs such as thyme or rosemary.

250 g/9 oz (1½ cups) coarse or medium semolina
1 teaspoon salt
butter, cut into pieces, to serve
honey, to serve

Bring 1.5 litres (50 fl oz/generous 6 cups) water to the boil in a large, sturdy saucepan. Stir in the semolina and salt and cook, stirring frequently with a wooden spoon, until tender and it has the consistency of a thick porridge, about 20 minutes. Add a touch more water if needed to keep it loose. Transfer to a wide serving bowl or individual bowls, generously dollop butter on top and drizzle over some honey. Serve hot with spoons.

White Assida with Honey

ALGERIA, LIBYA, TUNISIA
PREPARATION TIME: 10 minutes
COOKING TIME: 25 minutes
SERVES: 4

Known as *assida bidha* or *assida blanche* ('white *assida*'), this popular dish was traditionally made with semolina, but now it is usually prepared with plain (all-purpose) flour. It is served with honey, sugar or a date syrup known as *ruub*.

250 g/9 oz (1⅔ cups) plain (all-purpose) flour
1 teaspoon salt
15 g/½ oz (1 tablespoon) butter
extra-virgin olive oil, for oiling and to serve
honey, sugar or date syrup (*ruub*, page 402), to serve

Put the flour and salt into a large bowl and pour in 500 ml (18 fl oz/2 cups) water. Whisk well until smooth, then leave to stand for a few minutes. Whisk again, then pour through a sieve into a large saucepan, working out any lumps from the sieve. Cook over a medium heat, stirring constantly with a wooden spoon until it begins to thicken. Reduce the heat to low and cook until it is smooth and thick, about 20 minutes in total. Stir in the butter, then remove from the heat.

Generously oil a serving bowl and spoon the *assida* into the bowl. Using the back of a spoon and some of the oil from the bowl, smooth into a gentle dome. Make a well in the centre and add some oil to the well. Drizzle honey over the top and into the well. Serve hot from the bowl with spoons.

Barley Flour Dough
with Tomato Sauce

LIBYA, TUNISIA
PREPARATION TIME: 5 minutes
COOKING TIME: 45 minutes
SERVES: 3–4

Bazeen (or *bazin*) is one of Libya's national dishes and a staple in the west of the country, where the sauce tends to be more orange in tone from the turmeric. It is also prepared in southeastern Tunisia, near the Libyan border. Barley flour is cooked in boiling water, worked to a firm dough and then shaped into a dome. Covered with a spicy tomato sauce, it is eaten from a communal bowl by pinching off pieces with the fingers. (Some home cooks today blend in some wheat flour to make it more elastic.) The classic, simple version has a spicy tomato sauce with potatoes, often pumpkin and sometimes dried pulses, and is sometimes served with hard-boiled eggs. For guests, cooks might add in a few pieces of bone-in lamb, too. (To include lamb in this recipe, add at the beginning with the onions and stew for about 45 minutes before adding the potatoes and pumpkin.)

- 250 g/9 oz (2 cups) barley flour
- 3 tablespoons olive oil
- 2 red or white onions, finely chopped
- 2 cloves of garlic, finely chopped
- 2 heaped tablespoons double concentrated tomato purée (paste)
- 1 teaspoon ground turmeric
- 1 teaspoon sweet paprika
- cayenne pepper, to taste
- 2 white potatoes, peeled and halved
- 2 generous pieces of pumpkin or butternut squash, with the peel (about 500 g/1 lb 2 oz)
- salt and pepper
- 2 Hard-boiled Eggs (page 443), peeled, to garnish, optional

Put the barley flour into a large bowl, season with salt and work in about 200 ml (7 fl oz/generous ¾ cup) water with your fingers to form a soft dough. Set aside.

Heat the oil in a large pot, saucepan or casserole dish (Dutch oven) over a medium heat, add the onions and cook for about 10 minutes, or until tender. Stir in the garlic, tomato purée (paste) and 4 tablespoons water, the turmeric, paprika and cayenne pepper. Season with salt and pepper and cook for 2–3 minutes. Stir in 500 ml (18 fl oz/2 cups) water, bring to the boil and add the potatoes and pumpkin. Cover with a lid and simmer until tender,

about 30 minutes. Uncover or add some water as needed so that it is saucy but not watery. Remove from the heat and keep covered until ready to serve.

Meanwhile, bring a large, heavy pot or saucepan of water to the boil and season with salt. Cut the barley flour into 6 or 8 pieces and flatten into discs. Add to the pot and boil for about 30 minutes. They should float. Drain, reserving some of the water. Return the dough to the dry pot, off the heat, holding the pot firmly, and begin working it into a thick, compact paste with a sturdy wooden spoon, adding the reserved water back in as needed, 5–10 minutes.

Transfer the dough to a clean work counter and roll under the palms of your hands until it is a smooth ball without any lumps. Shape by pressing down to form a cone. Set on a large serving dish, smooth out as needed and form a well in the centre. Spoon over the sauce and arrange the potatoes, pumpkin and hard-boiled eggs (if using) around the dish. Eat directly from the bowl with your fingers or use a spoon.

RED
MEAT

Sweet Lamb
with Prunes and Dried Apricots

ALGERIA
PREPARATION TIME: 5 minutes,
plus soaking time
COOKING TIME: 1 hour 40 minutes
SERVES: 6

Known as *lham lahlou* ('sweet meat'), this Algerian lamb stew is prepared with prunes, usually apricots and sometimes also raisins, lending sweetness to the savoury flavours of the dish. It is a tradition for many families to prepare it on the first day of Ramadan, when home cooks usually leave out the salt to avoid making people thirsty. Add 80 g (3 oz/½ cup) seedless raisins with the other dried fruits, if desired.

> 40 g/1½ oz (3 tablespoons) butter
> 1.5 kg/3¼ lb bone-in lamb, cut into stewing-size pieces
> 1 teaspoon ground cinnamon
> 4 tablespoons honey or sugar
> pinch of salt
> 1 red or yellow onion, grated
> 175 g/6 oz (1 cup) prunes
> 125 g/4¼ oz (¾ cup) dried apricots
> 1 tablespoon orange blossom water
> 35 g/1¼ oz (¼ cup) fried or roasted almonds
>   (page 445), to garnish

Melt the butter in a low, heavy, wide pot or braiser pan over a medium-high heat, add the meat and brown on each side, about 10 minutes. Stir in the cinnamon, 2 tablespoons of the honey and the salt. Add the onion and pour in 250 ml (8 fl oz/1 cup) water. Bring to a simmer, then reduce the heat to low and simmer, partly covered, for 45 minutes.

Meanwhile, put the prunes and apricots into a large bowl of hot water and leave to soak for 30 minutes. Drain.

Add the soaked prunes, apricots, orange blossom water and remaining 2 tablespoons of the honey to the pot and cook until the meat and dried fruit are tender, about 45 minutes. Add more water if needed. There should be some syrupy sauce.

Arrange the lamb in a serving dish, top with the sauce, prunes and apricots and garnish with the almonds. Serve.

SLOW-COOKED STEWS

Slow-cooked stews form the heart of many North African meals. In Morocco, the classic method of cooking meat is to braise it with very little liquid in a tagine – a low, round terracotta pot with a conical lid. The moisture from the stew condenses on the cool part of the lid and falls back down into the stew. Cooking in this distinctive pot lends the dish its name. (See page 250 for more on cooking with tagines.) In Algeria and Tunisia, a braised stew or ragoût is called a *marka* and cooked with equal patience to equal tenderness. (Note that in Algeria, *tajine* is the name for the round ridged griddle pan used for cooking bread, although the term is now also sometimes used synonymously with *marka*. In Tunisia, *tajine* is a frittata-like egg dish, see page 177.)

These stews generally call for bone-in cuts of meat. These become the most tender and also give the stew more flavour. Lamb leg or shoulder is common, although saddle and neck are excellent choices. For beef, generous pieces of cross-cut shanks with bone and marrow are succulent and delicious. Chicken should also be bone-in, with legs (drumsticks and thighs) particularly well suited for this style of cooking. And fish is either whole or, if it is a large species, then ideally cut into generous steaks rather than fillets.

Cooked to such tenderness, the pieces of meat in these stews pull easily away from the bone. Served alongside is plenty of bread – ideally, traditional round loaves with crusts firm enough to carry morsels to the mouth and inside soft enough to soak up the rich sauce.

COOKING WITH A TAGINE

'Tagine' is the name for the two-part cooking utensil in Morocco that consists of a round, shallow terracotta casserole and a tall, conical lid that fits into the base's grooved rim, forming a closed chimney. The cool part of the lid captures the moisture of the simmering food, condensing and returning it to the stew below to keep it moist and retain all the flavours. The top of the lid is knob-shaped, which makes it easy to lift (and to not burn your fingers).

'Tagine' is also the name for any dish cooked in the vessel. From vegetables to meat to fish, tagines can be made from just about anything, and they frequently exhibit Moroccan cuisine's fondness for marrying bold and often disparate flavours.

Serving: The base of the tagine acts as a serving dish. It is traditionally set at the centre of the table and people eat directly from it. When setting on the table, do not remove the lid until it is time to eat.

Sizes: Tagines for stews range from 20 cm/8 inches in diameter for 1–2 people to about 40 cm/16 inches, which will serve 8 or more. The most practical size is 25–32 cm/10–12½ inches, perfect for 4–6 people.

Materials: Traditional Moroccan tagines are earthenware. They come both glazed and unglazed. A number of international brands sell ceramic tagines, as well as ones with sturdy cast-iron bases.

Glazing: Unglazed tagines are 'earthier' and darken deeply over time with use. More common are glazed tagines, which are more resistant and less likely to crack. These are especially recommended for those who cook with them infrequently, as they store better between longer gaps of use. They age with use and take on a deeper-coloured sheen.

Seasoning: An earthenware tagine should be seasoned before using for the first time. Submerge in water for at least 2 hours if glazed and overnight if unglazed. Remove from the water, leave to dry, then generously rub with olive oil. Ideally, the tagine should be placed in a cold oven, the oven turned on to 180°C/350°F/Gas Mark 4 and the tagine left in the hot oven for 2 hours. Turn off the oven and let the tagine slowly cool. If it goes unused for a number of months, soak again in water before using.

Ornamental serving tagines: Lightweight and usually ornately painted tagines are often sold as 'serving tagines' or for decorative – not cooking – purposes. Be sure that a tagine is heat resistant before using it on the stove.

Diffuser: On a gas stove, a metal diffuser will help ensure even cooking and prolong its lifespan.

While cooking: Stews made in a tagine usually need less water than in frying pans as the conical lid traps the moisture. Begin with a small amount and add if needed to keep the ingredients from going dry. The final texture should be saucy but not watery. Prop open the lid with the end of a wooden spoon during cooking if needed to help reduce. (Or if you see it bubbling around the base of the lid. Some tagine lids have a small hole in them, making this unnecessary.) Remove the lid completely towards the end to evaporate liquid if required.

Brazier: While most use tagines today on gas stoves, the traditional method is to cook with them over charcoal using a clay brazier, called *kanun* or *majmar*. Low and squat, they usually stand about 20 cm/8 inches high with a basin bowl-like top that holds the charcoal and measures about 30 cm/12 inches across. A trio of inset prongs hold the tagine in place on top. A barbecue with the grate just above the embers will also work.

Care: Handwash the tagine in warm, soapy water after use, rinse, then dry with a soft cloth. Be careful not to subject earthenware tagines to sudden temperature changes, such as setting a hot tagine onto a cold surface or putting it into cold water. Store with the lid slightly ajar to allow air flow between the bottom and lid.

To substitute: A heavy, shallow flameproof casserole dish (Dutch oven), braiser pan or a frying pan with a heavy lid will all produce excellent, succulent results.

Lamb Tagine with Sweet Cinnamon-scented Onions and Tomatoes

MOROCCO
PREPARATION TIME: 15 minutes
COOKING TIME: 2 hours 15 minutes–
2 hours 45 minutes
SERVES: 4

Using canned tomatoes, you can make this sumptuous sweet-and-savoury tagine from the western foothills of the High Atlas Mountains any time of the year. But if tomatoes are in season, replace the canned ones in the recipe with thick slices of large, ripe ones; lay them between the lamb and the onions.

2 × 400-g/14-oz cans whole peeled tomatoes
3 large red or yellow onions
2 tablespoons finely chopped flat-leaf parsley
2 tablespoons finely chopped coriander (cilantro)
2 cloves of garlic, minced
½ teaspoon ground turmeric
½ teaspoon ground ginger
1 teaspoon ground cinnamon
3 tablespoons olive oil
1 kg/2¼ lb bone-in leg of lamb, cut crosswise into
    pieces about 4 cm/1½ inches thick
2 teaspoons sugar
salt and pepper
toasted sesame seeds, to garnish

Drain the tomatoes in a sieve. Using a paring knife, make a small incision in each tomato and gently press out and discard any excess juice and seeds; set the tomatoes aside. Chop 1 of the onions.

Put the chopped onion, parsley, coriander (cilantro), garlic, turmeric, ginger and ¼ teaspoon of the cinnamon into a large tagine (see page 250) and mix together, then season with salt and pepper. Add the oil and 2 tablespoons water and mix. One by one, add the lamb pieces to the marinade and turn to coat. Arrange the lamb in a snug, single layer. Arrange the tomatoes around the lamb, then sprinkle 1 teaspoon of the sugar and ¼ teaspoon of the cinnamon over the tomatoes.

Cut the remaining 2 onions crosswise into 5-mm-/¼-inch-thick circles; do not separate the rings. Carefully lay the onion circles on top of the lamb, then sprinkle with the remaining 1 teaspoon of sugar, ½ teaspoon of cinnamon and a pinch of salt.

Cook, uncovered, over a medium heat, nudging the lamb occasionally to keep it from sticking, until the chopped onion is translucent, about 15 minutes.

Pour 60 ml (2 fl oz/¼ cup) water around the edges without disturbing the sugar and cinnamon. Cover with the lid, reduce the heat to low and gently cook, nudging the lamb from time to time to prevent sticking, until the lamb is very tender and the sliced onions are soft, 2–2½ hours. Drizzle in a few spoonfuls of water as necessary during cooking to keep the sauce loose or prop open with the end of a wooden spoon to reduce. Remove the lid at the end of cooking to evaporate and thicken the sauce if watery. Sprinkle with sesame seeds to garnish and serve from the tagine.

Lamb Tagine with Sweetened and Spiced Pears

MOROCCO
PREPARATION TIME: 10 minutes
COOKING TIME: 2 hours 15 minutes
SERVES: 6

This is a delicious sweet-and-savoury tagine. The sweetened pears, scented with clove, ginger and cinnamon, are cooked apart and served atop the lamb. The final combination of flavours is simply sublime.

2 red or yellow onions, sliced
1¼ teaspoons ground ginger
½ teaspoon ground turmeric
pinch of saffron threads, crumbled
4 tablespoons olive oil
1.5 kg/3¼ lb bone-in leg or shoulder of lamb, cut into 8–10 generous pieces
25 g/1 oz (2 tablespoons) butter
1 cinnamon stick, broken in half, or 2 pieces of cinnamon bark
3–4 firm pears (about 800 g/1¾ lb total)
6–8 cloves
100 g/3½ oz (½ cup) sugar
1 teaspoon orange blossom water, optional
salt and pepper
sesame seeds, to garnish

Add the onions, 1 teaspoon of the ginger, the turmeric and saffron to a large tagine (see page 250), then season with salt and pepper. Add the oil and mix well. Add the meat, piece by piece, turning to coat. Add the butter and cook over a medium heat, stirring from time to time, until the meat has browned, about 15 minutes. Add half of the cinnamon stick and 120 ml (4 fl oz/½ cup) water. Reduce the heat to medium-low and cook, moving the meat from time to time, for 1 hour. Reduce the heat to its lowest setting, cover with a lid and cook until the meat is very tender, about 1 hour. Add more water if necessary to keep the sauce loose, or prop open or remove the lid to evaporate and reduce it.

Meanwhile, peel the pears, halve lengthwise and core. Pierce each piece with a clove. Put the pears, the remaining cinnamon stick half and remaining ¼ teaspoon of the ginger into a frying pan or sauté pan and pour in 500 ml (18 fl oz/2 cups) water. Simmer, uncovered, over a medium heat for 30 minutes, gently turning and basting the pears from time to time. Add the sugar and cook for 10 minutes until syrupy. If needed, transfer the pears with a slotted spoon to a bowl and reduce the liquid in the pan over a high heat for a few minutes. Stir in the orange blossom water (if using), then remove from the heat and cover the pan to keep the pears warm until ready to serve.

Arrange the pears around the meat, drizzle some syrup over the top and sprinkle with sesame seeds. Serve.

Lamb Tagine
with Caramelized Quince

MOROCCO
PREPARATION TIME: 20 minutes
COOKING TIME: 1 hour 35 minutes
SERVES: 6

In a stunning, sophisticated combination of sweet
and savoury, tender lamb is topped with quince that
has been steamed, then lightly caramelized in butter
with sugar. Garnish with chopped fried or roasted
almonds (page 445).

    1 clove of garlic, minced
    1 teaspoon ground ginger
    1 teaspoon ground cinnamon
    generous pinch of saffron threads, crumbled
    4 tablespoons olive oil
    1.5 kg/3¼ lb bone-in leg or shoulder of lamb, cut into
        8–10 generous pieces
    2 red or yellow onions, chopped
    10 sprigs flat-leaf parsley
    10 sprigs coriander (cilantro)
    1 cinnamon stick or piece of cinnamon bark
    2 ripe quince (about 600 g/1 lb 5 oz total)
    25 g/1 oz (2 tablespoons) butter
    150 g/5 oz (¾ cup) sugar
    juice of ½ lemon
    salt and pepper
    chopped fried or roasted almonds (page 445),
        to garnish

Put the garlic, ginger, cinnamon and saffron into
a large tagine (see page 250), season with salt and
pepper and moisten with the oil. Mix. Add the lamb,
turning the pieces in the mixture. Sprinkle over
the onions, then cover with a lid and cook over a
medium-high heat until the onions are translucent
and the meat browned, about 10 minutes. Tie the
parsley and coriander (cilantro) together into a
bouquet with kitchen string and add together with
the cinnamon stick and 120 ml (4 fl oz/½ cup) water.
Reduce the heat to low, cover and cook until the
meat is very tender and the sauce reduced, about
1 hour 20 minutes. Add a touch more water during
cooking if needed, or remove the lid and evaporate
at the end.

Meanwhile, fill a large pot fitted with a steamer
basket or a couscoussier with at least 5 cm/2 inches
water and bring to the boil. While it comes to the
boil, fill a medium bowl with water. Peel, quarter
and core the quince, dropping them into the water
as you work to keep them from turning brown.
When done, drain and put into a steamer basket.
Lightly season with salt and steam until tender, about
45 minutes. Set aside some of the liquid from the
bottom of the steamer.

Melt the butter with the sugar, 4 tablespoons of
the reserved liquid from steaming the quince and
the lemon juice in a medium frying pan or sauté pan.
Add the quince and cook, gently turning from time
to time, over a medium-low heat until caramelized,
10–15 minutes.

To serve, arrange the quince on top of the lamb,
drizzle over some sweet syrup from the quince and
cook for a final few minutes to combine the flavours.
Scatter some almonds over the top to garnish and
serve from the tagine.

Roasted Lamb Quarter

MOROCCO
PREPARATION TIME: 10 minutes,
plus standing time
COOKING TIME: 2 hours 30 minutes–
3 hours
SERVES: 4

Mechoui – slow-roasted lamb basted with butter
and spices, traditionally done on a spit – is one of
North Africa's great dishes. In Morocco, where it
is especially popular, the succulent pieces of lamb
get pulled away and dipped into dishes of ground
cumin and salt. It is a country dish that has been
adapted by urban folks as a ceremonial one and
served at large and important festivities, including
weddings. The name is usually used to mean a
whole or half lamb, but a quarter – preferably the
front quarter with shoulder and ribs – carries the
same tag if roasted and served as a single piece.
Cover the lamb shoulder for the first two hours
or so in the oven, and then finishing roasting it
uncovered for 30 minutes or so to allow it to take
on that lovely crust. It shouldn't require any cutlery
to eat, just fingers.

> 40 g/1½ oz (3 tablespoons) butter, melted, or olive oil
> ground cumin, for seasoning and to serve
> sweet paprika, for seasoning
> 1 bone-in lamb shoulder with ribs (about 2.5 kg/5½ lb)
> salt

Put the melted butter into a small bow, very
generously season with cumin, paprika and salt
and stir to blend well. Generously rub about
three-quarters of the mixture on both sides of the
lamb, then set the remaining mixture aside. Lay the
lamb in a large roasting pan and leave to stand for
20–30 minutes.

Preheat the oven to 150 °C/300 °F/Gas Mark 2.

Cover the shoulder with baking (parchment)
paper, then cover the pan with some sheets of
aluminium foil. Crimp down along the edges to
make a good seal.

Roast in the hot oven until very tender,
2–2½ hours, turning about halfway through. Uncover
the meat, turn the oven to the grill (broiler) setting
and roast for 30 minutes, turning a few times, basting
with the reserved butter-spice mixture and allowing
the meat to take on a rich golden colour. The meat
should come away easily with a fork. Serve with
individual small dishes of cumin mixed with salt
for dipping the lamb.

Lamb Tagine with Fennel

MOROCCO
PREPARATION TIME: 15 minutes
COOKING TIME: 2 hours 20 minutes
SERVES: 4

Fennel finds its way into many dishes across North
Africa, including this Moroccan tagine. When in
season, add some freshly shelled green peas to the
tagine towards the end of cooking.

> 2 red or yellow onions, coarsely chopped
> 1.2 kg/2½ lb bone-in leg or shoulder of lamb, cut into
>   8–10 generous pieces
> ½ teaspoon ground ginger
> ½ teaspoon ground turmeric
> 2 cloves of garlic, minced
> 3 tablespoons extra-virgin olive oil
> 3 tablespoons vegetable oil
> 4 fennel bulbs (about 1 kg/2¼ lb total), quartered
> 2 tablespoons finely chopped flat-leaf parsley
> 2 tablespoons finely chopped coriander (cilantro)
> juice of ½ lemon
> salt and pepper
> black olives, to garnish, optional

Scatter the onions across the bottom of a large tagine
(see page 250) and arrange the pieces of meat on
top. Sprinkle the ginger, turmeric and garlic over
the top, then season with salt and pepper. Drizzle
over the olive and vegetable oils. Do not mix the
ingredients in the tagine. Cover with a lid and cook
over a medium heat for 15 minutes. Turn the meat,
add 120 ml (4 fl oz/½ cup) water around the edges,
reduce the heat to low and cook until the meat
is tender and nearly done, about 1 hour, turning
the meat from time to time. Add a touch of water
if needed.

Add the fennel to the tagine, gently working the
fennel between the pieces of lamb. Drizzle (4 fl oz/
½ cup) water around the edges, cover again and
cook until the meat is very tender and the fennel
done, 45 minutes–1 hour, nudging the lamb from
time to time to prevent it from sticking. Add a touch
more water during cooking if needed or remove the
lid to evaporate at the end if watery.

Add the parsley, coriander (cilantro) and lemon
juice and cook for a final 5 minutes. Garnish with
black olives (if using), then serve from the tagine.
Alternatively, arrange the meat in the centre of a
large serving dish, surround with the fennel and
spoon the sauce over the top.

Spicy Honeyed Lamb with Raisins and Almonds

MOROCCO
PREPARATION TIME: 25 minutes,
plus marinating and soaking time
COOKING TIME: 2 hours 30 minutes–
3 hours
SERVES: 4–6

Mrouzia is one of Morocco's great festive dishes and traditionally prepared after Eid al-Adha – 'feast of the sacrifice' (see page 34) – when there is plenty of lamb to cook. It is often made with bony cuts, such as saddle, neck and shoulder. These cuts give plenty of flavour as they slowly cook to extreme tenderness. The honey and raisins add sweet notes that perfectly contrast the ras al hanout spice blend. The final sauce should be deep brown, rich and glazy.

2 teaspoons ras al hanout (page 446)
1 teaspoon ground ginger
pinch of saffron threads, crumbled
1.5 kg/3¼ lb mix of bone-in lamb neck, saddle and/or
    shoulder, cut into 8–10 generous pieces
4 tablespoons olive oil
25 g/1 oz (2 tablespoons) butter
2 red or yellow onions, finely chopped
200 g/7 oz (scant 1½ cups) seedless raisins
100 g/3½ oz (⅔ cup) whole almonds
neutral oil, for frying
1 teaspoon ground cinnamon
120 ml/4 fl oz (½ cup) honey
salt and pepper

Put the ras al hanout, ginger and saffron with 2 tablespoons water into a large bowl and mix together, then season with salt and pepper. Add the pieces of lamb, one by one, turning to coat. Cover with cling film (plastic wrap) and leave to marinate at room temperature for 30 minutes.

Put the meat and all of the marinade into a large, heavy pot or casserole dish (Dutch oven). Add the olive oil, butter and onions and cook over a medium-high heat for 5 minutes, turning the meat. Pour in 250 ml (8 fl oz/1 cup) water, loosely cover with a lid and cook over a low heat until the meat is tender and the water evaporated, 2–2½ hours. Add a touch of water if needed during cooking or remove the lid.

Meanwhile, put the raisins into a small heatproof bowl of lukewarm water and leave to soak for 10 minutes. Drain and set aside. Put the almonds into a medium saucepan of water, bring to the boil and boil for 3–5 minutes, then drain. Once cool enough to handle, slip off the skins with your fingers. Spread the almonds out on paper towels to dry.

Line a medium plate with paper towels. Heat about 7 mm/⅓ inch of neutral oil in a small frying pan over a medium heat until the surface shimmers. Add the almonds and fry for 1–2 minutes until just golden. Transfer with a slotted spoon to the paper towels to drain. Set aside.

Add the soaked raisins, cinnamon and honey to the lamb, and cook, uncovered, over a very low heat until the sauce has reduced and the meat comes away easily from the bone, about 30 minutes. Arrange the lamb on a serving platter, cover with the glazy sauce and scatter over the almonds. Serve.

HONEY

While *assal* (honey) has been replaced by refined sugar as a cooking ingredient in many instances, it remains indispensable at the stove for cooks in North Africa.

Offering more heightened flavours and deeper aromas than sugar, as well as giving a dish more texture, it is used to caramelize vegetables for salads and sweeten slow-cooked tagines and stews that blend meat and fresh or dried fruits.

Honey is key to making caramelized onion and raisin *tfaya,* which tops couscous and fish tagines. Countless sweet confections call for it, while biscuits (cookies) are frequently dipped in warmed honey to give them a final sticky sweetness.

Bees gather nectar from various plants. Thyme, sage, lavender, mint, rosemary, orange blossom, almond, acacia and juniper are all popular in the region. Each imparts a slightly different flavour, colour and texture to the honey. Merchants sell honeys in a range of densities and in colours from pale wheat to luminous amber to nearly black.

Beekeeping is widespread across the region, both on small and large scales. One of the most unique systems can be found in the village of Argana, northeast of the Moroccan coastal city of Agadir, which houses the largest traditional collective apiary in the world.

Steamed Lamb with Vegetables

MOROCCO
PREPARATION TIME: 10 minutes
COOKING TIME: 2–3 hours
SERVES: 4–6

Steaming lamb in the basket of a large couscoussier is a popular way to get good, succulent meat at home without much effort. The key here is the quality of the lamb. If the lamb is good, then this dish will be, too. Lining the steamer basket with fresh mint or other herbs will give the lamb some lovely aromas. This recipe adds potatoes and carrots to the basket with the lamb to steam for the final 30 minutes–1 hour to make a complete meal. Serve with cumin and salt to dip the tender pieces of lamb.

   sprigs mint, flat-leaf parsley or coriander (cilantro),
      for lining the steamer basket, optional
   1.5–2.5 kg/3¼–5½ lb generous bone-in lamb pieces
   6 white potatoes, peeled and halved
   3 carrots, halved lengthwise
   salt
   ground cumin, to serve

Fill a large pot fitted with a steamer basket or a large couscoussier with salted water to just below the steamer basket and bring to the boil.

Line a steamer basket with mint (if using). Season the lamb with salt and set in the basket. Cover snugly with aluminium foil and then the lid so that no steam escapes. Set on top of the pot and steam until the lamb is very tender, 1½–2 hours. Arrange the potatoes and carrots around the lamb, cover snugly with a lid and steam until the meat is falling off the bone and the vegetables done, 30 minutes–1 hour. Check occasionally to make sure that the pot has enough water and doesn't go dry.

The meat should come away easily. Serve immediately with individual small dishes of cumin and salt for dipping the lamb.

Lamb Tagine with Potatoes and Olives

MOROCCO
PREPARATION TIME: 10 minutes
COOKING TIME: 2 hours 15 minutes
SERVES: 5–6

A popular dish in the south of Morocco, this tagine offers a pleasing tanginess from the olives and preserved lemon. It can be prepared with beef instead of lamb. Use bone-in cuts.

   2 red or yellow onions, cut crosswise into thin circles
   1.2 kg/2½ lb bone-in leg or shoulder of lamb, cut into
      about 10 pieces
   1 teaspoon ground ginger
   1 teaspoon ground turmeric
   1 clove of garlic, minced
   2 tablespoons finely chopped flat-leaf parsley
   2 tablespoons finely chopped coriander (cilantro)
   1 teaspoon ground cumin
   3 tablespoons extra-virgin olive oil
   3 tablespoons vegetable oil
   5 white potatoes (about 800 g/1¾ lb total), peeled
      and quartered lengthwise
   ½ preserved lemon (page 410)
   100 g/3½ oz (generous ¾ cup) green or red olives
   salt and pepper

Scatter the onions across the bottom of a large tagine (see page 250) and arrange the pieces of meat on top. Sprinkle with the ginger and turmeric and season with salt and pepper. Add the garlic, parsley and coriander (cilantro) and finally the cumin. Drizzle over the olive and vegetable oils. Do not mix the ingredients in the tagine. Cover with a lid and cook over a medium heat for 20 minutes. Turn the meat, add 60 ml (2 fl oz/¼ cup) water around the edges, reduce the heat to low and cook until the meat is becoming tender, about 45 minutes.

Arrange the potatoes across the top, add 60 ml (2 fl oz/¼ cup) water around the edges, cover again and cook until the meat is very tender and the potatoes are done, about 1 hour, nudging the lamb from time to time to prevent sticking. Add a touch more water during cooking if needed, or remove the lid to evaporate at the end.

Halve the preserved lemon, scrape out the pulp and discard. Cut the peel into strips and add to the tagine with the olives. Cook for a final 5–10 minutes, then serve from the tagine.

Lamb Tagine
with Okra and Quince

MOROCCO
PREPARATION TIME: 20 minutes
COOKING TIME: 2 hours 35 minutes
SERVES: 4

In autumn, when the end of the okra season overlaps with the beginning of the season for small, local quince called *lqim*, cooks prepare this classic lamb tagine from Fès. To keep the okra from getting viscous, do not chop them – only trim the very tips and end of the stems.

8 cloves of garlic, minced
1 teaspoon ground ginger
1 teaspoon ground cinnamon
1 teaspoon ground turmeric
5 tablespoons olive oil
1 kg/2¼ lb bone-in leg or shoulder of lamb, cut into 8 pieces
2 tablespoons finely chopped flat-leaf parsley
2 tablespoons finely chopped coriander (cilantro)
2 red or yellow onions, chopped
1 tomato, halved crosswise and grated, peel discarded (see page 445)
2 ripe small quince (about 250 g/9 oz each)
500 g/1 lb 2 oz fresh okra
salt and pepper

Put the garlic, ginger, cinnamon and turmeric into a large tagine (see page 250) or casserole dish (Dutch oven), season with salt and pepper and moisten with 4 tablespoons of the oil. Mix. Add the lamb, turning the pieces in the mixture. Sprinkle over the parsley, coriander (cilantro) and onions. Cover the tagine with a lid and cook over a medium-high heat until the onions are tender and the meat browned, about 10 minutes. Add the tomato and 120 ml (4 fl oz/½ cup) water. Reduce the heat to low, cover again and cook until the meat is very tender, about 1½ hours. Add a touch more water during cooking if needed, or remove the lid to evaporate at the end if watery. Transfer the lamb to a platter, cover with aluminium foil and keep warm.

Meanwhile, fill a large bowl with cool water. Scrub the quince, then quarter and core but do not peel, dropping the pieces into the water as you work. Leave in the water until ready to use.

Drain the quince and put into the tagine skin-side up. Add a touch of water if needed, then cover with a lid and cook until tender, about 45 minutes.

Meanwhile, trim just the very tips of the okra and the ends of the stem, but do not cut the pods themselves. Bring a large pot of water to the boil,

add the okra and immediately drain. Put the okra into a clean saucepan, add the remaining 1 tablespoon oil, a spoonful of sauce from the tagine and about 500 ml (18 fl oz/2 cups) water. Cover with a lid and cook over a medium heat until tender but not mushy, about 10 minutes. Remove from the heat and drain off the liquid.

To serve, return the lamb to the tagine to warm, letting it cook over a low heat for a few minutes if needed. Be careful to avoid breaking the quince. Place the lamb in the centre of a large serving dish and surround with quince. Arrange the okra around the dish and spoon over any sauce from the tagine.

Braised Lamb with Artichokes

ALGERIA
PREPARATION TIME: 30 minutes
COOKING TIME: 1 hour 25 minutes
SERVES: 5–6

A subtle, tasty Algerian lamb and artichoke *marka* (ragoût) with pleasing aromas of cinnamon. Add some freshly shelled peas to the pan towards the end of cooking, if desired.

3 tablespoons olive oil
40 g/1½ oz (3 tablespoons) butter
1 kg/2¼ lb bone-in leg or shoulder of lamb, cut into 6–10 pieces
2 red or yellow onions, finely chopped
½ lemon
2 kg/4½ lb artichokes
1 teaspoon ground cinnamon
salt and pepper

Add the oil, butter, lamb and onions to a large pot or casserole dish (Dutch oven). Season with salt and pepper and cook over a medium heat until the lamb is browned on each side and the onions pale and softened, about 10 minutes. Add 120 ml (4 fl oz/½ cup) water, partly cover with a lid, reduce the heat to low and cook for 45 minutes, stirring from time to time. Add a touch more water if needed to keep it from drying out.

Meanwhile, fill a large bowl with cool water. Squeeze in the lemon and then drop into the water. Working with 1 artichoke at a time, cut or pull away the toughest outer petals, then cut off the stem and trim away the top section. Quarter lengthwise, then remove the choke and drop into the lemon water to keep from discolouring. Repeat with the remaining artichokes. Leave in the water until ready to use.

Drain the artichokes and add to the pot with the cinnamon. Cover with a lid and cook until the meat and artichokes are tender, about 30 minutes. Serve.

Lamb Tagine with Okra and Quince   ➤➤

Lamb Cooked in a Sealed Clay Pot

TUNISIA
PREPARATION TIME: 10 minutes
COOKING TIME: 3 hours
SERVES: 4–6

A *gargoulette* is an unglazed, somewhat squat terracotta jug or urn used in the Tunisian kitchen to cook lamb or chicken or even fish slowly within their own juices. It comes in two sizes: the smaller version, often for fish, typically found in Djerba, Sfax and the Kerkennah Islands; and the larger, more common size made in Nabeul and found around the country. Most cooks use the larger ones to prepare this dish, known locally as *allouch fel kola* or *kola allouch* (both referring to lamb inside a pot), with lamb, potatoes, tomatoes and spices – rosemary, saffron (or nowadays often turmeric instead) and plenty of black pepper being most typical. A piece of aluminium foil is tied over the mouth and then a flour paste smeared around it to ensure that not a whiff of flavours can escape. Traditionally, *gargoulette* are cooked on embers, although today cooking in an oven is more common. It is a similar concept to the better-known Moroccan *tangia* (Marrakech Tangia with Beef and Preserved Lemons, page 271) with equally succulent results. If using a traditional unglazed *gargoulette*, the night before using for the first time, place upright in a large pot of water, fill and soak overnight. The next day, pour out the water, rinse and dry.

1.5 kg/3¼ lb bone-in leg or shoulder of lamb, cut into about 8 pieces and trimmed of fat
4 tablespoons olive oil, plus extra for coating
pinch of saffron threads, crumbled, or ground turmeric
4 small red or yellow onions, quartered
8 cloves of garlic, lightly crushed
3 tomatoes, quartered
6 small white potatoes, peeled and halved
2 sprigs thyme
1 sprig rosemary
3 tablespoons plain (all-purpose) flour
salt and pepper

Preheat the oven to 180 °C/350 °F/Gas Mark 4.

Put the lamb, oil and saffron into a large bowl, season with salt and pepper and turn to coat. Add the onions, garlic, tomatoes and potatoes and turn over to mix.

Rub the inside of a *gargoulette* with oil, or oil a large ovenproof casserole dish (Dutch oven) with a tight-fitting lid. Put the lamb, vegetables, sprigs of thyme and rosemary and all the marinade into the *gargoulette*. Add 120 ml (4 fl oz/½ cup) water to the bowl, swirl to get any remaining spices and pour into the *gargoulette*.

Fold a piece of aluminium foil into quarters and cover the opening. Tie with kitchen string. Put the flour into a small bowl with about 4 tablespoons water and mix to form a thick paste. Smear around and over the foil to get a perfect seal. (For other pots, cover with a heavy lid.) Cook in the hot oven for 3 hours. Remove from the oven, then very carefully break the seal and cut away the foil. Pour out into a deep serving bowl and serve.

Grilled Lamb Ribs with Harissa

ALGERIA, TUNISIA
PREPARATION TIME: 5 minutes
COOKING TIME: 8 minutes
SERVES: 3–4

Cooking lamb ribs over coals is a Mediterranean tradition. During the Eid al-Adha celebrations, when there is plenty of lamb meat, grilling them is hugely popular. Many simply season them with salt and pepper and cook. In Tunisia, some like to slather the ribs with harissa before eating. Loosen the harissa with some olive oil to make it easier to spread.

16 lamb ribs (about 1 kg/2¼ lb)
olive oil, for oiling and loosening the harissa
harissa (page 409)
salt and pepper

Generously season the ribs with salt and pepper.

If using a stovetop grill pan, large frying pan or griddle, oil the pan and heat over a high heat. If using a barbecue, prepare the coals. Put harissa into a small bowl and stir in some oil to loosen.

Grill the ribs, turning 1 or 2 times, until done and nicely browned, 6–8 minutes. If using a barbecue, wait until the embers die down and turn white before grilling. Serve immediately with the harissa to generously slather on top.

Marinated Lamb Cutlets

MOROCCO
PREPARATION TIME: 10 minutes,
plus marinating and standing time
COOKING TIME: 25 minutes
SERVES: 2–3

This version of marinated and grilled lamb cutlets (chops) is prepared under an oven grill (broiler). The cutlets could also be cooked on a barbecue instead. Either way, this dish is always a treat.

  2 tablespoons olive oil
  1 tablespoon fresh lemon juice
  1 teaspoon sweet paprika
  1 teaspoon ground cumin
  2 cloves of garlic, thinly sliced
  1 heaped tablespoon finely chopped flat-leaf parsley
  1 heaped tablespoon finely chopped coriander
    (cilantro)
  1 red onion, thinly sliced
  8 lamb cutlets (chops)
  salt and pepper

Put the oil, lemon juice, paprika and cumin into a large bowl and mix together. Add the garlic, parsley, coriander (cilantro) and onion, then season with salt and pepper and stir well. Add the lamb, turning to coat. Cover with cling film (plastic wrap) and leave to marinate for at least 1 hour in the refrigerator.

Preheat the oven grill (broiler). Line a baking sheet or roasting pan with baking (parchment) paper. Remove the bowl from the refrigerator and let the lamb return to room temperature.

Arrange the lamb and onion on the prepared baking sheet. Place the tray on a high oven rack and grill (broil) until done, nicely browned and the onion is tender, about 25 minutes, turning from time to time. Serve immediately.

Braised Goat with Peas

TUNISIA
PREPARATION TIME: 5 minutes
COOKING TIME: 1 hour
SERVES: 4–6

The name of this ragoût is *marka jelbana*, literally 'stew with peas'. But there are almost always artichoke hearts in the casserole dish (Dutch oven), too. It is often done with lamb, but in summer goat has become a favourite meat, as it is considered lighter (and healthier). There is an excellent coastal version of this dish prepared with cuttlefish on page 345.

  4 tablespoons olive oil
  1 kg/2¼ lb bone-in goat leg, shoulder or neck, cut into
    8–12 pieces
  1 red or yellow onion, finely chopped
  4 tomatoes, halved crosswise and grated,
    peel discarded (see page 445)
  2 tablespoons double concentrated tomato purée
    (paste)
  harissa (page 409) or cayenne pepper, to taste
  1 teaspoon sweet paprika
  ½ teaspoon ground turmeric
  500 g/1 lb 2 oz shelled fresh or thawed frozen peas
    (about 4 cups)
  8–12 fresh artichoke hearts
  salt and pepper

Add the oil, goat and onion to a large pot or casserole dish (Dutch oven). Season with salt and pepper and cook over a medium heat until the meat is browned on each side, about 10 minutes. Add the tomatoes, tomato purée (paste) and 4 tablespoons water, the harissa, paprika and turmeric, cover with a lid and cook for 20 minutes. Add the peas, cover and cook until the peas have lost their vibrant green colour and the meat is becoming tender, about 15 minutes. Add the artichoke hearts, cover again and cook until the artichokes and goat are tender, about 15 minutes. Add a touch of water if needed. It should be a bit saucy. Ladle into a serving dish and serve.

Goat Tagine
with Dried Figs and Walnuts

MOROCCO
PREPARATION TIME: 15 minutes
COOKING TIME: 2 hours
SERVES: 4

There are two main types of dried figs found in North African markets, flattened (often called Turkish) or ones that retain the original shape of fresh figs. The flattened ones, often sold in strands, are preferable for this goat tagine. They are cooked separately with butter and cinnamon in this recipe, but they can also be tucked around the goat in the tagine itself. This tagine can also be prepared with lamb or beef.

  2 red or yellow onions, finely chopped
  2 tablespoons finely chopped flat-leaf parsley
  2 tablespoons finely chopped coriander (cilantro)
  2 cloves of garlic, minced
  1 teaspoon ground turmeric
  1 teaspoon ground ginger
  pinch of saffron threads, crumbled
  4 tablespoons olive oil
  1.2 kg/2½ lb bone-in kid goat leg or shoulder, cut into
      8 or so pieces
  1 cinnamon stick or piece of cinnamon bark
  12–16 dried flattened figs (about 200 g/7 oz)
  15 g/½ oz (1 tablespoon) butter
  ½ teaspoon ground cinnamon
  2 tablespoons honey
  12–16 walnut halves
  salt and pepper

Add the onions, parsley, coriander (cilantro), garlic, turmeric, ginger and saffron to a large tagine (see page 250) and season with salt and pepper. Pour over the oil and 2 tablespoons water and mix well. Add the meat, piece by piece, turning to coat. Cook over a medium-high heat until the onions are translucent and the meat browned, 20 minutes. Add 60 ml (2 fl oz/¼ cup) water around the edges and the cinnamon stick. Cover the tagine with a lid, reduce the heat to low and gently simmer, nudging the meat from time to time to prevent it sticking, until the meat is very tender, about 1½ hours. Add a few spoonfuls of water as needed during cooking, or prop open the lid with the end of a wooden spoon to reduce. Remove the lid at the end of cooking to evaporate and thicken the sauce if watery.

Meanwhile, put the figs, butter and ground cinnamon into a small saucepan, then pour in 350 ml (12 fl oz/1½ cups) water. Bring to a simmer over a medium heat, partly cover with a lid and gently simmer until plump and tender, about 15 minutes. Stir in the honey and cook, swirling the pan from time to time, until the sauce becomes a touch syrupy and the figs very tender but not falling apart, 10–15 minutes. Remove from the heat and keep covered.

Stir a few tablespoons of the syrup into the tagine and cook for a final 3–5 minutes.

To serve from the tagine, place the figs on top of the meat. Drizzle over some sauce from the figs, then top each with a walnut half. Alternatively, arrange the pieces of goat on a large serving platter and spoon over the sauce from the tagine, then from the saucepan. Place the figs on top and set a walnut atop each one.

Beef Tagine with Quince

MOROCCO
PREPARATION TIME: 15 minutes
COOKING TIME: 2 hours
SERVES: 4

In winter, fragrant quince are a delightful addition to a savoury stew. The quince here are sweetened in a simple syrup. For caramelized quince, see the version with lamb on page 254.

- 1.2 kg/2½ lb cross-cut veal or beef shanks, cut into 6–8 pieces, with bone and marrow
- 1 heaped teaspoon ground ginger
- 1 heaped teaspoon ground turmeric
- 1 heaped teaspoon ground cinnamon
- 2 tablespoons finely chopped flat-leaf parsley
- 2 tablespoons finely chopped coriander (cilantro)
- 4 tablespoons olive oil
- 1 large red or yellow onion, sliced
- 2 ripe quince (about 600 g/1 lb 5 oz total)
- 100 g/3½ oz (½ cup) sugar
- salt and pepper

Add the meat to a large tagine (see page 250), then sprinkle over the ginger, turmeric, cinnamon, parsley and coriander (cilantro) and season with salt and pepper. Drizzle over the oil and turn the pieces until coated. Add the onion and turn to mix. Cover the tagine with a lid and cook over a medium-high heat for 20 minutes, turning the meat from time to time. Add a few tablespoons of water around the edges if needed. Reduce the heat to low and cook until the meat is very tender and the sauce reduced, about 1½ hours. Add a little water during cooking if needed, or remove the lid to evaporate at the end.

Meanwhile, fill a wide pot with about 750 ml (25 fl oz/3 cups) water and a generous pinch of salt. Begin heating while peeling, quartering and coring the quince, dropping the pieces into the water as you work to keep them from turning brown. Bring the water to the boil, cover with a lid and gently boil the quince until just tender, about 15 minutes. Scoop out most of the water, leaving about 250 ml (8 fl oz/1 cup) in the pot. Add the sugar and simmer, uncovered, until syrupy, about 10 minutes, being careful not to break the quince when stirring. Remove from the heat and keep covered until ready to serve.

To serve, arrange the quince on top of the lamb, drizzle over some syrup from the pan, cover the tagine and cook for 5–10 minutes to combine the flavours and reheat the quince. Serve from the tagine.

Beef Tagine with Aubergine

MOROCCO
PREPARATION TIME: 10 minutes
COOKING TIME: 2 hours–
2 hours 30 minutes
SERVES: 4

In making a beef tagine with aubergine (eggplant), some Moroccan cooks prepare the aubergine in a separate pan with garlic, tomatoes, coriander (cilantro) and parsley, mashing it to a paste (in the manner of a zaâlouk salad, see pages 87–88), which they spread on top of the meat before serving. This version cooks the aubergine in the tagine itself, allowing it to take all the flavours of the tagine. There is a similar Algerian marka (ragoût) with lamb on page 260.

- 2 red or yellow onions, sliced
- 1 kg/2¼ lb cross-cut bone-in veal or beef shanks, cut into 6–8 pieces, with bone and marrow
- 1 teaspoon ground ginger
- 1 teaspoon ground turmeric
- 1 teaspoon sweet paprika
- ½ teaspoon ground cinnamon
- 1 clove of garlic, minced
- 2 tablespoons finely chopped flat-leaf parsley
- 2 tablespoons finely chopped coriander (cilantro)
- 4 tablespoons olive oil
- 2 aubergines (eggplant) (about 750 g/1⅔ lb total), quartered lengthwise
- salt and pepper

Scatter the onions across the bottom of a large tagine (see page 250) and arrange the pieces of meat on top. Sprinkle over the ginger, turmeric, paprika and cinnamon and season with salt and pepper. Add the garlic, parsley and coriander (cilantro) and drizzle over the oil. Do not mix. Cover with a lid and cook over a medium-low heat for 1 hour, turning the meat only once the pieces begin to brown. If it is starting to look too dry, add about 4 tablespoons water during cooking.

Arrange the aubergines (eggplant) on top of the meat like spokes with the skin-side up. Cover the tagine and cook for 1–1½ hours until the meat is very tender and comes easily away from the bone and the aubergines are done. Add a touch more water during cooking if needed or remove the lid to evaporate at the end. Serve from the tagine.

Beef Tagine with Carrots

MOROCCO
PREPARATION TIME: 10 minutes
COOKING TIME: 2 hours–
2 hours 30 minutes
SERVES: 4–6

To add another level of sweetness to this tagine, toss in a small handful of raisins towards the end of cooking. Soak them first in a small heatproof bowl of lukewarm water for 10 minutes to soften.

2 red or yellow onions, finely chopped
1 kg/2¼ lb cross-cut bone-in veal or beef shanks, cut into 8 pieces with bone and marrow
250 g/9 oz bone-in beef ribs
½ teaspoon ras al hanout (page 446)
½ teaspoon ground ginger
½ teaspoon ground turmeric
½ teaspoon sweet paprika
1 clove of garlic, minced
2 tomatoes, halved crosswise and grated, peel discarded (see page 445)
2 tablespoons finely chopped flat-leaf parsley
2 tablespoons finely chopped coriander (cilantro)
½ teaspoon ground cumin
4 tablespoons olive oil
2 white potatoes, peeled and quartered lengthwise
4 carrots, halved lengthwise and then quartered lengthwise
salt and pepper

Scatter the onions across the bottom of a large tagine (see page 250) and arrange the pieces of meat on top. Sprinkle over the ras al hanout, ginger, turmeric and paprika and season with salt and pepper. Add the garlic, tomatoes, parsley and coriander (cilantro) and finally the cumin. Drizzle over the oil. Do not mix. Cover with a lid and cook over a medium heat for 30 minutes, turning the meat once the pieces begin to brown.

Set the potatoes along the edge of the tagine and lay the carrots across the centre. Cover the tagine and cook for 1½–2 hours until the meat is very tender and comes easily away from the bone and the potatoes and carrots are soft. Add a touch more water during cooking if needed, or remove the lid to evaporate at the end. Serve from the tagine.

Beef Tagine with Peas

MOROCCO
PREPARATION TIME: 10 minutes
COOKING TIME: 2 hours 15 minutes
SERVES: 4–6

In the south of Morocco, this recipe is sometimes prepared using camel meat. The peas here are cooked in the tagine, though they can be boiled in a saucepan of lightly salted water until just tender (about 5 minutes), then drained and scattered across the top of the tagine for the final 5 minutes of cooking. This works particularly well if preparing the tagine in advance.

4 tablespoons olive oil
1.5 kg/3¼ lb cross-cut bone-in veal or beef shanks, cut into 8 or so large pieces with bone and marrow
2 red onions, chopped
3 ripe tomatoes, seeded and chopped
2 tablespoons finely chopped flat-leaf parsley
2 tablespoons finely chopped coriander (cilantro)
3 cloves of garlic, minced
1 teaspoon ground turmeric
1 teaspoon sweet paprika
½ teaspoon ground cinnamon
200 g/7 oz (1½ cups) shelled fresh peas or thawed frozen petits pois
¼ teaspoon ground cumin
salt and pepper

Add the oil to a large tagine (see page 250), then add the meat, cover with a lid and brown on each side over a medium heat for about 10 minutes, turning from time to time. Add the onions and cook for 5 minutes, turning the meat a couple of times. Add the tomatoes, parsley, coriander (cilantro), garlic, turmeric, paprika and cinnamon and season with salt and pepper. Cover and cook over a medium-low heat, turning the pieces from time to time, for 45 minutes. Add a touch of water if needed. Reduce the heat to low, prop open the lid with the end of a wooden spoon and cook until the meat is tender and comes easily away from the bone, about 1 hour. Add a touch more water during cooking if needed, or remove the lid to evaporate at the end.

Scatter the peas over the top, add the cumin, cover and cook until the peas are tender, about 20 minutes. Serve from the tagine.

Beef Tagine
with Prunes and Fried Almonds

MOROCCO
PREPARATION TIME: 20 minutes
COOKING TIME: 1 hour 50 minutes
SERVES: 4

This Moroccan classic called *lham bel barkouk* ('meat with prunes') is regarded as a festive dish. For some in the south, for instance, where beef is far less common (and much more expensive) than lamb, it is considered special enough to serve at weddings.

3 red or yellow onions, finely chopped
1.2 kg/2½ lb cross-cut veal or beef shank, cut into
    6–8 pieces, with bone and marrow
1½ teaspoons ground ginger
1½ teaspoons ground turmeric
generous pinch of saffron threads, crumbled
2½ teaspoons ground cinnamon
2 tablespoons finely chopped flat-leaf parsley
2 tablespoons finely chopped coriander (cilantro)
½ teaspoon ground cumin
3 tablespoons extra-virgin olive oil
3 tablespoons vegetable oil
16 prunes with stones (pits)
100 g/3½ oz (½ cup) sugar
1 cinnamon stick or piece of cinnamon bark
75 g/2¾ cup (½ cup) whole almonds
neutral oil, for frying
salt and pepper
toasted sesame seeds, to garnish

Scatter the onions across the bottom of a large tagine (see page 250) and arrange the pieces of meat on top. Sprinkle the ginger, turmeric, saffron and 1½ teaspoons of the ground cinnamon evenly over the top and season with salt and pepper. Add the parsley and coriander (cilantro) and finally the cumin. Drizzle over the olive and vegetable oils. Do not mix. Cover with a lid and cook over a medium heat for 20 minutes. Turn the meat, add a few tablespoons of water around the edges if needed, reduce the heat to low and cook until the meat is very tender and the sauce reduced, about 1½ hours. Add a touch more water during cooking if needed, or remove the lid to evaporate at the end.

Meanwhile, put the prunes, sugar, cinnamon stick and remaining 1 teaspoon of ground cinnamon into a small saucepan, pour in 250 ml (8 fl oz/1 cup) water and bring to the boil. Reduce the heat to low and simmer, uncovered, until tender but not mushy and the sauce has been reduced to a syrup, about 30 minutes. Remove from the heat.

Meanwhile, put the almonds into a small saucepan of water, bring to the boil and boil for 3–5 minutes, then drain. Once cool enough to handle, slip off the skins with your fingers. Spread the almonds out on paper towels to dry. Heat about 7 mm/⅓ inch of neutral oil in a small frying pan over a medium heat until the surface shimmers. Line a plate with paper towels. Add the almonds and fry until just golden, 1–2 minutes. Transfer with a slotted spoon to the paper towels to drain.

To serve, arrange the prunes around the lamb in the tagine and drizzle over some glaze. Put a generous pinch of sesame seeds onto each of the prunes, scatter the almonds around the tagine and serve.

Marrakech Tangia
with Beef and Preserved Lemons

MOROCCO
PREPARATION TIME: 10 minutes
COOKING TIME: 3½–4 hours
SERVES: 4–5

Tangia – not to be confused with *tagine* – is one of Marrakech's most famous dishes. It takes its name from the tall, two-handled earthen pot used to cook it. Traditionally, it was considered something of a bachelor's dish. On Fridays it was common to drop the *tangia* filled with chunks of beef or lamb and seasonings – no vegetables here – at a *hammam* (Turkish or steam bath) and then pick it up once it had slowly cooked in the ashes of the furnace. Unsealed, the succulent meat, aromatic with spices and preserved lemon, falls off the bone with the marrow, giving a rich, fragrant sauce and lovely unctuousness. This home version prepared in the oven can be prepared in an upright *tangia* or a casserole dish (Dutch oven) with a heavy lid.

1 teaspoon ground ginger
1 teaspoon ground cumin
½ teaspoon ground turmeric
generous pinch of saffron threads, crumbled
3 tablespoons olive oil
1.5 kg/3¼ lb cross-cut bone-in veal or beef shanks
    or leg or shoulder of lamb, cut into generous pieces
    with bone and marrow
15 g/½ oz (1 tablespoon) butter or *smen* (page 412)
1 small preserved lemon, quartered, seeded and finely
    chopped
10 cloves of garlic, lightly crushed in the skin
1 small bouquet coriander (cilantro), tied together
1 small bouquet flat-leaf parsley, tied together
salt and pepper

Preheat the oven to 150 °C/300 °F/Gas Mark 2.

Add the ginger, cumin, turmeric and saffron to a large bowl. Season with salt and pepper and moisten with the oil. Mix well. Add the meat and turn to coat.

Add the meat, butter, preserved lemon, garlic, coriander (cilantro) and parsley to a *tangia* or ovenproof casserole dish (Dutch oven) with a tight-fitting lid. Pour in 300 ml (10 fl oz/1¼ cups) water into the bowl, swirl to get any remaining spices and pour into the *tangia*. If using a *tangia*, cover the opening with 2 large pieces of baking (parchment) paper and tie tightly with kitchen string, neatly tucking the excess paper under the string. For other pots, tightly cover with a lid. Cook in the hot oven until the meat is extremely tender and falling off the bone, 3½–4 hours.

Transfer the meat and all the sauce to a large serving bowl. Remove and discard the coriander (cilantro) and parsley and serve.

Spiced Beef Kebabs

ALGERIA, MOROCCO, TUNISIA
PREPARATION TIME: 20 minutes,
plus soaking (optional) and marinating time
COOKING TIME: 10 minutes
SERVES: 4

Marinated cubes of beef threaded onto skewers and grilled are a perennial treat, especially during Eid festivities. Many home cooks like to add some pieces of onions and fresh peppers between the pieces of meat. For a Tunisian touch – and more spice – loosen some harissa chilli (chile) paste with some water and blend into the marinade.

750 g/1⅔ lb boneless beef, trimmed and cut into
    2-cm/¾-inch cubes
1 teaspoon ground cumin
1 teaspoon sweet paprika
generous pinch of cayenne pepper
3 tablespoons olive oil
1 teaspoon fresh lemon juice
1 long sweet green or red pepper, cored, seeded and
    cut into 2-cm/¾-inch pieces
1 onion, cut into 2-cm/¾-inch pieces
salt and pepper

If using wooden skewers, put them into a large bowl of water and leave to soak for 30 minutes to prevent them burning during cooking.

Put the beef into a large bowl, add the cumin, paprika and cayenne pepper and season with salt and pepper. Moisten with the oil, lemon juice and 1–2 tablespoons water if needed and mix well. Add the peppers and onion and mix again. Cover and leave to marinate in the refrigerator for at least 1 hour. Slide cubes of meat interspersed with pieces of onion or pepper onto skewers so that they are just touching but not tightly packed together.

Heat a stovetop grill pan over a medium heat or prepare a charcoal grill or barbecue.

Cook the skewers, turning from time to time and brushing with any remaining marinade, until the meat is cooked through, the edges charred and inside a touch juicy, 8–10 minutes, turning as needed. If cooking on a charcoal grill or barbecue, wait until the embers die down and turn white.

Grilled Kebabs with Suet

MOROCCO
PREPARATION TIME: 20 minutes,
plus soaking (optional) and marinating time
COOKING TIME: 10 minutes
SERVES: 4

In this popular dish, pieces of marinated meat are threaded onto skewers together with some suet, the hard fat found around the kidneys, that give extra flavour. Be patient in allowing the embers to burn down before grilling the skewers. They are ideally served with a pot of Mint Tea (pages 417–421).

    1 kg/2¼ lb boneless beef or lamb, trimmed and cut
        into 2.5-cm/1-inch cubes
    250 g/9 oz suet, cut into 2.5-cm/1-inch cubes
    1 onion, grated
    4 tablespoons finely chopped flat-leaf parsley
    3 tablespoons olive oil
    1½ teaspoons ground cumin
    1½ teaspoons sweet paprika
    generous pinch of cayenne pepper
    salt and pepper

If using wooden skewers, put them into a large bowl of water and leave to soak for 30 minutes to prevent them burning during cooking.

Put the beef and suet into a large bowl, add the onion, parsley, oil, cumin, paprika and cayenne pepper, then season with salt and pepper and mix well. Cover and leave to marinate in the refrigerator for at least 1 hour. Slide 6 cubes of meat interspersed with 2 pieces of suet onto skewers so that they are just touching but not tightly packed together.

Prepare the charcoal grill or barbecue.

Once the embers die down and turn white, cook the skewers, turning from time to time, until the meat is cooked through, the edges charred and inside a touch juicy, 8–10 minutes, turning as needed.

Grilled Kefta Skewers

ALGERIA, MOROCCO
PREPARATION TIME: 20 minutes,
plus soaking (optional) and marinating time
COOKING TIME: 10 minutes
SERVES: 4; MAKES: 12 skewers

Many cooks and butchers have their unique version of seasoned minced (ground) meat known as *kefta*, with their special blend of herbs and spices. To the standard flavourings – paprika, cumin, cinnamon, parsley, coriander (cilantro) – some add ground coriander, mace or, in places such as Azrou in Morocco's Middle Atlas, fresh mint. If the meat is lean, add some olive oil. Or blend in some suet (the fat from around the kidney of a lamb) or even some lamb kidney itself. As with Grilled Kebabs with Suet (see left), these skewers are excellent with Mint Tea (pages 417–421).

    600 g/1 lb 5 oz minced (ground) beef or lamb,
        preferably a bit fatty
    1 red or yellow onion, grated
    3 tablespoons finely chopped flat-leaf parsley
    3 tablespoons finely chopped coriander (cilantro)
    3 tablespoons finely chopped mint
    1 teaspoon sweet paprika
    1 teaspoon ground cumin
    ¾ teaspoon ground cinnamon
    ¾ teaspoon ground ginger
    olive oil, for brushing
    salt and pepper

If using wooden skewers, put them into a large bowl of water and leave to soak for 30 minutes to prevent them burning during cooking.

Add the minced (ground) meat, onion, parsley, coriander (cilantro), mint, paprika, cumin, cinnamon and ginger to a large bowl. Season with salt and pepper and mix to a smooth mixture. Cover with cling film (plastic wrap) and leave to marinate in the refrigerator for at least 30 minutes.

Form the skewers about 10 cm/4 inches in length by taking an egg-size amount of meat, 55 g (2 oz/¼ cup), with moistened or oiled hands and packing around a skewer. Pinch both ends down around the skewer.

Heat a stovetop grill pan over a medium heat. Brush the skewers with oil and cook, turning from time to time, until the meat is cooked through, about 10 minutes. Serve immediately.

Lamb with Meatballs

ALGERIA
PREPARATION TIME: 20 minutes,
plus overnight soaking time
COOKING TIME: 1 hour 30 minutes
SERVES: 4

The name of this Algerian dish is *mechmachiya*,
which means 'apricot'. It refers to the size and shape
of these meatballs and their golden colour.

100 g/3½ oz (½ cup) dried chickpeas (garbanzo beans)
2 tablespoons olive oil
25 g/1 oz (2 tablespoons) butter or 15 g/½ oz
    (1 tablespoon) *smen* (page 412)
2 cloves of garlic, minced
1 red or yellow onion, chopped
750 g/1⅔ lb bone-in lamb shoulder, cut into 6 pieces
500 g/1 lb 2 oz minced (ground) beef or lamb
3 large eggs
generous pinch of ground cinnamon
6 tablespoons plain (all-purpose) flour
1 teaspoon baking powder
neutral oil, for frying
salt and pepper

Put the dried chickpeas (garbanzo beans) into a large
bowl, cover with abundant water and leave to soak
overnight. The next day, drain and rinse.

Add the olive oil, butter, garlic, onion and lamb to
a heavy pot or casserole dish (Dutch oven). Season
with salt and pepper and cook over a medium-high
heat until the meat is browned on each side, about
10 minutes. Add the chickpeas, then pour in 250 ml
(8 fl oz/1 cup) water. Cover with a lid, reduce the
heat to low and simmer for 1 hour.

Meanwhile, prepare the meatballs. Add the minced
(ground) meat, 1 of the eggs and the cinnamon to a
large bowl. Season with salt and pepper and blend
to a smooth mixture. Using moistened hands, roll
generous meatballs from 2 tablespoons of mixture.
Set in the pot and simmer until cooked through,
15–20 minutes. Using tongs, transfer the meatballs
to a plate to cool and continue to cook the lamb over
a low heat, adding a touch more water if necessary.

Put the remaining 2 eggs into a large bowl and,
using a fork, beat together. Add the flour and baking
powder and whisk to form a smooth batter. Line a
plate with paper towels. Heat about 1.5 cm/⅔ inch of
neutral oil in a large frying pan over a medium heat
until the surface shimmers. Working in batches as
needed, coat the meatballs in the batter and fry until
golden brown, about 1½ minutes per batch. Transfer
with a slotted spoon to the paper towels
to briefly drain.

Return the meatballs to the pot and cook for a
final 2–3 minutes. To serve, put the lamb, chickpeas
and sauce onto a large platter and surround with
the meatballs.

Kefta Meatball Tagine in Tomato Sauce with Eggs

MOROCCO
PREPARATION TIME: 30 minutes
COOKING TIME: 50 minutes
SERVES: 5

This extremely popular dish is something of a
standby in small restaurants. It is also typical to
prepare at home as comfort food.

2 tablespoons olive oil
5 ripe tomatoes, halved crosswise and grated,
    peel discarded (see page 445)
2 cloves of garlic, minced
2 tablespoons finely chopped flat-leaf parsley
2 tablespoons finely chopped coriander (cilantro)
1 teaspoon sweet paprika
¾ teaspoon ground cumin
750 g/1⅔ lb minced (ground) beef
1 onion, grated
4 large eggs
salt and pepper

Add the oil, tomatoes, 1 of the cloves of garlic, 1 heaped
tablespoon of the parsley, 1 heaped tablespoon of
the coriander (cilantro), ½ teaspoon of the paprika
and ¼ teaspoon of the cumin to a large tagine (see
page 250), then season with salt and pepper. Cover
with a lid and cook over a medium-low heat until
darker and reduced, about 15 minutes. Add a few
spoonfuls of water if needed to keep it moist.

Meanwhile, add the meat, onion, remaining
clove of garlic, parsley, coriander (cilantro), paprika
and cumin to a large bowl and season with salt
and pepper. Mix into a consistent, smooth paste.
Using moistened or oiled hands, roll meatballs
about 3 cm/1¼ inches in diameter from 1 heaped
tablespoon (25 g/1 oz) of the mixture.

Set the meatballs in the sauce, cover the tagine
and cook over a low heat until the meatballs are
cooked through, about 30 minutes, turning in the
sauce from time to time. Add some water if necessary
to keep the tomato sauce loose.

Make 4 spaces among the meatballs and crack the
eggs directly into the tagine. Cover and cook until
the egg whites are set but the yolks still runny, about
5 minutes. Serve immediately.

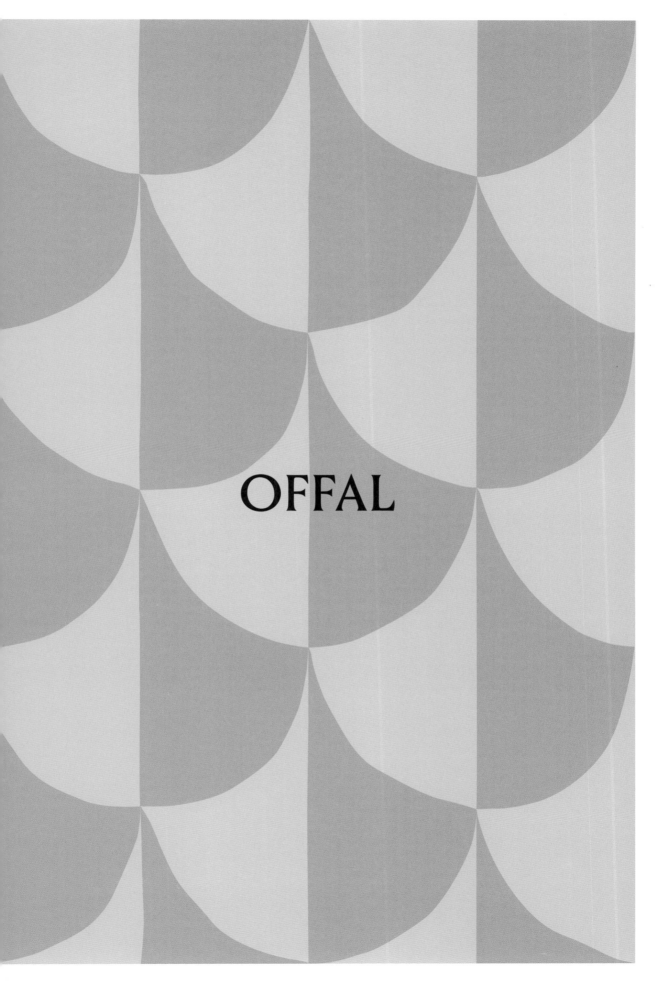

OFFAL

Lamb Kebabs with Kidneys

TUNISIA
PREPARATION TIME: 20 minutes,
plus marinating time
COOKING TIME: 10 minutes
SERVES: 4

While these skewers of lamb and kidney can be cooked in a frying pan, grilling them over charcoal is preferred. Interspersing pieces of fresh pepper makes a nice addition.

250 g/9 oz lamb kidneys
5 tablespoons olive oil
juice of 1 lemon
1 yellow onion, grated
generous pinch of dried oregano
generous pinch of cayenne pepper
800 g/1¾ lb boneless leg of lamb, cut into
    2-cm/¾-inch cubes
½ red bell pepper, cored, seeded and cut into
    2-cm/¾-inch pieces
½ green bell pepper, cored, seeded and cut into
    2-cm/¾-inch pieces
½ yellow bell pepper, cored, seeded and cut into
    2-cm/¾-inch pieces
½ large sweet onion, cut into 2-cm/¾-inch pieces
salt and pepper

Remove the silvery outer membrane of the kidneys and trim any white fat. Cut in half and snip out the white core. Rinse thoroughly under cold running water. Put the oil, lemon juice, grated onion, oregano and cayenne pepper into a large bowl and mix together. Put the kidneys and lamb cubes into the marinade, turn to coat, cover with cling film (plastic wrap) and leave to marinate in the refrigerator for at least 1 hour.

Meanwhile, prepare the charcoal grill or barbecue. If using wooden skewers, put them into a large bowl of water and leave to soak for 30 minutes to prevent them burning during cooking.

Thread the skewers with 4–6 pieces of lamb and 1–2 pieces of kidney interspersed with pieces of bell pepper and sweet onion. The pieces should be touching but not packed tightly together. Season with salt and pepper.

Once the embers die down and turn white, cook the skewers, turning them from time to time, until the meat is done, about 10 minutes. Serve hot.

Veal Liver in Chermoula

ALGERIA, MOROCCO
PREPARATION TIME: 15 minutes,
plus marinating time
COOKING TIME: 15 minutes
SERVES: 4

While *kebda mchermla* is delicious warm, you can also let this liver dish cool and then refrigerate to serve it as a chilled starter. Be mindful to not overcook the liver, which will toughen if left too long in the pan. In Algeria, it is common to dash it with vinegar just before removing from the heat. It is best when served with homemade Frites (fries, page 164).

1 tablespoon olive oil
1 tablespoon fresh lemon juice or white vinegar
½ preserved lemon, seeded and cut into thin strips
2 cloves of garlic, minced
2 tablespoons finely chopped flat-leaf parsley
2 tablespoons finely chopped coriander (cilantro)
1 teaspoon ground cumin
1 teaspoon sweet paprika
500 g/1 lb 2 oz veal liver, trimmed and cut into
    2-cm/¾-inch cubes
salt
12 red or purple olives, to garnish

Put the oil, lemon juice, 1 tablespoon water, preserved lemon, garlic, parsley, coriander (cilantro), cumin and paprika into a large bowl and mix together. Season with salt, add the liver and turn to coat. Cover with cling film (plastic wrap) and leave to marinate in the refrigerator for 1 hour.

Add the liver and all of the marinade along with 60 ml (2 fl oz/¼ cup) water to a large frying pan or sauté pan and cook over a medium-low heat until the liver is cooked through and the sauce reduced, 12–15 minutes. Transfer to a serving dish, garnish with the olives and serve.

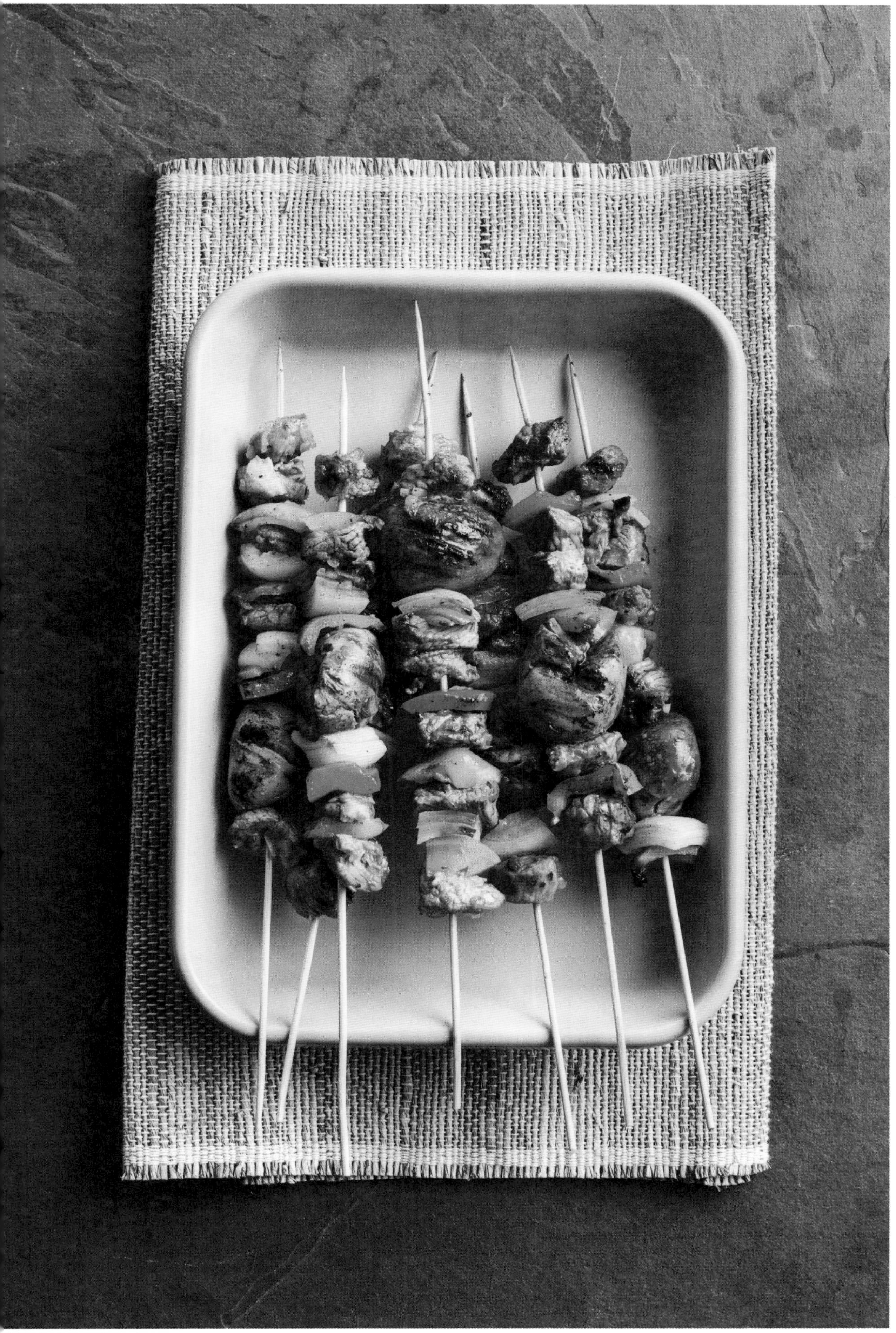

Skewers of Liver Wrapped in Caul Fat

MOROCCO
PREPARATION TIME: 45 minutes,
plus soaking (optional) and drying time
COOKING TIME: 10 minutes
SERVES: 4; MAKES: about 12 skewers

Much-beloved grilled skewers called *boulfaf* are pieces of liver wrapped in caul fat (known as *crépine* in French), the webby membrane around certain organs. This is classic Moroccan street food and popular to prepare on the first day of Eid al-Adha, when organ meat from the slaughtered lamb is cooked. This is a dish that takes time – so you may want help to prepare it – but it's delicious eaten straight off the skewer or stuffed into bread. Serve with hot Mint Tea (pages 417–421). Because of its size, it is easier to evenly slice the liver of veal after first searing it on each side. That is not necessary with lamb liver, which is smaller.

> 500 g/1 lb 2 oz sheep's caul fat
> 1 kg/2¼ lb lamb or veal liver
> 1 tablespoon ground cumin, plus extra to serve
> 1 tablespoon sweet paprika, plus extra to serve
> generous pinch of cayenne pepper
> salt

Prepare the charcoal grill or barbecue. If using wooden skewers, put them into a large bowl of water and leave to soak for 30 minutes to prevent them burning during cooking.

Rinse the caul in water, stretch out and leave to dry. Cut the caul into a dozen or so strips about 2 cm/¾ inch wide and 10 cm/4 inches in length by rolling up a sheet of the caul and slicing into the correct width, then unrolling and trimming the length as needed.

Remove any membrane that surrounds the liver with the help of the tip of a sharp knife. Rinse and cut into 2-cm/¾-inch cubes. If using veal liver, sear first for 1 minute on each side to firm up the pieces and make them easier to cut. Put into a large bowl, season with salt and toss with the cumin, paprika and cayenne pepper.

Wrap each cube of liver in a strip of caul (covering 4 of the 6 sides) and thread onto a skewer where the strip of caul fat overlaps in order to hold into place. Thread 6–8 pieces per skewer. They should be touching but not packed tightly together.

Once the embers die down and turn white, grill the skewers over the coals until the caul has turned transparent, the liver is cooked through and the texture is spongy, 5–8 minutes. Serve hot with small bowls of cumin, paprika and salt to season as desired.

Liver in Cumin Sauce

TUNISIA
PREPARATION TIME: 10 minutes
COOKING TIME: 25 minutes
SERVES: 4

In Tunis, it is common to prepare liver with cumin sauce – *kamounia*. The cumin is added at the end to retain its strong flavour. Some cooks like to prepare the liver with other *abats* (heart, lungs, etc.) or pieces of leg of lamb. You can find similar coastal versions of the dish with cuttlefish (page 345) or octopus.

> 4 tablespoons olive oil
> 1 yellow onion, grated
> 2 cloves of garlic, finely chopped
> 2 tomatoes, halved crosswise and grated,
>   peel discarded (see page 445)
> 1 heaped tablespoon double concentrated tomato
>   purée (paste)
> 1 tablespoon sweet paprika
> 1 teaspoon ground turmeric
> 1 lamb liver (about 450 g/1 lb), trimmed and cut into
>   2-cm/¾-inch cubes
> 1 tablespoon ground cumin
> salt and pepper
> flat-leaf parsley, to garnish

Heat the oil in a sauté pan or frying pan over a medium-high heat, add the onion and cook for about 8 minutes, or until soft. Stir in the garlic, then add the tomatoes, tomato purée (paste) and 4 tablespoons water, the paprika and turmeric. Season with salt and pepper and cook for 10 minutes, stirring frequently.

Add the liver, turn to coat with the sauce, then add 120 ml (4 fl oz/½ cup) water. Reduce the heat to medium and cook until the liver is cooked through and still tender, 12–15 minutes. Stir in the cumin and cook for a final 2 minutes. Transfer to a serving dish, garnish with parsley and serve.

Saucy Stewed Lamb Liver

ALGERIA
PREPARATION TIME: 10 minutes
COOKING TIME: 15 minutes
SERVES: 3–4

This liver dish in a spicy sauce based on the garlic-laden *dersa* chilli (chile) paste is widely popular across Algeria, and frequently found on home tables. Serve with plenty of bread.

    3 cloves of garlic, peeled
    ½ teaspoon sweet paprika
    ½ teaspoon cayenne pepper
    ½ teaspoon ground caraway
    4 tablespoons olive oil
    1 lamb liver (about 450 g/1 lb), trimmed and cut into
        2-cm/¾-inch cubes
    1 tablespoon white vinegar
    salt and pepper

Make a *dersa* paste by putting the garlic, paprika, cayenne and caraway into a mortar and pounding with a pestle. Stir in 2–3 tablespoons water to make it paste-like.

Heat the oil in a large sauté pan or frying pan over a high heat. Season the liver with salt and pepper and cook until browned, about 2 minutes. Reduce the heat to low, stir in the garlic paste, add 120 ml (4 fl oz/½ cup) water and simmer until the liver is cooked through and the sauce reduced, about 10 minutes. Remove from the heat, stir in the vinegar and serve hot.

Sautéed Lamb Hearts

ALGERIA, TUNISIA
PREPARATION TIME: 5 minutes
COOKING TIME: 3 minutes
SERVES: 2

During Eid al-Adha ('feast of the sacrifice', see page 34), lamb is butchered across North Africa in observance of the important Islamic holiday. The traditional lunch for many families is grilled heart and liver. With such freshness, the heart is often cooked with little spicing, allowing its flavour – akin to liver but milder – to come through.

    6 lamb hearts (about 400 g/14 oz)
    2 tablespoons olive oil
    salt and pepper

Cut the hearts open lengthwise, then cut each into a few pieces. Generously season with salt and pepper.

Heat the oil in a frying pan over a medium-high heat, add the hearts and quickly sauté until cooked through, about 3 minutes. Serve immediately.

Veal Trotters with White Beans

ALGERIA, MOROCCO, TUNISIA
PREPARATION TIME: 15 minutes,
plus overnight soaking time
COOKING TIME: 4 hours 15 minutes
SERVES: 6–8

This regional classic is related to *dafina* and *hergma*, North African Jewish dishes slow-cooked over Friday night for the sabbath meal on Saturday. It uses the bottom of the foot (but not the hoof), which usually comes singed and cleaned. Ask your butcher to cut it crosswise into pieces with a saw. The feet have little meat but give excellent flavour as well as a silky, gelatinous texture to the dish. There are many variations of this dish. In Morocco, some cooks use chickpeas (garbanzo beans), others blend chickpeas and white beans, while others add whole wheat berries. Sometimes raisins are added for sweetness. In Tunisia, this dish is often cooked with spinach or chard (then called *madfouna*). Serve with plenty of bread.

- 400 g/14 oz dried white beans, such as cannellini or white haricot (navy) (about 2 cups)
- 2 tablespoons olive oil
- 2 onions, chopped
- 1 veal trotter (foot), cleaned and cut crosswise into about 3-cm/1¼-inch-thick pieces by the butcher, rinsed
- 4 cloves of garlic, minced
- 2 tomatoes, halved crosswise and grated, peel discarded (see page 445)
- 2 tablespoons double concentrated tomato purée (paste)
- 2 teaspoons ground cumin
- 1 teaspoon sweet paprika
- 1 teaspoon ground turmeric
- 1 teaspoon ground ginger
- 1 bay leaf
- salt and pepper

Put the beans into a large bowl, cover with abundant water and leave to soak overnight, or for at least 8 hours. The next day, drain and rinse. Set aside.

Add the oil and onions to a large, heavy pot and cook for 2 minutes. Add the trotter (foot) and garlic and cook for about 5 minutes, or until the onions begin to soften. Add the tomatoes, tomato purée (paste) and 4 tablespoons water, 1 teaspoon of the cumin, the paprika, turmeric and ginger. Season with salt and pepper and cook for 5 minutes. Pour in 1 litre (34 fl oz/4¼ cups) water, bring to the boil, cover with a lid, reduce the heat to low and cook for 2½ hours.

Add the beans and bay leaf, pour in 500 ml (18 fl oz/2 cups) water, cover and gently boil until the trotters and beans are tender, about 1½ hours. Add water if needed, or uncover towards the end. It should be loose but not watery. Add the remaining 1 teaspoon of cumin about 15 minutes before it is done. Using a slotted spoon, skim off some fat from the surface if the sauce is greasy. Divide among bowls and serve very hot.

Spicy Stewed Tripe with Courgettes

ALGERIA
PREPARATION TIME: 15 minutes
COOKING TIME: 1 hour 25 minutes
SERVES: 4

Bakbouka is a popular way to prepare tripe – either just tripe or sometimes with pieces of lung and heart as well – with courgettes (zucchini). You can substitute the courgettes with artichokes and green peas, if desired.

350 g/12 oz cleaned and ready-to-cook sheep tripe
3 tablespoons olive oil
2 cloves of garlic, minced
½ teaspoon sweet paprika
½ teaspoon ground caraway
cayenne pepper, to taste
1 tablespoon double concentrated tomato purée (paste)
1 red or yellow onion, finely chopped
2 courgettes (zucchini), halved lengthwise and then crosswise
2 tablespoons finely chopped coriander (cilantro)
2 tablespoons finely chopped flat-leaf parsley
salt and pepper

Clean the tripe extremely well under cold running water and by scraping with a knife as needed. Cut into 2–4-cm/¾–1½-inch pieces or thin strips with kitchen scissors.

Put the oil, garlic, paprika, caraway, cayenne pepper, tomato purée (paste) and 4 tablespoons water into a large saucepan and mix together. Season with salt and pepper, then add the onion and tripe and turn to coat. Cover with a lid and cook over a medium heat for 10 minutes. Add 1 litre (34 fl oz/4¼ cups) of hot water, bring to the boil, cover, reduce the heat to low and simmer for 45 minutes. Add the courgettes (zucchini) and cook for a final 30 minutes, or until the tripe is tender. It should be a touch saucy. Add more water as needed. Stir in the coriander (cilantro) and parsley and serve.

Lamb Tripe with Chickpeas, Preserved Lemon and Olives

MOROCCO
PREPARATION TIME: 20 minutes
COOKING TIME: 1 hour 25 minutes
SERVES: 5–6

This Moroccan tripe dish of chickpeas (garbanzo beans) and preserved lemon is boldly flavoured and usually served with hot, sweet Mint Tea (pages 417–421). The tripe should be fresh and white.

500 g/1 lb 2 oz cleaned and ready-to-cook sheep tripe
3 tablespoons olive oil
1 red or yellow onion, finely chopped
3 cloves of garlic, minced
1 teaspoon sweet paprika
1 teaspoon ground cumin
1 heaped tablespoon finely chopped coriander (cilantro)
1 heaped tablespoon finely chopped flat-leaf parsley
250 g/9 oz (1½ cups) canned chickpeas (garbanzo beans), rinsed, or cooked dried chickpeas (page 443)
1 preserved lemon
about 18 olives
salt and pepper

Clean the tripe extremely well under cold running water and by scraping with a knife as needed. Cut into 2–4-cm/¾–1½-inch pieces or thin strips with kitchen scissors.

Put the tripe, oil, onion, garlic, paprika, cumin, coriander (cilantro) and parsley into a large saucepan and season with salt and pepper. Cook, uncovered, over a medium heat for 10 minutes, stirring frequently. Add 250 ml (8 fl oz/1 cup) water, reduce the heat to low, cover with a lid and cook until the tripe is tender, about 1 hour. Add the chickpeas (garbanzo beans) and cook for another 5 minutes.

Quarter the lemon, scrape out the pulp and discard. Finely chop the peel, then add to the pan with the olives and cook for a final 5–10 minutes. Serve.

Lamb Brains
in Tomato Sauce with Eggs

ALGERIA, MOROCCO, TUNISIA
PREPARATION TIME: 15 minutes
COOKING TIME: 35 minutes
SERVES: 6

Lamb brains (*moukh*) in tomato sauce with eggs is a regional classic and popular in Fès and Algiers. Beaten eggs are stirred into the pan at the end and cooked for just a couple of minutes. Be sure to rinse the brains in various changes of cold water. Tunisians call this *ojja bel moukh* and usually add a dollop of harissa to the sauce.

- 2 lamb brains (about 100 g/3½ oz each)
- 2 tablespoons olive oil
- 2 cloves of garlic, minced
- 4 ripe tomatoes, peeled (see page 445) and finely chopped
- 1 tablespoon finely chopped flat-leaf parsley
- ½ teaspoon ground cumin
- ½ teaspoon sweet paprika
- 2 large eggs, beaten
- salt and pepper

Rinse the brains under cold running water, then put into a large bowl of cold water and leave to soak for a few minutes, swishing around. Using your fingers, carefully remove the outer membrane and sinews, then separate the lobes and cut each into 2 pieces. Set aside.

Add the oil and garlic to a medium frying pan or sauté pan and cook over a medium heat for about 1 minute, or until fragrant. Add the tomatoes, parsley, cumin and paprika and season with salt and pepper. Cover with a lid and cook over a low heat for 15 minutes to thicken the sauce. Add the brains, cover and cook without stirring for 10 minutes. Gently turn the brains and cook until they are cooked through and the sauce reduced, about 5 minutes. Pour in the eggs, lightly stir and cook until set, about 3 minutes. Serve warm or leave to cool to room temperature before serving.

Spicy Lamb Brains

ALGERIA
PREPARATION TIME: 15 minutes
COOKING TIME: 20 minutes
SERVES: 4

While lamb brains prepared in tomato sauce with some eggs scrambled into the sauce at the end (see left) is a popular dish found across the region, there are other ways to prepare brains, including this Algerian version known as *chtitha moukh* – brains in sauce. The sauce itself is very simple and heady with garlic, paprika and as much spice as you desire. Some homes use caraway and others cumin – the former tends to be a touch sweeter, though both are excellent. To use whole dried chillies (chiles) instead of cayenne pepper, cut them open, shake out the seeds and soak in a heatproof bowl of hot water for a few minutes to soften, before pounding in the mortar.

- 2 lamb brains (about 100 g/3½ oz each)
- 5 cloves of garlic, peeled
- 1 teaspoon ground caraway or cumin
- 1 teaspoon sweet paprika
- cayenne pepper, to taste
- 2 tablespoons olive oil
- salt and pepper
- finely chopped flat-leaf parsley, to garnish, optional

Rinse the brains under cold running water, then put into a large bowl of cold water and leave to soak for a few minutes, swishing around. Using your fingers, carefully remove the outer membrane and sinews, then separate the lobes and cut each into 2 pieces. Set aside.

Put the garlic, caraway, paprika, cayenne pepper and salt and pepper into a mortar and pound with a pestle. Stir in 2–3 tablespoons water to give it a paste-like consistency.

Add the oil and paste to a medium frying pan or sauté pan and cook, stirring frequently, over a medium-low heat for about 2 minutes, or until fragrant. Stir in 60 ml (2 fl oz/¼ cup) water, set the brains in the pan, partly cover with a lid, reduce the heat to low and cook for 10–15 minutes until they are cooked through and have absorbed the flavours of the sauce. Turn carefully a few times as they cook. Add a touch more water if needed. Spoon into a serving dish, scatter over the parsley (if using) and serve.

Steamed Sheep's Head

ALGERIA, MOROCCO, TUNISIA
PREPARATION TIME: 15 minutes
COOKING TIME: 1 hour 30 minutes–
2 hours
SERVES: 2

While it can be a laborious process to clean a sheep's head, many butchers have them ready to cook, making this a simple – although somewhat lengthy – dish to prepare. To make it a fuller meal, add some onions, carrots, turnips and/or potatoes to the steamer basket. In many Morocco homes, it is served with salt and cumin to dip the hot pieces. Some Algerian cooks rub the head with a paste of pounded garlic, cumin and salt before steaming. The sheep's head is split in half, although some prefer to have their butcher cut it into six or eight pieces. The cheeks and tongue are particularly tender. It is typical to prepare during Eid al-Adha.

- 1 cleaned sheep's head, rinsed and cut in half
- ground cumin for seasoning, plus extra to serve
- ½ bulb of garlic, unpeeled
- 1 bunch flat-leaf parsley, tied together into a bouquet, optional
- 2 onions, halved
- salt and pepper

Fill a large pot fitted with a steamer basket or a large couscoussier with salted water to just below the steamer basket and bring to the boil.

Generously season the lamb with cumin, salt and pepper and set in the steamer basket. Add the garlic, then arrange the parsley (if using) on top. Cover snugly with aluminium foil and then the lid so that no steam escapes. Set on top of the pot and steam for 1 hour. Arrange the onions around the lamb, cover again and steam until the lamb is very tender and can be easily pulled away from the bone, 30 minutes–1 hour. Check occasionally to make sure that the pot has enough water and doesn't go dry.

Transfer to a platter and serve with individual small dishes of cumin and salt for dipping the lamb.

Veal Tongue with Garlic Tomato Sauce and Capers

TUNISIA
PREPARATION TIME: 20 minutes
COOKING TIME: 1 hour 45 minutes
SERVES: 6

The name of this dish is *methaouma*, which refers to the garlic in the tomato sauce where the tongue simmers. The tongue is briefly boiled, the tough outer skin peeled away and then the tongue is stewed directly in the sauce. It is more work peeling the tongue in this method than after boiling it for 2 hours (as in recipe for Veal Tongue with Olives, page 289), but cooking the tongue in the sauce makes for a richer final dish.

- 1 veal tongue (1–1.2 kg/2¼–2½ lb)
- 2 tablespoons olive oil
- 4 tomatoes, halved crosswise and grated, peel discarded (see page 445)
- 1 heaped tablespoon double concentrated tomato purée (paste)
- tabil spice blend (page 446), optional
- 4 cloves of garlic, minced
- 3 heaped tablespoons capers, rinsed
- salt and pepper

Bring a large pot or saucepan of water to the boil, add the tongue and blanch for 5 minutes. Remove, then while still warm, peel off the skin and discard. Trim away the fat, gristle and any tough sections at the root end. Cut crosswise into finger-thick slices with a sharp knife. Towards the base, cut it in half crosswise so that the pieces are roughly the same size.

Add the oil to a large casserole dish (Dutch oven) and heat for about 1 minute, or until aromatic. Stir in the tomatoes, tomato purée (paste) and 4 tablespoons water and cook for 10 minutes, stirring frequently. Add a touch more water if needed. Season the tongue with salt, pepper and tabil (if using), then lay in the sauce and turn the pieces to coat. Cook gently until tender, about 1 hour 15 minutes. Add a touch more water if needed. It should be saucy but not watery. Add the garlic and cook for 10 minutes. Scatter over the capers and cook for a final 5 minutes. Arrange the tongue slices on a platter, cover with the sauce and serve.

Veal Tongue with Olives

ALGERIA
PREPARATION TIME: 20 minutes
COOKING TIME: 2 hours 30 minutes
SERVES: 4–6

In this recipe, the tongue is boiled apart, peeled and sliced and then briefly simmered in the sauce. Add a carrot cut into thin circles to the sauce, if desired. It is typical to serve this dish topped with Frites (fries, page 164).

    1 veal tongue (1–1.2 kg/2¼–2½ lb)
    1 bulb of garlic
    1 teaspoon black peppercorns
    1 bay leaf
    3 cloves of garlic, peeled
    1 teaspoon sweet paprika
    cayenne pepper, to taste
    ½ teaspoon ground cumin
    2 tablespoons olive oil
    1 red or yellow onion, thinly sliced
    2 tomatoes, halved crosswise and grated,
        peel discarded (see page 445)
    1 heaped tablespoon double concentrated tomato
        purée (paste)
    1 heaped tablespoon finely chopped coriander
        (cilantro), plus extra to garnish
    200 g/7 oz (1⅔ cups) pitted green olives, rinsed in
        hot water
    salt and pepper
    Frites (page 164), to serve

Rinse the tongue under cold running water, prick it in a few places with the tines of a fork, then put it into a large pot with the garlic bulb, peppercorns, bay leaf and 1 teaspoon of salt. Cover with abundant water and bring to the boil. Gently boil until tender and the tines of a fork can easily pierce it, about 2 hours. Transfer to a plate and leave until cool enough to handle. Peel off the skin and discard. Trim away the fat, gristle and any tough sections at the root end. Cut crosswise into finger-thick slices. Towards the base, cut it in half crosswise so that the pieces are roughly the same size.

Put the peeled cloves of garlic, paprika, cayenne pepper, cumin and a pinch of salt into a mortar and pound to a paste with a pestle.

Add the oil and onion to a large saucepan and cook over a medium heat for about 5 minutes, or until the onion is pale and soft. Stir in the garlic paste, then add the tomatoes, tomato purée (paste), 4 tablespoons water and the coriander (cilantro). Season with salt and pepper and simmer until the sauce has thickened, about 10 minutes. Lay the

tongue in the sauce and turn over to coat. Add the olives and a few spoonfuls of water if needed. Cover with a lid and cook for 5–10 minutes to allow the tongue to absorb the flavours in the pan. Arrange the tongue slices on a platter, cover with the sauce and scatter over some coriander. Serve with the Frites strewn on top of the tongue.

Saucy Chicken Giblets

ALGERIA
PREPARATION TIME: 10 minutes
COOKING TIME: 1 hour 15 minutes
SERVES: 4

One delicious way to prepare giblets – the hearts, gizzards and livers of chicken – is in this rich tomato sauce. If using livers, remove them after browning and do not return to the pan until the end as they cook quicker than the other giblets.

    500 g/1 lb 2 oz cleaned chicken giblets
        (hearts, gizzards and livers)
    2 tablespoons olive oil
    4 cloves of garlic, minced
    2 large ripe tomatoes, halved crosswise and grated,
        peel discarded (see page 445)
    1 heaped tablespoon double concentrated tomato
        purée (paste)
    1 teaspoon ground cumin
    1 teaspoon sweet paprika
    salt and pepper

Rinse the giblets under cold running water, then cut the gizzards and livers into 2 or 3 pieces. Generously season with salt and pepper.

Heat the oil in a large frying pan over a medium-high heat, add the giblets and cook until browned, about 5 minutes. Remove the livers and set aside. Add the garlic, tomatoes, tomato purée (paste), 6 tablespoons water, the cumin and paprika. Reduce the heat to low, cover with a lid and cook until the sauce has thickened and the giblets are tender, about 1 hour. Add some tablespoons of water as needed during cooking to keep it saucy. Return the livers to the pan and cook for a final 5–10 minutes. Serve immediately.

POULTRY,
RABBIT
AND SNAILS

Chicken Tagine
with Preserved Lemons and Olives

MOROCCO
PREPARATION TIME: 20 MINUTES,
PLUS MARINATING TIME
COOKING TIME: 1 hour
SERVES: 4

For many visitors to Morocco, chicken tagine with preserved lemons and olives is the most iconic of all tagines, and it is offered at nearly every eatery catering to visitors. It is a sublime and classic combination of flavours.

1 small preserved lemon (page 410)
3 cloves of garlic, minced
2 tablespoons finely chopped flat-leaf parsley
2 tablespoons finely chopped coriander (cilantro)
1 teaspoon ground ginger
1 teaspoon ground turmeric
¼ teaspoon white pepper
2 tablespoons olive oil
2 tablespoons fresh lemon juice
1.5 kg/3¼ lb bone-in chicken legs (drumsticks and thighs) or breasts, skin on
15 g/½ oz (1 tablespoon) butter or *smen* (page 412)
2 red or yellow onions, chopped
175 g/6 oz (1½ cups) green olives with stones (pits)
salt

Quarter the preserved lemon lengthwise, rinse and remove the seeds. Without breaking the peel, scrape away the pulp and reserve; set the peel aside. Finely chop the pulp. Add the lemon pulp and any juices, the garlic, parsley, coriander (cilantro), ginger, turmeric and white pepper to a small bowl. Lightly season with salt, then moisten with the oil, lemon juice and 2 tablespoons water and blend well. Using a sharp knife, pierce the pieces of chicken to better absorb the marinade. Add the chicken, piece by piece, turning to coat. Cover and leave to marinate in the refrigerator for 30 minutes, turning from time to time.

Add the chicken, all of the marinade and the butter to a large tagine (see page 250), then spread the onions over the top. Cover and cook over a medium heat until the chicken is browned, about 20 minutes, turning occasionally. Finely chop half of the reserved preserved lemon peel and add to the tagine. Drizzle in 120 ml (4 fl oz/½ cup) water, cover, reduce the heat to low and cook, moving the chicken from time to time to keep it from sticking, until done but not falling off the bone, about 30 minutes. Stir in some water if necessary or remove the lid and reduce the sauce, which should be loose but not watery.

Trim the remaining preserved lemon peel into attractive shapes, such as leaves with serrated edges. Lay on top of the chicken, add the olives and cook, uncovered, for 5–10 minutes until the sauce has thickened. Serve.

PRESERVED LEMONS

The tight, tart flavour of preserved lemons give a pungent kick to a range of dishes from cooked salads to meat and fish stews. Among the most famous is Chicken Tagine with Preserved Lemons and Olives (see above). Preserved lemons are an iconic trademark of the Moroccan kitchen, where they are called *hamd markad* or (in French) *citrons confits*. Algerian and Tunisian cooks also use them in certain dishes.

Lemons are easy to preserve at home (page 410), and only require patience for them to be ready. The typical way to prepare them is to slice lemons into quarters leaving the bottom connected, pack the insides with salt and then put them into a sterilized mason jar (see page 462). Cover with lemon juice, seal with a lid and leave for 3–4 weeks to soften and the flavours intensify.

As the peel is part of the preserved lemon most often called for – along with sometimes the pulp – use untreated or organic lemons and scrub well before salting. Thinner-skin varieties are preferable. Thick-skinned lemons should be soaked in water for a couple of days before salting, changing the water regularly. Preserved lemons will keep for around 6 months. Before using, rinse under cold running water.

In Tunisia, it is more common to preserve lemons whole in a salt water solution (page 410). They are easier to prepare this way but take longer – about 6 months – for them to be ready.

To substitute: While a comparable replacement is hard to find, adding lemon zest at the end of cooking will give a stew a hint of tangy pungency.

Chicken Tagine with Caramelized Tomato Compote

MOROCCO
PREPARATION TIME: 20 minutes,
plus marinating time
COOKING TIME: 1 hour 30 minutes
SERVES: 5

Djaj mdarbel is one of the Moroccan kitchen's tastiest tagines. The sweet tomato compote is cooked separately and then dolloped on the deeply savoury chicken when serving. That compote is equally excellent atop a similarly flavoured beef or lamb tagine.

2 cloves of garlic, minced
½ teaspoon ground ginger
½ teaspoon ground turmeric
3 tablespoons olive oil
1.5 kg/3¼ lb bone-in chicken pieces, skin-on
2 red or yellow onions, finely chopped
12 sprigs flat-leaf parsley, tied together
12 sprigs coriander (cilantro), tied together
½ teaspoon ground cinnamon
35 g/1¼ oz (¼ cup) whole almonds
neutral oil, for frying
salt and pepper
toasted sesame seeds, to garnish

For the caramelized tomato compote:
1.5 kg/3¼ lb ripe tomatoes, halved crosswise and
   grated, peel discarded (see page 445)
3 tablespoons olive oil
4 tablespoons sugar
4 tablespoons honey
1 teaspoon ground cinnamon
salt

Add the garlic, ginger and turmeric to a large bowl. Season with salt and pepper and moisten with the olive oil. Mix well. Add the chicken, piece by piece, turning to coat. Cover with cling film (plastic wrap) and leave to marinate in the refrigerator for 30 minutes, turning from time to time.

MEANWHILE, BEGIN PREPARING THE CARAMELIZED TOMATO COMPOTE: Add the tomatoes and a pinch of salt to a sauté pan or frying pan with a lid. Cover and cook over a medium heat for 30 minutes. Stir in the olive oil, sugar, honey and cinnamon and cook, uncovered and stirring frequently, until the tomatoes are caramelized and jammy, about 45 minutes. Spoon into a bowl and set aside.

Meanwhile, begin cooking the chicken. Add the chicken and all of the marinade to a large tagine (see page 250). Spread the onions over the top, cover and cook over a medium heat until the chicken is browned on each side, about 10 minutes. Add the parsley, coriander (cilantro), cinnamon and 120 ml (4 fl oz/½ cup) water. Cover and cook over a medium-low heat, moving the chicken from time to time to keep it from sticking, until done but not falling off the bone, about 30 minutes. Remove the lid and reduce the sauce for a few minutes. Remove and discard the herb bouquets.

Meanwhile, bring a medium saucepan of water to the boil, add the almonds and boil for 3–5 minutes; drain. Once cool enough to handle, slip off the skins with your fingers. Spread the almonds out on paper towels to dry. Line a medium plate with paper towels. Heat about 7 mm/⅓ inch of neutral oil in a small frying pan over a medium heat until the surface shimmers. Add the almonds and fry for 1–2 minutes until just golden. Transfer with a slotted spoon to the paper towels to drain.

To serve from the tagine, spoon the tomato compote over the chicken pieces, sprinkle with sesame seeds and scatter the almonds across the top. Alternatively, arrange the pieces of chicken on a large platter, cover with sauce and spoon over the tomato compote. Sprinkle with sesame seeds, scatter over the almonds and serve.

Chicken Tagine with Dried Apricots and Caramelized Walnuts

MOROCCO
PREPARATION TIME: 20 minutes,
plus marinating and cooling time
COOKING TIME: 1 hour 15 minutes
SERVES: 4

This tagine is a refined example of blending flavours, with the sweet-tartness of the dried apricots offsetting the savoury saffron, garlic and fresh herbs of the tender chicken. Lightly caramelizing the walnuts in honey gives the dish an added decorative touch and a welcome crunch.

  3 cloves of garlic, minced
  1 tablespoon finely chopped flat-leaf parsley
  1 tablespoon finely chopped coriander (cilantro)
  generous pinch of saffron threads, crumbled
  1 teaspoon ground ginger
  2 tablespoons extra-virgin olive oil
  4 bone-in chicken drumsticks, skin-on
  4 bone-in chicken thighs, skin-on
  3 red or yellow onions, halved lengthwise and thinly
    sliced crosswise
  25 g/1 oz (2 tablespoons) butter, cut into pieces
  120 g/4 oz (¾ cup) dried apricots
  4 tablespoons honey
  ½ cinnamon stick or piece of cinnamon bark
  dash of orange blossom water, optional
  65 g/2½ oz (½ cup) walnut halves
  salt and pepper

Add the garlic, parsley, coriander (cilantro), saffron and ginger to a large bowl. Season with salt and pepper and moisten with the oil and 2 tablespoons water. Mix well. One by one, add the chicken pieces to the marinade, turning to coat. Cover with cling film (plastic wrap) and leave to marinate in the refrigerator for 30 minutes, turning the pieces from time to time.

Arrange the chicken in a single layer in a large tagine (see page 250) and spoon over the remaining marinade. Scatter the onions around and dot with 15 g (½ oz/1 tablespoon) of the butter. Cook over a medium heat, turning the chicken occasionally, until the onions are translucent, about 15 minutes. Add 60 ml (2 fl oz/¼ cup) water. Cover with a lid, reduce the heat to low and gently cook, nudging the chicken from time to time to prevent it sticking, until cooked through and tender but not falling off the bone, about 45 minutes. Drizzle in a few spoonfuls of water as necessary during cooking to keep the sauce loose, or prop open the lid with the end of a wooden spoon to reduce. If necessary, remove the lid at the end of cooking to evaporate and thicken the sauce if watery.

Meanwhile, put the apricots, 2 tablespoons of the honey, the cinnamon stick, orange blossom water (if using) and 175 ml (6 fl oz/¾ cup) water into a medium saucepan. Bring to a simmer over a medium heat, then reduce the heat to low and gently simmer until the apricots are tender and the liquid is reduced to 2–3 tablespoons of syrup, about 15 minutes. Add a touch more water if needed to keep it from drying out. Take the pan off the heat, then remove and discard the cinnamon stick.

Melt the remaining 15 g (½ oz/1 tablespoon) of the butter in a medium non-stick frying pan over a medium-low heat. Add the remaining 2 tablespoons of honey and the walnuts and cook, slowly turning the walnuts in the honey until they have a light, chewy coating, 4–5 minutes. Transfer to a plate, spread out into a single layer and leave to cool. Once cool, separate any walnuts that are stuck together.

When the chicken is done, arrange the apricots around the chicken, drizzle with the apricot syrup and cook, partially covered, over a low heat for 5–10 minutes, adding a touch more water if needed to keep the sauce loose. Scatter the walnuts over the top and serve from the tagine.

Chicken Tagine
with Green Beans and Olives

MOROCCO
PREPARATION TIME: 10 minutes,
plus marinating time
COOKING TIME: 1 hour 5 minutes
SERVES: 4

Simple and delicious, this is one of the many
Moroccan tagines that combines chicken with a
seasonal vegetable. Add some preserved lemon
(see page 410) to give the sauce a hint of tartness.

  2 red or yellow onions, finely chopped
  3 cloves of garlic, minced
  1 heaped tablespoon finely chopped flat-leaf parsley
  1 heaped tablespoon finely chopped coriander
    (cilantro)
  1 teaspoon ground ginger
  1 teaspoon ground turmeric
  4 tablespoons olive oil
  4 bone-in chicken drumsticks, skin removed
  4 bone-in chicken thighs, skin removed
  3 ripe tomatoes, halved crosswise and grated, peel
    discarded (see page 445)
  120 g/4 oz (1 cup) pitted green olives
  450 g/1 lb *haricots verts* (thin French green beans), cut
    into 5–7.5-cm/2–3-inch lengths
  salt and pepper

Add the onions, garlic, parsley, coriander (cilantro),
ginger and turmeric to a large bowl. Season with
salt and pepper and moisten with the oil. Mix well.
Add the chicken pieces and turn to coat. Cover with
cling film (plastic wrap) and leave to marinate in the
refrigerator for 1 hour.
   Add the chicken and all of the marinade to a tagine
(see page 250). Cover and cook over a medium-high
heat until the chicken is browned on each side,
about 10 minutes. Add the tomatoes and 120 ml
(4 fl oz/½ cup) water, loosely cover and cook over
a medium-low heat, moving the chicken from time
to time to keep it from sticking, about 15 minutes.
Add the olives and arrange the green beans across
the top. Cover the tagine and cook until the beans
are done but still a bit crunchy and the chicken
very tender, 35–40 minutes. Stir in some water if
necessary to keep the sauce loose or remove the lid
to evaporate and thicken it at the end. Serve from
the tagine.

Braised Chicken with Green Beans

ALGERIA
PREPARATION TIME: 10 minutes
COOKING TIME: 1 hour 15 minutes
SERVES: 4

This Algerian *marka* (ragoût) is straightforward,
naturally sweet from the green beans, onions and
tomatoes and carries the lovely aromas of cinnamon.
Add a few sliced potatoes with the green beans to
make it heartier and more filling.

  3 tablespoons olive oil
  4 bone-in chicken legs (drumsticks and thighs),
    skin-on
  2 red or yellow onions, thinly sliced
  2 cloves of garlic, finely chopped
  3 ripe tomatoes, peeled (see page 445) and finely
    chopped
  2 tablespoons finely chopped flat-leaf parsley
  750 g/1⅔ lb *haricots verts* (thin French green beans),
    cut in half if desired
  ½ cinnamon stick or piece of cinnamon bark
  salt and pepper

Heat the oil in a large pot or casserole dish (Dutch
oven) over a medium heat, add the chicken legs
and onions, season with salt and pepper and cook
until the chicken is browned on each side, about
10 minutes. Add the garlic, tomatoes and parsley,
partly cover the pan, reduce the heat to low and
cook for 20 minutes, stirring from time to time. Add
the green beans and cinnamon stick, then moisten
with a few tablespoons of water if needed. Cover
with a lid and cook until the chicken is very tender
and the beans done, about 45 minutes. Add a touch
more water if needed, or remove the lid towards the
end to reduce the sauce. Serve.

Braised Chicken,
Lentils and Fenugreek
on a Bed of Shredded Pastry

MOROCCO
PREPARATION TIME: 1 hour, plus
soaking marinating and resting time
COOKING TIME: 1 hour 50 minutes
SERVES: 6

Rfissa (also called *trid*) is a festive Moroccan dish
of chicken, onions and lentils, and is often served
to women after childbirth, in part because of the
restorative *hilba* (fenugreek) that flavours the sauce.
The chicken and rich sauce are served on a bed
of shredded *msemen* flatbread (page 65) or *trid* (a
very thin pastry usually bought in the market) or
even bread. While hand-shredding may be the most
traditional way, most cooks now roll up the *msemen*,
cut using kitchen scissors and unfurl into strips.
Some like to put a top layer of shredded pastry over
the chicken and decorate with cinnamon and icing
(confectioners') sugar. If you do, serve with a small
pot of honey to add as desired.

For the chicken:
2 tablespoons fenugreek seeds
100 g/3½ oz (½ cup) dried brown lentils
1 teaspoon ground ginger
1 teaspoon ground turmeric
1 teaspoon ras al hanout (page 446)
pinch of saffron threads, crumbled
4 tablespoons olive oil
1 whole chicken (about 1.8 kg/4 lb), cut into
    6–8 pieces and skin removed
25 g/1 oz (2 tablespoons) butter or *smen* (page 412)
2 red or yellow onions, sliced
4 cloves of garlic, peeled
12 sprigs flat-leaf parsley
12 sprigs coriander (cilantro)
salt and pepper

For the msemen:
125 g/4¼ oz (¾ cup) fine semolina
125 g/4¼ oz (generous ¾ cup) plain (all-purpose)
    flour, plus extra for dusting
½ teaspoon salt
pinch of sugar
coarse or medium semolina, for sprinkling
vegetable oil, for oiling hands and brushing dough

FOR THE CHICKEN: Rinse the fenugreek, put
into a small bowl, cover with water and leave to
soak for 3 hours; drain. Pick over the lentils for any

debris, rinse, then put into a large bowl, cover with
water and leave to soak for 2 hours; drain.

Meanwhile, add the ginger, turmeric, ras al hanout
and saffron to a large bowl, then season with salt and
pepper and moisten with the oil. Mix well. Pierce
the pieces of chicken so that they can better absorb
the marinade, then add the chicken, piece by piece,
turning to coat. Cover with cling film (plastic wrap)
and leave to marinate in the refrigerator for 1 hour,
turning from time to time.

**MEANWHILE, BEGIN PREPARING THE
MSEMEN:** Follow the directions on page 65,
halving the quantity of water and omitting the
butter and using only oil for brushing. It need not
be perfect as it will be shredded. While still warm,
pull apart to open the layers, then roll each up and
cut into strips using kitchen scissors. Toss with your
fingers to separate the layers. Set aside.

Put the chicken, all of the marinade, the butter and
onions into a large pot or casserole dish (Dutch
oven) and cook over a medium heat to brown the
chicken, about 10 minutes. Add the garlic, lentils
and fenugreek, then pour in 750 ml (25 fl oz/3 cups)
water. Tie the parsley and coriander (cilantro)
together and add to the pan. Bring to the boil, cover
with a lid, reduce the heat to low and cook until the
chicken and lentils are tender, 45 minutes–1 hour.
The sauce should be loose but not watery. Remove
the lid as needed.

To serve, put the shredded *msemen* into a steaming
basket over a large pot of water or in a couscoussier
and steam until soft and warm, about 5 minutes.
Transfer to a wide, shallow serving dish and moisten
the *msemen* with a few ladlefuls of sauce. Arrange
the chicken on top, then spoon over the onions and
lentils. Drizzle with more sauce and serve with the
remaining sauce in a bowl on the side.

Braised Chicken in Chtitha Sauce with Chickpeas

ALGERIA
PREPARATION TIME: 10 minutes,
plus soaking time
COOKING TIME: 1 hour
SERVES: 4–6

Chtitha is one of the most popular Algerian sauces – especially common with chicken and chickpeas (garbanzo beans). It is generally prepared with a simple Dersa Garlic-chilli Paste (page 441) as its base. While it typically uses dried chillies or cayenne pepper, you can also use a fresh red chilli in the *dersa* if desired.

    2 dried red chillies (chiles)
    4 cloves of garlic, peeled
    1 teaspoon sweet paprika
    ½ teaspoon ground cumin
    2 tablespoons olive oil
    15 g/½ oz (1 tablespoon) butter or *smen* (page 412)
    4 bone-in chicken legs (drumsticks and thighs)
        or 1 kg/2¼ lb bone-in chicken, skin on
    2 red onions, finely chopped
    250 g/9 oz (1½ cups) canned chickpeas
        (garbanzo beans), rinsed, or cooked dried
        chickpeas (page 443)
    salt and pepper
    finely chopped coriander (cilantro), to garnish

To make a *dersa* paste, cut the chillies (chiles) open, shake out the seeds and put the flesh into a small bowl. Cover with hot water and leave to soak for 30 minutes; drain. Transfer to a mortar with the garlic, paprika and cumin and using a pestle, pound to a paste. Season with salt and pepper and stir in 60 ml (2 fl oz/¼ cup) water to loosen. Set aside.

Heat the oil and butter in a large pot or casserole dish (Dutch oven) over a medium-high heat, add the chicken and onions, season with salt and pepper and cook until the chicken is browned on each side, about 10 minutes. Stir in the dersa paste and turn the chicken to coat. Add the chickpeas (garbanzo beans) and 175 ml (6 fl oz/¾ cup) water, mostly cover the pot with a lid, reduce the heat to medium and cook until the chicken is tender, about 45 minutes. It should be saucy. Add a touch of water if needed. Scatter over the coriander (cilantro) to garnish and serve.

Grilled Marinated Chicken Skewers

MOROCCO
PREPARATION TIME: 20 minutes,
plus soaking (optional) and marinating time
COOKING TIME: 10 minutes
SERVES: 4

Marinated chicken cubes remain a favourite to thread onto skewers and cook over charcoal. Turkey, though, has become a popular option today, as it is meatier and less expensive.

    3 cloves of garlic
    60 ml/2 fl oz (¼ cup) olive oil
    juice of ½ lemon
    2 tablespoons finely chopped flat-leaf parsley
    2 tablespoons finely chopped coriander (cilantro)
    2 teaspoons ground cumin
    1 teaspoon sweet paprika
    generous pinch of cayenne pepper or chilli (red
        pepper) flakes, optional
    1 kg/2¼ lb skinless, boneless chicken or turkey thighs
        or breasts, cut into 2.5-cm/1-inch cubes
    salt and pepper

If using wooden skewers, put them into a large bowl of water and leave to soak for 30 minutes to prevent them burning during cooking.

Put the garlic into a mortar with a generous pinch of salt and, using a pestle, mash into a paste. Put into a large bowl and add the oil, lemon juice, parsley, coriander (cilantro), cumin, paprika and cayenne pepper. Season with salt and pepper and mix well. Add the chicken pieces, spoon over the marinade and turn to coat well. Cover with cling film (plastic wrap) and leave to marinate in the refrigerator for at least 1 hour, turning occasionally.

Thread the skewers with 6–8 cubes of chicken so that they are touching but not packed tightly together. Brush with the remaining marinade.

Prepare the charcoal grill or barbecue. Once the embers die down and turn white, cook the skewers, turning from time to time, until the meat is cooked through and firm to the touch, 5–10 minutes. Serve hot.

Chicken with Coriander

ALGERIA
PREPARATION TIME: 10 minutes
COOKING TIME: 55 minutes
SERVES: 4

This dish of chicken and fresh coriander (cilantro) – *djaj kesbour* – calls for lots of the fresh herb. It is added once the chicken is partway cooked in order to not lose all its fresh, pungent and somewhat citrusy flavours. Garnish this dish with more coriander when serving, if desired.

- 4 bone-in chicken legs (drumsticks and thighs), or 1 kg/2½ lb bone-in chicken, skin on
- 3 tablespoons olive oil
- 15 g/½ oz (1 tablespoon) butter
- 1 large onion, finely chopped
- 3 cloves of garlic, minced
- pinch of saffron threads, crumbled
- 65 g/2½ oz coriander (cilantro), finely chopped (about 1½ cups loosely packed)
- ½ lemon or preserved lemon (page 410), cut into slices
- 100 g/3½ oz (generous ¾ cup) green or purple olives
- salt and pepper

Put the chicken, oil, butter and onion into a large pot or casserole dish (Dutch oven) and cook over a medium heat until the chicken has browned and the onion softened, about 10 minutes. Add the garlic and cook for about 1 minute, or until aromatic. Season with salt and pepper, sprinkle in the saffron and add 120 ml (4 fl oz/½ cup) water. Cover with a lid and cook over a medium-low heat for 15 minutes. Add the coriander (cilantro) and cook for 15 minutes, or until the chicken is tender. Add the lemon and olives, and cook, uncovered, for a final 10 minutes, or until the chicken is done and the sauce reduced. Serve.

Fès-style Chicken in Buttery Onion Sauce with Almonds

MOROCCO
PREPARATION TIME: 20 minutes
COOKING TIME: 2 hours
SERVES: 4

Djaj khadra is one of Fès's greatest (and richest) chicken dishes. *Djaj* means 'chicken' and *khadra* refers to the onion confit with almonds. The almonds are blanched but not fried, so they have a firm, brittle texture rather than a more familiar crunchiness. The onion sauce spiced with saffron and white pepper is enriched with plenty of butter plus often *smen* (page 412), which gives the dish an extra savoury punch.

- 150 g/5 oz (1 cup) whole almonds
- 1 whole chicken (about 1.8 kg/4 lb), cut into 8 pieces, skin-on
- 6 red onions, finely chopped
- 12 sprigs flat-leaf parsley, tied together
- 2 pinches of saffron threads, crumbled
- ¼ teaspoon white pepper
- 40 g/1 ½ oz (3 tablespoons) butter
- 1 teaspoon *smen* (page 412), optional
- salt

Bring a medium saucepan of water to the boil, add the almonds and boil for 3–5 minutes, then drain and leave to cool. Once cool enough to handle, slip off the skins with your fingers and leave to dry on paper towels.

Add the chicken, 2 of the onions, the parsley, saffron, white pepper, 25 g (1 oz/2 tablespoons) of the butter, the *smen* (if using) and reserved almonds to a large tagine (see page 250) or heavy pot or casserole dish (Dutch oven) and season with salt. Loosely cover with a lid and cook over a medium heat until the chicken is browned, about 10 minutes, turning the pieces from time to time. Add 120 ml (4 fl oz/½ cup) water and cook, mostly covered, over a medium-low heat, moving the chicken from time to time to keep from sticking, until done but not falling off the bone, about 45 minutes. Transfer the chicken to a serving platter and cover with aluminium foil to keep warm. Remove and discard the parsley.

Add the remaining 4 onions to the tagine with the remaining 15 g (½ oz/1 tablespoon) of butter. Cover and cook until the onions are tender, about 45 minutes. Return the chicken to the tagine, cover with some sauce and cook for 5–10 minutes to warm the chicken. Serve.

Chermoula Roasted Chicken

MOROCCO
PREPARATION TIME: 25 minutes
COOKING TIME: 1 hour 40 minutes
SERVES: 4

The chicken in this classic dish known as *djaj mcharmel* is finished under the oven grill (broiler) to give it a lively golden brown colour. While the chicken is in the oven, the sauce gets reduced to almost a relish in the tagine.

    1 whole chicken (about 1.5 kg/3¼ lb)
    1 small preserved lemon (page 410)
    2 cloves of garlic, minced
    2 packed tablespoons finely chopped coriander
        (cilantro)
    2 packed tablespoons finely chopped flat-leaf parsley
    1 teaspoon sweet paprika
    1 teaspoon ground ginger
    ½ teaspoon ground turmeric
    pinch of saffron threads, crumbled
    juice of ½ lemon
    15 g/½ oz (1 tablespoon) butter or *smen* (page 412),
        plus extra for rubbing
    2 red or yellow onions, chopped
    red or purple olives, rinsed
    salt and pepper

Trim the chicken of excess fat that can be reached without tearing the skin. Quarter the preserved lemon and seed. Scrape out the pulp, chop and set aside. Chop the peel and set aside.

Prepare a marinade by mixing the garlic, coriander (cilantro), parsley, reserved lemon pulp, paprika, ginger, turmeric and saffron together in a large bowl. Season with salt and pepper. Moisten with the lemon juice and 2 tablespoons water.

Working over a large, heavy pot or casserole dish (Dutch oven), coat the outside and inside of the chicken with the marinade, gently pushing some under the edges of the skin. Set the chicken breast-side up in the pan and tie the feet with kitchen string. Spoon over the remaining marinade, add the butter and scatter the onions around the chicken. Cover with a lid and cook over a medium heat for 15 minutes. Turn the chicken breast-side down, cover, reduce the heat to low and cook for 15 minutes. Pour in 250 ml (8 fl oz/1 cup) water, loosely cover and cook until the chicken is very tender, about 1 hour. Drizzle in more water if necessary to keep the sauce loose.

Preheat the oven grill (broiler). Transfer the chicken to a large baking dish. Rub with butter and place under the grill until the skin is golden and slightly crispy, 5–10 minutes. Set on a serving platter.

Meanwhile, add the olives and reserved preserved lemon peel to the pan, increase the heat to medium and reduce the sauce to almost a relish. Spoon the sauce over the chicken and serve.

Roasted Chicken Legs

TUNISIA
PREPARATION TIME: 15 minutes
COOKING TIME: 50 minutes
SERVES: 6

This recipe calls for *tabil* (page 446), the classic Tunisian spice blend that contains ground caraway, ground coriander and dried garlic. Substitute with some ground caraway and coriander seeds and either dried or fresh garlic, if desired.

    4 white potatoes, peeled and thinly sliced crosswise
    3 red or yellow onions, sliced
    3 tomatoes, quartered and seeded
    2 long sweet green peppers, quartered lengthwise,
        cored and seeded
    2 bay leaves
    6 bone-in chicken legs (drumsticks and thighs),
        skin removed
    1 teaspoon sweet paprika or cayenne pepper
    1 teaspoon tabil spice blend (page 446)
    ½ teaspoon ground turmeric
    3 tablespoons olive oil
    salt and pepper

Preheat the oven to 200 °C/400 °F/Gas Mark 6.

Spread out the potatoes and onions in a large roasting pan, then arrange the tomatoes, peppers and bay leaves on top. Lay the chicken legs across the top of the vegetables.

Add the paprika, tabil and turmeric to a medium bowl. Season with salt and pepper and stir in the oil and 4 tablespoons water. Brush the chicken with the mixture, then pour the remainder over the vegetables.

Roast the chicken, uncovered, until the juices of the chicken run clear and a thermometer poked into the thickest part of the thigh reads 75 °C/165 °F and the potatoes are tender, about 45 minutes, turning the pieces and basting as needed. If the potatoes are not yet done, transfer the chicken to a plate, cover with aluminium foil and keep warm, and continue cooking until the potatoes are tender.

Turn the oven to the grill (broil) setting and grill (broil) the chicken and potatoes until the chicken takes on a nice brown colour, about 5 minutes. Serve.

Stewed Chicken with Croquettes

ALGERIA
PREPARATION TIME: 20 minutes
COOKING TIME: 40 minutes
SERVES: 4

A classic from Algiers, *sfiriya* adds croquettes made from old or dried bread to chicken stewed in an aromatic 'white sauce' with a pinch of ground cinnamon.

3 tablespoons olive oil
15 g/½ oz (1 tablespoon) butter or *smen* (page 412)
1 kg/2¼ lb bone-in chicken pieces, such as legs, thighs or breasts, skin on
1 large red or yellow onion, grated
175 g/6 oz (1 cup) canned chickpeas (garbanzo beans), rinsed, or cooked dried chickpeas (page 443)
½ teaspoon ground cinnamon
2 tablespoons orange blossom water, optional
2 large eggs
75 g/2¾ oz (packed ¾ cup) shredded white cheese, such as Emmental or Gruyère
100 g/3½ oz (scant 1½ cups) dry breadcrumbs
½ teaspoon baking powder
2 tablespoons milk or water, or as needed
neutral oil, for frying
salt and white pepper
lemon wedges, to serve

Heat the olive oil and butter in a large frying pan over a medium-high heat, add the chicken and onion, then season with salt and white pepper and cook until the chicken is browned on each side, about 10 minutes. Add the chickpeas (garbanzo beans), ¼ teaspoon of the cinnamon, 1 tablespoon of the orange blossom water (if using) and 350 ml (12 fl oz/1½ cups) water. Reduce the heat to low and simmer, uncovered, until the chicken is done and tender and the sauce reduced, about 30 minutes.

Meanwhile, prepare the croquettes. Put the eggs into a large bowl and beat with a fork. Mix in the cheese, the remaining 1 tablespoon of the orange blossom water (if using) and the remaining ¼ teaspoon of cinnamon, then season with salt and white pepper. Work in the breadcrumbs, baking powder and milk, adding a touch more milk as needed until it is a slightly sticky paste. With moistened hands, roll balls about 2.5 cm/1 inch in diameter from 1 tablespoon of paste.

Heat at least 1 cm/½ inch of neutral oil in a small, deep frying pan over a medium heat until the surface shimmers. Line a plate with paper towels. Working in 2 batches, fry the croquettes until golden on the outside and cooked through, turning frequently,

about 5 minutes. Transfer to the paper towels to drain.

To serve, put the chicken into the centre of a wide serving dish, arrange the croquettes around the edges and ladle over the sauce. Serve hot with lemon wedges.

High Atlas Turkey Tagine

MOROCCO
PREPARATION TIME: 10 minutes,
plus soaking time
COOKING TIME: 1 hour 45 minutes–
2 hours 15 minutes
SERVES: 4

Turkey cooked with baby (pearl) onions and raisins is a delicious dish. Add some butter or *smen* (page 412) to the sauce to give it a silky richness.

2 cloves of garlic, minced
2 tablespoons finely chopped flat-leaf parsley
2 tablespoons finely chopped coriander (cilantro)
1 teaspoon ground ginger
½ teaspoon ground turmeric
pinch of saffron threads, crumbled
4 tablespoons olive oil
4 small turkey legs or drumsticks, skin-on
1 red or yellow onion, chopped
3 tomatoes, cut into wedges
500 g/1 lb 2 oz baby (pearl) onions or shallots, peeled
1 small cinnamon stick or piece of cinnamon bark
115 g/4 oz (generous ¾ cup) seedless raisins
salt and pepper

Add the garlic, parsley, coriander (cilantro), ginger, turmeric and saffron to a large tagine (see page 250). Season with salt and pepper and moisten with the oil and 2 tablespoons water. Blend well. Add the turkey, turning to coat. Scatter around the chopped onion and cook over a medium heat, turning from time to time, until the turkey is browned and the onion is softening, about 10 minutes. Add the tomatoes, baby (pearl) onions, cinnamon stick and 120 ml (4 fl oz/½ cup) water. Reduce the heat to low, cover the tagine and cook until the turkey is done and the baby onions tender, about 1½–2 hours. Drizzle in a few spoonfuls of water as necessary during cooking to keep the sauce loose, or remove the lid at the end of cooking to evaporate and reduce the sauce if watery.

Meanwhile, put the raisins into a small heatproof bowl, cover with lukewarm water and leave to soak for 10 minutes; drain. Add the raisins to the tagine and cook for a final 5 minutes. Serve from the tagine or arrange the turkey on a serving platter covered with the sauce.

Braised Rabbit with Olives

ALGERIA
PREPARATION TIME: 10 minutes
COOKING TIME: 1 hour 5 minutes
SERVES: 4

This braised rabbit dish with olives captures the rustic flavours of the countryside. Add carrots, mushrooms or other vegetables, and some fresh thyme or other herbs, if desired, with the onions and garlic.

  1 cleaned rabbit (about 1.2 kg/2½ lb)
  3 tablespoons olive oil
  2 yellow onions, finely chopped
  3 cloves of garlic, crushed in the skin
  140 g/5 oz (generous 1 cup) green olives, rinsed
  salt and pepper

Cut the rabbit into 8–10 pieces (or have your butcher do it). Trim the excess fat. Generously season with salt and pepper.

Heat the oil in a large, deep frying pan with a lid or casserole dish (Dutch oven) over a high heat, add the rabbit and cook until richly browned on each side, about 10 minutes. Add the onions, reduce the heat to medium and cook until they begin to turn translucent, about 10 minutes. Add the garlic, olives and 120 ml (4 fl oz/½ cup) water, reduce the heat to low, mostly cover with a lid and cook for 45 minutes, or until the rabbit is very tender. Add more water if needed during cooking to keep it from drying out. It should be a bit saucy. Serve.

Rabbit with Peppers

ALGERIA
PREPARATION TIME: 10 minutes
COOKING TIME: 1 hour 20 minutes
SERVES: 4

This rabbit dish comes from Oran where it is often called *frita*, which takes the Spanish name for 'fried', highlighting the city's Spanish culinary influences. It's simple and delicious, with a lovely sweetness from the peppers.

  1 cleaned rabbit (1.2–1.5 kg/2½–3¼ lb)
  4 tablespoons olive oil
  1 red bell pepper, cored, seeded and cut into
    2–3-cm/¾–1¼-inch pieces
  1 long sweet green pepper or ½ green bell pepper,
    cored, seeded and cut into 2–3-cm/¾–1¼-inch
    pieces
  4 cloves of garlic, minced
  4 ripe tomatoes, peeled (see page 445) and finely
    chopped
  salt and pepper

Cut the rabbit into 8–10 pieces (or have your butcher do it) and trim any excess fat. Season generously with salt and pepper.

Heat the oil in a large frying pan with a lid or casserole dish (Dutch oven) over a high heat, add the rabbit and cook until richly browned on each side, about 10 minutes. Transfer to a plate. Add the peppers to the pan, reduce the heat to medium and cook until they begin to soften, about 8 minutes. Stir in the garlic, then add the tomatoes. Return the rabbit to the pan, reduce the heat to low, cover and cook until the rabbit is very tender, 45 minutes–1 hour. Remove the lid towards the end if the sauce is too runny. Serve.

Stewed Rabbit with New Potatoes

ALGERIA
PREPARATION TIME: 10 minutes
COOKING TIME: 1 hour 20 minutes
SERVES: 4

Rabbit dishes are more common in Algeria – especially in places like Algiers, Oran and Annaba that had large populations of French and Spanish before 1962 independence. Add fresh herbs – rosemary, oregano, thyme – to the pan if desired.

1 cleaned rabbit (about 1.2 kg/2½ lb)
2 tablespoons olive oil
25 g/1 oz (2 tablespoons) butter
2 red or yellow onions, finely chopped
2 cloves of garlic, minced
500 g/1 lb 2 oz small new potatoes
salt and pepper
finely chopped flat-leaf parsley, to garnish

Cut the rabbit into 8–10 pieces (or have your butcher do it) and trim any excess fat. Season generously with salt and pepper.

Heat the oil in a large frying pan with a lid or casserole dish (Dutch oven) over a high heat, add the rabbit and cook until richly browned on each side, about 10 minutes. Transfer to a platter. Add the butter and onions, reduce the heat to medium and cook until pale and soft, about 10 minutes. Stir in the garlic.

Return the rabbit to the pan, turning to coat with the onions. Add the potatoes and 120 ml (4 fl oz/½ cup) water, cover the pan with a lid and reduce the heat to low. Cook until the rabbit is very tender and the potatoes are done, 45 minutes–1 hour. Remove the lid at the end to reduce the sauce if needed or add a touch more water. Transfer to a platter, garnish with parsley and serve.

Snails with Ajwain and Thyme

ALGERIA
PREPARATION TIME: 35 minutes
COOKING TIME: 1 hour 40 minutes
SERVES: 4–6

One of Oran's most famous dishes is *babbouche be nounkha we zaâtar* – snails with ajwain (or ajowan, also called carom) and thyme. *Nounkha* has an aroma that recalls thyme but is stronger and more bitter. It is common to use the seed-like fruits of *nounkha* as well as whole sprigs of the dried plant. Citrus peels and some cayenne pepper or a chilli (chile) add flavour to the aromatic broth.

1 kg/2¼ lb fresh (live) snails or snails in brine
3 tablespoons dried thyme (*zaâtar*)
1 tablespoon ajwain (*nounkha*)
1 sprig thyme
1 teaspoon cayenne pepper or 1 small chilli (chile), optional
peel of ½ orange, white pith scraped away
peel of ½ lemon, white pith scraped away
1 red or yellow onion, quartered
salt and pepper

Follow the directions for preparing snails on page 444 (fresh or in brine). Once boiled, drain and rinse the snails.

Put the thyme, ajwain, thyme, cayenne pepper (if using), the orange and lemon peels and onion into a large clean pot or saucepan. Season with salt and pepper and cover with 2 litres (68 fl oz/generous 2 quarts/8½ cups) water. Bring to the boil, add the prepared snails, loosely cover with a lid and simmer until the snails are tender (not chewy) and can be easily extracted from their shells, about 45 minutes. Ladle the snails into bowls with some broth and serve hot with cocktail sticks (toothpicks) to extract the snails from their shells.

Snails in Tomato Sauce

ALGERIA
PREPARATION TIME: 40 minutes
COOKING TIME: 2 hours 5 minutes
SERVES: 4

Djeghlellou (snails) combine well with tomatoes, and this recipe for stewing them in tomato sauce is popular, especially in north Algeria.

750 g/1⅔ lb fresh (live) snails or snails in brine
1 bay leaf
generous pinch of dried thyme
piece of orange peel, white pith scraped away
3 tablespoons olive oil
3 cloves of garlic, minced
1 teaspoon sweet paprika
cayenne pepper, to taste
4 ripe tomatoes, peeled (see page 445) and finely chopped
1 tablespoon double concentrated tomato purée (paste)
salt and pepper

Follow the directions for preparing snails on page 444 (fresh or in brine). Once boiled, drain and rinse the snails.

Put the prepared snails into a large clean pot or saucepan and cover with 1.5 litres (50 fl oz/generous 6 cups) water. Add the bay leaf, thyme and orange peel. Season with salt and pepper and bring to the boil. Reduce the heat to medium-low, loosely cover with a lid and simmer until the snails are tender and can be easily extracted from their shells, about 45 minutes. Remove from the heat and leave in the water until ready to add.

Add the oil, garlic, paprika, cayenne pepper, tomatoes, tomato purée (paste) and 4 tablespoons of the liquid from the snails to a casserole dish (Dutch oven) or large pot and season with salt and pepper. Cook over a medium heat for 10 minutes. Transfer the snails with a slotted spoon to the sauce, add a touch of broth from the snails and cook until the sauce is reduced, 10–15 minutes. Serve with cocktail sticks (toothpicks) to extract the meat.

Snails in Spice-laden Broth

MOROCCO
PREPARATION TIME: 35 minutes
COOKING TIME: 1 hour 45 minutes
SERVES: 4–6

At busy spots in many Moroccan cities, carts sell bowls of snails (*babbouche*). They come with a ladle of aromatic broth seasoned by an array of herbs and spices (plus green tea leaves to help aid digestion). White with distinctive chocolate brown whirls, Moroccan snails are smaller than their classic French escargot cousins. Allow plenty of time to clean and prepare them. Traditionally washed with abundant water seven times in a row, the snails in this recipe are cleaned and prepared (see page 444 for details), rinsed, then added to the flavourful broth to cook. The spices are preferably tied in a piece of muslin (cheesecloth).

1 kg/2¼ lb fresh (live) snails or snails in brine
1 tablespoon dried mint
1 teaspoon dried thyme (*zaâtar*)
1 teaspoon dried oregano
10 sprigs mint
1 teaspoon aniseed
½ teaspoon caraway seeds
2 cloves
1 bay leaf
1 liquorice root, about 7.5 cm/3 inches in length
½ teaspoon loose leaf Chinese gunpowder green tea or 1 tea bag of green tea
peel of ½ orange, white pith scraped away
1 small dried hot chilli (chile)
salt

Follow the directions for preparing snails on page 444 (fresh or in brine). Once boiled, drain and rinse the snails.

Put the prepared snails into a large clean pot or saucepan and cover with 2 litres (68 fl oz/generous 2 quarts/8½ cups) water. Tie all the herbs and spices (except the hot chilli/chile), tea leaves and orange peel in a piece of muslin (cheesecloth) and add to the pan. Season with salt. Bring to the boil, loosely cover the pan with a lid and gently simmer over a medium-low heat until the snails are tender and can be easily extracted from their shells, about 45 minutes. Add the chilli and simmer for 5 minutes. Ladle the snails into bowls with some broth and serve hot with cocktail sticks (toothpicks) to extract the snails from their shells.

FISH AND
SEAFOOD

Fish Tagine with Caramelized Onion and Raisin Tfaya

MOROCCO
PREPARATION TIME: 20 minutes,
plus marinating and soaking time
COOKING TIME: 50 minutes–1 hour 25 minutes
SERVES: 4–5

This is a sublime sweet-and-savoury combination of spiced fish cooked atop caramelized onions. Monkfish and conger eel are excellent choices to use for this dish, although any bone-in white fish will work. If using conger, remove the skin before adding. (Pouring boiling water over the conger helps in this task.) Conger takes a bit longer to cook, so allow 30–45 minutes. While the *tfaya* topping can be prepared separately and served atop the fish, cooking the fish and the *tfaya* in the same pan yields more flavourful results.

   5 tablespoons olive oil
   2 small cloves of garlic, grated
   1 tablespoon finely chopped flat-leaf parsley
   1 tablespoon finely chopped coriander (cilantro)
   1 teaspoon ground ginger
   pinch of saffron threads, crumbled
   1 kg/2¼ lb monkfish, conger eel, hake or another
      white-fleshed fish, cut crosswise into 5-cm/2-inch
      steaks
   200 g/7 oz (scant 1½ cups) seedless raisins
   15 g/½ oz (1 tablespoon) butter or *smen* (page 412)
   1 kg/2¼ lb red or yellow onions, cut into rings, rings
      separated
   1 tablespoon sugar
   1 teaspoon ground cinnamon
   salt and pepper

Put 1 tablespoon of the oil, the garlic, parsley, coriander (cilantro), ½ teaspoon of the ginger and half of the saffron into a large bowl and mix to combine, then season with salt and pepper. Add the fish, turning to coat. Cover with cling film (plastic wrap) and leave to marinate in the refrigerator for 1 hour.

Meanwhile, put the raisins into a small bowl, cover with lukewarm water and leave to soak for 10 minutes; drain.

Add the remaining 4 tablespoons of the oil, the butter, onions, raisins, the remaining ½ teaspoon of ginger and remaining half of the saffron to a large tagine (see page 250) over a medium-high heat. Cook, stirring frequently, until the onions soften and begin to brown, 30–45 minutes. Stir in the sugar and cinnamon. Arrange the fish in a single layer on top of the onions. Cover the tagine with a lid and cook until the onions are caramelized and the fish

cooked through, 20–40 minutes, depending on the fish, carefully turning the fish once after a couple of minutes. Add a touch of water if needed or remove the lid to evaporate. Serve.

Oven-roasted Fish Tagine with Tomatoes and Potatoes

MOROCCO
PREPARATION TIME: 30 minutes
COOKING TIME: 1 hour
SERVES: 4

Fish tagines in Morocco are frequently not cooked in a tagine on the stove, rather roasted in the oven, yet they retain that name. This recipe comes from the Atlantic coast.

2 whole sea bream (about 450 g/1 lb each) or another firm-fleshed white fish
4 cloves of garlic, minced
2 heaped tablespoons finely chopped coriander (cilantro)
2 heaped tablespoons finely chopped flat-leaf parsley
2 teaspoons sweet paprika
2 teaspoons ground cumin
2 tablespoons fresh lemon juice
3 tablespoons olive oil
4 ripe tomatoes
2 carrots, thinly sliced crosswise
2 celery stalks, halved lengthwise
4 white potatoes, peeled and cut crosswise into thin slices
salt

◇ Preheat the oven to 200 °C/400 °F/Gas Mark 6.

Scale the fish by holding it by the tail and scraping at the scales with the back edge of a knife, then remove and discard the entrails and rinse the fish under cold running water. Set aside.

Make 2 parallel gashes to the bone on each side of each fish. Put the garlic, coriander (cilantro), parsley, paprika, cumin, lemon juice and oil into a large bowl and mix together, then season with salt. Rub the fish all over with half of the marinade. Set the remaining marinade aside.

Cut the top one-third off of each tomato. Arrange the tomato tops, carrots and celery stalks in a single layer over the bottom of a large baking dish or roasting tray, then spread the potatoes out across the top. Lay the fish across the potatoes. Slice the remaining tomatoes and arrange around the fish. Stir 175 ml (6 fl oz/¾ cup) water into the remaining marinade and drizzle over the top.

Cover with aluminium foil and roast in the hot oven for 40 minutes. Uncover and cook until the potatoes are tender and the fish is done, about 20 minutes. Check for doneness behind the gills with the tip of a knife. It should be opaque and flaky. If the fish is done before the potatoes, gently transfer to a platter, cover to keep warm and return the dish to the oven until the potatoes are done. Add a touch more water if needed. Serve.

CUMIN

While impossible to pinpoint the precise location of its origin, cumin is native to the Eastern Mediterranean or Upper Nile Valley. It was prevalent in the ancient world and spread early and widely. Arab traders carried it down to India, and from there it went throughout South Asia. Phoenicians took it to their outposts in Spain and North Africa, and the Spanish eventually to their colonies in the Americas. It travelled the Silk Road to China and to Europe, while desert Berbers took cumin along the trans-Saharan trade routes.

Cumin not only reached the far corners of the globe, but inserted itself deeply into various local cuisines. In some places, cumin has become more associated with its adopted home than its native homeland. That is the case with North Africa, where it is called *kammun*.

Algerian cooks frequently use the spice with fish, certain stews and dried pulses. In Libya, cumin is most associated with fish dishes, whether being added to bream for the grill or added halfway through cooking a fish couscous. In Tunisia, a heady, cumin-laden sauce called *kamounia* with liver (page 281), goat or cuttlefish (page 345) is a popular favourite. Cumin is added at the end so that the flavour is at the forefront of the dish's taste.

In Morocco, cumin grown in the foothills of the Anti-Atlas Mountains is prized for its high quality and intense aromas. Almost always ground, cumin goes into a wide range of popular Moroccan dishes. So beloved and common is *kammun* in Morocco that in many homes there is a small dish of it on the table alongside salt.

Tangy Fish Tagine with Preserved Lemons, Olives and Vegetables

MOROCCO
PREPARATION TIME: 30 minutes,
plus marinating time
COOKING TIME: 1 hour
SERVES: 4

Moroccan cooks traditionally build savoury
fish tagines, such as this one, on a base of fresh
vegetables. Because the vegetables take longer to
cook than the fish steaks or fillets, parcook some of
the vegetables before adding to the tagine in order
to not overcook the fish.

- 1 small preserved lemon (page 410)
- 2 tomatoes, halved crosswise and grated,
  peel discarded (see page 445)
- 2 tablespoons finely chopped flat-leaf parsley
- 2 tablespoons finely chopped coriander (cilantro)
- 1 clove of garlic, minced
- ½ teaspoon ground cumin
- ½ teaspoon sweet paprika
- 4 tablespoons olive oil
- 4 × 2.5-cm-/1-inch-thick skinless monkfish, swordfish or
  bream steaks, or fillets (170–225 g/6–8 oz each)
- 3 carrots, cut into 5-mm-/¼-inch-thick circles
- 4 white potatoes, peeled and cut crosswise into
  5-mm/¼-inch-thick slices
- 1 red or green bell pepper, cored, seeded and sliced
  lengthwise into thin strips
- 1 red or yellow onion, thinly sliced
- 50 g/2 oz olives (about ½ cup)
- salt and pepper

Cut the preserved lemon into wedges, rinse thoroughly
and remove any seeds. Using a spoon or paring
knife, separate the pulp from the peel. Finely chop
the pulp and set aside. Finely chop half of the peel.
Set the remaining peel aside.

Add the lemon pulp and finely chopped peel,
tomatoes, parsley, coriander (cilantro), garlic, cumin
and paprika to a large bowl, then season with salt
and pepper. Moisten with 2 tablespoons of the oil
and 2 tablespoons water and blend well. Add the
fish, turning to coat. Cover and leave to marinate in
the refrigerator for 30 minutes, turning the fish from
time to time.

Meanwhile, put the carrots and potatoes into a
large pot or saucepan of lightly salted water and gently
boil for 6–10 minutes until they begin to soften; drain.

Put the bell pepper strips into a medium frying
pan, add 60 ml (2 fl oz/¼ cup) water, cover with a
lid and steam over a medium heat until the peppers
begin to soften, about 5 minutes. Watch that the pan
does not scorch. Set aside.

Coat the bottom of a medium tagine (see
page 250) with the remaining 2 tablespoons of oil.
Evenly arrange the carrots and potatoes across the
bottom of the tagine. Separate the onion slices and
scatter on top. Put the fish over the vegetables.
Add 2 tablespoons of water to the marinade, swirl
the bowl and spoon over the top. Arrange the bell
pepper strips and reserved lemon peel on top, and
dot with the olives.

Cover the tagine with a lid and cook over a medium-
low heat for 30–45 minutes, gently nudging the
vegetables from time to time to prevent sticking,
until the fish is opaque throughout. Drizzle in a few
tablespoons of water as necessary during cooking to
keep from drying out, or remove the lid at the end
of cooking to evaporate and thicken the sauce if it's
watery. Serve from the tagine.

Marinated Fish Skewers

MOROCCO
PREPARATION TIME: 15 minutes,
plus soaking (optional) and marinating time
COOKING TIME: 5 minutes
SERVES: 4

Skewers of marinated fish are popular along
Morocco's Atlantic coast. The range of species used
depends on what the fishing boats have brought in
that day to the market: *courbine* (known in English
as meagre or croaker, a large, elongated silvery fish
with a golden mouth), swordfish, monkfish, conger
eel and even shark. For added flavour and attractive
presentation, it is common to intersperse the fish
with pieces of fresh green pepper.

    1 kg/2¼ lb skinless monkfish or swordfish steaks or
      another firm-fleshed white fish
    4 cloves of garlic, minced
    2 tablespoons finely chopped flat-leaf parsley
    2 tablespoons finely chopped coriander (cilantro)
    1 teaspoon sweet paprika
    ½ teaspoon cayenne pepper
    ½ teaspoon ground cumin
    1 tablespoon olive oil, plus extra for oiling
    juice of 1 lemon
    salt and pepper

If using wooden skewers, put them into a large bowl
of water and leave to soak for 30 minutes to prevent
them burning during cooking.

Trim the fish and cut into 2–2.5-cm/¾–1-inch cubes.
Add the garlic, parsley, coriander (cilantro), paprika,
cayenne pepper and cumin to a large bowl. Season
with salt and pepper and moisten with the oil and
lemon juice, then blend together. Add the fish,
turning to coat. Cover with cling film (plastic wrap)
and leave to marinate in the refrigerator for at least
30 minutes, turning occasionally. Thread skewers
with 4–5 pieces of fish on each. The pieces should
be touching but not packed tightly together.

If using a stovetop grill pan, frying pan or griddle,
lightly oil and heat over a high heat. Or prepare
a charcoal grill or barbecue. Cook the skewers,
turning as needed with a spatula, until the fish
is opaque throughout and firm to touch, about
5 minutes. If cooking on a charcoal grill or barbecue,
wait until the embers die down and turn white.
Serve immediately.

Spiced Fishcakes

TUNISIA
PREPARATION TIME: 30 minutes
COOKING TIME: 30 minutes
MAKES: about 12 fishcakes

Fishcakes are easy to prepare with leftover pieces of
fish. When preparing fishcakes from uncooked fish,
as in this recipe, a popular choice is whiting (*merlan*
in French), as they are easy to debone. Serve with
homemade Tomato Dipping Sauce (page 442).

    500 g/1 lb 2 oz fish fillets, preferably whiting, bream
      or another white fish
    2 small white potatoes, quartered
    1 red or yellow onion, grated
    ½ teaspoon ground cumin
    ½ teaspoon sweet paprika
    3 tablespoons finely chopped flat-leaf parsley
    2 eggs
    50 g/2 oz (¾ cup) dry breadcrumbs, plus extra
      for coating
    neutral oil, for frying
    salt and pepper
    Tomato Dipping Sauce (page 442), to serve

Bring at least 5 cm/2 inches water to the boil in the
bottom of a steamer pot. Put the fish into the steamer
basket, cover with a lid and steam until opaque
throughout, about 5 minutes. Or boil in a large pot
of lightly salted water for about 5 minutes. Transfer
the fillets to a platter to cool and drain. Remove and
discard the skin of the fish if needed, check for any
bones and break the flesh up into pieces.

Meanwhile, put the potatoes into a medium pot or
saucepan of lightly salted water and boil until tender,
about 20 minutes; drain and return to the pan. Once
cool enough to handle, peel and mash with a fork.

Put the potatoes, onion, cumin, paprika and parsley
into a large bowl. Season with salt and pepper and blend
well. Fold in the eggs, breadcrumbs and flaked fish.

Put enough breadcrumbs for coating into a wide
dish. Roll the mixture into golf ball-size (about 4 cm/
1½ inches in diameter), slightly flatten with the
palms of your hands and roll in the breadcrumbs
until they are lightly coated all over. Set aside.

Heat at least 1 cm/½ inch of oil in a large frying
pan over a medium heat until the surface shimmers.
Line a plate with paper towels. Gently and carefully
set the fishcakes into the pan and fry, turning, until
golden on the outside and hot at the centre, about
1½ minutes. Gently transfer to the paper towels to
briefly drain. Serve hot with the dipping sauce.

Fish Stuffed with Fennel

MOROCCO
PREPARATION TIME: 15 minutes
COOKING TIME: 20 minutes
SERVES: 3

Stuffing fish with fresh fennel gives lovely sweet, anise notes. This recipe is for roasting in the oven, but it can be done by laying the aluminium foil-wrapped packages of stuffed fish directly on embers. The recipe calls for individual serving-size fish.

- 3 whole sea bass (about 450 g/1 lb each) or gilthead sea bream
- 1 large fennel bulb (about 450 g/1 lb), fronds trimmed and set aside
- 1 lemon, halved
- 1 tablespoon olive oil, plus extra for drizzling
- 2 tablespoons finely chopped flat-leaf parsley
- 2 tablespoons finely chopped coriander (cilantro)
- salt and pepper

Preheat the oven to 200 °C/400 °F/Gas Mark 6.

Scale the fish by holding it by the tail and scraping at the scales with the back edge of a knife, then remove and discard the entrails and rinse the fish under cold running water. Set aside.

Finely slice the fennel and put into a large bowl. Juice half of the lemon and thinly slice the other half. Add the olive oil, lemon juice, parsley and coriander (cilantro) to the fennel and toss together. Season with salt and pepper.

Make 3 parallel diagonal incisions on each side of the fish. Lay each fish on a large, individual sheet of aluminium foil. Rub the fish with oil and season with salt and pepper. Generously stuff the cavities with the fennel mixture, scatter the fennel fronds across the top and arrange 1 or 2 lemon slices on top. Fold the foil packages closed. Put onto a baking sheet and bake in the hot oven until opaque and the fish flakes easily when pierced with the tip of a knife, about 20 minutes. Carefully open the foil packages and transfer the fish to plates. Serve immediately.

Grilled Whole Sea Bass

LIBYA, TUNISIA
PREPARATION TIME: 10 minutes
COOKING TIME: 10 minutes
SERVES: 2

Stalls, cafés and restaurants offering an assortment of grilled lamb cuts, merguez sausages and fish are very popular across the region. In Libya and Tunisia, the fish usually gets a series of incisions cut into the sides, and then is seasoned with cumin and salt before being laid on the grill.

- 2 whole sea bass (about 450 g/1 lb each) or gilthead sea bream
- 2 tablespoons olive oil
- 1 teaspoon ground cumin
- 1 teaspoon salt

Scale the fish by holding it by the tail and scraping at the scales with the back edge of a knife, then remove and discard the entrails and rinse the fish under cold running water. Set aside.

Put the oil, cumin and salt into a small bowl and whisk together. Using a sharp knife, make 4 or 5 parallel diagonal incisions to the bone on each side of the fish, then generously brush with the spiced oil, rubbing into the incisions.

Prepare the charcoal on a barbecue or heat a stovetop grill pan, large frying pan or griddle over a medium-high heat.

Grill the fish, carefully turning once with a wide spatula, until opaque throughout, about 10 minutes. Check for doneness behind the gills with the tip of a knife. If cooking on a charcoal grill or barbecue, wait until the embers die down and turn white. Serve immediately.

Grilled Sea Bream

TUNISIA
PREPARATION TIME: 10 minutes
COOKING TIME: 12 minutes
SERVES: 2

Wild sea bream swimming off Tunisia's Sahel shore are much sought-after for their firm meat and fine flavours. This recipe uses a simple marinade. The fish is ideally served with Frites (page 164) and Tomato Dipping Sauce (page 442).

2 whole gilthead sea bream (about 450 g/1 lb each)
3 tablespoons olive oil
1 teaspoon ground cumin
1 teaspoon sweet paprika
1 teaspoon salt
Frites (page 164), to serve
Tomato Dipping Sauce (page 442), to serve

Scale the fish by holding it by the tail and scraping at the scales with the back edge of a knife, then remove and discard the entrails and rinse the fish under cold running water. Set aside.

Put the oil, cumin, paprika and salt into a small bowl and whisk together. Make 2 parallel diagonal incisions on each side of the fish and generously brush with the spiced oil.

Heat a stovetop grill pan, large frying pan or griddle over a medium-high heat or prepare a barbecue.

Grill the fish, carefully turning once with a wide spatula, until opaque throughout, about 12 minutes. Check for doneness behind the gills with the tip of a knife. If cooking on a charcoal grill or barbecue, wait until the embers die down and turn white. Serve immediately with Frites and the dipping sauce.

Roasted Sea Bream with Lemon and Tomato Slices

TUNISIA
PREPARATION TIME: 10 minutes
COOKING TIME: 20 minutes
SERVES: 2

These roasted fish are brushed with oil, topped with a couple of thin circles of lemon and tomato and sprinkled with cumin. It's simple and the fish is tasty, tender and moist.

2 whole gilthead sea bream (about 400 g/14 oz each)
olive oil, for drizzling
1 lemon, cut crosswise into thin slices
1 tomato, cut crosswise into thin slices
ground cumin, for dusting
salt

Preheat the oven to 200 °C/400 °F/Gas Mark 6. Line a large baking sheet with baking (parchment) paper.

Scale the fish by holding it by the tail and scraping at the scales with the back edge of a knife, then remove and discard the entrails and rinse the fish under cold running water. Set aside.

Rub both sides of the fish with oil and season with salt. Set on the prepared baking sheet and place a couple of lemon slices in each cavity of the fish. Lay 2 slices of lemons and 2 slices of tomatoes across the top of each fish and generously dust with cumin.

Roast in the hot oven and until opaque and the fish flakes easily, about 20 minutes. Check for doneness behind the gills with the tip of a knife. Serve immediately.

Marinated Fried Fish

MOROCCO
PREPARATION TIME: 15 minutes,
plus marinating time
COOKING TIME: 10 minutes
SERVES: 4

In southern Spain, one of the most famous dishes is *pescadito frito,* small fish coated in flour and deep-fried. Across the Strait of Gibraltar in northern Morocco, fish are often fried in a similar way – although usually marinated first in *chermoula.*

1 kg/2¼ lb mixed small whole fresh fish, such as small hake, sole, fresh anchovies and red mullet
2 cloves of garlic, peeled
½ teaspoon salt
2 teaspoons sweet paprika
1 teaspoon ground cumin
½ teaspoon cayenne pepper, optional
2 heaped tablespoons finely chopped coriander (cilantro)
2 heaped tablespoons finely chopped flat-leaf parsley
1 tablespoon olive oil
1 tablespoon fresh lemon juice
neutral oil, for frying
plain (all-purpose) flour, for dusting
lemons wedges, to serve
Tomato Dipping Sauce (page 442), to serve

Rinse the fish under cold running water and clean, removing the innards and, if desired, the heads. Lay out on paper towels to dry, then put into a large bowl.

Put the garlic and salt into a mortar and using a pestle, pound to a paste. Add the paprika, cumin, cayenne pepper (if using), coriander (cilantro) and parsley, then stir in the olive oil and lemon juice. Rub the mixture over the fish. Cover with cling film (plastic wrap) and leave to marinate in the refrigerator for at least 30 minutes, turning occasionally.

Heat at least 1 cm/½ inch of neutral oil in a large, deep frying pan over a medium heat until the surface shimmers. Line a plate with paper towels. Put enough flour for coating into a wide bowl.

Working in batches, dip the fish into the flour until lightly coated all over, then shake off the excess and carefully slip into the hot oil with tongs. Fry until golden and slightly crispy, 45 seconds–2 minutes, depending on the size of the fish. Using tongs or a slotted spoon, transfer the fish to the paper towels to briefly drain. Fry the remaining fish. Serve immediately with lemon wedges and small bowls of Tomato Dipping Sauce.

OLIVE OIL

Zeyt – olive oil – has long been key to the region's cuisine. Remains at ancient sites such as Carthage show that olive oil pressing in North Africa goes back thousands of years. The Phoenicians introduced the olive tree and developed the technology for pressing the oil. Romans expanded cultivation and the use for the oil, and in the centuries following the arrival of the Arabs, techniques of irrigation and production were improved and gradually perfected.

In Algeria, Kabylia is the best-known olive oil region.

Small producers with often just a handful of trees dominate production. They pick the ripe fruits beginning in November and take them to the mill to be pressed. The main variety in Kabylia is called Chemlal, which is well adapted to being planted in difficult terrains and on steep slopes. Chemlal represents about 40 per cent of the country's total olive crop. In the centre of Algeria, the Azeradj variety is popular, while Sigoise dominate western groves. Comprising about a quarter of the country's trees, Sigoise also make excellent table olives –

about two-thirds of the crop is for that purpose.

Key olive oil areas in Morocco are around Marrakech, Fès, Meknès and, in the north, especially around the Rif Mountains. Most of Morocco's olive oil comes from the hearty, highly productive Picholine Marocaine variety, an elliptical, medium-size and late-ripening olive similar to Algerian Sigoise. Used for both the table and for pressing oil, Picholine Marocaine makes up as much as 96 per cent of Morocco's olive groves.

Fried Whiting with Cumin, Garlic and Semolina Breading

ALGERIA, TUNISIA
PREPARATION TIME: 15 minutes,
plus marinating time
COOKING TIME: 12 minutes
SERVES: 3–4

Whiting have lovely light and firm flesh when fried. (If cooked too slowly, they can turn mushy.) They are perfect to rub with this paste of pounded garlic and cumin before coating in flour or semolina and frying. Whiting range in size, but in the market they are often about 30 cm/12 inches in length. Remove the head and entrails before rubbing with the spice paste. Some cooks in Algeria use lemon juice rather than oil to loosen the spice rub, and even add in some fresh coriander (cilantro) and grated onion for more flavour.

  1 kg/2¼ lb whole whiting
  4 cloves of garlic, peeled
  2 teaspoons cumin seeds
  1 teaspoon sweet paprika or cayenne pepper
  2 teaspoons olive oil
  neutral oil, for frying
  fine semolina or plain (all-purpose) flour, for dusting
  salt and pepper
  lemon wedges, to serve

Remove the heads and entrails of the whiting, and carefully rinse under cold running water. Put the garlic and cumin seeds into a mortar, and using a pestle, pound until crushed. Add the paprika, generously season with salt and pepper and stir in the olive oil to form a paste. Rub the fish with the paste, then put into a large bowl, cover with cling film (plastic wrap) and leave to marinate in the refrigerator for about 15 minutes.

Heat at least 1 cm/½ inch of neutral oil in a large, deep frying pan over a medium heat until the surface shimmers. Line a plate with paper towels. Put enough semolina for coating into a wide bowl.

Working in batches, dip the fish into the semolina until lightly coated all over, then shake off the excess and carefully slip into the oil with tongs. Fry until golden brown and cooked through, about 4 minutes. Using a slotted spoon or tongs, transfer the fish to the paper towels to briefly drain. Fry the remaining fish. Serve immediately with lemon wedges.

Fried Red Mullet

TUNISIA
PREPARATION TIME: 10 minutes,
plus marinating time
COOKING TIME: 15 minutes
SERVES: 4–5

While it is enough to simply season the *trilia* with salt and maybe a bit of cumin before dusting in flour and frying until they turn a tinny-reddish-orange colour, many Tunisians prefer to marinate them in a headier blend of spices first. This mullet dish is excellent served with Frites (page 164).

  1 kg/2¼ lb whole red mullet
  1 teaspoon ground cumin
  2 teaspoons sweet paprika
  harissa (page 409) or cayenne pepper, to taste
  2 heaped tablespoons finely chopped flat-leaf parsley
  1 tablespoon olive oil
  1 tablespoon fresh lemon juice
  neutral oil, for frying
  plain (all-purpose) flour, for dusting
  salt and pepper
  lemons wedges, to serve

Rinse the fish under cold running water and clean, trimming the bottom fins and removing the innards. Lay out on paper towels to dry, then put into a large bowl.

Put the cumin, paprika, harissa and parsley into a small bowl and mix together. Season with salt and pepper, then stir in the olive oil and lemon juice. Add 1–2 teaspoons water if needed to further loosen. Rub the mixture over the fish. Cover with cling film (plastic wrap) and leave to marinate in the refrigerator for at least 30 minutes, turning occasionally.

Heat at least 1 cm/½ inch of neutral oil in a large, deep frying pan over a medium heat until the surface shimmers. Line a plate with paper towels. Put enough flour for coating into a wide bowl.

Working in batches, dip the fish into the flour until lightly coated all over, then shake off the excess and carefully slip into the hot oil with tongs. Fry until golden and nicely crispy, 1–2 minutes per batch, depending on the size of the fish. Using tongs, transfer the fish to the paper towels to briefly drain. Fry the remaining fish. Serve immediately with lemon wedges.

Skate in Tomato Sauce

ALGERIA
PREPARATION TIME: 20 minutes
COOKING TIME: 35 minutes
SERVES: 4

Skate are a cartilaginous fish – their skeletons are made of strong cartilage rather than bones – with fine, pinkish flesh that turns white when cooked. The flavour is mild and the texture pleasing. Skate is usually sold ready-skinned and often as 'wings'. Add 1 tablespoon of double concentrated tomato purée (paste) to boost flavour of the sauce, if desired.

> 1 kg/2¼ lb skinned skate wings
> neutral oil, for frying
> plain (all-purpose) flour, for dusting
> 3 tablespoons olive oil
> 3 cloves of garlic, minced
> 4 tomatoes, peeled (see page 445) and finely chopped
> 2 heaped tablespoons flat-leaf parsley
> 1 teaspoon sweet paprika
> ½ teaspoon ground cumin, optional
> 1 heaped tablespoon capers, rinsed, optional
> salt and pepper

Trim the skate into 6 or so pieces.

Heat at least 5 mm/¼ inch of neutral oil in a large, deep frying pan over a medium heat until the surface shimmers. Line a plate with paper towels. Put enough flour for coating into a wide bowl and season with salt. Working in batches, dip the fish into the flour until lightly coated, then shake off the excess and carefully slip into the hot oil with tongs. Fry until golden, about 5 minutes. Using a slotted spoon or tongs, transfer the fish to the paper towels to drain. Fry the remaining fish.

Heat the olive oil in a wide pot or saucepan over a medium heat, add the garlic and cook for about 30 seconds, or until aromatic. Add the tomatoes, parsley, paprika and cumin (if using) and season with salt and pepper. Reduce the heat to low and cook until the tomato is darker and reduced, about 15 minutes. Set the skate in the sauce, add the capers (if using) and 4 tablespoons water. Cook until the fish is cooked through, 5–10 minutes. Loosen with a touch more water if needed. Arrange the fish on a serving platter and cover with the sauce. Serve.

Fried Skate

ALGERIA, TUNISIA
PREPARATION TIME: 5 minutes
COOKING TIME: 20 minutes
SERVES: 4

With its mild flavour and tender-yet-firm texture, sometimes the best way to prepare skate is to just flour and fry it in oil, then serve it immediately with lemon wedges. Dusting the skate with fine semolina will give the coating slightly more texture than with plain (all-purpose) flour.

> 1 kg/2¼ lb skinned skate wings
> neutral oil, for frying
> fine semolina or plain (all-purpose) flour, for dusting
> salt and pepper
> lemon wedges, to serve

Cut the skate into generous pieces and season with salt and pepper.

Heat at least 2 cm/¾ inch of oil in a large, deep frying pan over a medium heat until the surface shimmers. Line a plate with paper towels. Put enough semolina for coating into a wide bowl.

Working in batches that don't crowd the pan, dip the fish into the semolina until lightly coated, then shake off the excess and slip into the hot oil with tongs. Fry until golden and cooked through, 5–8 minutes per batch, depending on the thickness of the piece. Transfer to the paper towels to briefly drain. Fry the remaining fish. Serve immediately with lemon wedges.

CAPERS

Most capers you can buy in the Mediterranean are sold already salted or preserved in vinegar. In Tunisia they are also found fresh in late spring and early summer, that is April, May and June. Capers grow abundantly in the wild across northern Tunisia, and people pick the immature flower buds from the thorny shrubs in the forests or buy them in the markets. The thorns make gathering them difficult.

In Tunis's nineteenth-century Marche Central, which occupies an entire city block just outside the main entrance of Tunis's dense, ancient medina, numerous stalls sell the fresh buds that are vibrant green and tinged with purple. When preserved at home, the fresh green capers are spread out in layers with coarse salt and then stored in salt or, sometimes, in a blend of vinegar and salted water.

In the Tunisian kitchen, cured capers give a tang to numerous starters, soups, salads, pastas and stews. A spoonful gets added to spicy *hsou* soup with meatballs (page 128), also to *lablabi*, a dish of chickpeas (garbanzo beans) ladled over day-old bread and topped with a range of condiments (page 147), and even to tongue simmered in a garlic-rich tomato sauce (page 288). One characteristic (and extraordinary) dish that calls for them is *kabkabou*, fish with preserved lemons, smoky olives and capers in a tomato sauce (see below).

In Algeria, capers are particularly widespread in the area around Béjaïa, to the east of Algiers, where they thrive in the sunny, dry climate. While most capers in Algeria are foraged in the wild, Morocco has a large industry of cultivated capers and is a major exporter. In Morocco, capers grow largely around Fès, Safi and Marrakech.

From adding a few to a cucumber salad (page 88) to topping skate stewed in tomato sauce (page 327), a small spoonful of pungent buds has the power to immediately transform a dish.

Tuna with Olives, Preserved Lemon and Capers in Tomato Sauce

TUNISIA
PREPARATION TIME: 15 minutes
COOKING TIME: 35 minutes
SERVES: 4

One of Tunisia's iconic dishes, *kabkabou* is a sublime combination of fish in a tomato sauce with olives, lemon and capers. Tuna steaks are the classic choice for fish, but even stronger fish such as mackerel or shark work well, too. Whole sea bream or sea bass make for impressive presentations.

2 tablespoons olive oil
4 tuna steaks, about 1.5-cm/⅔-inch thick (about 150 g/5 oz each)
1 onion, halved lengthwise and thinly sliced
2 tomatoes, halved crosswise and grated, peel discarded (see page 445)
1 tablespoon double concentrated tomato purée (paste)
1 teaspoon sweet paprika
harissa (page 409), to taste
½ preserved lemon (page 410), pulp scraped out and peel cut into thin strips
2 tablespoons capers, rinsed
12 pitted black or green olives
white vinegar, for dashing
salt and pepper

Heat the oil in a large, wide saucepan over a medium heat, add the tuna steaks and sear for about 30 seconds on each side. Transfer to a plate. Transfer to the plate and set aside. Add the onion to the pan and cook until pale and soft, about 5 minutes. Stir in the tomatoes, tomato purée (paste) and 3 tablespoons warm water, then add the paprika and harissa and season with salt and pepper. Cook for 2–3 minutes, then stir in 250 ml (8 fl oz/1 cup) water. Reduce the heat to low and cook until it has thickened but is still moist, about 15 minutes. Add the preserved lemon and capers, then gently set the tuna in the pan. Spoon over some sauce, add the olives, cover the pan with a lid and cook until the tuna is opaque throughout, about 5 minutes. Dash with vinegar. Carefully transfer the fish with a wide spatula to individual plates and serve topped with sauce from the pan.

Tuna in Olive Oil with Onions and Capers

TUNISIA
PREPARATION TIME: 10 minutes,
plus cooling time
COOKING TIME: 10 minutes
SERVES: 2

A generous hunk of high-quality canned tuna fish with olive oil is a favourite starter. Topping it with some sweet, grilled onions and tangy capers turns it into a perfect combination of disparate flavours.

2 tablespoons olive oil
1 red onion, cut crosswise into thin rings
1 × 100–150 g/3½–5 oz piece of drained high-quality canned tuna
extra-virgin olive oil, for drizzling
2 tablespoons capers, rinsed
10–15 pitted black olives, sliced in half
minced flat-leaf parsley, to garnish, optional

Heat the olive oil in a medium stovetop grill pan, frying pan or griddle over a high heat. Add the onion and cook, stirring frequently, until tender and turning brown on the edges, about 10 minutes. Transfer to a bowl and leave to cool.

Put the piece of tuna onto a large plate. Generously drizzle with extra-virgin olive oil, then spoon the onion over the top and scatter over the capers and olives. Sprinkle over some parsley (if using) and serve.

Fresh Bonito in Chunky Tomato and Onion Sauce

ALGERIA
PREPARATION TIME: 15 minutes
COOKING TIME: 40 minutes
SERVES: 4–6

Small Atlantic bonito (*Sarda sarda*) are exquisite, with oily dark meat that is slightly less firm than tuna. One popular way to prepare them in Algeria is in an oil-and-vinegar escabeche (see page 335 for Sardines in Escabeche); another is like this recipe with plenty of onions and tomatoes. This dish is best using whole, smallish bonito that weigh about 750 g/1⅔ lb.

2 small whole bonito tuna (about 750 g/1⅔ lb each)
4 tablespoons olive oil
3 red or yellow onions, halved lengthwise and thinly sliced
3 cloves of garlic, minced
5 ripe tomatoes, peeled (see page 445) and coarsely chopped
½ teaspoon ground cumin
1 tablespoon finely chopped parsley or coriander (cilantro)
1 lemon, quartered
salt and pepper

Remove and discard the entrails of the bonito, but leave on the heads and tails. Rinse the fish under cold running water. Cut each bonito crosswise into 3 large pieces and generously season with salt and pepper.

Heat the oil in a casserole dish (Dutch oven) or large, wide pot over a high heat, add the onions and cook until they begin to brown, about 10 minutes. Stir in the garlic, tomatoes and 4 tablespoons water and cook for 10 minutes to reduce. Stir in the cumin and parsley, squeeze over the lemon quarters and drop them into the sauce. Set the pieces of bonito in the pan, reduce the heat to low and cook, gently turning the pieces just once, until cooked through and the sauce thickened, about 20 minutes. Serve from the pan.

Grilled Sardines

ALGERIA, LIBYA, MOROCCO, TUNISIA
PREPARATION TIME: 10 minutes
COOKING TIME: 20 minutes
SERVES: 6

The smell of sardines grilling over embers is one of North Africa's summer pleasures. But they can also be prepared inside under an oven grill (broiler). Baking sheets lined with baking (parchment) paper helps keep the skin intact when turning the fish. The sardines are generally neither cleaned nor scaled; larger ones may be cleaned (but not scaled), if desired. Calculate 6–8 sardines per person. Some like to squeeze over some lemon juice before eating.

36–48 fresh sardines
coarse sea salt
lemon wedges, to serve, optional

IF USING A BARBECUE: Prepare the coals. Once the embers die down and turn white, arrange the sardines close but not touching in a grill basket. Liberally sprinkle both sides with salt. Place the rack just above the coals and set the grill basket on the rack. Grill the sardines, fanning the embers to keep them hot, until the skin is buckled and charred and the eyes have gone white, turning various times, 6–8 minutes total, depending on the size of the sardines. Carefully remove the fish from the grill basket. Grill the remaining sardines in batches.

IF USING AN OVEN GRILL (BROILER): Preheat to high. Line a baking sheet with baking (parchment) paper. Place the sardines on the sheet, spacing them about 2.5 cm/1 inch apart to make turning easier and liberally sprinkle with salt. Place the oven rack as close as possible under the grill. Grill (broil) the fish, gently turning once with a spatula, until the skin is buckled and charred and the eyes have gone white, 6–8 minutes total, depending on the size of the sardines. Carefully transfer to a platter. Re-line the sheet with baking (parchment) paper and grill the remaining sardines in batches, changing the paper each time.

Serve immediately with lemon wedges (if using).

SARDINES

Morocco is the world's largest producer of sardines. Its boats haul in about 70 per cent of the global sardine catch. The industry processes about 600,000 tons of fresh *Sardina pilchardus* each year, largely from its Atlantic ports. The sardine is also an important catch for Algerian, Tunisian and Libyan fleets in the Mediterranean.

Atlantic sardines tend to be larger than their Mediterranean cousins, with smaller heads and bulkier bodies. While much of the region's catch goes into cans, fresh sardines remain perhaps the most popular (and economical) fish and many families eat them frequently. Although commercially fished all year round, sardines are most abundant in local markets during warmer months. Highly perishable, they come directly from the port to be eaten the same day. Sardines are nutrient rich in calcium, protein and omega-3 fatty acids and, thanks to being far down on the food chain, low in mercury. But they are devoured with great gusto for their healthfulness and flavour.

There are numerous beloved sardine dishes across the region. Butterflied open, smeared with a garlic- and herb-laden *chermoula* marinade, pressed together and deep-fried (page 335). Marinated with a harissa-laden concoction and grilled. Arranged in a radial fashion on a bed of potatoes and tomatoes and cooked in a tagine. Conserved in an escabeche marinade (page 335) or with vinegar and plenty of fresh mint (page 332). Despite the effort involved in filleting and deboning the sardines, one of the popular ways to prepare them is as fish balls stewed in sauce. The Moroccan version of sardine balls in tomato sauce (page 336) is a favourite for families to take to the beach for a picnic.

Sardines, though, are best when simply grilled over embers (see above), their flavours robust, their flesh sparkling, briny and shaded with smoky oils. They are cooked for just a couple of minutes on each side until the skin turns crispy gold and the eyes go white. Sprinkled with a pinch of sea salt and sometimes given a squeeze of lemon juice, they are devoured with the fingers just as soon as they can be handled.

Marinated Sardines with Fresh Mint

ALGERIA
PREPARATION TIME: 20 minutes,
plus cooling and chilling
COOKING TIME: 5 minutes
SERVES: 3–4

Sardines are one of the most popular fish in Algeria. One delicious way to prepare them is to marinate for a few hours in vinegar with plenty of mint. They make a delicious filling for a baguette sandwich. For a version in a bolder marinade, see Sardines in Escabeche (page 335).

    18 small–medium fresh sardines
        (about 450 g/1 lb total)
    neutral oil, for frying
    plain (all-purpose) flour, for dusting
    4 heaped tablespoons finely chopped mint
    120 ml/4 fl oz (½ cup) white vinegar
    salt and pepper

Clean, scale and remove the heads and entrails of the sardines following the directions on page 444. Rinse under cold running water and pat dry with paper towels. Season the sardines with salt and pepper.

Heat at least 1.5 cm/⅔ inch of oil in a large, deep frying pan over a medium heat until the surface shimmers. Line a plate with paper towels. Put enough flour for coating into a wide bowl and season with salt.

Working in batches, dip the sardines into the flour until lightly coated, then shake off the excess and carefully slip them into the hot oil with tongs. Fry until golden brown and cooked through, about 1½ minutes. Using a slotted spoon or tongs, transfer the sardines to the paper towels to briefly drain. Fry the remaining fish.

Arrange the sardines in layers in a medium rectangular dish, while generously sprinkling with the mint.

Pour the vinegar into a large bowl, pour in 250 ml (8 fl oz/1 cup) water and whisk together. Pour over the sardines, then leave to cool, cover with cling film (plastic wrap) and refrigerate for 30 minutes, or until chilled. Eat chilled. Store in the refrigerator and eat within 3 days.

Fried Sardines in Dersa Red Chilli Paste and Semolina Breading

ALGERIA
PREPARATION TIME: 20 minutes,
plus marinating time
COOKING TIME: 10 minutes
SERVES: 4–6

A delicious way of preparing these silvery packages of flavour, *sardines bel dersa*, is an Algerian classic. *Dersa* (page 441) is a garlic paste made with either dried or fresh chillies (chiles). As with other fried fish, coating with fine semolina gives a particularly pleasing texture.

    3 tablespoons Dersa Garlic-chilli Paste (page 441)
        or Dersa Garlic and Fresh Red Chilli Paste
        (page 441)
    36 fresh sardines
    neutral oil, for frying
    fine semolina or plain (all-purpose) flour, for coating
    white vinegar, for dashing, optional
    salt

Clean and remove the heads and entrails of the sardines following the directions on page 444. Rinse under cold running water and pat dry with paper towels. Rub the outside and inside of the sardines with the dersa paste and leave to marinate for at least 15 minutes.

Heat at least 1.5 cm/⅔ inch of oil in a large, deep frying pan over a medium heat until the surface shimmers. Line a plate with paper towels. Put enough semolina for coating into a wide bowl and season with salt.

Working in batches, dip the fish into the semolina until lightly coated, then shake off the excess and carefully slip into the hot oil with tongs. Fry until golden brown, 30 seconds–1 minute. Transfer with a slotted spoon or tongs to the paper towels to briefly drain. Fry the remaining fish.

Put the sardines onto a serving plate, dash with vinegar (if using) and serve immediately.

Stuffed Sardine Pairs

MOROCCO
PREPARATION TIME: 30 minutes
COOKING TIME: 10 minutes
SERVES: 4–6

Known as *sardine chrayek* (*chrayek* means 'coupled' or 'partnered'), these stuffed sardine pairs are a favourite street food. Atlantic sardines are often slightly larger than Mediterranean ones and may require a touch more marinade.

    24 fresh sardines
    4 cloves of garlic, minced
    3 tablespoons finely chopped flat-leaf parsley
    3 tablespoons finely chopped coriander (cilantro)
    1 teaspoon ground cumin
    1 teaspoon sweet paprika
    1 generous pinch of cayenne pepper
    1 tablespoon olive oil
    2 tablespoons fresh lemon juice
    neutral oil, for frying
    plain (all-purpose) flour, for dredging
    salt and pepper
    2 lemons, cut into wedges, to serve

Butterfly open the sardines. To do this, remove the heads and entrails. Using a thumbnail or knife, open along the stomach. Loosen the central spine by pressing around it with your thumb. Clip the spine towards the tail with kitchen scissors, then take the end and pull up the spine. Remove any remaining bones, then spread open into a single, butterflied fillet. Rinse under cold running water and pat dry with paper towels. Repeat with the remaining fish.

Add the garlic, parsley, coriander (cilantro), cumin, paprika and cayenne pepper to a large bowl. Season with salt and pepper and moisten with the olive oil and lemon juice. Blend well.

Lay half of the sardines, skin-side down, on a large plate. Spread about 1 teaspoon of the paste on each, then place a second sardine on top, skin-side up, and gently press together.

Heat at least 1.5 cm/⅔ inch of neutral oil in a large, deep frying pan over a medium heat until the surface shimmers. Line a plate with paper towels. Put enough flour for coating into a wide bowl and season with salt.

Working in batches, fry the sardines. Holding a pair together, dust with the flour and carefully set in the hot oil with tongs. Fry until golden and cooked through, 1–2 minutes, turning as needed. Using tongs, transfer to the paper towels to drain. Fry the remaining fish. Serve immediately with the lemon wedges.

Sardines in Escabeche

ALGERIA
PREPARATION TIME: 15 minutes,
plus cooling and 1 day marinating time
COOKING TIME: 20 minutes
SERVES: 4

Skabitch is an herby, oil-and-vinegar marinade found in various places around the Mediterranean, including Algeria.

    16 fresh sardines (about 500 g/1 lb 2 oz total)
    plain (all-purpose) flour, for dusting
    360 ml/12 fl oz (1½ cups) olive oil, plus extra if needed
    6 cloves of garlic, lightly crushed in the skin
    1 small red onion, cut crosswise into thin slices
    2 bay leaves
    1 heaped tablespoon finely chopped flat-leaf parsley
    1 teaspoon black peppercorns
    120 ml/4 fl oz (½ cup) white vinegar
    salt

Scale, clean and remove the heads and entrails of the sardines following the directions on page 444. Rinse under cold running water and pat dry with paper towels. Season with salt and lightly flour.

Heat 60 ml (2 fl oz/¼ cup) of the oil in a medium, deep frying pan or sauté pan over a medium heat. Working in batches, fry the sardines until the skin is golden, about 2 minutes. Without breaking the skin, turn them over with a wide spatula and cook on the other side until golden, 1–2 minutes. Transfer to a medium rectangular earthenware, ceramic or glass dish, arranging the sardines side by side in the dish, alternating head-tail direction so that they fit snugly together.

Put the remaining 300 ml (10 fl oz/1¼ cups) of the oil, the garlic, onion, bay leaves, parsley and peppercorns into a large saucepan and bring to the boil. Cook until the onion and garlic have softened but not turned brown, about 5 minutes. Remove from the heat, leave to cool for a few minutes, then carefully stir in the vinegar and 60 ml (2 fl oz/¼ cup) water. Return the saucepan to the heat and simmer for 5 minutes.

Stir the marinade and pour over the sardines. If the marinade does not cover the fish, top up with more olive oil. Leave to cool to room temperature. Cover with cling film (plastic wrap) and refrigerate for at least 1 day to fully absorb the flavours.

Remove the sardines from the refrigerator at least 1 hour before serving. Serve at room temperature with some of the marinade drizzled over the top of the sardines. Store in the refrigerator and use within 4 days.

Stewed Sardine Balls in Tomato Sauce

ALGERIA, MOROCCO
PREPARATION TIME: 45 minutes
COOKING TIME: 35 minutes
SERVES: 4–6

Sardine balls stewed in tomato sauce is a popular dish, and a particular favourite for Moroccan families to take to the beach on a summer's day. Fresh sardines – inexpensive, readily available and naturally oily to be less dry – are the most typical fish to use in these popular *boulettes*, but *merlan* (whiting) are another excellent option. If the mixture feels too pasty to form into balls, add a few tablespoons of dry breadcrumbs. This dish is called *kefta de sardines* or sometimes *sardine kwari* (from the plural for *kora*, which means 'ball'). In Algeria, cooks also prepare a version of this classic that they call *dolma sardines*, often with rice in the mixture, plenty of garlic in the tomato sauce and chickpeas (garbanzo beans). No matter where it is prepared, it is a dish served with plenty of bread.

For the fish balls:
1 kg/2¼ lb fresh sardines or whiting
2 cloves of garlic, minced
1 heaped tablespoon finely chopped flat-leaf parsley
1 heaped tablespoon finely chopped coriander (cilantro)
1 teaspoon ground cumin
1 teaspoon sweet paprika
1 tablespoon fresh lemon juice
salt and pepper

For the tomato sauce:
2 tablespoons olive oil
3 cloves of garlic, minced
6 ripe tomatoes, halved crosswise and grated, peel discarded (see page 445)
1 tablespoon double concentrated tomato purée (paste)
2 tablespoons finely chopped flat-leaf parsley
2 tablespoons finely chopped coriander (cilantro)
1 teaspoon ground cumin
1 teaspoon sweet paprika
salt and pepper

PREPARE THE FISH BALLS: Scale, wash and clean the sardines. To do this, remove the heads and entrails, and, using a thumbnail or knife, open along the stomach. Loosen the central spine by pressing around it with your thumb. Clip the spine towards the tail with kitchen scissors, then take the end and pull up the spine. Remove any remaining bones. Snip off the tails and rinse under cold running water. Check to be sure there are no bones. Pat dry on paper towels.

Put the sardines into a food processor and grind to a coarse paste using quick pulses. Spoon into a large bowl, add the garlic, parsley, coriander (cilantro), cumin, paprika and lemon juice. Season with salt and pepper and work into a smooth paste. Moisten your hands with water to keep the paste from sticking and roll smooth balls about 3 cm/1¼ inches in diameter from 1 tablespoon of paste. There should be about 32.

PREPARE THE TOMATO SAUCE: Heat the oil in a large tagine (see page 250) or casserole dish (Dutch oven) over a medium heat, add the garlic, tomatoes, tomato purée (paste) and 4 tablespoons water, the parsley, coriander (cilantro), cumin and paprika, then season with salt and pepper. Cover with a lid and cook over a medium-low heat until the tomatoes are pulpy and deeper red, about 15 minutes.

Set the sardine balls in the sauce, jiggling the tagine to evenly settle. Drizzle in 60 ml (2 fl oz/ ¼ cup) water, cover and cook over a medium-low heat until the fish balls are nearly done, about 10 minutes. Remove the lid and cook for a final 10 minutes to reduce the sauce. Serve.

Marinated Fresh Anchovies

ALGERIA
PREPARATION TIME: 20 minutes,
plus marinating time
SERVES: 4

Marinated fresh anchovies covered in olive oil and given a generous grinding of pepper makes an ideal starter. Lemon juice gives the anchovies a tangy kick, but you can use instead a white vinegar, which yields slightly smoother, less sharp flavours. If using vinegar, allow about 1 hour to marinate.

16 fresh anchovies (about 12 cm/5 inches in length)
3–4 ripe lemons
extra-virgin olive oil, for drizzling
salt and pepper

Butterfly open the anchovies by removing the heads and entrails. Using a thumbnail or knife, open each fish along the stomach. Loosen the central spine by pressing around it with your thumb. Clip the spine towards the tail with kitchen scissors, then take the end and pull up the spine. Remove any remaining bones. Either leave the fillets joined along the back or separate. Rinse under cold running water and pat dry with paper towels.

Lay the fillets in a wide, shallow bowl so that they are not overlapping and juice enough lemons over the top to cover. Cover with cling film (plastic wrap) and leave to marinate in the refrigerator for about 1½ hours. Swirl the dish from time to time so that they marinate evenly. The fillets will turn white. Drain, then gently but thoroughly pat the fillets dry with paper towels. Arrange the fillets, skin-side down, in a clean dish or shallow bowl. Drizzle with oil, season with a pinch of salt and a generous grating of pepper and refrigerate until ready to serve.

Middle Atlas Trout with Fried Almonds

MOROCCO
PREPARATION TIME: 15 minutes
COOKING TIME: 15 minutes
SERVES: 2

The town of Azrou, 82 km/50 miles south of Fès in the Middle Atlas, is the centre of Morocco's trout industry. The French introduced trout in the local streams and pisciculture in the area when they governed the country during the Protectorate era (1912–1956). One popular local way to prepare trout is fried with butter and topped with almonds, which makes it simple and tasty.

2 whole trout (about 275 g/9¾ oz each)
50 g/2 oz (⅓ cup) whole almonds
2 tablespoons neutral oil
plain (all-purpose) flour, for dusting
25 g/1 oz (2 tablespoons) butter
2 tablespoons fresh lemon juice
salt and pepper

Clean the fish by removing and discarding the entrails. Leave the heads and tails on.

Blanch and peel the almonds following the directions on page 445. Line a plate with paper towels. Heat the oil in a small frying pan over a medium heat, add the almonds and cook, stirring occasionally, until golden, 1–2 minutes. Transfer with a slotted spoon to the paper towels to drain. Put the almonds into a small bowl and season with a pinch of salt. Coarsely chop half of the almonds and set both aside.

Rinse the fish under cold running water and pat dry with paper towels. Season the inside and outside with salt and pepper, then dust with flour.

Melt the butter with the lemon juice in a large non-stick frying pan over a medium-high heat. Lay the fish in the pan and cook for 4–5 minutes until golden. Using a wide, thin spatula, gently turn the fish and cook for another 3–4 minutes until done. Check for doneness behind the gills with the tip of a knife. Transfer to a platter, scatter all the almonds over the top and serve.

Sautéed Prawns with Garlic and Parsley

ALGERIA
PREPARATION TIME: 15 minutes
COOKING TIME: 5 minutes
SERVES: 4

Simple, timeless and popular, sautéed prawns (shrimp) make for a quick and delicious meal. There is little here in this recipe to cover the flavours of the excellent prawns caught off Algeria's coast. Serve with bread.

    1 kg/2¼ lb large raw prawns (shrimp) with heads and
        shells, or 500 g/1 lb 2 oz peeled
    4 tablespoons olive oil
    4 cloves of garlic, finely chopped
    2 heaped tablespoons finely chopped flat-leaf parsley
    salt and pepper
    bread, to serve

Peel the prawns (shrimp), removing the heads, but leaving the tails on. Rinse under cold running water.

Heat the oil in a large frying pan or sauté pan over a medium-high heat, add the prawns, season with salt and pepper and cook until they change colour, about 2 minutes. Add the garlic and parsley and cook, stirring frequently, until the garlic is aromatic and the prawns cooked through, about 30 seconds. Transfer to a bowl with all the oil and serve immediately with bread.

Prawns in Tomato Sauce

ALGERIA
PREPARATION TIME: 10 minutes
COOKING TIME: 30 minutes
SERVES: 4–6

This prawn (shrimp) dish from Algeria is usually served with plenty of bread. Add 1 tablespoon of sugar to the sauce if the tomatoes are not so sweet. If you want it saucier, increase the amount of water added with the prawns.

    3 tablespoons olive oil
    4 cloves of garlic, finely chopped
    4 ripe tomatoes, halved crosswise and grated,
        peel discarded (see page 445)
    1 tablespoon double concentrated tomato purée
        (paste)
    1½ teaspoons sweet paprika
    1 kg/2¼ lb large raw prawns (shrimp) with heads and
        shells
    1 bay leaf
    salt and pepper
    finely chopped flat-leaf parsley, to garnish
    lemon wedges, to serve

Heat the oil in a large frying pan or sauté pan over a medium heat, add the garlic and cook for about 30 seconds, or until fragrant. Add the tomatoes, tomato purée (paste) and 4 tablespoons water, and the paprika, then season with salt and pepper. Reduce the heat to medium-low and cook until pasty and reduced, about 20 minutes. Add a touch of water if needed to keep the sauce from drying out.

Meanwhile, remove the heads from the prawns (shrimp) and rinse under cold running water. Add the prawns, bay leaf and 60 ml (2 fl oz/¼ cup) water to the pan and cook until the prawns are cooked through, 5–8 minutes. Transfer to a serving dish, scatter with parsley to garnish and serve with lemon wedges.

Prawns in Spicy Tomato Sauce

TUNISIA
PREPARATION TIME: 10 minutes
COOKING TIME: 25 minutes
SERVES: 3–4

Many dishes in Tunisia are cooked in a harissa-spiced tomato sauce, including prawns (shrimp) caught off its lengthy coastline. Serve with plenty of bread.

3 tablespoons olive oil
3 ripe tomatoes, halved crosswise and grated, peel discarded (see page 445)
3 cloves of garlic, grated
2 tablespoon double concentrated tomato purée (paste)
harissa (page 409), to taste
¼ teaspoon ground caraway
¼ teaspoon ground coriander
500 g/1 lb 2 oz peeled large raw prawns (shrimp)
2 tablespoons finely chopped coriander (cilantro)
salt and pepper
bread, to serve

Heat the oil in a large frying pan with a lid or sauté pan over a medium-high heat, add the tomatoes and cook until they begin to darken, 8–10 minutes. Stir in the garlic, tomato purée (paste) and 6 tablespoons water, the harissa, caraway and ground coriander, then season with salt and pepper. Reduce the heat to low, cover with a lid and cook, stirring from time to time, until the sauce has thickened, 8–10 minutes. Put the prawns (shrimp) into the pan and cook until cooked through, about 5 minutes, turning from time to time. Stir in the coriander (cilantro), then transfer to a platter and serve with bread.

Grilled Prawns with Tomato Dipping Sauce

ALGERIA
PREPARATION TIME: 2 minutes
COOKING TIME: 10 minutes
SERVES: 4

Sometimes the best way to eat fresh seafood is simply grilled. For prawns (shrimp) in Algeria, cooks like to use a stovetop grill pan or, if preparing outside over coals, put them onto a metal plate rather than on the flames themselves. Serve with a Tomato Dipping Sauce (page 442).

1 kg/2¼ lb large raw prawns (shrimp) with heads and shells
olive oil, for brushing
salt and pepper
Tomato Dipping Sauce (page 442), to serve

Brush the prawns (shrimp) with oil and season with salt and a generous amount of pepper. Heat a stovetop grill pan over a medium heat or a metal grilling plate over embers. Lightly brush the pan with oil. Working in batches, lay the prawns in the grill pan and cook, turning once, until opaque throughout, 2–3 minutes. Serve immediately.

Prawn Tagine
in Spicy Pil-pil Sauce

MOROCCO
PREPARATION TIME: 5 minutes
COOKING TIME: 25 minutes
SERVES: 4

This spicy tagine is a popular way to eat prawns (shrimp) in Morocco, especially in the north. The tomato sauce has plenty of garlic and hot cayenne pepper. Home cooks usually prepare it using whole peeled prawns. The tails are often left on larger prawns.

- 2 tablespoons olive oil
- 4 cloves of garlic, minced
- 5 ripe tomatoes, halved crosswise and grated, peel discarded (see page 445)
- 2 heaped tablespoons finely chopped coriander (cilantro)
- 1 teaspoon sweet paprika
- ½ teaspoon ground cumin
- ½ teaspoon cayenne pepper, or more to taste
- 500 g/1 lb 2 oz peeled raw prawns (shrimp), tails left on if desired
- salt and pepper
- lemon wedges, to serve

Add the oil, garlic and tomatoes to a tagine (see page 250), heavy frying pan or sauté pan and cook, uncovered, over a medium heat until the tomatoes are pulpy and a deeper red, about 15 minutes. Stir in the coriander (cilantro), paprika, cumin and cayenne pepper, then season with salt and pepper. Add the prawns (shrimp) and turn to coat with the sauce. Cover the tagine with a lid and cook until the prawns are done, about 10 minutes. Serve with lemon wedges.

Tagine of Mussels in Tomato Sauce

MOROCCO
PREPARATION TIME: 30 minutes
COOKING TIME: 30 minutes
SERVES: 4

This mussel tagine is especially popular in the far north and far south of Morocco, where the Spanish influence runs stronger. It uses a classic Spanish tomato *sofrito* but is distinctively Moroccan with cumin. Serve it with plenty of bread. Today, some cooks serve it over pasta or boiled white rice.

- 1.5 kg/3¼ lb large live mussels, rinsed
- 2 tablespoons olive oil
- 1 long sweet green pepper or ½ green bell pepper, cored, seeded and finely chopped
- 2 large cloves of garlic, minced
- 8 ripe medium–small tomatoes (about 1 kg/2¼ lb), halved crosswise and grated, peel discarded (see page 445)
- 1 bay leaf
- 1 teaspoon sweet paprika
- ½ teaspoon ground cumin
- 2 tablespoons finely chopped flat-leaf parsley, plus extra to garnish
- salt and pepper
- bread, to serve

Trim and debeard the mussels, then scrape the outside of the shell with a paring knife if needed. Rinse under cold running water.

Bring 120 ml (4 fl oz/½ cup) water to the boil in a large pot or saucepan over a high heat. Add the mussels, cover with a lid and steam for 3–5 minutes until the mussels have opened, shaking the pot from time to time. Drain in a colander, reserving the liquid. Strain the liquid through a sieve and set aside. Remove and discard any mussels that did not open. Once cool enough to handle, shuck the mussels and discard the shells. Trim the beards with scissors.

Heat the oil in a large tagine (see page 250), sauté pan or frying pan over a medium heat, add the green pepper and cook for 5 minutes. Stir in the garlic, then add the tomatoes, bay leaf, paprika and cumin. Season with salt and pepper and cook until darker and reduced, about 15 minutes, stirring frequently. Add a couple of tablespoons of the reserved liquid from the mussels to keep it moist. Add the mussels, parsley and 2–3 tablespoons of the reserved mussel liquid, then cover with a lid and cook for 5 minutes. Garnish with parsley and serve from the tagine with bread.

Prawn Tagine in Spicy Pil-pil Sauce ➤➤

Sautéed Cuttlefish with Garlic and Cumin

TUNISIA
PREPARATION TIME: 10 minutes
COOKING TIME: 10 minutes
SERVES: 4

Quick and tasty, this Tunisian staple adds the cumin at the end to ensure its flavour remains strong. So key is cumin that it gives the dish its name, *kamounia*. Use smaller cuttlefish, ideally ones that weigh no more than 100 g/3½ oz each. Also use a large frying pan to avoid overcrowding the pan, or cook in batches. There is a popular version of this cumin-rich dish with liver (page 281).

3 tablespoons olive oil
600 g/1 lb 5 oz cleaned small cuttlefish, sliced lengthwise into 2-cm/¾-inch-wide pieces
2 small red onions, thinly sliced and segments separated
4 cloves of garlic, chopped
ground cumin, for seasoning
salt
finely chopped flat-leaf parsley, to garnish

Heat the oil in a large frying pan or sauté pan over a high heat, add the cuttlefish and season with salt. Sauté until they have sweated out all their liquid and are tender, about 5 minutes. Scatter the onions around the pan and cook, stirring frequently, until the onions lose their rawness, about 2 minutes. Stir in the garlic, generously season with cumin and remove from the heat. Transfer to a serving platter, garnish with parsley and serve immediately.

Stewed Cuttlefish with Peas

TUNISIA
PREPARATION TIME: 15 minutes
COOKING TIME: 1 hour 10 minutes
SERVES: 3–4

Marka jelbana bel soubia – cuttlefish stew with peas (and plenty of cumin) – is a popular Tunisian *marka* (ragoût). Similar versions are made with lamb, goat (page 263) and chicken as well. If the cuttlefish are small, they can be left whole or cut in half. The cumin should be noticeable and is added at the end to not lose its potency.

3 tablespoons olive oil
400 g/14 oz cleaned cuttlefish, cut into generous bite-size pieces
1 onion, finely chopped
3 ripe tomatoes, halved crosswise and grated, peel discarded (see page 445)
1 tablespoon double concentrated tomato purée (paste)
½ teaspoon cayenne pepper
150 g/5 oz (1¼ cups) shelled fresh or thawed frozen peas
1 teaspoon ground cumin
salt and pepper

Heat the oil in a large casserole dish (Dutch oven) or large frying pan over a high heat, add the cuttlefish, season with salt and pepper and cook until they have thrown their moisture, about 5 minutes. Add the onion, reduce the heat to medium and cook until it begins to turn translucent, about 5 minutes. Add the tomatoes, tomato purée (paste) and 3 tablespoons water, and the cayenne pepper, and cook for 5 minutes to reduce the sauce. Stir in 350 ml (12 fl oz/1½ cups) water, reduce the heat to low and cook until the cuttlefish is tender, about 45 minutes. Add more water if needed to keep it loose and saucy. Scatter the peas over the top and cook until just done, 5–10 minutes. Stir in the cumin and remove the pan from the heat. Serve from the pan or spoon into a serving bowl.

Cuttlefish Tagine

MOROCCO
PREPARATION TIME: 15 minutes
COOKING TIME: 1 hour 25 minutes
SERVES: 2–3

This is an excellent and simple seafood dish from the Atlantic coastline of Morocco's desert south, which was occupied and ruled by the Spanish. This tagine shows some Spanish roots, with its sofrito-like tomato base and light spicing, so the flavour of the stewed cuttlefish comes through. Some toss in a handful of raisins for a (decidedly un-Spanish) sweet touch.

  600 g/1 lb 5 oz cleaned cuttlefish or squid (calamari)
  3 tablespoons olive oil
  1 red or yellow onion, finely chopped
  5 ripe tomatoes (about 700 g/1 lb 8½ oz), halved crosswise and grated, peel discarded (see page 445)
  generous pinch of ground ginger
  generous pinch of saffron threads, crumbled
  salt and pepper
  finely chopped flat-leaf parsley, to garnish

If using cuttlefish, cut into bite-size pieces. If using squid (calamari), clean it following the directions in the Stuffed Squid recipe (see right) but leave the arms whole.

Add the oil and onion to a medium tagine (see page 250), sauté pan or heavy frying pan and cook over a medium heat until pale, about 10 minutes. Add the tomatoes, ginger and saffron, season with salt and pepper and cook, stirring frequently, until darker and reduced, about 15 minutes. Add the cuttlefish, reduce the heat to low, mostly cover the tagine and cook until the cuttlefish is tender, 45 minutes–1 hour. Drizzle in some water if necessary to keep it moist. Garnish with parsley and serve.

Stuffed Squid

ALGERIA
PREPARATION TIME: 30 minutes
COOKING TIME: 1 hour 15 minutes
SERVES: 4

Among the popular ways to prepare squid (or calamari) is to stuff the tubes with a mixture of minced (ground) meat, chopped tentacles, rice and spices. Serve this Algerian version with plenty of bread.

  450 g/1 lb whole squid (calamari), with tubes about 10 cm/4 inches in length
  100 g/3½ oz minced (ground) beef
  2 red or yellow onions, grated
  100 g/3½ oz (½ cup) uncooked white rice, preferably short- or medium-grain
  1 egg
  2 tablespoons finely chopped flat-leaf parsley
  2 tablespoons finely chopped coriander (cilantro)
  pinch of ground caraway or cumin
  3 tablespoons olive oil
  2 cloves of garlic, minced
  3 tomatoes, halved crosswise and grated, peel discarded (see page 445)
  1 heaped tablespoon double concentrated tomato purée (paste)
  1 teaspoon sweet paprika
  1 sprig thyme
  1 bay leaf
  salt and pepper
  bread, to serve

Clean the squid (calamari) or ask your fishmonger to do so. Trim off the tentacles and set aside. Remove the hard, clear quill from inside the tubes and any innards that remain. Wash the tubes well and set aside. Finely chop the arms.

Add the chopped arms, minced (ground) beef, half of the onions, the rice, egg, parsley, coriander (cilantro) and caraway to a large bowl, then season with salt and pepper. Mix well. Stuff the tubes with the mixture and secure with a cocktail stick (toothpick). There might be some stuffing leftover.

Heat the oil in a large frying pan or sauté pan over a medium heat, add the remaining onion and cook until soft, about 5 minutes. Stir in the garlic, then add the tomatoes, tomato purée (paste) and 4 tablespoons water, the paprika, thyme and bay leaf, then season with salt and pepper. Reduce the heat to low and cook for 10 minutes. Set the stuffed squid in the pan, pour in 300 ml (10 fl oz/1¼ cups) water, partly cover with a lid and simmer for 45 minutes. Remove the lid and cook until the rice inside the squid is tender and the sauce reduced, about 15 minutes.

Arrange the squid on a serving plate, cover with sauce, carve into slices and serve with bread.

CONFECTIONS, DESSERTS AND FRUITS

SWEET DELICACIES

It is impossible to understate the importance of pastries and sweet confections in North Africa.

Sweets appear in such force at every important moment as symbols of welcome and celebration. Their role feels both unparalleled and constant. Kitchens during the last days of the holy month of Ramadan convert to pastry workshops, preparing for visitors during the Eid al-Fitr holiday that follows. It is a time when these delicacies have an unparalleled position.

Even in places where frugality rather than excess marks the food there is also a deep love for often elaborate – or at least laborious – sweets. Cooks generously sweeten with sugar or honey, add almonds, pistachios and walnuts with little sense of frugality, and liberally aromatize with cinnamon and the essences of rose petals, orange blossoms or young rose geranium. Some sweet pastries then get dipped in honey or syrup as a final step in their preparation. Twice-baked Sesame Seed

Biscuits (*fekka*, page 370), Date-filled Semolina Cookies (*makrout*, page 362) and chewy Almond Ghriba Cookies (page 369) are among the hundreds of beloved options.

Certainly, a culture of hospitality and sharing drive such abundance. Guests are offered sweets confections – usually heaped trays – with tea or coffee. It speaks not only to presentation but also to abundance. There is pleasure in decoration – and in plenty.

Sweet Pastry Triangles Stuffed with Milky Rice

MOROCCO
PREPARATION TIME: 30 minutes
COOKING TIME: 30 minutes
MAKES: 15–18 stuffed pastries

Briouats (crispy fried pastries) filled with meat, vegetables or cheese are popular starters in Morocco. There are also sweet versions, such as these with milky rice. They are excellent with coffee as a snack or served as a starter.

  100 g/3½ oz (½ cup) short- or medium-grain
    white rice
  120 ml/4 fl oz (½ cup) milk
  1 tablespoon sugar
  1 teaspoon orange blossom water, optional
  1 small cinnamon stick or piece of cinnamon bark
  warka, *brick* or *dioul* leaves (see page 56), spring roll
    wrappers or filo (phyllo) sheets
  1 egg yolk, beaten
  neutral oil, for frying
  icing (confectioners') sugar, for dusting
  ground cinnamon, for dusting
  salt

Bring 500 ml (18 fl oz/2 cups) water to a rolling boil in a large saucepan over a high heat. Add the rice, stir and boil until the rice has absorbed the water, about 15 minutes. Stir in the milk, sugar and orange

blossom water (if using), then add the cinnamon stick and a pinch of salt. Bring to the boil, reduce the heat and simmer, stirring frequently, until the rice is tender and creamy but not mushy and the milk absorbed, about 5 minutes. Stir in a touch more milk if necessary. Spoon into a wide bowl to cool. Remove and discard the cinnamon stick.

Unroll a few pastry sheets on a clean, flat work counter, then cut into strips about 10 cm/4 inches wide and about 25 cm/10 inches in length. Arrange a couple of the strips facing away from you; cover the remaining strips with cling film (plastic wrap) to keep from drying out.

Place 1 heaped tablespoon of the filling on the end of each strip closest to you and fold over the end. Fold over to form a triangle, then turn again to form another triangle and so on to the end. At the end, brush the side of the triangle with egg yolk and fold over the final end. Place the triangles on a plate without touching. Repeat with the remaining filling and pastry sheets.

Heat at least 1 cm/½ inch of oil in a large frying pan over a medium heat until the surface shimmers. Line a plate with paper towels. Working in batches, gently place the rolls in the oil and fry, turning once, until golden brown, 30 seconds–1 minute. Using a slotted spoon, transfer to the paper towels to drain.

Arrange 2 or 3 rolls on each plate. Dust with icing (confectioners') sugar and sprinkle a pattern of cinnamon across each just before serving. Store in the refrigerator in airtight containers. They are best eaten within 1 week.

Serpent Pastries Stuffed with Almond Paste

ALGERIA, MOROCCO
PREPARATION TIME: 40 minutes,
plus drying time
COOKING TIME: 30 minutes
MAKES: 24 pastries

The name of this popular coiled pastry is *mhencha*, which means 'snake' or 'serpent'. It is prepared both as a long, single coiled pastry of joined links, or, as in this recipe, individually. While individual ones are often fried in oil, brushing with butter and baking in the oven until golden leaves them less greasy.

500 g/1 lb 2 oz (3⅓ cups) whole almonds
200 g/7 oz (1 cup) sugar
85 g/3 oz (6 tablespoons) butter, melted, plus extra
   for greasing and brushing
1 teaspoon ground cinnamon, plus extra for dusting
2 tablespoons orange blossom water
12–14 round *warka*, *brick* or *dioul* leaves (see page 56),
   spring roll wrappers or filo (phyllo) sheets
neutral oil, for brushing
250 g/9 oz (⅔ cup) honey
chopped toasted or fried almonds, to decorate

Bring a medium saucepan of water to the boil, add the whole almonds and boil for 3–5 minutes; drain. Once cool enough to handle, slip off the skins with your fingers. Spread the almonds out on a baking sheet to dry completely for at least 1 hour.

Put the almonds and sugar into a food processor and finely grind. Spoon into a large bowl, add the butter, cinnamon and orange blossom water and mix well with your hands to a smooth, sticky paste.

Take 1 pastry sheet and fold it in half, then cut it in half. Take 1 piece and trim off the rounded edge. Open on a clean work counter perpendicular to you with the longer edge at the top and brush with oil.

Butter a large baking dish. Take a piece of the almond paste about the size of an egg and roll gently under the palms of your hands and fingers to form a snake about 1 cm/½ inch thick. It should be about the same length as the short end of pastry; pinch off any excess. Lay on the lip (short end) and roll the almond paste up into the pastry sheet to form a smooth tube. Coil one end around and loosely wind into a coil, tucking over the end piece and slipping it between a roll to secure. Carefully put into the prepared baking dish. Roll up the remaining pastries and brush them with butter.

Preheat the oven to 180°C/350°F/Gas Mark 4. Bake in the hot oven until golden, about 20 minutes.

Put the honey into a medium saucepan and heat over a low heat for a few minutes until warm. Or warm in a microwave. Drizzle the honey over the pastries. Sprinkle each with a pinch of cinnamon and scatter over the chopped almonds. Store in airtight containers. They are best eaten within 2 weeks.

Honeyed Triangles Stuffed with Almonds

ALGERIA, LIBYA, MOROCCO, TUNISIA
PREPARATION TIME: 30 minutes
COOKING TIME: 15 minutes,
plus drying and cooling time
MAKES: 20 stuffed pastries

Popular across North Africa, these pastry triangles filled with almonds and dipped in honey are known as *samsa bel louz* in Algeria and Tunisia and *briouat bel louz* in Morocco. It is common to mix fried almonds with ones that have only been blanched. The directions here are for triangles, but they can be rolled like cigars by following the directions on page 388. Add some cinnamon or finely grated orange zest to the filling, if desired.

    125 g/4¼ oz (generous ¾ cup) whole almonds
    neutral oil, for frying
    30 g/1 oz (¼ cup) icing (confectioners') sugar
    25 g/1 oz (2 tablespoons) butter, melted
    1 tablespoon orange blossom water or water
    warka, *brick* or *dioul* leaves (see page 56), spring roll
        wrappers or filo (phyllo) sheets
    1 egg yolk, beaten
    270 g/9½ oz (¾ cup) honey, for soaking
    sesame seeds, for sprinkling

Bring a medium saucepan of water to the boil, add the almonds and boil for 3–5 minutes; drain. Once cool enough to handle, slip off the skins with your fingers. Spread the almonds out on paper towels to dry. Set half aside. Line a medium plate with paper towels. Heat about 7 mm/⅓ inch of neutral oil in a small frying pan over a medium heat until the surface shimmers. Add the almonds and fry for 1–2 minutes until just golden. Transfer with a slotted spoon to the paper towels to drain and cool completely.

Put all the almonds and sugar into a food processor and grind using pulses. Add the butter and orange blossom water and grind again. It should be oily and compact.

Unroll a few pastry sheets on a clean, flat work counter and cut into strips, about 5–6 cm/2–2½ inches wide and about 25 cm/10 inches in length. Arrange a couple of the strips facing away from you; cover the remaining strips to keep them from drying out.

Roll ½ tablespoon of the filling (10 g/¼ oz) into a ball and place on the end of each strip closest to you. Fold over to form a triangle, then turn again to form another triangle and so on to the end. At the end, brush the side of the triangle with egg yolk and fold over the final end. Place the triangles on a plate without touching. Repeat with the remaining almond filling and pastry sheets.

Put the honey into a large saucepan and heat over a low heat for about 5 minutes, or until warm. Place a colander over a bowl.

Heat at least 1 cm/½ inch of oil in a large frying pan over a medium heat until the surface shimmers. Line a plate with paper towels. Working in batches, gently put the triangles into the hot oil and fry, turning once, until golden brown, about 30 seconds. Transfer with a slotted spoon to the paper towels to briefly drain.

Set the pastries in the honey, turning them over to coat and absorb the honey for about 1 minute. Transfer to the colander to drain. Lay the pastries on a wide platter without touching and sprinkle with some sesame seeds. Serve while still warm or at room temperature. Store in airtight containers. They are best eaten within 2 weeks.

Crispy Pastilla with Orange Blossom Water Custard

MOROCCO
PREPARATION TIME: 25 minutes,
plus cooling and chilling time
COOKING TIME: 15 minutes
SERVES: 4

Pastilla is a celebratory dish in Morocco. Stacked crisp sheets of delicate *warka* pastry layered with cream are cut into pieces and served for dessert. *Pastilla jouhara* is the custard version of this popular dessert. Prepare the stacked dessert just before serving to keep the discs crispy.

1½ tablespoons cornflour (cornstarch)
400 ml/14 fl oz (1⅔) cups cold milk
55 g/2 oz (¼ cup) sugar
1 small cinnamon stick or piece of cinnamon bark
1 tablespoon orange blossom water
warka, *brick* or *dioul* leaves (see page 56), spring roll
    wrappers or filo (phyllo) sheets
olive oil, for brushing
60 g/2¼ oz (generous ⅓ cup) chopped almonds
ground cinnamon, for dusting
icing (confectioners') sugar, for dusting, optional

Put the cornflour (cornstarch) into a medium bowl, add 50 ml (2 fl oz/¼ cup) of the milk and whisk until combined. Set aside.

Bring the remaining 350 ml (12 fl oz/1½ cups) milk to a simmer in a large saucepan over a low heat (do not allow it to boil). Stir in the sugar, then the reserved cornflour mixture. Add the cinnamon stick and orange blossom water and simmer, stirring, until it thickens and coats the back of a wooden spoon, about 5 minutes. Pass through a fine-mesh sieve or chinois into a bowl; remove and discard the cinnamon stick and any solids. Leave to cool. The custard should be thick enough to spoon onto the pastry discs without running off. Lay a piece of cling film (plastic wrap) across the top of the custard to stop a skin forming on the surface and chill in the refrigerator until ready to serve.

Preheat the oven to 180 °C/350 °F/Gas Mark 4.

Cut the pastry sheets into 8–10-cm-/3–4-inch-diameter discs using a cutter or by tracing a knife around an inverted glass. There should be at least 24 discs plus a few extra. Cover with cling film (plastic wrap) until ready to use.

Line a pair of baking sheets with baking (parchment) paper. Brush the discs on each side with oil and arrange in layers of 2 on the prepared baking sheets. Cover with another layer of baking paper, then place a baking sheet on top of each to keep the discs from curling as they bake. Bake until golden and crispy, 3–6 minutes. Carefully transfer the discs to a wire rack to cool and then to paper towels to wick away some of the oil.

To assemble, place a disc on a dessert plate. Working quickly, dollop 1 tablespoon of custard and some almonds onto the disc. Place another disc on top, then more custard and almonds and so on to form 4 layers, ending with a top layer of custard and almonds. Add a generous pinch of cinnamon and some icing (confectioners') sugar (if using) and serve immediately.

Crispy Pastilla with Whipped Cream and Fresh Fruit

MOROCCO
PREPARATION TIME: 20 minutes
COOKING TIME: 10 minutes
SERVES: 4

This is a lighter, fresher version of Crispy Pastilla with Orange Blossom Water Custard (*pastilla jouhara*, page 355), made with whipped cream and fresh fruit instead of custard. While some like to fry large pastry sheets whole and make a single dessert, this recipe is for smaller discs, which are more manageable to prepare and serve. Frying two small discs pressed together (rather than individually) will keep them from curling too much and make them easier to stack when assembling. (To bake in the oven, follow the directions for *pastilla jouhara* on page 355.) Prepare a couple more discs than needed in case of breakage. To keep the important crunch of the dish, assemble just before serving.

- *warka*, *brick* or *dioul* leaves (see page 56), spring roll wrappers or filo (phyllo) sheets
- neutral oil, for frying
- 500 ml/18 fl oz (2 cups) double (heavy) whipping cream, chilled
- 2 tablespoons sugar
- 2 tablespoons orange blossom water
- 225 g/8 oz (2 cups) finely sliced or chopped mixed fresh fruit, such as strawberries, peaches, nectarines, apples and bananas
- 30 g/1 oz (scant ¼ cup) chopped or sliced toasted almonds, to decorate

Cut the pastry sheets into 10-cm/4-inch diameter discs using a cutter or by tracing a knife around an inverted glass. There should be at least 24 discs plus a few extra. Cover with cling film (plastic wrap) until ready to use.

Heat at least 1 cm/½ inch of oil in a large frying pan over a medium heat until the surface shimmers. Line a plate with paper towels. Pressing 2 discs together, carefully lower into the oil and fry until golden brown, about 30 seconds. Using a slotted spoon, transfer the discs to the paper towels to drain and fry the remaining discs.

Put the cream, sugar and orange blossom water into a large bowl and, using electric beaters, beat on high speed until it begins to thicken. Reduce the speed and continue beating until smooth and the cream forms soft peaks. Or use a stand mixer fitted with a whisk attachment.

To assemble, place 1 disc on a dessert plate. Working quickly, spread 1 tablespoon of cream and some fruit on top. Place another disc on top, then more cream and fruit, and so on to form 3 or 4 layers, ending with a top layer of cream and fruit. Scatter some almonds over the top and serve immediately.

Toasted Semolina with Melted Butter and Honey

ALGERIA
PREPARATION TIME: 5 minutes,
plus cooling time
COOKING TIME: 15 minutes
SERVES: 6–8

Hailing from western Algeria, this simple – and extremely rich – dish of toasted semolina with melted butter and honey is served with coffee or tea. It goes by the name of *tamina* or *taknetta*. It is popular to serve to mothers just after giving birth, and at the *aqiqah* ceremony for a child seven days after birth where his or her name is announced. It is also often prepared on the Mawlid al-Nabi, the birthday of the Prophet Muhammad. While quantities vary, the common ratio is two parts semolina to one part butter and one part (or slightly less) honey, although some like it moister and increase those last two measures. The orange blossom water is optional, although certain families would never consider omitting it.

- 250 g/9 oz (1½ cups) medium semolina
- 150 g/5 oz butter
- 120–150 g/4–5 oz (⅓–scant ½ cup) honey
- pinch of salt
- 1–2 teaspoons orange blossom water, optional
- ground cinnamon, to decorate

Put the semolina into a large non-stick frying pan and dry-toast over a medium-low heat until nutty golden and aromatic, about 10 minutes. Transfer to a bowl and leave to cool to room temperature.

Put the butter and honey into a large saucepan and melt over a low heat for 2 minutes. Add the salt and orange blossom water (if using), then gradually mix in the toasted semolina. Cook over a low heat for 1 minute, stirring until it is slightly firm but still jiggles when shaken.

Spoon onto a serving plate and smooth to flatten. Leave to cool, then dust with cinnamon. Serve at room temperature with spoons.

Sellou

MOROCCO
PREPARATION TIME: 20 minutes,
plus drying and cooling time
COOKING TIME: 15 minutes
SERVES: 6–8; MAKES: 450 g/1 lb (3 cups)

Sellou (or *sfouf*) is a Moroccan mixture of ground nuts and toasted flour, sweetened and flavoured with cinnamon and aniseed, and bound with butter or (allowing for longer storage) clarified butter. It is widely popular across the country, especially during Ramadan. As well, new mothers often get a dish of it after giving birth for energy. This recipe uses the standard equal ratios of oven-toasted flour, dried almonds and toasted sesame seeds. This is a drier, sandy version of *sellou*. Some add honey rather than sugar and more butter to make it pastier. While families tend to make large batches and use over the month of Ramadan, this is a smaller batch that can easily serve 6–8 people. Scale up as desired. Toasting brings out a nutty rich flavour.

125 g/4¼ oz (generous ¾ cup) whole almonds
neutral oil, for frying
125 g/4¼ oz (generous ¾ cup) sesame seeds
125 g/4¼ oz (generous ¾ cup) plain (all-purpose) flour
50 g/2 oz (scant ½ cup) icing (confectioners') sugar, plus extra to decorate
½ teaspoon ground aniseed
1 teaspoon ground cinnamon
60 g/2¼ oz (4 tablespoons) butter

Bring a medium saucepan of water to the boil, add the almonds and boil for 3–5 minutes; drain. Once cool enough to handle, slip off the skins with your fingers. Spread the almonds out on paper towels to dry. Line a medium plate with paper towels. Heat about 7 mm/⅓ inch of neutral oil in a small frying pan over a medium heat until the surface shimmers. Add the almonds and fry for 1–2 minutes until just golden. Transfer with a slotted spoon to the paper towels to drain and cool completely.

Put most of the almonds and the sesame seeds into a food processor and grind. Spoon into a large bowl, then add the flour, sugar, aniseed and cinnamon and mix well.

Put the butter into a small saucepan and slowly melt over a low heat to clarify, skimming off the foam as it rises to the surface with a slotted spoon. Cook until transparent and the solids have sunk to the bottom, about 5 minutes. Do not stir or let the solids darken. Remove from the heat and let the whitish solids settle. Carefully pour off the liquid through a muslin cloth (cheesecloth) or fine-mesh sieve into a bowl. Discard the solids.

Begin adding the clarified butter to the dry mixture, patiently mixing until it is well absorbed and has somewhat firmed up.

Place it in a dish or on individual plates and loosely heap into a pyramid or dome. Sprinkle with icing (confectioners') sugar and decorate with the reserved almonds. Serve with spoons. Store in an airtight container in the refrigerator for 1 month, or in the freezer for longer.

Almond Dip
with Argan Oil and Honey

MOROCCO
PREPARATION TIME: 15 minutes
COOKING TIME: 10–15 minutes
MAKES: 250 ml/8 fl oz (1 cup)

Amlou is a perfect, spreadable combination of three local ingredients that are specialities of the southwestern Moroccan region of Sous, between Agadir and Essaouira: almonds, honey and argan oil. Ground together they become a gritty, earthy-sweet dip that is eaten with bread for breakfast or as a snack. Endemic to the region, argan trees produce a hard, oil-rich seed. The oil is often sold as a beauty product, so be sure to use culinary-grade argan oil. Walnut oil or some very full-bodied extra-virgin olive oil make excellent substitutions. Serve with bread.

200 g/7 oz (1⅓ cups) whole almonds with skins
120 ml/4 fl oz (½ cup) culinary argan oil or walnut
    or extra-virgin olive oil
2 tablespoons honey, or as needed
salt
bread, to serve

Preheat the oven to 180 °C/350 °F/Gas Mark 4.

Scatter the almonds across an ungreased baking sheet and roast, shaking the pan occasionally, until darker brown and crunchy, 10–15 minutes. Transfer immediately to a plate to cool. (They will get crunchier as they cool.)

Put the almonds into a food processor and grind on high speed to a gritty paste. Season with salt, then while blending on low speed, gradually add the oil.

Spoon into a bowl and mix in the honey with a fork. Taste and add more if desired. It should be loose and runny. Serve or cover with cling film (plastic wrap) and store in the refrigerator for a few days. Serve with bread.

ARGAN OIL

Argan trees are indigenous to the Sous region of Morocco's Anti-Atlas Mountains. The thorny, sprawling trees produce a bright yellow fruit in summer that is left to fall to the ground and shrivel before being collected. The nut on the inside is removed and cracked open to a reveal an almond-like kernel. These kernels are ground to extract a rich, deep golden oil that is nutty with hints of hazelnuts. Argan oil is one of Morocco's most prized – and expensive – products.

Made nowadays almost exclusively in women's cooperatives, the extraction process is low-yielding and labour-intensive. A 500-ml/18-fl oz bottle of oil requires around 50 kg/110 lb of fresh argan fruits or about 1.5 kg/3¼ lb of argan kernels.

Argan oil is most famously blended with honey and ground almonds into a thick, gritty dip called *amlou* (Almond Dip with Argan Oil and Honey, see above). Locals like to add some drops of oil to couscous, fish or meat tagines or salads for flavour (it is lovely, for instance, on the salad of oranges and black olives, page 105), or dip bread into it for breakfast or as a snack with Mint Tea (pages 417–421). Restaurants in Morocco have begun to use it in contemporary cooking. In the area where argan grows, a few drops are given to newborn babies as their first food.

Exceptionally hearty and able to withstand droughts, the argan tree can live for up to two hundred years. Every part of its fruit gets used, not just the inner kernels. Goats are fed the outer fruits while the dried nut shells can be used to fire bread ovens or *hammams* (Turkish baths).

Outside of Morocco, most argan oil is sold for cosmetic use as a skin moisturizer and used in facials and massages. When purchasing, make sure it is the edible, culinary argan oil. Store argan oil in a cool, dry place.

As a substitute, walnut, almond or extra-virgin olive oil can be used instead.

Fried Fritters in Rose Water Syrup

LIBYA
PREPARATION TIME: 20 minutes,
plus rising time
COOKING TIME: 25 minutes
MAKES: about 24 golf ball-size
(4-cm/1½-inch) fritters

The name of these popular bite-size Libyan fried fritters is *luqmet al-qadi*, which translates to something like 'the judge's bite'. The golden balls are soft on the inside and a little crunchy on the outside, and they are drenched in syrup.

300 g/11 oz (2 cups) plain (all-purpose) flour
2 teaspoons instant yeast or fast-action active dry yeast granules
½ teaspoon salt
neutral oil, for frying and oiling

For the syrup:
440 g/15½ oz (2¼ cups) sugar
1 tablespoon fresh lemon juice
1 tablespoon rose or orange blossom water

Put the flour, yeast and salt into a large bowl and stir to combine. Add 250 ml (8 fl oz/1 cup) water and mix into a thick, sticky and gooey dough. Cover with cling film (plastic wrap) and leave in a warm place for 1 hour. Stir the dough, cover again and leave to stand in a warm place for another 30 minutes.

MEANWHILE, PREPARE THE SYRUP: Put the sugar, lemon juice and 250 ml (8 fl oz/1 cup) water into a large saucepan and bring to the boil, then lower the heat and reduce until syrupy and it can coat the back of a spoon, about 15 minutes. Stir in the rose water, pour into a bowl and leave to cool.

Heat at least 2.5 cm/1 inch of oil in a large, deep saucepan over a medium heat until the surface shimmers. Line a plate with paper towels. Using 2 oiled spoons, take slightly rounded tablespoons (20 g/¾ oz) of the batter and carefully slip into the hot oil. Fry until golden on the outside, 5–8 minutes, moving them around with a slotted spoon to cook evenly. Using the slotted spoon, transfer them to the paper towels to briefly drain. While still warm, set in the syrup and coat, turning with a spoon. Arrange on a plate. Serve warm.

DISTILLATIONS

The food of North Africa is often defined by spices: the earthy heat of Tunisia's ubiquitous harissa; the complex use of both sweet and savoury spices in a Moroccan tagine; cinnamon added at the end to certain savoury Algerian dishes; or some dried mint to a bowl of spicy *chorba* (soup) (page 127) in Libya and Tunisia.

But it is a trio of distilled aromatics that frequently make these cuisines distinctive. Across the Maghreb, orange blossom water, rose water and geranium water go into countless sweet and savoury dishes as well as drinks. All three can easily overpower all other ingredients and the unaccustomed should use in moderation. They are all to be stored in a cool, dry place.

Orange blossom water (*ma zhar*): Distilled from the essence of bitter or Seville orange blossoms in spring, orange blossom (or orange flower) water gives pleasing and bright citrusy notes to a wide range of dishes from cooked pumpkin salad (page 83) to brioche buns (page 52) and jams to traditional coffee (page 425). Across the region, it is spritzed onto the hands of guests in welcome. Its importance goes further in the north of Morocco, where it is dashed into milk offered to newly-weds alongside dates, and splashed onto mourners at funerals.

Rose water (*ma ward* or *ouard*): This is distilled from pink petals of the Damask rose. Dashed onto a bowl of pomegranate seeds (page 395), added to the dough of Crunchy Vanilla Biscuits (*bachkoutou*, page 372) or stirred into *mhalbi* (Rice Flour Pudding, page 380), rose water gives a frequent floral touch to desserts, pastries and creamy puddings. This important industry in Morocco is focused in the Valley of the Roses on the eastern slopes of the High Atlas.

Geranium water (*ma atershiya*): The least common of the trio of essences today, geranium water is also the most expensive. Different varieties of geranium – including rose-scented – are cultivated for the essence. It is most commonly used in various Tunisian creamy desserts and long-simmered 'bricklayer's tea' (page 424).

Doughnuts Soaked in Orange Blossom Syrup

TUNISIA
PREPARATION TIME: 30 minutes,
plus resting time
COOKING TIME: 15 minutes
MAKES: about 18 doughnuts

Youyou are popular Tunisian mini-doughnut-like cookies glazed in syrup. Sometimes called *kaak youyou*, they are highly popular – and perfect for dipping into the morning *café au lait*.

350 g/12 oz (2⅓ cups) plain (all-purpose) flour, sifted, plus extra for dusting
2 teaspoons baking powder
60 g/2¼ oz (⅓ cup) sugar
3 tablespoons milk
3 tablespoons olive oil, plus extra for oiling
2 large eggs
neutral oil, for frying
sesame seeds, to decorate

For the syrup:
200 g/7 oz (1 cup) sugar
1 tablespoon fresh lemon juice
1 tablespoon orange blossom water

Put the flour and baking powder into a large bowl and stir to combine, then add the sugar, milk and olive oil. Mix in the eggs one at a time until a dough comes together, adding extra milk if needed. Turn out onto a lightly floured work counter and knead to a soft, slightly sticky dough. Put into a large, lightly oiled bowl, cover with cling film (plastic wrap) and leave to rest for 1 hour at room temperature.

MEANWHILE, PREPARE THE SYRUP: Put the sugar, lemon juice and 250 ml (8 fl oz/1 cup) water into a large saucepan and bring to the boil over a high heat, stirring to dissolve the sugar. Reduce the heat to low and simmer until it has reduced to a light, clear syrup, about 5 minutes. Stir in the orange blossom water and remove from the heat.

Roll out the dough on a lightly floured work counter to about 1 cm/½ inch thick. Using small cookie cutters, cut the dough into doughnut shapes. Or use a glass (5–6 cm/2–2½ inches in diameter) and a cap to press out into doughnut shapes. You should have about 18 doughnuts in total.

Heat at least 2 cm/¾ inch of neutral oil in a large, deep frying pan over a medium heat until the surface shimmers. Line a plate with paper towels.

Working in batches, gently set the doughnuts in the hot oil and fry until golden, 2–4 minutes, turning halfway through. Remove with a slotted spoon and leave to drain on the paper towels.

If needed, warm the syrup. Set a large sieve or colander over a bowl. Set the doughnuts in the syrup and turn to coat. Drain the excess syrup, then arrange the doughnuts on a serving plate. They are best eaten fresh. For maximum freshness, store the doughnuts uncoated for up to 4 days in an airtight container, glazing them in syrup just before serving.

Deep-fried Fritters

ALGERIA, MOROCCO
PREPARATION TIME: 15 minutes,
plus rising time
COOKING TIME: 20 minutes
MAKES: 10–12 fritters

Sfenj means 'sponge', a fitting description for the imperfect shape of these fried fritters. Sticky, unsweetened dough is deep-fried and then looped together with a strip of palm leaf and knotted in a loop to carry, especially loved by kids on the way to school. When prepared at home they tend to have more irregular shapes, though are just as delicious.

400 g/14 oz (2⅔ cups) plain (all-purpose) flour
2 teaspoons instant or fast-action active dry yeast granules
½ teaspoon salt
neutral oil, for frying and oiling
icing (confectioners') sugar, for dusting, optional

Sift the flour into a wide bowl and add the yeast and salt. Using your hands, gradually and vigorously mix in 250–300 ml (8–10 fl oz/1–1¼ cups) warm water to form a moist, smooth and sticky dough. Cover the bowl with cling film (plastic wrap), place in a warm spot in the kitchen and leave the dough to rise for about 3 hours to double or triple in size.

Heat at least 2.5 cm/1 inch of oil in a large, deep frying pan over a medium heat until the surface shimmers. Line a plate with paper towels.

Moisten your hands with oil. Pull off a piece of dough the size of an apricot (about 60 g/2¼ oz). Flatten with your hands, poke a hole in the centre with your thumb and stretch into a ring. Carefully lower into the hot oil and fry until golden, 3–5 minutes. Remove with a slotted spoon and leave to drain on the paper towels. Repeat with the remaining dough. Dust with icing (confectioners') sugar (if using) and serve hot.

Date-filled Semolina Cookies

ALGERIA, LIBYA, MOROCCO, TUNISIA
PREPARATION TIME: 30 minutes,
plus resting time
COOKING TIME: 40 minutes
MAKES: about 32 cookies

Makrout are arguably the region's most iconic cookie. After frying, these date-filled semolina cookies are dipped in warmed, runny honey or, more common today, a simple syrup. To use honey instead, warm gently in a small saucepan over a low heat for a few minutes until runny. Add melted butter to the date paste to soften, or a bit of orange zest for citrus notes. Some bakers add a touch of saffron or ground turmeric to the dough for a yellowish colour.

500 g/1 lb 2 oz (3 cups) medium semolina
125 ml/4 fl oz (½ cup) melted butter
pinch of salt
neutral oil, for oiling and frying
sesame seeds, to decorate

For the syrup:
500 g/1 lb 2 oz (2½ cups) sugar
juice of 1 lemon

For the date paste:
250 g/9 oz date paste or pitted and chopped ripe dates
15 g/½ oz (1 tablespoon) butter, melted
½ teaspoon ground cinnamon
2 tablespoons orange blossom water

Put the semolina in a large bowl, add the butter and salt and mix in with your hands to coat. Knead while gradually adding in warm water a little at a time as needed to form a smooth dough that holds together. Cover with cling film (plastic wrap) and let rest for about 1 hour.

MEANWHILE, PREPARE THE SYRUP: Pour 500 ml (18 fl oz/2 cups) water into a large saucepan, add the sugar and lemon juice and bring to the boil. Lower the heat and reduce to a syrup that when cooled is just sticky between your fingers when pinched together, 20–30 minutes. To test whether the syrup is ready, remove the pan from the heat and let the syrup cool a little, returning the pan to the heat and continuing to reduce if the syrup is not just sticky. Leave in the saucepan and keep warm.

TO MAKE THE DATE PASTE: Put the date paste, butter, cinnamon and orange blossom water into a large bowl and mix together. If using pitted dates, put them into a steaming basket over a pot of water and steam over a low heat until very soft, about

1 hour, then mash with the butter, cinnamon and orange blossom water. Set aside.

Divide the dough into 4 pieces. On a well-oiled work counter, roll out each piece in the form of a baguette. Make a central furrow along the length of the 'baguettes'. Divide the date paste into 4 pieces, then roll out the paste into finger-thick snakes and place in the furrows. Pinch the tops over to close and gently roll under the palms of your hands to 2–3 cm/¾–1¼ inches in diameter. Slightly flatten, trim the ends off and cut into diamond-shaped lozenges, 2–3 cm/¾–1¼ inches in length. You should have about 32 cookies in total.

Heat at least 2 cm/¾ inch of oil in a large, deep frying pan over a medium heat until the surface shimmers. Line a plate with paper towels. Set a large sieve or colander over a bowl.

Working in batches, carefully set the cookies into the oil and fry until just golden, 2–3 minutes per batch, turning halfway through. Using a slotted spoon, transfer to the paper towels to drain. Repeat with the remaining cookies.

While still warm, dip the cookies in the syrup, leave them to stand for a few moments and then put them into the colander to drain. Arrange on a platter and sprinkle with sesame seeds. Store in airtight containers. They are best eaten within 2 weeks.

Pan-cooked Semolina Date Bars

ALGERIA
PREPARATION TIME: 30 minutes,
plus resting time
COOKING TIME: 20 minutes
MAKES: 16–20 cookies

Bradj are an Algerian favourite to serve with coffee and tea, and to offer to guests during Eid al-Fitr visits. Made with medium semolina, many now add a spoonful of plain (all-purpose) flour to give the dough a suppleness. As for the date paste, it can be seasoned in various ways. Many cooks knead some butter and ground cinnamon, perhaps orange blossom water, occasionally a pinch of ground cloves and sesame seeds into the paste.

500 g/1 lb 2 oz (3 cups) medium semolina
1 heaped tablespoon plain (all-purpose) flour
150 g/5 oz butter, melted and cooled
2 tablespoons extra-virgin olive oil
salt

For the date paste:
250 g/9 oz date paste
15 g/½ oz (1 tablespoon) butter or neutral oil
¼ teaspoon ground cinnamon
generous pinch of ground cloves

Put the semolina into a wide bowl and mix in the flour, then season with salt. Pour over the cooled melted butter and oil and work in well with your fingers. Cover with cling film (plastic wrap) and leave to rest for 30 minutes to fully absorb.

MEANWHILE, PREPARE THE DATE PASTE:
If the date paste is stiff, put it into a steamer basket over a pot of water and steam over a low heat for a few minutes. Put the paste, butter, cinnamon and cloves onto a clean work counter and knead to a smooth, pliable paste. Set aside.

Sprinkle 60 ml (2 fl oz/¼ cup) of tepid water over the dough and work in with your fingers. Cover with cling film (plastic wrap) and leave to rest for 15 minutes at room temperature. Sprinkle over 60 ml (2 fl oz/¼ cup) water. Without kneading, work to form a smooth, compact and sandy-textured dough. Divide into 2 equal-size balls.

Press or roll out one of the balls on baking (parchment) paper or cling film to about 1 cm/½ inch thick. Set aside. On another sheet of baking paper or cling film, roll out the remaining ball to the same size and thickness. Flatten the date paste and roll out to the same size as the other pieces. Lay on top of the flattened piece of dough,

then gently lay the reserved piece of dough on top. Press out with a rolling pin to 2 cm/¾ inch thick. Using a pastry cutter or knife, cut into diamond or square shapes, 5–7.5 cm/2–3 inches in size. You should have 16–20 cookies in total. Decorate the top with patterns as desired by gently pressing the knife against the top.

Heat a medium ungreased frying pan over a medium heat. Working in batches, with the help of a spatula, lift pieces, one at a time, and set in the pan. Cook for about 5 minutes, carefully turning only once, until brown on both sides. Store in airtight containers. They are best eaten within 2 weeks.

No-bake Date and Semolina Cookies

ALGERIA, TUNISIA
PREPARATION TIME: 15 minutes
COOKING TIME: 10 minutes
MAKES: 20 cookies

In Algeria, these no-bake treats are called *rfiss tounsi*, which basically means 'Tunisian cookies'. In El Kef, in western Tunisia, an hour's drive from the Algerian border, they go by the same name, although some places in Tunisia call them *rfiss tmer* (*tmer* means 'date'). Many cooks use equal amounts of semolina and dates and about half the amount of butter, plus a touch of honey if needed. This recipe calls for soft dates that can easily be mashed into a paste. If using less-soft dates, stone (pit) and steam until soft.

200 g/7 oz soft dates, such as deglet nour, medjool or *ghars*, or date paste
200 g/7 oz (1¼ cups) medium semolina
75 g/2¾ oz (5 tablespoons) salted butter, softened
1 teaspoon honey, optional

Wipe the dates with paper towels and stone (pit). Finely chop, then mash the dates into a smooth paste with the back of a fork or potato masher.

Put the semolina into a medium, ungreased frying pan and dry-toast over a low heat, stirring frequently with a wooden spoon, until a rich, golden colour, about 10 minutes. Do not scorch. Transfer to a large bowl, add the date paste, butter and honey (if using) and knead to a smooth paste. Form the paste into a single ball and press out on a chopping (cutting) board until it is 1.5 cm/⅔ inch thick. Cut into rectangular pieces about 3 × 5 cm/1¼ x 2 inches. You should have about 20 cookies in total. Leave to cool to room temperature before serving. Store in airtight containers. They are best eaten within 2 weeks.

Gazelle Horns

ALGERIA, LIBYA, MOROCCO, TUNISIA
PREPARATION TIME: 30 minutes,
plus resting time
COOKING TIME: 20 minutes
MAKES: about 24 cookies

Among the most famous sweets in North Africa is
the almond paste-stuffed cookie known as *kaab el
ghazal*. The name translates to 'gazelle ankles' but
the sweets are always called 'gazelle horns' for their
curving shape. Pricking a few times with a needle
allows the steam to escape and the cookies to retain
their shape and texture. Bake only until a very light
golden colour, and do not overbake. Once cooled,
they will become chewy.

For the dough:
300 g/11 oz (2 cups) plain (all-purpose) flour, sifted,
   plus extra for dusting
25 g/1 oz (2 tablespoons) butter, softened
2 large eggs
2 tablespoons orange blossom water, plus extra for the
   egg wash
generous pinch of salt

For the almond paste:
250 g/9 oz (1⅔ cups) whole almonds
100 g/3½ oz (½ cup) sugar
25 g/1 oz (2 tablespoons) butter, softened
¼ teaspoon ground cinnamon
2 teaspoons orange blossom water

TO MAKE THE DOUGH: Sift the flour into a
large bowl, add the butter, one of the eggs, the
orange blossom water and salt and mix together.
Patiently knead for 10 minutes to a smooth, firm
dough, adding about 60 ml (2 fl oz/¼ cup) water
as needed, until it is the consistency of bread dough.
Divide the dough into 4 pieces, wrap in cling film
(plastic wrap) and leave to rest in the refrigerator
for 1–2 hours.

MEANWHILE, PREPARE THE ALMOND PASTE:
Bring a medium saucepan of water to the boil, add
the almonds and boil for 3–5 minutes; drain. Once
cool enough to handle, slip off the skins with your
fingers. Spread the almonds out on paper towels to
dry. Put the almonds and sugar into a food processor
and grind to a powdery mixture. Add the butter,
cinnamon and orange blossom water and work to a
soft, smooth paste with your fingers. Make small balls
from about 10 g (¼ oz/2 teaspoons) of the mixture
and roll into tapered, little-finger-thick cylinders
about 7.5 cm/3 inches in length. Set aside.

Preheat the oven to 180 °C/350 °F/Gas Mark 4. Line
1–2 baking sheets with baking (parchment) paper.

Using a rolling pin, roll out a piece of dough
on a lightly floured work counter until very thin,
turning over as needed. Cut into ribbons about
10 cm/4 inches wide. In the centre of each ribbon,
place pieces of almond paste 3–4 cm/1¼–1½ inches
apart. Fold over the pastry to cover the almond paste
and seal the edges by pinching with your fingertips.
Cut out each one into a semi-circle using a fluted
pastry wheel. Cup your hand around each pastry
and shape to a crescent using your thumb. Arrange
on the prepared baking sheet and repeat with the
remaining dough.

Put the remaining egg and a dash of orange
blossom water into a small bowl and whisk together.
Brush the egg mixture across the top of each cookie,
then prick the tops along the ridge a few times with
a needle or cocktail stick (toothpick). Bake in the
hot oven until just golden brown, 10–15 minutes.
Remove from oven and leave to cool before serving.
Store in airtight containers. They are best eaten
within 2 weeks.

Almond Ghriba Cookies

ALGERIA, MOROCCO
PREPARATION TIME: 20 minutes,
plus drying and chilling time
COOKING TIME: 20 minutes
MAKES: about 18 cookies

The name of these cookies is *ghriba* (or its diminutive *ghouriba*), which means 'mysterious'. They stand out for their cracked surface and rich, chewy texture. This recipe is gluten-free and made with ground raw almonds, but there are other popular versions with semolina or flour blended with walnuts, sesame seeds or coconut (see right).

250 g/9 oz (1⅔ cups) whole almonds
75 g/2¾ oz (⅓ cup) sugar
1 large egg
25 g/1 oz (2 tablespoons) butter, softened, or neutral oil
1 teaspoon baking powder
pinch of salt
icing (confectioners') sugar, for coating

Bring a medium saucepan of water to the boil, add the almonds and boil for 3–5 minutes; drain. Once cool enough to handle, slip off the skins with your fingers. Spread the almonds out on paper towels to dry. Put the almonds and sugar into a food processor and grind to a powder. Transfer to a large bowl, add the egg, butter, baking powder and salt and work into a smooth paste. Cover with cling film (plastic wrap) and refrigerate until chilled.

Preheat the oven to 180°C/350°F/Gas Mark 4. Line a baking sheet with baking (parchment) paper. Put enough icing (confectioners') sugar for coating into a medium bowl.

With moistened hands, roll the dough into 3.5-cm/1⅓-inch balls, then roll in the icing sugar until coated all over and arrange on the prepared baking sheet, leaving space around each.

Bake in the hot oven until the cookies are golden and firm at the edges and cracked on the surface but soft in the centre, about 12 minutes. Remove from the oven and leave to cool on the baking sheet for 10 minutes, then transfer to a wire rack to cool completely. Store in airtight containers. They are best eaten within 2 weeks.

Coconut and Semolina Ghriba Cookies

ALGERIA, MOROCCO
PREPARATION TIME: 20 minutes
COOKING TIME: 10–15 minutes
MAKES: about 20 cookies

Another popular version of *ghriba* cookies is made with dried coconut and semolina rather than ground almonds (see left). Some cooks in Algeria add a dollop of apricot jam to the dough, which gives it a lovely, fruity-sweet touch.

2 large eggs
160 g/5¾ oz (generous ¾ cup) sugar
120 ml/4 fl oz (½ cup) neutral oil
pinch of salt
finely grated zest of 1 small lemon
1 tablespoon baking powder
250 g/9 oz (scant 3¼ cups) desiccated (unsweetened shredded) coconut
125 g/4¼ oz (¾ cup) medium semolina
100 g/3½ oz (generous ¾ cup) icing (confectioners') sugar
orange blossom water or water, for moistening

Preheat the oven to 180°C/350°F/Gas Mark 4. Line a baking sheet with baking (parchment) paper.

Put the eggs and sugar into a large bowl and beat together with electric beaters, then beat in the oil, salt, lemon zest and baking powder. Or use a stand mixer fitted with a whisk attachment. Fold in the coconut, then work in the semolina to form a smooth and sticky dough.

Put the icing (confectioners') sugar into a wide bowl. Pour some orange blossom water or water into a small bowl.

Moisten your hands with orange blossom water, then roll the dough into 4-cm/1½-inch balls. You should have about 20 cookies in total. Carefully roll in the icing sugar until coated all over and arrange on the prepared baking sheet at least 5 cm/2 inches apart.

Bake in the hot oven until the cookies are light golden, firm at the edges and cracked on the surface but still very soft in the centre, 10–15 minutes. Remove from the oven and leave to cool on the sheet for 10 minutes, then transfer to a wire rack to cool completely. Store in airtight containers. They are best eaten within 2 weeks.

Bitter Almond Macaroons

LIBYA
PREPARATION TIME: 20 minutes,
plus chilling and resting time
COOKING TIME: 12 minutes
MAKES: 12–15 cookies

A speciality of Tripoli, Libyan *abambar* are akin
to classic almond macaroons but with a signature
flavour of essence of bitter almonds. Some cooks
like to affix an almond atop of each cookie with a
drop or two of orange blossom water before baking.
Leaving the shaped dough to stand before putting
in the oven helps the distinctive texture form on the
cookie surface during baking.

  175 g/6 oz (scant 1½ cups) ground almonds
  120 g/4 oz (1 cup) icing (confectioners') sugar
  pinch of salt
  ½ teaspoon bitter almond essence
  2 large egg whites
  12–15 blanched and peeled whole almonds
    (see page 445)

Put the ground almonds, sugar, salt and bitter almond
essence into a large bowl and mix to combine. Put
the egg whites into another large bowl and beat to
stiff peaks with electric beaters, or use a stand mixer
fitted with a whisk attachment, then gradually fold
into the almond mixture, working from the bottom
upwards. Do not overwork. Cover with cling film
(plastic wrap) and refrigerate for 30 minutes, or
until chilled.
  Line 1–2 baking sheets with baking (parchment)
paper.
  Roll the dough into golf ball-size balls (about
4 cm/1½ inches) and arrange on the baking sheet
leaving a space between each as they will spread.
Press to slightly flatten. Place a whole almond on
top. Leave to stand for 1 hour.
  Preheat the oven to 180 °C/350 °F/Gas Mark 4.
  Bake in the hot oven until lightly golden and
still soft to touch, about 12 minutes. Remove from
the oven and leave to cool for 5 minutes before
transferring to wire racks to cool completely. Store
in airtight containers in the refrigerator. They are
best eaten within 2 weeks.

Twice-baked Sesame Seed Biscuits

MOROCCO
PREPARATION TIME: 30 minutes,
plus cooling time
COOKING TIME: 25–35 minutes
MAKES: about 60 small biscuits (cookies)

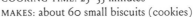

Crunchy, twice-baked, biscotti-like biscuits (cookies)
known as *fekkas* are extremely popular in Morocco.
This version with sesame seeds is so beloved that
it is usually called *fekkas beldi*, *beldi* meaning 'local'
or 'of this country'. The key is to allow the log to
completely cool after the first baking, ideally under
a moist cloth, so it slices without crumbling.

  2 large eggs
  150 g/5 oz (1¼ cups) icing (confectioners') sugar
  90 ml/3 fl oz (6 tablespoons) neutral oil, plus extra
    for oiling
  35 g/1¼ oz (¼ cup) toasted sesame seeds
  1 tablespoon orange blossom water, optional
  2 teaspoons baking powder
  pinch of salt
  400 g/14 oz (2⅔ cups) plain (all-purpose) flour
  1 egg yolk, beaten

Preheat the oven to 180 °C/350 °F/Gas Mark 4. Line
1–2 baking sheets with baking (parchment) paper.
  Put the eggs and sugar into a large bowl and beat
with a fork until frothy. Using your fingers, work
in the oil, sesame seeds, orange blossom water (if
using), baking powder and salt. Begin working in the
flour to form a smooth, moist and somewhat sticky
dough. With oiled hands to keep the dough from
sticking, divide into 3–4 pieces and roll under the
palms of your hands into logs about 4 cm/1½ inches
in diameter. Place on the prepared baking sheet and
brush with beaten egg yolk.
  Bake the logs in the hot oven until golden, still
somewhat spongy and a cocktail stick (toothpick)
comes out dry, about 15 minutes. Transfer the logs
to a wire rack, cover with clean, moist dish towels
and leave to cool completely.
  Preheat the oven to 180 °C/350 °F/Gas Mark 4.
Line 2 baking sheets with baking paper.
  Using a bread knife, cut the logs diagonally into
1-cm-/½-inch-thick slices, watching that they do not
break. Spread out flat on the prepared baking sheets
and bake in the hot oven until golden, carefully
turning once if needed, 10–15 minutes. Remove
from the oven and leave to cool on wire racks. Store
in airtight containers. They are best eaten within
2 weeks.

Crunchy Vanilla Biscuits

TUNISIA
PREPARATION TIME: 15 minutes,
plus chilling time
COOKING TIME: 15 minutes
MAKES: about 24 biscuits (cookies)

While pâtisseries abound selling pastries and cookies, there are a couple of favourites that people like to make at home. In Tunis, the most popular is a simple, baton-shaped one called *bachkoutou*, or just *biscuit*. The thick dough is often put through a small, hand-cranked meat grinder, which blends and gives a ridged shape. They can be pressed through a sturdy spritzer or piping (pastry) bag, or hand cut.

3 large eggs
125 g/4¼ oz (generous ½ cup) sugar
1 teaspoon vanilla sugar or dash of vanilla extract
1 tablespoon orange blossom or rose water, optional
120 ml/4 fl oz (½ cup) neutral oil
400 g/14 oz (2⅔ cups) plain (all-purpose) flour, plus extra for dusting (optional)
1½ tablespoons baking powder

Put the eggs, sugar, vanilla sugar and orange blossom water (if using) into a large bowl and beat with electric beaters until it has doubled in volume. Or use a stand mixer fitted with a whisk attachment. While continuing to beat, add the oil in a slow, steady stream. Put the flour and baking powder into another bowl and mix together, then fold in to form a smooth and not overly sticky dough. Cover with cling film (plastic wrap) and refrigerate for 15 minutes.

Preheat the oven to 180 °C/350 °F/Gas Mark 4. Line 2 baking sheets with baking (parchment) paper.

Fill a sturdy pastry spritzer or piping (pastry) bag fitted with a wide fluted tip. Working directly over the baking sheets, force the dough through the tip and cut with a knife or scissors into baton-shaped biscuits (cookies) about 7.5 cm/3 inches in length. Alternatively, roll out the dough on a lightly floured work counter to about 1 cm/½ inch thick and cut into batons about 1 cm/½ inch wide and 7.5 cm/3 inches in length.

Bake in the hot oven until golden and firm, about 15 minutes. Remove from the oven and leave to cool on wire racks. Store in airtight containers. They are best eaten within 2 weeks.

Sablés with Jam

ALGERIA
PREPARATION TIME: 30 minutes,
plus chilling time
COOKING TIME: 10–12 minutes
MAKES: about 24 cookies

A favourite cookie to bake at home in Algeria, *sablés à la confiture* are two-layer cookies with jam in the middle. (The name means 'sandy', referring to their crumbly texture.) Many home bakers use a special serrated cookie cutter that can cut out the circular cookies as well as the hole in the middle for the top piece. (Nowadays, that hole can be all types of shapes.) Watch that the cookies don't brown in the oven – they should be ivory to pale golden in colour. As for jam, apricot (page 406) and fig (page 405) are popular choices, but use any that aren't too runny or chunky. If desired, dust the top layer with icing (confectioners') sugar before assembling the cookies.

225 g/8 oz butter, softened
225 g/8 oz (generous 1 cup) sugar
2 large eggs
2 teaspoons baking powder
pinch of salt
500 g/1 lb 2 oz (3⅓ cups) plain (all-purpose) flour, plus extra for dusting
apricot, fig or another smooth jam (pages 402–406), for filling

Put the butter and sugar into a large bowl and beat with electric beaters until creamy. Or use a stand mixer fitted with a whisk attachment. Add the eggs, one by one, beating until the mixture is pale. Add the baking powder and salt, and gradually work in the flour to form a firm dough. Wrap with cling film (plastic wrap) and refrigerate for at least 30 minutes to chill.

Preheat the oven to 180 °C/350 °F/Gas Mark 4. Line several baking sheets with baking (parchment) paper.

Roll out the dough on a lightly floured work counter to 5 mm/¼ inch thick or thinner. Press out discs using a round or fluted cookie cutter, about 7 cm/2¾ inches in diameter. With a smaller cutter (about 2.5 cm/1 inch in diameter), press out a hole in the centre of half of them.

Arrange on the baking sheets and bake in the hot oven until pale golden, 10–12 minutes. Remove from the oven and leave to cool completely on wire racks. Spread jam on the bottom halves, then top with the circular pieces. Store in the refrigerator in airtight containers. They are best eaten within 2 weeks.

Coconut Snowballs with Orange Blossom-scented Apricot Jam

ALGERIA, MOROCCO
PREPARATION TIME: 25 minutes,
plus cooling time
COOKING TIME: 15 minutes
MAKES: about 20 biscuits (cookies)

These biscuits (cookies), which get coated in apricot jam and rolled in shredded coconut, go by various (usually French) names, from *boules de neige* (snowballs) to *boules de noix de coco* (coconut balls).

2 large eggs
150 g/5 oz (¾ cup) sugar
1 teaspoon vanilla sugar or dash of vanilla extract
175 ml/6 fl oz (¾ cup) neutral oil
350 g/12 oz (2⅓ cups) plain (all-purpose) flour
14 g/½ oz (1½ tablespoons) baking powder
300 g/11 oz (1 cup) Apricot Jam (page 406)
1 tablespoon orange blossom water, optional
200 g/7 oz (2½ cups) desiccated (unsweetened shredded) coconut

Preheat the oven to 180°C/350°F/Gas Mark 4. Line several baking sheets with baking (parchment) paper.

Put the eggs, sugar and vanilla sugar into a large bowl and beat with electric beaters, then beat in the oil. Or use a stand mixer fitted with a whisk attachment. Put the flour and baking powder into a large bowl and mix together, then fold into the mixture to form a smooth dough. Roll tablespoonfuls of the dough into small balls about 2 cm/¾ inch in diameter and place on the prepared baking sheets.

Bake in the hot oven until very light golden and still quite soft, 10–12 minutes. Remove from the oven and leave to cool on wire racks.

Put the jam into a small saucepan and heat over a low heat for about 5 minutes, or until liquid. Strain into a bowl to remove any large pieces of fruit, then stir in the orange blossom water (if using). Put the coconut into a wide bowl.

Set a pair of biscuits (cookies) in the jam and turn to coat well. Gently press the two flat ends together to form a sphere, then set in the coconut and turn until generously coated. Place on a plate to dry and fully absorb the jam. Store in the refrigerator in airtight containers. They are best eaten within 2 weeks.

Lemon Cut-out Cookies

ALGERIA
PREPARATION TIME: 20 minutes
COOKING TIME: 8–10 minutes
MAKES: about 30 cookies

Called *torno* in Oran from the Spanish that refers to turning (as a lathe) for their circular shape, these lemon and vanilla-flavoured cookies are another favourite to bake at home. They are also known as *halwat tabaa* in Algerian Arabic, or 'cookie cutter sweet', as they are made using a cookie cutter. Shapes such as moons, stars and hearts have become popular for kids, as have decorating the cookies with colourful sprinkles.

2 large eggs
110 g/3¾ oz (½ cup) sugar, plus extra for sprinkling
finely grated zest of 1 lemon
1 teaspoon vanilla sugar or dash of vanilla extract
120 ml/4 fl oz (½ cup) mild olive oil
500 g/1 lb 2 oz (3⅓ cups) plain (all-purpose) flour, plus extra for dusting
2 teaspoons baking powder
1 egg yolk
2 teaspoons milk

Preheat the oven to 180°C/350°F/Gas Mark 4. Line several baking sheets with baking (parchment) paper.

Put the eggs into a large bowl and beat with electric beaters. Or use a stand mixer fitted with a whisk attachment. Beat in the sugar, lemon zest, vanilla sugar and finally the oil. Put the flour and baking powder into another bowl and mix together, then gradually work into the mixture to form a firm dough.

Roll out the dough on a lightly floured work counter to 5 mm/¼ inch thick, then cut out circles using a round 8-cm/3¼-inch cookie cutter. Arrange on the prepared baking sheets. Put the egg yolk and milk into a cup and beat together. Brush each cookie with the egg mixture, then sprinkle with a generous pinch of sugar.

Bake in the hot oven until golden, 8–10 minutes. Remove from the oven and leave to cool on wire racks. Store in airtight containers. They are best eaten within 2 weeks.

Lacy Honey-soaked Cookies

ALGERIA, TUNISIA
PREPARATION TIME: 45 minutes,
plus resting time
COOKING TIME: 10 minutes
MAKES: about 24 large cookies

These generously sized, floral-shaped twists of pastries known as *griwach* are fried and then soaked in honey, giving them a lovely crunchy-yet-chewy texture. (Their name comes from a word meaning 'crunchy' or 'to crunch'.) They are one of the most important sweets during Ramadan in Algeria. They are also popular in Tunisia, where they are often a touch smaller.

    100 g/3½ oz (7 tablespoons) butter
    1 large egg
    1 tablespoon sugar
    1 teaspoon white vinegar
    1 tablespoon orange blossom water
    1 teaspoon salt
    500 g/1 lb 2 oz (3⅓ cups) plain (all-purpose) flour,
        sifted, plus extra for dusting
    1 teaspoon baking powder
    250 g/9 oz (⅔ cup) honey
    neutral oil, for frying
    sesame seeds, to decorate

Gently melt the butter in a small saucepan over a low heat for a couple of minutes without letting it boil and bubble. Pour into a large bowl, add the egg, sugar, vinegar, orange blossom water and salt and mix together. Add the flour and baking powder to form a ball. Turn out onto a lightly floured work counter and patiently knead for 10 minutes to a supple dough, adding 60–120 ml (2–4 fl oz/¼–½ cup) lukewarm water as needed, until it is the consistency of bread dough. Cover with cling film (plastic wrap) and leave to rest in the refrigerator for 30 minutes.

Put a piece of dough onto a lightly floured work counter and form it into a ball the size of an orange. Using a rolling pin, roll out until very thin, turning over as needed. Using a fluted pastry wheel, cut out rectangle-shaped pieces about 12 × 10 cm/5 × 4 inches. Into each, make 5 parallel lengthwise incisions, leaving uncut along each end. Slip a finger through every other one, then take the end corner and pull through the gap and out the other side to form a plait (braid). Set on a plate and repeat with the rest of the dough.

Put the honey into a medium saucepan and warm for a few minutes over a low heat. Line a plate with paper towels. Set a large sieve or colander over a bowl.

Heat at least 2 cm/¾ inch of oil in a large, deep frying pan over a medium heat until the surface shimmers. Working in batches, set in the cookies and fry until just golden, 1–2 minutes per batch. Using a slotted spoon, transfer the cookies to the paper towels to drain. Repeat with the remaining cookies.

While still warm, dip the cookies into the honey and leave to stand for a moment, then transfer to the sieve to drain. Arrange on a platter and sprinkle with sesame seeds while warm. Store in airtight containers. They are best eaten within 2 weeks.

Aromatic Tea Biscuits with Sesame Seeds

TUNISIA
PREPARATION TIME: 20 minutes,
plus resting time
COOKING TIME: 20 minutes
MAKES: 12 biscuits (cookies)

Tunisia has a variety of ring-shaped biscuits (cookies) known as *kaak*, including stuffed ones such as *kaak warka* (stuffed with marzipan) and *kaak tmar* (stuffed with date paste). These are the classics ones, unstuffed, and flavoured with sesame seeds, ground aniseed, fennel and some orange blossom water.

    250 g/9 oz (1⅔ cups) plain (all-purpose) flour
    60 g/2¼ oz (⅓ cup) sugar
    35 g/1¼ oz (¼ cup) toasted sesame seeds, plus extra
        to decorate
    2 teaspoons baking powder
    1 teaspoon ground fennel
    1 teaspoon ground aniseed
    pinch of salt
    2 large eggs
    1 teaspoon orange blossom water, optional
    60 ml/2 fl oz (¼ cup) vegetable or mild olive oil

Put the flour, sugar, sesame seeds, baking powder, fennel, aniseed and salt into a large bowl and mix together. Add one of the eggs and the orange blossom water (if using). Work in the oil and a few tablespoons of water to form a smooth dough.

Cover 2 baking sheets with baking (parchment) paper. Put the remaining egg into a small bowl and beat with a fork. Set aside.

Take golf ball-size pieces of the dough (4 cm/ 1½ inches in diameter, about 50 g/2 oz) under the palms of your hands and roll into finger-thick ropes 1 cm/½ inch in diameter and about 25 cm/10 inches in length. Shape by connecting the ends into a circle and placing on the prepared baking sheet. Brush with beaten egg and sprinkle with some sesame seeds. Leave the biscuits to rest for 15 minutes.

Preheat the oven to 180 °C/350 °F/Gas Mark 4.

Bake in the hot oven until golden, about 20 minutes. Remove from the oven, then transfer to wire racks and leave to cool. They will get crunchier as they cool. Store in airtight containers. They are best eaten within 2 weeks.

Basbousa Semolina Cake with Almonds

ALGERIA, LIBYA, TUNISIA
PREPARATION TIME: 20 minutes,
plus soaking time
COOKING TIME 50 minutes
MAKES: about 16 smallish slices

Basbousa is a beloved semolina cake that gets soaked in a light syrup after baking. It's popular across much of the region, and goes by different names, from *harissa hloua* ('sweet harissa') in Tunisia to *kalb el louz* ('heart of almonds') in Algeria. While basic versions all have semolina and an almond on top of each piece, it has become common to include other ingredients, such as ground almonds, yoghurt or thick *lben* (buttermilk), vanilla sugar or dried coconut. Prepare the syrup first, as it should be cool when added to the warm cake.

For the syrup:
200 g/7 oz (1 cup) sugar
juice of ½ lemon
1 tablespoon orange blossom water, geranium water or rose water, optional

For the cake:
250 g/9 oz (1½ cups) medium semolina
50 g/2 oz (scant ½ cup) ground almonds
100 g/3½ oz (½ cup) sugar
1 teaspoon baking powder
pinch of salt
120 ml/4 fl oz (½ cup) plain yoghurt
90 ml/3 fl oz (6 tablespoons) olive oil or melted butter
16 blanched whole almonds

TO MAKE THE SYRUP: Put the sugar, lemon juice and 500 ml (18 fl oz/2 cups) water into a large saucepan and bring to the boil, stirring to dissolve the sugar. Boil for 10 minutes to a light syrup. Add the orange blossom water (if using), then remove from the heat and leave to cool.

TO MAKE THE CAKE: Preheat the oven to 180 °C/350 °F/Gas Mark 4. Line a 20 × 20-cm/8 × 8-inch square or 23-cm/9-inch round cake pan with baking (parchment) paper.

Put the semolina, ground almonds, sugar, baking powder, salt and yoghurt into a large bowl. Add the oil and blend until very smooth. Spread the batter evenly in the prepared pan. With a knife, pre-cut into 16 square- or diamond-shaped pieces without removing from the pan. Place an almond at the centre of each piece.

Bake in the hot oven until golden and firm, 30–40 minutes. Remove the cake from the oven. (Turn off the oven but keep it warm.) Slowly pour about a third of the syrup over the warm cake and allow it to absorb. Pour over a third more and leave it to absorb, then begin pouring over the final third, leaving some extra if the cake appears saturated. Set in the warm oven with the door open for about 10 minutes to fully absorb the syrup. Remove from the oven and leave to cool to room temperature still in the pan. Serve. The cake can be stored in an airtight container in a cool place for up to 7 days.

Orange Cake with Orange Glaze

TUNISIA
PREPARATION TIME: 15 minutes
COOKING TIME: 30 minutes
SERVES: 8

This wonderfully aromatic orange cake from Tunisia is a classic. It is a favourite to serve guests, and a leftover slice is perfect with the morning *café au lait*. It is also lovely when made with blood oranges.

    butter, for greasing
    300 g/11 oz (2 cups) plain (all-purpose) flour,
        plus extra for dusting
    3 large eggs
    180 g/6 oz (generous ¾ cup) sugar
    1 tablespoon baking powder
    pinch of salt
    100 ml/3½ fl oz (generous ⅓ cup) mild olive oil
    finely grated zest and juice of 2 oranges

    For the orange glaze:
    2 oranges
    100 g/3½ oz (½ cup) sugar

Preheat the oven to 180 °C/350 °F/Gas Mark 4. Grease a 25-cm/10-inch round cake pan with butter and dust with flour, shaking out the excess.

Put the eggs into a large bowl and vigorously beat with electric beaters, then add the sugar and beat until pale yellow. Or use a stand mixer fitted with a whisk attachment. Sift in the flour and baking powder, then add the salt, oil, orange zest and juice and mix until combined but not overly worked. Pour the batter into the prepared cake pan.

Bake in the hot oven until done but still spongy and a cocktail stick (toothpick) poked into the centre comes out clean, about 30 minutes. Remove from the oven and leave to cool before turning out of the pan.

MEANWHILE, PREPARE THE ORANGE GLAZE: Juice the oranges and add to a medium saucepan with the sugar. Cook, uncovered, over a medium heat, stirring from time to time, until the liquid is reduced to a syrupy glaze, about 15 minutes. Remove from the heat and leave to cool slightly. Pour the glaze over the top of the cake. Serve. Store in an airtight container for up to 3 days.

Sponge Cake

ALGERIA
PREPARATION TIME: 10 minutes,
plus cooling time
COOKING TIME: 25 minutes
SERVES: 8

Mouskoutchou is a simple, everyday cake. Light and spongy, it resembles a genoise sponge. Usually prepared in a round Bundt pan or ring mould, it's easy to make, delicious and frequently served to guests.

    butter, for greasing
    225 g/8 oz (1½ cups) plain (all-purpose) flour,
        plus extra for dusting
    3 large eggs
    180 g/6 oz (generous ¾ cup) sugar
    2 teaspoons baking powder
    pinch of salt
    100 ml/3½ fl oz (generous ⅓ cup) mild olive oil
    100 ml/3½ fl oz (generous ⅓ cup) full-fat (whole)
        milk at room temperature
    finely grated zest of ½ orange or 1 lemon
    icing (confectioners') sugar, for dusting

Preheat the oven to 180 °C/350 °F/Gas Mark 4. Grease a 25-cm/10-inch Bundt, Savarin or round fluted cake pan with butter and dust with flour, shaking out the excess.

Put the eggs into a large bowl and vigorously beat with electric beaters, then add the sugar and beat until light and fluffy. Or use a stand mixer fitted with a whisk attachment. Put the flour, baking powder and salt into another bowl and mix together, then sift into the egg and sugar mixture, add the oil, milk and orange zest and mix until combined but not overly beaten. Pour the batter into the prepared pan.

Bake in the hot oven until done but still spongy and a cocktail stick (toothpick) poked into the centre comes out clean, about 25 minutes. Remove from the oven and leave to cool for 10–15 minutes before turning out of the pan on to a wire rack to cool completely. Dust with icing (confectioners') sugar. Serve. Store in an airtight container for up to 3 days.

Jam Cake

ALGERIA
PREPARATION TIME: 15 minutes
COOKING TIME: 30 minutes
SERVES: 8

A speciality of eastern Algeria, this jam-covered cake called *mderbel* has a texture similar to shortbread. The name refers to being nonchalant or casual, which is a good description of this cake's appearance. One thing that makes it stand out is the topping it often gets. A piece of the dough is set aside, stiffened with some flour and grated over the top. For jam, choose a smooth one, without large pieces of fruit. Apricot Jam (page 406) is the classic choice.

120 g/4 oz butter, melted, plus extra for greasing (optional)
350 g/12 oz (2⅓ cups) plain (all-purpose) flour, plus extra for dusting (optional) and the topping
150 g/5 oz (¾ cup) sugar
2 large eggs
2 teaspoons baking powder
2 pinches of salt
150 g/5 oz (generous ⅓ cup) smooth fruit jam

Preheat the oven to 180°C/350°F/Gas Mark 4. Line a 23-cm/9-inch round or square 20 × 20-cm/ 8 × 8-inch cake pan with baking (parchment) paper, or grease the pan with butter and dust with flour, shaking out the excess.

Put the butter and sugar into a large bowl and cream until light and fluffy, then add the eggs, one at a time. Add the baking powder and salt, sift in the flour and lightly work to a soft dough that doesn't stick to your fingers. Set aside a quarter of the dough.

Spread the dough evenly across the bottom of the prepared pan. Loosen the jam with a touch of warm water if necessary and spread evenly and generously over the top.

With the reserved piece of dough, work in a touch more flour to make it stiffer, then using a box grater, coarsely grate the dough in an even layer over the jam.

Bake in the hot oven until cooked through and golden, about 30 minutes. Serve. Store in an airtight container for up to 3 days.

Kabyle Omelette Cake with Honey

ALGERIA
PREPARATION TIME: 10 minutes
COOKING TIME: 20 minutes
SERVES: 4–6

Mchewcha (or *tahboult timlaline* in Berber) is a cross between a cake and omelette from Algeria's Kabylia region that traditionally was served to a woman after giving birth, and to those who came to visit her. It is egg-rich – one egg per heaped tablespoon of flour is a standard ratio – cooked in a frying pan and flipped. At the end it is soaked in honey, hence its French moniker *omelette au miel*. It should rise as it cooks and be soft. Serve as a snack or for breakfast with Mint Tea (pages 417–421).

6 large eggs
pinch of salt
2 tablespoons sugar
¼ teaspoon vanilla extract or 1 teaspoon vanilla sugar
75 g/2¾ oz (6 heaped tablespoons) plain (all-purpose) flour
2 teaspoons baking powder
1 tablespoon olive oil, plus extra for oiling
honey, for drizzling

Put the eggs and salt into a large bowl and vigorously beat with electric beaters until pale and fluffy. Or use a stand mixer fitted with a whisk attachment. Mix in the sugar and vanilla. Put the flour and baking powder into another bowl and mix together, then gradually sift into the egg mixture while beating to a smooth and airy batter.

Heat the oil in a deep 23–25-cm/9–10-inch non-stick frying pan over a medium heat. Pour in the batter. Reduce the heat to its lowest, cover with a lid and cook until the top is just set and can be flipped, about 15 minutes. Oil a plate. Loosen the sides with a spatula, cover with the plate and carefully turn. Slide back into the pan. Cover again and cook until golden on the other side, about 2 minutes. Transfer to a plate. Cut into wedges, then drizzle honey over the slices and serve.

Rice Flour Pudding with Pistachios

ALGERIA, LIBYA, TUNISIA
PREPARATION TIME: 5 minutes,
plus cooling and chilling time
COOKING TIME: 5 minutes
SERVES: 3–4

Mhalbi is a favourite creamy dessert to serve during Ramadan after the fast-breaking *iftar* meal in the evening. This easy-to-make version uses rice flour, while other popular ways to prepare use broken rice (see right). Some add rose water or orange blossom water, to give the pudding an aromatic touch. In Algeria it is also called *satladj*.

    500 ml/18 fl oz (2 cups) full-fat (whole) milk
    3 tablespoons sugar
    50 g/2 oz (⅓ cup) rice flour
    2 tablespoons rose water or orange blossom water
    ground cinnamon, to decorate
    chopped pistachios or toasted almonds, to decorate

Put the milk, sugar and rice flour into a large saucepan and whisk together. Heat over a medium heat and cook, while stirring constantly, until bubbles begin forming and the pudding is creamy, thickened and coats the back of a wooden spoon, 4–5 minutes total. Stir in the rose water and remove from the heat. Pour into ramekins or small dessert bowls, leave to cool and refrigerate until chilled. Before serving, decorate with cinnamon and pistachios.

Rice Pudding with Orange Blossom Water

ALGERIA, LIBYA
PREPARATION TIME: 10 minutes,
plus cooling and chilling time
COOKING TIME: 35 minutes
SERVES: 6

This version of *mhalbi* is made using ground or broken rice (rather than rice flour, see left) and decorated with chopped almonds and cinnamon. When grinding the rice at home, the particles generally lack perfect uniformity in size. While that means cooking times might vary, the dish has a lovely texture to it.

    100 g/3½ oz (½ cup) uncooked short- or medium-
        grain white rice
    75 g/2¾ oz (generous ⅓ cup) sugar
    1 sachet (7.5 g/¼ oz) vanilla sugar (1½ teaspoons) or
        dash of vanilla extract and 1½ teaspoons sugar
    1 litre/34 fl oz (4¼ cups) full-fat (whole) milk
    1 tablespoon orange blossom water
    ground cinnamon, to decorate
    chopped almonds, to decorate

Put the rice into a food processor and grind to a gritty powder. Put into a large saucepan with the sugar and vanilla sugar, then pour in the milk and stir. Bring to a simmer over a medium heat, reduce the heat and cook, stirring almost constantly to keep from scorching, until thick and creamy and all of the rice particles are tender, 20–30 minutes, depending on how finely ground the rice is. Stir in the orange blossom water and remove from the heat. Pour into ramekins or small dessert bowls, leave to cool and refrigerate until chilled. Before serving, decorate with cinnamon and chopped almonds.

Cinnamon-scented Rice Pudding

MOROCCO
PREPARATION TIME: 5 minutes,
plus cooling and chilling time
COOKING TIME: 40 minutes
SERVES: 6

This version of rice pudding is, firstly, not cloyingly sweet, and secondly, delightfully aromatic. The final consistency when cooking should be somewhat creamy and runny, as it will thicken when it cools. Stir in more milk if needed as different rice varieties have various levels of absorption.

200 g/7 oz (1 cup) short- or medium-grain white rice
1.5 litres/50 fl oz (generous 6 cups) full-fat (whole) milk
1 cinnamon stick or piece of cinnamon bark
peel of ½ orange, preferably unwaxed or organic, white pith scraped away
peel of ½ lemon, preferably unwaxed or organic, white pith scraped away
pinch of salt
55 g/2 oz (¼ cup) sugar
15 g/½ oz (1 tablespoon) butter, cut into pieces
1 teaspoon orange blossom water, optional
ground cinnamon, for dusting

Put the rice into a large saucepan and cover with 250 ml (8 fl oz/1 cup) water. Bring to the boil and boil for 1–2 minutes until the water is nearly absorbed. Immediately stir in the milk. Add the cinnamon stick, orange and lemon peels and salt, and bring to a simmer over a medium-high heat. Reduce the heat to low, cover with a lid and gently boil until the rice is tender and the milk creamy, about 25 minutes. Stir frequently to keep from scorching on the bottom or a skin forming on the surface. Stir in the sugar and butter and cook for a final 5 minutes. Stir in the orange blossom water (if using) and remove from the heat. Remove and discard the cinnamon stick and citrus peels. Leave to cool, stirring from time to time. Once cool, transfer to a bowl, cover with cling film (plastic wrap) and refrigerate until well chilled.

Divide among bowls and dust with cinnamon before serving.

Orange Blossom Water Custard

TUNISIA
PREPARATION TIME: 10 minutes
COOKING TIME: 20 minutes
SERVES: 6

This *crème* is especially popular in the northeast of Tunisia around Nabeul, Cap Bon and Sousse, the heart of the country's citrus industry and the main area for distilling orange blossom water. A typical modern touch is to add some cornflour (cornstarch) to help thicken the custard. Serve chilled or even warm.

1 litre/34 fl oz (4¼ cups) full-fat (whole) milk
2 tablespoons orange blossom, rose or geranium water
4 egg yolks
150 g/5 oz (¾ cup) sugar
3 tablespoons cornflour (cornstarch)

Pour the milk into a large saucepan and gently heat over a low heat until it reaches a simmer (don't allow it to boil). Remove from the heat and leave to cool for a few minutes. Stir in the orange blossom water.

Put the egg yolks, sugar and cornflour (cornstarch) into a large bowl and beat with a wooden spoon or fork until pale yellow. Very slowly, while whisking the milk, pour into the pan, then cook over a low heat, stirring constantly in the same direction to avoid any lumps, until it thickens and easily coats the back of a spoon, about 10 minutes. Do not let the milk boil. Strain through a fine-mesh sieve or chinois into dessert bowls. Serve warm or leave to cool, cover with cling film (plastic wrap) and refrigerate until chilled.

Milk Pudding with Steamed Dried Apricots and Chopped Almonds

ALGERIA, LIBYA, TUNISIA
PREPARATION TIME: 5 minutes,
plus cooling and chilling time
COOKING TIME: 30 minutes
SERVES: 4

A classic milky pudding thickened with cornflour (cornstarch), *palouza* has a freshness to it that makes it a favourite on Ramadan evenings. This version is aromatized with orange blossom water or rose water and decorated with dried apricots softened by steaming. Allow time for the pudding to fully chill before serving.

  4 tablespoons cornflour (cornstarch)
  1 litre (34 fl oz/4¼ cups) cold full-fat (whole) milk
  4–6 tablespoons sugar
  1 tablespoon orange blossom water or rose water
  6 dried apricots
  chopped almonds

Put the cornflour (cornstarch) and milk into a large saucepan and stir to dissolve, then add the sugar and cook over a low heat, stirring constantly with a wooden spoon, until thickened, about 20 minutes. It should be light and velvety and coat the back of the spoon. Stir in the orange blossom water, then pour into the ramekins. Leave to cool, then refrigerate for at least 2 hours until well chilled.

Bring a medium steamer pot or couscoussier to the boil with about 7.5 cm/3 inches water, put the apricots into the steamer basket, snugly cover with a lid and steam until soft, 6–8 minutes. Remove from the heat and once cool enough to handle, chop into small pieces.

Before serving, sprinkle the apricots and almonds over the top of the pudding.

Sorghum Pudding with Hazelnuts and Sesame Seeds

TUNISIA
PREPARATION TIME: 15 minutes
COOKING TIME: 30 minutes
SERVES: 6–8

Bouza is a popular dessert made from gluten-free sorghum flour (*droo*) and ground nuts. You can make it with either hazelnuts or sesame seeds, though the classic version uses both. Grind the nuts very well. It can be served chilled as a cream to eat with a spoon or warm as a thick drink. This is the loose, almost liquidy version served in glasses. It is especially popular during Ramadan.

  125 g/4¼ oz (¾ cup) sorghum flour
  100 g/3½ oz (⅔ cup) hazelnuts
  75 g/2¾ oz (½ cup) toasted sesame seeds
  500 ml/18 fl oz (2 cups) milk
  100 g/3½ oz (½ cup) sugar
  rose water or geranium flower water, to dash, optional
  ground pistachios and/or almonds, to decorate

Put the sorghum flour and 750 ml (25 fl oz/3 cups) water into a large bowl and whisk thoroughly until smooth and combined. Set aside.

Put the hazelnuts into a medium ungreased frying pan and dry-toast over a low heat until warm and aromatic, 3–4 minutes. Rub off the skins if needed with your fingers or a clean dish towel and leave to cool. Put the hazelnuts into a food processor and grind into a fine, oily paste, then spoon into a large bowl. Put the sesame seeds into the food processor and grind to a fine and oily paste, then spoon into the bowl. Add 4–5 tablespoons water and blend with a whisk.

Add the milk, sugar, sorghum mixture and the hazelnut-sesame seed mixture to a large saucepan and bring to a gentle boil over a medium heat, stirring constantly, about 20 minutes. It should be loose and semi-liquidy. Dash with rose water (if using). Pour into glasses and top with ground nuts. Serve warm or leave to cool.

Orange Blossom- and Cinnamon-scented Flan

ALGERIA, MOROCCO
PREPARATION TIME: 15 minutes, plus
steeping, cooling and chilling time
COOKING TIME: 1 hour 30 minutes
SERVES: 6

Flan is popular across much of North Africa and
that might show some European influence, but
the dessert often gets a local twist, such as being
scented with orange blossom water (*ma zhar*).
Cooks prepare either a single, family-size flan
or individual ramekins, as in this recipe. (The
150–175 ml-/5–6 fl oz-size ramekins are ideal here.)
When adding warm milk to the egg mixture, do
so very slowly, whisking constantly to keep the
eggs from curdling. The orange blossom water
can be replaced by infusing citrus peels in the milk.
Remove and discard the peels before whisking into
the egg mixture.

500 ml/18 fl oz (2 cups) full-fat (whole) milk
½ cinnamon stick or piece of cinnamon bark
1½ teaspoons orange blossom water
220 g/7½ oz (generous 1 cup) sugar
5 large eggs

Preheat the oven to 150 °C/300 °F/Gas Mark 2.
Arrange 6 ramekins or custard cups in a medium
baking pan.

Bring the milk and cinnamon to a simmer in a
medium saucepan over a low heat; do not let it
boil. Remove from the heat and leave to steep for
15 minutes. Remove and discard the cinnamon and
stir in the orange blossom water.

Meanwhile, put 110 g (3¾ oz/½ cup) of the
sugar and 60 ml (2 fl oz/¼ cup) water into a small
saucepan and cook over a medium-high heat, stirring
just until the sugar dissolves. Reduce the heat to
medium and let the sugar syrup simmer, without
stirring, until it turns a deep amber caramel, about
15 minutes. Immediately pour the caramel into the
ramekins, tilting them to evenly coat the bottoms
before the caramel sets.

Put the eggs and remaining 110 g (3¾ oz/½ cup)
of sugar into a large bowl and beat together with
electric beaters. Slowly whisk in the warm milk,
avoiding creating bubbles. Strain through a fine-
mesh sieve into a bowl, then ladle into the ramekins.

Bring a kettle or saucepan of water to the boil and
pour enough hot water into the baking pan to reach
at least halfway up the sides of the ramekins. Bake in
the hot oven until a knife inserted into a flan comes
out clean, 50 minutes–1 hour. Remove the ramekins
from the oven and leave to cool to room temperature
on a wire rack. Refrigerate until well chilled.

To serve, run a thin knife around each flan. Cover
each flan with an inverted dessert plate and, jiggling
to release the flan, gently unmould, letting the caramel
run over the flans.

Hazelnut Pudding
with Rose Water Crème

TUNISIA
PREPARATION TIME: 30 minutes, plus
resting, cooling and chilling time
COOKING TIME: 30 minutes
SERVES: 6–8

For Mawlid al-Nabi (the birthday of the Prophet
Muhammad), Tunisians traditionally prepare *assida
zgougou*, a dessert made from the black seeds of
Aleppo pine (page 387). But there are other creamy
puddings often served for the occasion as well,
including this one made of ground hazelnuts called
assida boufriwa. The hazelnut version is sweeter and
particularly popular with children. It is two layers
– the top a classic *crème pâtissière* (pastry cream)
scented with rose water or geranium water.

For the hazelnut pudding:
250 g/9 oz (2 cups) hazelnuts
100 g/3½ oz (⅔ cup) plain (all-purpose) flour
100 g/3½ oz (½ cup) sugar
500 ml/18 fl oz (2 cups) milk
whole, chopped and ground nuts (pine nuts, almonds,
　hazelnuts, etc), to decorate

For the rose water crème:
2 tablespoons cornstarch (cornflour)
250 ml/8 fl oz (1 cup) milk
1 large egg yolk
3 tablespoons sugar
1 teaspoon rose water or geranium water, or more
　to taste

TO MAKE THE HAZELNUT PUDDING: Put
the hazelnuts into a large ungreased frying pan and
dry-toast over a low heat until warm and aromatic,
3–4 minutes. Rub off the skins if needed with your
fingers or a clean dish towel and leave to cool. Put
the hazelnuts into a food processor and grind into
a fine, oily paste, then spoon into a large bowl. Add
the flour, sugar and 750 ml (25 fl oz/3 cups) water
and mix well using an electric beater or blender.
Leave to stand for 1 hour, then add the milk and
mix again.

　Transfer the mixture to a large saucepan and
cook over a low heat, stirring constantly in the same
direction, until the cream thickens and can easily
coat the back of a spoon, about 15 minutes. Divide
among dessert cups or bowls, leaving room for a top
layer of cream, and leave to cool.

PREPARE THE ROSE WATER CRÈME: Put the
cornflour (cornstarch) and a couple of tablespoons
of the milk into a small bowl and whisk together
until smooth, then set aside. Put the egg yolk, sugar
and remaining milk into a large saucepan and whisk
together. Stir in the cornflour mixture and cook over
a low heat, stirring constantly in the same direction
to avoid any lumps, until it thickens and easily coats
the back of a spoon, about 8 minutes. Do not let it
boil. Stir in the rose water, remove from the heat and
leave to cool for a few minutes while stirring.

　Strain through a fine-mesh sieve or chinois, then
pour a layer of cream on top of each cup. Cover with
cling film (plastic wrap) and refrigerate until chilled.
Decorate the top of each cup with nuts. Serve.

Cream of Aleppo Pine Nuts

TUNISIA
PREPARATION TIME: 30 minutes,
plus cooling and chilling time
COOKING TIME: 40 minutes
SERVES: 10

Assida zgougou (Aleppo pine nut pudding) is one the most famous Tunisian desserts, and practically required for Mawlid al-Nabi (the birthday of the Prophet Muhammad). It is also one of the most laborious when making from the tiny black seeds of the Aleppo pine tree, an irregular-shaped, native conifer that grows across Mediterranean North Africa. Today, more home cooks are using commercially sold Aleppo pine paste – look for packages that read 'Pâte de Graines de Pin d'Alep Zgougou' or just 'Pâte Zgougou'. The sugar should be added at the end, as it will keep the pudding a darker colour instead of a greyish hue.

For the nuts:
500 g/1 lb 2 oz Aleppo pine paste
250 g/9 oz (1⅔ cups) plain (all-purpose) flour
225 g/8 oz (generous 1 cup) sugar
toasted almonds, whole or ground, to decorate
toasted hazelnuts, whole or ground, to decorate
pistachios, whole or ground, to decorate

For the pastry cream:
1 large egg yolk
3 tablespoons sugar
2 tablespoons cornflour (cornstarch)
250 ml/8 fl oz (1 cup) milk
geranium water, for dashing, optional

PREPARE THE NUTS: Put the pine paste and 2 litres (68 fl oz/generous 2 quarts/8½ cups) water into a blender and blend well. Strain twice through a sieve into a large saucepan. Pour 500 ml (18 fl oz/2 cups) water into a large bowl and whisk in the flour, then add to the saucepan. Cook over a low heat, while stirring constantly, until it thickens and can coat the back of a wooden spoon, about 30 minutes. Stir in the sugar and cook for another 1–2 minutes. Remove from the heat. Divide among dessert cups, glasses or bowls, leaving room at the top for a layer of cream, and leave to cool.

PREPARE THE PASTRY CREAM: Put the egg yolk and sugar into a large bowl and beat together with electric beaters. or use a stand mixer fitted with a whisk attachment. Put the cornflour (cornstarch) into a small bowl, add a couple of tablespoons of the milk and whisk together until smooth, then whisk it into the egg-sugar mixture. Whisk in the remaining milk and pour into a large saucepan. Cook over a very low heat, stirring constantly in the same direction to avoid any lumps, until it thickens and easily coats the back of a wooden spoon, about 8 minutes. Do not let it boil. Remove from the heat, add the geranium water (if using) and leave to cool for a few minutes while stirring. Strain the pastry cream through a fine-mesh sieve or chinois.

Pour a layer of cream on top of each cup and leave to cool. Cover with cling film (plastic wrap) and refrigerate until chilled. Before serving, decorate the top of each cup with almonds, hazelnuts and pistachios. Serve very cold.

Creamy Pudding with Fried Cigars

TUNISIA
PREPARATION TIME: 30 minutes
COOKING TIME: 25 minutes
SERVES: 4

Another classic Tunisian dessert, *zriga* is prepared
in two parts: creamy pudding and fried cigars. It
is very popular during Ramadan, when it is made
during the day and put in the refrigerator to chill
fully for the evening. It is standard to place a couple
of 'cigars' upright in the dessert glasses before
pouring in the pudding, although some like to cut
up a few cigars and also put pieces into the bottom
of the glasses.

For the cigars:
melted butter, for greasing and brushing
50 g/2 oz (scant ½ cup) ground almonds
50 g/2 oz (scant ½ cup) ground hazelnuts
50 g/2 oz (scant ½ cup) icing (confectioners') sugar
1 tablespoon geranium water or rose water
3 round *warka*, *brick* or *dioul* leaves (see page 56),
    spring roll wrappers or filo (phyllo) sheets

For the pudding:
2 large egg yolks
3 tablespoons sugar
3 tablespoons cornstarch (cornflour)
500 ml/18 fl oz (2 cups) milk
1 teaspoon geranium water or rose water
ground pistachios, to decorate, optional

PREPARE THE CIGARS: Preheat the oven to
180 °C/350 °F/Gas Mark 4. Butter a small–medium
baking dish and set aside. Put the almonds, hazelnuts
and sugar into a large bowl and mix together. Add
the geranium water while forming a compact paste
that can hold together. Unroll the pastry sheets on
a clean, flat work counter and cut into quarters.
Arrange a couple of the pieces with the wide, round
end facing you and generously brush with melted
butter. Take 1 tablespoon of the filling (15 g/½ oz),
roll it into an oblong shape about 7.5 cm/3 inches in
length and place at the bottom of a piece. Fold the
sides overlapping to meet in the centre, then roll
like a cigar to the end. Repeat with the remaining
pastry pieces and filling. You should have 10–12
cigars in total. Place the rolls in the prepared baking
dish and bake in the hot oven until golden, about
15 minutes. Place 1 or 2 cigars upright in each dessert
glass and set the remainder aside.

PREPARE THE PUDDING: Put the egg yolks and
sugar into a large saucepan and beat together, then
add the cornflour (cornstarch). Whisk in the milk
and cook over a very low heat, stirring constantly
in the same direction to avoid any lumps, until it
thickens and easily coats the back of a spoon, about
8 minutes. Do not let it boil. Stir in the geranium
water, remove from the heat and leave to cool
for a few minutes while stirring. Pour into the
dessert glasses, then leave to cool. Refrigerate until
chilled. Serve chilled, decorated with some ground
pistachios (if using) and with the remaining cigars
on the side.

Fresh Figs with Orange Glaze

MOROCCO
PREPARATION TIME: 10 minutes
COOKING TIME: 20 minutes
SERVES: 4

This lovely dessert is as delicious as it is colourful, blending the deep orange of orange juice with some of the figs' purple hue. The simmered figs are excellent with plain yoghurt as well as vanilla ice cream.

250 ml/8 fl oz (1 cup) fresh orange juice
1½ tablespoons honey
8 ripe fresh figs
unsweetened plain yoghurt, to serve

Put the orange juice into a medium saucepan and stir in the honey. Set the figs in the pan and bring to a gentle boil. Reduce the heat to medium and gently simmer until tender but not falling apart, about 8 minutes. Carefully transfer the figs with a slotted spoon to a plate. There should be about 250 ml (8 fl oz/1 cup) of liquid. Increase the heat to high and reduce it by half to a runny glaze, 6–8 minutes.

Arrange the figs on 4 dessert plates and drizzle over the glaze. Serve warm with yoghurt.

Whole Stewed Figs in Syrup

ALGERIA
PREPARATION TIME: 5 minutes,
plus cooling time
COOKING TIME: 15 minutes
SERVES: 4–5

When they hit peak season, the bounty of figs is enjoyed fresh but also preserved, as jam (page 405) for instance. This fig dish is the simplest of the preserving ones. The figs are stewed whole in a syrup and meant to be eaten within a week.

50 g/2 oz (¼ cup) sugar
10 ripe fresh figs (about 450 g/1 lb total)

Sterilize a 1-litre (34-fl oz) wide-mouthed glass canning jar and lid (see page 462).

Bring 250 ml (8 fl oz/1 cup) water to the boil with the sugar in a medium heavy saucepan, stirring to dissolve. Reduce the heat to medium-low. Gently set the figs in the pan and cook, turning carefully with a pair of spoons just a few times, until the figs are tender but not splitting apart, about 10 minutes. Remove the figs with a slotted spoon and place on a plate to cool. Remove the pan from the heat and leave the syrup to cool.

Carefully put the figs into the glass jar and pour over the syrup. Wipe the jar clean and, once completely cooled, close with the lid. Store in the refrigerator and use within 1 week. Serve the figs with some syrup spooned over the top.

Candied Oranges in Syrup

ALGERIA
PREPARATION TIME: 15 minutes, plus
overnight soaking and cooling time
COOKING TIME: 1 hour 25 minutes
SERVES: 4

These stewed orange quarters take time to make, as they require overnight soaking. But they are delicious, especially when served with plain yoghurt or a simple cake, such as Sponge Cake (page 376).

2 thick-skinned oranges
450 g/1 lb (2¼ cups) sugar

The day before, completely remove the zest from the oranges with either a knife or citrus zester and discard. Do not peel. Rinse under cold running water. Put the oranges into a large pot of water and leave to soak overnight, changing the water a couple of times. The next day, drain and rinse.

Bring a large pot or saucepan of water to the boil, add the oranges and boil until tender to the touch and before they split, about 20 minutes. Drain and once cool enough to handle, cut lengthwise into quarters. Remove any pips and trim the ends and tough cores.

Bring 250 ml (8 fl oz/1 cup) water and the sugar to the boil in a large, heavy saucepan, stirring to dissolve the sugar. Carefully set the oranges into the pot, reduce the heat to low and cook until the quarters are tender and the liquid syrupy, 45 minutes–1 hour. Remove from the heat and leave to cool.

Transfer to a bowl and leave to cool completely. Cover with cling film (plastic wrap) and store in the refrigerator. Eat within 1 week.

Spicy Stewed Pears

MOROCCO
PREPARATION TIME: 10 minutes,
plus cooling time
COOKING TIME: 25 minutes
SERVES: 4–6

The heady flavours of the spice market come through in these sweetened pears. With hints of cardamom, cloves, cinnamon and ginger, these pears make for a perfect dessert.

    6 ripe but firm large pears (about 1.2 kg/2½ lb total),
        peeled, halved lengthwise and cored
    120 ml/4 fl oz (½ cup) fresh orange juice
    6 tablespoons sugar
    6 cardamom pods, gently crushed
    4 cloves
    ½ cinnamon stick or piece of cinnamon bark
    generous pinch of ground ginger
    2 tablespoons fresh lemon juice

Put the pears into a large saucepan, add 120 ml (4 fl oz/½ cup) water, cover with a lid and bring to the boil. Steam until they soften, 5–15 minutes, depending on their firmness. Add more water if necessary to keep the saucepan from drying out. Transfer with a slotted spoon to a dish.

Bring 250 ml (8 fl oz/1 cup) water to the boil in a large sauté pan that will hold the pears in a single layer. Add the orange juice, sugar, cardamom, cloves, cinnamon and ginger and cook, stirring frequently, over a high heat until reduced by half, about 10 minutes. Stir in the lemon juice and remove from the heat.

Gently set the pears into the pan, turning to coat with the syrup. Leave to cool, basting the pears from time to time. Serve in shallow bowls drizzled with the aromatic syrup.

Stewed Prunes and Dried Apricots

ALGERIA
PREPARATION TIME: 5 minutes,
plus soaking time
COOKING TIME: 35 minutes
SERVES: 4–6

While not exactly a dessert, prunes and dried apricots stewed in an aromatic syrup are often served towards the end of the meal in parts of Algeria. The name of the dish is fitting: *tajine hlou* or *marka hlou*, 'sweet stew'. Dipping bread into the rich, golden sauce is a deep pleasure. They are particularly famous for following *berkoukès* (Stewed Pasta Pellets, page 228) to give the needed burst of sugar to fight off the sleepiness that this type of filling, comforting dish can induce.

    200 g/7 oz (1½ cups) dried apricots
    200 g/7 oz (1½ cups) prunes, preferably with stones
        (pits)
    2 tablespoons sugar
    50 g/2 oz (3⅓ tablespoons) butter
    1 teaspoon ground ginger
    pinch of saffron threads, crumbled
    ½ teaspoon ground cinnamon
    juice of 1 orange
    1 tablespoon orange blossom water

Put the apricots into a large bowl, cover with warm water and leave to soak for 30 minutes to soften; drain.

Put the apricots, prunes, sugar, butter, ginger, saffron, cinnamon and orange juice into a large saucepan and add 120 ml (4 fl oz/½ cup) or just enough water to cover. Bring to the boil, reduce the heat and simmer until the apricots and prunes are tender and the sauce glazy, about 30 minutes. Add a touch more water if needed during cooking. Stir in the orange blossom water, then spoon into a large bowl and serve.

Pomegranate Seeds with Tangerine Juice and Rose Water

ALGERIA, LIBYA, MOROCCO, TUNISIA
PREPARATION TIME: 15 minutes,
plus chilling time
SERVES: 4–6

When pomegranates are in season in October, a bowl of seeds moistened with rose (or orange blossom) water is one of the most common desserts on the table of many homes in North Africa, especially in Tunisia and Libya. Sometimes, as it is also the season for citruses, the juice of tangerines, clementines or an orange is added, too. While some use a heavy hand with rose water or orange blossom water, the unaccustomed should be more prudent.

- 2 ripe pomegranates
- 2 tangerines or clementines or ½ orange
- ½ lemon
- dash of rose water or orange blossom water
- 1–2 teaspoons icing (confectioners') sugar, optional

Seed the pomegranates and remove any pieces of white pith. Put into a large bowl. Juice the tangerines and lemon, add the rose water and icing (confectioners') sugar (if using) and toss to blend. Cover with cling film (plastic wrap) and refrigerate for at least 30 minutes to chill and allow the flavours to meld. Toss again, spoon into individual bowls and serve.

Pomegranate Seeds with Orange Blossom Water

ALGERIA
PREPARATION TIME: 15 minutes,
plus chilling time
SERVES: 4–6

In eastern Algeria, this way of serving fresh pomegranate seeds is popular. While some like to prepare a light syrup, it is enough to simply moisten the grains with orange blossom water, sprinkle with icing (confectioners') sugar and leave them to macerate and chill. Note that if you do make a syrup, leave it to cool before pouring over the pomegranate seeds. This will ensure that the seeds remain firm and fresh without turning a brownish colour from the heat.

- 2 ripe pomegranates
- 1–2 tablespoons icing (confectioners') sugar
- 1–2 tablespoons orange blossom water
- mint leaves, to decorate

Seed the pomegranates and remove any pieces of white pith. Put into a small bowl, sprinkle with the icing (confectioners') sugar and drizzle with orange blossom water. Toss well. Cover with cling film (plastic wrap) and refrigerate for at least 30 minutes to chill and macerate. Toss again, spoon into individual bowls, decorate with a few mint leaves and serve.

Fruit Salad with Orange Blossom Water

ALGERIA, TUNISIA
PREPARATION TIME: 15 minutes,
plus chilling time
SERVES: 6

This macerated fruit salad adds a touch of orange blossom water to lift the aromas. You can use whatever fruits are in season, including apricots, peaches, oranges, apples, pears, bananas and strawberries.

- 1 kg/2¼ lb assorted seasonal fresh fruit
- 2 tablespoons sugar
- 1 tablespoon fresh lemon juice
- 1 tablespoon orange blossom water
- mint leaves, to decorate

Peel and stone (pit) the fruit as needed. Cut into bite-size pieces and put into a large bowl. Sprinkle with the sugar, lemon juice and orange blossom water and toss well. Cover with cling film (plastic wrap) and refrigerate for at least 30 minutes to chill and macerate. Toss again, spoon into individual bowls, decorate with mint and serve.

Aromatic Orange Slices with Golden Sultanas

MOROCCO
PREPARATION TIME: 10 minutes,
plus chilling and soaking time
SERVES: 4–6

This is one of the most popular desserts in Morocco. It's simple, refreshing and an ideal way to finish a meal. Add a dash of orange blossom water for an extra punch. Morocco's orange growers favour two varieties. Maroc Late is a late-maturing orange with a thick, easy-to-peel rind and high rate of sweet juice. Classic soft and sweet navel oranges are also used.

    4 ripe sweet oranges
    juice of ½ lemon
    1 teaspoon sugar
    pinch of ground cinnamon, plus extra for dusting
    35 g/1¼ oz (¼ cup) golden sultanas (golden raisins)
    mint leaves, to decorate

Trim off the top and bottom ends of the oranges and reserve. Working over a large bowl to catch any juices, peel and remove the white pith. Cut crosswise into 5 or so slices about 1 cm/½ inch thick and transfer to a large bowl.

In a bowl, juice the reserved ends, then add the lemon juice, sugar and cinnamon and whisk until the sugar is dissolved. Pour over the orange slices, turning to coat. Cover with cling film (plastic wrap) and refrigerate until chilled.

Put the golden sultanas (golden raisins) into a small bowl, cover with lukewarm water and leave to soak for about 10 minutes to soften; drain.

Divide the oranges slices among dessert plates, overlapping as needed. Spoon any remaining juice over the top and dust with cinnamon. Scatter over the sultanas and decorate with a couple of mint leaves. Serve.

Oranges with Cinnamon and Orange Blossom Water

ALGERIA
PREPARATION TIME: 10 minutes,
plus chilling time
SERVES: 4

This is another version of the popular North African dessert that is simple and a perfect way to end a hearty meal. It's both fresh and refreshing. A dash or two of orange blossom water should be enough.

    3 ripe sweet oranges
    orange blossom water, for dashing
    icing (confectioners') sugar, for dusting
    ground cinnamon, for dusting

Trim off the top and bottom ends of the oranges and reserve. Working over a large bowl to catch any juices, peel and remove the white pith. Cut the oranges crosswise into 5 or so slices about 1 cm/½ inch thick. Pull the segments into triangular pieces, then drop into the bowl. Squeeze the reserved ends over the top and dash with orange blossom water. Cover with cling film (plastic wrap) and refrigerate until chilled.

Toss the orange segments and arrange in a serving dish. Drizzle over all the juices from the bowl, generously dust with icing (confectioners') sugar and cinnamon and serve.

Orange Slices in Syrup

ALGERIA
PREPARATION TIME: 10 minutes,
plus cooling and chilling time
COOKING TIME: 1 hour 5 minutes
SERVES: 4

From Algeria – a country of oranges, growing over
1.2 million tons of the fruit a year – comes these
quick candied orange slices. They are delightful
served with plain yoghurt.

4 ripe oranges, preferably unwaxed or organic
150 g/5 oz (¾ cup) sugar
2 cloves

Scrub the peels of 3 of the oranges. Trim the top and
bottom ends and reserve. Cut crosswise into 1-cm-
/½-inch-thick slices. Remove any pips. Juice the
reserved ends and remaining orange.

Add the orange juice, sugar and 120 ml (4 fl oz/
½ cup) water to a wide pan and bring to the boil,
stirring to dissolve the sugar. Gently set the orange
slices into the pan with the cloves, then reduce the
heat to low and simmer, uncovered, until tender and
the syrup thickened, about 1 hour. Add more water if
needed to keep it from drying out. Remove from the
heat and leave to cool in the pan. Spoon into a large
bowl and refrigerate until chilled. Serve chilled in
small dessert bowls.

Dates Stuffed with Almond Paste

ALGERIA, MOROCCO, TUNISIA
PREPARATION TIME: 10 minutes
MAKES: 12 stuffed dates

One of North Africa's best-known sweet treats,
dates stuffed with almond paste are a staple. Some
like to give them a more festive presentation by
colouring the almond paste with drops of red, green
or yellow food colouring or pressing pine nuts into
the top of the paste in a pattern. Medjool dates are
the ideal variety here. Large (up to 30 g/1 oz each),
soft and very sweet, they are considered the king
of the dates. While traditionally the stuffing goes
lengthwise across the side of the date, it has become
trendy lately to stuff the dates from the end.

12 large sweet dates, such as the medjool variety
100 g/3½ oz (generous ¾ cup) ground almonds
3 tablespoons icing (confectioners') sugar
2 teaspoons orange blossom water
sugar, for rolling, optional

Without completely opening the dates, make an
incision lengthwise along the side of each date or
at the end and remove the stone (pit) and stem.

Put the ground almonds, icing (confectioners')
sugar and orange blossom water into a medium bowl
and mix together. Add 2–3 teaspoons water and work
into a slightly moist paste.

Make 12 spherical pellets a touch smaller than
the dates, then tuck inside the dates so that the
filling bulges out of the opening. Put enough sugar
for rolling (if using) into a small dish and roll the
dates in it until well coated. Arrange on a plate
and serve. Store in an airtight container in the
refrigerator. Allow the stuffed dates to return to
room temperature before serving. They are best
eaten within 1 week.

Chocolate-covered Dates

TUNISIA
PREPARATION TIME: 15 minutes,
plus chilling time
COOKING TIME: 5 minutes
MAKES: 12 covered dates

From the southern oases that grow dates to the
capital Tunis in the north, chocolate-covered dates
have become a popular, energy-filled family snack.
The butter filling makes them especially rich.

12 large sweet dates, such as the deglet nour
    or medjool variety
butter, softened, for filling
125 g/4¼ oz dark (semisweet) chocolate, broken
    into pieces

Wipe the dates with a clean dish towel. Without
completely opening the dates, make an incision
across the top of each date and remove the stone
(pit) and stem. Fill each with butter and gently press
closed. Line a plate with baking (parchment) paper.

Put the chocolate into a small heatproof bowl set
over a saucepan of simmering water, making sure
the bottom of the bowl doesn't touch the water, and
melt, about 5 minutes, then remove from the heat.
Or melt in a bowl in the microwave. Using skewers
or a pair of spoons, dip each date into the chocolate
to coat, letting the excess fall back into the pan. Set
the covered dates on the baking paper. Refrigerate
for at least 30 minutes to harden the chocolate. Store
in an airtight container for 1 week.

PRESERVES

Date Syrup

ALGERIA, MOROCCO, LIBYA, TUNISIA
PREPARATION TIME: 30 minutes,
plus cooling
COOKING TIME: 1 hour 30 minutes
MAKES: about 175 ml/6 fl oz (¾ cup)

Known as *ruub* (and frequently also spelled *robb*
or *rob*), date syrup is the rich, caramelly sweetness
extracted from dates. It is also called date honey or
date molasses. While it is prepared in various date-
producing areas of the region, *ruub* is particularly
popular in Libya. Along with being eaten with *assida*
(a thick porridge) for the Mawlid, Libyans also
spread it on bread and use it to sweeten warm milk
(page 428). Because it takes 1 kg/2¼ lb of dates to
get about 350 ml (12 fl oz/1½ cups) of syrup, it is
often made with second-class dates. The traditional
test to see when the syrup is ready was to dribble
a few drops onto white sand: if the droplets kept
their shape and remained on the sand, they were
ready. If they entered the sand easily, they were not.
This test also works with flour. Note that the syrup
will thicken as it cools. If too thick, stir in a small
amount of boiling water.

500 g/1 lb 2 oz dates with stones (pits)

Wash the dates under cold running water and pat
dry with paper towels. Remove the stones (pits)
and tops. Sterilize a 250-ml (8-fl oz) jam jar and
lid (see page 462).

Put the dates into a large, heavy saucepan and
pour in 1 litre (34 fl oz/4¼ cups) water. Bring to
the boil over a high heat. Cover the pan with a lid,
reduce the heat to low and simmer until the dates
are very soft and have begun to dissolve, about 1 hour.
Stir from time to time, and add more water if needed
to keep the dates just covered.

Line a sieve with a large piece of muslin
(cheesecloth) and place over a clean saucepan.
Carefully spoon the mixture into the muslin, then
leave to strain and cool. Once cool enough to handle,
twist the muslin and patiently twist, squeeze and
press as needed in order to extract all of the liquid.

Put the saucepan over a medium heat and simmer
the liquid for 20–30 minutes until it is a shiny, dark
burgundy colour and can coat the back of the spoon.

Pour the syrup into the sterilized jar while still warm,
making sure there is a 1-cm/½-inch head space, then
leave to cool, seal, label and store in the refrigerator.
Use within a few weeks.

Date Jam

ALGERIA, MOROCCO, TUNISIA
PREPARATION TIME: 10 minutes,
plus soaking time
COOKING TIME: 35 minutes
MAKES: 1 × 250-ml/8-fl oz jam jar

Date jam is modern and popular. While adding
orange juice is fairly standard, other seasonings vary
from kitchen to kitchen and can include cinnamon,
nutmeg or cardamom and orange zest to balance
out the sweetness. This is an easy version for a
small batch that can be kept in the refrigerator for
up to a month. If using a very soft and sticky date
variety such as medjool, reduce the amount of sugar
and skip the soaking step. Add a pinch of ground
cloves for more spice, and after removing from the
heat, add a good dash of orange blossom water for
citrusy aromas.

200 g/7 oz pitted dates
100 g/3½ oz (½ cup) sugar
finely grated zest of ½ orange
120 ml/4 fl oz (½ cup) fresh orange juice
generous pinch of cinnamon or grated nutmeg
1 teaspoon orange blossom water, optional

Wipe the dates clean with paper towels, then finely
chop. Put the dates into a large heatproof bowl, pour
in 120 ml (4 fl oz/½ cup) warm water and leave to
soak for 30 minutes. Meanwhile, sterilize a 250-ml
(8-fl oz) jam jar and lid (see page 462).

Put the dates and liquid from the bowl, the sugar,
orange zest and orange juice into a large, heavy
saucepan and bring to a simmer. Reduce the heat to
low and cook, stirring and mashing frequently, until
jammy, about 30 minutes. Remove from the heat and
stir in the cinnamon and orange blossom water.

Spoon the jam into the sterilized jar while still
warm, making sure there is a 1-cm/½-inch head space.
Leave to cool, cover with a lid, label and store
in the refrigerator. It is best used within 1 month.

Chunky Fig Jam

ALGERIA, MOROCCO, TUNISIA
PREPARATION TIME: 10 minutes,
plus macerating time
COOKING TIME: 30 minutes
MAKES: 2 × 250-ml/8-fl oz jam jars

Fig jam is widespread across the Mediterranean arc of North Africa. If the figs are very sweet, use a touch less sugar than called for in the recipe here. Some prefer a smoother jam and purée the figs before cooking, but the chunks in this version are delightful.

500 g /1 lb 2 oz ripe fresh figs
225 g/8 oz (generous 1 cup) sugar
finely grated zest and juice of ½ small lemon
2 cloves

Rinse and wipe the figs with paper towels. Trim the stems and quarter. Put the figs into a large, heavy saucepan, sprinkle over the sugar, lemon zest and juice and then pour in 60 ml (2 fl oz/¼ cup) water. Stir, cover with cling film (plastic wrap) and leave to stand for 1–2 hours.

Meanwhile, sterilize 2 × 250-ml (8-fl oz) jam jars and lids (see page 462). If you don't have a sugar (candy) thermometer, put a few saucers into the freezer to chill to test the jam.

Bring the mixture to the boil over a medium heat, reduce the heat to low and boil for 20–25 minutes until jammy and it reaches the setting temperature of 105 °C/221 °F on a sugar thermometer. Alternatively, check for doneness by putting a dollop onto a cold saucer, leave it to cool for 1 minute, then push the jam with your finger to see if it 'wrinkles'. If it does not, boil for a few more minutes before testing again.

Remove from the heat. Carefully remove the cloves with a spoon, then spoon into the sterilized jars while still warm, making sure there is a 1-cm/½-inch head space. Leave to cool, cover with a lid, label and store in the refrigerator. It is best used within 1 month.

Watermelon Jam

ALGERIA
PREPARATION TIME: 15 minutes,
plus macerating time
COOKING TIME: 1 hour
MAKES: 1 × 280-ml/9-fl oz jam jar

Watermelon jam is a popular homemade *confiture* in Oran, where it is made with classic watermelon in summer and in autumn using a pale-green-fleshed variety called *gingérine*. It is excellent on yoghurt or ice cream, and with simple cakes. For some home cooks it is a combination of frugality, practicality and *goût* (taste); they don't use only the prime red flesh of the fruit, but once wedges have been eaten, they cut away the remaining bits of red and the white flesh and use that in the jam. This recipe makes enough for a single jar. Double the amounts if desired. Calculate about half the weight of the trimmed flesh in sugar.

500 g/1 lb 2 oz seeded watermelon flesh
250 g/9 oz (1¼ cups) sugar
finely grated zest and juice of ½ lemon

Sterilize a 280-ml (9-fl oz) jam jar and lid (see page 462). If you don't have a sugar (candy) thermometer, put a few saucers into the freezer to chill to test the jam.

Trim the watermelon, avoiding the hardest white or green parts of the rind, then finely chop. Put into a large bowl, cover with the sugar, then cover with cling film (plastic wrap) and leave to stand for at least 2 hours, stirring from time to time.

Transfer the watermelon and all of its liquid to a large, heavy saucepan with the lemon zest and juice and bring to the boil over a medium heat. Boil for 45 minutes–1 hour until the white pieces turn transparent, the reddish ones darken and the juice coats a spoon with a shiny film. It should reach the setting temperature of 105 °C/221 °F on a sugar thermometer. Alternatively, check for doneness by putting a dollop onto a cold saucer, leave it to cool for 1 minute, then push it with your finger to see if it 'wrinkles'. If it does not, boil for a few more minutes before testing again.

Remove from the heat and leave to cool for a few minutes. Spoon into the sterilized jar while still warm, making sure there is a 1-cm/½-inch head space. Leave to cool, cover with a lid, label and store in the refrigerator. It is best used within 1 month.

Apricot Jam

ALGERIA, TUNISIA
PREPARATION TIME: 15 minutes,
plus macerating time
COOKING TIME: 45 minutes
MAKES: 3 × 300-ml/10-fl oz jam jars

This is one of the most popular jams in the region, especially in Algeria and Tunisia. It should be sweet with a soft punch of tartness and plenty of perfumed aromas. You can add a couple of cloves at the end. Some cooks like to split the apricot stones (pits) and add them at the beginning of cooking. Add these to the jar – they have a pleasing bitter taste. In Tunisia, it is popular to enjoy apricot jam for breakfast with bread and some good extra-virgin olive oil.

1 kg/2¼ lb ripe apricots
juice of 1 lemon
750 g/1⅔ lb (3¾ cups) sugar

Gently wash the apricots, then remove the stems and stones (pits). Cut each into 4–6 pieces and put into a large bowl. Add the lemon juice and cover with the sugar. Stir, cover with cling film (plastic wrap) and leave to stand for 6–8 hours, stirring from time to time, to draw out the juices and soften the fruit.

Sterilize 3 × 300-ml (10-fl oz) jam jars and lids (see page 462). If you don't have a sugar (candy) thermometer, put a few saucers into the freezer to chill to test the jam.

Add the fruit and everything from the bowl to a large, heavy saucepan and bring to the boil over a medium heat, stirring and skimming off some of the foam that rises to the surface with a slotted spoon. Reduce the heat to medium-low and simmer for 10–15 minutes until the fruit is soft, then turn up the heat, bring to a boil and cook for 10–15 minutes, or until it reaches the setting point of 105 °C/221 °F on a sugar thermometer. Alternatively, check for doneness by putting a dollop of jam onto a cold saucer, leave it to cool for 1 minute, then push the jam with your finger to see if it 'wrinkles'. If it does not, boil for a few more minutes before testing again.

Remove from the heat and spoon into the sterilized jars while still warm, making sure there is a 1-cm/½-inch head space. Leave to cool, cover with a lid, label and store in the refrigerator. It is best used within 1 month.

Spiced Carrot Jam

ALGERIA
PREPARATION TIME: 15 minutes,
plus macerating time
COOKING TIME: 50 minutes
MAKES: 2 × 300-ml/10-fl oz jam jars

The carrots of this jam are more akin to soft, candied grated carrots, and don't need to set like a classic marmalade. Quite versatile, it can be served like a jam or as a relish with cheeses or meats.

500 g/1 lb 2 oz carrots, coarsely grated
    (about 3¾ packed cups)
finely grated zest and juice of 2 clementines
    or tangerines or 1 orange
finely grated zest and juice of 1 lemon
350 g/12 oz (1¾ cups) sugar
4 cloves
4 cardamom pods
⅛ teaspoon ground cinnamon, optional
pinch of salt

Put the carrots, clementine zest and juice and lemon zest and juice into a large bowl. Add the sugar, stir well and leave to stand for 1 hour. Sterilize 2 × 300-ml (10-fl oz) jam jars and lids (see page 462).

Put the mixture into a large, heavy saucepan, add the cloves, cardamom, cinnamon (if using) and salt, then stir in 120 ml (4 fl oz/½ cup) water. Bring to the boil over a medium heat, reduce the heat to low and cook until the carrots are a shiny, ruddy orange and the liquid is syrupy, about 40 minutes.

Remove from the heat and spoon into the sterilized jars while still warm, making sure there is a 1-cm/½-inch head space. Leave to cool, cover with a lid, label and store in the refrigerator. It is best used within 1 month.

There are different methods to preserve the seasonal spoils from the field, farm or sea. Prolonging the life of fresh ingredients to allow them to be stored and used throughout the year, on a voyage or at least before they can go bad has been a challenge from the beginning of humankind.

Using salt is one way. It dehydrates food by drawing out water, which all living things need. For Phoenicians and Romans, developing salt pans went hand-in-hand with their settlements along the North Africa coast. So key was salt that trans-Sahara caravans carried it to trade for gold. Seasoned, sun-dried strips of meat (see page 206), fish or octopus are obvious examples of using it to preserve today. Preserved lemons (page 410), harissa chilli paste (see below) and preserved butter known as *smen* (page 412) also rely on the natural preservative properties of salt.

Olive oil is another way. Among the ample range of items preserved in the region's olive oil are roasted peppers (page 412) and in the Rif Mountains, wild mushrooms. In Algeria, one popular method for preserving sardines (page 335) or aubergine (eggplant, page 153) for a handful of days is *skabitch* (escabeche), an herby, spice-laden vinegar-and-olive oil marinade. While helping to keep these items longer, it also imbues them with deep flavours.

These ancient methods were born out of necessity and honed over centuries to prolong the life of products. And while freezers, easier availability of fresh goods and plenty of commercially canned ones on store shelves have largely rendered away their need, homemade preserves remain hallmarks of the cuisine for the distinctive flavours they offer.

Harissa

TUNISIA
PREPARATION TIME: 30 minutes, plus soaking time
MAKES: 200 g/7 oz (¾ cup), enough for 1 × 250-ml/8-fl oz jar

Tunisia's defining ingredient is harissa, a dense, often tongue-withering paste that is ubiquitous both as an ingredient and a condiment. It calls for dried red chillies (chiles) that are seeded and de-ribbed (this helps tone down some of the heat) and then soaked in water to soften. The name 'harissa' comes from the Arabic word meaning to break into pieces or crush. Tunisians once laboriously pounded the peppers in a mortar to make 'harissa' but today they generally use a hand-crank grinder or food processor. While spices are ground with the chillies, purists only add olive oil to cover the paste once in the jar. This recipe is for a small batch, enough for a 250-ml/8-fl oz jar. Serve it alongside couscous, on *fricassé*, with *bricks* (page 58) or just about any other Tunisian savoury dish. Harissa has become widely popular elsewhere in the Maghreb. See page 98 for more on harissa.

125 g/4¼ oz dried medium-hot red chillies (chiles)
3 cloves of garlic, central germs removed
1 tablespoon ground coriander
2 teaspoons ground cumin
1 teaspoon ground caraway
2 tablespoons salt
olive oil, for covering

Sterilize a 250-ml/8-fl oz glass jar and lid (see page 462). Wearing rubber gloves, wipe the chillies (chiles) with a clean, damp cloth. Stem, seed and tear into pieces, then put into a medium heatproof bowl, cover with boiling water and leave to soften for 30 minutes. Drain well and spread out to dry on paper towels for a few minutes. Purée the chillies (chiles) in a food processor with the garlic, or pound into a paste in a mortar with a pestle. Mix in the coriander, cumin, caraway and salt, and purée or grind again if needed into a smooth paste. Spoon the mixture into the jar and cover with a generous layer of oil, making sure there is a 1-cm/½-inch head space. Close tightly with a lid and label. The harissa will keep in the refrigerator for some months if the paste remains covered with oil.

Preserved Lemons

MOROCCO
PREPARATION TIME: 20 minutes,
plus pickling time
MAKES: 6 preserved lemons

Salt-preserved lemons are one of the iconic
ingredients that define Moroccan cuisine and make
it stand out. Some like to add flavourings when
preserving – such as bay leaves and coriander
seeds. Use thin-skinned, unwaxed organic lemons
because the peel will be used in cooking and they
are easier to pack into wide-mouthed jars. Rinse
thoroughly before using. It is important that they
remain covered in lemon juice. You need to wait
about three weeks before using. They are also used
in Algeria and Tunisia, though less frequently.

  225 g/8 oz (1 cup) fine or pickling salt, or as needed
  10 thin-skinned lemons, preferably unwaxed or
     organic

Sterilize a 1-litre (34-fl oz) wide-mouthed glass canning
jar and lid (see page 462), then sprinkle the bottom
with about 2 tablespoons of salt until covered.

Scrub 6 of the lemons, rinse under cold running
water and dry well with paper towels. Leaving the
bottoms attached, cut lengthwise into quarters.
Gently open, pack with 2–3 heaped teaspoons of salt
and then reshape. Put the lemons into the jar and
press down with a wooden spoon to release some
of their juices. Depending on the size of the lemons
and shape of the jar, you may not use all the lemons.

Leaving a 1-cm/½-inch head space, juice the remaining
lemons into the jar to cover the lemons completely.
Sprinkle over about 2 tablespoons of salt. Cover with
a lid and invert the jar a few times to mix. Label.

Keep in a cool, dark place, turning the jar from
time to time. After a few days, once the lemons have
softened, press down and cover with more lemon
juice if needed. Leave to mature for 3–4 weeks
before using, opening the lid from time to time to
release any pressure that has built up. Remove from
the jar with a clean, dry spoon and rinse the lemons
well before using. Add lemon juice to the jar as needed
to keep the lemons covered. Once opened, store in
the refrigerator for up to 6 months.

Preserved Whole Lemons

TUNISIA
PREPARATION TIME: 5 minutes,
plus pickling time
COOKING TIME: 2 minutes
MAKES: 4–6 preserved lemons

In Tunisia, the traditional way to preserve lemons is
to soak smallish ones whole in a saline solution for
a number of months. The brine should have about
a 10 per cent salt solution. The number of lemons
that will fit depends on their size and the shape of
the jar.

  4–6 smallish, thin-skinned lemons, preferably
     unwaxed or organic
  3 generous tablespoons fine or pickling salt

Sterilize a 1-litre (34-fl oz) wide-mouthed glass canning
jar and lid (see page 462).

Scrub the lemons, rinse under cold running water
and dry well. Put the lemons into the jar.

Pour 500 ml (18 fl oz/2 cups) water into a large
saucepan, add the salt and stir over a low heat until
dissolved. Pour over to completely cover the lemons,
making sure there is a 1-cm/½-inch head space. There
might be some liquid remaining. Close the jar with
a lid and label.

Keep in a cool, dark place, opening the lid
occasionally to release any gases that build up,
especially during the first few weeks. They will be
ready in 6–9 months. They should be darker yellow
and soft. Add more salted water if needed to keep
covered. Once opened, store in the refrigerator for
up to 6 months.

Smen

ALGERIA, MOROCCO
PREPARATION TIME: 10 minutes, plus
overnight resting and maturing time
COOKING TIME: 15 minutes
MAKES: 225 g/8 oz (1 cup)

This clarified and preserved salted butter is used
as a cooking ingredient (rather than a spread on
its own) in couscous, tagines, soups and so on.
The distinctive flavour deepens with time. Always
remove *smen* from the jar with a clean, dry spoon
to prevent bacteria from forming. See page 120 for
more information on *smen*.

> 250 g/9 oz unsalted butter, at room temperature
> 1 tablespoon salt

The night before, put the butter and salt into a
large bowl and knead together with your fingers
or a spoon. Cover with cling film (plastic wrap)
and refrigerate.

The next day, sterilize a 250-ml (8-fl oz) jar and
lid (see page 462). Put the salt butter into a small
saucepan and very slowly melt over a low heat,
skimming off the foam as it rises to the surface with
a slotted spoon. Cook until transparent and the
solids have sunk to the bottom, about 5 minutes.
Do not stir or let the solids darken. Remove from
the heat and let the whitish solids settle. Strain
through muslin (cheesecloth) into the jar, leaving a
1-cm/½-inch head space. Leave to cool completely,
then tightly close the jar with a lid and label. It will
be ready for use after about 1 month. Stored in the
refrigerator, it will keep for 1 year or longer.

Preserved Grilled Red Peppers

ALGERIA, TUNISIA
PREPARATION TIME: 20 minutes,
plus cooling and draining time
COOKING TIME: 40 minutes
MAKES: 1 × 500-ml/18-fl oz jar

This recipe grills (broils) the fresh peppers in the
oven, but you can cook them directly on coals for
pleasing smoky flavours. Letting the peppers cool
while covered or inside a plastic bag makes peeling
them easier. The preserved peppers are lovely with
bread, in salads and as a side to grilled meat. Serve
with chopped garlic and some oil from the jar.

> 1 kg/2¼ lb red bell peppers, or another variety
> 150 ml/5 fl oz (⅔ cup) olive oil, or as needed
> salt
> minced garlic, to serve

Preheat the oven grill (broiler). Arrange the peppers
on a baking sheet and grill (broil), turning as
needed, until charred in places and tender, about
40 minutes. Remove from the grill, put into a large
bowl and snugly cover with cling film (plastic wrap).
Leave to cool in the steam to make peeling easier.

Working one by one, peel, core and seed the
peppers, leaving them in as large pieces as possible.
Place in a colander to drain for 1 hour.

Sterilize a 500-ml (18-fl oz) mason or glass canning
jar and lid (see page 462).

Put the peppers into the jar, season with salt and
cover with olive oil, leaving a 1-cm/½-inch head
space. Close the jar with a lid and label. Store in the
refrigerator and use within 1 month, making sure that
the peppers remain completely submerged in oil. To
serve, place on a dish, scatter over garlic and spoon
over some oil from the jar.

Preserved Roasted Tomatoes with Thyme

ALGERIA
PREPARATION TIME: 20 minutes,
plus cooling time
COOKING TIME: 4–5 hours
MAKES: 2 × 500-ml/18-fl oz jars

This recipe is redolent of a Mediterranean summer on Algeria's coast with a quartet of quintessential local ingredients – tomatoes, garlic, thyme and olive oil. They are slow-roasted without rush to heighten the season's taste.

　1 kg/2¼ lb ripe but firm Roma tomatoes or another
　　variety
　250 ml/8 fl oz (1 cup) plus 3 tablespoons olive oil
　2 tablespoons sugar
　1 teaspoon salt
　8 cloves of garlic, lightly crushed in the skin
　sprigs of thyme

Preheat the oven to 90 °C/194 °F/lowest gas setting. Wash and dry the tomatoes with paper towels, then trim. Cut them in half lengthwise. If the tomatoes are large, remove the seeds with a spoon. Put them into a large bowl.

In a small bowl, whisk together the 3 tablespoons of olive oil with the sugar and salt, then pour over the tomatoes and toss well.

Arrange the tomatoes, skin-side up, in a baking dish. Scatter around the garlic, then strip some thyme leaves from a few branches and generously sprinkle over the top.

Roast in the hot oven for 2 hours. Turn the tomatoes skin-side down and roast until deep red and tender but not collapsing, 2–3 hours. Turn off the oven and leave the tomatoes to gradually cool in the oven.

Meanwhile, sterilize 2 × 500-ml (18-fl oz) wide-mouthed glass canning jars and lids (see page 462).

Gently set the tomatoes in the jars, while layering in the cloves of garlic and pieces of thyme sprigs. Completely cover with the oil, making sure there is a 1-cm/½-inch head space. Close with lids and label the jars. Store in the refrigerator and use within 3 weeks, making sure that the tomatoes remain completely submerged in oil. Serve with some of the oil from the jar.

Preserved Nuts in Honey

TUNISIA
PREPARATION TIME: 15 minutes
MAKES: 1 × 350-ml/12-fl oz jar

Preserving nuts in honey is popular in Tunisia – most commonly walnuts, hazelnuts, cashews and whole almonds with their skins. These are eaten alone by the spoonful in the morning or as a snack in the afternoon with a cup of coffee. It has become popular to add them to yoghurt.

　100 g/3½ oz (1 cup) nuts, or as needed
　225 ml/7¾ fl oz (scant 1 cup) honey, or as needed

Sterilize a 350-ml (12-fl oz) glass canning jar and lid (see page 462).

Wipe the nuts clean with a clean cloth. If using hazelnuts, remove the skins by rubbing them with a cloth and then break in half. If using cashews, split in half lengthwise.

Add the nuts to the jar, jiggling to settle while doing so. Slowly dribble in the honey, jiggling to settle. Close the jar tightly with a lid and label. Store in a cool, dark place. They are best used within 1 month.

DRINKS

MINT TEA

If couscous or a tagine symbolizes Morocco on the plate, then mint tea does so in the glass: scalding hot and golden-amber in colour, sufficiently sweetened to make you a touch thirsty and with enough mint to make the mouth tingle.

Mint tea starts and ends a day, is sipped as a mid-morning and afternoon break, precedes and finishes a meal. With certain heavy dishes – roast lamb, skewers of lamb liver individually wrapped in caul fat (*boulfaf*, page 281), *kefta* (spiced minced/ground meat, page 272) cooked on the barbecue, fried eggs with strips of *khlii* (a confit of dried meat, page 206) – mint tea is served with the meal. Tea is a symbol of generosity and hospitality, sipped when meeting friends and prepared without fail for guests.

There are a number of ways to prepare mint tea, and each house has its own specific method. All are brewed without hurry, eventually pouring the tea back and forth between the pot and a glass as the flavours blend and bloom. Once the perfect balance of strength, sweetness and mintiness is achieved, the silver teapot is held high and the tea poured into small, ornately patterned glasses.

The tea itself is loose leaf Chinese gunpowder green, with its tight, granular roll. To that, Moroccans add sugar (once and still occasionally in chunks broken from conical loafs) and stuff generous handfuls of fresh herbs into the teapot (skipping milk). The key ingredient is mint – technically spearmint, *Mentha spicata*, with narrow, brilliant green leaves.

Often mint is only one of the herbs in the pot. In winter it is typical to also include pale, silvery absinthe leaves (wormwood), marjoram, sage and/or vervain (page 421). Another winter touch is floating some fragrant, brilliant white bitter orange blossoms on the surface of the tea.

In the north of Morocco, people tend to prepare more golden, aromatic versions, lighter toned and more subtle, while Berbers in the High Atlas prepare a bolder brew with plenty of wild herbs. In the deep south, the tea is stronger, darker and served in smaller glasses. Tradition once required drinking three glasses, each getting progressively mellower, as the local proverb goes:

The first glass is as bitter as life,
The second is as strong as love,
The third is as soothing as death.

Although ingredients used in preparing tea tend to be added with a generous hand, they are not simply dumped into the teapot and steeped. Patient and measured, sometimes ceremonious and always artful, the ritualistic preparation in Morocco becomes particularly stylized, as the tea is at last poured into glasses from high above.

But the dramatic pour is more than just a neat trick. Some argue that boiling 'flattens' the water and this is a way to re-aerate it and give it body. Others say it is done to cool the scalding tea, while there are those that claim it's for the small bubbles that form on the surface and cling to the inside curve of the glass and give the tea 'texture' when drunk.

If first we eat with our eyes, then we first drink with our noses. The aroma of mint tea precedes it, and before tasting with the tongue, the nose has already gathered up the bouquet of mint and slightly caramelized aromas from the sugar. But it seems that it is as much for the soothing, cascading sound which adds another sensory layer to the experience. Like a gentle nudge, that sound is a way of saying, 'Attention. Your tea is ready!'

Mint Tea (Steeped Version)

ALGERIA, MOROCCO
PREPARATION TIME: 10 minutes
COOKING TIME: 5 minutes
SERVES: 2–3

Making a pot of *atay bel naânaâ* (mint tea) in Morocco consists of more than dunking a tea bag into a mug of lukewarm water and garnishing with a few leaves of mint. There is ritual and ceremony – plus a generous amount of fresh mint. The most common mistake for those outside the region is using too little of the fresh herb. The mintiness in the tea should leave an almost medicinal tingle in the mouth, and the sweetness a hint of thirst. There are various common methods to prepare mint tea, and every home has its own preferred way. This is a simplified one that just steeps the mint. In springtime, float a few orange blossoms on the surface, if possible.

> 1 tablespoon loose leaf Chinese gunpowder green tea
> 50 g/2 oz mint leaves (about ½ bunch)
> 2 tablespoons sugar, or more to taste

Bring about 750 ml (25 fl oz/3 cups) water to the boil in either a kettle or large saucepan.

Rinse the inside of a stovetop teapot or large saucepan with some of the hot water to warm. Spoon in the tea. Add 120 ml (4 fl oz/½ cup) of the boiling water, swirl for a moment and pour out without letting any leaves escape. Add 500 ml (18 fl oz/2 cups) of the boiling water and simmer for 4–5 minutes. Add the mint leaves, pressing down with a spoon to slightly crush, then add the sugar. Remove the pot from the heat, cover with a lid and leave to steep for 4–5 minutes. Pour some tea into a heatproof glass and return it to the pot to begin blending flavours. Repeat 2 or 3 times. Taste for sweetness and strength. Add more sugar if desired, or leave to steep longer. When the balance is right, immediately pour into tea glasses and serve.

Mint Tea (Simmered Version)

ALGERIA, MOROCCO
PREPARATION TIME: 5 minutes
COOKING TIME: 5 minutes
SERVES: 2–3

While some say you should only steep the mint in tea and never simmer it, as it will give the herb a slightly soured taste, there are those that do exactly that.

> 1 tablespoon loose leaf Chinese gunpowder green tea
> 2 tablespoons sugar, or more to taste
> 50 g/2 oz mint leaves (about ½ bunch)

Rinse the inside of a stovetop teapot or large saucepan. Spoon in the tea. Add 120 ml (4 fl oz/½ cup) water, bring to the boil, swirl and pour out without letting any leaves escape and discard. Add the sugar and mint leaves, pressing down with a spoon to slightly crush. Add 500 ml (18 fl oz/2 cups) water. Bring to a slow boil over a medium-low heat, then simmer for about 3 minutes. Pour some tea into a heatproof glass and return it to the pot to begin blending the flavours. Repeat 2 or 3 times. Taste for sweetness and strength. Add more sugar if desired or leave to simmer longer. When the balance is right, pour into tea glasses and serve.

Mint Tea (Ceremonial Version)

MOROCCO
PREPARATION TIME: 15 minutes
COOKING TIME: 5 minutes
SERVES: 2–4

This is the ceremonial way to prepare mint tea in Morocco, and especially for guests. This method keeps the first rinse of tea leaves known as 'the spirit of the tea' to add it back in later. A second rinse gets discarded. Doing this allows the tea to steep longer without becoming bitter.

- 2 heaped tablespoons loose leaf Chinese gunpowder green tea
- 75 g/2¾ oz mint leaves (about ¾ bunch)
- 4 tablespoons sugar, or more to taste

Bring about 1 litre (34 fl oz/4¼ cups) water to the boil in a large saucepan and keep it boiling.

Rinse the inside of a large stovetop teapot or saucepan with some of the boiling water. Spoon in the tea and cover with 175 ml (6 fl oz/¾ cup) of the boiling water. Wait for 1 minute without disturbing, then pour off into a heatproof glass without letting any leaves escape; set aside. Add 175 ml (6 fl oz/¾ cup) of the boiling water to the teapot, swirl and immediately pour off without letting any leaves escape and discard the liquid.

Return the reserved glass of liquid to the teapot along with 500 ml (18 fl oz/2 cups) of the boiling water. Simmer over a low heat for 5 minutes. Remove the teapot from the heat. Stuff the mint leaves into the pot, pressing down with a spoon to slightly crush, then add the sugar. Close the lid and leave to steep for 4–5 minutes.

Pour some tea into a glass and return it to the pot to begin blending the flavours. Repeat 2 or 3 times. Taste for sweetness and strength. Add more sugar if desired or leave to steep longer. When the balance is right, pour into tea glasses from as high as possible and serve.

Mint Tea with Toasted Pine Nuts

TUNISIA
PREPARATION TIME: 10 minutes
COOKING TIME: 3 minutes
SERVES: 2–3

While synonymous with Morocco, mint tea is also common in Tunisia. It has one major difference: some pine nuts are added to the glass. Some Tunisians prefer to add whole almonds with their skins slipped off (see page 445).

- 10 g/¼ oz (2 teaspoons) pine nuts
- 1 heaped teaspoon loose leaf Chinese gunpowder green tea
- 1 tablespoon sugar, or more to taste
- 50 g/2 oz mint (about ½ large bunch), plus extra sprigs to garnish

Put the pine nuts into a small ungreased frying pan and lightly dry-toast over a low heat for 2–3 minutes without letting them change colour, shaking the pan from time to time. Divide among 2–3 tea glasses.

Bring about 750 ml (25 fl oz/3 cups) water to the boil in a large saucepan. Rinse a teapot with some of the boiling water to warm it. Put the tea and sugar into the pot. Crush the mint and stuff it into the pot. Pour in 400 ml (14 fl oz/1⅔ cups) of the boiling water, cover with a lid and leave to steep for 5 minutes. Pour some tea into a heatproof glass and return it to the pot to begin blending the flavours. Repeat 2 or 3 times. Taste for sweetness and strength. Add more sugar if desired or leave to steep longer. Pour into the glasses, garnish with a few sprigs of mint and serve.

Mint Tea with Fresh Almonds

TUNISIA
PREPARATION TIME: 20 minutes
COOKING TIME: 5 minutes
SERVES: 2–3

This is another way to prepare tea in Tunisia. The almonds are a delightful touch. Use whole – raw and untoasted – almonds. It only takes a few minutes of soaking in boiling water to easily remove the almond skins.

12–16 whole almonds
1 heaped teaspoon loose leaf Chinese gunpowder green tea
1 tablespoon sugar, or more to taste
50 g/2 oz mint (about ½ large bunch), plus extra sprigs to garnish

Put the almonds into a small heatproof bowl, cover with boiling water and leave to soak for about 5 minutes, or until the skins easily slip off. Drain and peel off the skins. Divide among 2–3 tea glasses.

Rinse the inside of a stovetop teapot or large saucepan with boiling water. Spoon in the tea. Add 120 ml (4 fl oz/ ½ cup) water, bring to the boil, swirl, then pour out without letting any leaves escape and discard. Pour in about 500 ml (18 fl oz/2 cups) water, bring to the boil over a medium-low heat, then simmer for about 5 minutes, or until the desired strength of the tea is reached. Remove from the heat, stir in the sugar and add the mint, pressing down with a spoon to slightly crush it. Leave to steep for a few minutes, then begin pouring the tea into a heatproof glass and returning it to the pot to blend the flavours. Repeat a number of times. Taste for sweetness and strength. Pour into the tea glasses and serve ganrished with mint sprigs.

High Atlas Tea with Fresh Herbs

MOROCCO
PREPARATION TIME: 10 minutes
COOKING TIME: 5 minutes
SERVES: 2–3

Especially in the Atlas, and especially during winter, mint is only one of the fresh herbs in the pot. Marjoram, sage, vervain and a sprig of absinthe (*shiba*) go in alongside a generous handful of mint.

1 sprig absinthe (wormwood), optional
1 tablespoon loose leaf Chinese gunpowder green tea
25 g/1 oz mint leaves
sprigs vervain
sprigs sage
sprigs marjoram
3 tablespoons sugar, or more to taste

Bring about 1 litre (34 fl oz/4¼ cups) water to the boil in a large saucepan and keep it boiling.

Meanwhile, put the absinthe (if using) into a heatproof glass, cover with 120 ml (4 fl oz/½ cup) of the boiling water and leave to steep for 2–3 minutes to remove the bitterness. Drain, discarding the liquid.

Rinse out a stovetop teapot or large saucepan with some of the boiling water to warm. Put the tea into the pot, add 120 ml (4 fl oz/½ cup) of the boiling water, swirl for a moment, then pour out without letting any leaves escape and discard. Add 750 ml (25 fl oz/3 cups) of the boiling water to the pot and gently boil over a medium heat for 3–4 minutes. Add the mint, vervain, sage, marjoram and the steeped absinthe (if using). Push the herbs down with a spoon to slightly crush and sprinkle over the sugar. Remove from the heat, cover with a lid and leave to steep for 3–4 minutes. Pour some tea into a heatproof glass and return it to the pot to begin blending the flavours. Repeat 2 or 3 times. Taste for sweetness and strength. Add more sugar if desired or leave to steep longer. When the balance is right, pour into tea glasses and serve.

Tea with Fresh Absinthe

MOROCCO
PREPARATION TIME: 10 minutes
COOKING TIME: 5 minutes
SERVES: 2–3

Tea with a sprig of absinthe (*shiba*) is a winter favourite, as the silvery-green herb has warming properties. It also has a bitter aftertaste and is usually steeped in some boiling water first before adding. Simmer the tea until the foam changes colour.

> 1 sprig absinthe (wormwood)
> 2 tablespoons loose leaf Chinese gunpowder green tea
> 3 tablespoons sugar, or more to taste

Bring 1 litre (34 fl oz/4¼ cups) water to the boil in a large saucepan or kettle.

Meanwhile, put the absinthe (wormwood) into a large heatproof glass, cover with 250 ml (8 fl oz/1 cup) of the boiling water and leave to steep for 2–3 minutes to remove the bitterness. Drain, discarding the liquid.

Rinse out a stovetop teapot or large saucepan with some of the boiling water to warm. Put the tea and sugar into the teapot, add the remaining 750 ml (25 fl oz/3 cups) boiling water and simmer over a medium heat until the foam changes to a caramel-brown colour, about 5 minutes. Remove from the heat. Add the absinthe, cover with a lid and leave to steep for 2 minutes. Pour some tea into a heatproof glass and return it to the pot to begin blending the flavours. Repeat 2 or 3 times. Taste for sweetness and strength. Add more sugar if desired or leave to steep longer. When the balance is right, pour into tea glasses and serve.

Green Tea with Geranium Leaves and Rosemary

MOROCCO
PREPARATION TIME: 10 minutes
COOKING TIME: 5 minutes
SERVES: 2–3

This is another favourite winter tea, especially in the Drâa Valley in the south of Morocco. Use a scented geranium, such as rose-scented – just enough to hold in the palm of your hand for a small pot of tea. Simmer until the foam changes colour, then add the geranium and rosemary.

> 2 tablespoons loose leaf Chinese gunpowder green tea
> 3 tablespoons sugar, or more to taste
> scented geranium leaves
> 1 sprig rosemary

Bring about 750 ml (25 fl oz/3 cups) water to the boil in a large saucepan or kettle.

Put the tea and sugar into a stovetop teapot or large saucepan and pour over the boiling water. Simmer over a medium heat until the foam changes to a caramel-brown, about 5 minutes. Remove from the heat. Add the geranium and rosemary, cover with a lid and leave to steep for 4–5 minutes. Pour some tea into a heatproof glass and return it to the pot to begin blending the flavours. Repeat 2 or 3 times. Taste for sweetness and strength. Add more sugar if desired or leave to steep longer. When the balance is right, pour into tea glasses and serve.

Saffron Tea

MOROCCO
PREPARATION TIME: 5 minutes
COOKING TIME: 10 minutes
SERVES: 4

While *thé à la menthe* is Morocco's national drink, saffron tea (*atay bel zaâfrane*) is a winter-time favourite around the saffron-producing area of Taliouine (see page 183). It should be bold, sweet and aromatic. Serve in clear tea glasses to fully appreciate its golden colour.

> 10 saffron threads, plus extra to garnish
> 1 tablespoon loose leaf Chinese gunpowder green tea
> 2 tablespoons sugar, or more to taste

Crumble the 10 saffron threads into a stovetop teapot or large saucepan, then pour in 750 ml (25 fl oz/3 cups) cold water. Bring to the boil, remove from the heat and leave to steep for 1 minute. Add the tea and simmer over a low heat for 5 minutes. Remove from the heat and stir in the sugar.

Pour some tea into a heatproof glass and return it to the pot to begin blending the flavours. Repeat 2 or 3 times. The colour should be deep gold. Taste for sweetness and add more sugar if needed. Strain the tea into tea glasses. Place 1 or 2 saffron threads in each glass and serve hot.

Foamy Desert Tea

LIBYA
PREPARATION TIME: 10 minutes
COOKING TIME: 30 minutes
SERVES: 2–3

Libya's famous tea is served with a layer of foam known as *reghwa*, created by pouring the tea back and forth between the pot and a large enamel or steel mug or two mugs. That frothy top is key to successful brewing. It is a Berber tradition from the desert and mountains that can be found around the country. The tea is traditionally served in small glasses in three rounds. For the third round, many like to add some whole almonds (soaked in boiling water for a few minutes until their skins can easily be slipped off), toasted almonds or peanuts. These are served alongside or are added to the tea glasses.

    2 tablespoons loose leaf Chinese gunpowder green tea
    3 tablespoons sugar, or more to taste
    peanuts, toasted almonds or whole almonds with the
        skins slipped off, to serve

Add the tea to a large stovetop teapot or saucepan, pour in 500 ml (18 fl oz/2 cups) water and bring to a simmer over a medium-high heat. Cover with a lid and simmer over a low heat for 15–20 minutes. Stir in the sugar and simmer for another 1–2 minutes. Taste for sweetness and strength. Add more sugar if desired or leave to simmer for longer. Strain the tea into a clean teapot or a large mug. Pour it back and forth 20–30 times between the top of the teapot (rather than from the spout) and mug (or between 2 mugs) held at a distance to create a foam. Pour into small tea glasses and spoon some foam on the top. Serve in 3 rounds. On the third round, add some peanuts to the glasses and pour the tea over the top.

Bricklayer's 'Red' Tea with Geranium Water

TUNISIA
PREPARATION TIME: 2 minutes
COOKING TIME: 20 minutes
SERVES: 2–3

Tey ahmar, 'red tea', is made from black tea leaves, long-brewed and heavily sweetened, and given a dash of *ma atrichiya* (geranium water) before serving. The red tea is often called *tey el khedema* or (in French) *thé des maçons*, names that translate to 'bricklayers' or 'construction workers' tea, because a pot is left brewing on the embers of a brazier while they work. That long brew turns the tea a reddish tint. Today, orange blossom water is more common to add than geranium water, largely because it is more readily available and less expensive.

    2 tablespoons loose leaf black tea leaves
    3 tablespoons sugar, or more to taste
    geranium water or orange blossom water, for dashing

Put the tea into a stovetop teapot or medium saucepan, pour in 500 ml (18 fl oz/2 cups) water and bring to a simmer. Cover with a lid and simmer over a low heat for 15–20 minutes. Towards the end, stir in the sugar. Taste for sweetness and strength. Add more sugar if desired or leave to simmer for longer. Strain into tea glasses, dash with geranium water and serve.

AHWA (COFFEE)

It is not language that marks the borders of the old Ottoman Empire today – as a singular one never spread throughout the disparate range of places under its rule – but coffee. From Istanbul to Cairo to Sarajevo and across most of North Africa, the Ottoman period left a taste for thick, almost muddy coffee prepared in small, long-handled, hourglass-shaped pots and served in demitasses. Unfiltered and made with very finely ground coffee, with the sugar added to the dry grounds before boiling (rather than just before drinking), it is an intense and velvety coffee with a slight foam on the surface. The grounds need to settle before drinking.

The love for this type of traditional coffee is particularly strong in Tunisia, where it is called *kahoua arbi*. The name literally means 'Arabic coffee', but the *arbi* is often used to mean 'ours', or a local version. (*Makrouna arbi*, or Pasta with Chicken, Potato and Chickpeas, on page 223, is another example.)

Dating back 500 years to Yemen and spread by the Ottomans, the method for making this style of coffee remains similar around the lands of the old Ottoman Empire. In Turkey, the small pots used to prepare it are called *cezve* or *ibrik*. In Tunisia, they are called *zezwa* (also frequently spelled *zazoua* and *zézoua*), which sometimes lends the coffee its name (*ahwa zezwa*).

Rather than any of these names, many Tunisians call it *café*
maure, Moorish coffee, because cups get a generous dash of orange blossom water before being served. Originally brought from Andalucía by Spanish Muslims expelled during the Christian Reconquista, orange blossom water is a key flavouring for both sweet and savoury dishes in the kitchen. Kept in a special silver container called a *siniya*, it is also a symbol of luck and welcome, and spritzed onto the hands of visitors when entering a home.

The style of coffee might have been an import, but Tunisians gave it a distinct local touch to make it their own.

Moorish Coffee with Orange Blossom Water

ALGERIA, TUNISIA
PREPARATION TIME: 1 minute
COOKING TIME: 4 minutes
SERVES: 1

A legacy from the Ottomans, this traditional coffee in Tunisia and Algeria is prepared in small pot with a long handle called a *zezwa* and served in demitasses. The coffee grind is superfine, almost powder. Sugar and any spices are added to the dry preparation – rather than after the coffee has been boiled. Traditional coffee in Tunisia frequently gets a dash of orange blossom water, leading some to call it Moorish coffee. In Algeria, some of the older generation also like to perfume their *café arabe* with, alongside a dash of orange blossom water, a touch of cinnamon or even a pinch of pepper. Be sure to let the sludgy grounds settle before drinking.

1½ teaspoons very finely ground coffee
1 teaspoon sugar, or more to taste
2 cardamom pods, lightly crushed, optional
orange blossom water, for dashing

Add the coffee, sugar and cardamom pods (if using) to a traditional *zezwa* (or Turkish *cezve*) coffee pot or mini saucepan, then add 90 ml (3 fl oz/ 6 tablespoons) cold water. Stir lightly. Heat the coffee over a medium heat until a ring of foam begins to build around the edges, about 3 minutes. Watch carefully towards the end that it does not foam over. When the ring closes and the foam rises, remove the pot from the heat and let the foam fully recede, about 15 seconds. Return the pot to the heat and leave the foam to rise and recede twice more, removing it from the heat before it can boil over. Slowly pour the coffee into a small cup, taking care to keep as much foam as possible. Dash with orange blossom water and serve. Allow the sludgy grounds to completely settle before drinking.

Arabic Coffee with Cardamom

LIBYA
PREPARATION TIME: 1 minute
COOKING TIME: 4 minutes
SERVES: 1

In Libya, cups of thick coffee are a key element of hospitality. Traditional Arabic (or Turkish) coffee here usually gets boiled with ground cardamom. If possible, have some whole cardamom ground with the coffee beans. In general, Libyans tend to prefer their Arabic coffee a touch less sweet than their Tunisian neighbours.

  1½ teaspoons very finely ground coffee
  ½ teaspoon sugar, or more to taste
  2 generous pinches of ground cardamom, or to taste

Add the coffee, sugar and cardamom to a traditional Turkish coffee pot or mini saucepan, then add 90 ml (3 fl oz/6 tablespoons) cold water. Stir lightly. Heat the coffee over a medium heat until a ring of foam begins to build around the edges, about 3 minutes. Watch carefully towards the end that it does not foam over. When the ring closes and the foam rises, remove the pot from the heat and let the foam fully recede, about 15 seconds. Return the pot to the heat and leave the foam to rise and recede twice more, removing it from the heat before it can boil over. Slowly pour the coffee into a small cup, taking care to keep as much foam as possible. Allow the sludgy grounds to completely settle before drinking.

Spiced Coffee

MOROCCO
PREPARATION TIME: 10 minutes
COOKING TIME: 1 minute
SERVES: 2

The most basic spiced coffee in Morocco usually includes cinnamon, cardamom and ground ginger – and then whatever the *attar* (spice merchant) or client wants, from aniseed to sesame seeds, for a nutty touch. While *café épicé* has been largely replaced in cafés by espresso, it remains popular in many homes, where a pan of the simmering coffee fills the kitchen with heady aromas. Ideally, have the coffee and spices ground together in small amounts so it is fresh when preparing.

  2 heaped tablespoons ground coffee
  2 pinches of ground cinnamon
  2 cardamom pods, crushed
  2 pinches of ground ginger
  2 pinches of ground aniseed
  pinch of ground white or black pepper
  pinch of grated nutmeg
  sugar, for sweetening

Mix the coffee and spices together in a small bowl. Bring 400 ml (14 fl oz/1⅔ cups) water to the boil in a large saucepan. Stir in the coffee mixture and gently boil for 1 minute, watching that it does not foam over. Remove from the heat, stir and cover the pan with a lid. Leave to stand undisturbed for 5 minutes. Gently pour the coffee through a fine-mesh sieve or coffee filter into 2 cups. Serve hot with sugar to sweeten as desired.

Cinnamon and Pepper Coffee

MOROCCO
PREPARATION TIME: 5 minutes
COOKING TIME: 10 minutes
SERVES: 4

This Moroccan coffee adds two perfectly paired spices, cinnamon and black pepper: sharp back notes coupled with aromas from cinnamon. A typical way to prepare at home is to bring a large saucepan of water to the boil, add the coffee grounds and spices, simmer for a few minutes, remove from the heat and leave to stand and the grounds settle before pouring through a fine-mesh sieve into cups.

  1 cinnamon stick or piece of cinnamon bark
  3 tablespoons ground coffee
  1 teaspoon ground black pepper
  sugar, for sweetening

Bring 1 litre (34 fl oz/4¼ cups) water and the cinnamon stick to the boil in a large saucepan. Reduce the heat to low and simmer for 5 minutes. Stir in the coffee and pepper and simmer for 3 minutes. Remove from the heat and leave the grounds to settle for 2–3 minutes. Pour the coffee through a fine-mesh sieve or coffee filter into 4 cups. Serve hot with sugar to sweetened as desired.

'Half-half' Coffee

MOROCCO
PREPARATION TIME: 3 minutes
COOKING TIME: 5 minutes
SERVES: 2

In Morocco, *nous-nous* – literally 'half-half', sometimes written as *nusnus* – is the local coffee of choice. It is half coffee and half steamed milk. It should be quite strong. In cafés, the milk goes into the glass first, then the glass is set directly under the spout of the espresso machine to pour directly into it. At a café, *nous-nous* is meant to be sipped and lingered over.

150–175 ml/5–6 fl oz (⅔–¾ cup) full-fat (whole) milk
espresso coffee
sugar, for sweetening

Using an espresso coffee machine, steam the milk until foamy. Divide among 2 small heatproof glasses. They should be about half-full.

Prepare the espresso. If using an espresso machine, put the glasses directly under the spout. If using a stovetop moka pot, slowly pour into the glasses as soon as the coffee is ready. Serve with sugar to sweeten as desired.

Vervain-infused Hot Milk

MOROCCO
PREPARATION TIME: 2 minutes,
plus steeping time
COOKING TIME: 3 minutes
SERVES: 1

Moroccans claim that the best dried vervain (*louiza* in Maghrebi Arabic, *verveine* in French) comes from around Marrakech. In that city on cold winter evenings, it is common to infuse hot milk with some dried vervain leaves. It is considered a relaxing drink and is commonly prepared for a cold. Some like to infuse peppermint in hot milk in wintertime as well.

1 handful dried vervain leaves
250 ml/8 fl oz (1 cup) milk
sugar, for sweetening

Rinse the vervain with boiling water. Bring the milk to the boil in a large saucepan, then remove from the heat. Add the vervain leaves, cover with a lid and leave to steep for 8–10 minutes. Strain into a cup and sweeten with sugar to taste.

Warm Milk with Date Syrup

LIBYA
PREPARATION TIME: 2 minutes
COOKING TIME: 5 minutes
SERVES: 2

Dates are one of Libya's traditional staples, with date syrup (page 402) being a popular product derived from them. Among its many uses is as a sweetener – ideal to stir into a warm glass of another of the country's key staples, milk. It turns the milk a pink-purple colour, and gives it a lovely fruity sweetness.

500 ml/18 fl oz (2 cups) milk
1 tablespoon date syrup (*ruub*, page 402), or to taste

Bring the milk to a gentle simmer in a large saucepan, then remove from the heat. Stir in the date syrup until dissolved. Divide among glasses and serve.

Milk with Orange Blossom Water

MOROCCO
PREPARATION TIME: 2 minutes
SERVES: 4–6

A glass of cold, unsweetened milk perfumed with orange blossom water is offered ceremoniously at various occasions (often alongside dates). It is given to newly-weds and guests at the entrance of weddings, for hajj pilgrims returning from Mecca or to a special guest at one's home. This tradition is more common in northern Morocco.

1 litre/34 fl oz (4¼ cups) cold milk
1 teaspoon orange blossom water, or more to taste

Put the milk into a large jug (pitcher) and stir in the orange blossom water. Pour into glasses and serve cold.

JUICES

Mint tea cascading into a small, ornate glass and a tiny cup of thick sweet coffee dashed with orange blossom water are emblems of North African culture that get served at every conceivable occasion. Juice is their chilled counterpart.

The abundance of fresh juices is striking. A vast array of fruit orchards across the region supplies a bounty of options in the market. But the incredible frequency of drinking juice also stems from Islam's prohibition of alcohol, warm summers and Ramadan, when juice revitalizes after a day without eating or drinking. While the juices vary from season to season – strawberry in spring, watermelon in summer, pomegranate in autumn, orange in winter – jugs (pitchers) of freshly made juices sit on Ramadan *iftar* tables every night after the fast is broken, and again for the pre-dawn *suhur* meal before the fast begins again.

But just as notable as the amount and frequency of juice is the variety of combinations and flavours that fill glasses. Orange juice is blended with beetroot (beets) (page 437), carrots (page 437) or strawberries (page 433). Lemonade is classic (page 430), but not always prepared with only lemons, sugar and water – it often gets combined with fresh mint (page 430), strawberries (page 433) or watermelon (page 430) and even a touch of milk to balance its acidity. Juice sweetened with vanilla sugar is also common. Avocado has become common to thicken fruit drinks (page 438), and dates and raisins are sometimes puréed with fruits as a natural sweetener. These rich and filling avocado smoothies have become incredibly popular at juice stalls and *mahlaba* (dairy stores), and to make at home during Ramadan.

◇

Watermelon Juice

MOROCCO
PREPARATION TIME: 10 minutes, plus chilling time
SERVES: 2; MAKES: 500 ml/18 fl oz (2 cups)

Fresh and sweet, this popular juice is a summer favourite. It is exquisite with a dash of orange blossom water. Morocco is a major producer of watermelon and has become the largest supplier to the European market. They are grown in the south of the country.

500 g/1 lb 2 oz peeled and seeded watermelon, cut into cubes (about 4 cups)
2 tablespoons sugar
1 tablespoon fresh lemon juice
orange blossom water, for dashing, optional

Put the watermelon into a large bowl, sprinkle with the sugar and lemon juice, turn over and let the sugar dissolve for a few minutes. Transfer the watermelon and all the juices to a blender and purée until very smooth. Pour into a large jug (pitcher), cover with cling film (plastic wrap) and refrigerate until chilled. Dash with orange blossom water (if using) and serve.

Watermelon Juice with Fresh Mint Leaves

ALGERIA
PREPARATION TIME: 10 minutes, plus infusing time
SERVES: 2; MAKES: 500 ml/18 fl oz (2 cups)

This is a simple but deeply refreshing juice of watermelon aromatized with mint. It is perfect on a hot summer's day. Leave the juice to infuse and fully take on the minty flavours for at least a couple of hours.

500 g/1 lb 2 oz peeled and seeded watermelon, cut into cubes (about 4 cups)
1 teaspoon fresh lemon juice
small handful mint leaves, plus extra to garnish

Put the watermelon into a blender and purée until very smooth. Pour into a large jug (pitcher), stir in the lemon juice and add the mint leaves. Cover with cling film (plastic wrap) and refrigerate for at least 2 hours. Remove the mint leaves, pour into glasses, garnish with fresh mint leaves and serve chilled.

Watermelon Lemonade

MOROCCO
PREPARATION TIME: 15 minutes,
plus chilling time
SERVES: 4; MAKES: 1 litre/34 fl oz
(4¼ cups)

Among the array of juices, this combination of
watermelon and lemonade is particularly lovely and
offers the essence of summer. Watermelon's sweet
freshness perfectly complements the tartness of
the lemons.

100 g/3½ oz (½ cup) sugar
120 ml/4 fl oz (½ cup) fresh lemon juice
600 g/1 lb 5 oz watermelon flesh, seeded
1 sprig mint leaves
½ ripe lemon, preferably unwaxed or organic,
    thinly sliced
ice cubes, to serve

Put the sugar and 100 ml (3½ fl oz/generous ⅓ cup)
of hot water into a large bowl and stir to dissolve.
Stir in the lemon juice and set aside.

Put the watermelon into a blender and purée. Strain
through a sieve into a large jug (pitcher). Add the
sweetened lemon juice. Thin with about 250 ml
(8 fl oz/1 cup) cold water or as desired. Add the
mint leaves and lemon slices. Cover with cling film
(plastic wrap) and chill in the refrigerator before
serving. Serve in glasses over ice cubes.

Lemonade with Fresh Mint

TUNISIA
PREPARATION TIME: 10 minutes,
plus chilling time
SERVES: 4; MAKES: 1 litre/34 fl oz
(4¼ cups)

Refreshing, soothingly tart and deeply aromatic,
this lovely, emerald-coloured *citronade à la menthe*
is Tunisia's twist on fresh lemonade served across
the Mediterranean. The southern part of the
Cap Bon peninsula grows most of the country's
citruses, with the fields around beachside
Hammamet – a traditional walled town overlooking
a fifteenth-century kasbah (citadel) – the centre of
lemon production.

100 g/3½ oz (½ cup) sugar
6–8 ripe lemons
1 handful mint leaves, plus 4 sprigs to garnish
ice cubes, to serve

Put the sugar and 250 ml (8 fl oz/1 cup) of hot water
into a large bowl and stir to dissolve. Pour into a
blender, scraping any remaining sugar from the bowl
with a spatula.

Juice the lemons. There should be about 250 ml
(8 fl oz/1 cup) of juice. Pour into the blender. Add
the mint leaves and 250 ml (8 fl oz/1 cup) cold
water and blend well using quick pulses. Pour
through a fine-mesh sieve into a large jug (pitcher),
pressing out all the liquid with the back of a spoon.
Discard the solids. Dilute the juice with 250 ml
(8 fl oz/1 cup) cold water or as desired. Cover
with cling film (plastic wrap) and chill until ready
to serve.

Stir and pour into ice cube-filled glasses. Garnish
with sprigs of mint and serve.

Classic Lemonade

ALGERIA, MOROCCO, TUNISIA
PREPARATION TIME: 10 minutes,
plus macerating and chilling time
SERVES: 4; MAKES: 1 litre/34 fl oz
(4¼ cups)

This bold *citronade* uses the juice of the lemon
and the zest, where the essence of the fruit resides.
Some Moroccans like to add a dash of orange
blossom water for fragrance.

4 ripe lemons, preferably unwaxed or organic
100 g/3½ oz (½ cup) sugar, plus extra as needed
ice cubes, to serve

Zest the lemon, removing only the yellow part.
Put it into a large bowl, cover with the sugar, blend
well and leave to macerate for 30 minutes. Juice
the lemons and add to the bowl. Pour through a
fine-mesh sieve into a large jug (pitcher). Return the
solids to the bowl, pour in 750 ml (25 fl oz/3 cups)
water, stir and strain into the jug, pressing out all the
liquid with the back of a spoon. Discard the solids.
Taste for sweetness and stir in more sugar if needed.
Cover with cling film (plastic wrap) and chill until
ready to serve. Serve over ice cubes.

Strawberry Juice

TUNISIA
PREPARATION TIME: 10 minutes,
plus macerating and chilling time
SERVES: 2

Nearly all of Tunisia's strawberries are grown in Nabeul, on the south side of the Cap Bon peninsula. Whether enjoying a glass from a stall, on a café terrace or at home, Tunisians love the tall glasses of deep red juice while strawberries are in season from March to July. Some strain out the seeds.

    250 g/9 oz (2 cups) ripe strawberries, hulled
    2 tablespoons sugar
    1 teaspoon fresh lemon juice
    ice cubes, to serve
    sprigs mint, to garnish, optional

Halve or quarter the strawberries, depending on their size. Put into a large bowl, cover with the sugar, stir and leave to stand for 20 minutes for the sugar to dissolve. Transfer the strawberries and all the juices to a blender, scraping any remaining sugar from the bowl with a spatula. Add the lemon juice and begin blending, gradually adding 175–250 ml (6–7 fl oz/¾–1 cup) water to your desired consistency. Strain through a fine-mesh sieve into a large jug (pitcher), using the back of a spoon to patiently press out anything that isn't seeds. Cover with cling film (plastic wrap) and refrigerate until chilled. Stir and serve over ice cubes with a sprig of mint (if using).

Strawberry and Orange Juice

MOROCCO
PREPARATION TIME: 10 minutes,
plus macerating time
SERVES: 4; MAKES: 1 litre/34 fl oz
(4¼ cups)

In Morocco, juice made from strawberries and oranges is popular. There is a range in the proportions between the two, with some preferring theirs thicker and more dominated by strawberries, while others add more orange juice into the blend.

    500 g/1 lb 2 oz (4 cups) ripe strawberries, hulled
    1 tablespoon sugar
    500 ml/18 fl oz (2 cups) fresh orange juice

Halve or quarter the strawberries, depending on their size. Put into a large bowl, cover with the sugar, stir and leave to stand for 15 minutes for the sugar to dissolve. Transfer the strawberries and all the juices to a blender, scraping any remaining sugar from the bowl with a spatula. Add the orange juice and blend well. Divide among glasses and serve.

Strawberry Lemonade

TUNISIA
PREPARATION TIME: 10 minutes,
plus macerating and chilling time
SERVES: 4; MAKES: 1 litre/34 fl oz
(4¼ cups)

This tangy, delicious juice combines the bold tartness of whole lemons with the jamminess of the strawberries. It is a delicious spring and early summer beverage.

    2 ripe unwaxed organic lemons (350 g/12 oz in total)
    225 g/8 oz (generous 1 cup) sugar
    500 g/1 lb 2 oz (4 cups) ripe strawberries, hulled

Trim the ends off the lemons and discard. Working over a medium bowl to catch any juices, cut the lemons into pieces, remove any pips and put into a large bowl. Cover with the sugar, turn the mixture, then stir to blend and leave to stand for 30 minutes. Transfer the mixture to a blender, add 250 ml (8 fl oz/1 cup) water and blend to a coarse mixture. Pour through a fine-mesh sieve into a large jug (pitcher), pressing out all of the liquid with the back of a spoon.

Put the strawberries into the blender, pour in 175 ml (6 fl oz/¾ cup) water and purée. Pour into the jug with the lemon juice mixture and stir to blend. Cover with cling film (plastic wrap) and refrigerate until chilled. Serve chilled.

Pomegranate Juice

ALGERIA, LIBYA, MOROCCO, TUNISIA
PREPARATION TIME: 10 minutes,
plus chilling time
SERVES: 2

When pomegranates are in season in autumn, the vibrant scarlet-red arils can be found in various guises, from studding couscous (page 220) to being moistened with some rose water or orange blossom water (page 395) and served after a meal. They are also pressed into juice. Tunisians and Moroccans, in particular, love to add a dash of orange blossom water. The key is to only pulse the arils until the juice is released and the seeds inside remain intact.

> 2 ripe pomegranates
> juice of ½ lemon
> orange blossom water, for dashing
> caster (superfine) sugar, to taste

Working over a large bowl, remove the arils of the pomegranates and discard any pieces of white membrane. Put the arils into a blender or food processor and pulse only until they begin to release their juice. Pour through a fine-mesh sieve into a jug. Patiently press the juice from the pulp with the back of a large spoon. Pour into a large jug (pitcher), stir in the lemon juice, dash with orange blossom water and sweeten with sugar. Thin with 120 ml (4 fl oz/½ cup) cold water or as desired. Cover with cling film (plastic wrap) and refrigerate until chilled. Pour into tall glasses and serve cold.

Orangeade with Fresh Orange Blossoms

ALGERIA
PREPARATION TIME: 10 minutes,
plus chilling time
SERVES: 4; MAKES: 1 litre/34 fl oz
(4¼ cups)

When orange blossoms arrive in the market in March, homemade *orangeade* (orange squash, or concentrate) with a pinch of ground cinnamon and topped with fragrant white flowers is a springtime treat. Dilute the concentrate with cold water just before serving.

> 4 tablespoons sugar, or more to taste
> 500 ml/18 fl oz (2 cups) fresh orange juice
> orange blossom water, for dashing

ground cinnamon, for dusting
fresh orange blossoms, optional

Put the sugar and 250 ml (8 fl oz/1 cup) warm water into a large bowl and stir until the sugar has dissolved. Add a little more sugar, if it's not sweet enough. Pour into a large jug (pitcher), scraping any lingering sugar from the bowl with a spatula. Add the orange juice, stir well, cover with cling film (plastic wrap) and refrigerate until well chilled.

Before serving, dilute with 250 ml (8 fl oz/1 cup) cold water or as desired, dash with orange blossom water and stir well. Divide among glasses. Add a small pinch of ground cinnamon to each and garnish with fresh orange blossoms (if using).

Lemon Granita

TUNISIA
PREPARATION TIME: 20 minutes,
plus cooling and freezing time
COOKING TIME: 5 minutes
SERVES: 6–8; MAKES: about 1.25 litres/
42 fl oz (5¼ cups)

Lemon granita, known as *granite au citron*, is refreshing on a hot day. It is easy to make by breaking up the mixture with a fork as it freezes. Some like to add vanilla sugar to the mixture. Served in glasses, it melts a bit as you enjoy.

> 225 g/8 oz (generous 1 cup) sugar
> 300 ml/10 fl oz (1¼ cups) fresh lemon juice
> white of 1 large egg
> mint leaves, to garnish, optional

Bring 1 litre (34 fl oz/4¼ cups) water and the sugar to the boil in a large saucepan, stirring until the sugar has fully dissolved. Pour into a flat-bottomed glass, stainless-steel or plastic container and leave to cool to room temperature. Stir in the lemon juice. Cover the container with cling film (plastic wrap) or a lid and put into the freezer. After 1–2 hours, when it begins to freeze, remove from the freezer, uncover and stir with a fork.

Put the egg white into a large clean bowl and beat with electric beaters on medium speed to medium peaks. Or use a stand mixer fitted with a whisk attachment. Fold into the frozen mixture. Return to the freezer and freeze for another 2–3 hours, stirring and breaking up the ice crystals with a fork, about every 30 minutes. Stir again just before serving.

Spoon into glasses, garnish with a couple of mint leaves (if using) and serve with spoons or straws.

Beetroot and Orange Juice

MOROCCO
PREPARATION TIME: 20 minutes,
plus cooling and chilling time
COOKING TIME: 50 minutes
SERVES: 6

Moroccans like to prepare assorted combinations of juices, often with orange juice as a base mixer. The combination with beetroot (beets) is lovely. While it takes longer to prepare than most juices, it is worth the effort.

    2 beetroot (beets), unpeeled
    250 ml/8 fl oz (1 cup) fresh orange juice
    2 teaspoons sugar

To prevent the beetroot (beets) from 'bleeding' while cooking, leave at least 2.5 cm/1 inch of stem and do not trim the root ends. Put the beetroot into a large pot, cover with water and bring to the boil. Reduce the heat and gently boil until tender and a knife tip can easily penetrate, about 45 minutes. Drain in a colander and leave to cool.

Peel the beetroot, cut into a few pieces, then put into a blender with the orange juice and sugar and purée. Pour into a large jug (pitcher) and thin with about 500 ml (18 fl oz/2 cups) water or as desired. Cover with cling film (plastic wrap) and refrigerate until well chilled. Pour into tall glasses and serve cold.

Carrot and Orange Juice

ALGERIA
PREPARATION TIME: 15 minutes,
plus cooling and chilling time
COOKING TIME: 20 minutes
SERVES: 4; MAKES: 1 litre/34 fl oz
(4¼ cups)

This recipe is a lovely carrot juice for those without a juicer. It is popular during Ramadan, especially when it falls during the orange season. These days, many add yoghurt, either plain or fruit flavoured (peach and apricot are top choices), to give the juice some body.

    6 carrots (about 450 g/1 lb), cut into circles
    juice of 4 ripe oranges
    juice of 1 lemon
    1 tablespoon caster (superfine) sugar, or to taste
    120 ml/4 fl oz (½ cup) plain or fruit-flavoured yoghurt
    dash of orange blossom water, optional

Put the carrots and about 750 ml (25 fl oz/3 cups) water into a large saucepan, bring to the boil and boil until tender, about 15 minutes. Drain, setting the liquid aside. Leave to cool. Put the cooled carrots into a blender with 500 ml (18 fl oz/2 cups) of the reserved liquid and purée. Pour through a fine-mesh sieve, patiently pressing out all of the liquid from the carrots with a ladle or the back of a spoon. Return the liquid to the blender. Discard the solids. Add the orange and lemon juice, sugar, yoghurt and orange blossom water (if using) to the blender and blend well. Pour into a large jug (pitcher), cover with cling film (plastic wrap) and refrigerate until well chilled. Pour into glasses and serve cold.

Orange Juice with Cinnamon

MOROCCO
PREPARATION TIME: 5 minutes,
plus chilling time
SERVES: 2; MAKES: 500 ml/18 fl oz
(2 cups)

The juice stalls in Marrakech's Jemaa el-Fna square are legendary. Among the bountiful concoctions that they offer are freshly squeezed orange juices. A dash of orange blossom water and a pinch of ground cinnamon makes it even more enjoyable.

    500 ml/18 fl oz (2 cups) fresh orange juice
    icing (confectioners') sugar, to taste
    orange blossom water, for dashing
    ground cinnamon, for dusting

Pour the juice into a large jug (pitcher) and stir in sugar as needed. Dash with orange blossom water, cover with cling film (plastic wrap) and refrigerate until well chilled. Pour into glasses, add a pinch of ground cinnamon to each and serve.

Cinnamony Raisin Juice

ALGERIA, MOROCCO
PREPARATION TIME: 5 minutes,
plus cooling and chilling time
COOKING TIME: 25 minutes
SERVES: 4; MAKES: about 1 litre/
34 fl oz (4¼ cups)

This refreshing juice known as *khchaf* is made from raisins simmered with a cinnamon stick. Replace the cinnamon with a generous dash of orange blossom water if desired. In Morocco, some like to infuse with mint as it cools. Serve very cold.

200 g/7 oz (scant 1½ cups) dark raisins, rinsed
1 cinnamon stick or piece of cinnamon bark
2 tablespoons sugar, or to taste

Put the raisins into a large saucepan, add the cinnamon stick and pour in 1.5 litres (50 fl oz/ generous 6 cups) water. Bring to the boil, then reduce the heat to low, cover with a lid and gently simmer for 20 minutes. Take off the heat, remove the cinnamon stick, stir in the sugar and leave to cool.

Pour into a large jug (pitcher), cover with cling film (plastic wrap) and refrigerate until chilled. Strain through a fine-mesh sieve, gently pressing out the moisture from the raisins. Serve with some of the raisins left in the sieve in the glass.

Avocado Smoothie

MOROCCO
PREPARATION TIME: 5 minutes
SERVES: 3; MAKES: 750 ml/25 fl oz
(3 cups)

Soothing, nutritious smoothies made with avocados have become enormously popular in Morocco, especially during Ramadan. They are thick, rich and filling. The texture and sweetness of this drink depends on the ripeness of the avocado.

1 ripe avocado, peeled and stoned (pitted)
1½ tablespoons caster (superfine) sugar
500 ml/18 fl oz (2 cups) cold milk, or extra as needed
dash of orange blossom water, optional
ice cubes, to serve

Add the avocado, sugar and milk to a blender and purée at high speed. Add a touch more milk if desired. Stir in the orange blossom water (if using) and serve immediately in tall glasses over ice.

Avocado, Date and Almond Smoothie

MOROCCO
PREPARATION TIME: 10 minutes,
plus soaking time
SERVES: 4–6

This smoothie is naturally sweetened with dates and raisins, and it calls for whole almonds with their skins still on. Serve immediately, as it will turn brownish from the avocado.

35 g/1¼ oz (¼ cup) seedless raisins, optional
8 large stoned (pitted) dates
1 ripe avocado, peeled and stoned (pitted)
30 g/1 oz (¼ cup) whole almonds or ground almonds
750 ml/25 fl oz (3 cups) cold milk
dash of orange blossom water

Put the raisins (if using) into a small bowl, cover with hot water and leave to soak for 10 minutes to soften, then drain. Put the dates, soaked raisins, avocado, almonds, milk and orange blossom water into a blender and purée at high speed until very smooth. Divide among glasses and serve immediately.

Almond Milk

MOROCCO
PREPARATION TIME: 15 minutes,
plus standng and chilling time
SERVES: 2–4; MAKES: 750 ml/25 fl oz
(3 cups)

Festive and satisfying, *sharbat bel louz* (literally 'almond juice') is popular during Moroccan festivities and parties.

100 g/3½ oz (generous ¾ cup) ground almonds
55 g/2 oz (¼ cup) caster (superfine) sugar
500 ml/18 fl oz (2 cups) full-fat (whole) milk
orange blossom water or rose water, for dashing

Put the almonds into a large heatproof bowl and cover with 250 ml (8 fl oz/1 cup) boiling water. Stir and leave to stand for 10 minutes. Strain through a very fine-mesh sieve, tea strainer or muslin (cheesecloth) into a large jug (pitcher), pressing all of the liquid from the almonds with the back of a spoon. Discard the solids. Stir in the sugar and add the milk. Refrigerate until well chilled. Before serving, generously dash with orange blossom water and stir again. Pour into glasses and serve very cold.

Avocado Smoothie ➤➤

BASICS

Dersa Garlic-chilli Paste

ALGERIA
PREPARATION TIME: 5 minutes
MAKES: about 4 tablespoons

The Algerian spice mixture *dersa* forms the base of all manner of dishes. Unlike harissa (page 409) that is prepared to be stored, this is generally made when needed and incorporated into the dish. Pounded in a *mehraz* (mortar) with a pestle to a paste, it is garlic-rich, usually seasoned with cumin or caraway, and has a blend of sweet paprika and hot red pepper (called *felfla driss* or *felfla gnawa*). While it can be prepared with fresh chillies (chiles) (see below), it is more commonly made with dried chillies or ground cayenne pepper. If using a dried chilli, cut open, remove the seeds and soak in a small bowl of water for a few minutes before pounding. As *dersa* is frequently cooked in some olive oil at the beginning of a dish, it should be thinned with some water to keep the garlic from scorching.

    4 cloves of garlic, peeled, halved lengthwise
       and germ removed
    ¼ teaspoon ground cumin or caraway
    ¼ teaspoon sweet paprika
    cayenne pepper, to taste
    ½ teaspoon salt
    pinch of pepper

Put the garlic with the cumin, paprika, cayenne pepper, salt and pepper into a mortar and pound with a pestle to a smooth paste. Stir in 3–4 tablespoons water to loosen.

Dersa Garlic and Fresh Red Chilli Paste

ALGERIA
PREPARATION TIME: 5 minutes
MAKES: about 3 tablespoons

This version of *dersa* uses fresh hot red peppers rather than dried ones (or ground cayenne pepper). *Dersa* flavours sauces and stews and gets rubbed onto fish before being floured and fried (page 332). This just makes enough to enliven a dish or as a base to a simple marinade.

    1 small fresh red chilli (chile), cored, seeded
       and coarsely chopped
    4 cloves of garlic, halved lengthwise and germ
       removed
    1 teaspoon sweet paprika
    1 teaspoon ground cumin
    ½ teaspoon cayenne pepper
    ½ teaspoon salt
    2 tablespoons olive oil

Put the chilli (chile), garlic, paprika, cumin, cayenne pepper and salt into a mortar and pound with a pestle to a smooth paste. Stir in the oil. Spoon into a bowl. Cover and store in the refrigerator, and use within 3 days.

Chermoula Fish Marinade

MOROCCO
PREPARATION TIME: 10 minutes
MAKES: 120 ml/4 fl oz (½ cup)

Variations of this popular Moroccan fish marinade differ from house to house and region to region. In Tangier and northern Morocco, home cooks might add thyme and parsley, while in Marrakech and the south they may blend in ground ginger and possibly a little parsley, or just plenty of coriander (cilantro).

    4 cloves of garlic, minced
    3 tablespoons olive oil
    juice of 1 ripe lemon
    6 tablespoons finely chopped coriander (cilantro)
    4 tablespoons finely chopped flat-leaf parsley
    1 tablespoon sweet paprika
    1 tablespoon ground cumin
    ½ teaspoon cayenne pepper, optional
    salt

Put all the ingredients into a large bowl and mix together. For a less chunky marinade, first pound the garlic with salt to a paste in a mortar using a pestle before mixing with the other ingredients. For a smooth marinade, blend in a food processor or blender using quick pulses. Cover and store in the refrigerator, and use within 3 days.

Chermoula Chicken Marinade

MOROCCO
PREPARATION TIME: 10 minutes
MAKES: 175 ml/6 fl oz (¾ cup)

This is the classic Moroccan *chermoula* marinade for chicken and it has onion and saffron.

    4 cloves of garlic, minced
    3 tablespoons extra-virgin olive oil
    juice of 1 lemon
    1 red onion, finely chopped
    6 tablespoons finely chopped coriander (cilantro)
    4 tablespoons finely chopped flat-leaf parsley
    1 tablespoon sweet paprika
    2 teaspoons ground cumin
    ½ teaspoon cayenne pepper, optional
    pinch of saffron threads, crumbled
    salt

Put all the ingredients into a large bowl and mix together. Cover and store in the refrigerator, and use within 3 days.

Tomato Dipping Sauce

ALGERIA, MOROCCO, TUNISIA
PREPARATION TIME: 10 minutes
COOKING TIME: 20 minutes
MAKES: about 500 ml/18 fl oz (2 cups)

In eateries across the region, a dish of runny tomato sauce frequently accompanies fried fish (page 324), fishcakes (page 319) grilled seafood (page 341) or *kefta* skewers, kebabs, grilled lamb, roast chicken and even tagines. It is primarily there to eat with the bread on the side. The Tunisian version often contains harissa.

    3 tablespoons olive oil
    3 cloves of garlic, grated
    6 ripe tomatoes, halved crosswise and grated, peel
        discarded (see page 445)
    2 tablespoons double concentrated tomato purée
        (paste)
    harissa (page 409), optional
    salt and pepper

Heat the oil in a sauté pan over a medium heat, add the garlic and cook for about 30 seconds, or until aromatic. Add the tomatoes, tomato purée (paste) and 6 tablespoons water, and harissa (if using), then season with salt and pepper. Cook, uncovered, stirring frequently, until the sauce has thickened

and the tomato lost its acidity, 10–15 minutes. Stir in 120 ml (4 fl oz/½ cup) water or more as desired to loosen. Serve. It's best eaten on the day it is made.

Tomato Sauce

TUNISIA
PREPARATION TIME: 5 minutes
COOKING TIME: 40 minutes
SERVES: 4; MAKES: 500 ml/18 fl oz
(2 cups)

This sauce is used for topping pasta or rice. To make a fuller version, add some minced (ground) or finely chopped beef or lamb at the beginning with the onion. If the tomatoes are a touch acidic and not fully ripe, sprinkle in a touch of sugar.

    3 tablespoons olive oil
    1 yellow onion, finely chopped
    4 cloves of garlic, minced
    3 ripe tomatoes, halved crosswise and grated,
        peel discarded (see page 445)
    2 heaped tablespoons double concentrated tomato
        purée (paste)
    harissa (see page 409), to taste, optional
    1 bay leaf, optional
    salt and pepper

Heat the oil in a sauté pan over a medium heat, add the onion and cook for 5–10 minutes until soft and pale. Add the garlic and cook for about 30 seconds, or until aromatic. Stir in the tomatoes, tomato purée (paste) and 6 tablespoons water, and harissa (if using), then season with salt and pepper and cook for 2–3 minutes. Stir in 250 ml (8 fl oz/1 cup) water and cook until the sauce has thickened and the tomato lost its acidity, about 20 minutes. Stir in 250 ml (8 fl oz/1 cup) water, add the bay leaf (if using) and bring to the boil. Simmer for a few minutes if desired for a slightly less runny sauce.

Hard-boiled Eggs

ALGERIA, LIBYA, MOROCCO, TUNISIA
PREPARATION TIME: 5 minutes,
plus resting and cooling time
COOKING TIME: 5 minutes
MAKES: 6 hard-boiled eggs

Wedges of hard-boiled eggs accompany numerous dishes across the Maghreb, from salads to tagines to pasta and couscous. A good hard-boiled egg should have whites that are supple not rubbery, a creamy, brilliant golden yolk and no trace of greenish-grey rings. Hard-boiled eggs are a classic snack or breakfast with some salt and cumin.

6 large eggs, at room temperature

Put the eggs into a medium saucepan and cover with 2.5 cm/1 inch water. Bring to the boil over a high heat, then remove from the heat, cover the pan with a lid and let the eggs sit in the hot water for 12 minutes. Meanwhile, fill a large bowl with ice water. Transfer the eggs with a slotted spoon to the ice water to cool, then drain. Gently roll under the palms to crack the shells and peel.

Cooked Dried Chickpeas

ALGERIA, LIBYA, MOROCCO, TUNISIA
PREPARATION TIME: 5 minutes,
plus overnight soaking time
COOKING TIME: 1 hour 35 minutes–
2 hours 5 minutes
MAKES: 1.1 kg/2½ lb (generous 6 cups)
cooked chickpeas

Dried chickpeas (garbanzo beans) need to be soaked before cooking, preferably overnight. If the water is 'hard' or chlorinated, adding some bicarbonate of soda (baking soda) will help them soften during the soaking stage.

500 g/1 lb 2 oz (3 cups) dried chickpeas (garbanzo beans)
1½ teaspoons bicarbonate of soda (baking soda), optional
1 small onion, peeled and left whole
1 clove of garlic, unpeeled
1 teaspoon salt

Rinse the chickpeas (garbanzo beans) under cold running water. Put the bicarbonate of soda (baking soda) (if using) into a large bowl, pour in abundant cold water, stir to dissolve the bicarbonate of soda

and add the chickpeas. Leave to soak overnight. The next day, drain and rinse thoroughly.

Bring a generous amount of water to the boil in a large, heavy pot or saucepan over a high heat, then add the chickpeas, onion and garlic. Once the water returns to the boil, reduce the heat to low, cover with a lid and cook without losing the boil until tender, 1½–2 hours. Once the chickpeas begin to soften, add the salt. If the pot needs more water during cooking, add boiling water. Remove the pot from the heat and leave the beans in the water until ready to use. Drain and discard the onion and garlic.

Cooked Dried White Beans

ALGERIA, LIBYA, MOROCCO, TUNISIA
PREPARATION TIME: 5 minutes,
plus soaking time
COOKING TIME: 1 hour 35 minutes–
2 hours 5 minutes
MAKES: about 1.5 kg/3¼ lb (6 cups)
cooked beans

Gently boil the dried white beans, such as cannellini beans or white haricot (navy) beans, with only a limited amount of water to keep them from breaking. Season with salt at the end. The cooking time depends on the type, size and age of the beans.

500 g/1 lb 2 oz dried white beans (about 2½ cups)
1 clove of garlic, unpeeled
1 bay leaf, optional
salt

Rinse the beans under cold running water, then put into a large bowl and cover with abundant cold water. Leave to soak for 8 hours in a cool place. Drain the beans and rinse away any fermenting odours.

Put the beans, garlic and bay leaf (if using) into a large pot or saucepan and cover with about 5 cm/2 inches of cold water. Bring to a simmer, skimming off the foam that rises to the top with a slotted spoon. Reduce the heat to low, cover with a lid and gently boil until tender but not mushy, 1½–2 hours. Add a few generous pinches of salt towards the end of cooking. Add cold water during cooking if needed. Remove the pot from the heat and leave the beans in the water until ready to use. Drain and discard the garlic and bay leaf.

Cleaned and Prepared Fresh Snails

ALGERIA, MOROCCO, TUNISIA
PREPARATION TIME: 30 minutes
COOKING TIME: 50 minutes

Live snails are traditionally left for a time without feeding before preparing, in order to clean out their systems. (In Tunisia, they feed on rosemary to give them aroma.) Nowadays, snails are often sold in net baskets ready to be prepared. Before using in a recipe, they should be scrubbed clean and boiled in a large pot of water for about 5 minutes. When added to boiling water, live snails retract inside their shell and make it harder to remove later to eat, but bringing snails to a slow boil will make them easier to extract when serving.

fresh (live) snails
white vinegar
salt

Patiently clean the snails with abundant water, using salt to scrub the shells and a touch of vinegar.

Put the snails into a large pot or saucepan and cover with abundant water. Bring to a slow boil over a medium heat, watching to keep the snails inside the water, about 45 minutes. When the water reaches the boil and foam comes to the surface, reduce the heat and boil for 5 minutes. Drain the snails in a colander and rinse thoroughly. They are now ready to use in a recipe.

Prepared Snails in Brine

ALGERIA, MOROCCO, TUNISIA
PREPARATION TIME: 2 minutes
COOKING TIME: 10 minutes

Snails are also sold in brine. As they have already been cleaned, they take much less time to prepare. Drain and discard the brine.

snails prepared in brine

Drain and rinse the snails well. Put the snails into a large pot and cover with water. Bring to the boil over a high heat and boil for 5 minutes. Drain the snails in a colander and rinse thoroughly. They are now ready to use in a recipe.

Cooked Octopus

ALGERIA, LIBYA, MOROCCO, TUNISIA
PREPARATION TIME: 5 minutes,
plus thawing and cooling time
COOKING TIME: 35 minutes–
1 hour 5 minutes

You can tenderize fresh octopus by freezing it for 24–48 hours and then thawing before using. The length of boiling varies greatly – from 20 or 30 minutes to 60 minutes for a medium octopus. Prick the upper part of a tentacle with the tip of a knife. When the knife slides in with little resistance, it is ready.

1 medium octopus (about 1 kg/2¼ lb), frozen

Thaw the octopus gently in the refrigerator. Rinse thoroughly under cold running water and remove any grit in the tentacles.

Put the octopus into a large pot or saucepan and cover with cold water, then bring to the boil. Gently boil until tender and the tip of a knife pricked quite deep into the upper part of a tentacle enters with little resistance, 20 minutes–1 hour, beginning to check after about 20 minutes. Remove the pot from the heat, cover with a lid and let the octopus sit in the water to cool. Remove the octopus and place on a large platter to fully cool.

Prepared Fresh Sardines

ALGERIA, LIBYA, MOROCCO, TUNISIA
PREPARATION TIME: 10 minutes

Cleaning sardines is very quick once you achieve the technique.

fresh sardines

If needed, gently scale the sardines with a fish scaler or dull knife. Remove the innards by holding the body of a sardine with one hand and the head with the other, rocking the head upwards to break the neck downwards and then firmly pulling it away to draw out the entrails. Run a finger through the cavity to clean and then rinse under cold running water.

Filleted Fresh Anchovies and Sardines

ALGERIA, LIBYA, MOROCCO, TUNISIA
PREPARATION TIME: 10 minutes

While it can be tedious, it is important to be sure that all bones are removed when filleting fresh anchovies or sardines.

fresh anchovies or sardines

Make an incision at the base of the tail to the bone, slide a thumbnail under the fillet and gently pull it away from the spine. Repeat on other side. Check closely for any bones, rinse under cold running water and pat dry with paper towels.

Grated Tomatoes

ALGERIA, LIBYA, MOROCCO, TUNISIA
PREPARATION TIME: 10 minutes

Grating tomatoes is easier than peeling and dicing them. This method will work with round or pear-shaped tomatoes.

fresh ripe tomatoes

Cut the tomatoes in half crosswise. (If using a plum tomato or similar smaller variety, cut across the top.) Gently squeeze the seeds into a bowl and run a finger through the seed cavity to remove the seeds. Cupping a tomato half, grate on a box grater until the skin peels back and all the flesh has been grated away. Discard the flattened skin. Strain the liquid from the seeds and add to the grated pulp.

Blanched and Peeled Tomatoes

ALGERIA, LIBYA, MOROCCO, TUNISIA
PREPARATION TIME: 5 minutes
COOKING TIME: 1 minute

It is sometimes preferable to not have pieces of tomato skin in a dish. The easiest way to peel a tomato before chopping is to blanch it in boiling water.

fresh ripe tomatoes

Remove the stem of each tomato and score an X in the bottom with the tip of a knife. Fill a large bowl with cold water and set aside. Bring enough water

to cover the tomatoes to a rolling boil in a large saucepan. Add the tomatoes and boil until the skins begin to split, 20 seconds–1 minute, depending on the ripeness of the tomatoes. Using a slotted spoon, plunge the tomatoes into the bowl of cold water. Drain and peel once the tomatoes have cooled.

Blanched, Peeled and Fried Whole Almonds

ALGERIA, LIBYA, MOROCCO, TUNISIA
PREPARATION TIME: 15 minutes
COOKING TIME: 10 minutes

Fried almonds are ingredients in numerous dishes and they top countless ones. For small amounts of almonds, it is enough to cover them in a small heatproof bowl of boiling water and leave them to soak for a few minutes until the skins can be slipped off with your fingers.

whole almonds
neutral oil, for frying

Bring a medium saucepan of water to the boil, add the almonds and boil for 3–5 minutes, then drain. Once cool enough to handle, slip off the skins with your fingers. Spread the almonds out on paper towels to dry.

Line a medium plate with paper towels. Heat about 5 mm–1 cm/¼–½ inch of neutral oil in a small frying pan over a medium heat until the surface shimmers. Add the almonds and fry for 1–2 minutes until just golden. Transfer with a slotted spoon to the paper towels to drain.

Roasted Whole Almonds

ALGERIA, LIBYA, MOROCCO, TUNISIA
COOKING TIME: 8–10 minutes

Almonds can be roasted in the oven. Be careful to not over-roast, as they will continue to cook a bit more after they are removed from the oven.

peeled whole almonds

Preheat the oven to 200°C/400°F/Gas Mark 6. Put the almonds into a medium ungreased pie or cake pan and roast, shaking the pan occasionally, until golden, crunchy and fragrant, 8–10 minutes. (Do not let them get too dark, as the almonds continue to cook a bit more after being removed from the oven.) Transfer immediately to a plate to cool.

Ras al Hanout Spice Blend

MOROCCO
PREPARATION TIME: 5 minutes
MAKES: 2 tablespoons

The name of this legendary spice blend literally means 'head of shop' or 'top of shop' and can include dozens of different spices. Every *attar* (spice merchant) blends it differently and combines the common (black pepper) with the exotic (local wild 'Sufi's' cumin known as *kamûne es sûfi*) and deeply aromatic (dried rosebuds or lavender), to concoct a distinct mixture added to tagines, stews, marinades or fish. This recipe is a pared-down version of more readily available ingredients. Add rosebuds or lavender for more aroma, long pepper for some muskiness and heat, and so on. Dry-toasting the whole spices before grinding will help draw out their flavours. While famous in Morocco, this blend is also found in Algeria. Scale up and adjust measurements as desired.

I teaspoon ground cumin
I teaspoon ground ginger
½ teaspoon ground cinnamon
½ teaspoon ground turmeric
½ teaspoon ground coriander
½ teaspoon cayenne pepper
½ teaspoon ground fennel
½ teaspoon ground black pepper
½ teaspoon ground white pepper
¼ teaspoon ground nutmeg
pinch of saffron threads, crumbled
generous pinch of ground cloves

Put all the spices into a medium bowl and mix together. For optimal flavour, store in an airtight container in a cool, dry place and use within 6 months.

Tabil Spice Blend

TUNISIA
PREPARATION TIME: 5 minutes
COOKING TIME: I minute
MAKES: 2 tablespoons

The most popular Tunisian spice blend is called *tabil* (or *tabel*), the name for coriander seeds, the blend's main ingredient. They are traditionally ground with caraway seeds, chilli (red pepper) flakes, often dried garlic and salt and occasionally a bit of dried onion. The ratios here are standard and can be scaled up as desired. This blend is often used in stews and with meat dishes. Note that some people in Tunisia refer to *tabil* as *ras al hanout*, meaning a blend.

I tablespoon coriander seeds
½ tablespoon caraway seeds
¼ tablespoon dried garlic or garlic powder
cayenne pepper or chilli (red pepper) flakes, to taste
pinch of salt

Put the coriander and caraway seeds into a small sauté pan or frying pan and dry-toast over a medium heat until warm and aromatic, tossing occasionally, about I minute. Remove from the heat and leave to cool. Transfer the cooled spices to a spice grinder, add the garlic, cayenne pepper and salt and grind to a powder. For optimal flavour, store in an airtight container in a cool, dry place and use within 6 months.

Bzaar Spice Blend

LIBYA
PREPARATION TIME: 5 minutes
MAKES: 3 tablespoons

Turmeric is at the forefront of Libya's most famous spice blend. If possible, grind the spices just before blending. *Hararat* is a similar blend, although less dominated by turmeric.

I tablespoon ground turmeric
I teaspoon ground ginger
I teaspoon ground galangal
I teaspoon ground cinnamon
I teaspoon ground black pepper
½ teaspoon ground cloves
½ teaspoon ground coriander
½ teaspoon ground caraway seeds
½ teaspoon grated nutmeg, optional

Put all the spices into a medium bowl and mix together. For optimal flavour, store in an airtight container in a cool, dry place and use within 6 months.

Agourram, Touria. *De mère en fille: La cuisine marocaine*. Paris: Albin Michel, 2000.

Alami, Fouziya, and Souâd El Mansouri. *Cuisine pour Ramadan et fêtes*. Casablanca: Najah El Jadida, 1996.

Amhaouche, Rachida. *Cuisine marocaine*. Casablanca: Chaaraoui, 2005.

–. *Jus de fruits et boissons chaudes*. Casablanca: Chaaraoui, 2009.

–. *L'herire du thé*. Casablanca: Chaaraoui, 2007.

–. *Pâtisserie marocaine*. Casablanca: Chaaraoui, 2005.

–. *Petits Fours Sucrés*. Casablanca: Chaaraoui, 2005.

–. *Tajines*. Casablanca: Chaaraoui, 2007.

Bellahsen, Fabien, and Daniel Rouche. *Délices du Maroc*. Paris: Éditions de Lodi, 2005.

Bellakhdar, Jamal. *Plantes Médicinales au Maghreb et soins de base*. Casablanca: Le Fennec, 2006.

Benayoun, Aline. *Casablanca Cuisine: French North African Cooking*. London: Serif, 1998.

Benkirane, Fettouma. *Délices de Ramadan*. Mohammedia (Morocco): Librairie Nationale, 2006.

–. *Salés et sucrés marocains*. Mohammedia (Morocco): Librairie Nationale, 2006.

Bennani-Smirès, Latifa. *La cuisine marocaine*. Casablanca: Al Madariss, 2004.

–. *Les saveurs d'Algérie*. Paris: Bachari, 2002.

Ben Jemaa, Zouhair. *La cuisine tunisienne: Patrimoine et Authenticité*. Tunis: Simpact, 2010.

Bismuth, Jacqueline. *Tunisie gourmande: Le carnet de cuisine*. Paris: Éditions de La Martinière, 2017.

Bouayed, Fatima-Zohra. *La Cuisine Algérienne*. Algiers: ENAG, 2019.

–. *Le Livre de la cuisine d'Algérie*. Algiers: ENAG, 2005.

Boubezari, Karimène. *Ma cuisine algérienne*. Aix-en-Provence: Édisud, 2002.

Boucherite, Madame L. *Le Guide du cuisinier algérien*. Algiers: Baghdadi, 2003.

Boughalous, Nadia. *Spécial plats traditionnels Chahrazed*. Algiers: Édition La Plume, n.d.

Bouhamed, Mme. *Cuisine Kabyle: Les spécialités montagnardes inconquises*. Algiers: Les Éditions El Manel, 2003.

Certain, Christophe. *Cuisine pied-noir*. Aix-en-Provence: Édisud, 2001.

Chakor, Salah. *Traité de gastronomie marocaine*. Tangier: Le Journal de Tanger, 2008.

Choumicha. *Choumicha Ch'hiwate: cuisine marocaine*. Casablanca: Librairie Al Ouma, 2005.

Cocina marroquí. Madrid: H. Kliczowski-Onlybook, 2003.

Cocina tunecina. Madrid: H Kliczowski-Onlybook, 2003.

Correnti, Pino. *Cuscus: storia, ricette, tradizioni*. Palermo (Sicily): Dario Flaccovio, 2002.

Cuisine algéroise. Algiers: El Morchid, n.d.

Cuisine kabyle. Algiers: El Morchid, n.d.

Dammak, Sarra. *Les délices des soirées ramadanesques*. Tunis: Maison Yamama, 2022.

Danan, Simy, and Jacques Denarnaud. *La nouvelle cuisine judéo-marocaine*. Paris: ACR Édition, 1994.

Délices du Maroc. Barcelona: EDL, 2005.

Delicias de Túnez. Madrid: H Kliczowski-Onlybook, 2003.

Desbordes, Christaine. *Cuisine tunisienne*. Aix-en-Provence: Édisud, 2003.

Dunlop, Fiona. *Medina Cooking: Home Cooking from North Africa*. London: Mitchell Beazley, 2007.

El Kouch, Noufissa. *Bricks*. Paris: Al Kitab, 2009.

–. *Couscous*. Paris: Al Kitab, 2009.

–. *Plats Noufissa: Viandes*. Casablanca: Taoufik, 2007.

–. *Tajines*. Paris: Al Kitab, 2009.

El Mahdi, Lilia and Sarra Dammak. *La cuisine tunisienne*. Tunis: Maison Yamama, 2022.

El Mahdi, Lilia and Touba Achour. *Tajines et entrées tunisiennes*. Tunis: Maison Yamama, 2022.

Eléxpuru, Inés. *La cocina de al-Andalus*. Madrid: Alianza, 1994.

Fedel, Mohamed. *Saveurs du Maroc*. Paris: Éditions de Lodi, 2006.

Ferhi, Youcef. *Grandes recettes de la cuisine algérienne*. Paris: Bordas, 1969.

Gobert, E.G. *Usages et rites alimentaires des Tunisiens*. 2nd edition facsimile of 1940 edition. Tunis: Éditions Sahar, 2003.

Guinaudeau, Madame. *Traditional Moroccan Cooking: Recipes from Fez*. Translated by J.E. Harris. London: Serif, 2003.

Hadj Hammou, Zuleikha. *Le Livre de la cuisine algérienne*. Algiers: Éditions Mimouni, 1991.

Hal, Fatema. *The Food of Morocco*. Singapore: Periplus, 2002.

Hemphill, Ian. *Spice Notes: A Cook's Compendium of Herbs and Spices*. Sydney: Macmillan, 2000.

Jah, Cherif Abderrahman. *Los aromas de al-Andalus*. Madrid: Alianza, 2001.

Jamal, Salah. *Aroma árabe: Recetas y relatos*. Barcelona: Zendrera Zariquiey, 2011.

Jenkins, Nancy Harmon. *The Essential Mediterranean*. New York: HarperCollins, 2003.

Kaâk, Zeinab. *La Sofra: Cuisine tunisienne traditionnelle*. Tunis: Cérès Éditions, 1995.

–. *La Sofra: Cuisine tunisienne traditionnelle*. New Edition. Tunis: Cérès Éditions, 2016.

Khelifi, Lalia. *Gâteaux d'or*. Algiers: Dar El Hadith Lil-Kitab, 2004.

Koehler, Jeff. *Morocco: A Culinary Journey with Recipes from the Spice-Scented Markets of Marrakech to the Date-Filled Oasis of Zagora*. San Francisco: Chronicle, 2012.

–. *Rice Pasta Couscous: The Heart of the Mediterranean Kitchen*. San Francisco: Chronicle, 2009.

Koenig, Leah. *The Jewish Cookbook*. New York: Phaidon Press, 2019.

Kouki, Mohamed. *La pâtisserie tunisienne d'Ommok Sannafa*. Tunis: Relié, 1971.

–. *Tunisian Gastronomy*. Translated by Najoua Kouki. Tunis: Wafa, 2000.

La Maison Arabe. *Moroccan Cooking: Our Dadas' Recipes*. Marrakech: La Maison Arabe, 2013.

–. *Moroccan Recipes: Prepared in less than 1 hour*. Marrakech: La Maison Arabe, 2016.

Lhomme, Valérie, and Bouchra Derraqui. *Les Carnets de Cuisine marocaine de Bouchra*. Paris: Solar, 2006.

Mallos, Tess. *A Little Taste of Morocco*. Sydney: Murdoch, 2006.

Mardam-Bey, Farouk. *La cocina de Ziryâb: El gran sibarita del Califato de Córdoba*. Translated by Sylvia Oussedik. Barcelona: Editorial Zendrera Zariquiey, 2002.

Morsy, Magali. *Recettes de couscous*. Aix-en-Provence: Édisud, 1996.

Norman, Jill. *Herbs & Spices: The Cook's Reference*. New York: DK, 2002.

Plats Traditionnels Samira. Algiers: Édition La Plume, n.d.

Reguieg, Rachi. *Saveurs d'Algérie*. Algiers: El Morchid, n.d.

Rezki, Mokhtaria. *Le Couscous algérien*. Algiers: ENAG, 2003.

Roden, Claudia. *Arabesque: A Taste of Morocco, Turkey, and Lebanon*. New York: Alfred A. Knopf, 2006.

–. *The New Book of Middle Eastern Food*. New York: Alfred A. Knopf, 2000.

Saïda-Ben Mouhoud, Guimini. *Plats Chaouí. Cuisine Facile de A à Z. 30 Recettes*. Édition La Plume: Algiers, 2013.

Sekili, Zined, and Mehdi Adjaoud. *30 menus traditionnels pour le ramadham*. Algiers: Tamgout, 2004.

Sijelmassi, Abdelhaï. *Les plantes médicinales du Maroc*. Casablanca: Éditions La Fennec, 2008.

Tamzali, Haydee. *La cuisine en Afrique du Nord*. Paris: Tomkinson, 2000.

Tayaba, Ommi. *La cuisine tunisienne*. Tunis: MC-Éditions, 2008.

Túnez. Madrid: H Kliczowski-Onlybook, 2003.

Véhel, Jacques. *La véritable cuisine tunisienne*. Original: 1922. Tunis: MC-Éditions, 2008.

Wolfert, Paula. *Couscous and Other Good Food from Morocco*. New York: Harper & Row, 1973.

–. *The Food of Morocco*. New York: Ecco, 2013.

Wright, Clifford A. *A Mediterranean Feast*. New York: William Morrow, 1999.

Yasmina, M., and M. Fodil. *Les meilleurs plâts traditionels*. Algiers: El Hana, 2003.

Yerasimos, Marianna. *500 Years of Ottoman Cuisine*. Translated by Sally Bradbrook. Istanbul: Boyut, 2005.

Zeitoun, Edmond. *250 recettes classiques de cuisine tunisienne*. Paris: J. Grancher, 1977.

Index

Page numbers in *italics* refer to the illustrations

451

Recipe Notes

Butter is salted butter, unless otherwise specified.

Eggs are UK size medium (US size large), unless otherwise specified.

Herbs are fresh, unless otherwise specified.

Milk is whole (full-fat) or semi-skimmed (reduced-fat) milk, unless otherwise specified.

Olives can be pitted or unpitted, unless otherwise specified.

Pepper is freshly ground black pepper, unless otherwise specified.

Salt is fine sea salt, unless otherwise specified.

Sugar is white granulated or table sugar, unless otherwise specified.

Individual vegetables and fruits, such as carrots and apples, are assumed to be medium, unless otherwise specified, and should be peeled and/or washed unless otherwise specified.

Where neutral oil is specified, use vegetable, rapeseed (canola), grapeseed, sunflower, corn or light olive oil.

Metric, imperial and cup measurements are used in this book. Follow one set of measurements throughout, not a mixture, as they are not interchangeable.

All tablespoon and teaspoon measurements given are level, not heaped, unless otherwise specified.

1 teaspoon = 5 ml; 1 tablespoon = 15 ml. Australian standard tablespoons are 20 ml, so Australian readers are advised to use 3 teaspoons in place of 1 tablespoon when measuring small quantities.

When no quantity is specified, for example of oils, salts and herbs used for finishing dishes or for deep-frying, quantities are discretionary and flexible.

Cooking and preparation times are for guidance only. If using a convection (fan) oven, follow the manufacturer's directions concerning oven temperatures.

When deep-frying, heat the oil to the temperature specified, or until a cube of bread browns in 30 seconds. After frying, drain fried foods on paper towels.

When sterilizing jars for preserves, wash the jars in clean, hot water and rinse thoroughly. Heat the oven to 140°C/275°F/Gas Mark 1. Place the jars on a baking sheet and place in the oven to dry.

Exercise a high level of caution when following recipes involving any potentially hazardous activity including the use of high temperatures and open flames and when deep-frying. In particular, when deep-frying, add food carefully to avoid splashing, wear long sleeves and never leave the pan unattended.

Some recipes include raw or very lightly cooked eggs, meat or fish, and fermented products. These should be avoided by the elderly, infants, pregnant women, convalescents and anyone with an impaired immune system.

About the Author

Jeff Koehler, winner of a James Beard award, two International Association of Culinary Professionals (IACP) awards and two Gourmand World Cookbook Award 'Best in the World' prizes, is an American writer, cook and culinary historian. He is the author of seven critically acclaimed books, including *Where the Wild Coffee Grows*; *Darjeeling: A History of the World's Greatest Tea*; *Spain: Recipes and Traditions*; *Morocco: A Culinary Journey with Recipes*; *Rice, Pasta, Couscous*; and *La Paella*.

His writing and recipes have appeared in the *Washington Post*, NPR.com, *Wall Street Journal*, *Saveur*, *Food & Wine*, *Gourmet*, Eater.com, *Fine Cooking*, *Taste*, NationalGeographic.com, *Afar*, *Dwell*, *Tin House*, the *Times Literary Supplement*, *South China Morning Post* and many other publications. Originally from the Seattle, Washington, area, he did his postgraduate studies in London and has lived in Barcelona since 1996. He divides his time between Barcelona, Menorca and North Africa.

Acknowledgements

To those across North Africa who, for the last 25 years, have been welcoming me into their homes and shops, at their stoves and around their tables, I want to say thank you for your hospitality and generosity – and for sharing secrets to your marvellous cuisine.

Certainly, one of the great things about writing on the topic of food is that everyone is an expert in their own cooking and culinary traditions. That means conversations with quite literally everyone yield clues to a project like this book. It also means that in the many years of questions that have gone into these recipes, answers often came from people whose names I never learned – from produce stall owners and butchers to waiters and people sitting at a nearby café table to cooks cajoled from the kitchen. So, to this unnamed brigade of help, *shukran*.

There is a core group of people I want to particularly thank for their help on this book: Ahmed Agouni, Aziz Begdouri, Myriam Ben Farhat, Hakim Bouguettaya, Warda Bouguettaya, Chakib Ghadouani, Jaber El Hababi, Noor El Ouni and Syrine Saddoud. Your assistance was truly invaluable.

Among the many others whose help was significant, insightful or particularly useful at some point during the long span of working on this book: Habiba Abdelkéfi, José Abete, Ali Amrou, Mounir Arem, Fouad el Awam, Hamza Ayari, Zoubida Azouzi, Souhail Basli, Khadija Benchaalal, Abed Bekaddour, Fatiha Bekaddour, Jacqueline Bismuth, Hugues Blin, Fatiha Boudjema, Aïcha Boutkhoum, Ami Cherif, Meryem Cherkaoui, Imed Chorfi, Vincent Coppée, Khadija Dilali, Rachid El Ouariti, Malika Essaidi, Dada Fatiha, Ahmed Gatnash, Ahmed Ghadouani, Taoufik Ghaffouli, Ghazi Gherairi, Philippe Guiguet-Bologne, Abderrazak Haouari, Siham Hatta, Ian Hemphill, Valeria Judkowski, Rachid Kandy, Zohra Kanfoud, Meriem Khercouf, Ismail Kherradji, Dada LaAziza, Sid Ali Lahlou, Abdelmajid Mahjoub, Souad Maidja, Aicha Muniga, Mohammed Nahir, Sanae Nouali, Khadija Oualili, Pascal Poignard, Helen Ranger, Catherine Rophé, Fabrizio Ruspoli, Fredj Saddoud, Bilel Wechtati and Mustafa Zaizoun.

Thanks goes also to the many cookbook authors, food writers and scholars whose works have been so valuable. See pages 448–449 for a selection of recommended culinary titles.

I also want to thank the various magazine and newspaper editors who commissioned pieces about North Africa from me over the years and not only sustained me professionally but made me a better writer: Joe Yonan, Maria Godoy, Jocelyn Zuckerman, Stacy Adimando, Derk Richardson, April Fulton, Dana Bowen, Christopher Hill, Justin Paul, Marika Cain, Richard Doughty, Jennifer Mathlouthi, Alva Robinson, Michelle Wildgen, Matt Rodbard, Jennifer Armentrout, Kate Krader, Corie Brown, Catharine Hamm, Maureen Murphy, Kemp Minifie, Jeanne McManus, Allison Cleary, Patsy Jamieson, Jennifer Wolcott, Amelia Newcomb and Amy Treadwell.

Thanks to Kim Witherspoon and Maria Whelan at InkWell Management, who shared their enthusiasm for this project from the very beginning.

At Phaidon, my deepest thanks to Emily Takoudes who commissioned the book and has been its champion from the beginning, project editor Clare Churly, culinary managing editor Ellie Smith, Emilia Terragni, the meticulous copyeditor Kathy Steer, Ellie Levine, Alex Coumbis, photographer Simon Bajada and designer Paco Lacasta.

I was fortunate to have a strong group of support for my writing about food when I first started out, and I want to acknowledge how important that was to me back then, and how important it was in the years that followed: Eva Borràs, Joanne Koehler, Naomi Duguid, Rebecca Staffel, Doe Coover, Leslie Jonath and Jodi Liano.

And to Eva, Alba and Maia, for all they bring to our family table, for tasting everything in this book and for always asking for more.

Finally, to my father, Bill, who passed away just weeks after I finished the first draft of this manuscript. While he didn't get to see the final version of the book, he did join me a few times in North Africa while I worked on it, and for that I am fortunate.

Phaidon Press Limited
2 Cooperage Yard
London E15 2QR

Phaidon Press Inc.
65 Bleecker Street
New York, NY 10012

phaidon.com

First published 2023
© 2023 Phaidon Press Limited
Text © 2023 Jeff Koehler

ISBN 978 1 83866 626 2

A CIP catalogue record for this book is available from the
British Library and the Library of Congress.

Photography by Simon Bajada

Commissioning Editor: Emily Takoudes
Project Editor: Clare Churly
Production Controller: Lily Rodgers
Designed by Lacasta Design

Printed in China

Phaidon would like to thank Ahmed Agouni, Mounir Arem,
Hilary Bird, Warda Bouguettaya, Houda Ghadouani, Julia
Hasting, João Mota, Jo Murray, Ellie Smith, Caroline Stearns,
Kathy Steer, Maria Whelan, Kim Witherspoon.